A History of Music and Musical Style

A History of
Music and Musical Style

 HOMER ULRICH

Professor and Head, Department of Music, University of Maryland

 PAUL A. PISK

Professor of Music, University of Texas

NEW YORK · CHICAGO · SAN FRANCISCO · ATLANTA

Harcourt, Brace & World, Inc.

FRONT ENDPAPER: Interior of a Bavarian church, showing the musicians' gallery. Engraving by J. A. Corvinus (1683–1738), from a drawing by M. Diesel. [THE METROPOLITAN MUSEUM OF ART, GIFT OF HARRY G. FRIEDMAN, 1956]

BACK ENDPAPER ILLUSTRATION: "The Music Room," by Gerard Terborch (1617–81). [STAATLICHE MUSEEN BERLIN, GEMÄLDEGALERIE]

TITLE PAGE ILLUSTRATION: Woodcut from the title page of Pierre Phalèse, *Des chansons réduits en tablature de luth* (Louvain, 1546).

To Miriam and Martha

ISBN: 0-15-537720-5

Library of Congress Catalog Card Number: 63-13512

PRINTED IN THE UNITED STATES OF AMERICA

Contents

Preface

THE AUTHORS' purpose in writing this history of music has been to offer a clear, straightforward presentation of historical developments in musical style. The men who contributed ideas, principles, and compositions are of course brought into the account, but the emphasis is on the contributions and not on the men. Thus the book is "music-centered" rather than "composer-centered."

In any large historical period general aspects of style are common to many categories of works, but each category (such as sacred, operatic, or orchestral music) is characterized by a particular combination of style elements. Within a given period, therefore, we consider each such category separately through whatever time span it remains dominant. For example, Baroque opera is treated in a single place and as an organic entity—even though it embodied Italian, French, English, and German elements and though its course spanned a century and a half. This plan makes possible fuller consideration of chamber music and the smaller vocal forms, which are treated sketchily in many books; it also permits description of their stylistic evolution and discussion of their intrinsic value as literature. Occasionally deviations from this plan are necessary, notably in the period after about 1860, when many composers in effect represented individual styles.

Another aim of this book has been to restore an equitable balance among the various eras. Without slighting the earlier music, we have attempted to do justice to the Romantic period and to give full coverage to the music of our own time. In addition, a lengthy chapter is devoted to music in America from colonial times to the present.

We have sought throughout to keep in mind the needs of the general reader to whom the book is directed. In several places, for example, we have made wide-ranging summaries and generalizations without describing all the sources and detailed research on which the generalizations are founded. Such musicological details have been omitted in the interest of clarity and concise presentation; they belong properly in works for the specialist.

In a collaboration such as the one undertaken here, it is difficult to determine the extent of each author's contributions. Paul A. Pisk wrote the first drafts of Chapters 1, 2, 22, 26, 29, and 30, as well as portions of other chapters, but also contributed to chapters for which Homer Ulrich is primarily responsible. Each of us gladly recognizes the other's large share in giving the book whatever virtues it possesses.

Dr. Bryce Jordan evaluated the manuscript from the standpoint of an experienced teacher and suggested many improvements in the form and clarity of the presentation. Dr. Harold Spivacke and the capable staff of the Music Division of the Library of Congress were generous with their assistance at many points. The staffs of the Music Division of the New York Public Library and the Print Division of the Metropolitan Museum of Art were particularly helpful in the preparation of the illustration program. Mr. Maxwell Weaner's excellent work in copying the musical examples is recognized with thanks. Much of the manuscript was written during a sabbatical leave granted to Homer Ulrich, who is grateful to Dr. R. Lee Hornbake for making that leave possible. Mrs. Karen E. Jones deciphered reams of illegible manuscript and emerged with a flawless typescript; her devotion to the task is sincerely appreciated. She and other members of our families encouraged, supported, and actively assisted in many details of the writing. Individually they will know how much they have contributed to this book; their help is gratefully recognized.

HOMER ULRICH
PAUL A. PISK

January 17, 1963

A History of Music and Musical Style

ABBREVIATIONS USED IN FOOTNOTES

GMB: Schering, *Geschichte der Musik in Beispielen*

HAM: Davison-Apel, *Historical Anthology of Music*

MoM: Parrish-Ohl, *Masterpieces of Music Before 1750*

SRMH: Strunk, *Source Readings in Music History*

TEM: Parrish, *A Treasury of Early Music*

I

Introduction

THE FIELD of music history is ideally concerned with the art of music in all its myriad manifestations since the dawn of human consciousness. A book in this field may give an account of the origins of music in the remote past, to the extent that such origins can be deduced from the music of existing primitive cultures. It may discuss the several functions of music in different ages, and the cultural, political, philosophical, or even climatic conditions which gave rise to those functions. It may attempt to relate developments in music to other parallel cultural phenomena. It may include accounts of the lives of men, great and small, who were responsible for those developments. It may justifiably pay attention to the origins of musical instruments, to musical organizations and the ways in which music was performed. It may refer to musical documents, whatever their form—not only manuscripts, sketches, printed works, and treatises, but also paintings, sculpture, and inscriptions on monuments. It may consider legends, myths, and references to music in the writings of the various religions. But above all, it must focus on the music itself.

Mentioning the areas of investigation within the province of a book

Drawing from a bas-relief from the royal palace at Nineveh, *c.* 700 B.C.

on music history may well suggest that there is more than enough material for a number of volumes. The music historian preparing to write a single volume, therefore, must select out of this vast amount of material that which reflects his purpose, illuminates his approach, and meets the needs of his potential readers. His first obligation is to state his purpose and outline his approach. He is then in a position to set limits to his material, eliminating the areas which do not directly contribute to that purpose. It is only fair to warn the reader at the outset that no single book can do justice to the many important and fascinating aspects of the field.

This book approaches music history through musical style. Music comes into being when musical material is meaningfully manipulated, when the resources of music are employed to establish communication between human beings, especially between creative and receptive minds. At any one time in the long course of music through human experience a particular aspect of the material is organized in a particular way, and most of the music originating during that time has certain characteristics in common. At another time the organization of the material proceeds along different lines; that music in turn develops characteristics which make it distinguishable from other music—earlier, later, and even music of the same period written under different conditions—and which allow it to be considered separately.

In this way the concept of *style* arises. Musical style may be thought of as the set of elements which on the one hand gives a piece of music its identity and on the other allows it to be related to something outside itself: to a particular period of time, to a particular country of origin, to a type, to a function, to a composer, or to another piece of music. Elements of style may include the principles of tonal organization, ways of combining single melodic lines, ways of employing instruments, uses of certain rhythmic patterns, ways of treating the vertical components of music, ways of assembling tones and phrases to form larger musical entities. They may also include the manner in which a piece of music is performed, the uses to which it is put, its ritualistic or social or aesthetic purposes, and a variety of other aspects. As a result, the concept of style permits a piece of music to be examined with respect to all the elements mentioned above, to be compared with others, and to be classified according to its place in the history of the art.

Musical style, then, will dictate the scope and content of this book, and certain aspects of style will be in the forefront of the discussion throughout. Biography, cultural history in general, philosophy, and many other fields can richly support the study of music history and will be brought in when they illuminate the style element or style history under consideration at the moment. Such fields, however, cannot substitute for the music itself; they must remain on the periphery. Further, the contributions of such fields to the central core of music history can be properly evaluated only after the music itself has been seen in historical perspective.

The concept of musical style, in turn, leads directly to another large concept, that of *style periods*. A style period may be defined simply as the period of time in which certain style elements dominate or in which those elements significantly affect the sound and shape of most of the music then being composed. The concept of style periods provides a convenient and workable framework upon which the historian can construct the large-scale generalizations that are needed to survey the mass of material with which he is confronted. In naming the style periods, music history has traditionally made use of a terminology borrowed from the histories of literature and the other arts—even though dates do not exactly coincide in the various fields and the contents of the various periods are not always analogous. Thus such terms as Gothic, Medieval, and Renaissance, found in historical writings generally, will be employed throughout the following chapters.

We live in the complex of cultural patterns, heritages, and institutions which together make up Western civilization. In spite of many diverse facets and extreme contradictions, that civilization has characteristics which differentiate it from the Orient, Near East, and other parts of the world. More especially, Western music has a structure, meaning, and history quite unlike those of other kinds of music. In its types of organization and its place in the culture, it shows little relationship to, let us say, Chinese, Indian, or Polynesian music. The few references to non-Western music in the pages that follow will serve to show the extent of these differences, as well as the few relationships and influences which that music has had on the West, especially in antiquity and in the early Middle Ages. An extended discussion of that music would have few points in common with the main approach adopted here.

Style Periods and Centers

MORE than two thousand years are involved in the history of Western music, during which time a number of radical changes in style have taken place. It is significant to note that, although differing in their scope and effect, the changes have come about at approximately equal intervals of time. A major style change has been followed by a less far-reaching change after about 150 years, and after an equal interval of approximately 150 years another major style change has occurred. This regular sequence has taken place several times in the past ten or eleven centuries.

It may further be pointed out that Western musical developments spread across the European continent in a unique way. They began in the general area of the eastern and central Mediterranean and gradually, during the first eight or nine centuries of the Christian era, made their effects felt across the entire face of Europe. Thereafter, however, and beginning roughly in the tenth century, certain localities rose above surrounding areas in the significance of their musical accomplishments. Such localities may be called musical centers, and it is interesting to observe that each new style period had its origin in a different musical center.

The progression of these centers began in central Europe about A.D. 900.

By 1150 musical activities had moved to the northwest and were centered in the neighborhood of Paris. The years after 1300 saw a new center arise southeast of Paris in the general area of Burgundy, after which, about 1450, the Flemish and Dutch regions became most influential. By 1600 the main center of musical activity had moved southward to Italy, but toward 1750 it moved northward again, to Germany and Austria. The general proliferation of musical centers since about 1900 makes it diffi- cult to determine which twentieth-century center will loom largest in the minds of later historians, but it cannot be denied that a large amount of significant musical activity today takes place in the United States.

The discussions in the chapters that follow will necessarily take these geographical facts into account. After a preliminary review of the theories concerning the origins of music generally and a brief description of Ori- ental and Near Eastern music, the place of Greece as the starting point for music in the Western world will be considered.

Theories and Origins

WRITERS on music in the early centuries of Western civilization ex- pounded many theories about the origins of the art. They usually at- tempted to link the beginnings of music to Biblical heroes and to the exalted figures of Greek mythology. Today we know, however, that the origins of music lie much farther back, and that they can be traced to the utterances of men in a culturally primitive state. From the eighteenth century onward many philosophers and sociologists attempted to formu- late theories which explained these beginnings, but their conflicting and divergent theories can be refuted because they were not based on actual research.

As early as the 1750's, philosopher Jean-Jacques Rousseau suggested that music was an elevated form of speech, and Herbert Spencer later elaborated this premise. Charles Darwin, on the other hand, saw the root of musical activity in the imitations of animal cries (bird songs, mating calls, and the like). Carl Stumpf, an eminent German tone psychologist, reverted to the older hypothesis that music originated in the emphatic calling of words on certain pitches.[1] In the twentieth century an entirely new science, comparative musicology (ethnomusicology), seems to have arrived at a more valid theory: music began with singing, independent of language. Scientific investigations of the music of primitive tribes in Africa, Asia, and the South Pacific islands, and the assumption that that music is similar to the music of thousands of years ago, permit the fol- lowing observations to be made.

The range of this primitive music is two or three tones. Its intervals are mainly seconds, but it has a tendency to use larger intervals in descend- ing passages.[2] At an early stage genuine musical instruments did not exist, but sticks or other solid bodies were used to reinforce the rhythm. The opinion that rudimentary forms of polyphony existed as early as this

1 Stumpf, *Die Anfänge der Musik.*
2 Sachs, *The Rise of Music in the Ancient World*, pp. 25–28.

stage has been corroborated. The forms include *parallelism,* the singing of melodic segments in octaves or other intervals (including dissonances); *heterophony,* the appearance of melodic variants which occur when two or more groups sing the same tune simultaneously; and *drones,* sustained long tones above or below the melody. In addition, alternation between two groups of singers was employed by certain Polynesian tribes.[3] Music at that time had no connotation with art, but functioned as an element of magic in rituals. Only gradually did the relationship to magic fade, and it is still prevalent in the highly developed cultures of east Asia, notably China and India, and to a lesser extent in the Semitic cultures.

Music of the Far East

China. Writings on music as well as on the practice of music in China can be traced back approximately four thousand years. In these early writings, however, scale structures and pitch levels are not given definitely. One may gather that one principal tone, the "yellow bell," was established as emanating from a pipe of fixed length. By overblowing, and by selecting pipes of different length, the player obtained a series of tones. Each tone, called a *lü,* lay at the interval of a fifth from its neighbors. These tones, not identical with the tones of our system, formed only the raw material for the basic Chinese scale, which was a five-tone row without half-steps, arranged like the black keys of the piano. At a later date, smaller intervals, called *pien tones* and not definitely standardized as to pitch, were inserted between the five tones of the main row. According to the magic connotations of the music the five main tones could be related to colors, celestial bodies, seasons, times of day, ages of man, and even emotions. Thus a relationship between music, human life, and celestial forces was established.

The music was performed in connection with court ceremonies, but folk music and theatrical music are mentioned also. We know that rhythm was strictly organized and that accompaniments were performed on traditional instruments: zithers, lutes, and many kinds of bell-like chimes made of wood, stone, and metal. In the historical documents various types of orchestras are mentioned. All this music had great influence on the life of the nation, and Confucius, a century before Plato, spoke of its ethical qualities and its importance in general education.

India. In the music of India two epochs can be distinguished. The music of the first, pre-Buddhistic epoch (about 600 B.C. and earlier), consisted mostly of the cantillation of the holy books of the Veda. Two methods of performing that chant existed; the earlier employed only three notes, and the later used several intervals in the range of a sixth. These intervals do not coincide in pitch with those of Western music, although steps which are roughly diatonic and chromatic may be distinguished.

The musical system of the second epoch of Indian music, which has

3 For further details see Schneider, *Geschichte der Mehrstimmigkeit.*

continued to the present, is a complicated one by Western standards. There is no scale as such; instead, the octave is divided into twenty-two microtones, each of which is called a *sruti*. From the twenty-two *srutis* a number of intervals are selected for practical use. These may be, in our terminology, whole-tones and half-tones, but they are without tonal function and do not coincide with the familiar intervals of our scale. Two types of these selected patterns of *srutis* are characteristic, corresponding to the authentic and plagal modes of Western music (see page 42). Music moved not in these scales, however, but in *ragas*. A *raga*, literally a "color," is a melodic pattern which has characteristic intervals at the beginning, middle, and end; and every *raga*—there are over a hundred—has its concomitant rhythm. Some *ragas* use seven tones, others use fewer; still others avoid certain intervals and consist of exactly prescribed ornamentation or modes. The musician improvises in or on these *ragas*, and such improvisation is more than an artistic endeavor, for each of the *ragas* has extramusical connotations. Secret relationships with the periods of

Spring festival in honor of Krishna, showing musicians with barrel drum (*mrdanga*), lute (*sitar*), and tambourine. Mid-seventeenth-century Indian painting.

the day (certain *ragas* can be sung only early in the morning, for example, and others at dusk), with specific emotions, with physical states of being, and even with weather conditions are implied. However, these qualities are by no means uniformly defined.

The instrumental or vocal melodic line is usually accompanied by one or more percussion instruments or by a pedal tone (drone). The rhythm is most complicated when compared with Western rhythm. Groups containing up to twelve time units, but with an irregular number of notes of different length in each group, patterns with subdivisions into five, seven, or nine units—such complex structures are common. The drones may use cross-rhythm in still other irregular groupings to fill out gaps.[4] In spite of the improvisational character of Indian music, certain formal considerations having to do with the lengths of sections are noticeable. Influences of this art were felt not only in the countries where Buddhism spread (for example, Japan and the Malayan countries), but to a lesser extent in the Near East also.[5]

Music of the Near East

Egypt. Among the oldest cultures of the Near East is that of Egypt. In contrast to India, however, where elaborate treatises on music theory exist, Egyptian sources include only pictorial relics, some instruments, and a few literary records concerned with performance practices. The art works date from different epochs, and the assumption is made that the variously shaped instruments pictured in them are the results of innovations or imports from Asiatic countries rather than the results of development within Egypt itself.

As early as the Old Kingdom (about 3000 B.C.) a highly developed musical culture existed. On various pieces of sculpture we find reliefs of harpists and flutists taking part in religious ceremonies and social entertainments. The instruments pictured there have been measured in an attempt to gauge their acoustical characteristics, and the results permit the conjecture that the musical scale was a five-tone row consisting of major thirds and half-steps, in the pattern A-F-E-C-B (reading downward). In the New Kingdom (about 1500 B.C.) a definite change apparently took place. A number of new instruments appeared: the lyre, a different kind of harp, an oboe-like instrument, the lute, various kinds of drums imported from Asia, and the typical Egyptian *sistrum* (rattle). Again, exact measurements suggest that the intervals of the scale became smaller at that time. There are a number of murals showing singers and instrumentalists performing, some with the right arms of certain performers extended in a gesture that suggests conducting. According to reports of writers about 500 B.C., a reaction leading toward a resumption of more

4 Olivier Messiaen, a contemporary French composer, has introduced Indian rhythms into his music, with results that are scarcely comprehensible to Western listeners.

5 For further details see Lachmann, *Die Musik des Orients*, and Fyzee-Rahamin, *The Music of India*.

Ancient Egyptian instruments: arched harp, lute, double oboe, and lyre. Tomb painting, *c.* 1420–1411 B.C.

dignified ancient techniques took place. It is likely that Egyptian influences determined the educational and ethical aspects of Greek music.

Sumer and Babylonia. The records of music in Sumer, the oldest cultural group in Mesopotamia, are very scanty. It is known that between 3000 B.C. and 2300 B.C. organized temple music with singers and players existed. Several instruments have been found in excavations: harps, lutes with small sound boxes and long, sticklike fingerboards, double oboes, and others; the same instruments were later used by the Babylonians. Written records do not exist.

Knowledge of conditions in Babylonia is almost as scanty, except that the instruments were more numerous than in Sumer, and the Greek historian Plutarch reported that the Chinese concept of identifying the basic musical intervals (octave, fifth, and fourth) with the seasons of the year was prevalent in Babylonia also. The connotations are not identical, however, for the Babylonians calculated their intervals in a different way than the Chinese. Certain accents in Babylonian script were once believed to represent musical notation, but this hypothesis proved to be erroneous. It may be that some of the signs which are later found in different forms in Assyrian and other relics from Asia Minor represent note groups such as those found in Hindu notation.[6]

Music of the Hebrews. Because of the political interrelations between the Hebrews and the Semitic nations (Babylonia, Assyria, and the empire

6 Sachs, "The Mystery of Babylonian Notation," in *The Musical Quarterly,* XXVII (1941).

of the Hittites), certain facets of the musical culture of the Judean people are similar to those of the others. Jewish music began in the early
years of tribal life, and the references to music in the Bible are numerous. As the political development of the Jewish people proceeded from
the nomadic state to the occupation of Palestine and the gradual establishment of a kingdom, musical activities were increased. These activities
may be divided into three periods: the time of the patriarchs and judges,
that of the kings, and that after the return from the Babylonian exile.
The post-Biblical events in the musical history of the Jews and their
influence on the music of the Christian church belong in a later chapter.

The Bible mentions many types of music and musical instruments. We
find songs of praise, songs of victory, songs of mourning, and above all
the Psalms. Dances are also mentioned, and the coupling of vocal and
instrumental music is typical. At a later time purely vocal music prevailed. The following principal types of Hebrew music may be established: [7] (1) *Cantillation*, used when parts of the Bible were read during
the service. It customarily employed only two or three tones, and the text
was sung or chanted in a rapid *parlando* style (see EXAMPLE 1). (2) *Antiph-*

E X A M P L E   1

Hebrew cantillation

Niš - mat kol hoj te - wo- resh at šim - ho   a - du- noj e - lu hej - nu

we - ru - ah Kol - bo - sor   te - fo - ejr ut - rum- ejm   zih - re - ho etc.

onal or *responsorial singing*. Since Hebrew poetry is based on parallelism (the expression of one thought in two different ways), several types
of performance are possible. The parallel lines of poetry are sung either
by two half-choruses or by one soloist alternating with the chorus. Conforming to the text, the second statement is usually amplified in the
music also; the principle of variation and the elaboration of motives
may be implied. (3) *Hymn singing* within the service, performed either
by a soloist (cantor) or by groups. Some of the hymns are motivic throughout; others are freely organized, with groups of melodic motives and their
variants connected by transitional motives (called "binders") so that a
continuous melodic chant results. This type could be either syllabic or
rich in melismatic ornamentation.

Music played an important part in both the secular and the religious
life of the Hebrews. Kings and other leaders of the people were cus-

7 For detailed information see Idelsohn, *Jewish Music in its Historical Development*.
(Idelsohn also edited the critical collection of original Jewish melodies, *Hebräisch-
Orientalischer Melodienschatz*.)

tomarily acclaimed in songs and fanfares, and very elaborate musical services in the Temple, described in the Bible, were important parts of the worship. A description of an orchestra is given, consisting of nine lutes, two harps, and a cymbal. Certain numbers, for which the tribe of Levites was responsible, appear in connection with the accounts of the music: the numbers 12, 9, and 7, for example, indicate that magical or mystical qualities were ascribed to the music. The problem of rhythm in the music of the Hebrews is still open to discussion. According to Sachs, the Hebrews employed the classical meter of qualitative measurement (long-short) and not the accented rhythmic groupings (heavy-light) as asserted by other authorities.[8] A gradual development from stricter to freer organization can be traced, however. The musical accounts in the Bible, before the establishment of the Temple, describe choral singing combined with dancing and percussion accompaniments, in all of which women took part. At a later period a still freer rhythmic organization, approaching declamation, prevailed.

An exact musical notation in our sense did not exist. The Hebrew alphabet consists of consonants and half-consonants; vowels were indicated by dots and dashes above and below the letter symbols. In addition to these vowel signs, a number of other signs used to indicate musical rendition are found. These signs, called "masoretic" (which implies "traditional"), referred not to single notes but to melodic particles or groups. The particles were handed down by oral tradition among singers for centuries. When they were finally codified, in the sixteenth century, the discrepancies between the interpretations of Jewish communities in Europe, north Africa, and Asia were so great that a definitive interpretation was impossible to achieve. The recently discovered Dead Sea Scrolls contain signs similar to those in the liturgical script of early Christian sects in the Orient, strengthening the conjecture that a common musical heritage is shared by the people of related cultures, no matter how widely separated geographically.

Musical instruments of the Hebrews of Biblical times have not been recovered. The few instruments mentioned in the Bible can be identified by analogy with similar instruments found in other Oriental cultures. They include string instruments, primarily a harp (played with the fingers) and a lyre (played with a plectrum); wind instruments, including the *shofar* (the horn of a ram, used for liturgical purposes), silver trumpet, and double oboe; and percussion instruments, among them hand drums, tambourines, and cymbals. Later references also mention the use of the Greek hydraulic organ in the temple service. The majority of the instruments mentioned here are of Egyptian or Babylonian ancestry.

This more detailed presentation of the music of the Hebrews seems appropriate here, since the music was of direct and immediate influence on the musical practices of the early Christian church. The connections between Hebrew and Christian chant have been scientifically investigated and proved.[9]

8 Sachs, *The Rise of Music in the Ancient World*, pp. 89–90.
9 See Eric Werner, *The Sacred Bridge*.

$\mathscr{e}\mathscr{y}\mathscr{O}$ 2 $\mathscr{e}\mathscr{y}\mathscr{o}$

Music in Greece and Rome

G REEK music, like Greek culture in general, had its roots in the Orient. Its theoretical system, the development of its instruments, and even its connotations with magic (which later were refined and incorporated into the doctrine of *ethos*) give evidence of an Oriental heritage. Two difficulties stand in the way of obtaining a clear picture of Greek music, however: the scarcity of musical compositions and the problem of transcribing what few there are in accordance with available information about performance practices. We do possess knowledge of Greek notation and of an elaborate system of music theory. The latter, fundamental to all the musical speculations of the Medieval period, became in turn basic to Western tonal organization.

Music in Greece

M USIC in Greece was not an art (in the modern sense) but a science closely related to mathematics and astronomy; nevertheless, it was of

Attic vase, 6th c. B.C. [THE METROPOLITAN MUSEUM OF ART, ROGERS FUND, 1907]

supreme importance in the cultural development of the people. A strong belief in the influence of music on human behavior assured it a vital place in religious, political, and personal life. Music could affect the personality in a variety of ways and became, therefore, a required subject in general education. About the fourth century B.C., Plato (in the *Republic*) and Aristotle (in his *Metaphysics* and *Politics*) gave music an extensive place in their writings, especially the aspect of music dealing with *ethos*.[1]

Doctrine of ethos. Ethos may be simply defined as an innate characteristic in music (and, since Greek music was inextricably tied to poetry, drama, and the dance, in these as well), varying according to pitch, tonal pattern, or function, and believed to influence human behavior. The quality of *ethos* is different in each of the modes (scale types) which together form the body of Greek musical theory. The modes are named after various Greek tribes and may be taken to reflect the different emotional or temperamental characteristics of those peoples. (Significantly, the names of two of the modes, Phrygian and Lydian, refer to Greek colonies in Asia Minor.) For example, the Dorian mode evokes firm or even harsh, vivid, and virtuous reactions; it stands for mental equilibrium enabling man to withstand his fate. Phrygian melodies are of sensual, passionate, and ecstatic character. Lydian tunes are melancholy, tender, and more intimate than the others.

Origins. It is probably impossible to reconstruct an accurate history of Greek music, for its origins are clouded by mythological references and legends such as those of Orpheus, who through music delivered his wife from the realm of the shades, and of Amphion, who brought stones to life through his lyre playing. The early Homeric epics mention professional singers and instrumentalists. The *aulos* (a double-reed instrument) is prominent in accounts of the music of Olympos, a half-legendary, half-historical figure who came from Phrygia to the Greek mainland, possibly in the eighth century B.C. Olympos was considered by later Greeks to be the father of their art music.

From about the seventh century a few historical figures appear. Terpander, who flourished about 675 B.C. and is associated with the island of Lesbos, introduced the accompaniment of the *kithara* (a type of lyre) to vocal music. The names of composers and performers are mentioned in connection with the many athletic contests which were a feature of Hellenic life. The Olympic games, the Delphic festivals in honor of Apollo, and the gymnastic assemblies in Sparta and Athens all included music among their activities. The *paean* performed in memory of Apollo, the *dithyrambus* in honor of Dionysus, various cultic songs which were danced—these are among the known forms of the time. Archilochos of Paros (flourished *c.* 650 B.C.) is mentioned as a composer who contributed new stylistic elements to some of these types. For the Pythian games at

1 Selections from Plato's *Republic* and Aristotle's *Politics* are in *SRMH*, pp. 4–12 and pp. 13–24, respectively.

Delphi in 586 B.C., one Sakadas composed a piece for the aulos commemorating Apollo's victory over the dragon; this piece, probably the
first known example of program music, remained a famous work for
centuries. Finally, Sappho of Lesbos and Anacreon of Samos (both *c.* 525
B.C.) were known not only as poets but as musicians.

The place of music in the Greek drama cannot be definitely established,
but it seems that the drama itself was an outgrowth of the dithyrambs
performed in honor of Dionysus. Dialogues and monologues were probably spoken or declaimed (a monologue performed by Thespis in 534
B.C. is reputed to be the first such example), while dramatically elevated
passages were most likely sung. The chorus combined singing with acting
and dancing, and in the works of the three giants of Greek drama,
Aeschylus (525–456 B.C.), Sophocles (496–406 B.C.), and Euripides (484–
406 B.C.), the chorus—and hence the music—dominated. About the middle
of the fifth century B.C. the nature of musical activity seems to have
changed. Professional musicians and virtuoso performers became active
and dominated the fields of vocal and instrumental music. The character

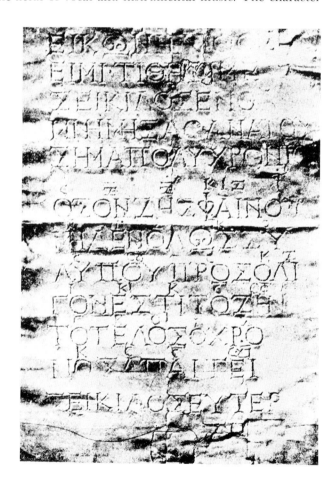

One of the few
extant examples
of Greek music:
the *skolion* (drink-
ing song) on the
tomb of Seikilos,
c. 100 B.C.

of the music changed also, although few details of the change are known, and the artistic level of music gradually declined. The last period of Greek music history is shrouded in darkness.

Surviving examples. Less than a dozen examples of Greek music have survived, encompassing a period of almost eight centuries. Some are fragmentary and at least one is of doubtful authenticity; a transcription of the entire group occupies scarcely four pages. With so flimsy a foundation, it is understandable that speculation occupies a large place in an account of Greek music.

The earliest of the pieces are a Pythian ode, about 478 B.C., attributed to Pindar of Thebes (this is probably spurious), and a fragment of a choral song from Euripides' *Orestes* of 408 B.C. After a gap of some two and a half centuries, in about 150 B.C., come two hymns to Apollo, found on the walls of the treasury at Delphi, and slightly later, about 100 B.C., a *skolion* (drinking song) carved on the tomb of one Seikilos in Asia Minor. Another gap of some two hundred and fifty years elapses between those relics and three hymns of Mesomedes of Crete, ascribed to the years about A.D. 150 and dedicated to Helios (the sun god), Nemesis (the goddess of vengeance), and the Muse. A Christian hymn from the third century A.D., but in Greek notation, was found as late as 1922 in the famous Egyptian Oxyrhynchos papyrus. A few undistinguished fragments which cannot be dated even approximately complete the meager list of surviving examples of Greek music.

Music Theory

IN CONTRAST to the scarcity of musical fragments and historical facts, there exist a number of treatises in which elements of Greek music have been worked out in great detail. The theoretical system, the pitch levels, and the notation are discussed. Because of ambiguous terminology and changes in musical concepts across the centuries, however, these sources contain many inconsistencies.

Mathematical speculation plays an important role in Greek music theory. Pythagoras, philosopher and mathematician of Samos in the sixth century B.C., is usually credited with the discovery and measurement of the vibrations which give rise to tone. His principal apparatus, and one which served generations of musical scientist-philosophers, was the monochord, an instrument with one string and a movable bridge that allowed the length of the segments of the vibrating string to be varied at will. Although his contributions to music are considered minor by Curt Sachs, one of the foremost authorities on Greek music, it seems probable that Pythagoras expressed the divisions of the string by numerical ratios. Applications of the Pythagorean ratios, which formed the scientific basis of music theory in the Middle Ages, were not restricted to actual sounds; they were also extended to mathematical relationships within the structure of the cosmos. Thus arose the "harmony of the spheres," or theory of celestial music, which also supposedly developed from the theories of Pythagoras.

It seems likely that the theory of vibration and vibration rates was perfected about two hundred years later (*c.* 380 B.C.) by Archytas of Tarentum (modern Taranto, in southern Italy) and built by the neo-Pythagorean school into an exact mathematical system. The definition of music as a "movement of numbers" continued to be valid for musical philosophers for many centuries. Ptolemy's famous musical treatise, *Harmonikè,* dating from about A.D. 130–140, became the standard work of this school.

Aristoxenus of Tarentum represents another school of musical theorists.[2] As early as the third century B.C. he recognized the principle that music and its relationships could be determined not only by numbers and string lengths, but also by ear. This almost aesthetic way of reasoning was influential as late as the Middle Ages. Yet another theorist, Aristides Quintilianus, summed up the entire music theory of antiquity in three books, *Peri mousikes* ("About Music"), written about A.D. 150. The last great theorists of Greek music were Boethius (*c.* 480–524), philosopher, statesman, and counselor to King Theodoric, and his associate at the court, the long-lived Cassiodorus (*c.* 485–*c.* 580). Boethius' five books, collectively entitled *De institutione musica,*[3] dominated the theoretical literature for a thousand years. But since the sixth century no longer knew Greek music in its pure classic form, many discrepancies and misunderstandings found their way into Boethius' work, adding to the confused and contradictory state of our knowledge of the period.

The Greek system of scales. All scale patterns in Greek music employ the *tetrachord* as a basic unit. The tetrachord is a group of four tones in which the outer tones are a perfect fourth apart and the inner tones are variably spaced. Three types of inner spacing gave rise to three different genera: (1) counting downward from the top tone, the spacing of whole-step, whole-step, and half-step constitutes the *diatonic* genus; (2) the spacing of a minor third and two half-steps forms the *chromatic* genus; (3) the spacing of a major third and two quarter-steps forms the *enharmonic* genus (see EXAMPLE 2). The discussion that follows will be based on the uses made of the diatonic genus only.

E X A M P L E   2

Types of tetrachords

Diatonic   Chromatic   Enharmonic

---

2 A section of his *Harmonic Elements* is given in *SRMH,* pp. 25–33.

3 A selection from Boethius' work is given in *SRMH,* pp. 79–86; and from Cassiodorus', pp. 87–92.

A scale pattern or mode consists of a series of two tetrachords which can be combined in either of two ways: *disjunct,* in which one tetrachord lies next to the other; or *conjunct,* in which the two tetrachords overlap by one tone (see EXAMPLE 3). One basic mode, the Dorian, consists of two

EXAMPLE 3

Combinations of tetrachords

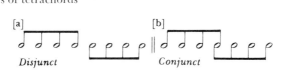

disjunct tetrachords (always reading downward): E-D-C-B and A-G-F-E. The octave formed by these two tetrachords is the principal octave of the Greek system; presumably most vocal and instrumental music was performed in that range.

It is possible, however, to change this arrangement by placing the second tetrachord above (*hyper*) the first, or by placing the first tetrachord below (*hypo*) the second. Thus two additional forms of the Dorian scale pattern emerge; however, the tetrachords must now be employed conjunctly and the missing tone added to fill out the octave, as shown below.

Dorian: ⌐E   D   C   B⌐⌐A   G   F   E⌐

Hyperdorian: (B) ⌐A   G   F ⌐E⌐ D   C   B⌐

Hypodorian: ⌐A   G   F ⌐E⌐ D   C   B⌐ (A)

The complete tonal system (called the Greater Perfect System), used for theoretical purposes, consists of two additional tetrachords placed conjunctly above and below the principal octave, plus one added tone to complete a two-octave span (see EXAMPLE 4). The Greek name of the

EXAMPLE 4

The Greater Perfect System

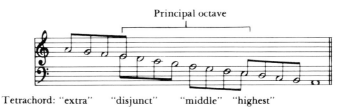

Tetrachord: "extra"   "disjunct"   "middle" "highest"

fourth tetrachord (*hypaton,* "of the highest") may call attention to the position assumed by the kithara in playing the tones of the system; presumably the instrument was turned on its vertical axis so that the bottom strings were higher (in relation to the ground) than the top strings.

Another theoretical configuration, called the Lesser Perfect System, consisted of three tetrachords, all conjunct, plus the added tone (see EXAMPLE 5).

EXAMPLE 5

The Lesser Perfect System

Tonoi. As we have seen, each of the various modes, comprising a different pattern of whole- and half-steps within its octave span, was considered to have the power to affect its hearers differently; the *ethos* of the Dorian mode differed from that of the Lydian, for example. While the Greek theorists are in agreement on this point and even on the particular pattern of each mode, they do not agree on the method whereby each pattern was determined. Nor do later theorists find common ground upon which to base an explanation.[4]

The point of departure in all accounts of the Greek modes is the Dorian octave species or mode, which consists of the tones of the principal octave, e'–e, of the Greater Perfect System (see EXAMPLE 4) and is comprised of two disjunct diatonic tetrachords (see EXAMPLE 2*a*) as follows:

$$\overline{\text{E} \quad \text{D} \quad \text{C} \quad \text{B}} \quad \overline{\text{A} \quad \text{G} \quad \text{F} \quad \text{E}}$$

$$1 \quad 1 \quad \tfrac{1}{2} \quad 1 \quad 1 \quad 1 \quad \tfrac{1}{2}$$

Other modes were theoretically based on other segments of the Greater Perfect System. The ranges of the voices and of the early Greek musical instruments, however, were seldom greater than an octave. In the interest of convenience and practicability, the Dorian octave (e'–e) was used as a pitch standard. Consequently the other modes were necessarily transposed or adjusted to conform to that standard. A scale segment of this kind, when adjusted to the e'–e octave span, was called a *tonos* (plural, *tonoi*).

Each of the *tonoi* was based on a different intervallic pattern or formula. The following diagram will illustrate several of the patterns:

Phrygian:	E	D	C♯	B	A	G	F♯	E
	1	½	1	1	1	½	1	
Lydian:	E	D♯	C♯	B	A	G♯	F♯	E
	½	1	1	1	½	1	1	
Mixolydian:	E	D	C	B♭	A	G	F	E
	1	1	1	½	1	1	½	

4 Compare, for example, Adler, *Handbuch der Musikgeschichte*, I, pp. 41–42, and Sachs. *The Rise of Music in the Ancient World*, pp. 225–37.

The formulation of each of the *tonoi* other than the Dorian may be explained in a number of ways; the Phrygian can serve as an example. (1) In the first explanation, the Phrygian *tonos* is formed by changing the spacing of the intervals within each of the tetrachords comprising the scale—from the normal Dorian spacing of 1-1-$\frac{1}{2}$ to the spacing of 1-$\frac{1}{2}$-1; the pattern shown above for the Phrygian illustrates the change. (2) In another explanation, it is the result of using the octave segment d′–d (that is, the tones d′-c′-b-a-g-f-e-d) and transposing the segment a whole-step upward. That result is given in the following diagram, which may be compared with that given in the other method, above.

Segment d′–d: D   C   B   A   G   F   E   D

                        1 $\frac{1}{2}$ 1 1 1 $\frac{1}{2}$ 1

Transposed to e′–e: E   D C♯ B   A   G F♯ E

                        1 $\frac{1}{2}$ 1 1 1 $\frac{1}{2}$ 1

(3) According to a third explanation, the Phrygian *tonos* results from duplicating the basic Dorian pattern a step higher (to embrace the F♯ octave span) and converting the new pattern to fit the range of the principal octave. This conversion is done not by simple transposition, however, but by removing whatever tones lie above e′ and adding appropriate tones at the lower end of the pattern to complete the octave e′–e. This process is illustrated in the following diagram and in Example 6.

Dorian pattern on F♯ segment: F♯ E   D C♯ B   A   G F♯

                                    1 1 $\frac{1}{2}$ 1 1 1 $\frac{1}{2}$

Altered to conform to e′–e range: ( ) E   D C♯ B   A   G F♯ (E)

                                        1 $\frac{1}{2}$ 1 1 1 $\frac{1}{2}$ 1

EXAMPLE 6

The Phrygian *tonos*

This tone is removed
This tone is added
The result is the Phrygian *tonos*

In each of these three cases the final result (namely, the pattern of the Phrygian *tonos*) is identical; only the methods of arriving at the result differ. These different theoretical explanations account for some of the difficulties usually experienced in comprehending Greek music theory. Apparently theorists of antiquity differed among themselves (understandably so, for the period of Greek musical activity covered almost eight centuries), and more recent writers have adopted one or another of the methods discussed here. For example, one point of view formulated in the late nineteenth century, discussed as (2) above, explained the Phrygian as an original mode on the white-key octave d′–d; another mode, the Lydian, on the white-key octave c′–c, and so on.

The most recent investigations of Greek music make possible the explanation discussed under (3) above. That explanation, which is the one adopted here, has the virtue of conforming to what is known about Greek string instruments and their various tunings. It aids in resolving certain inconsistencies found among the earlier theorists and seems to come closer to the actual musical practices of antiquity. It makes it possible to extend the system of *tonoi* to the eight most commonly mentioned.

In addition to the three *tonoi* mentioned above (Dorian, Phrygian, and Lydian), the system included the *hypo* forms of those three (Hypodorian, Hypophrygian, and Hypolydian) as well as the Mixolydian and eventually the Hypermixolydian. The system of eight *tonoi* is given in EXAMPLE 7. If each *tonos* in that example is compared with the *tonoi* above and below it (by observing only the tones given in whole-note symbols), the relationship of its pattern to that of the Dorian is seen; the formula of whole- and half-steps is identical in each, namely 1-1-½-1-1-1-½. If the diagonal lines are observed, however, each *tonos* is seen to embrace the range e′–e and to have an individual pattern of whole- and half-steps. It is this essential difference between one *tonos* and the others which contributes to the differences in *ethos* that the philosophers of antiquity ascribed to them.

At some undetermined time in the period of Greek music, an alternate tuning was adopted. This tuning had the effect of shifting the whole corpus of the modes a half-step higher; the basic octave e′–e became f′–f in the new tuning, and all *tonoi* were adjusted accordingly. Apparently the "F-series," as it is called, did not entirely supplant the E-series, but was used along with the latter. There is even some evidence that the F-series is the older of the two. In any case, the presence of two systems eventually made it possible and desirable to increase the number of modes to fifteen.

Texture. None of the Greek writings on music permit us to conclude that more than one independent melodic line was used in any of their music. In other words, it is highly questionable whether harmony or counterpoint, in their modern senses, existed. All performance was in unison, or in octaves whenever high and low voices were used together in choruses. References exist to an ancient harp, the *magadis*, which could be played in octaves. The term "magadizing," which refers to playing or singing in octaves, is derived from the name of that instrument. No Greek sources, however, permit the conclusion that more than one *independent* line was ever used. As in Oriental music, heterophony (see page 7) could occur when two performers departed from a unison, or when tones of a melody were either repeated or omitted in an accompaniment. In regard to harmony in our sense, it is likely that two or more tones must have sounded together on occasion, but there is no evidence that the sounds were organized. The terms "concord" and "discord" appear, but the term "harmony" had different meanings in Greek music than in our own; in one definition, harmonies are the modes themselves.

Rhythm and meter. The question of rhythm in Greek music is equally problematical. Meter was determined by the succession of long and short syllables in the lines of verse. The familiar patterns of dactyl, iamb, and all the others resulted; a group of two beats formed a metrical foot con-

EXAMPLE 7

The eight *tonoi*

ANTIKENSAMMLUNGEN GLYPTOTHEK UND MUSEUM ANTIKER KLEINKUNST, MUNICH

Women playing harp, kithara, and lyre. Southern Italian volute cup, 5th c. B.C.

sisting of *arsis* ("lifting" or upbeat) and *thesis* ("dropping" or downbeat). Combinations of beats into different feet were permitted, for example, an iambic foot (short-long) and a trochaic foot (long-short); larger combinations of three and four feet, resulting in irregular combinations of accents, were also common. The metrical accents did not always coincide with the word accents; the latter were indicated by acute, grave, and circumflex symbols and were associated with the pitch inflections and pitch levels of the language.

It seems that in actual musical performance a combination of the two accentual systems was achieved, leading to a complete flexibility of rhythm. Large deviations from a basic tempo probably did not occur, if only because of the static character of the melodies. Since Greek music had no emotional connotations which would justify fluctuations in tempo and dynamics for the sake of expression, it is also likely that no striking deviations in dynamic level took place.

Instruments. The most common musical instruments used by the Greeks have already been mentioned. The oldest was the lyre. It consisted of a round resonant body to which two yokelike arms were fixed, with strings attached to a bar which ran between the arms of the yoke. The strings were plucked either with the fingers or with a plectrum. The older pentatonic tuning (without half-steps) was later modified when more strings were added. The lyre was gradually superseded by the kithara, a younger, more refined instrument of Oriental ancestry. Similar to the lyre in general construction, its complement of strings was more variable; from four strings it was expanded to seven, later twelve, and finally as many as eighteen.

The aulos, as mentioned above, was a woodwind instrument, also of Oriental origin, and was brought to Greece within historical times, roughly 800 B.C. It is a double-reed instrument, resembling two oboes joined as a pair and played by one performer. The aulos was primarily used for the drama, for martial purposes, and for accompaniments to dancing.

Although the musical remains of Greece are minimal, its performance practices uncertain, and its theoretical system not always understandable, Greek music exerted a tremendous influence on music of the West. The mathematical components of musical intervals and the construction and naming of the modes (retained with significant changes in the Medieval period's church modes) remained a heritage upon which the Middle Ages built.

Woman playing double flute. Detail from marble krater, Roman adaptation of Greek model. 1st c. A.D.

Music in Rome

THE ROMAN empire, politically and economically superior to Hellas, never attained a comparable cultural independence in its music. The earliest influences came from the Etruscans, who contributed brass instruments for military uses. Greek musical culture was imported later, mainly by way of Sicily, which remained within the orbit of Greek civilization. There are no Roman musical monuments extant, and literary references to music are scanty. While many poets and other writers decried the noisy aspects and low standards of Roman music, they mentioned orchestras and musical instruction. There are also references to music for social entertainment, and explicitly for funerals. Extensive musical activity took place among musical amateurs, among whom Nero (Roman emperor from A.D. 54 to 68) must be included.

More kinds of instruments and more varied ones were used in Rome than in Greece. The ancient dramas and comedies, some of them translated from the Greek, mention music played on pipes. Both wind and percussion instruments were employed; the performers, active in groups or as virtuosi soloists, were principally Greeks. Representative of the brass instruments are the *tuba,* a long cylindrical trumpet; the *cornu,* a conical hornlike instrument; and the *bucina,* probably made of animal horn. The aulos (named *tibia* in Latin) and the kithara were employed as in Greece. Among the percussion instruments are the Egyptian *sistrum* or rattle, and the *scabellum,* a wooden instrument attached to the sandals of actors to help them keep time.

In summary, nothing resembling the Greek doctrine of *ethos* appeared in Rome, nor has any treatise on musical theory survived—if indeed any was ever written. Rome was too much occupied with building and maintaining a political empire to engage extensively in musical activities.

ৼঌ 3 ৵

Music in the Early Church

Few products of artistic activity have had more influence upon the course of Western civilization than the liturgical music of the early Christian church. It served as a source of cultural stability during the chaotic centuries that saw the death of one great historical epoch and the birth of another. It expedited—and in some cases it may have made possible—the diffusion of Christianity to the furthermost corners of the Western world.

This liturgical music began by bending Roman patricians and northern barbarians alike to its mystical purposes. It continued for over a thousand years to illuminate the sacred texts and carry their meanings deep into the hearts of all who heard them. In spite of having been composed in a highly sophisticated idiom, in spite of running counter to the musical impulses of the people it sought to enthrall, it eventually conquered all its opponents and became the fundamental artistic expression of the entire Christian world.

In turn, having reached its widest distribution and its greatest vitality, it then became a source of musical supply for Gothic and Renaissance composers. Musicians from the eleventh century onward developed new techniques of composition and applied them to the material of the earlier liturgical music, building various new polyphonic forms on this substructure. In the early fifteenth century, when polyphonic choral music emerged, it too was largely derived from the old melodies. Even the refined language of Renaissance sacred music derived vocabulary and structure from these sources. And these developments led, in turn, to new musical forms and textures which are still vital today.

Detail of drawing from Velislav's Bible, 1340. [UNIVERSITY LIBRARY, PRAGUE]

But even while Roman liturgical music was providing so generous a supply of melodic material for the creation of new sacred repertoires, it lost ground as an independent musical literature and eventually went into a long period of decline. Only recently has it been partially restored to its ancient place. Its religious validity, however, its expressive potency, and its musical strength are scarcely less today than they were almost two thousand years ago. Remarkably enough, this power can make itself felt to sensitive listeners regardless of their church affiliations, for the melodic beauty of the music transcends religious lines.

Plainsong

THE LITURGY of the early Roman church, taking shape across a dozen centuries, contained many elements drawn from other forms of Christian worship. Some elements may be traced to the Near Eastern branches of the Church, while others had much in common with pre-Christian and Oriental elements.. An essential point of similarity between the Roman and other liturgies was in the style of the music that accompanied the delivery of the sacred texts. Identified by a number of different names during the first thousand years of its existence, it eventually came to be known as *cantus planus* (plainchant or plainsong).

The tendency of the Christian liturgy to be influenced by the past is not an isolated phenomenon in the history of the Western world. The dwellers in early Christian Europe inherited many strong and enduring cultural elements from the declining ancient civilizations. For well over a thousand years European aesthetic concepts were those that pre-Christian philosophers had recorded and clarified. The musicians and churchmen of the first millennium were content to utilize and be led by those concepts simply because their force was still vital and present.

The various plainsong repertoires consist of thousands of monophonic, rhythmically free melodic lines to which the liturgical texts are set.[1] This large body of chant, always linear and unaccompanied, may be divided into two basic types. (1) A recitativelike declamation, usually set with one note to a syllable and with a small compass of two to six tones, was called *accentus*. It was employed mainly in the recitation of Psalms and prayers and appeared in nine "psalm tones" or formulas—one for each of the church modes (see below, page 42) and one called *tonus peregrinus* ("wandering tone" or "strange tone") because it did not conform to any of the eight modes. (2) A more melodic type with a wider range and set in three different styles was called *concentus*. The three styles, which often appeared in combination within a single chant, were: (a) syllabic, in which each syllable of the text was set to a single tone; (b) neumatic, in which several tones were sung to one syllable; (c) florid or melismatic, in which a larger number of tones or groups of tones were provided for one syllable (see EXAMPLE 8). A florid melodic line set to a single syllable of text is consequently called a "melisma."

1 See *HAM*, Nos. 10–15, for examples.

EXAMPLE 8

Styles of *concentus*

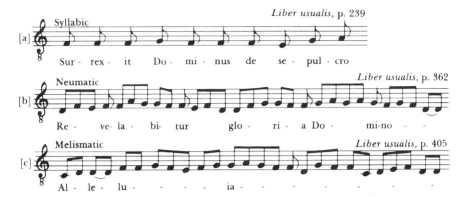

During the first centuries of the Christian era, churches in various geographical regions developed their own liturgies and their own plainsong "dialects." Among these dialects or versions was one centered in Milan, another developed by the Visigoths in Spain and the later Spanish Christians, yet another taking root in the Frankish empire, and a fourth identified with the practice in Rome. The Milanese version, traditionally associated with the name of Ambrose, Bishop of Milan from 374 to 397, is called Ambrosian chant. More ornate than the Roman version, it is still used for certain services in the diocese of Milan. The Spanish version, called Mozarabic chant, retained its integrity and liturgical position until about the eleventh century. Even today some of its melodies are used in the cathedrals of Toledo and Valladolid. Gallican chant, as the Frankish version is known, was abolished after the time of Charlemagne in the ninth century, and only a few fragments were transferred to the Roman repertoire (but see below, page 29). It remained for the Roman dialect to emerge as the most influential; Roman chant is in general use today in all Roman Catholic churches.[2]

Gregorian Chant

EARLY in the Christian era Rome became the dominant ecclesiastical authority in Europe. The chant repertoire emanating from that city eventually spread across most of the European continent, and it is the Roman chant with which the majority of Western musicians in later centuries concerned themselves. Documentary materials covering the first six or seven centuries of the chant's existence are scant. It is known, however, that all Christian chant had its roots in the Jewish liturgy, and that several textual elements (for example, *Amen, Alleluia,* "Holy, Holy,

2 Examples of Ambrosian, Gallican, and Mozarabic chant are given in *TEM*, Nos. 1–3, *Redde mihi, Popule meus, Gaudete populi.*

Holy" of the *Sanctus,* and others) were derived from that liturgy. It is likely, further, that Byzantine and Greek influences were at work in Christian chant, but at a time after the beginning of the Christian era.[3] The surviving documents give some details of performance and some steps in the growth of the liturgy, but not in sufficient quantity to allow a detailed presentation to be made.[4]

According to traditions extending back to about the eighth century, Roman chant was organized and codified during the pontificate of Gregory I, pope from 590 to 604. For over a thousand years, as a consequence, Roman plainsong has been called Gregorian chant. Periodically, however, doubt has been cast upon the historical validity of this term. The latest authorities call attention to a variety of historical evidence which suggests that "Gregorian chant" was developed in France and Germany in the eighth and ninth centuries, and thus is only related to (rather than derived from) the old Roman chant dialect.[5] According to this view, the chant in its Franco-German or Gallican form eventually spread to Rome and displaced the indigenous Roman chant, which may indeed have been codified by Pope Gregory and others. Thereupon the imported chant became standard for virtually all of Europe; and subsequently it became identified with the Gregorian tradition and name.

The tradition linking Pope Gregory's name with the Roman repertoire will most probably endure, in spite of continuing historical research. The term Gregorian chant does serve to distinguish the present official repertoire of the Roman Catholic church from other bodies of plainsong. And even if, as some authorities claim, that repertoire has been misnamed for over a thousand years, it has been transmitted without essential change from at least the ninth century to the present.

Classification. The chants themselves, whose texts are drawn largely from the Book of Psalms,[6] include almost three thousand items. They vary according to their liturgical position and function, and also as to their method of performance. In some cases an entire Psalm is chanted; in others, only a single verse or group of verses. Selected verses of different Psalms are sometimes combined to form a new whole. Hymns, mostly nonmetrical religious poems, are found also. Liturgical requirements are responsible for the selection and arrangement of the text in each case.

---

3 See *HAM,* No. 6b, *Wajigra moše* . . . ; 6c, *Ledovid boruh* . . . ; and 8, *Essose laon.* . . . Other examples are given in *MoM,* Nos. 1, *Laus Deo* . . . , and 2, *Alleluia;* and *TEM,* No. 4, *Veni Creator.* . . .

4 See Apel, *Gregorian Chant,* pp. 38–41.

5 Apel, *Gregorian Chant,* pp. 74–83.

6 The numbering of the Psalms in the Latin Bible does not agree with that in the Protestant (King James) Bible. Psalms I–VIII of the Latin = Psalms 1–8 of the King James; IX = 9 and 10; X–CXII = 11–113; CXIII = 114 and 115; CXIV and CXV = 116; CXVI–CXLV = 117–146; CXLVI and CXLVII = 147; CXLVIII–CL = 148–150. References to Psalms in musical writings are generally made in the following form: the Catholic number is given in Roman numerals, followed in parentheses by the Protestant number in Arabic.

Consequently a classification of the principal items in the Roman liturgy must precede a discussion of the chants.

Eight services, held at intervals through the day, form the series of Divine Office (Office hours and Canonical hours are other terms). These are Matins, before dawn; Lauds, at sunrise; Prime, at six o'clock; Terce, at nine; Sext, at noon; None, at three; Vespers, at sunset; and Compline, after dark. The chants assigned to these Offices are of various types— antiphons, hymns, and Psalms among them. The Chants of the Offices form one of the two major classes of Gregorian chant. In the early Middle Ages the Divine Offices constituted the main part of the liturgy, but at the present time they are observed in their entirety only in monasteries. A few items drawn from the Offices have been incorporated into the general Catholic service, however.

The Chants of the Mass constitute the other major class. This part of the liturgy commemorates the Eucharist, the mystical transubstantiation of the elements into the body and blood of our Lord. Originally the Mass was sung after the hour of Terce, but it could be celebrated after the hour of Sext on ferial days (ordinary weekdays on which there was no feast) or after None on fast days. The Mass grew steadily in importance and structural complexity, gradually becoming independent of the Offices. At the present time it has all but replaced them.[7]

The Mass has a complex structure, in that it contains twenty liturgical items, eleven of which are sung or chanted and nine of which are recited or spoken. Five of the eleven chanted items have texts which vary according to the liturgical year or the special occasion (Marian holidays, feasts of saints, and the like); that is to say, their texts are *proper* to a particular event. Hence these five chanted items with variable texts are called Chants of the Proper of the Mass. Only the remaining six have unvarying texts; they are the Chants of the Ordinary of the Mass.[8] Likewise, the texts of the recited items are either variable (hence associated with the Proper) or fixed (parts of the Ordinary).

A tabular view of the complete Mass in its normal form may clarify the foregoing description (see Table 1). The texts for the Chants of the Mass (both of the Proper and the Ordinary) may in large part be found in the *Liber usualis*.[9]

7 See articles "Gregorian chant," "Mass," and "Offices" in Apel, *Harvard Dictionary of Music;* further, see Apel, *Gregorian Chant,* p. 14.

8 The term "Mass" is derived from the last item of the Ordinary: *Ite, missa est*—"Go, it is dismissed."

9 The *Liber usualis* is perhaps the most useful book for approaching the study of Gregorian chant. It includes chants of the Mass (both Proper and Ordinary) as well as of some Offices, arranged in order for the entire year. Of particular value is the long introduction which explains Gregorian notation, gives directions for performing the chant, and describes the psalm tones. The *Liber usualis* also contains, in the rubrics that accompany its several sections, a variety of liturgical information that is not easily found elsewhere. The book is available with either Gregorian or modern notation.

The *Saint Andrew Daily Missal* contains, in parallel Latin and English columns, the variable (Proper) texts of the Mass—both the sung and the spoken items. The Missal will be useful to those seeking translations of the various liturgical items.

TABLE 1: The Mass in its normal form

Sung (*Concentus*)		Recited (*Accentus*)	
PROPER	ORDINARY	PROPER	ORDINARY
1 Introit			
	2 *Kyrie*		
	3 *Gloria*		
		4 Collects, prayers, etc.	
		5 Epistle	
6 Gradual			
7 *Alleluia*, or Tract (in Lent) with Sequence			
		8 Gospel	
	9 *Credo*		
10 Offertory			
			11 Prayers
		12 Secret	
		13 Preface	
	14 *Sanctus* (including *Benedictus*)		
			15 Canon
			16 *Pater noster*
	17 *Agnus Dei*		
18 Communion			
		19 Post-communion	
	20 *Ite, missa est* or *Benedicamus Domino*		

Three points must be emphasized. One is that the chant classification as set forth here represents the culmination of a long historical process. The Divine Offices, adopting some items from pre-Christian liturgies, arrived at approximately their present-day form about the fifth or sixth century. The Mass, on the other hand, remained in a fluid state for the first thousand years of the Christian era. The Chants of the Proper found their place in the liturgy about the sixth century, whereas those of the Ordinary became standardized at widely varying times. The *Sanctus*, for example, dates back possibly to the second century; the *Kyrie* and *Gloria* were introduced about the sixth, and the *Agnus Dei* late in the seventh; and the *Credo*, finally, did not become an official part of the Roman liturgy until the first decades of the eleventh century.

Another point is that, while details of the Roman liturgy are meticulously prescribed in the official liturgical books, the whole gives the effect of being flexible and free. It is subject to large or small modification on particular days or in special seasons, especially in the observance of the

Mass. For example, the *Gloria* is not sung from the first Sunday of Advent until Christmas, except on feasts, and it is never sung during the Lenten season. On days when the *Gloria* is omitted, the phrase *Benedicamus Domino* replaces the closing *Ite, missa est.* And during Lent the *Alleluia* gives way to the Tract. These are but a few departures from the "normal" Mass; they serve to indicate that the above table of Mass organization gives but an approximation of the fluid and carefully worked out liturgical ceremony that stands at the center of Roman Catholic rites.

The third point in this connection is that the general musical use of the word "Mass" differs widely from the liturgical one. From the fifteenth century onward, musicians composing in the polyphonic style applied themselves to setting the invariable chants of the Ordinary—possibly because such compositions could be performed virtually throughout the Church year and not only on a particular day. Thus the well-known later Mass settings such as Palestrina's *Missa Papae Marcelli,* Bach's Mass in B Minor, and Beethoven's *Missa solemnis,* to name but a few, contain only the texts given in the second column in Table 1 (excluding the last item), and are by no means complete Masses in the liturgical sense. The term "Mass" will be used in this book in the musical sense, referring only to the five chants of the Ordinary: *Kyrie, Gloria, Credo, Sanctus* with *Benedictus,* and *Agnus Dei.*

Notation

Pitch notation. The Gregorian manuscripts which reveal the earliest stages of musical notation date from about the ninth century. They show, above the lines of text, symbols of different shapes and sizes which were probably derived from the Latin or Greek grammatical accents similar to or identical with the acute, grave, and circumflex which survive in modern French. Such symbols, called "neumes" (from the Greek *neuma,* sign or nod), represent single pitches or groups of pitches. A series of neumes usually gives an indication of the general melodic contour or direction of the melody. Exact or even approximate intervals could not be indicated, however; the supposition is that the singer had the chant virtually committed to memory, and that the neumes served only to recall it to his mind as the conductor indicated with his hand the intervallic progression of the melody. At this level of development the system is called "staffless" or "cheironomic" notation. ("Cheironomic" refers to the gestures of the conductor.)

About the year 1000 the practice arose of placing the neumes at various heights above the text, in order to indicate more accurately the distances between the tones. Neumes were also used in conjunction with letter notation to define pitches still more accurately. Simultaneously, many manuscripts of the time reveal that the copyist imagined or actually wrote in one or more horizontal lines above the text. Each line represented a definite pitch (f, c′, and f′, for example); the neumes were then placed higher or lower in relation to the (often imaginary) lines, and a closer suggestion of actual melodic contour and actual intervals was given. This procedure, to which the terms "heighted neumes" or "diastematic notation" are applied, marks the beginning of our modern staff.

The form that Gregorian notation attained about the thirteenth century was made possible by the establishment of a four-line staff, with adjoining lines and spaces representing intervals of a second. This development, attributed to Guido d'Arezzo (*c.* 990–1050), was the result of experiments carried out by many musicians in western Europe across several centuries. It provides a flexible system of staff notation which meets all the requirements of Gregorian chant and is still used in modern chant books.

The system employs the four-line staff and two clefs which indicate the positions of C and F, respectively. The C-clef may appear on any of the three upper lines of the staff, while the F-clef is usually placed on the third line from the bottom. The tones used are restricted to the natural tones C, D, E, F, G, A, B, plus B♭. One leger line may be used above or below the staff; if the notation of a wide-ranging melody would make an additional leger line necessary, the clef is shifted within the chant so that the staff limits will not be exceeded. Vertical divisions (the later measure lines or bars) are of four kinds and are used to mark phrase subdivisions, divisions, and endings.[10]

The more than two dozen neumes employed in the system have shapes which only partially recall the shapes of the neumes at earlier levels of development. They are of three main types: (a) simple neumes, representing one, two, or three notes each; (b) compound neumes, of four or more notes; (c) a group of special, liquescent neumes which, in addition to indicating pitch, imply expressive performance—legato or glissando delivery, a slight retard or delay, different degrees of stress, and the like (see EXAMPLE 10, page 39).

Guido d'Arezzo is known not only for the development of the four-line staff but for his work as a theorist and teacher. The system of solmization he invented proved invaluable in the process of sight-singing, and is still in use today with only minor changes. It involves the association of tones with easily remembered syllables. Guido selected the famous *Hymn to St. John,* each phrase of which (except the last) began on a successively higher tone, thus: C, D, E, F, G, A, G. Further, each of the first five phrases contained a different vowel in its first syllable. The text of the hymn is as follows:

> *Ut* queant laxis
> *Re*sonare fibris
> *Mi*ra gestorum
> *Fa*muli tuorum,
> *Sol*ve polluti
> *La*bii reatum,
> Sancte Joannes.

10 Two kinds are shown in EXAMPLE 10, p. 39; the other kinds were still shorter and extended across only one or two spaces.

34

I. Staffless neumes.

STEPS IN THE DEVELOPMENT OF
GREGORIAN NOTATION

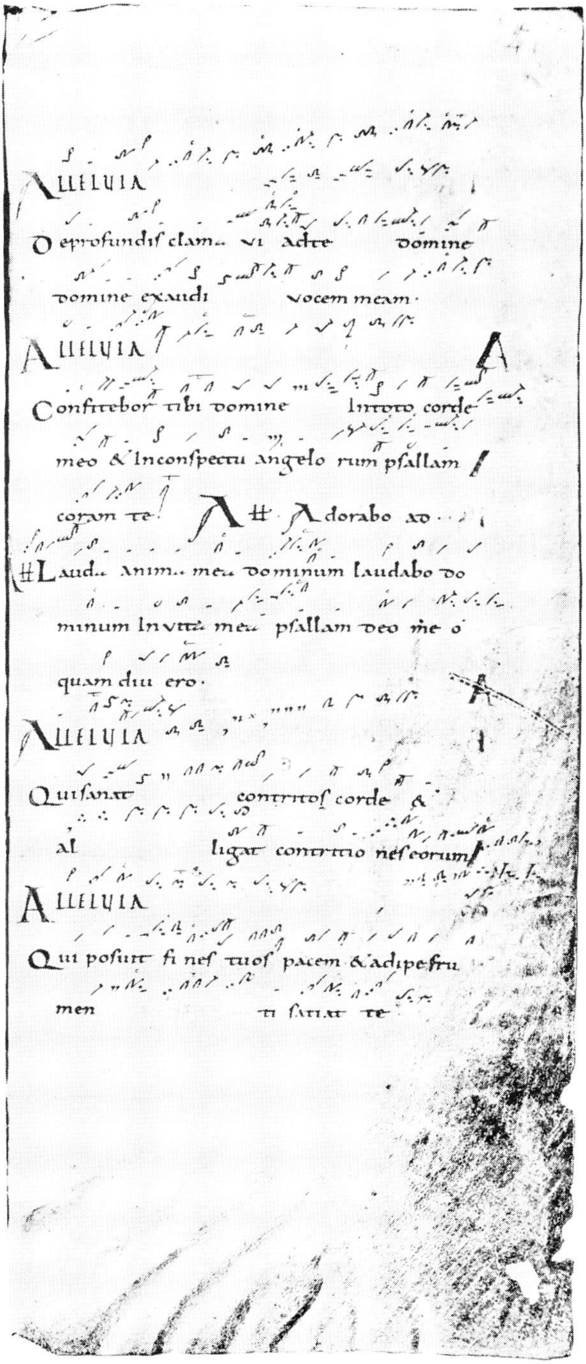

Alleluia

De profundis clamavi ad te Domine
Domine exaudi vocem meam·

Alleluia

Confitebor tibi Domine in toto corde
meo & in conspectu angelo rum psallam
coram te.   Adorabo ad...

Laudat anima mea Dominum laudabo Do
minum in vita mea psallam Deo meo
quam diu ero·

Alleluia

Qui sanat contritos corde &
al   ligat contritiones eorum

Alleluia

Qui posuit fines tuos pacem & adipe fru
men   ti satiat te

II. Heighted neumes.

36

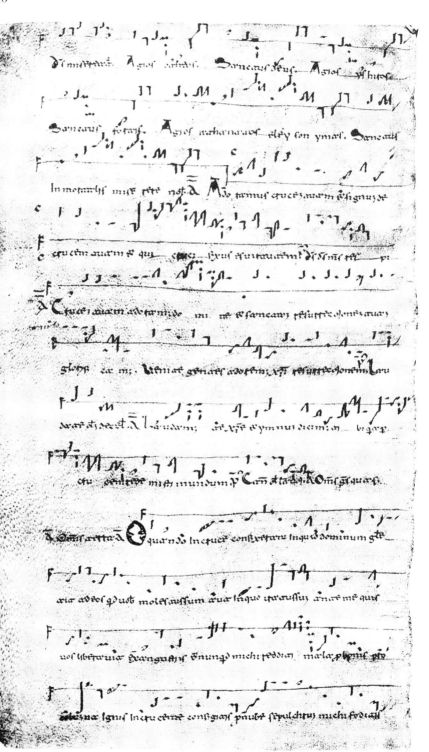

III. One-line notation.

IV. Staff notation.

The six tones, C to A, called a *hexachord,* had an easily remembered structure: whole-steps separated all but the third and fourth (*mi-fa*). The hexachord could be transposed to begin on G, or, through the substitution of B♭ for B, to begin on F. In each case the same pattern of whole- and half-steps occurred; the three positions of the hexachord embraced all the notes recognized in Guido's time. Each note, consequently, could be identified with one, two, or three syllables. When the hexachord system was adjusted to begin with the lowest tone employed in Medieval theory, the result was the pattern in EXAMPLE 9. Guido's system of solmization based

EXAMPLE 9

Naming of tones in hexachords

Hexachord on F: Ut re mi fa   sol la   etc.
Hexachord on C: Ut re mi fa sol la
Hexachord on G: Ut re mi fa sol la

on hexachords is employed today with only two minor changes: the syllable *do* has replaced *ut,* and *ti* has been added to identify the seventh scale step.

Rhythmic notation. It will be seen that insofar as pitch is concerned, Gregorian notation offered few problems. The rhythmic aspects of the notation, however, are still subject to discussion. Three different interpretations are offered: those held by the Accentualists, the Mensuralists, and the Benedictine monks of Solesmes, respectively. Real agreement between them has not yet been reached. The Accentualists hold that the word accents determine the rhythm of the chant: when a melisma occurs, the first note of each neume group should be stressed. The Mensuralists believe that the notes of the chant represent certain unequal rhythmic values: two or three different durations, therefore, should apply in performance. The Solesmes interpretation, however, is the one adopted in the Vatican edition of the liturgical books and therefore in most widespread use.[11]

The principal elements of the Solesmes theory are as follows. Gregorian rhythm is free (unmetrical, as prose is unmetrical). Every note of plainsong, whether notated as a single neume or in a group, has the same value as every other and is equivalent to an eighth note in modern notation. The notes, representing small rhythmic pulses, are thought of as belonging to binary or ternary groups. The first note of each group receives an "ictus," which may be thought of as a mental accent, but which

11 The Vatican-approved interpretation of the rhythmic problem, together with a fuller explanation of the notation, is given in *Liber usualis,* pp. xvii–xxxix. Reese, in *Music in the Middle Ages,* gives a summary of the notation (pp. 130–40) and details of the three rhythmic interpretations (pp. 140–48). See also Apel, *Gregorian Chant,* pp. 126–32.

may not always coincide with the word accent; the groups themselves are combined into the larger divisions of phrase member, phrase, and period.

The Introit for the Fourth Sunday in Lent is given in EXAMPLE 10

EXAMPLE 10

Gregorian and modern notation compared

Liber usualis, p. 559

in both Gregorian and modern notation and may serve to illustrate the elements discussed above.

Performance

AS EARLY as the third century, psalm-singing was a well-established part —perhaps the main element—of the Christian ritual. The writings of the early Church Fathers are filled with references to the use of psalms in Christian communities ranging from northern Africa to the Near East. Models offered by the psalmody of the Hebrew liturgy cannot have been without influence upon the emerging Christian forms of worship. In fact, two large groups of Gregorian chants—responsorial and antiphonal, respectively—may owe their forms to the various ways in which psalms were performed in the Synagogue.

A typical psalm consists of a number of unmetrical verses (that is, verses of different lengths and with different numbers of syllables), each of which is divided into halves. In the Hebrew version of responsorial psalmody, the leader or cantor sang a half or whole verse (V), after which the congregation interpolated a short sentence in the manner of a refrain or response (R); this was continued throughout the psalm, the response being unchanged. In antiphonal psalmody, found especially in the Syrian church, the congregation or choir was divided into halves; apparently one group sang verses or half verses in alternation with the other.

Responsorial performance. In the slowly developing Roman ritual, to about the sixth century, the above methods of singing psalm texts were used but were later altered to meet new liturgical needs. In one group of chants—those which became the responsorial type—the interpolated refrain or response became longer and more elaborate; its performance passed from the congregation to the choir and it was customarily sung not only within the psalm but at the beginning and end as well. Further, and following a directive issued by St. Benedict about 530, the "lesser Doxology" (*Gloria Patri*) was added as a final verse to each psalm.[12] But lengthening the response and adding the *Gloria* made it desirable to shorten the chant as a whole; often the psalm text was cut to a single verse or group of verses. And finally, the response after its first appearance was repeated in part only, the opening phrase or phrases being cut on successive hearings.

With such modifications, the truncated psalm-chants were assigned particular liturgical positions and functions. The Graduals (in the Proper of the Mass) form one group of such responsorial chants, the many florid *Alleluia*s form another. The various components—response (R), modified response (R'), psalm verse or verses (V), and *Gloria Patri* (D)—were combined in a number of ways that allowed the responsorial chant to develop a flexible form. In many cases the form R-V-R' resulted, or R-V-R'-D-R. A short response (*responsorium breve*) from the Office of Prime [13] shows the following form: R-R-V_1-R'-D-R-V_2-R.

In the performance of responsorial chants, the verse or verses and the Doxology were sung by the unison choir. The responses were begun by a soloist (hence often became somewhat florid), but the choir joined in after the soloist had sung the first phrase or portion, called the *incipit*. In modern chant books the point at which the choir enters is marked by an asterisk (see the asterisk after *Laetare* in EXAMPLE 10, page 39).

The group of *Alleluia* chants early developed one characteristic that was destined to be of considerable importance in the later evolution of vocal forms. The opening response of this type of chant consists only of the word *Alleluia,* sung first by the soloist, then repeated by the choir; but the choral repetition is extended by means of a long melisma, called the *jubilus* (j), on the final vowel of the word. The form of the *Alleluia* chant is thus R-R-j-V-R-j. It will be seen later that the presence of the long melismatic *jubilus* was a factor in the development of tropes, sequences, and, indirectly, the motet.

Antiphonal performance. Antiphonal chants developed in the Roman liturgy somewhat later than the responsorial type. Like the latter, antiphonal chants owe much to ancient psalmodic practices. In an early, pre-Gregorian version of psalm performance, a refrainlike sentence, called "antiphon," was attached before and after the set of psalm verses itself,

12 The "greater Doxology" is the *Gloria* of the Mass; its text begins *Gloria in excelsis Deo.* Neither of these is to be confused with the stanza beginning "Praise God from whom all blessings flow," which is often called the Doxology in the Protestant church.
13 See *Liber usualis,* p. 229.

and usually was interpolated after each verse or pair of verses as well. The diagram A-V_1-V_2-A-V_3-V_4-A . . . represents this stage. And as in the responsorial psalm, the *Gloria Patri* was sung as a final verse.

In adopting antiphonal psalmody to the requirements of the Gregorian liturgy, however, the various components—antiphon (A), verse (V), and *Gloria Patri* (D)—were not employed rigidly. The psalms as sung in the Offices usually appear in the form A-V_1-V_2 . . . V_n-D-A, and only in a few chants is the old pre-Gregorian pattern to be traced.

In those chants of the Proper of the Mass that grew out of the antiphonal tradition, an even briefer form developed. The Introit, for example, is usually in the form A-V-D-A. In the Communion (as also in the responsorial Offertory) only the antiphon is left; the psalm verses have been eliminated entirely. Further, many of the antiphonal chants adopted the responsorial method of performance, the soloist singing the *incipit* and the choir entering at the point marked with an asterisk in modern chant books. In certain cases in the Proper of the Mass (as well as in the chants of the Ordinary), an option is provided: after the *incipit* either the responsorial or the antiphonal method of performance is permitted. With the antiphonal method, the choir is divided into two parts and each half sings in alternation the verses that follow.[14]

Modal Theory

LIKE all other factors of Gregorian chant, the systematization of its melodic materials into definite patterns—and eventually into the eight ecclesiastical modes of the Medieval period—required several centuries. Chant melodies were composed and sung for hundreds of years before any attempt was made to classify them as to basic tonal materials (half- and whole-steps) and thus to emerge with a theory of music that accounted for them.

A series of developments from about the sixth century to the eleventh marked the formulation of the theory. Explanations and misunderstandings of Greek music played a part in the developments, along with changing concepts of what constituted the basic scale-structure—whether hexachord (six-tone group) or octave. Theorists such as Boethius (*c.* 480–524), the four or five anonymous authors of a tenth-century treatise called *Alia musica,* Guido d'Arezzo (*c.* 990–1050), and Herman Contractus (1013–1054) contributed to the evolution of the modal theory.[15] The stage of development described here was reached about the eleventh century and served until the middle years of the sixteenth, when a few additions to the modal system and some new terminology brought the theory to its definitive form.

Diatonic scale-segments, each spanning an octave, are constructed on the tones D, E, F, and G. Each segment consists of an overlapping pentachord (five-tone group) and tetrachord (four-tone group). Thus, in the

14 See *Liber usualis,* pp. xv–xvi, for details.
15 Reese, in *Music in the Middle Ages,* pp. 149–64, gives a comprehensive summary; see the bibliographical references given there for additional information.

octave segment beginning on D, the pentachord is D, E, F, G, A, the tetrachord is A, B, C, D. Such an octave segment is called an "authentic mode." The lowest tone of the pentachord, called the *finalis* (final), becomes an important element of the modal structure. Reversing the sequence of the groups, that is, placing the tetrachord below (*hypo*) the pentachord, gives rise to a "plagal mode"; but the *finalis* of the plagal form is still the lowest tone of the pentachord. In some cases the permissible range of the mode is extended downward by one tone (the *subtonium*). The complete system of eight modes, together with the names given in the system, is shown in EXAMPLE 11.

EXAMPLE 11

The system of eight modes

> The octave segment spans the normal range; the note in parentheses gives the usually accepted *subtonium,* and the whole note shows the *finalis.*

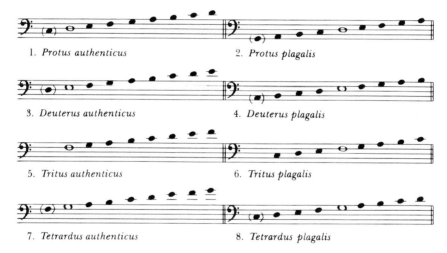

1. *Protus authenticus*   2. *Protus plagalis*

3. *Deuterus authenticus*   4. *Deuterus plagalis*

5. *Tritus authenticus*   6. *Tritus plagalis*

7. *Tetrardus authenticus*   8. *Tetrardus plagalis*

Gregorian chants are classified, in the liturgical books, according to these eight modes. The number of the mode is found at the beginning of the chant, thus: **Grad. 5.** Two factors enter into the classification: the *finalis,* which is normally the tone on which the chant ends, and the *ambitus* or range, which in the normal chant is either from the final to an octave above (in an "authentic" chant), or from a fourth below the final to a fifth above (in a "plagal" chant).

It must be pointed out that in the early stages of development the chants were looked upon as traditional melodic groups or formulas not necessarily related to scale-segments. Apparently not until about the ninth century were systems of classification regularly attempted, and contrary to later practice, it was often the beginning formula of the chant rather than its end that determined the mode to which it belonged.

4

Monophonic Music

In the centuries after the liturgy became virtually standardized and the introduction of new chant types came to an end, composers connected with the Church found little outlet for their creative impulses. The chant repertoire was increased considerably through the addition of many new feast days to the liturgical calendar, it is true, but the texts required by each new feast were set to chants which were either modifications of the existing melodies or in the same general style. In their official capacities, Church musicians became in effect arrangers of melodic formulas.

Interpolations

Unofficially, however, and especially in the monasteries, the impulse to compose was not stifled. From about the ninth century a group of texts and melodies was added to the repertoire—if not sanctioned, at least condoned. These interpolations were of two types, called "tropes" and "sequences." It is likely that an interest in ornamenting or embellishing the chant was basic to the idea of chant interpolations, growing out of the thwarted desire to compose new chants. This may account for the

Woodcut from a French edition of St. Augustine's *The City of God,* 1485.

rapid spread of the practice of interpolation, which eventually was responsible for the creation of many thousands of additions or supplements to the chant that eventually took root in both the Offices and the Mass.

Trope. One element of Gregorian chant lent itself especially well to the new practice, namely, the sections of the chant text that were set in a florid or melismatic style. During the eighth and ninth centuries such sections were often extended to considerable length, and melismatic phrases were added before or after the chant as well. At a time when the chant was notated only with staffless neumes and was transmitted virtually from memory, the extended melismata had been difficult to remember. The custom therefore arose of adding new texts to the melismata, usually commentaries on the chant texts themselves. Often they expanded the sense of the text or amplified it: thus a *Kyrie eleison* ("Lord, have mercy upon us") could become *Kyrie, fons bonitatis, eleison*

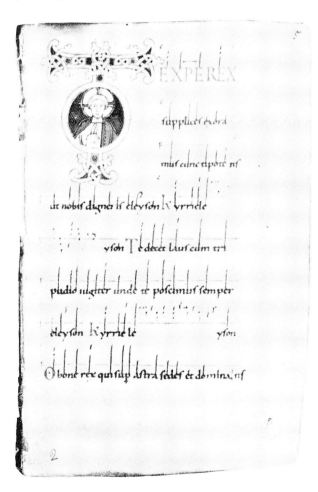

Kyrie trope,
from *Troparium
Sequentiarium
Nonantulanum*
(Cod. Casanatense
1741).

("Lord, fountain of goodness, have mercy upon us"; see EXAMPLE 12).
Thereby the erstwhile florid chant, now syllabic in its newly texted por-

EXAMPLE 12

Kyrie and trope

FROM *Gregorian Chant* by Willi Apel. Reprinted by permission of Indiana University Press.

tions at least, became easier to remember. An addition of this kind is
called a "trope." [1] It is probable that chants on the *Kyrie* text were troped
more frequently than the other chants of the Ordinary.

In another kind of trope, even earlier than the type just discussed, a
commentary with its own new melody was interpolated in the chant;
the new melody might be a paraphrase of the chant into which it was
inserted, or it might be entirely original. EXAMPLE 13a gives a portion of
a *Gloria* chant, and 13b a trope based on that portion. The chant itself
is in Mode 4 (*Deuterus plagalis*); in the example it has been transposed
up a fourth in order to show its relationship to the trope more clearly.

The name of Tuotilo (died 915), a monk at St. Gall in Switzerland, is
usually associated with the invention of troping, but there is evidence that
the process existed before Tuotilo's time and that he was only among the
early composers in the new species. The popularity of the trope continued
for about two hundred years, well into the twelfth century. Troping
apparently ceased to interest composers about that time, for a new kind
of chant elaboration, which was to lead to singing in parts, had begun
to be practiced. Few new tropes were composed, and the existing ones
were gradually removed from the liturgy, where they had enjoyed an

---

1 For examples of various types of tropes, see *HAM*, Nos. 15, *Kyrie* . . . and *Om-*
nipotens . . . ; and 16, *Alleluia* . . . , *Victimae* . . . . and *Jubilemus*. . . .

unofficial status. Their use was finally forbidden by the Council of Trent (1545–1563), but the *Kyries* in modern liturgical books are still named according to the trope texts that were once attached to them.[2]

EXAMPLE 13

Gloria and trope

TRANSLATION:
Glory to God in the highest, to whom citizens of Heaven, crying "Holy," sing their praises; and on earth peace to men of good will, which the angels of God . . . etc.

Liturgical drama. The practice of troping had a direct influence upon the formation of a new class of monophonic song. For high festive occasions tropes with appropriate texts were arranged in dialogue form and sung just before the Introit (the first item of the Mass). Among the first tropes of this kind is one attributed to Tuotilo about the year 900. The lengthy text begins: *Ministers:* "Today we sing of a Child . . . born of a virgin mother." *Singers:* "Who is this Child . . . ?" *Ministers:* "He it is of Whom the Prophet David has spoken. . . ." The trope then leads directly into the Introit for Christmas Day; its closing words, identical with the first phrase of the Introit, begin: "A Child is born to us. . . ."[3]

2 See, for example, *Kyrie lux et origo, Kyrie fons bonitatis*, etc., in *Liber usualis*, pp. 16–62.

3 A portion of this trope is reprinted in *GMB*, No. 3. Another Christmas trope is given in *TEM*, No. 5, *Infantem vidimus*.

A similar trope, *Quem quaeritis*, from about the tenth century, is similarly attached to the Introit for Easter. Here, in dialogue form, is the account of the three Marys before the tomb of Jesus. Across the following centuries this trope was lengthened, new parts and entire scenes were added, and eventually a liturgical drama took shape that became the prototype for other liturgical dramas attached to other festivals of the Church year. Until well into the fourteenth century, stories of the saints, events from both the Old and New Testaments, and many related subjects were dramatized—that is, cast in dialogue form and supplied with music. The music was derived from chant, chant paraphrases, hymns, and even secular songs. This mixture of heterogeneous elements was further compounded by the use of two languages, Latin and the vernacular. During the fourteenth century, the liturgical dramas lost their connections with the liturgy and began to be performed outside the church. Subsequently they were elaborated still further and provided the roots of the so-called mystery plays; as such they were the direct ancestors of European drama and played a part in the evolution of oratorio and sacred opera after the seventeenth century.

Sequence. The other type of interpolation is still represented by a few examples in the liturgy. In this type, the melisma on the final vowel of the *Alleluia* (that is, the *jubilus*) was lengthened and supplied with a text set in syllabic style. This process is similar to standard troping, of course. But in the new type, the melisma was divided into sections which

A copyist monk offering his gradual to St. Gall. Drawing from a St. Gall manuscript.

the singer could perform in one breath, and each section except the first and last was repeated in performance. In applying words, therefore, it seemed natural to set rhyming texts to the paired melodic sections. Thus arose a form which may be diagrammed *a bb cc dd . . . n*. Since the new form followed the *Alleluia* in the liturgy, it became known as a "sequence" (from *sequor,* to follow); the form is often called *prosa* in France. (*Prosa* is an abbreviation of the term "*pro* sequentia" and is a possible source of the word "prose.")

Notker Balbulus (died 912), a contemporary of Tuotilo's at St. Gall, has often been given credit for inventing the sequence. But Notker's own account shows that he adopted the methods of an earlier monk and did no more than continue and expand the process. In any event, sequences became enormously popular. They were composed in all parts of western Europe and in time threatened the standard observance of the liturgy. The Council of Trent (1545–1563), dealing with that and related problems, abolished all but four of the sequences. Later, in the early eighteenth century, a fifth one was admitted to the liturgy. These five sequences are assigned to a position in the Proper of the Mass, following the item (either *Alleluia* or Tract) that occurs after the Gradual (see TABLE 1, page 31).[4]

The process of troping had mixed effects on the integrity of Gregorian chant. On the one hand, it made the florid melismata easier to learn and to remember, thus easier to transmit from one generation to the next. On the other hand, it destroyed the uniformity and universality of the liturgy by adding unsanctified local texts. It kept alive the creative spirit of composers during an age when few other creative outlets were available to Church musicians. It turned attention away, however, from the ritualistic meaning of the text and toward the musical implications of the melody. Not until the middle of the sixteenth century did the Church fully recognize the mixed blessings that troping brought in its train and assign to the Council of Trent the task of purifying the chant repertoire. But by that time the golden age of the chant had long passed and other forms of music had largely usurped the chant's function.

Secular Monophonic Song

A FEW remnants of a secular and of a nonliturgical religious vocal literature, dating from at least the seventh century, are known to music history and suggest that the secular musical impulse in Christian Europe reaches far back into the past. Chief among these remnants is the *Song of Sybil,* a musical setting of a passage from St. Augustine, found in sev-

4 The five sequences are: *Dies irae,* assigned to the Mass for the Dead, and found on p. 1810 of *Liber usualis; Lauda Sion,* the Feast of Corpus Christi, p. 945; *Veni Sancte Spiritus,* the Feast of Pentecost and the week thereafter, p. 880; *Victimae paschali,* Easter Sunday, p. 780; and the eighteenth-century newcomer to the list, *Stabat Mater,* the Feast of the Seven Sorrows, p. 1634v. The Easter sequence. *Victimae paschali,* is given in modern notation in *MoM,* No. 3.

eral manuscripts from Spain, France, and Italy. A large part of this literature, which includes the type later called *planctus* or *plainte,* consists of laments on the death of kings and queens. Included also are settings of Latin texts by Horace and other Roman poets. In the majority of cases the melodies are notated in staffless neumes and hence cannot be transcribed accurately.

The secular song of the eleventh to the fourteenth centuries, however, is in a different category. In many ways it reflects the changes in society brought about by the advent of feudalism. The feudal system had permitted a feeling of security to be born. Barbarian raids from the north and east had ceased temporarily, local governments had come into being, and the Church became active as an arbiter of peace. Society, to some extent unified by the expanding Church, became international: knightly institutions imposed a uniform code of conduct on all men of gentle birth. The relationship of the knight to his lady underwent a change; the symbol of woman idealized was celebrated in a new kind of chivalric poetry. And in the unfolding of that poetry music played a vital part, for the poets were themselves musicians and some of them wrote both melody and text for their songs. Several groups of men were involved in the creation and spread of these secular songs.

Goliards. One group of songs is attributed to the wandering students, minor members of religious orders, who were as much at home on the highways and in the inns as they were in the newly founded universities with which they were ostensibly connected. The goliards, as they were called, were looked upon by the Church as emissaries of Satan, for they often mocked the liturgy with their parodies and satirical songs. But they also paraphrased verses by poets of classical antiquity and brought a fresh, graceful air to literature. Most of the manuscripts (in Latin) contain melodies notated in staffless neumes; thus the tunes they sang remain in the field of conjecture. The poems found in one thirteenth-century goliard manuscript were used in 1937 in an oratorio, *Carmina Burana,* by the contemporary German composer, Carl Orff.

Jongleurs. Of higher repute were the professional singers and instrumentalists called *jongleurs* by their age (whence the English word "juggler") but often referred to as minstrels today. A typical jongleur played or sang for coins tossed by the crowds which assembled in market place and courtyard to hear him. He might also exhibit trained animals, perform juggling and sleight-of-hand tricks, and act as all-round entertainer. He brought news and court gossip to his listeners and sang epic songs dealing with the exploits of past heroes.

Troubadours and trouvères. Late in the eleventh century a new type of poet-musician emerged in southern France, writing in the *langue d'oc,* the language of the region which included Provence. Within a few decades the art of the *troubadours,* as these men were called, had spread across western Europe, especially to northern France. There the poet-musician was called *trouvère*, and writing in the *langue d'oïl*,[5] he added greatly to the emerging song repertoire.

The new movement included men of noble birth in its ranks: Guillaume IX (about 1100), Duke of Aquitaine, Richard the Lion-Hearted (1157–1199), and Thibaut IV (1201–1253), King of Navarre, are notable examples. But men of humble birth—including such names as Marcabru (about 1140), Bernart de Ventadorn (about 1175), and Adam de la Halle (about 1270)—were active also. The probability is strong that often jongleurs accompanied their masters in their travels and did the actual performing. The era of the troubadours and trouvères ended toward the close of the thirteenth century, when the Inquisition, established by the Church to stamp out the remains of the Albigensian heresy, altered the tone of the relaxed, courtly society in which they had flourished.

The new secular activity had its parallels in other countries. The Austrian and German counterparts of the trouvères were called *minnesingers*. They too sang of chivalric love (*Minne*), and they too were drawn from both noble and humble ranks. Among them, in the late twelfth and early thirteenth centuries, were Walther von der Vogelweide, a nobleman who for a time traveled as a jongleur; Neidhart von Reuenthal; Tannhäuser and Wolfram von Eschenbach, both immortalized by Richard Wagner; and many others.

Two other branches of the large and varied monophonic song literature of the Middle Ages may be mentioned. In Italy, in the late eleventh century, a popular religious movement arose as a result of wars and general suffering. A mood of penitence was in the air; people marched in procession, scourging themselves and singing. The movement spread to Germany and became intensified about 1350, when the Black Death was rampant. The songs of these penitents and flagellants were called *laude* in Italy and *Geisslerlieder* in Germany.

Monophonic songs are represented in Spain by a large collection of *cantigas*, assembled by Alfonso X, king of Castile and Leon from 1252 to 1284. The texts of the *cantigas*, written in Galician-Portuguese, are concerned with miracles wrought by the Virgin Mary. It is likely that these songs were influenced by the troubadours, many of whom were active in Spain in the thirteenth century.

Texts. Like the poems of the jongleurs, those of the troubadours and trouvères dealt with many subjects. Courtly love was well represented, but songs in praise of God, songs that tell of the Crusades, songs of fealty and service (called *sirventes*), spinning songs (*chansons de toile*), laments (*plaintes*), drinking songs, and political satires are also found. Indeed, these songs range so widely in subject matter that they seem to anticipate the flowering of the humanistic movement of the fifteenth century.

5 *Oc* and *oïl* were two French dialect forms of the word "Yes" (compare the modern French *oui*). Thus *langue d'oc* refers to the language in which "yes" is *oc*; and *langue d'oïl*, in which it is *oïl*. Modern French eventually grew out of the latter.

Troubadours visiting a chateau. Fifteenth-century painting.

Melodies. Although the melodies have not been preserved in as great numbers as the texts, and many are still undecipherable, they are sufficiently numerous to give a clear picture of the time in which they flourished. In virtually the entire body of monophonic song written across three centuries in France, Germany, Spain, and Italy, Gregorian chant and folk music provide the strongest influences. The melodies seldom exceed an octave in range. Many fit perfectly into one of the ecclesiastical modes and contain typical modal patterns, while others fit equally well into a major or minor scale and have a decidedly modern sound. Yet the modal influence may have been accepted unconsciously; Johannes de Grocheo, whose *Theoria* (written about 1300, presumably at Paris) is one of the principal sources of information about the secular music of his time, pointed out that modes had no bearing on music of the people (*musica vulgaris*), even though the melodies seemed to be modal. The melodies in general are well defined as to phrases, most of which are of even length (corresponding to four measures in modern notation), although longer and shorter phrases are found.

While exact details of performance are not known, it is likely that the songs were not fully accompanied. An instrumental prelude, interlude between stanzas, or postlude may be surmised, for many of the jongleurs and other performers are pictured with instruments. Further, in some cases an approximation of accompaniment in unison (heterophony) may have been attempted. But this was primarily a vocal art. The melodies dating after the late eleventh century, unlike those of the jongleurs, are given in plainsong notation; thus pitch reconstruction offers few problems. But the rhythmic and metrical aspects of the melodies are still sources of discussion and controversy.

Meter. Manuscripts of the twelfth-century St. Martial school give evidence that a system of rhythmic modes (see page 61) existed and that at the same time a desire to bring metrical regularity to music was abroad. It happens that some of the secular melodies under discussion here are found in later manuscripts which also include two-voice compositions written in the rhythmic modes. This fact has led many scholars to assume that the secular melodies were also designed with the rhythmic modes in mind. A great amount of confusion has resulted from this assumption, and various experts in the field find themselves in complete disagreement. Even where general understanding of the principles has been reached, transcription of details may vary widely. The result is that often a single melody transcribed by various scholars emerges in widely different versions.[6]

Perhaps a solution to the problem of the metrical aspects of these melodies lies in the compromise put forward by Handschin and others. In this view, some melodies can be cast in the rhythmic modes and others cannot. In many melodies a rhapsodic, free expression is most suitable, in others a metrical rhythm akin to the dance seems appropriate. The confusion arises from overlooking individual rhythmic characteristics in the melodies.

Forms. The texts of the songs are characterized by short lines, usually from five to ten syllables in length, arranged in stanzas seldom less than six lines long or more than ten. Rhyme schemes are of several kinds, with couplets and distichs predominating.[7] And the rhyme scheme of one stanza is not necessarily carried out in all the stanzas of a poem. Finally, a refrain, which may be as short as three syllables or longer than the longest line of the stanza, is often present. The refrain may be sung before as well as after or within the stanza, and it may vary from stanza to stanza.

The troubadours, trouvères, and all the others were both authors and composers; in many cases they probably conceived text and melody to-

6 See, for example, in *HAM*, No. 18c, *Reis glorios*, a *canzo* by Guiraut de Bornelh as transcribed by Anglès, Gérold, and Besseler, respectively.

7 A couplet is a pair of lines in a series rhyming *aa, bb, cc,* etc.:

> Nature and Nature's laws lay hid in night:
> God said, "Let Newton be!" and all was light.
> —POPE.

A distich is a pair of lines in a series rhyming *ab, ab,* etc.:

> The rain set early in tonight,
> The sullen wind was soon awake,
> It tore the elm-tops down for spite,
> And did its worst to vex the lake.
> —ROBERT BROWNING.

gether. Thus there is likely to be an intimate relationship between the two. And in view of the variety of forms in the texts, it is not surprising that a large number of formal patterns appear in the melodies. The melodic fragments or phrases with which the composer worked were often repeated for successive couplets; the same phrases were often used later in the stanza, or in the refrain. Thus, with a minimum of melodic material, the composer created subtle, highly organized, and often symmetrical songs.

Simplest among the forms are those in which repetition is the guiding principle. The *chanson de geste,* sung by the jongleurs, was of this type. A short melodic fragment was repeated for each line of the text, and a new fragment was sung at the end of each stanza; the entire stanza was called a *laisse.* The diagram *a a a a* . . . *b* illustrates the type. When the final line (*b*) was sung as a refrain (*B*) by the audience, in the form

E X A M P L E 14

Anon., *Lai*   [Beck, *Cent Chansons*

TRANSLATION:
It is fitting that in song I rid myself of the grief and ill caused by love, which has wounded me shamefully but has promised that I will soon be comforted. If I suffer, I shall be ready; if I die, I shall be cured. If it please God, I shall love the fair one; for which fidelity I shall serve without wakening. But in speaking ill, they have killed themselves; they are quite conscious of having injured me; and if God wills, they shall be given the lie. (*Translated by Leon P. Smith*)

a a a a . . . bB, the form was called a *rotrouenge.* Other variants of refrain-form appear also.

Many other applications of the principle of repetition also exist. The *lai,* modeled upon the sequence (see page 47), had the form *aa bb cc dd . . . n;* each of a series of couplets was given its own melodic phrase, and a single fragment called *cauda* ("tail") ended the stanza. EXAMPLE 14 illustrates the type.[8] In some cases the song is composed of only one couplet and an unrepeated phrase longer than the couplet, thus: *aa b———;* then the refrain is not employed. In this case the form is called *chanson,* and is similar to the *Bar* of the minnesinger.

Repetition plus symmetry is found in a number of forms of which the *virelai* is the best-known representative. In the *virelai* a refrain (*AB*) is followed by a couplet (*cc*) and by the refrain melody in a distich with a new text (*ab*), after which the refrain is repeated; the entire form is *AB cc ab AB.*[9] A variant of the *virelai* form is seen in EXAMPLE 15, in

E X A M P L E   15

Colin Muset (?), *Chansonnette*   [Beck, *Cent Chansons*

TRANSLATION:
When I see winter returning I should like to settle, if I could find a big-hearted host who would not wish to tell that he had pigs, cows, sheep, drakes, pheasants, venison, fat hens, capons, and good cheese in baskets.
(*Translated by Leon P. Smith*)

which the middle sections are reversed and no specific mention is made of a refrain; the form is thus *ab ab cc ab.* The Italian *ballata* and *lauda* of the thirteenth and fourteenth centuries are similar to the *virelai,* as

8 Another example is found in *HAM,* No. 18d, *Kalenda maya;* here it is called *estampie,* a term which properly belongs in the field of dance music. Note that the melodic couplet sometimes has a different cadence at the repetition, hence the first and second endings.

9 *HAM,* No. 19f, *C'est la fin,* provides an example. In this example line 1 is the refrain (*AB*), lines 2 plus 3 form the couplet (*cc*), line 4 is the distich (*ab*), and line 5 repeats the refrain (*AB*). Another *virelai* is given in *MoM,* No. 4, *Or la truix.*

are the *Geisslerlieder* of fourteenth-century Germany. In most of these cases, a refrain begins and ends the stanza, and new material appears in the middle.

Among the most graceful and charming of the forms is the *rondeau*. Its text is six or eight lines long, and its melodic material consists of two fragments (*a* and *b*) sometimes sung by the soloist and sometimes by the audience as a refrain (*A* and *B*). The complete *rondeau* in the six-line version is in the form *a A ab AB;* in the eight-line version the refrain is sung at the beginning of the stanza also.[10] Given two melodic fragments (see EXAMPLE 16) and the formal diagram *AB a A abAB*, the entire melody can be constructed.

EXAMPLE 16

Fragments of a *Rondeau*

An older form of troubadour song is represented by the *vers*, whose distinguishing mark is that the melodic phrases do not repeat but differ with each line. Thus a *vers* is a through-composed form for which the diagram *a b c d e . . .* is appropriate.[11]

The last class includes a popular troubadour form (called *canzo*), which was widely imitated by the trouvères (as *ballade*) and the minnesingers (as *Bar*). In essence it consists of a phrase once repeated and followed by a contrasting phrase, thus: *aa b.* In practice, the end of the second phrase often included a portion of the first, and sometimes the entire first phrase was included in the second.[12] In other examples the two melodic phrases are combined in yet other ways as well, so that a general air of improvisation is suggested.

---

10 Example 19d in *HAM*, a *rondeau* with the title *En ma dame,* is of the eight-line type.

11 *HAM*, No. 18a, *Pax in nomine Domini*, by Marcabru, and No. 20a, *Swa eyn vriund*, by Spervogel, a twelfth-century minnesinger, are examples.

12 See *HAM*, No. 18b, *Be m'an perdut*, for a *canzo* by Ventadorn which ends with the last three measures of phrase *a;* and No. 20b, *Nu al 'erst*, a *Bar* by Reuenthal, in the form *aa b a.* Another version of the Ventadorn *canzo* is given in *TEM*, No. 6.

The Beginnings of
Polyphony

PLAINSONG was in many essentials an importation from the East, imposed upon the newly converted people of western and northern Europe by the developing Roman church. It is not surprising, therefore, that it often ran counter to the latent musical instincts of those people. A conflict of tastes developed; and the history of music in the Middle Ages in large part reflects that conflict.

One of the aspects of this conflict may be seen in the rise of troping, discussed in the previous chapter. Another is seen in the introduction of what may be called vertical troping, that is, the practice of adding new material above or below instead of within the Gregorian chant. This practice, beginning at some undetermined time about the ninth century, brought about significant changes in the manner of performing the chant that in turn led to a new practice of singing in parts and the beginnings of polyphony. Part-singing of this kind is the unique possession of the Western world.

Illustration from Rodericus Zamorensis, *Der Spiegel des menschliches Lebens.* Printed at Augsburg, 1479. [THE METROPOLITAN MUSEUM OF ART]

Part-singing

THE NAMES of the inventors of singing in parts are not known to history, nor are all the steps which led from monophonic plainsong to the simultaneous performance of two or more independent melodies. There is, in fact, considerable doubt as to whether such "steps" even existed; whether singing in parts was not simply an application of an old secular practice to Gregorian chant. Deviations from a unison melody sometimes occurred in Oriental music and in the music of primitive cultures—possibly by accident when different vocal groups performed the same melody together, or possibly when an instrumentalist ornamented the vocal line he was accompanying. Among the Greeks two different versions of a melody had sometimes been sung together, with a consequent dissolution of the unison at the points where the versions differed; this practice was called "heterophony." A number of treatises, commentaries, and other writings, dating after the fifth century, contain obscure passages which, if the accepted interpretation is correct, suggest that singing in parts was practiced. Among such writings are the sixth-century *De institutione musica,* by Boethius; the ninth-century *De divisione naturae,* by Johannes Scotus (Erigena); and a twelfth-century treatise, *Descriptio Cambriae,* by Giraldus Cambrensis.[1]

Organum. Not until about the end of the ninth century, however, is a way of singing part-music described in sufficient detail to serve as the beginning of an historical account. Two of the treatises in which this far-reaching departure from the monophonic tradition is described are the *Musica enchiriadis* (handbook or manual of music) and the *Scholia enchiriadis,* both of uncertain authorship.[2] The new process is called "organum." In its simplest manifestation, it consists of a chant sung at one pitch level by one group, and sung simultaneously at a fifth below by another. The first group sings the *vox principalis* (principal voice), and the second the *vox organalis* (organal voice). Each voice may be doubled, the *principalis* an octave below and the *organalis* an octave above, resulting in a texture comprising four parallel lines. Such doubling might be useful if, for example, a choir of boys and men (both tenors and baritones) were entrusted with the chant performance. In both the simple (two-voice) and compound (four-voice) types, the principle of parallel writing is observed. EXAMPLE 17 shows a portion of chant treated in parallel organum.

Organum at the fourth below is also possible, according to the author of the *Musica enchiriadis,* and the principle of doubling at the respective octaves may again apply (see EXAMPLE 18). But now the forbidden tritone or augmented fourth (marked with an arrow in EXAMPLE 18) occurs, and

---

1 See Handschin, "Zur Geschichte der Lehre vom Organum," in *Zeitschrift für Musikwissenschaft,* VIII (1926); Handschin, "Ein mittelalterlicher Beitrag zur Lehre von der Sphärenharmonie," *ibid.,* IX (1927); and Hibberd, "Giraldus Cambrensis and English 'Organ' Music," in *Journal of the American Musicological Society,* III (1955).

2 A section from the *Scholia enchiriadis* is given in *SRMH,* pp. 126–38.

EXAMPLE 17

Parallel organum

EXAMPLE 18

Organum at the fourth

the avoidance of that interval may become one reason for departing from strict parallel writing. A free type of organum results, one that employs unisons as well as other intervals, and one that may even include contrary motion (indicated by the brackets in EXAMPLE 19) to approach a unison.

EXAMPLE 19

Free organum

The approach (*occursus*) to a unison at a cadence is discussed at length by Guido d'Arezzo in the *Micrologus,* which would seem to indicate that oblique and even contrary motion and their "resolutions" were of considerable interest to theorists of the time (about 1025). It is also significant that the interval of the third (see the syllable -*runt* and other syllables in EXAMPLE 19) is represented in many examples of free organum. The major third, considered a dissonance at that time, and the major second occur mostly in the *occursus,* where they represent mere passing tones between the fourth and the unison. The third, of course, was to dominate the music of later centuries and eventually to cancel out the Medieval preoccupation with the fourth and fifth. In this free type of organum, the possibility of achieving two independent melodic lines is somewhat greater than in the parallel type.

It is easy to overlook the significance of these early examples of part-writing. Ears accustomed to the full and rich polyphony of later centuries may hear in organum only a primitive attempt to ornament a pre-existent chant. In reality, organum marks a radical change in the nature and status of melody itself. For in a melody heard alone, single tones are subordinated to the general contour and rhythmic sweep of the whole. When a second melody is added to the first, however, each tone achieves a vertical relationship to the tone above or below it. The two tones sounding together form a musical interval, perceived not merely as the sum of the two tones but as a new, integrated tonal phenomenon. Attention is diverted from the flow and contour of the first melody to the effect of the vertical sound-complex. This is equivalent to saying that a new musical ingredient—namely harmony—enters musical consciousness.

While it is true that almost every example of organal treatment given in the sources employs a liturgical melody as *vox principalis*, one must not assume that organum originated and was practiced entirely within the Church. The device may first have been used in folk singing, and there is evidence that it was applied to secular texts generally.[3] It was most completely documented and consistently worked out in sacred music, however, and it is in that field that organum eventually developed into polyphony.

Organum, once having captured the attention of the theorists, was referred to more frequently from the eleventh century on. In Guido's *Micrologus,* in the *Musica,* about 1100, by Johannes Affligemensis (formerly referred to as "John Cotton"), as well as in other treatises both earlier and later, further relaxations from parallel writing are sanctioned. The following are important developments in the increasing independence of the *vox organalis:* (1) the traditional consonant intervals of the unison, fourth, fifth, and octave are mixed and not used only in parallel-isms; (2) dissonant intervals, especially major thirds and minor sixths, appear in increasing numbers; (3) contrary motion becomes more frequent, not only at cadence points but within phrases also; (4) crossing of parts becomes a feature to be exploited; (5) in cases where the tritone F–B would appear, the B is replaced by B♭ (this practice had been mentioned by Guido d'Arezzo earlier). Finally (6), as seen not in the theoretical treatises but in compositions themselves, notably in one of the Winchester *Tropers,* the *vox organalis* sometimes appears above rather than below the principal voice—a feature which was to play an important part in the later development of the polyphonic structure; and (7) short melismatic groups in the *vox organalis* may be composed over a single tone of the *vox principalis* (mentioned also by Johannes).[4]

3 See Reese, *Music in the Middle Ages,* pp. 249, 252, 255–58, and 264.
4 See *HAM*, Nos. 25–27, for a series of examples showing the evolution of organum types thus far described. Additional examples will be found in *MoM*, Nos. 6 and 7.

St. Martial School

THE LAST two points mentioned above were destined to be of immediate significance in the formulation of a new repertoire. The expansion of the principles implied there is reflected in a number of compositions dating from the early years of the twelfth century and found in several manuscripts from the monasteries of St. Martial in Limoges, France, and Santiago de Compostela in Spain. In those manuscripts, instead of a short melisma above a single tone of the Gregorian chant (that is, above the *vox principalis*), whole chains of melismata were used. The tone below the melisma was stretched out to an inordinate length, and each tone of the chant could be thus lengthened and sustained (see EXAMPLE 20; the rhythmic notation of this example is arbitrary and uncertain, even as to the exact place where the tenor changes from one note to the next).

E X A M P L E   20

St. Martial: Organum; *Benedicamus*

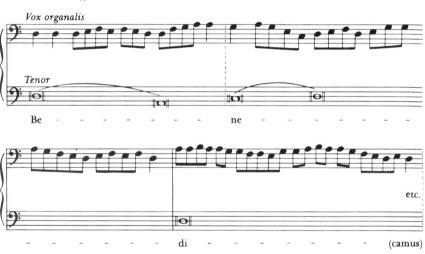

F R O M *Handbuch der Musikgeschichte*, by Guido Adler.
Reprinted by permission of Verlag Hans Schneider, Tutzing,
Germany.

Because of this characteristic prolongation, the *vox principalis* acquired the name *tenor* (from *tenere,* to hold; compare the English "tenure" or "tenant"). The tenor—which, used in this sense, has no connection with the high male voice of later times—became one of the most important technical features of Medieval composition. At about the same time the *vox organalis* acquired the name *duplum.*

The other, older, and simpler style of setting note against note is also represented in the St. Martial repertoire. Indeed, the two styles—note-against-note and melismatic—existed side by side through much of the twelfth century. And even after later developments in the art of music had made the two styles as such obsolete, certain of their characteristics were carried over into the newer music. Indeed, chordal writing, florid melodies, and sustained basses have remained standard musical effects to the present day.

In the interest of clarifying references to style in the pages that follow, a summary of the descriptive terms will be given here: The style illustrated in EXAMPLES 17, 18, and 19, in which one note is placed above ("against") another, bears the name "note-against-note"; at a later time that term became virtually synonymous with "discant style" and was closely allied with "conductus style" (see page 69). EXAMPLE 20, on the other hand, illustrates a style in which long notes in the lower voice and melismata in the upper voice are characteristic. At one stage this was called "melismatic style" or "tenor style"; and about the twelfth century the term "organum style" was usual. We shall hereafter adopt the terms "discant style" and "organum style" for these two contrasting types of texture.

The devices of organum were often applied to those portions of the Mass in which troping had been most frequent, for example, the *Kyrie, Gloria,* and *Benedicamus Domino.* They were also applied to the sequence, the syllabic style of which was well suited to vertical embellishment. Organum appeared also, but in a somewhat restricted sense, in *Alleluia* chants as well as those with other texts. In the main, only the solo portions (see page 40) were set in organum style; that is, the *incipit* (but not the *jubilus*) of *Alleluia* chants, the first phrase or phrases of the response or the antiphon, or the verse in other types. The remaining sections (that is, those appearing after the asterisk in modern chant books) were then sung in choral unison as unembellished plainsong. Other practices appear also in the manuscripts, but the combination of organum (sung by two soloists) and monophony (by a unison choir) as described here was destined to be the longest lasting.

It must not be inferred that the steps in the development of organum from the strict type to the freely melismatic were necessarily taken in the order in which they have been set down here. The various theorists may have done no more than observe the performance practices of their respective times, some of them perhaps centuries old and existing at different stages in different regions (France, Spain, England, and perhaps Germany), and abstract from them the common elements upon which they constructed a theory of evolving organum.

Rhythmic Modes

IN THE St. Martial settings the rhythm of the upper voice (*duplum*) is not precisely indicated. The necessity of determining the length of the notes in that voice became increasingly pressing as the need for proper ensemble with the tenor became apparent. Further, the short note values were difficult for a group of singers to perform together. It was probably out of a desire to regularize the florid upper voice that a new method of rhythmic organization came into use late in the twelfth century. Perhaps "desire" should be replaced by "need," for the increasing rhythmic complexity of the music made a systematic, measured approach necessary—measured, hence metrical.

The first attempt to solve this problem was the system of *rhythmic modes.* Several basic rhythmic patterns were established (although the rhythmic values of individual notes were not exactly determined) and used in certain groupings. Gradually, then, rules for the metrical relationships between longer and shorter notes were introduced. These modes, not to be confused with the church modes (scales) which form the theoretical basis of Gregorian chant, were first used at Notre Dame in Paris, and are associated in particular with the names of Leonin and Perotin (see below, page 65). The rhythmic modes reflect perhaps the first musical application of a theory of rhythm propounded by St. Augustine (354–430) in his treatise, *De musica,* a work which was long thought to deal with poetic meters rather than with music itself.[5] The influence of Augustine's theory can be traced in several of the later manuscripts that deal with rhythm and notation; among them are the *De musica mensurabili positio* by Johannes de Garlandia (about 1240), and the *Tractatus de musica,* by Jerome of Moravia (about 1250), which is in part a compilation of several other and earlier manuscripts. In these sources, the relationships which can exist between long and short tones (and which are fundamental both to the rhythmic modes and to later mensural music) are derived from the metrical feet of classical poetry and reflect various combinations of accented and unaccented syllables in the poetic meters.[6]

The basic principle of modal rhythm concerns the repetitions of a pattern of long and short tones; the pattern is analogous to a poetic foot. In the early stages of modal notation the exact time values were not yet indicated. At a later period the values were implied in or could be deduced from the way in which single note symbols were combined. Only in the last decades of the operation of the system was the measure of duration actually expressed in the symbols.

In the music of the last stage the short tone has the value of a single brief unit of time, called *tempus;* the long tone is normally understood to last through two such units, or two *tempora.* The note symbols for these two tones are called *recta brevis* and *recta longa,* respectively ("correct short" and "correct long"). These two note values added together form a *perfectio* ("perfection"), a unit of three beats. When a perfection contains tones of other than normal length (for example, a long of three *tempora* or a brevis of two *tempora*), the normal relationship within the perfection is necessarily altered. The exact way in which this was to be done was not codified; therefore the term *ultra mensuram* ("beyond measurement") was applied to such perfections.

Out of these patterns, each of which consists of a particular combination of long and short tones, six rhythmic modes are formed. Each mode

5 See Reese, *Music in the Middle Ages,* p. 64, and an opposite point of view in Waite, *The Rhythm of Twelfth Century Polyphony,* pp. 29–31.

6 Another view of metrical relationships is held by Apel; see his *The Notation of Polyphonic Music, 900–1600,* 2nd ed., p. 230.

contains a series of repetitions of the pattern; the last pattern is incomplete, and the equivalent of the missing tone (whether long or short) is provided by a rest which completes the pattern. The rest will thus be equivalent to one *tempus,* or two *tempora,* and so on. A melody written in one of the rhythmic modes is consequently divided into groups of tones, the groups separated by rests. Each group, called an *ordo* (plural, *ordines*), thus consists of at least two recurrences of a pattern and is equivalent to two or more metrical feet. If an *ordo* contains three patterns or feet, it is a "second *ordo*"; if four patterns, a "third *ordo,*" and so on. EXAMPLE 21 will illustrate these points in modern notation.

EXAMPLE 21

The rhythmic modes

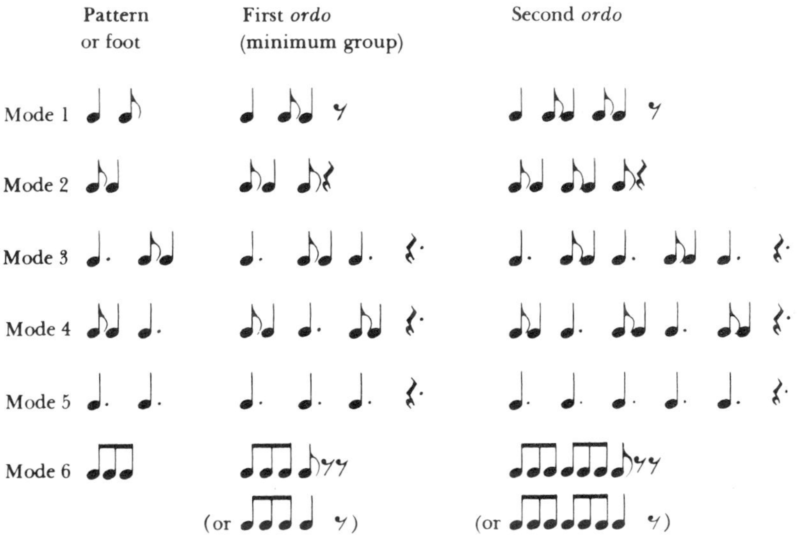

Pattern or foot	First *ordo* (minimum group)	Second *ordo*

The modes are classified either as *recti* (Modes 1, 2, and 6) or as *ultra mensuram* (Modes 3, 4, and 5). The latter are beyond measure (the implication is: "incorrect") because they contain longs which are of more than two *tempora.* The practice of borrowing a pattern from one mode and using it in another, called *fractio modorum,* was also employed. The pattern of the sixth mode, for example (three eighth notes in modern notation), could be used in the first mode, where it replaced the pattern of long-short (quarter note plus eighth); or in the second mode (eighth note plus quarter).[7]

In working out a system of notation that would adequately express the relationships of long and short in the rhythmic modes, the composers of the Notre Dame school (see below) made use of note symbols derived from Gregorian chant as well as several types of ligatures which represent

7 See Waite, *The Rhythm* . . . ., pp. 38–55, for further details.

two or more notes bound together in a definite metrical relationship [8] (see EXAMPLE 22). It must be stressed that although these symbols out-

EXAMPLE 22

Types of ligatures

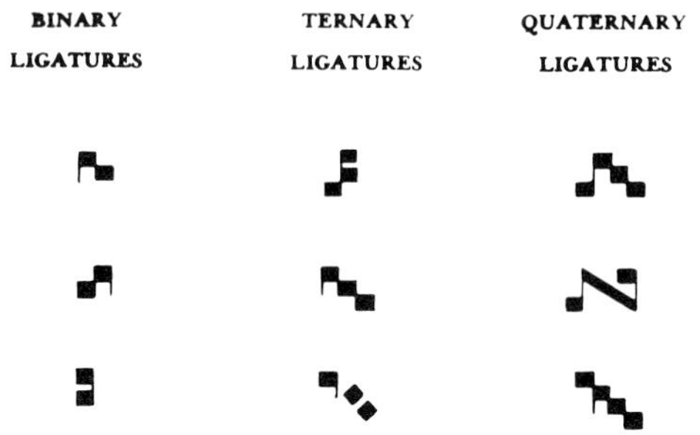

BINARY LIGATURES	TERNARY LIGATURES	QUATERNARY LIGATURES

wardly resemble those used in Gregorian plainsong, they bear certain definite metrical values which the Gregorian symbols did not have—or had lost by the twelfth century.

Definite rules for the relative length of notes in the ligatures were set down by the theorists: by the unknown author (called Anonymous III) of *Discantus positio vulgaris* (about 1230), by Garlandia in *De musica* (about 1240), and many others. The respective modes were recognized by the shapes of the ligatures and the relative positions of the notes and stems.[9] The exact value of a single note had not yet been determined, however. It seems likely that the Notre Dame composers were among the first to assign these specific values to the notes in their music, and that the theorists merely drew conclusions from what the music of those composers actually contained.

The Notre Dame School

THE TYPE of melismatic organum illustrated in the St. Martial manuscripts was carried to a high degree of elaboration by composers associated with the Cathedral of Notre Dame in Paris later in the twelfth century. With the emergence of that school, one can speak of organum both as a way of composing and as a musical form. Earlier pieces had usually been sequences or chant *incipits* set in organum or discant style. From the time of the Notre Dame school, the pieces employ the rhythmic modes and disclose the use of structural principles to such an extent that they became well-rounded, self-enclosed compositions of considerable length. And it is out of the organa forms that several later Medieval musical forms were developed.

8 Such a relationship is seen in the following: ". . . When, however, three notes are joined together, if a rest precedes them the first note is long, the second is a brevis, and the third a long"; from Anonymous IV, quoted by Waite, *The Rhythm* . . . , p. 61.

9 See Waite, *The Rhythm* . . . , pp. 61, 62.

The first important composer of the school to be encountered was Leonin (or Leoninus), who flourished about 1160–1180 but about whom little else is known. The work ascribed to Leonin in manuscript sources is the *Magnus liber organi de gradali et antiphonario,* a cycle of almost 100 two-voice settings of graduals and antiphons for the Offices and the Mass.[10] The two styles seen in the works of the St. Martial school are represented in Leonin also, but they are considerably modified. In Leonin's discant-style organa, for example, the tenor may be broken into a series of notes of even length, and the upper voice may consist of melismata set in a rhythmic mode. In the organum style, the notes of the tenor are extended to many times their original value (similar to tenor treatment in St. Martial); in addition, however, the upper voice, again consisting of a chain of melismata, is cast in a rhythmic mode (see EXAMPLES 23*a* and 23*b*).[11]

While Mode 1 predominates in the *Magnus liber,* Modes 5 and 6 are present in a rudimentary or tentative form, as EXAMPLE 23 reveals. The breaking-up of each foot of Mode 1 into three breves is a step toward the regularization of Mode 6, and the ternary longs (dotted quarter notes) of the tenor similarly anticipate Mode 5.

Clausulae. In a typical composition of the Leonin school, the two styles (discant and organum) often occur side by side to form contrasting sections. The section in discant style is called a *clausula.* The liturgical text was applied only to the notes of the tenor, of course, and in typical cases a single syllable was drawn out across several notes. The singers of the melismatic upper part sang the same syllable as the tenor. Often two sections, sung by the soloists, are separated by a section in unadorned plainsong which is performed in the old manner by a unison choir. There is also a strong likelihood that the *clausulae,* in one or all of their parts, were performed by instruments on occasion.

One composition, which cannot be reproduced here because of space limitations, may be discussed nevertheless: the organal setting of *Haec dies,* the Gradual of the Mass for Easter Sunday.[12] This organum contains eight contrasting sections: three *clausulae* with the upper voices set in a rhythmic mode; three organal sections with greatly extended tenors and free-flowing melismata above the tenors; and two sections in plainsong.

10 The title may loosely be rendered as "great book of organal graduals and antiphons," although pieces in discant style appear also. The original manuscript is not extant, but Leonin's work has been preserved in several later manuscripts. One of these, Wolfenbüttel 677, has been transcribed by Waite in *The Rhythm of Twelfth Century Polyphony,* and several facsimile pages of it are reproduced in Parrish, *The Notation of Medieval Music,* Plates 25, 26, 27*a,* and 28. It may be noted (Plate 25) that the scribe in various parts employed four-, five-, and six-line staves; the choice was determined apparently by the range of the melody being notated.

11 Waite's application of the rhythmic modes in the *organa dupla* of Leonin is not accepted by some contemporary scholars. According to them, only those in discant style are strictly measured. Another example of Leonin is given in *TEM,* No. 9, *Viderunt omnes.*

12 The chant itself is found in *Liber usualis,* page 778; the entire transcription is in *HAM,* No. 29. A setting of this Gradual as a motet is discussed on page 79.

EXAMPLE 23

Leonin, *Magnus liber organi*

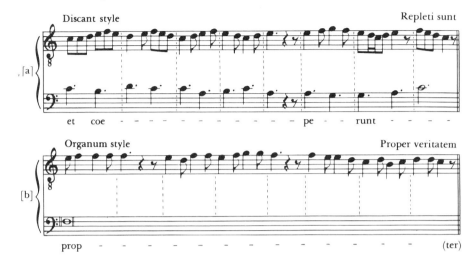

The arrangement of the eight sections is: organum-plainsong-organum-discant-discant-organum-discant-plainsong. EXAMPLE 24 gives the beginning of the fifth (discant) and sixth (organum) sections. The entire composition illustrates the degree to which chant elaboration was carried out in the Notre Dame school; comprising almost two hundred "measures" of ⁶⁄₈ and ⁹⁄₈ meter, exclusive of the plainsong sections, it requires approximately six minutes to perform. The Gradual itself, in its original Gregorian version, required less than two minutes.

Several of the manuscripts that contain music from the *Magnus liber* contain also a number of later *clausulae* and organal sections which are designed to substitute for or replace the corresponding portions of Leonin's pieces. Many of these substitute *clausulae* are attributed to

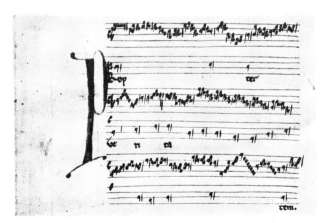

Fragment of
Propter veritatem,
from Leonin's
Magnus liber.
See EXAMPLE 23*b*.

EXAMPLE 24

School of Leonin, *Haec dies*

Leonin's successor, Perotin, whose activity began about in the 1190's and who was perhaps the principal composer of the Notre Dame school. Occurring in both the discant and organum styles, these *clausulae* represent Perotin's chief contributions to the organum repertoire.

There are certain important differences, however, between a *clausula* of the Perotin type and one by Leonin. Leonin in general confined himself to Modes 1 and 3. Modes 5 and 6 are present by implication only, and the modal writing is most often confined to the upper voice in both discant and organum styles. In Perotin's substitute *clausulae,* on the other hand, Modes 5 and 6 are used more consistently, and Modes 1, 2, and 3 are freely employed. Both tenor and duplum are usually written modally. It must be emphasized that the modes were frequently mixed: a pattern from one mode could, on occasion, be used in another; and two modes could be used simultaneously, one in the discant tenor, for example, and another in the duplum.

The characteristic reiteration of modal patterns in both voices of the *clausulae,* the well-planned rhythmic organization of sections in organum style, and the frequent mixing of modes in sections of either style—these became Perotin's trademarks. This disciplined rhythm, so to say, contributed to the later creation of the rhythmic flow that was to become a major factor in the formation of a true polyphonic style.

It may be convenient at this point to adopt the nomenclature of Perotin's time and refer to the lower voice of a two-part *clausula* as "tenor" and the upper voice as "duplum," which we have done several times heretofore. This is especially appropriate here in view of the fact that Perotin composed a number of three-part *clausulae* (see EXAMPLE 25), in which the third voice becomes the "triplum" (from which the word "treble" was

EXAMPLE 25

School of Perotin, *Haec dies*

Haec - - - - - - - - - - - - - - - - (dies)

eventually derived).[13] And a few four-part *clausulae* exist also; the new voice, following the pattern of nomenclature, is the "quadruplum." Perotin's organa for more than two voices contain, in embryonic form, a technical device that prepared the way for imitative writing and even canonic writing in later centuries. Called *Stimmtausch* (exchange of voices) in German musicological writings, it consists of placing in one voice what

EXAMPLE 26

Perotin, *Viderunt*

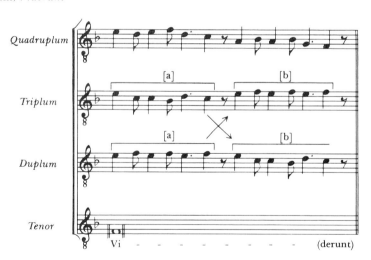

Vi - - - - - - - - (derunt)

another voice has had previously, and vice versa. EXAMPLE 26, a fragment taken from the organum quadruplum *Viderunt,* illustrates the use of the

13 Another example of an organum triplum by Perotin is given in *MoM*, No. 9, *Alleluia.*

device.[14] It is clear that if one voice is consistently given what another voice has had a moment before, the technique of canon is at hand, and that if the practice is carried out not quite so consistently, imitative passages result. Such possibilities took a century or two to be fully realized, however.

Perotin's contributions to stylistic development may be summarized as follows: (1) rhythmic organization of all voices; (2) the use of more than one mode in the same voice part; (3) the increase in the number of voices from two to four; (4) the use of *Stimmtausch* and the rudiments of canonic writing. It is not too much to say that the rhythmic independence of the voices in Perotin's music marks the beginning of real polyphony.

The Notre Dame school continued to dominate music well into the thirteenth century. But technical practices and new forms were often subject to modification in regions distant from Paris. In general, a more conservative style existed in the French provinces; the compositions contained less florid writing, and the tenors of the organum-style compositions were not often stretched out to the extent that was typical of Notre Dame.[15] Later, in works of the thirteenth century, one sees that the only real distinction between the two styles lies in whether the notes of the tenor are shortened and arranged in rhythmic patterns (thus in discant style), or greatly extended (thus illustrating the sustained nature of the organum-style lower part).

Conductus. The term "conductus style" has been used in reference to St. Martial compositions, and has been equated with the term "discant style." While the term has little bearing on the evolution of musical forms, it does bear upon the subject of musical textures. The conductus apparently originated as a monophonic melody about the time of the troubadours in the twelfth century. It was not an outgrowth of the chant repertoire, however, but a freely composed work in the general style of a hymn. The Latin text, usually metrical (that is to say, based on poetic meters), was set in syllabic style.

The function of a conductus at its early stage of development has not been completely determined. Nor do the surviving conducti clarify the point, for their texts may be either sacred or secular, and their musical forms range from simple phrases to complex structures in which phrase repetition and recapitulation play a part. The assumption is made that the conductus was sung during pauses in the liturgical ritual when the priest was required to move from one area of the church to another; in a sense, he was "conducted" by the music. Even that assumption, however, may be valid only for the period up to about 1175.

14 From Ludwig, in Adler, *Handbuch der Musikgeschichte*, Vol. 1, p. 229, where *Stimmtausch* is discussed more fully. See also *HAM*, Nos. 32c, *Deo confitemini*, and 33a, *Alle . . . , On panolè . . .* ; and Bukofzer, *Studies in Medieval and Renaissance Music*, pp. 24–33.

15 For further information concerning provincial developments, see Handschin, "Eine wenig beachtete Stilrichtung . . ." in *Schweizerisches Jahrbuch für Musikwissenschaft*, Vol. I (1924).

The monophonic conductus was treated to the kind of polyphonic elaboration that was applied to liturgical melodies; polyphonic conducti appear in the Notre Dame manuscripts. Major points of distinction between them and the various organa and *clausulae,* however, are that the tenor of a conductus was not based on a Gregorian chant and was not treated in the melismatic style typical of the Notre Dame organa. The text was usually metrical and was most often set in syllabic style with note-against-note writing in the parts above the tenor. And even though melismata sometimes appeared at certain points in the conductus—for example, at phrase endings or cadences—the syllabic style, with all the voices moving in essentially identical rhythmic patterns above the tenor, remained a characteristic feature (see EXAMPLE 27). It is in this sense that the term "conductus style" is used in musical writings.

EXAMPLE 27

Anon., Conductus: *Salve virgo*

English Developments

THE ENGLISH repertoire of polyphonic works is quite distinct from that found on the Continent. Part-singing was well established in England in the eleventh century, perhaps influenced by an even older Scandinavian practice. But instead of basing their polyphony on the perfect consonances of the fourth or fifth, as in the early stages of organum, English musicians displayed a fondness for writing in thirds. There are a number of compositions from the late twelfth century in which the voices are either in parallel thirds or in mixtures of thirds and unisons. The style may be illustrated by the following portion of a hymn in discant style, written in praise of St. Magnus, patron saint of the Orkney Islands (see EXAMPLE 28).[16]

EXAMPLE 28

Anon., Hymn: *Nobilis humilus*

16 Transcribed in full in Adler, *Handbuch der Musikgeschichte,* Vol. I, p. 167.

Writing in thirds existed as a characteristic element of English music as late as the fifteenth century. Known as *gymel* (twin) it may be considered a type of parallel organum in thirds. Gymel is important in its own right as a twelfth-century English variant of continental organum. Sometimes it was improvised instead of notated. In the fourteenth century sixths were often added to the thirds; thus the "English discant," which played a part in the evolution of continental fauxbourdon, arose. That style, in turn, became influential in transforming the basic texture of all polyphonic music. Fauxbourdon will be discussed in Chapter 7.

English organa, roughly contemporary with those of Notre Dame and found in the same manuscript (Wolfenbüttel 677) that contains the *Magnus liber,* also exhibit distinctive characteristics. Often the tenor is not derived from Gregorian chant; the sections between *clausulae,* which in the Notre Dame works are usually retained in plainsong, are in the English works often set in either discant or organum style. And the English organa are the only known works of the time that applied the new device to chants of the Ordinary as well as the Proper of the Mass; the Notre Dame works were associated largely with the Proper, of course.

The Motet

WE HAVE now reached the point at which the history of one of the most important Medieval and Renaissance forms begins. It will be remembered that tropes and sequences appeared about the ninth century as chant interpolations. The rise of troping can be attributed in part to the desire to embellish or ornament a liturgical item. The text of a typical trope served to amplify the sentiment of the chant in which it appeared, often providing a commentary or interpretation. Also about the ninth century, the process of organum was first described in detail. It was clearly stated by the early theorists that organum too was thought of as a kind of chant elaboration in the sense that the chant was sung together with one or more ornamented versions of itself.

Near the beginning of the thirteenth century some composers began to ornament the chant again, on yet another level; now the *clausula* provided the incentive. They gave to the duplum a text that paraphrased the text from which the tenor was chosen. A few of Perotin's *clausulae* are so treated. Upper voices, when they existed, were treated similarly; at first the triplum and quadruplum shared the text of the duplum, but at a later stage each voice was given its own text. Because of this transformation from a vocalized line into a text-carrying one, the duplum in all these cases became known as the *motetus* (compare the French *mot,* "word"), and soon "motet" became a generic term used to identify a *clausula* with texts in the upper parts. The chief sources of the thirteenth-century motets are a Wolfenbüttel manuscript (one of the sources of Leonin's *Magnus liber*), the famous Montpellier Codex, the Bamberg Codex, and other manuscripts from Darmstadt and elsewhere.

The tenor of a motet carried a portion of a Latin chant text, of course. The texts of the other voices could and did appear not only in Latin but,

in the later part of the thirteenth century, also in French or in both together (see EXAMPLE 29). And sometimes the text of the triplum as well as

EXAMPLE 29

Anon., Motet, *c.* 1250

Triplum: Pu-ce - le - te bele et a - ve - nant Jo - li - e - te, po- lie et plei- sant

Duplum: Je lan - guis des maus d'a - mours. Mieuz aim as - sez

Tenor: Do (mino)

of the duplum was of secular origin, derived perhaps from a troubadour
song and bearing not the slightest relationship to the sense of the liturgical
tenor or to its French or Latin paraphrase in the *motetus.* Apparently any
subject was felt to be worthy of treatment in the upper parts: the full
range of material found in secular song—love, conviviality, social satire,
and so on—is suggested. Even the tenors suffered in this regard; for a time
about 1250, a French translation of the Latin text could serve as a motet
tenor, as could a trouvère melody or a dance tune.[17] But toward the end
of the century, Latin again began to be the preferred language and the
bilingual motet declined in popularity although the multitextual feature
of the form was most often retained.[18]

Rhythm. Modern transcriptions of thirteenth-century music necessarily
fail to dramatize one of the major problems to which composers of the
time addressed themselves: mastering the rhythmic implications revealed
by the emergence of polyphonic writing. Obviously, the problem could
not have arisen much earlier. For a thousand years or more, musicians
had been concerned primarily with melody—first in monophonic and
later in polyphonic textures; any other musical problems arising with
Gregorian chant before about 1150 were subsidiary or were related to the

17 See *HAM*, No. 33b, *On panole* . . . , for a motet whose tenor is a French street
cry, "Fresh strawberries." Another example, in which the tenor was presumably performed instrumentally, is given in *MoM*, No. 10, *En non Diu!* . . .
    18 An example of this type is given in *TEM*, No. 10, *Ave gloriosa.* . . .

Motet, *Dame de valour—Hé Dieus!—Amoris,* from Montpellier manuscript.

setting of the texts. And several centuries were to elapse before harmony received consistent attention and rigorous development; the turn from preoccupation with the horizontal aspects of music to an abiding concern for the vertical may be placed roughly at the year 1600.

The long interval between those dates, however, was marked by a growing interest in rhythm as an essential ingredient of polyphonic textures. In the thirteenth century particularly, musicians were keenly alive to all manifestations of the rhythmic factor. Their attempts to explore the temporal possibilities provided by three- and four-part writing are reflected in their efforts to devise a comprehensive system of notation. The rhythmic modes mentioned on pages 61–64 represent only one of the steps taken to overcome what might be called the loose relationship between tone and time.

A number of thirteenth-century treatises record the practices of musicians who struggled with the problem of notating the new rhythm. Several of the treatises embodied in the *Tractatus de musica* by Jerome of Moravia deal with mensural music. The oldest is an anonymous *Discantus positio vulgaris*, from about 1230; the most influential is the *Ars cantus mensurabilis* by Franco of Cologne, from about 1280.

It must be stressed that modifications of the system of notation in the thirteenth century came into being because the music required them. (This is of course true of every change in the notation of music.) The thirteenth-century changes reflect not only the thought processes and musical purposes of the composers but also the practical difficulties experienced by the performers. Several performers in an ensemble work, for example, could scarcely stay together if they had no means of relating their individual performance speeds to each other. Every increase in the floridity of the writing, every increase in the rhythmic complexity of the texture, made it more urgent to develop a measured or mensural music.

Rhythmic modes were still employed in the thirteenth century, but as the century progressed, the mixing of modes became so general that the guiding principle of the modes—namely, rhythmic regularity—was in effect negated. Modal ligatures, which had been used for notating groups of tones in melismata, were found ambiguous and inadequate to notate the new music being composed, for in the new music, the texts in the upper parts were generally set one syllable to a note. The long and breve of the modes were now given distinctive shapes (a square with a stem and without a stem, respectively). Ligatures derived their metrical values from the values of the notes which surrounded them instead of from the metrical schemes of the modes themselves (this point will be amplified below). A new note, the semibreve, in the shape of a diamond, was used more often than in the previous century. These and many other new elements entered the notational system, each new element further complicating the task of writing music. The need for simplification became obvious.

It was Franco of Cologne, in his *Ars cantus mensurabilis*,[19] who showed that a logical and consistent rhythmic notation was possible. Even though

19 Translated in *SRMH*, pp. 139–59.

his system retained many elements that had been in use earlier in the century and was based on the rhythmic modes, it marked a large step forward in the establishment of mensural music—that is to say, music in which the length of the tones can be measured. It provided a structure in which later refinements were embodied, and it contained the ingredients of our own system of notation. The main provisions of Franco's system are as follows.

(1) The *brevis recta* had been one *tempus* in length; the *longa recta* had been twice as long, or two *tempora;* and the *longa ultra mensuram,* three *tempora.* In the thirteenth century the two values of the long were given different names: the long of three *tempora* became "perfect," and the long of two, "imperfect."

(2) Similarly, two types of breves were recognized: *brevis recta* ("correct") retained its value of one *tempus;* and *brevis altera* ("altered") had a value of two *tempora* (and was equivalent to an imperfect long).

(3) The semibreve was of two types also. A "major" semibreve equaled two-thirds of a breve; a "minor" semibreve, half as long as a major semibreve, equaled one-third of a breve.

(4) The same note symbol could stand for either type of long (perfect or imperfect); another symbol stood for either type of breve (correct or altered); and so on, according to the context in which it appeared. A special "sign of perfection" (a short vertical line in the staff), when placed after a note, modified this rule of context, as it may be called. Franco, illustrating rules already in effect earlier in the century, gave a set of examples.[20] A summary of the effect of the rules may be seen in EXAMPLE 30.

E X A M P L E   30

The rules of Franco summarized

(5) The binary ligature, which had been an essential element in the modal system, was now modified to permit a variety of relationships between breve (B) and long (L). The ligature was said to have "propriety" if its first note was a B, to have "perfection" if its last note was an L; and to be "without propriety" and "without perfection" if those values were

20 In *SRMH,* pp. 142–46. See also Apel, *The Notation of Polyphonic Music,* pp. 310–11, and p. 294.

reversed. For example, a ligature BL was with propriety and perfection, while LB was without either. The four possible combinations of note values (BL, LL, BB, LB) were given one set of symbols in ascending ligatures, and another set in descending ligatures (see EXAMPLE 31).

EXAMPLE 31

The Franconian ligatures

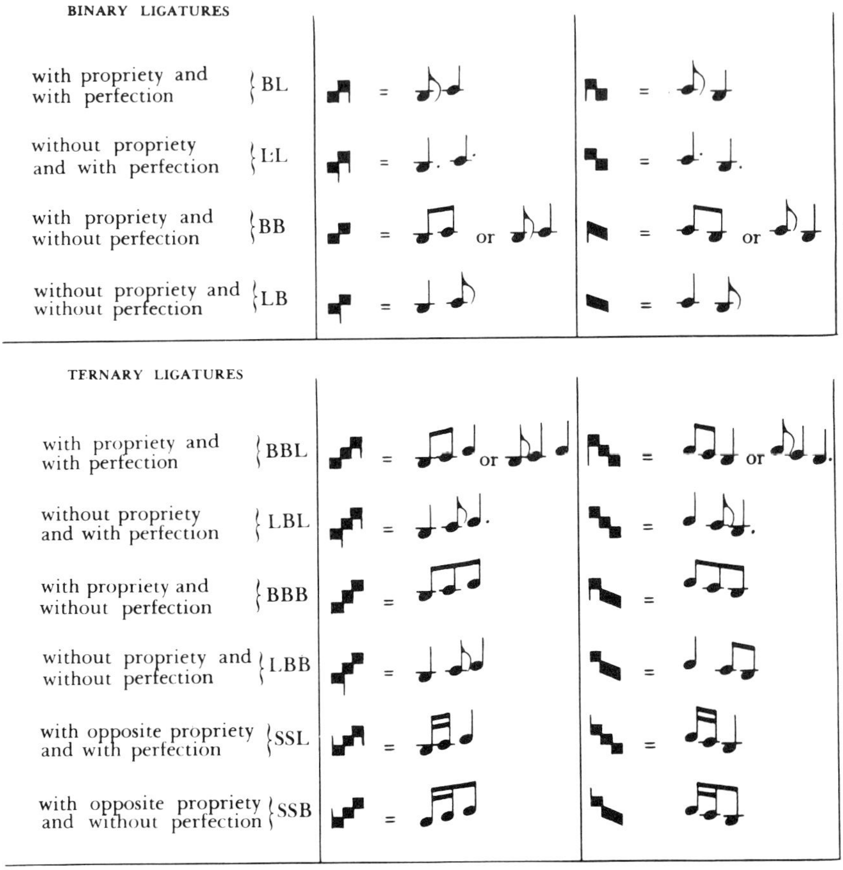

ADAPTED FROM Apel, *The Notation of Polyphonic Music.*

NOTE: the modern equivalents given here are valid in general; but the context in which a ligature is placed may in some cases affect the length of the ligature's last note.

(6) In ternary ligatures, provision was made for the semibreve (S), which had been introduced earlier in the century, by devising the attribute called "opposite propriety." Thus in a ligature with this attribute, the first two notes were semibreves; the last note was either with or without perfection according to the rule of the paragraph above.

(7) The middle note in ternary ligatures was always a breve, except in ligatures with opposite propriety, where of course the middle note was one of the two semibreves. Example 31 provides a summary of the chief symbols for ligatures.

Compositions embodying Franconian principles are relatively few in number; a manuscript from Las Huelgas in Spain and sections of the Montpellier Codex are the chief sources. It will be seen that the rational principle embodied in Franco's reforms is that "perfections" of three *tempora* carry the music forward; in other words, the music is essentially in triple meter. But the thirteenth century also saw the emergence of duple meter—a revolutionary new concept in mensural music. The earliest examples are found in the tenors of several motets in the Montpellier and Bamberg Codices.[21] In spite of the opposition of theorists such as Magister Lambertus, duple meter gained a strong foothold in the music of the time, and in the fourteenth century it appeared in ever increasing numbers of compositions.

Style characteristics. It is likely that many of the points contained in Franco's treatise are little more than observations, made in the 1280's, of what musicians had been doing for thirty years previously. Motets of the period after 1280 reveal greater rhythmic freedom in the voices above the tenor, and the triplum often became the most important part. With this step, modern four-part writing (that is, the texture that reached its first peak of development late in the sixteenth century) came appreciably closer.

Another style trait that led in the same direction is seen in the generally more lively upper parts. A somewhat heavy style had characterized motets earlier in the century; in many cases upper voices were held back by the ponderous, slow-moving tenor. But now, by breaking away from "tenor domination," as it is sometimes called, the motetus and triplum moved toward light and elegant expression. This is seen, near the end of the century, in motets composed by Pierre de la Croix (Petrus de Cruce) and by others who wrote in his style. A feature of these later motets is that the breve in the triplum is often broken up into many semibreves (as many as nine were allowed according to some sources, seven according to others), and a free declamation is at hand. Example 32 illustrates this style. But with this newly won freedom comes a strange lack of concern for the principles of proper textual accentuation, as even this example shows. (See, for example, in the second line, how cursorily the main thought of the fragment, *je m'en repent,* is treated.)

Theoreticians' pronouncements governing consonances and dissonances in multi-voiced music had been modified considerably since the early days of organum. While the octave and fifth were still firmly entrenched as the basic perfect consonances, the fourth had taken a less-favored position.

21 See Apel, *The Notation of Polyphonic Music,* pp. 290–94 and 303–04. Facsimiles of other duple-meter tenors are given in Parrish, *The Notation of Medieval Music,* Plates 40 and 41.

EXAMPLE 32

School of De la Croix, *Je cuidoie—Se j'ai—Solem*

Thirds and sixths were admitted as imperfect consonances—with the pro-
viso that minor thirds progress to the first step, major thirds and minor
sixths to the fifth step, and major sixths to the octave. And in general, a
composition was expected to begin and end with a perfect consonance,
even though many examples of beginnings with major or minor triads
can be found.

The sketchiest glance at thirteenth-century music, however, will disclose
occasional dissonances that ring uncomfortably even in modern ears accustomed to atonal and polytonal progressions. Passages such as those
shown in EXAMPLE 33 are by no means uncommon; they are the logical
outcome of the composing method generally employed by musicians of
the time.

A clue to that method is found in a statement by Franco—made in connection with the writing of a polyphonic *conductus,* true enough, but applicable to motet writing also. In effect Franco states that the tenor must

E X A M P L E 33

Cadences, 13th century

be written first, and next the duplum. A third voice may then be added, which should agree with either the tenor or the duplum.[22]

It is this practice of successive rather than simultaneous composing that is responsible for the characteristic thirteenth-century dissonances. We are dealing here not with three-part polyphony but with two-part polyphony to which a free voice has been added, or in some cases with two sets of two-part writing (duplum-tenor and triplum-tenor) superimposed upon each other. Harsh dissonances can scarcely be avoided under such conditions.

Performance. The ways in which motets were performed in the thirteenth century have not yet been completely determined. While its liturgical position can be established, it is not certain that the motet occupied that position in the Church service of the time. When the origin of the form is considered, the motet is seen to be actually a chant interpolation; the text of its tenor thus fixes its place in the liturgy. A motet whose tenor is derived, say, from the beginning of an Offertory could theoretically be performed in place of the *incipit* of that chant. Another motet based on a later portion of the same Offertory could also presumably have its liturgical place fixed by the same principle. The following table shows how three motets, each derived from a different portion of the Easter Gradual, *Haec dies,* are related to the complete text of that chant.[23] Following the old method of Gregorian chant performance, the three motets were sung by soloists and the plainsong sections were given to the unison choir.

	MOTET	PLAINSONG	MOTET	PLAINSONG	MOTET
Triplum:	Quant voi revenir		Deo confitemini		Trop sovent
Motetus:	Virgo virginum		Deo confitemini		Brunete, a qui
Tenor:	Haec dies	Quam fecit	Domino	Quoniam bonus	In saeculum

22 In *Ars cantus mensurabilis,* Section 11; reprinted in translation in *SRMH,* pp. 155–56.

23 See *Liber usualis,* p. 778, for the entire Gradual for Easter Sunday, and *HAM,* Nos. 32b, 32c, and 32d, *O mitissima . . . , Deo confitemini . . . ,* and *Trop sovent . . . ,* for the three motets. Translations of the motet texts are also in *HAM,* p. 244.

There is evidence, both pictorial and written, that the tenors of such motets were often performed instrumentally. Motets without tenor texts exist in some manuscripts and with such texts in others. The use of dance tunes—which are textless, of course—as motet tenors tells something about the popularity of this mixed type of performance. It is rather well established that instruments were sometimes used to support the soloist who sang the tenor; the practice of combining players and singers on the same part, which originated in twelfth-century organa performance and which existed until well into the seventeenth century, may have been used here in the thirteenth also. It could not have been a great innovation to dispense with the singer of that part entirely, on occasion, and thus to introduce instrumental performance of the tenor.

But now the liturgical propriety of such performance practices comes to question. With it may come another question about the propriety of these multi-textual motets themselves. It can scarcely be denied that some of the texts border on the sacrilegious or worse; yet it is often overlooked that the "profane" motets represent only a small if noteworthy part of the thirteenth-century motet repertoire. The larger part of that repertoire includes pieces whose Latin texts express sentiments that are thoroughly appropriate to the service. It is probable that when texts were obviously unsuitable, the motets were not sung in the service at all.

It is equally probable that the motet of this period was both a sacred and a secular form; in its worldly version, a trouvère tune as tenor is not amiss, nor are the lovesick verses that enliven the upper parts. In acting as a link between the Church and society, the motet greatly enriched the field of secular art, supplying secular composers with techniques, rhythmic devices, and melodic types. On the other hand, the intrusion of secular elements on a large scale did much to weaken the unique position of the motet. The fine balance between scriptural text and personal commentary on that text was lost. The motet was forced to compete with other, more vital secular forms and declined in importance. By the fifteenth century, however, it had largely cast off its secular traits and had returned to the precincts of the Church.

❧ 6 ❧

The *Ars Nova*

THE EARLY part of the fourteenth century marks one of the major turn-ing points in the history of music. Developments in the fields of rhythm and rhythmic notation were among the most notable of the contribu-tions made by that century. A new structural principle within the motet, new chord forms, and a new expressiveness in melody writing considerably altered the sound of the music. In addition, a growing interest in poly-phonic secular music and a new concept of the Mass as a musical unit added new forms to the repertoire.

The French musicians involved in these developments were quite con-scious of their extent. About 1320 Philippe de Vitry (*c.* 1290–1361) intro-duced a term, *ars nova* ("new art"), in the title of a treatise to describe the music that embodied the new developments. And driving the point home, other writers such as Johannes de Muris and Jacobus de Liége [1] referred to the music of Franco and Pierre de la Croix as *ars antiqua,* although in the music of Pierre de la Croix some of the changes were clearly antici-pated.

1 *SRMH,* pp. 172–79 and 180–90, respectively.

Later writers, however, applied the term *ars nova* to the music of the entire fourteenth century, and *ars antiqua* to that of the thirteenth. Thus a convenient date about 1300 is provided to mark the turn from the "antique art" to the "new art," or from the early Gothic period to the late.

The period of the development of the *ars nova* in France also saw a resurgence of musical creativity in Italy, where it had lain dormant for many centuries. An interest in secular music, paralleling that of the French, resulted in a number of new vocal forms. In both French and Italian music one can now begin to speak of national style characteristics, even though the "nations" did not yet exist in a political sense. The rhythmic characteristics of Italian music even brought into being a new system of notation that for a time existed side by side with the French. The Italian system contributed several innovations, though in the end the French system prevailed and led directly to the notation used in later centuries.

Notation

IN NOTATING the *ars nova,* musicians had three problems to deal with. (1) Use of the rhythmic modes had hampered the desire to increase the freedom and independence of the upper voices; the modes had declined in importance even in Franco's time and now in the fourteenth century they became virtually obsolete. (2) The greater flexibility and lightness of the upper parts, such as that seen in the music of Pierre de la Croix (see EXAMPLE 32, page 78), drove the semibreve into the background and forced the use and measurement of smaller note values. Minims and semiminims had existed earlier, of course, but had not yet found their proper and well-regulated places in the system. (3) The dominant position of triple meter, which was held to reflect the perfection of the Trinity, was now seriously threatened by the encroachment of binary meter—an indication that sacred concerns were losing ground and a period of secular thinking was at hand.

It is with these rhythmic factors that De Vitry proposed to deal. Some of the elements that had proved useful in the Franconian system he retained and extended. The long, for example, could still be divided into either three breves or two, these relationships being defined by the term *modus;* the proportion of three breves to one long was to be known as *modus perfectus,* while two to one was *modus imperfectus.* The same considerations of "perfect" and "imperfect" were projected downward to the divisions of the breve, except that the relationships were shown by the term *tempus* instead of *modus.* Thus *tempus perfectum* indicated that a group of three semibreves was equivalent to a breve; and *tempus imperfectum,* that a group of two sufficed. On a still lower level came the corresponding divisions of a semibreve into three or two minims; here the relating term was *prolatio,* but the internal division of the *prolatio* was known as "major" or "minor" instead of "perfect" or "imperfect." Thus in *prolatio maior* a semibreve contained three minims, and in *prolatio minor,* two minims.

83

BIBLIOTHÈQUE NATIONALE, PARIS

French *ars nova* notation. Ballade, *Dame de qui toute ma ioie vient,* by Guillaume de Machaut.

Each of the three relationships (mode, time, and prolation) in both of its aspects (ternary and binary) could exist independently on its own level. By the early fourteenth century, however, the increased use of smaller note values had caused the breve in effect to be lengthened; the long lost much of its usefulness and appeared only rarely. The *modus* relationship, concerned with the inner structure of the long (that is, whether it contained three breves or two), thus became of historical interest only. The breve, consequently, no longer served as a convenient basic unit; for all practical purposes the semibreve took its place.[2] *Tempus* (either perfect or imperfect) and *prolatio* (either major or minor) were the chief rhythmical relationships that the music of the time reflected.

Apparently De Vitry also devised symbols which served as metrical signatures and which were placed at the beginning of a composition or, if the metrical pattern was to be changed, at an appropriate place within. The sign that referred to *tempus* was a circle: unbroken to indicate a perfect division, and open at the right to indicate an imperfect division. The signs for *prolatio* were three dots (or more often, one) placed within the circle to denote major prolation; and two dots (or a vertical line) for minor prolation.

Those and other symbols and relationships, then, not only provided De Vitry and his French contemporaries with means to notate their music,

EXAMPLE 34

The *Ars nova* notation

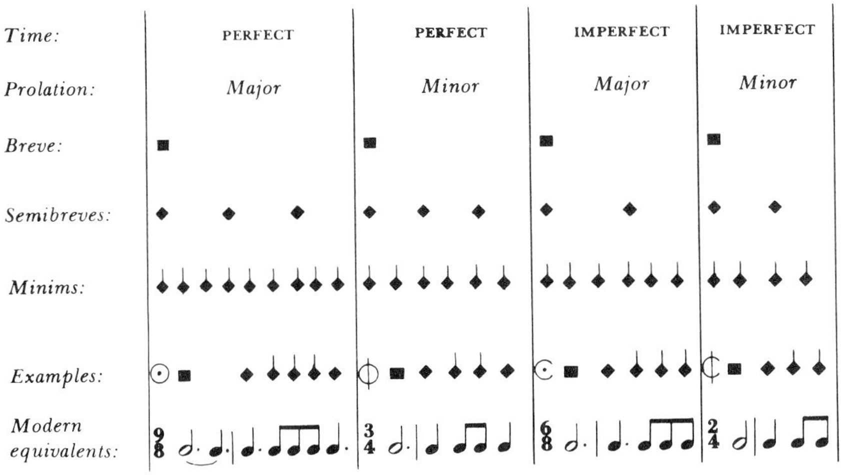

Time:	PERFECT	PERFECT	IMPERFECT	IMPERFECT
Prolation:	Major	Minor	Major	Minor
Breve:	■	■	■	■
Semibreves:	◆ ◆ ◆	◆ ◆ ◆	◆ ◆	◆ ◆
Minims:	♦♦♦♦♦♦♦♦♦	♦♦♦♦♦ ♦	♦♦ ♦♦♦ ♦	♦♦ ♦ ♦
Examples:	⊙ ■ ◆♦♦♦◆♦	⊘ ■ ◆ ♦♦♦♦	ℭ ■ ◆ ♦♦♦♦	ℭ̸ ■ ◆ ♦♦♦
Modern equivalents:	𝄴⁹⁄₈ ♩. ♩.|♩. ♫♫♩.	³⁄₄ ♩.|♩ ♫♫♩	⁶⁄₈ ♩.|♩. ♫♫♩.	²⁄₄ ♩|♩ ♫♩

ADAPTED FROM Apel, *The Notation of Polyphonic Music.*

2 This process was to be repeated at least twice more in subsequent centuries. The semibreve (modern whole-note) later gave way to the minim (modern half-note), and eventually to the semiminim (modern quarter-note) as the basic time unit. In each case, the increasing use of smaller note values made the dividing by two necessary.

but serve with only slight modification to reproduce the basic patterns of our own.[3] The foregoing paragraphs are summarized in EXAMPLE 34.

This account of *ars nova* notation does little more than set down the chief symbols and indicate the fundamental rhythmic relationships.[4] Many other symbols, also made necessary by the music of the time, were used as well. The dot, for example, had a variety of uses. Sometimes it served as do modern barlines, to separate metrical groups (*punctus divisionis*). The dot of addition (*punctus additionis*) was used to lengthen a note by half, in a way comparable to modern practice. The possibilities of syncopation revealed themselves to fourteenth-century musicians, and dots were used in particular ways to make the notation of this device practicable. EXAMPLE 35 shows the kind of writing that became possible.

E X A M P L E   35

Machaut, Motet

The color of the note symbols played an important part in the system also. Red notes—or when red ink was not available, white notes (that is, hollow or "vacant" notes)—had great significance in indicating proportional changes in note values. In general, three colored notes had the value of two blacks. This use of color could signify either a change to triplets in the imperfect group (see EXAMPLE 36a) or a change in the rhythm of the perfect group (EXAMPLE 36b). Another device using color was diminution, in which a part (usually the tenor) was performed as though it were written in smaller note values than it actually was. For example, each breve was read as a semibreve, each semibreve as a minim, but the proportions existing between notes were not altered.

3 It is of more than passing interest to observe that the two "imperfect" symbols, signifying the presence of binary meter, have been forwarded to our own system without change. The broken circle, which today resembles a "C," is often said to refer to "common time." And the broken circle cut by a vertical line has through the centuries become a symbol for *alla breve*; in view of its modern function, the term *alla minima* ("by the half-note") would be more nearly correct.

4 See Apel, *The Notation of Polyphonic Music*, pp. 338–60, for a full account of the system.

E X A M P L E 36

The effect of red (or white) notes

[a] ■ ■ = □ □ □   [b] ■ ■ = □ □ □

The *ars nova* notation gradually developed a high degree of complexity. In addition, when elements of that notation were adopted by Italian musicians (see below, page 97), the problem was further complicated. The transcription of works written in "mixed notation" or "mannered notation" is still among the most difficult of musicological tasks.[5]

5 See Apel, *Notation of . . .* , pp. 385–402 and 403–15, respectively, for accounts of these practices. Further, see his collection, *French Secular Music of the Late Fourteenth Century.*

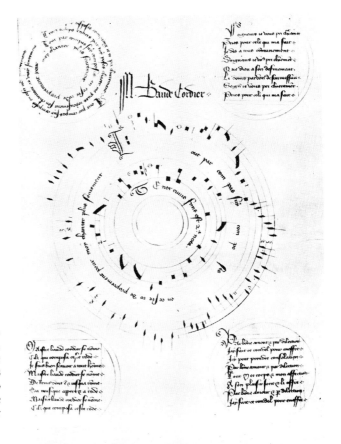

A perpetual canon by Baude Cordier, early 15th c. The outer circle calls for two voices to sing in canon; the inner circle is for an instrumental tenor.

Secular Music

IN DISCUSSING music of the fourteenth century, one easily runs the risk of overemphasizing the sacred field. Secular music, in the period covered by this chapter, reached an equally high level of significance; indeed, Guillaume de Machaut, the most important composer of the *ars nova,* was apparently as much interested in the world as he was in the Church.

To some extent, the growth of interest in secular music may have been accelerated by an edict issued by Pope John XXII in 1324 from the temporary papal seat at Avignon. The Pope virtually excluded polyphony from the Church and specifically forbade the addition of motetus and triplum parts to the chant.[6] Far-reaching as this papal bull was, it seems not to have had any lasting effect. In France, for example, single Mass movements and motets with chant tenors continued to be written, and a few examples of liturgical polyphony survive in England and Italy. Whatever Pope John's intention, there is no evidence that a Gregorian revival, such as was begun in the late nineteenth century, was instituted in the fourteenth.

There is much more reason to suppose that the waning interest in sacred music was but the latest step in the gradual decline of liturgical strictness generally. The secularization of the thirteenth-century motet, the lessening importance of chant tenors, and the introduction of the isorhythmic principle (see below, page 88), were all related to that decline. The final result, in the fifteenth and early sixteenth centuries, was the creation of a large body of secular vocal ensemble music that rivaled the sacred forms in vitality, expressive power, and artistic worth.

The growth of that literature had been a slow one, however. The secular musical impulse has probably existed as long as the religious, even though manuscripts attesting to its existence do not go much beyond the ninth century. For many hundreds of years, no clear distinction between the fields was possible. Hymns and other sacred melodies were often supplied with worldly texts, and often sacred and profane verses were combined in one poem which was then set to a melody drawn from either field. During this period the Church was the only custodian of learning and the principal patron of the arts. It is likely that the Church had no interest in copying and preserving music that did not serve its purpose.

The monophonic songs of the troubadours and trouvères had continued to represent a strong secular impulse through the thirteenth century. Late in that century polyphonic equivalents of the trouvères' *lais, ballades, rondeaux,* and *virelais* appeared. These two- or three-voice (seldom more) compositions gave rise to a rich and varied secular literature to which the generic term *chanson* is applicable and which flourished in the following centuries with ever increasing vigor. The secular works of Machaut, as representative of French accomplishments in this field, will be discussed below (see page 92).

6 See *Oxford History of Music,* I, pp. 294–96, for the Latin text and an English translation.

Musica Ficta

A TENDENCY to introduce new tones not found in the modal system is
noted in a number of theoretical treatises from about the tenth century
to the fourteenth. It is likely that the need for such tones first was felt
when it became necessary to transpose a Gregorian chant; for example,
the melodic line A-B-C, if transposed down a fourth, would have to become E-F♯-G. During the course of the centuries more and more such
tones were recognized—in theory at least—until by 1400 the entire chromatic scale was a possibility.

Among the uses made of the new tones were the following: substituting
B♭ for B when that tone was flanked by two A's (and at a later stage,
substituting E♭ for E when the tone appeared between two D's); altering
either tone of the augmented fourth, F-B (F♯-B or F-B♭) in both horizontal and vertical contexts. Gradually other uses were suggested in the music
itself: raising the seventh step in the seventh (later Mixolydian) mode,
for example, or lowering the fourth step in the fifth (later Lydian) mode.
The result of these practices was that the integrity of the modes was
threatened and the formation of modern major and minor scales came
appreciably closer.

For a number of reasons (objections by Church authorities are among
the most likely ones) the implied substitutions were not always indicated
in the music, but were generally understood among musicians and were
employed without being written. Thus arose the term *musica falsa* about
the thirteenth century, but the term *musica ficta,* introduced a century
later, gradually supplanted the earlier term. Composers differed in their
approach to the practice. In Landini's works, for example (see below,
page 100), as well as in many other fourteenth-century compositions, accidentals are indicated more freely than in works of the earlier generation;
by about 1450 they have again virtually disappeared, and the music requires of the performer a knowledge of the rules which govern their use.[7]

Isorhythm

PHILIPPE DE VITRY was highly esteemed by his contemporaries, not only
as a theorist and the author of the *Ars nova,* but as a composer as well.
Unfortunately, only a few of his works have survived. Five motets among
the musical interpolations in the famous *Roman de Fauvel*[8] are attributed to De Vitry, and a mid-century manuscript from Ivrea, near Turin,

---

7 In modern editions the suggested or implied accidentals are often written above
the notes to which they apply.

8 This Medieval poem was written by Gervais de Bus about 1310. It is essentially a
work of satirical criticism. Fauvel, a fawn-colored stallion in the poem, is a symbol for
the vices of *flatterie, avarice, vilenie, variété, envie,* and *lacheté;* throughout the poem
all men from commoners to kings, from friars to popes, pay homage to the beast, whose
name is derived from the initial letters of the vices it symbolizes. The musical interpolations number about 130, with Latin or French texts (sometimes both). The musical
forms include *conducti,* motets, and many other types. One motet is found in *HAM,*
No. 43, *Detractor est.*

contains half a dozen of De Vitry's motets, the authenticity of several of which is in doubt.

The principal distinguishing feature of De Vitry's motets is a new way of rhythmically organizing the tenors. It will be remembered that in the *clausula* of the Notre Dame period the notes of the tenor were often cast in a short rhythmic pattern which was subsequently repeated. Later, in compositions employing the rhythmic modes, the repeated use of *ordines* (see page 63) also gave rise to rhythmic patterns.

Now, in the first half of the fourteenth century, such patterns were lengthened and employed consistently, to the extent that a new organizing principle was created. This principle, called "isorhythm" (from the Greek *iso,* meaning "same"), contains two components, *talea* and *color.*

The *talea* is the rhythmic pattern of the tenor independent of the rhythm or the note values of the melody from which the tenor was derived; in other words, it is a free rhythmic creation and is composed according to musical laws only. In a typical motet the *talea* is repeated a number of times without reference to the melodic contour of its first statement. EXAMPLE 37 gives the tenor of a motet by De Vitry, and 37a abstracts the *talea.*

EXAMPLE 37

Talea and *color* in a motet tenor

The *color,* on the other hand, represents the melodic contour (or a portion of it) independent of the rhythm. If the tenor is a derived one, the *color* must necessarily show a resemblance to the melodic line of the chant from which the tenor is derived. EXAMPLE 37*b* shows the *color* of the De Vitry motet. It often happens that the *talea* and the *color* are of different lengths, as they are in EXAMPLE 37*c* (the *talea* comprises six "measures," the *color* thirteen tones). As a consequence, the successive reiterations of the two components overlap; then the isorhythmic tenor includes different melodic versions of a rhythmic pattern (seen in the recurrent *taleae*) as well as rhythmic versions of a melodic fragment (wherever the *colores* are repeated).

The device of diminution, mentioned on page 85, is also present in EXAMPLE 37*c.* In that example it is used as follows: beginning with the ninth statement of the *talea* (and the fourth return of the *color*) the rhythmic pattern is presented seven additional times, but now in note values half as long as formerly. The *color,* being concerned only with pitches and not with length of tones, is not affected by the diminution.

The unifying effect of isorhythm was probably not perceptible on first hearing to the audiences of the time. Many technicalities of composition make their appeal primarily to the trained performer and pass the casual listener by, and isorhythm was such a technicality. In fact, it was not discovered until the twentieth century, when music of the *ars nova* was thoroughly restudied; it may be considered an element of *Augenmusik* ("music for the eyes"). (It is interesting to note that a thoroughly twentieth-century development, the twelve-tone row of Arnold Schoenberg, is another example of an "inaudible" musical device.) Whatever its effect on the layman, isorhythm contained elements that only the singer was in a position to appreciate. The principle, in a word, made the motet into "singers' music." As such it was able to impart to that form, and to other forms which employed it, a degree of refinement, subtlety, and unity unmatched by other more universal or folk-minded forms.

The Organization of the Mass

IT IS of more than passing significance that the Ordinary of the Mass played little or no part in musical developments up to the time of the *ars nova.* As we have seen, certain portions of the chants of the Proper were set as organa in the twelfth century and as motets in the thirteenth, and some chants of the Offices were similarly treated. But the five chanted items of the Ordinary escaped such elaboration; they were presumably chanted in the early 1300's as they had been in the time of Tuotilo—except, of course, when the relatively few polyphonic settings of single Mass movements were substituted.[9]

9 See Ludwig, "Die Mehrstimmige Messe des 14. Jahrhunderts," in *Archiv für Musikwissenschaft,* VII (1925), pp. 421–24, for a description of the single Mass movements and pairs whose existence was known in his day. Since that time many more have been found: see Schrade, *Polyphonic Music of the Fourteenth Century.* Two such single movements, by Ciconia and Legrant, are given in *HAM,* Nos. 55, *Et in terra pax,* and 56, *Credo.*

About the middle of the fourteenth century, however, a new attitude toward the Ordinary began to make itself felt. The isorhythmic motet had shown that a tenor-based composition need not be bound by liturgical or textual restrictions, but could become an independent musical work. With this realization, composers gradually ceased to regard the prescribed liturgical observances as sacrosanct and gave greater weight to musical considerations in setting chant texts. They turned their attention especially to the chants of the Ordinary, which thus far had escaped consistent polyphonic elaboration.[10]

The chants of the Ordinary—*Kyrie, Gloria, Credo, Sanctus-Benedictus,* and *Agnus Dei*—have certain elements in common. Their place and function in the Mass, as well as the invariability of their texts, relate them to each other, even though they are separated in the actual rite.[11] One might expect that composers, inspired by this liturgical unity, would have superimposed the element of musical unity when setting the chants polyphonically. But such a far-reaching idea occurred to no one before the fourteenth century, as far as we know today. Two steps were taken, however, that were eventually to make the cyclical Mass—that is, one thematically unified in some planned fashion—a historical reality.

The first step went no further than collecting pre-existent Mass items and placing them together in a single manuscript. The second step was taken by Machaut (see below, page 95) when he set the texts of the Ordinary in a single composition. The first step is represented by the Mass of Tournai, dating from a time between 1300 and about 1350,[12] which contains six items (including a setting of the *Ite missa est*) possibly written at different times (see EXAMPLE 38). The Mass is for three voices throughout. It has no stylistic unity, but the tenors of all the movements except the *Credo* and the *Ite missa est* have much thematic similarity. Three movements are in the conductus style of the *ars antiqua*; the *Gloria* and *Sanctus* contain examples of hocketing;[13] the whole is predominantly in duple meter; and the *Ite missa est* is actually a motet with sacred Latin and secular French texts. Regardless of stylistic dis-

10 Ludwig, "Die Mehrstimmige Messe . . . ," pp. 432–35.

11 It must be admitted that this concept of a unified Ordinary is a late development even from a liturgical standpoint. The arrangement of the chants in many Medieval liturgical books (all the *Kyrie*s were placed in one group, all the *Gloria*s in another, and so on) strongly suggests that the concept had little validity before, say, the fifteenth century. Even today the various chants on the *Credo* text are grouped separately from the other chants of the Ordinary. See *Liber usualis*, pp. 16–63, and compare pp. 64–78.

12 Printed as *Messe du XIIIe siècle*, edited by Coussemaker, 1861. Subsequent research showed the editor to have been mistaken about the century of the work's origin. The Mass of Tournai may be found in Schrade, *Polyphonic Music of the Fourteenth Century*, Vol. I. The *Agnus Dei* from this Mass is given in *TEM*, No. 13.

13 Hocketing, in the thirteenth and fourteenth centuries, was the practice of dividing consecutive notes of a melody between two different voices. The device appeared in motets and other forms, and sometimes gave rise to a form known as "hocket," in which it was used extensively. For examples, see *HAM*, No. 32e, *In seculum*, the eighth and ninth measures of No. 35, and the second section of No. 58. An instrumental hocket is given in *TEM*, No. 12, *Je n'amerai*. . . . It is popularly supposed that the words "hocket" and "hiccup" have the same root; if so, this etymology illustrates the device admirably.

EXAMPLE 38

Mass of Tournai, *Kyrie*

similarities, however, the fact that an unknown scribe assembled the six items in one manuscript brings the concept of a unified Mass Ordinary appreciably closer.

Two other similar Mass sets from the fourteenth century are known: the so-called Mass of Toulouse and Mass of Barcelona. The Toulouse cycle lacks a *Gloria,* and the *Credo* is fragmentary.[14]

Machaut

GUILLAUME DE MACHAUT (*c.* 1300–1377) must be ranked as one of the foremost musicians of the fourteenth century. Active as cleric, poet, and composer, he held a number of positions during his lifetime: secretary to King John of Bohemia, with whom he traveled as far as Russia, member of the court of Charles V of France, and a number of church positions. From 1340 to his death he was canon at Rheims. His works include perhaps the largest and most important group of early polyphonic secular compositions, a number of motets, and the first known polyphonic setting of the complete Ordinary of the Mass.[15]

Secular works. Polyphonic equivalents of the songs of the troubadours and trouvères had appeared late in the thirteenth century. It is likely that the earliest of these were merely three-voice settings of pre-existing melodies, the original melody placed either in the lowest (tenor) or middle (contratenor) voice.[16] But works with original melodies soon ap-

14 The manuscripts are analyzed and described, and both works are given in modern notation, in Schrade, *Polyphonic Music of the Fourteenth Century.*

15 Published in modern notation in Schrade, *Polyphonic Music of the Fourteenth Century.*

16 In the first half of the century the naming of voices underwent significant changes. The term "contratenor" was used for the voice next to the tenor, occasionally at first

peared—some anonymous and some not. It is in this area that Machaut became active. Among his secular works are more than a hundred compositions in the old trouvère forms. In these works Machaut showed himself to be interested in both the old and the new; more than half of the *lais* and *virelais* are monophonic, whereas all the *rondeaux* and all but one of the *ballades* are polyphonic.

The *lais* deviate to some extent from the corresponding form of the troubadours, but the essential pairing of verses is present. Of special significance are two three-voice *lais:* one marked *chace,* alternately monophonic and polyphonic in texture, with the polyphonic sections written in canon; and the other in three-voice canon throughout. The French *chace* was a secular form with programatic intent in which canonic writing predominated. A few anonymous examples of the *chace* are known from the early fourteenth century. Usually lengthy pieces set as two-voice canons, they describe hunting scenes, scenes in a market place, and similar events, all in moods of excitement and humor. The two three-voice *chaces* found among Machaut's *lais* represent a more highly organized type.

The majority of Machaut's forty-one polyphonic *ballades* are for two or three voices, with a single text. The form in general corresponds to the earlier form: *ab ab cd E.* One exception, however, contains three different texts set to the same melody; in each part the melody begins at a different time, so that a three-part canon emerges. All the *ballades* have their main musical interest concentrated in the topmost melody, which in most cases is the only one supplied with text.[17] It is generally understood that in such cases instruments performed the lower voice or voices.

The *rondeaux* also show similarities with the corresponding thirteenth-century form. In general, they are of the eight-line type: *AB aA ab AB.* The majority are set for three voices, although a few two-voice and four-voice settings have been preserved.

One *rondeau* deserves closer attention. It is a three-voice setting of the text, "My end is my beginning, and my beginning, my end . . ." Here the tenor melody proceeds to the middle of the piece, after which it retraces its steps measure by measure; thus measures 21–40 are merely measures 1–20 sung in retrograde. At the same time the second voice proceeds directly from beginning to end (measures 1–40), while the third voice sings the second voice in retrograde. The direction of the voices can be traced in EXAMPLE 39*a,* which shows the midpoint of the tenor; and 39*b,* which gives the beginning and end of the upper voices.

and more frequently later in the century. The contratenor is roughly of the same range as the tenor, appearing sometimes above it and sometimes below. At about the same time the term *motetus* was often discarded in favor of *discantus.* Toward the end of the century, especially in Italian works, the term *superius* began to drive out *triplum* (or *quadruplum*) as a designation for the topmost voice; eventually the word "soprano" was formed out of *superius.* See p. 111 in this connection.

17 One is given in *HAM,* No. 45, *Je puis . . .* ; another is in *GMB,* No. 26a, *Ma chiere dame. . . .* For an example of a French *ballade* by an Italian composer, Antonello da Caserta, see *TEM,* No. 17, *Notes pour moi. . . .*

EXAMPLE 39

Machaut, *Ma fin est ma commencement*

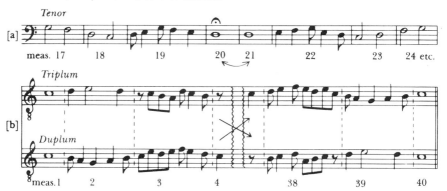

FROM *Polyphonic Music of the Fourteenth Century*,
edited by Leo Schrade. Reprinted by permission of Editions
de L'Oiseau-lyre, Monaco.

The *virelais* are composed in monophonic style; twenty-five are for voice alone, seven are accompanied by one instrument, and one is accompanied by two instruments.[18] Here again adherence to the trouvères' model is close; in general, the form *AB cc ab AB* for each of three stanzas results. With these works of Machaut the writing of monophonic music came virtually to an end. New sonorities, new rhythmic flexibility, and new lyric grace became factors of polyphonic style. The way was open for the development of new forms not modeled upon those of the twelfth and thirteenth centuries.

Motets. Twenty-three motets by Machaut are known. They are similar to the motets of De Vitry in their use of isorhythm, but they also reveal Machaut's appreciation of the consonances provided by triads—notably at cadences. One cannot yet speak of triadic harmony as having supplanted the older consonances of the fifth and the octave, but the music of Machaut, and of the *ars nova* in general, shows a strong tendency to move in that direction.

The motets are also comparatively free in rhythm, at least in those voices to which isorhythm is not applied, rhythmic independence having gradually taken the place of adherence to the rhythmic modes. Attempts to make the upper voice melodically more attractive had already been made by Pierre de la Croix and his school, as we have seen (see EXAMPLE 32, page 78). EXAMPLE 40, which may be compared with the mid-thirteenth-century motet fragment given in EXAMPLE 29 (page 72), represents a further stage of transition. The melodic sprightliness seen here soon developed into a kind of lyricism characterized by rhythmic diversity and

18 The types are illustrated in *HAM,* Nos. 46a, *Comment . . .* and 46b, *Plus dure . . .* , and in *GMB,* No. 26b, *Si je souspir. . . .*

EXAMPLE 40

Machaut, Motet

J'ay tant mon cuer et mon or-gueil cre - u Et te-nu cher ce qui m'a de-ce-

u Et en vil - te ce qui m'a - mait e - u Que j'ay fail - li

expressive contours and accompanied by a new interest in harmonies based on thirds.

The isorhythmic principle in Machaut's motets[19] in several cases was applied not only in the tenor but also in other voices and in freer form. In a few cases, upper voices are isorhythmic in part only; in others, one or both voices above the tenor in a three-voice motet employ the device throughout. Finally, a tenor may have two different *taleae,* each applied to the same *color.* The device of diminution, in which a tenor was performed in half the value of the indicated notation, is also found in about half of Machaut's motets. This feature apparently outlasted isorhythm itself, for it became an important element of fifteenth-century style.

The motet of the *ars nova,* while it may have had a sacred text in the tenor, was concerned more with secular matters than with liturgical. Texts glorifying the king, commemorating actions by the state, and reflecting warlike pursuits are typical. For example, in Machaut's four-voice motet, *Plange republica regni,* the text is in the form of a petition to end the civil chaos which had existed since the defeat of King John by the Black Prince in 1356. The text of the triplum outlines the duties of a leader of the people.[20]

Motets that are isorhythmic in all or most of their parts are unparalleled examples of concentration on a single technical device. Yet isorhythm had more than a technical aspect, and its concentrated use grew out of aesthetic considerations. First of all, it provided a new unifying principle to replace what the motet had lost when it abandoned the rhythmic modes. And in bringing the work into a connected whole, isorhythm had nothing to do with text or liturgy; it was a purely musical principle. It served to turn music in a new direction, to lead it toward a new status as a completely independent art divorced from word, rite, or externally imposed form.

The Mass. Machaut's famous Mass is of great historical importance; it is the first polyphonic setting of the complete Ordinary known to have

19 See *HAM,* No. 44, *S'il estoit nulz* . . . , and *GMB,* No. 27, *Trop plus.* . . .
20 Ficker, "Polyphonic Music of the Gothic Period," in *Musical Quarterly,* XV (1929), pp. 502–03.

been composed by one man.[21] The circumstances that led to its composition are not known; the date of 1364 is popularly assigned to it, but there is no supporting evidence. Machaut's attempts to achieve musical unity by using the same melodic material in several movements are recognized by some authorities, such as Machabey, and denied by others.[22]

With or without thematic unity, however, the broad conception of the work is unique in its period. The Mass contains the five chants of the Ordinary plus the *Ite missa est;* it is for four voices throughout and is stylistically varied. The isorhythmic principle is employed differently in each movement. Missing entirely in the *Gloria,* it appears in both the tenor and contratenor of the *Kyrie;* in the *Credo,* in the same two parts, it is confined to the final Amen; in the *Agnus Dei* it appears in the upper voices only; and in the *Ite missa est,* after the first few measures, all four voices are isorhythmic.

Extended sections of the Mass are in conductus style; others are freely polyphonic, with both syllabic and melismatic treatment strongly evident. The *Sanctus* exhibits a style which combines syncopation with hocketing; EXAMPLE 41 shows the type of treatment.

E X A M P L E   41

Machaut, *Sanctus*

FROM *Polyphonic Music of the Fourteenth Century,* edited by Leo Schrade. Reprinted by permission of Editions de L'Oiseau-lyre, Monaco.

The chants which underlie the several movements are paraphrased freely, occasionally in an effort to bring out the emotional significance

21 The edition in modern notation by Schrade has been mentioned. Other editions of the complete Mass include those by Machabey (1948), De Van (1949), and Besseler (1954). The *Agnus Dei* from the Mass is given in *MoM,* No. 13.

22 Machabey is quoted by Reese in *Music in the Middle Ages,* p. 356; Bukofzer takes the opposite point of view in *Studies in Medieval and Renaissance Music,* p. 218.

of the text. For example, the section of the *Credo* which speaks of the incarnation, birth, and crucifixion of Christ is treated more broadly and impressively than the sections surrounding it. Thus in possibly the very earliest polyphonic setting of the complete Ordinary of the Mass, the type of *Credo* treatment that later became traditional is already found.

The *Ars Nova* in Italy

ITALIAN musicians of the fourteenth century, like their French contemporaries, developed a keen interest in the field of polyphonic secular music. Whereas many of the French secular forms were derived from the songs of the troubadours and trouvères, however, and were in a sense the polyphonic equivalents of those forms, Italian secular music was derived independently. Three forms were especially cultivated by Italian composers: the madrigal, the *caccia,* and the *ballata.*

As if to emphasize their independence of French music, which had prevailed over the Italian for several centuries, Italian musicians also developed a system of notation which departs in several respects from the French notation described earlier in this chapter.

Italian notation. Early in the fourteenth century, probably as an offshoot of the notational devices introduced by Pierre de la Croix and his school, the distinctive Italian system of notation emerged. It is described in *Pomerium,* a treatise by Marchetto da Padua, written about 1318 [23] and also important as the first theoretical source in which duple meter is held to be the equal of triple.

In the Italian system the fundamental unit is the breve, which in effect corresponds to a measure of later music. The breve or its equivalent is marked off by dots. The principles of perfection and imperfection are still present by implication; the breve can be divided by two or three and by compounds of two or three (up to twelve). The smaller note values thus arrived at are technically semibreves, but they may be of different lengths according to the context. They appear in the shape of a diamond, a diamond with a descending stem, and one with an ascending stem. The latter is a later development; in earlier manuscripts all minims were written as semibreves.

The basic unit (*divisione*) of a composition is named according to the number of *semibreves minima* in each breve: *quaternaria, senaria imperfecta,* and so on. Abbreviations of these names (*q., i.,* and so on) are often used as time signatures to indicate the metrical pattern of the music. The various metrical types and the abbreviations for them, together with the divisions of the breve and their modern equivalents, are given in EXAMPLE 42.

When fewer than the required number of notes appear in a *divisione* (for example, only six notes in an *octonaria*), the first notes are considered of normal length and the last notes are lengthened to fill out the

23 Excerpts are in *SRMH,* pp. 160–71.

EXAMPLE 42

Italian notation

[a] Twofold division (analogous to *tempus imperfectum*)

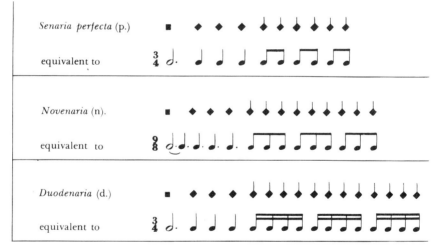

[b] Threefold division (analogous to *tempus perfectum*)

(Note: the upward stems on the *semibreves minima* represent a late development)

measure (see EXAMPLE 43*a*). Such lengthening was considered the "natural way" (*via naturae*) of proceeding. If longer notes were needed at the beginning of a measure, an "artificial way" (*via artis*) could be employed, recognized by the direction of the stems on the appropriate notes (see EXAMPLES 43*b* and 43*c*).

It will be seen that in the Italian system the semibreve could serve

EXAMPLE 43

Via naturae and *via artis*

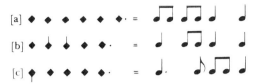

several functions. It could serve as a normal *semibrevis* (one-half or one-third of a breve), as a *semibrevis maior* (longer than normal), or as a *semibrevis minima* (one-half or one-third of a semibreve). In the latter capacity, as a *semibrevis minima,* it could also equal one-quarter of a breve in *quaternaria* or one-twelfth of a breve in *duodenaria* (as shown in EXAMPLE 42). The possibility of confusion here was eventually felt to be a defect of the system. Further, the system found it advantageous to use the *ars nova* "dot of addition" (to lengthen tones by half), but this made the Italian "dot of division" (whereby each *divisione* was identified) somewhat ambiguous. With its distinctive feature thus brought into question, the Italian system soon became obsolete. Its passing is deplored in a treatise by Prosdocimus, written about 1412.

Landini. Essential differences between the music composed north and south of the Alps have marked music history for centuries. In most cases the northern music has been more reserved, more formalized, and more "contrived" than that of the south. The latter in general has been more melodious, more spontaneous, and simpler in form and texture. The music of France and Italy in the fourteenth century provides early examples of these differences.

Just as Machaut is the outstanding representative of the *ars nova* in France, so Francesco Landini (1325–1397) stands for the music of Italy. Although blind from early youth, Landini mastered several instruments and became an outstanding organ virtuoso. He is associated principally with Florence, where he was active as a church organist and composer. His chief compositions are of three types: the *caccia,* similar to the French *chace;* the *ballata,* a form often associated with dancing; and the madrigal. The term "madrigal" [24] was to assume great importance in the sixteenth and early seventeenth centuries, but there it refers to a form that has little in common with its *ars nova* homonym.

The madrigal of Landini and of his Italian contemporaries had a text of several stanzas, each consisting usually of three lines; a rhythmically contrasting *ritornello* of two lines was attached at the end, resulting in the form *aab* or *aaab.* [25] It was most often set for two voices, the upper

24 The word, probably derived from *matricale,* originally referred to a poem in the mother tongue. It may also be connected with *mandriale,* the term used to designate an early fourteenth-century type of rustic poem.

25 See *HAM,* Nos. 49, *Non al suo . . . ,* and 50, *Nel mezzo,* for madrigals by Jacopo da Bologna and by Giovanni da Firenze; and No. 54, *Sy dolce . . . ,* for a madrigal by Landini. The latter, however, is through-composed and includes an isorhythmic tenor.

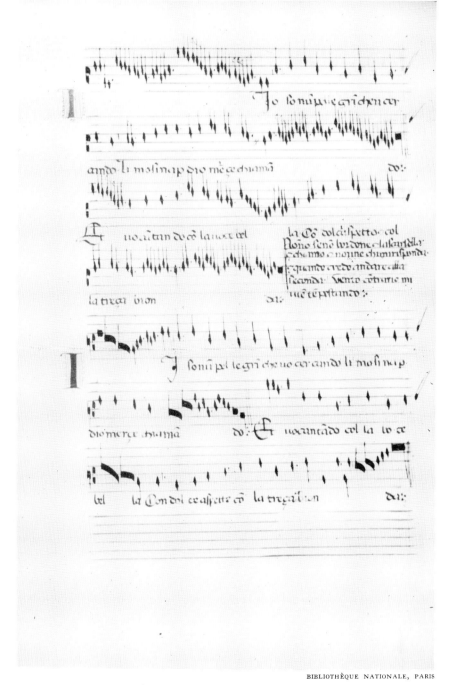

Italian *ars nova* notation. Ballata, *Io son un pellegrino,* by Giovanni da Firenze.

voice more florid than the lower, and it often contained internal changes of meter. The text was concerned with some aspect of romantic love, with an apostrophe to beauty, or something similar. Occasionally text phrases are set in imitative style or even in canon, reflecting the Italian interest in a more unified texture, one that avoids the extreme contrasts characteristic of much thirteenth-century music.

The device of canon was even more typical of the Italian *caccia,* a form related to the French *chace.* The *chace,* as we have seen, was a two-voice canonic piece with a programmatic content. The *caccia,* with a similar descriptive text, also had two voices in canon, but to them a third voice (tenor) not in canon with the others was added.[26] The canonic techniques developed here provided the foundations upon which fifteenth-century Flemish composers created their complex canonic puzzles.

A polyphonic form adapted from the *virelai* is also present in Italy, where it was known as the *ballata*. Landini composed about one hundred and fifty works in this form, which is characterized by external symmetry and internal repetition of parts, often in the form *AbbaA*. In one meter throughout and often in a lively style, the *ballata* was probably used for dancing on many occasions. The absence of a text in the lower part leads to the conclusion that it was performed as a solo song accompanied by two instruments.[27]

The Italian secular works in general reveal a marked feeling for tonality, similar to that reflected in many French *ars nova* works. Cadences comprising a half-step progression from leading tone to tonic are characteristic, and a single tonal center is sometimes in evidence. The so-called Landini cadence (with the sixth scale step inserted between the leading tone and the tonic, often with another leading tone a fourth below the upper one), which was once held to be the exclusive property of the Italian composer, is on the contrary found in French works even earlier than Landini's (see EXAMPLE 44). The appoggiatura is found in Landini's music to such an extent that it may be considered an element of his style. Italian composers used the device consistently in later centuries, and it was subsequently adopted by composers of the Classical period.

EXAMPLE 44

The "Landini cadence"

26 See *HAM,* No. 52, *Tosto che* . . . . , for an example. An earlier *caccia,* by Giovanni da Firenze (also known as Johannes de Florence or Giovanni da Cascia) is given in *TEM,* No. 16, *Con brachi assai.*

27 *HAM,* No. 51, *Io son* . . . , is a *ballata* by Giovanni da Firenze; No. 53, *Amor c'al* . . . , one by Landini. Another *ballata* by Landini is in *MoM,* No. 14, *Chi più.* . . .

The Early Fifteenth Century

Tʜᴇ ʏᴇᴀʀs after about 1400 were marked by a steady progress toward a musical texture in which the parts not only became independent but achieved equal importance. The contributions of Italian musicians to this development were small; music in Italy declined during this period and was to be of only minor importance for the next hundred years. A school of Burgundian composers arose, adopted many style elements from the French school of the fourteenth century, and made vital contributions to the music of the Renaissance period.

English composers made another of their periodic appearances on the stage of music history early in the fifteenth century. An interest in the consonance of the third had marked English music in earlier centuries and had given rise to the style known as *gymel* (see page 71). In the fourteenth century English composers seized upon those and other stylistic elements, creating a style which was to become influential in shaping the style of Burgundian music in the fifteenth.

Developments in England

IN FACT, indigenous music written in several parts must have flourished in England long before the fifteenth century. The sole surviving example is the famous *rota* or round, *Sumer is icumen in,* dated about 1240 by some authorities and about 1310 by others.[1] The first known example of a work in six parts, the piece consists of a four-part canon for unaccompanied voices, with both sacred and secular texts, below which is a *basso ostinato* for two additional voices on a separate text. This *ostinato* (called a *pes* or "foot"), itself a two-part canon, provides firm harmonic support and clearly anticipates tonality in the modern sense.

English discant. A group of English compositions, dating from the thirteenth to the fifteenth centuries, reveals that a modification of discant style (see page 61) was favored by English composers long after a different contrapuntal style had emerged on the continent. Called "English discant" because of its special features, this type of discant is often confused with another and apparently similar style introduced by Burgundian composers, a style that is properly called *fauxbourdon.*

The English discant style, characterized by a degree of parallelism between several voices, grew out of the practice of adding parts to a *cantus firmus* by improvisation. Most often two parts were added above the given melody; thirds and sixths were the basic intervals used in improvising the new parts, so that a succession of (in modern terminology) chords of the sixth or triads in the first inversion resulted. The two new upper parts were called "treble" (derived from *triplum*) and "meane" (or "middle"); the lowest voice, the *cantus firmus,* retained the old term, *tenor.*

Parallelism was not rigidly adhered to, however. The manuscripts of the time show departures from strict writing in rhythmic independence of the three voices, a degree of ornamentation particularly in the topmost voice, and parallel progressions at intervals other than thirds and sixths (see EXAMPLE 45). It will be noticed in the example that octaves and fifths are about as numerous as thirds and tenths; that the intervals are about equally divided between perfect and imperfect; and that, thirds and sixths once having been admitted to the list of consonances, only a single dissonance is present in the fragment (marked with an arrow in the example). These are among the factors which gave English music of the period about 1400 the sonority that was to influence Burgundian and Flemish composers of the following generation.[2]

It is evident that a full sonority based on vertical tonal combinations

1 See Bukofzer, *"Sumer is icumen in"—a Revision,* for a theory about the later date, and the article in *Grove's Dictionary* (5th edition, VII, pp. 186–87) for a defense of the earlier. The *rota* itself is given in *HAM,* No. 42.

2 Another example of the English discant style is given in *HAM,* No. 57b, *Gloria.* Conflicting theories of the origin and scope of the style are found in Bukofzer, *Geschichte des englischen Diskants und des Fauxbourdons nach den theoretischen Quellen,* and Kenney, " 'English Discant' and Discant in England," *Musical Quarterly,* XLV (1959), pp. 26–48.

Sumer is icumen in, the oldest known six-part composition.

EXAMPLE 45

Anon., Motet: *Ave miles*

(they cannot yet be called chords) made for a lessening of independence between voices. This seems not to have concerned English composers of the time; to some extent it is a mark of the conservative attitude one finds across long periods of English history. But the interest in full sonority, on the other hand, was definitely a forward-looking factor. It is seen not only in the considerable use of sixth chords but also in the few works that call for more than the usual three voices.

Dunstable. At the beginning of the fifteenth century English discant was only one of the styles available to English composers. The isorhythmic principle had long since crossed the English Channel, conductus style had not been forgotten, and a free, nonimitative texture was in the process of creation. Although most English composers of the time achieved only local renown, several English names and some English music are preserved in Continental manuscript sources. Isolated works of Cooke and Thomas Damett, about whom little is known, and Lionel (or Leonel) Power (?–1445) are found. The compositions of John Dunstable (*c.* 1370–1453) are available in larger quantity than those of any other English composer and give a clear picture of the stylistic variety that was possible to achieve.

Almost nothing is known about Dunstable's life. He is thought to have spent some years in Paris in the employ of John, Duke of Bedford and regent of France. The majority of his works, which consist of three *chansons* and about fifty sacred compositions, were found in Continental manuscripts, notably the famous Trent Codices and others from Modena, Aosta, and Bologna. Dunstable's contemporaries considered him their leader, and his few surviving compositions are enough to rank him among the most important composers of the late Medieval period. The expressiveness that permeates his music has often caused him to be called the "first composer"; but even without indulging in this false bit of sentimentality, one can find expressive qualities in abundance.

There is first of all a melodic charm in Dunstable's lighter works, of a type that no previous composer had achieved so consistently. A smoothly flowing line characteristic of his part-writing resulted largely from his way of outlining a triad in the melody, restricting dissonances to weak beats (for example, as passing notes) or using them in controlled effects (as in suspensions), and employing wide leaps in the melody for expressive purposes but avoiding leaps elsewhere. EXAMPLE 46 shows a typical short Dunstable phrase.[3]

E X A M P L E   46

Dunstable, *O rosa bella*

Equally important in Dunstable's works is the evidence of his feeling for harmony in the modern sense of the term. Vertical combinations of tones, both of the English discant and the French fauxbourdon types (see below), began to be sensed as having a relationship to other combinations, and melodic lines are often contrived so that their encounters produce a consonant effect and hence a high degree of mellifluous sound. An organized system of harmony lay two or more centuries beyond Dunstable's time, of course, but a suggestion of what was to come finds an early expression in his music and that of his colleagues.

The motet *Sancta Maria* illustrates a trend that, beginning perhaps in Dunstable's time, was to restore sacred music to its high place (see EXAMPLE 47). There is only a single text here; secular influences have disappeared, and the motet has again become a worthy representative of the music of the Church. In the following century a large and flourishing repertoire of sacred music reappeared, in which freely composed liturgical motets without *cantus firmi* became important items.

Other types of motets also occur; they too were to be of considerable influence on fifteenth-century composers. In one type, the *cantus firmus* was not only retained in the tenor but supplied with a partner: a second derived melody, usually more ornate than the first, was sung by the discant (*motetus*). This "double backbone" technique produced motets—by Dunstable as well as by his contemporaries—that contained imitative textures,

3 From *HAM*, No. 61. A motet by Dunstable, *Sancta Maria*, is given in No. 62; other motets will be found in *GMB*, No. 34, *Quam pulchra* . . . , and *TEM*, No. 18. *Veni Sancte*. . . .

E X A M P L E 47

Dunstable, *Sancta Maria*

melodic contrast, and considerable rhythmic diversity. And the technique itself, transferred to other forms, became one of the chief organizing principles of fifteenth-century sacred compositions, especially those pertaining to the Mass.

Dunstable also used the isorhythmic principle in his motets, but he seldom permitted it to interfere with the expressive quality of the music. In many cases he seems to have been guided by the verbal rhythms of his texts and to let that "natural" element shape the rhythms of his melodies. This resulted in a freshness of expression which became one of the characteristics of the forthcoming Renaissance period; and Dunstable in a sense must be considered a harbinger of that period.

Developments in Burgundy

M u c h of the important musical activity of the time from the late Gothic period to the period we are considering had taken place in what is now France. The schools of St. Martial and Notre Dame, the courts of the troubadours and trouvères, the various domiciles of De Vitry and Machaut, the towns in which Dufay and Binchois worked—all are within present-day French borders. On the other hand, many of the principal composers later than Dufay, composers who will be discussed in the following chapters, bear names which suggest Germanic origins; this fact often gives rise to the mistaken impression that musical culture had suddenly moved across the Rhine. In the interest of clarifying the relationships between composers and geography, a brief account of the roles of the duchy of Burgundy and the provinces of the Netherlands is in order.

Burgundy, a large area west of Switzerland and southeast of Paris and a part of the Holy Roman Empire since the eleventh century, had removed itself from French control in the mid-fourteenth. Under Duke Philip and members of his family, Burgundian influence was extended to the east and north and by about 1400 embraced the northern provinces of France as well. These provinces, which included Flanders and other parts of Belgium, adjoined Germanic Holland; thus the entire Netherlands enjoyed a mixed Gallic and Germanic culture. In 1477 the then Duke of Burgundy was killed in battle and the duchy was seized by Louis XI of France. Subsequently, however, the Netherlands came under the control of the Hapsburg line—first, the Austrian branch of that family (1477) and later, the Spanish (1507).

Thus the composers to be discussed in this and the following chapters —Burgundian, Flemish, Dutch—may be predominantly of French culture or of German; more probably, however, they may be simply representatives of the large geographical area now embracing northern France, Belgium, and the Netherlands, in which cultural lines are inextricably mixed.

By the beginning of the fifteenth century, passages in parallel motion had long since disappeared from the music of French composers. In the prevailing style in France, the rhythm of each voice contrasted greatly with those of the others. The ranges of the parts were not yet clearly defined, however, nor were the parts spaced in different registers. As a consequence, tenor and contratenor tended to cross each other to such an extent that it became difficult to determine which of the two was to be called the lowest voice of a piece. Often the individual voices entered one after the other instead of simultaneously. Contrasts in performing medium were also characteristic. One or more voices could be performed instrumentally instead of vocally, and directions for performance were sufficiently free so that a variety of performing media could be drawn upon.

A new style, *fauxbourdon,* also served to alter the sound of French music. In spite of external similarities between it and English discant, the two styles result from quite distinct processes. Fauxbourdon is first found in French compositions about 1430; unlike its English relative, therefore, it was not the result of long development. Further, in a piece in fauxbourdon style the *cantus firmus* was most often in the topmost voice; in English discant, as we have seen, it was usually at the bottom of the texture. Finally, there is a notable difference in the technical formulation of the two styles.

In early compositions employing fauxbourdon only the two outer voices

(*superius* and tenor) were written out; the singer of the (unwritten) contratenor or middle part was expected to sing the *superius* a fourth below
its written pitch. The tenor was so arranged that each of its tones was at
the distance of an octave or a sixth from the topmost tone (see EXAMPLE
48).

E X A M P L E 48

Dufay, *Missa Sancti Jacobi, Communion*

The importance of fauxbourdon in early fifteenth-century French music
was that it enabled composers to smooth out their harmonic textures. The
melodic line became less angular, and a closer rhythmic relationship between the two upper voices appeared. And while the smoother melodic
textures first appeared in pieces in fauxbourdon style, they were soon
taken over in compositions of other styles.

Dufay

IT SEEMS likely that fauxbourdon was the invention of Guillaume Dufay
(*c.* 1400–1474), the most prominent Burgundian composer of the fifteenth
century. Dufay was active in both Italy and France; he was a member of
the Papal choir for at least seven years and lived in Savoy about as long.
But he is identified most closely with the cathedral of Cambrai, in northern France. Held in great esteem by his contemporaries, he was proficient
in both secular and sacred music and contributed also to the literature of
the chanson.

Dufay's secular works include several three-voice songs on Italian texts.
Even these early works, possibly influenced by Landini, reveal the clear
texture and melodiousness that were to characterize all of Dufay's music.
Many of his later and similar songs on French texts (these may now be
called chansons) are free in form; that is, they are not modeled upon the
rondeau, virelai, or other forms employed by Machaut and his com-
patriots.[4]

4 See *HAM*, Nos. 67, *Mon chier amy,* and 68, *Adieu . . . ,* and *GMB*, No. 40, *Le
jour . . . ,* for examples.

The majority of Dufay's motets, for three to five voices, are isorhythmic and based on derived tenors. The tenor is usually the next-to-bottom voice in the four-voice settings, a practice found also in Dufay's Masses. In other motets the principal melody, set in the top voice, is original. Often a four-voice motet contains an extended passage for the two upper voices; this practice lends variety and lightens the texture of the whole. Occasionally, as in the motet based on the antiphon *Alma redemptoris mater*,[5] a long passage for solo voice begins the work, and a series of dramatic chords appears at the end. The great variety of textures, the freely moving rhythms, and the expressive melodies of Dufay's music brought it immediate acceptance, and even in his own day he was celebrated as the greatest composer of Burgundy.

Masses. In the time span between Machaut's Mass (about 1364) and the early Masses of Dufay (roughly 1430), no complete Masses are known to have been composed. A number of settings of single Mass movements have survived, however. These are written in a variety of styles: *cantus firmus* or motet style, with contrapuntal texture over a slow-moving tenor often based on a pre-existing melody; conductus style, composed of vertical groups of tones; and treble or *ballata* style, which contained parts for one or two voices and one or two instruments. And although works written in four parts exist, the majority were three-part. The works of Dufay include some two dozen single or pairs of Mass movements, in the styles described above.

Dufay was also one of the first composers since Machaut to compose complete settings of the Ordinary.[6] Eight Masses are definitely attributed to him, and three or four anonymous works of the period are also considered by some scholars to be his. It is in these works that Dufay went far to standardize a four-voice setting, as opposed to the three-voice setting that had dominated earlier. True, two of his early Masses are for three voices, and another, written about 1430 (the *Missa Sancti Jacobi*), contains some sections for three voices and others for four. But Dufay's later works in this form, as well as many of his motets, are set for four voices.

An important element of Dufay's style in the four-voice settings, in the Masses as well as in the motets, is that the tenor is the next-to-bottom voice. The lowest voice, often called *bassus*, provided something of a real bass function, in that it supplied a foundation upon which other counterpoints could be built. A full development of the bass register, however, was the work of the following generation. With these works of Dufay's the modern setting for four voices came appreciably closer. The following table calls attention to the developments in this area in the time of Dufay and also serves as a summary of earlier practices. It must be pointed out, however, that while the chart gives the usual *relative* disposition of voices, the voices do not necessarily conform to modern voices in pitch range.

5 Given in *HAM*, No. 65.
6 Perhaps a Mass for three voices by Arnold de Lantins predates all of Dufay's. See Reese, *Music in the Renaissance*, p. 39.

TABLE 2:   The naming of voices in polyphonic music

c. 950	c. 1050	c. 1150	c. 1250	c. 1350	c. 1450
			triplum (treble)	*discantus*	*superius* (soprano)
	vox organalis	*duplum*	*duplum* (*motetus*)	*contratenor*	*contratenor altus* (contralto)
vox principalis	*vox principalis*	*tenor*	*tenor*	*tenor*	*tenor* (tenor)
vox organalis					*contratenor bassus* (bass)

At least six of Dufay's Masses are of the *cantus firmus* type, which rose to great importance in the later fifteenth and sixteenth centuries. Many single Mass movements, notably by Dunstable and his contemporaries, as well as pairs of movements (*Gloria* and *Credo*, for example), illustrate a technique similar to that of the *cantus firmus*. And other types of Masses appear also. It will be well, therefore, to describe the principal Mass types.

Mass Types

Cantus firmus Mass. It will be remembered that as early as the ninth century the *vox principalis* (later called *tenor*) in an organum was often a section of a Gregorian chant which the other voice or voices in the piece served to embellish. Further, in the thirteenth century when the motet was created, an underlying tenor—again derived from a pre-existent melody—served as a foundation above which the other voices ran their separate courses. Most often that melody was stretched out, so to speak; a series of long tones, corresponding in pitch to the tones of the borrowed tune, then constituted the tenor. Finally, in the period with which this chapter is concerned, we have seen that such a derived melody came to be called a *cantus firmus*, which may be translated roughly as "fundamental melody." The principle of composition illustrated here—namely, that of embellishing, paraphrasing, or otherwise reworking a borrowed melody— was greatly respected in Medieval music. And we shall see in later chapters that it was employed widely in the Renaissance period as well.

In the time of Dufay, this principle was extended to the composition of an entire Mass. One borrowed melody appeared in all the movements, usually in the tenor, resulting in a unified, cyclical, or *cantus firmus* Mass. Over half of Dufay's known Masses are of this type. A related type is called a "plainsong Mass"; here a different *cantus firmus* was used in each movement—a Gregorian *Kyrie* in the first movement, a Gregorian *Gloria* in the second, and so on—hence this type is not cyclical.[7]

7 The terms are somewhat confusing, for the *cantus firmus* in the cyclical Mass is usually derived from plainsong, and the plainsongs in the noncyclical type are most often treated with *cantus firmus* techniques.

A typical setting for Burgundian church music: the Cathedral at Autun.

The *cantus firmus* was sometimes derived from the Gregorian reper-toire and sometimes not. It could be taken from a secular song, from two or more songs, or from a motet; later, it could be freely invented by the composer. Often the name by which a Mass is known gives the source of the borrowed tenor. Thus Dufay's *Missa Se la face ay pale* has a tenor borrowed from the same composer's chanson of that name. His *Missa Caput* employs the melody of a Gregorian antiphon, *Venit ad Petrum*. Conversely, one of Dufay's early Masses is identified as a *Missa sine nomine* (literally, "Mass without a name"); in this type the Mass is freely composed, that is, without a derived tenor.

Paraphrase Mass. Another somewhat related Mass type is called a "para-phrase Mass." Here again borrowed material is employed, but now it is most often in the topmost voice (*superius*), rhythmically altered to some extent, and sometimes embellished through the addition of short melodic turns, ornamental tones, and the like. Paraphrase techniques appear in Dufay's early Masses and in works by Okeghem and Josquin des Prez;

they form important ingredients of the style of Palestrina in the late Renaissance period.

Paraphrase Masses are sometimes called "discant Masses," possibly because the borrowed material is employed in the discant—which, it will be remembered, is one of the old names for the topmost voice. A special kind of paraphrase Mass is known as the "discant-tenor Mass"; in this kind the *cantus firmus* is employed not only in long notes in the tenor but also in embellished form with various note values in the discant.

Parody Mass. The parody Mass came into existence somewhat later than the types mentioned above. Again borrowed material is employed, but now more than one melody is reworked in the new composition. Entire sections of a pre-existing composition are embodied in the new work; or more properly, such sections are worked together with new material to create a new composition.

Binchois

A NUMBER of composers roughly contemporary with Dufay contributed to the fame of the Burgundian school early in the fifteenth century. Walter Frye, an Englishman, is presumably to be included, as are Jean Brassart and Jean Vide. The only composer of the school who even approached Dufay in musical excellence and charm, however, was Gilles Binchois.

Binchois (*c.* 1400–1460) was a native of Mons; there is a reference (in a motet by Okeghem) to his having been a soldier in his youth. He served the Burgundian court at Dijon in a variety of offices for about thirty years, eventually rising to the post of second chaplain. His works are preserved in many manuscripts, and the melodies of some of them served as *cantus firmi* for later composers, testifying to the esteem in which his music was held, both by his own generation and by later ones.

The number of Binchois's sacred compositions is not large: twenty-two motets, four Magnificats, and twenty-five Mass movements have been preserved. It is noteworthy that the *cantus firmus* style, employed extensively by Dufay, plays no part in the work of Binchois, his contemporary. Other stylistic devices are present in abundance—fauxbourdon, treble-dominated passages, and isorhythm, for example—and in a few cases, textures embodying contrapuntal imitation are found.

It is in Binchois's fifty or more chansons that the composer's true stature is seen. The term "chanson" is sometimes used to refer to any song with a French text. In this sense the various *rondeaux, virelais,* and similar monophonic songs of the troubadours and trouvères may also be called chansons. Likewise the polyphonic equivalents of such works, as seen in Machaut, can be grouped under this term. At the turn of the sixteenth century, however, the term took on a third, specialized meaning. A tendency arose to abandon the fixed forms which had survived without essential change since the twelfth century and to write in free forms, with textures based on the joint use of imitative counterpoint and chordal writing. It is to this sixteenth-century development that the term "chanson" is usually applied; works by Josquin, Lasso, and others will illustrate this use of the term (see below, Chapter 11).

The chansons of Binchois represent the second stage of development, in that they are usually in fixed forms (with the *rondeau* predominating) and set in three-part polyphony (see EXAMPLE 49). The main melody is

EXAMPLE 49

Binchois, Chanson: *Se la belle*

FROM Friedrich Blume, *Das Chorwerk*, Vol. 22, *Binchois, 16 weltliche Lieder*, edited by W. Gurlitt, Möseler Verlag, Wolfenbüttel and Zürich.

TRANSLATION:
If the beauty does not wish
to ease my pain . . .

most often set as the highest part, and in general it is the only one supplied with a text. Here, as with similar chansons by Dufay and others, one may assume that the lower voices were performed instrumentally. The tenor part of these chansons is often in the same melodic style as the upper parts and is capable of being performed vocally, forming a complement to the equally melodious topmost part; the contratenor, by contrast, serves primarily as a harmonic filler and is likely to be somewhat angular in

COURTESY FERNAND NATHAN, PARIS

A concert in the fields. Scene from a fifteenth-century Burgundian tapestry.

melodic contour. The melodious character of the tenor part can be taken as early evidence of a style trait that was to grow in importance in later centuries—namely, the approach of instrumental writing to a vocal idiom and vice versa.

It appears that with Binchois the old unity of poet and musician was lost, for he found his texts in poems written by his contemporaries. While the intimate relationship between text and music sometimes suffered thereby, the music gained in freedom, melodic charm, and independence. The presence of many triadic patterns in Binchois's melodies reflects the practices of Dunstable and Dufay. New ingredients, such as an unprepossessing folklike tone, simpler rhythms in triple meter, and clearly defined cadences, give Binchois's chansons a naturalness in which the last traces of *ars nova* artificiality and stylization disappear.[8]

8 Two chansons are reprinted in *HAM*, Nos. 69, *De plus* . . . , and 70, *Files* . . . ; and one is in *MoM*, No. 16, *Adieu*. . . .

8

Emergence of Renaissance Style

SHORTLY after the beginning of the fifteenth century, Franco-Flemish composers played a vital role in developing a new manner of vocal performance, choral polyphony. It will be remembered that to about the tenth century, certain sections of Gregorian plainsong had been sung by a soloist and others by a unison choir (see page 40). Later, in *organa*, *clausulae*, and some motets, only the sections which had been sung by the soloist were set in the new polyphonic style; the other sections were still sung by the unison choir. And in many fourteenth-century sacred polyphonic works, the lower voices were given to instruments and only the upper voice was sung—still by the unison choir. Finally, in compositions which contained text in all voices, it was understood that a group of soloists would sing the work.

"The Couple at the Fountain," design for a paten by Israhel van Meckenem, 15th c. [THE METROPOLITAN MUSEUM OF ART, DICK FUND, 1927]

Indications of the development of true choral polyphony are seen in a group of Italian manuscripts dating from the years about 1420–1430, principally of Burgundian or Franco-Flemish composers—Dufay and Binchois among them. The terms *unus* and *chorus* are used to identify the kind of performance desired, and a gradual differentiation in style is seen between the sections sung by an ensemble of soloists and those sung by a chorus. The most graphic indication of choral performance is the increase in the size of the manuscript pages themselves. These are frequently of a size (about twenty by twenty-eight inches) which would allow a chorus to read the music even at a distance; earlier manuscripts, designed for solo-ists, had seldom exceeded a normal page size.

The earliest known work in which choral polyphony is clearly distin-guished from solo-ensemble writing consists of a pair of movements, *Gloria* and *Credo*, by Guillaume Legrant, dated 1426.[1] Here the choral sections are in chordal style and the soloistic sections are free in rhythm and technically more demanding. The way once having been opened, the new manner of performance spread rapidly, principally in the Church. By

---

1 The *Credo* may be found in *HAM*, No. 56.

Choir singing from a large chorus book. Title page of Gafori's *Practica Musica*, 1512.

the middle of the century it had become standard practice, both on the Continent and in England. This development of polyphonic choral singing out of an essentially soloistic tradition constitutes one aspect of the transition from the late Gothic period to the Renaissance.[2]

Okeghem

THE GROUP of composers of Burgundian extraction headed by Dufay was succeeded by a line of Flemish composers which continued to be of vital significance for two centuries. Among the first and most important of these composers was Johannes Okeghem, born about 1430. Okeghem may have been a pupil of Dufay; he served as a choir singer in Antwerp, Cambrai, and in the Royal Chapel at Paris. He became chaplain and composer to three kings of France (Charles VII, Louis XI, and Charles VIII), and received a number of other ecclesiastical and royal honors. His travels took him to Spain and Flanders. He died in Tours about 1495, revered by his fellow musicians both as a composer and as a teacher.

Okeghem composed both secular and sacred music, but it is in the latter field that his full development as a composer is seen. About a dozen Masses, nine motets, and a few other sacred works have survived, in addition to about twenty chansons. The principal stylistic feature of the Masses is a smoothly flowing web of contrapuntal lines not derived from each other; in other words, Okeghem's counterpoint in general is nonimitative.[3] Characteristic opening motives, which could easily be imitated in other voices, do not usually appear. Internal cadences and phrase endings most often occur at different times in different voices, so that a spun-out, unbroken or continuous texture is most typical (see EXAMPLE 50). In some later works, however, imitative textures are occasionally employed.

It was Okeghem's general practice to write each part in a different rhythm—an almost necessary corollary of a nonimitative texture. He also expanded the range by placing the bass part lower than usual; the two middle voices (tenor and contratenor) are about equal in range, but the *superius* (soprano) is pitched lower than would be the custom today and corresponds roughly to the alto range. The result is a rather dark vocal color which enhances the mystic feeling prevailing in Okeghem's works in general. These works, in turn, went far to establish an austere choral style.

The majority of Okeghem's Masses are written for four voices, although some three- and five-voice Masses exist. *Cantus firmus* Masses predominate, but paraphrase and freely composed Masses are also found. The melodies used as *cantus firmi* are derived from *rondeaux* by Binchois and others, the long-popular song, *L'homme armé,* and material that has not yet been identified; some may be original. The writing generally includes parts for all the voices across long passages, resulting in a variety of sonorities.

---

2 See Bukofzer, "The Beginnings of Choral Polyphony," in *Studies in Medieval and Renaissance Music,* pp. 176–89, for details of this development.

3 See *HAM,* Nos. 73a, *Kyrie,* 73b, *Agnus Dei III,* 74, *Ma maitresse,* and 75, *Ma bouche rit,* and *GMB,* No. 52, *Ut heremita . . . ,* for examples of the style.

EXAMPLE 50

Okeghem, *Missa mi-mi, Credo*

et in - vi- si - bi - - - - - - li -um,

et in- vi - si - bi-li- um,

et in - vi - si - bi - li- um,

et in - vi - si - bi - li - um,

FROM *Collected Works of Johannes Okeghem*, Volume II, edited by Dragan Plamenac. Reprinted by permission of the American Musicological Society and Columbia University Press.

While a more or less free contrapuntal style (always unified by the *cantus firmus*) prevails in the majority of the Masses, canonic writing appears in others. Okeghem's unique *Missa prolationum* is one such work. It is a four-voice Mass, but only the first and third voices are notated. A second voice, not notated, is designed to be sung in canon with the first, at intervals ranging from the unison to the octave. The first voice begins in *tempus imperfectum,* the second in *tempus perfectum;* but both voices are in *prolatio minor.* Similarly, the fourth voice, not notated, forms a canon with the third; here both voices, one in *tempus imperfectum* and the other in *tempus perfectum,* are in *prolatio maior.* Thus the four prolations are provided for. The voices in imperfect time, however, move in shorter steps than those in perfect, and the distance between the halves of each canon constantly increases. Okeghem then resorts to other note values, and several types of canon as well as double canons with irregular augmentation result (see EXAMPLE 51). It must be admitted that the strict identity of the parts and the similarity of their melodic contours are not always perceived in performance because of the irregular augmentations.[4]

It has long been customary in musical writings to overemphasize the importance and frequency of works such as the *Missa prolationum* which employ cryptic canonic writing in one way or another. These works are called "puzzle canons"; the notation is given for only some of the voices and the other voices must be worked out (in crab, inverted, or a similar kind of canon) according to a set of cryptic directions. A typical directive of this type might include the phrase, "We adore the Trinity in unity";

4 A section of the *Sanctus* is given in *MoM*, No. 17.

EXAMPLE 51

Okeghem, *Missa prolationum*

FROM *Collected Works of Johannes Okeghem*, Volume II, edited by Dragan Plamenac. Reprinted by permission of the American Musicological Society and Columbia University Press.

this could indicate that the work was a triple canon in unison. Machaut's *Ma fin est ma commencement* was such a work (see p. 93). Puzzle canons are not numerous, however; they do no more than testify to the efforts made by fifteenth-century composers to realize fully the technical possibilities of unified contrapuntal writing. The intellectual effort which such works call forth does not usually affect the music adversely; indeed, Okeghem and his school took pains to establish the same melodiousness, sonority, and musical values in these works as in their less "contrived" ones.

Okeghem's Requiem Mass is the oldest that has yet been found (an earlier work known to have been written by Dufay has not been preserved). In his day the liturgy of the Requiem was not fixed; Okeghem's version consists of two-, three-, and four-part settings of the Introit, *Kyrie*, Gradual, Tract, and Offertory. (The *Dies irae*, usually treated as a highly dramatic episode by later composers, did not enter the Requiem Mass until about 1565.) The corresponding Gregorian chants are paraphrased, usually in the topmost voice, and the writing is in general nonimitative and conservative.

In summary, Okeghem's music shows a relationship to Dunstable's in its free-flowing polyphony, a continuation of the melodiousness found in Dufay, and a complete mastery of the contrapuntal techniques developed by the Burgundian school. The moods of his works, as indicated above, are quite different from those of the Burgundians—that is, they are darker in general. In his sacred music as in his secular, Okeghem emphasized rhythmic subtlety and variety, and he set his texts with regard for their

Sanctus and *Osanna* from Okeghem's *Missa prolationum,* showing the notated first and third voices. See EXAMPLE 51 for the realization of the unwritten second and fourth voices of the *Osanna.*

mood. The last traces of Gothic rigidity in text setting disappeared, and expression of emotion became an ideal to be sought.

Busnois

ANTOINE BUSNOIS (?–1492) was one of the many Flemish contemporaries of Okeghem whose compositions are of great charm. Very little is known of Busnois's life; he was in the chapel choir at the Burgundian court in 1467, at Mons in 1476, and some years later was appointed to a position at Bruges. His compositions are primarily in the secular field; some sixty or more chansons survive—some written for three voices and others for four, the latter setting soon becoming standardized. Other surviving works are in the fixed forms: *rondeaux, virelais,* and the like. The outstanding technical feature of Busnois's style is the considerable use of imitative counterpoint, especially in pairs of voices. Thus Busnois may be grouped with the forward-looking composers, for imitative counterpoint became an important stylistic element in the works of later fifteenth- and sixteenth-century composers.

Obrecht

FLEMISH composers of the generation after Okeghem may be roughly classified as either conservative or progressive. Conservative style elements include occasional textures based on free counterpoint (that is, nonimitative); a "seamless" form produced by overlapping phrases and characterized by the relative absence of internal cadences; and, at the ends of pieces, the cadence types that had served the composers of Dufay's and Okeghem's generations. The chief steps toward a new style, on the other hand, are the consistent use of imitative counterpoint, the creation of forms divided into sections (each such section was later called a "point of imitation"), sensitivity to contrasts of range and texture, and the introduction of new cadence types.

In this classification Jacob Obrecht (1452–1505) takes an intermediate position. Obrecht was Dutch rather than Flemish; his career was divided between Berg op Zoom, Cambrai, Bruges, and Antwerp, but he also lived and traveled in Italy for short periods, and he died in Ferrara. His preserved works include about two dozen motets, as many Masses, a setting of the Passion According to St. Matthew (the oldest polyphonic setting yet known), and about thirty secular compositions of various kinds. His general musicality, technical proficiency, and imaginative approach to his texts place him among the finest composers of the late fifteenth century; only Josquin des Prez looms higher.

Like Okeghem, Obrecht often relied upon nonimitative writing; much of the time his polyphony consists of free counterpoints. Other works, however, reveal the use of canonic writing, of which he was apparently quite fond, and in still others free imitation is used copiously. His melodic phrases in general are shorter and more concise than Okeghem's. Also unlike the older master, Obrecht most often created textures in which internal cadences in three of the (usually) four voices occur at the same time, providing moments of repose within the movements. Cadences in the late fifteenth century had often shown a dominant-tonic relationship (speaking in today's terms, which of course are not appropriate to that century), and Obrecht's music contains its share of such modern-sounding devices. On the other hand, the polytextual motets found occasionally in Obrecht are again reflections of old Gothic practices.[5]

In his use of *cantus firmus* techniques, especially in the Masses, Obrecht revealed considerable imagination. Often the *cantus firmus* was divided into short sections, each section used separately. In his *Missa super Maria zart*, for example, the twenty-seven-measure melody is divided into twelve sections, which are then distributed according to a well-planned scheme throughout the Mass movements. The *Kyrie* contains sections 1 and 2 of the *cantus firmus;* the *Gloria,* sections 3 to 6; the *Credo,* sections 6 to 9, and so on. Only in the *Agnus Dei* is the entire melody heard, and there it provides a climactic moment and unifies the entire Mass.[6] In certain other Masses, more than one *cantus firmus* is employed, and a few Masses are *sine nomine,* that is, freely composed.

Obrecht also approached the parody technique on occasion. It will be recalled that a parody Mass differs from a *cantus firmus* Mass in employ-

5 Two of Obrecht's motets are printed in *GMB*, No. 54, *O vos omnes*, and *MoM*, No. 18, *Parce . . .* ; neither of these is polytextual, however.
6 See Reese, *Music in the Renaissance,* p. 193, for details.

ing not only a pre-existent melody but entire polyphonic sections or entire compositions. Obrecht's *Missa Rosa playsant* makes use of a three-voice chanson of uncertain authorship.[7] At least once in each movement all three voices of a section of the chanson are heard simultaneously, in somewhat paraphrased form but clearly related to it. Much of the time, however, the various melodies are heard singly as *cantus firmi,* and to this extent Obrecht's work is not a true parody Mass.

In his tentative employment of the parody principle Obrecht anticipated the work of the next generation of Flemish composers. The parody Mass became a favorite form throughout the sixteenth century, when much ingenuity was expended on concealing and elaborating the borrowed material.

Josquin des Prez

OCCASIONALLY one composer succeeds in summing up all the techniques that existed before his time, bringing a high degree of refinement and skill to their use. At the same time, he impresses a new and individual style upon all that he writes and therefore stands at the beginning of a new style period. Such a composer was Josquin des Prez, born about 1450 in Hainault, near the present Belgian-French border. Josquin was reputedly a pupil of Okeghem's. He spent some years in Italy, in the Papal choir and at the court of Duke Galeazzo Sforza in Milan. Later he returned to Burgundy, where he died in 1521. Few other biographical details can be attested to with certainty, but his immense reputation as an inspired teacher and composer is well documented. Several of Josquin's works were included in the very first volume of printed part-music, which Ottaviano de' Petrucci of Venice produced in 1501, and books of Josquin's Masses were printed and reprinted by Petrucci between 1502 and 1516. This alone indicates that he was favorably known internationally even during his lifetime.

The style that had culminated in Okeghem, and that was present to a lesser extent in Obrecht, was a self-limiting one. Okeghem had carried the art of continuous, free, and consistent contrapuntal writing to a peak from which no further rise could be expected. A texture resulted in which all four voices were equal and intertwined, producing a serious, mystical mood. A less rigorous polyphony and an abandonment of technical consistency were unthinkable in the last decades of the fifteenth century. It remained for Josquin to create a new kind of music, to effect a rebirth of musical expression, and to provide models for a century of subsequent Renaissance composers. In his chansons, Masses, and motets, he revealed a keen awareness of the past, yet he also approached the future with imagination and boundless resource. The result was a body of music unsurpassed in the Renaissance period.

Solid contrapuntal writing, much figuration in the sonorous web, and a fascination for the technical possibilities of canon are evident in one

7 See Reese, *Music in the Renaissance,* pp. 111, 202.

group of Josquin's works—presumably his early ones. But his visits and studies in Italy brought a marked change in his style, adding lightness, clarity, and emotional richness to the great contrapuntal skill of the young composer, and a new style was born. The essential ingredients of this new style are polyphonic texture, emotional expressiveness, and a new interest in contrasting choral sonorities.

Chansons. Josquin's chansons embody a variety of forms, a wide range of expression, and a consistently high level of musical quality. Some of them retain the fixed forms of the older chanson (for example, the ballade, with a form *ab ab cd E*); others are through-composed and entirely free and subjective. They are written for three to six voices, in contrast to the predominant three-voice settings of the Dufay period. The texts themselves reflect the conventional themes: unrequited love, broken hearts, fidelity, and occasionally a more humorous subject. Josquin set himself the task of finding the exact shade of musical expression appropriate to each text. In his artistry he succeeded—but sometimes the result was a higher musical expressiveness than was called for by the text. This is seen, for example, in *Fault d'argent,*[8] where the eloquent melodies, the finely wrought imitations, and the symmetrical *aba* form seem wasted on the text, which is concerned with the evils arising from lack of money.

Josquin's chansons in general show the same care and technical mastery that are characteristic of his sacred works. Imitative counterpoint is perhaps the most consistently used device; what had in Okeghem appeared seldom and in Obrecht frequently now becomes a principal stylistic feature. Often this develops into canonic writing, but Josquin seldom used canon rigidly. Subtle changes in the distance of a canonic response, a shift of accent or interval, or a changed phrase ending—these help to invest the canonic chansons with a spontaneous, flexible mode of expression. Chanson texts are sometimes set in *cantus firmus* style, with the derived melody taken from a chanson by Okeghem or some other composer, or from a popular tune such as *L'homme armé.*

Motets. More than a hundred of Josquin's motets were printed between 1501 and 1564. In these, even more than in the chansons, imitative counterpoint became the chief structural feature, and perhaps as a consequence, *cantus firmus* devices became less evident. Josquin's practice was to divide a text into sentences or short paragraphs and to give each section (point of imitation) its own melodic material. This is seen in the motet *Dominus regnavit,* a setting of Psalm XCII (93).[9] Even within the sections, however, the type of imitation varies. In this four-voice motet, for example, the first section contains a passage for the two upper voices in canon, followed after fifteen measures by one for the two lower voices, again in canon; the second section begins and ends in four-part canon, but contains two short two-voice canons between the

8 In *HAM,* No. 91. The text is translated in *HAM,* p. 249.

9 Printed in *Das Chorwerk,* Vol. 33. Other motets are in *GMB,* No. 60, *O Domine . . . ,* and *MoM,* No. 19, *Ave Maria.*

four-part passages; the third section is in four-part canon throughout, and the succeeding sections have still other canonic plans.

Pairs of canons often appear in the motets. In *Ave Christe, immolate*, for example, tenor and bass are given one canon (at the fifth after one beat) for seven measures, after which soprano and alto enter with another canon (at the octave after six beats) for nine measures; this is followed by a four-voice passage in canonic imitation. Variety in canonic treatment is frequently in evidence (see EXAMPLE 52).

The line between canon and imitation is not easy to draw in Josquin's motets, for a canonic passage which is not strict (and Josquin's rarely are) tends to resemble a passage in which imitation is employed consist-

EXAMPLE 52

Josquin, *Ave Christe, immolate*

ently. And Josquin's canonic passages often resolve into imitative writing after a few measures.

The motets include some of the earliest polyphonic settings of Psalm texts. Scriptural texts had not in general found employment in motets until late in the fifteenth century, but after Josquin the practice became general. Some of the most moving of Josquin's works are in this category: Psalm CXXIX (130), *De profundis*, which occurs in two settings, and the turbulent Psalm XXXVII (38), as well as Psalm XCII (93), mentioned above. In these settings he often uses a psalm tone as *cantus firmus*, or paraphrases it. In Psalm XXXVII the contrapuntal style occasionally gives way to chordal declamation (see EXAMPLE 53), the sudden cessation of

EXAMPLE 53

Josquin, *Domine, ne in furore*

contrapuntal motion emphasizing the meaning of the chordally treated phrase, *domum tuam.*

The music thus becomes an instrument for expressing the inmost meaning of the text, and one aspect of Josquin's genius lies in his finding the proper musical expression for a great variety of texts. That variety seems to have challenged Josquin, for it is in the motets that the full range of his musical discernment is revealed.

Masses. A number of Masses, which are presumably among Josquin's early works in the form, reveal similarities to the motets: a variety of imitative devices, use of *cantus firmi,* and sectional structures in each movement. Changes in the thickness of the texture are equally characteristic: the Masses are all for four voices, yet passages for the top two, the bottom two, for all but the tenor, for the top three, and other combinations lend a degree of varied sonority to the music. The concept of vocal "orchestration" cannot have been far from Josquin's mind. Individual vocal ranges, too, are somewhat extended, voices are laid out further apart, and there is consequently less need for voice crossings. In spite of this, Josquin frequently permits one voice to cross over or under another, but for purely expressive reasons. Indeed, in these works as in all of Josquin's, musical expressiveness is the factor always to be looked for—and found.

Josquin's *cantus firmi* include a variety of types. The familiar *L'homme armé* is employed in two Masses. Josquin also drew upon Okeghem's chanson, *Malheur me bat,* a motet by Brumel, *Mater Patris,* and similar sources as well as the Gregorian chant repertoire, and occasionally he employed a series of solmization syllables, as in the *Missa La sol fa re mi.*[10]

In a few of Josquin's Masses the paraphrase technique is approached. In this technique, it will be recalled, the *cantus firmus* appears not in the tenor but most often in the upper voice, where it is freely elaborated (paraphrased). The *Missa Pange lingua* is Josquin's most famous Mass of this type; its borrowed material is drawn from the Vesper hymn for the Feast of Corpus Christi.[11] Here, in an extension of the paraphrase technique, the chant material pervades all voices in the entire Mass. Movements or sections frequently begin with paraphrased versions of the chant's first phrase (see Example 54); these versions are then treated imitatively. Elsewhere other phrases of the chant are similarly paraphrased and embodied in the contrapuntal texture. The Mass also contains passages in chordal style; indeed, the mixture of polyphonic and chordal style became a feature of Josquin's later and most profound works. This feature proved to be of great influence on the entire sixteenth-century sacred repertoire.

In the *Missa Pange lingua* as well as in other similar late compositions, the variety of textures enabled Josquin to set the text with regard for its emotional meaning. A subjective kind of writing resulted, of course;

10 A section of the *Credo* is reprinted in *GMB,* No. 59.

11 In *Liber usualis,* p. 957. The *Missa Pange lingua* itself is published in *Das Chorwerk,* Vol. 1.

EXAMPLE 54

Josquin, *Missa Pange lingua*

Josquin is among the first of the composers in whose works a subjective approach can be traced throughout. A new aesthetic principle, in which one of the functions of music was to parallel the rhetoric of the text, was in the process of being born in Josquin's time. One result was a strengthening of the *a cappella* concept, in which vocal music was not to be supported by instruments but was to be performed by voices alone. The idea that a composition had to be *interpreted*, that the notation could not bring out all the subtleties contained in the music, became a part of musical thinking. To this complex of principles and ideas the name *musica reservata* was given, and Josquin is credited with taking a major role in creating the new music in which the ideas came to expression. It must be said that all the implications of the term *musica reservata*, introduced by Josquin's pupil, Adrianus Coclico, are not yet known; it may be that the term in the early sixteenth century had yet other meanings not related to expressive content.[12]

Other Composers

A host of Franco-Flemish composers roughly contemporary with Josquin give evidence of solid musical accomplishments. If they did not rise above Josquin in the quality of the music they wrote, they at least showed comparable technical skill and versatility. Few of them remained at home during their entire lifetimes; in traveling to Italy, Germany, Spain, and elsewhere, they contributed to the dissemination of the Flemish contrapuntal arts and to the eventual formation, in the later sixteenth century, of a virtually international style compounded of Flemish, German, and Italian elements. A few of those composers may be mentioned briefly.

Isaac. Heinrich Isaac (*c.* 1450–1517) lived in Italy from about 1480 to 1497, when he moved to the court at Vienna. In 1514 he returned to Italy, where he remained. Isaac developed facility in the style of each country's music and was equally at home in all branches of composition. He composed chansons in the Flemish style with imitative counterpoint; his Italian secular music is largely chordal; and some of his Masses, most of them for four voices, are rhythmically alive in the best Italian style. Isaac's principal work is the *Choralis Constantinus,* commissioned by the Cathedral of Constance in 1508. Here his style is purely Flemish, abstract, and involved. The three books of this work contain motets on texts from the Proper of the Mass, from the Offices for the Feasts and Saints, and from the Ordinary; thus the work embraces the entire church year. The motets, preceded by chant intonations, employ the corresponding Gregorian melodies as *cantus firmi* in the most varied manner. Like his Masses, the *Choralis Constantinus* is written primarily for four voices. The borrowed material of the *cantus firmus* is used freely. Found in upper voices as well as in the tenor, and not always set in long notes, it is often as diverse rhythmically as the other voices. The continuous polyphonic textures in the work are somewhat reminiscent of Okeghem's. Isaac died before finishing the *Choralis Constantinus,* and his pupil, Ludwig Senfl, brought the work to completion.

Compère. Loyset Compère (*c.* 1455–1518) made the usual Flemish visits to Italy and France, but he is associated primarily with Flanders. In his Masses and motets he is related to the school of Okeghem, despite the fact that he belonged to a later generation. His chansons are in general built on the old fixed forms, but their textures are imitative in the more forward-looking Flemish tradition.

12 See Reese, *Music in the Renaissance,* pp. 511–17, for a summary; also Palisca, "A Clarification of 'Musica Reservata' in Jean Taisnier's 'Astrologiae,' " in *Acta musicologica,* XXXI (1959), pp. 133–61.

De La Rue. Pierre de La Rue (?–1518) was associated with the Burgundian court as well as with the city of Brussels. His works include about thirty-five Masses, among them a canonic Mass in six parts; an equal number of motets; and several chansons. His principal work, however, is a Requiem Mass, in which tonal effects and varieties of sonority are outstanding. De La Rue virtually completed the development of a true bass range, thus ending the series of steps that had been begun by Okeghem: in several passages in the Requiem, the bass descends to a low B♭. The Requiem is basically for four voices, but it contains many passages for two, three, and five. In keeping with the somber purpose of the Mass, the lower ranges and darker vocal colors predominate. At times de La Rue wrote with the fervor and eloquence of Josquin.

Mouton. Jean Mouton (c. 1470–1522) became a singer in the chapel of two kings of France, Louis XII and Francis I, but he was also professionally active in Flanders. His major interest seems to have been sacred music, which he modeled on the style of Josquin.[13] Mouton is also known as the teacher of Adrian Willaert.

The Renaissance

THE SERIES of developments discussed in this chapter, and more especially the new aesthetic outlook and musical content of the works of Josquin and others of his generation, were not removed from the general stream of culture. Many of them were, in fact, concomitants of developments in the arts, in literature, and in social life in general that mark the late fifteenth century as one of the turning points of cultural history. Those developments are reflected in a movement called humanism which gave rise to the cultural period of the Renaissance.

Humanism, so called because it stressed the powers and virtues of human beings, began as a literary movement in Italy. It concerned itself with the dignity of secular life, holding that life in the present was as important as life in the hereafter. The belief that the individual man— as opposed to Man, the abstraction—had rights, inner strengths, and worthy personal feelings made the search for happiness a valid motive for living. Inevitably, the renunciation of worldly pleasures for the sake of future salvation lost force as the mainspring of human behavior.

The search for beauty was another aspect of the new humanism. It is likely that the idea of abstract beauty as an attribute of human life had not entered the minds of Medieval artists and musicians; music and art existed primarily to glorify God and not to give pleasure to man. Now, in the late fifteenth century, beauty became an ingredient to be discovered and expressed.

North of the Alps, humanism took a more religious, mystical tone. Lay religious movements, having no connection with the Church, flourished in the Netherlands. Their members taught the virtues of reverence, love,

13 A mirror canon is printed in *GMB*, No. 66, *Salve Mater*.

and similar personal qualities. Mystics found a way to a direct relationship with the divine without need of clerical intermediaries; religion for them could become a personal, human experience. Thus in both the south and the north of Europe, man as an individual was born; but in the minds of fifteenth-century men it was a *rebirth,* for they knew that the men of the ancient world had had such individual worth. The concept of a rebirth, a renaissance, gradually became current, eventually giving its name to the cultural period itself. In a music-historical sense, the period runs roughly from the mid-fifteenth century to the end of the sixteenth.

It may now be seen in retrospect that Josquin's concern with subjective expression, with musical beauty itself, is one characteristic of the musical Renaissance. Further, the attention given by the humanists to the literature of Greece and Rome—that is, to the meanings and implications of the texts themselves—was soon extended to the meanings of all texts, and church musicians re-examined their liturgical texts with an eye to discovering for themselves whatever personal significance the texts could hold for them. Thus one may account for Josquin's preoccupation with textual meaning and his search for the musical means that would best express that meaning. With this concern for meaning came an appreciation of prosody and proper declamation; the insensitivity shown by many Medieval composers to the relationship between textual and musical ac-

PHOTO PAUL BLATEBIER

A detail of Jan and Hubert Van Eyck's altarpiece at Ghent, a fine example of the Renaissance spirit as it found expression in the Netherlands.

cents soon became a thing of the past, and in the sixteenth century the proper placing of musical accents became part of every competent composer's style.

In their encounters with the new concepts and in their assimilation of specific Italian elements, all the Flemish composers did not react alike. Okeghem remained a serious, mystical man of the north, seemingly unaffected by Italian contributions—if indeed he was aware of them. Obrecht's acquaintance with Italian style elements was probably greater, for his music shows clear rhythmic structures and warm expressiveness akin to the Italian. Isaac, more international than his contemporaries, knew the Italian *frottola*, an unassuming secular form in chordal style, gay in mood and breathing a vital musical air; at his hand the form became more refined and dignified. It remained for Josquin to bring about the complete fusion of the two styles: Flemish counterpoint, with its technical possibilities, intellectual appeal, and serious purpose; and Italian spiritedness, with its harmonic color, flexible rhythms, and charming directness. The result was a Renaissance style which became virtually universal in the sixteenth century and gave rise to some of the most refined, moving, and expressive works in the repertoire of Western music.

The Renaissance:
Vocal Music of Catholic
Composers

THE PERIOD of the Renaissance was marked by considerable activity on the part of music theorists. Classification of consonances and dissonances, mathematical ratios between the intervals of the octave, combinations of modes in polyphonic music, varieties of contrapuntal textures, rhythmic proportions, notation, and similar subjects were discussed at length. Johannes Tinctoris (c. 1435–1511) wrote twelve treatises in the years about 1475 to 1485, summarizing the music theory of his day. Franchino Gafori (1451–1522), in about ten treatises written between 1496 and 1518, contributed to the discussion of consonances and dissonances and established eight rules governing voice leadings, intervals, cadences, and the regulation of dissonances in various contexts. Other theorists summarized or clarified the writings of still others and con-

---

Triumphal procession of Maximilian. Engraving by H. Burgkmair, c. 1510.
[THE METROPOLITAN MUSEUM OF ART, DICK FUND, 1932]

tributed valuable information about composers, their works and styles, and performance practices and instruments.

A far-reaching work was the *Musica practica* by Bartolomé Ramos de Pareja (c. 1440–?), a Spaniard active in Bologna and Rome. Ramos was among the first to advocate replacing Guido's solmization syllables (based on the hexachord) with a set of syllables based on the octave. Further, he suggested a new division of the monochord which would result in intervals of approximately just intonation.[1] In his system, major and minor thirds were admitted to the list of consonances—and thus a practice which had long been followed by composers now became theoretically admissible. Ramos's work was considered revolutionary in his time and set off a controversy among theorists that raged for a generation. Pietro Aron (c. 1490–1545), an influential Italian theorist, advocated Ramos's views. In one of his treatises he called attention to the fact that composers had abandoned the old method of composing consecutively (see page 78) in favor of composing all voices simultaneously; he recommended the new process, along with a method of applying accidentals consistently.

Theorists up to about 1550 had closed their eyes to the fact that the eight ecclesiastical modes (see page 42) had long since been modified in practice (see page 88, in reference to *musica ficta*). A composition ostensibly in the Lydian mode could and did contain passages in which B, the fourth step, was replaced by B♭, and which thus corresponded to F major. Likewise, a piece in the Mixolydian mode sounded like G major whenever its seventh step became F♯ instead of F. And again, the presence of a B♭ instead of B on the sixth step of the Dorian mode gave rise to D minor in its natural form. Examples of this treatment abound in music of the fifteenth and sixteenth centuries; major and minor scales had actually existed for generations.

It remained for a Swiss theorist, Henricus Glareanus (1488–1563), to justify this fact theoretically and thus to modify the old theory of the eight ecclesiastical modes. In his treatise, *Dodecachordon* ("Twelve Modes" or "Twelve Keys"), published in 1547, Glareanus added authentic-plagal pairs of modes on the tones A and C. The natural minor modes on A were called Aeolian and Hypoaeolian and were numbered 9 and 10; the major modes on C became Ionian and Hypoionian, numbered 11 and 12. The presence of a pair of modes on B was theoretically recognized by Glareanus, but these (called Locrian and Hypolocrian by later theorists) were dismissed as being impracticable. The distinction between the authentic and plagal forms of a mode became virtually impossible to maintain in polyphonic compositions, in which both forms were present simultaneously. For all practical purposes the two forms merged and a system of six modes, each incorporating both authentic and plagal ranges, remained. By the 1570's Glareanus's numbering of the modes was modi-

---

1 See *SRMH*, pp. 201–04. "Just intonation" may be described as the result of a system of theory (or a performance) in which all the intervals are perfectly in tune. Just intonation is opposed to "tempered intonation," in which certain intervals are adjusted upward or downward to meet certain musical requirements.

fied; in later editions of Zarlino's *Istitutioni armoniche* (1562, 1573) the Ionian became Mode 1, and thus the important place later assumed by the major scale was fixed (see EXAMPLE 55).[2]

EXAMPLE 55

The system of six modes

Gioseffe Zarlino (1517–1590), one of the most important musicians of the Renaissance, was a pupil of Willaert (see page 153) and, after De Rore, succeeded to his teacher's position as *maestro di cappella* at St. Mark's in 1565. His principal writings are in the field of theory, the *Istitutioni* being his chief work. Published in 1558 and reprinted several times in the author's lifetime, it was translated into French and was liberally drawn upon by other theorists in other countries. Whereas earlier theorists, in discussing consonances and dissonances, had been concerned with intervals, Zarlino discussed triads as harmonic entities—the first theorist to do so. He recognized differences in the effect of major and minor triads and gave sound reasons for avoiding parallel octaves and fifths in polyphonic writing. Basing his rules on aesthetic grounds, he clarified the handling of dissonances and proposed rules for judiciously mixing consonances and dissonances. And with his ten rules for applying a text to music, he called attention to the late sixteenth-century musician's concern for proper text declamation. Zarlino dealt with other areas of music theory as well, in each showing himself to be an original thinker well informed about other theoretical writings as well as about contemporary practices.[3]

The Flemish Tradition

EVEN in the time of Josquin, when Flemish polyphonic style was the principal technical factor in European music, local or personal divergences from that style were common. From about 1525 the extent of each departure from the common style became more marked, and several different styles developed in the various countries. While the differences be-

2 It should be noted, however, that the old *protus authenticus* (that is, the Dorian mode) is still referred to as Mode 1 in modern chant books; these books do not recognize Glareanus's Modes 9–12.

3 An excerpt from Zarlino's *Istitutioni armoniche* is given in *SRMH*, pp. 229–61.

tween one style and another can perhaps be seen most clearly in the secular field, they also existed to a considerable degree in the sacred field. The parent style, as it may be called, continued to flourish among Flemish Catholic composers active in many countries of Europe, but two markedly different offshoots emerged in Rome and Venice.

Gombert. The traditions established by Josquin were upheld and widely disseminated by Nicolas Gombert (*c.* 1490–1556), one of his most eminent pupils. Gombert traveled extensively as a singer in the court of Charles V, visiting Spain, Austria, and Germany, but later he was active chiefly in Brussels and Tournai. His sacred works include about ten Masses and almost two hundred motets and related compositions.

A four-voice texture had become standardized in the generation of Obrecht and Josquin, as we have seen; toward the middle of the sixteenth century writing for five voices became popular, and by the latter part of the century it became most usual (exceptional works for two to eight or more voices are found throughout the century, of course). Gombert wrote primarily for five or six voices; like other composers of the time, he wrote more conservatively in the relatively few four-voice settings (possibly because they represented the traditional size) and reserved his most advanced writing for the larger settings. Imitative counterpoint, employed so effectively by Josquin, became a feature of Gombert's conservative four-voice writing,[4] but even in those works he seldom used a *cantus firmus* derived from Gregorian chant, which earlier generations had found indispensable.

In other compositions Gombert made full use of newer fashions. His five- and six-part settings contain both free counterpoint and imitative writing of the highest quality. The principle of the parody Mass, employed tentatively by Josquin's generation, found wide use; eight of Gombert's ten Masses are of this type. The model is usually a motet; as in the works of other composers of the time, each Mass movement begins with a transformation of the borrowed material. But thereafter the material is manipulated freely. Voices are added to or subtracted from the borrowed motet, parodied sections are separated by new material, and on occasion the writing is entirely original.

Gombert's motets, like his Masses, are composed of a continuously flowing polyphonic texture interrupted only occasionally by rests in the several voices or by chordal writing; a full, rich sonority results. In his contrapuntal writing Gombert seems to have been guided by linear rather than by harmonic considerations, for dissonances are controlled less rigorously than was customary later in the century. And in the interest of providing rhythmic vitality, he freely altered the rhythmic pattern of a phrase when it was imitated in another voice. Many syncopations and a variety of note values give his music a rhythmic animation not always equaled by that of his contemporaries. Gombert's works, widely dis-

4 See a four-voice motet in *HAM,* No. 114, *Super flumina.*

Celebration of the Mass. Engraving by Hans Weiditz, 16th c.

seminated throughout Europe, are among those that served as models of Flemish style and caused the style to be generally adopted.

One of Gombert's contemporaries was Claudin de Sermisy (*c.* 1490–1562), a singer in the French royal chapel. Known primarily as a composer of chansons (which will be described in Chapter 11), he was also active in the sacred field. Sermisy's sacred music differs from that of the Flemish in several respects. A simpler and more chordal texture is most usual, with melodies progressing stepwise rather than by leaps. Parallel writing between pairs of voices is also characteristic of Sermisy; the influence of the French chanson (see page 185) may be surmised from these attempts to lighten the texture and to let the texts stand out clearly. The relatively few sacred works of two other chanson composers, Janequin and Certon, may be included with the compositions of Sermisy as forming a somewhat distinct French school. The Masses of the French school in general were written for four voices. Individual movements were short, and texts were set primarily in syllabic style and in simple rhythm. Here too the influence of the chanson is apparent.

Clemens non Papa. The parody principle was employed by Jacobus Clemens[5] (*c.* 1510–*c.* 1556) even more extensively than by Gombert; fourteen of Clemens' Masses are of the parody type, and the other is a Requiem Mass. The majority of the Masses, set for five voices, reveal an increase in the proportion of chordal writing over contrapuntal, marking Clemens as a forward-looking composer. One may also distinguish the use of musical motives—short melodic phrases used repeatedly in different contexts (see EXAMPLE 56)—which was to become common later in the sixteenth century.

Over two hundred motets by Clemens have survived, the great majority

EXAMPLE 56

Clemens, *Vox in rama*

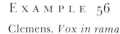

5 Apparently Clemens adopted the "non Papa" to remove any possibility of confusing him with a contemporary poet and cleric, Father Clemens (Clemens Papa in Latin).

of them for four or five voices. In these works, as in many other works of the time, extreme rhythmic contrasts between voices, which had characterized much fifteenth-century music, gave way completely; similar note values were employed in all voices, and unified rhythmic structures resulted. The use of imitative counterpoint in one or two voices had prepared the way for the new structures; when imitation was employed in all the voices, as it frequently was in the sixteenth century, the possibility of referring to one voice as the principal one, or as heavier or lighter than another, disappeared. The motets of Clemens were particularly evenly balanced in this respect. Even in passages based largely on notes of the same value, the judicious use of syncopations, cross accents, and polyrhythms provided a clear and flowing rhythm.[6]

Lasso. Orlando di Lasso, one of the most prolific composers of the sixteenth century, was also one of the most significant. In Lasso's music the contrapuntal arts of the Flemish school reached their culmination; his expressive power and variety of means were unmatched. Lasso, born in 1532 at Mons, spent his formative years in Italy as a singer. For a few years in his early twenties he was active in Antwerp; his first publications (madrigals and motets) appeared in 1555 in Venice and in the following year in Antwerp. In 1556 he was engaged by Duke Albert V of Bavaria and moved to Munich, remaining in the employ of the Bavarian court until his death in 1594.

Lasso's creative output was tremendous. He wrote more than fifty Masses, one hundred Magnificats, about 1200 motets, and about 650 secular compositions of various types. During the early part of his life, before about 1560, a typical Renaissance spirit found expression in a variety of Italian madrigals, French chansons, German *Lieder,* and many motets. In later works, written at Munich under the influence of the Jesuit Counter-Reformation, Lasso modified his style in the direction of seriousness and austerity. In whatever he composed his great mastery of counterpoint was always evident; he was at home in involved canonic writing as well as in simple imitation. He employed Gregorian chants frequently but just as frequently composed original *cantus firmi* or dispensed with them. The motets are usually in one of two forms: a sectional type, sometimes in *abba* form, and a type which may be diagramed *aba.* A great variety of style elements (see below) derived from Flemish, French, Italian, and German music was perfectly synthesized by Lasso; the result was a cosmopolitan, virtually universal style. Although his writing was not always as smooth as Palestrina's, it was more individual.

About fifty of Lasso's Masses have survived, most of them parody Masses on chansons, madrigals, and motets—his own as well as others. All the various parody techniques found in Masses by other Flemish composers are found in those of Lasso. Individual phrases of the model are lengthened or shortened; sometimes motives are derived from them, giving rise

6 A motet by Clemens is given in *HAM,* No. 125, *Vox in rama.*

to points of imitation. In longer movements of the Mass (*Gloria* and *Credo*) the material may appear more than once; in shorter movements it may not appear at all. And whether the material is sacred or secular in origin, it contributes to the formation of elegant, polished, and well-proportioned textures. The expressive possibilities inherent in the Mass texts seem not to have interested Lasso greatly, for while the Masses are technically flawless they are not always inspired.

The many hundreds of motets permit Lasso's great stature to be seen fully. In them the sense of the text and the expressiveness of the music form a unified whole. There is no standardized texture or technical approach in Lasso's motets. Each text was set to music in a style that brought out its meaning, significant words as well as large phrases being given the most appropriate musical expression. Lasso not only used all the familiar devices of word painting but even, when the sense of the text permitted, employed rhythms and textures in what might be called a symbolic manner.

A page from the Munich copy (*c.* 1570) of Lasso's *Seven Penitential Psalms.*

The stylistic devices which permeate Lasso's music may be seen in concentrated fashion in one set of his works: the famous *Seven Penitential Psalms*. The *Psalms* were written some time before 1565 in the course of Lasso's regular employment at the Bavarian court. Except in a few cases, each verse of each Psalm forms a separate section or motet; in addition, each Psalm closes with two supplementary motets set to the texts *Gloria Patri* and *Sicut erat in principio,* respectively. Thus the *Psalms* contain from ten to thirty-one motets each, for a total of 132. They vary from two-voice settings to six-voice, although the great majority are for five voices: soprano, alto, two tenors, and bass.

In certain respects Lasso's style is similar to that of his contemporaries. The range of his melodic line, the treatment of dissonance, the cadential devices and rhythmic practices are typical of the sixteenth century. A more forward-looking approach to tonality, however, is in evidence in Lasso's music than, say, in Palestrina's or Monte's. In many passages in the *Psalms* the bass has a purely harmonic function, leaping from one triad root-tone to another, often in connection with a circle-of-fifths progression (see EXAMPLE 57). Cross relations, normally characteristic of

EXAMPLE 57

Lasso, *Penitential Psalm III, No. 10*

modality and destructive of tonal feeling, are extremely rare in the *Psalms;* only nine cross relations occur in the 132 motets, and then they are used in connection with such textual thoughts as "change," "tribulation," "ire," and the like.

The expected contrapuntal, chordal, and mixed textures appear in the *Psalms,* but in addition there is a texture which is melodically and harmonically static, representing a kind of rhythmic counterpoint (see EXAMPLE 58). The contrapuntal textures are largely based on free imitation; canonic imitation is found, but in relatively few passages. The imitation is "free" in the sense that the interval of imitation (unison, third, or fifth, for example) and the distance (after one measure, after a half measure, and so on) are constantly shifted from one phrase to the next. In one extreme case the tenors sing alone for two full measures before another voice enters in imitation. The opposite extreme is seen in a passage in which all five voices enter imitatively within one and a half measures (see EXAMPLE 59).

EXAMPLE 58

Lasso, *Penitential Psalm VI, No. 1*

EXAMPLE 59

Lasso, *Penitential Psalm II, No. 9*

The floridity of the melodic lines in the *Psalms* marks what is probably Lasso's greatest departure from the style common to other composers of sacred music in the sixteenth century. Fully two thirds of the phrases in this work are melismatic, often to an extreme degree. Not only the simple filling-in of scale steps, but undulating contours, expressive leaps, rhythmic complexities, and other melismatic devices are represented. Melismata often occur in two or more voices simultaneously, illustrating counterpoint at its best (see EXAMPLE 60).

EXAMPLE 60

Lasso, *Penitential Psalm II, No. 6*

Finally, examples of imaginative text setting abound in the *Psalms.* In addition to the more obvious illustrative devices—a descending line or leap for *profundis* (deep), an agitated rhythmic passage to illustrate *velociter* (quickly), and the like—many more subtle examples occur. An outstanding case is seen in the second *Psalm,* over the text "Be not like a horse or a mule, without understanding . . . ," where the lack of understanding is shown graphically in a short passage characterized by great rhythmic confusion (see EXAMPLE 61). Whatever the sense or symbolism of the text, Lasso was able to find an appropriate musical counter-

EXAMPLE 61

Lasso. *Penitential Psalm II, No. 11*

part. In this, as well as in his complete technical mastery and refinement of expression, he showed himself to be one of the most consummate composers of all time.

The Roman School

ROME, with its churches closely under the eyes of worldly Renaissance popes, enjoyed a rich musical life through the late fifteenth century. The Papal Chapel choir, of which many of the leading Flemish composers were at times members, was known throughout Christendom. It is likely, however, that Rome, as the center of the Christian world, had to be conservative in attitude; it remained so through the entire sixteenth century. Perhaps because of the presence of many eminent foreign musicians —Flemish and Spanish for the most part—a distinct Roman school did not emerge until well into the 1500's. The Roman sacred style represents in a sense the amalgamation of many foreign styles (and came about in much the same way as the Viennese Classical style of the late eighteenth century).

Costanzo Festa (*c.* 1490–1545) was one of the first Roman composers of significance. Festa was a member of the Papal Chapel for almost thirty years, but he also contributed to the development of the Italian madrigal (see Chapter 11). In his sacred music, of which almost a hundred items survive, he favored a style which was basically Flemish in its contrapuntal elements but infused with the melodiousness characteristic of Italy. Free counterpoint, rather than imitative writing on the Flemish model, became characteristic of Festa's writing, and to vary the textures further, he wrote chordally as well.

Among a group of Spanish composers active in Rome in the early years of the century, Cristóbal de Morales (*c.* 1500–1553) was outstanding. Morales sang in the Papal choir for about ten years, though he began and ended his career in his native Spain. Most of his twenty-one Masses and many of his motets were published during his Roman stay and were presumably written in Italy. Morales was a reserved composer; an air of mysticism surrounds his music, especially in works whose texts express somber thoughts. In the motet *Emendemus in melius,*[7] for example, while the four outer voices proceed with the main text, the tenor reiterates six times on a severe, stark melodic line "Remember, man, that thou art dust. . . ." Elsewhere, in those of his Mass settings which embody Gregorian plainsongs, Morales uses the chant strictly, composing the other voices in such a way that the contours of the chant melodies are not obscured.

The Council of Trent. The increasing use of imitative counterpoint, the appearance of secular songs in parody Masses, and the frequent employment of melismata for purely musical rather than textual reasons had for half a century caused purists in the Catholic church to look askance at much sixteenth-century sacred music. The sanctity of the liturgy had lost ground in the sense that the music itself became more attractive to the mind and ear—or so the purists felt. When an ecumenical or general council was convened at Trent in 1545 to consider various matters affecting the Catholic church, the relationship of music to the liturgy was among the subjects considered, and much of the Council's final year (1562–1563) was devoted to a discussion of the problem. At one stage in the Council's deliberations the very existence of contrapuntal music was threatened, but the final recommendations called merely for greater intelligibility of the text and a less florid style of writing. As a consequence, Gregorian chant with its many melismata suffered a further decline in its liturgical position; a short, simple, and often chordal type of Mass setting known as a *Missa brevis* came to be preferred, and secular pieces appeared in sacred forms less frequently.

In formulating its recommendations, the Council was probably influenced to a considerable degree by the works of Jacob van Kerle (*c.* 1531–1591). Kerle, of Flemish birth, spent several years in and near Rome and held a respected position among church musicians. The style of his Masses, motets, and other sacred works was relatively simple and direct, avoiding contrapuntal complexity and extravagance. One such work, his *Preces speciales* ("Special Prayers"), consisting of ten motets, was written especially for the Council and given several performances at its sessions;

7 Reprinted in *HAM,* No. 128.

it may have disposed the delegates to modify their opposition to counterpoint. The general style of this work came to serve as a model of proper church music.

Palestrina. The Roman school reached its culmination in the works of Palestrina. So important were Palestrina's musical accomplishments, and so consistent and appropriate his style, that it is customary to look upon him as the greatest representative of late Renaissance sacred music. If this tends somewhat to obscure the towering figure of Lasso, especially in the field of the motet, it serves to focus on the fact that Italian musicians had come to the fore and that the dominant position of Flanders had declined.

Giovanni Pierluigi was born in about 1525 at Praeneste (Palestrina); he later added the name of his birthplace to his own. As a boy he was sent to Rome to study. In about his twentieth year he returned to his native city as organist and singer, but in 1551 he was called to Rome as *maestro di cappella* of the Julian Chapel. For a short time in 1555 he sang in the Papal choir but was dismissed because he was married; he was then employed as choirmaster at St. John Lateran (a position that Lasso had held until the previous year) until about 1560, after which he served in a similar position at Santa Maria Maggiore up to 1567. In 1566 he also became musical director of a new Roman seminary and about the same time took on a secular position as director of concerts for Cardinal Ippolito d'Este. But within five years (1571) Palestrina returned to church music as *maestro* of the Julian Chapel, the position he had held twenty years earlier, and there he remained until his death in 1594.

Palestrina composed more than a hundred Masses, about 260 motets, and a large number of related works (thirty-five Magnificats, thirteen Lamentations, forty-five hymns, sixty-eight Offertories, and others). The term "consistency of style" is perhaps more applicable to the works of Palestrina than to those of any other major composer. His style had vari-

EXAMPLE 62

Palestrina, *Ecce quomodo moritur*

[a] Tan - quam a - gnus co - ram ton-den - te se ob - mu - tu - it.

[b] Et re - sur - re - cti - o no stra, et re - sur - re - cti -

o - no - stra.

ous sources: Flemish polyphony and Italian melodiousness were its principal ingredients, but so perfectly blended were they, and employed with so much restraint and taste, that a personal, unique "Palestrina style" resulted. It is quite possible to use that style as a measuring stick for all other Renaissance styles, for in technical excellence and musical appropriateness it is unmatched.

Palestrina's melodies are based almost entirely on the modes; the kinds of chromatic inflection found in other music are noticeably absent in his (except, of course, for the usual *musica ficta* treatment). The melodies are predominantly stepwise; when leaps occur, especially near the beginnings of phrases, they usually outline triads. A broad, sweeping melodic curve is most usual, with the point of greatest melodic concentration near the midpoint of the phrase. Syllabic settings are more frequent in Palestrina than in many of his contemporaries, and florid writing is characteristically confined to cadence points (see EXAMPLE 62).

The rhythmic aspects of Palestrina's music—and indeed of large quantities of Renaissance music in general—are often obscured by the practice

Palestrina and
Pope Julian III.
After a woodcut,
1554.

EXAMPLE 63

Palestrina, *Missa Papae Marcelli*

in modern editions of setting a barline after every fourth beat in duple meter. This creates the impression that the music is cast in regular measures and that the first note of each measure receives an accent. It was the practice in the Renaissance, however, to consider the word accents in composing each phrase—that is, to give to the accented syllable a prominent place (a high pitch or a long note or a melisma) in the tonal structure. A syllable so treated attracted attention to itself, and created a "psychological accent." In a contrapuntal texture the result of this practice was an unmetrical rhythm for the word accents did not necessarily coincide in the various parts, nor were the words or phrases of the text set to equally long musical phrases in each part. As a consequence, a typical Renaissance contrapuntal work is composed of a number of overlapping phrases, each with its own scheme of textual accents; a "counterpoint of meters" takes place, and a conflict results between the rhythms of the individual phrases and the composite rhythm of the whole.[8]

EXAMPLE 63*a* shows a typical passage in which the barring is carried out in the usual way. The normal accents of the text (*Ple*-ni sunt *coe*-li et *ter*-ra), appearing on weak beats, are obscured, and any sense of the rhythmic counterpoint involved in the passage is lost in the notation as it stands. If, however, the regular barlines are removed and each phrase is barred according to its true accentual pattern, the rhythmic complexity of the passage is revealed (see EXAMPLE 63*b*).

In this respect, Palestrina resembles his contemporaries and immediate predecessors. One point of difference may be noted: his tendency to use a narrower range of time values. The majority of Palestrina's melodies are composed of notes of even length, mainly minims (which are transcribed as quarter notes in the examples in this chapter); longer and shorter note values appear, of course, at cadences and within melodies themselves, but the restlessness and rhythmic variety which characterize the music, say, of Gabrieli and Lasso are largely missing. Here is another example of the restraint and proportion that shine through all of Palestrina's music.

Palestrina's treatment of dissonance provides perhaps the most revealing evidence of refinement and economy of means. Working at a time when the expressive dissonances of the madrigalists had to some extent found employment in sacred music as well, he resisted all extremes and retained a conservative style of great consonance. His use of dissonance was regulated to such an extent that a number of basic principles can be abstracted from a few of his works and applied to virtually all of them. In Palestrina's music, dissonance is always related to note length; the longer the note, the less likely it is to be dissonant. Hence it rarely or never appears in note-against-note writing with minims; with semiminims it is somewhat more common (see EXAMPLE 64*a*). Unprepared dissonances rarely appear on accented beats. Suspensions, which are of course dis-

---

8 See Jeppesen, *The Style of Palestrina and the Dissonance*, pp. 18–30, for an elaboration of this point.

EXAMPLE 64

Palestrina, Examples of dissonance

sonant, are prepared, since the suspended note first appears (on the previous weak beat) as a consonance (see EXAMPLE 64b). And dissonance is almost never used as an expressive, subjective device.[9]

Palestrina was similarly conservative in his treatment of melodic line. He proceeded from the principle that the attention-attracting force of a leap is conditioned by its size, its location within the range of the part in which it appears, and its place in the total texture. Thus if two consecutive upward leaps in the same direction occur, the second is smaller than the first. Leaps are more common in the lower voices than in the upper, and they are generally avoided in the highest range of the voice. It has been mentioned that Palestrina's melodies generally progress in stepwise motion; leaps in the body of a phrase are in the minority. The following melodies show his practices in this regard (see EXAMPLE 65).

The textures in which these several elements are embodied are not confined to the contrapuntal; indeed, the smooth alternation of contrapuntal and chordal passages is one of the characteristic features of the Palestrina style. Strict imitation or even canonic writing often gives way

9 The whole matter of dissonance is treated exhaustively in Jeppesen, *The Style of Palestrina.* . . .

EXAMPLE 65

Palestrina. Examples of melodic line

Nos autem gloriari

[a] In quo est sa - lus, vi - ta, et re - su - re - cti - o no - -

O crux ave

[b] In hoc pas - cha - - - li tem - po - re, tem - po - re

O crux ave

[c] Re - is - que do - na, ve - ni - am, re - is - que do - - - na.

to a measure or two of chordal writing,[10] and occasionally two voices in counterpoint are accompanied by three voices arranged chordally. The purely imitative passages are consistently so; Palestrina went far beyond the usual practice of employing imitation only at phrase beginnings, and within a passage he frequently introduced short motives which were themselves imitated. Canonic writing, too, is more common than in many other works of the time; in this area, as in all others, Palestrina revealed his complete mastery over all aspects of composition.

Whereas Lasso seems to have been inspired to do his best work in the motet, Palestrina excelled in the composition of Masses. His 105 works in this form summarized and brought to completion a line of development that extended back more than three centuries to the time of Machaut. All the main types are represented, including the *cantus firmus* Mass, which had become virtually obsolete in the sixteenth century. A tabulation [11] shows the following division: five canonic Masses, six *sine nomine*, seven *cantus firmus*, thirty-five paraphrase, and fifty-two parody. Forty-one are for four voices, thirty-eight for five, twenty-two for six, and four for eight. Each type reveals the composer's complete dedication to one purpose: to set the liturgical texts in an illuminating and comprehensible manner. The services for which these Masses were designed were of two different kinds: the simple service, for which a *Missa brevis* or *Missa sine nomine* was suitable, and the service for feast and ceremonial days, for which one of the longer Masses was appropriate.

Even in the canonic and *cantus firmus* Masses, in which contrapuntal textures dominate, the successive text entrances are so arranged that the words can be clearly heard. A serene and truly reverent tone far removed from virtuosic expression animates these works; and the technical mastery of canon, especially in the *Missa Repleatur os meum*, is skillfully concealed in the interest of developing a quiet, unassuming setting. In many

10 See *HAM*, Nos. 140, *Agnus Dei* I, and 141, *Sicut cervus*, for examples.
11 Given in Reese, *Music in the Renaissance*, pp. 470–72.

of the Masses of other types, notably the freely composed *Missa Papae Marcelli* (despite its title a *sine nomine* Mass, for it is not based on pre-existing material), the amount of chordal writing is relatively greater and clear text declamation is even less of a problem.

The fifty-two parody Masses are based on a variety of borrowed material. Almost half of them are parodies of Palestrina's own works, primarily motets; another third utilize motets of other composers, and the remainder are parodies of secular material. It seems obvious that even in his choice of pre-existing music Palestrina felt more closely drawn to the sacred field than to the secular. The same is true of the thirty-five paraphrase Masses, the sources of which were Gregorian chants, hymns, and the like, and in only a few cases secular material.

A reserved, unspectacular, and balanced kind of expression is common to virtually all of Palestrina's music. One senses that an objective composer was at work here, striving constantly to refine his music to make it worthy to glorify God. Every detail of rhythm, melismatic writing, dissonance treatment, texture, and text declamation was subjected to the closest scrutiny; contour, accent, cadence, and other details were treated in accord with Palestrina's sense of economy and proportion. The result was a body of music ideally suited to its sacred purpose and approaching technical and expressive perfection.

Other composers. The Roman school included a number of Palestrina's pupils, notably Giovanni Maria Nanino (c. 1545–1607). Nanino showed his fondness for writing in canon by composing thirty canonic settings of a single *cantus firmus*. He also set another *cantus firmus* no fewer than 157 times for groups of voices ranging from two to eleven. These works, illustrating all the possibilities of the art, were probably used for pedagogical purposes. Felice Anerio (c. 1560–1614), Palestrina's successor as composer for the Papal Chapel, wrote in a style that resembled the older composer's; a number of works formerly attributed to Palestrina are now known to be by Anerio. Several other composers, Netherlanders and Italians by birth, contributed works in the Palestrina style without remotely approaching the expressiveness or excellence of his music.

Tomás Luis de Victoria (c. 1549–1611) was the only member of the Roman school whose work can be compared to Palestrina's. Victoria, of Spanish birth, lived in Rome from 1565 to about 1594, after which he returned to his homeland. He was befriended by Palestrina and may have studied with him; in 1571 he succeeded the older composer as *maestro* of the Roman seminary and thereafter held a series of positions as organist and choirmaster in several Roman churches. He was ordained a priest in 1575.

Several books of motets, twenty Masses, and many more of his sacred works were published during Victoria's lifetime. As far as is known, he composed no secular music. In technical mastery and devotion to a religious ideal, Victoria's works resemble Palestrina's; a dignified and reserved tone is common to many motets of the two men. But Victoria also

brought a degree of fervor and drama to his writing,[12] often using striking leaps in his melodic line to eloquent effect. Among his works are several motets and Magnificats for antiphonal choruses, with organ accompaniments. This approach to the lavishness of the Venetian school is in
general foreign to the Palestrina style. It may serve to indicate that of all
the members of the Roman school Palestrina wrote most economically
and with the greatest reserve.

The Venetian School

THE CATHEDRAL of St. Mark in Venice has long been one of the most
important churches in Europe. It is distinguished by having two choir
lofts facing each other, each with its own organ. There, possibly as a last
remnant of a Byzantine tradition in Italy, polychoral writing flourished
about the middle of the sixteenth century. The name of Adrian Willaert
is generally associated with the development of the polychoral style, but
earlier examples than Willaert's first compositions for two choruses are
known. The fifteenth-century Italian manuscripts spoken of in connection with the rise of choral singing (see page 117) include some Flemish
polychoral compositions; a number of similar works by obscure composers working at Padua likewise predate the earliest Venetian works of
this type; and other compositions also exist.[13] The Venetian school headed
by Willaert made a feature of the device, however, and gave rise to a
distinctive Venetian style.

Willaert (*c.* 1490–1562) became *maestro di cappella* at St. Mark's in
1527. Quite apart from his worth as a composer was his influence as a
teacher. To his pupils (including De Rore, Zarlino, Andrea Gabrieli, and
many others) he imparted the Franco-Flemish contrapuntal techniques
of which he was a master, especially in the field of sacred music. He provided models for the antiphonal treatment of liturgical texts, and he made
evident his concern for proper text declamation, following the example
of Josquin.

Willaert's surviving Masses number less than ten, written for four, five,
and six voices; the antiphonal principle is not employed. The influence
of Josquin is strongly felt: works of the older composer are parodied, the
familiar canonic devices and imitative techniques are employed, and a
high level of technical competence is evident throughout.

It is in certain of Willaert's psalms and other motets that antiphonal
writing, which usually implies a polychoral medium, appears.[14] A set of
psalms published in 1550 includes some works by Willaert in which two

12 A motet is given in *HAM*, No. 149, *O vos omnes.*
13 See Bukofzer, "The Beginnings of Choral Polyphony," in *Studies in Medieval
and Renaissance Music,* p. 181, for details. Lang, in *Music in Western Civilization,*
p. 1032, note 4, gives a brief account of the Byzantine influence at St. Mark's. See Reese,
Music in the Renaissance, pp. 174, 285, and 349 for additional information.
14 But not in all: see a polyphonic motet by Willaert in *HAM*, No. 113, *Victimae.* . . .

The Cathedral of St. Mark, Venice. One of the choir lofts is shown, upper right.

four-voice choirs sing alternately and, at the end of the psalm, join in singing eight-voice passages together. The tradition of antiphonal chanting was still remembered in Willaert's day, and he probably knew the works of Josquin in which quasi-antiphonal effects were suggested within four-voice textures. With the two opposed choir lofts at St. Mark's providing the physical setting, writing for double chorus was a natural result. Psalms and canticle texts in general lent themselves to antiphonal treatment. It will be recalled that a typical text of this type contains a number of verses in prose rhythm, each of which is divided into halves; in many cases the half verse itself was treated in antiphonal fashion (see EXAMPLE 66).

A number of eminent composers served at St. Mark's in the second half of the sixteenth century, either as Willaert's successor in the position of *maestro di cappella* (De Rore) or as first or second organist (Merulo and the two Gabrielis). The presence of so many musicians of high quality is testimony to the commanding position enjoyed by the cathedral; it attracted Italy's finest composers and performers making possible the establishment of a school of composition that represents one of the peaks of sixteenth-century Italian culture. Elements of the Venetian style included, in addition to polychoral writing, a concern with both instrumental and vocal color, a dramatic approach to texts, occasional use (in sacred music) of the advanced chromatic touches developed primarily in the madrigal,

EXAMPLE 66

Willaert, *Magnificat*

and a texture in which block chords replaced contrapuntal writing.

Possibly because the text of the Mass provided relatively little opportunity to indulge a feeling for color and drama, the later Venetian composers wrote most characteristically in the motet. Masses by De Rore, Merulo, and the two Gabrielis exist, but only in a few cases—notably in a set of four Mass movements by Giovanni Gabrieli—do the colorful Venetian style elements appear. In the motets and related compositions, on the other hand, a variety of sonorous effects is obtained. For example, in two motet collections by Andrea Gabrieli, published in 1565 and 1576 respectively, the upper or lower voices are sometimes omitted in order to achieve a darker or lighter vocal color. Further, instruments are specified, and on occasion the use of instruments and voices on independent parts is implied.

The culmination of the Venetian style was reached in the music of Giovanni Gabrieli (*c.* 1557–1612), who composed accompanied motets and other sacred compositions for two, three, and even four choruses. Gabrieli's works, which make up several collections, were published at intervals from 1587 to 1615. In his compositions for single chorus he sometimes wrote for as many as eight voices—treated not antiphonally but as a unit. In the larger polychoral works the number of vocal parts in each chorus seldom exceeded four; in the smaller ones, five or six parts were usually required. Gabrieli's desire to explore the possibilities of diverse vocal colors in these polychoral works led him at times to abandon counterpoint entirely and write in a chordal style throughout. The problem of manipulating up to sixteen vocal lines, plus the acoustic and ensemble difficulties involved in choral groups physically separated from one another, were perhaps additional factors in the development of a chordal style rather than a contrapuntal one.

The Venetian love of drama, pomp, and display also led to a greater use of instruments with the choirs. The presence of the two organs at St. Mark's has been noted. Gabrieli employed them, but in addition he wrote for wind and string instruments. The instrumental parts for a motet did not merely support the voices; often they included independent melodic lines. Voices, organs, and "orchestra" were employed in various ways to create a texture combining color, sumptuousness, and stateliness in magnificent fashion. An outstanding example of this treatment is seen in Gabrieli's motet *In ecclesiis.* The first section begins with the sopranos of Chorus I accompanied by the organ, then heard antiphonally with the entire Chorus II; next the tenors of Chorus I are treated similarly, and an interlude for instruments alone (called *sinfonia*) follows; the inner voices of Chorus I are then heard in counterpoint over instrumental accompaniment; and finally, the section rises to a climax with both choruses and the orchestra performing the last phrase. The second section of the motet is treated even more elaborately.[15] Certain aspects of this and similar works—notably the writing for organ bass and the inclusion of the instrumental *sinfonia*—bring them to the border of Renaissance style and beyond. Gabrieli, in raising the Venetian style to its highest point, also transcended that style and became one of the earliest masters of the seventeenth-century Baroque.

15 The motet is given in *HAM*, No. 157.

The Renaissance:
Music of the Reformation

THE DEVELOPMENTS discussed in the previous chapter took place entirely within the Roman Catholic church and brought Catholic sacred music to its highest level of technical achievement and expressive power. At the same time another series of musical developments was taking place, brought about by the needs of the emerging Protestant church. Composers of the Protestant faith gradually abandoned the composition of Masses and music for the Offices. A long interval elapsed, however, before a Protestant order of service was established. The first decades of the Reformation were tentative at best. It was well into the seventeenth century before the styles of Protestant church music emerged, soon thereafter reaching a high level of expressiveness.

The Protestant Reformation was the result of long-standing objections to certain practices of the Catholic church. Some of the clergy stressed worldly matters at the cost of spiritual concerns, many were corrupt and abused their power; as a result, others of the clergy and some laymen began to lose their respect for the Church and its ruling hierarchy. The growth of humanism, with its emphasis on individual dignity and free-

Woodcut from *Le Baston pour chasser les loups,* a Protestant tract condemning the sale of indulgences, printed at Lyons, 1518.

dom, strengthened the desire of many people to reform the Church; leaders among the humanists, notably Philip Melanchthon and Ulrich von Hutten, were closely associated with the leaders of the reform movement itself. Political considerations also entered into the complex situation, for with the rise of monarchies many of the new kings wished to be absolute within their realms, even to the extent of controlling the church.

The central figure of the Reformation was Martin Luther (1483–1546). In 1517 Luther posted his famous statement of principles on the door of the castle church in Wittenberg, setting in motion a chain of events that led to the establishment of the several Protestant denominations and to a century of wars fought in the name of religion. More immediately, Luther's principles were influential in bringing about significant changes

Martin Luther.
Portrait by Lucas
Cranach, c. 1526.

in the body of church music and in preparing Germany for the important musical role it was to play from the seventeenth century onward.

Parallel to the musical developments within the Lutheran movement itself was another series of developments which took place primarily in Switzerland under the leadership of Jean Calvin, as well as in France and the Netherlands. The Calvinist view of music in the church differed in many respects from the Lutheran; it gave rise to a body of music based on psalm- and hymn-singing which is still influential in the Protestant church today.

About the middle of the sixteenth century England too established its own church. This event had been prefaced by the action of Henry VIII in breaking with the Pope and setting himself up as the head of an English Catholic church (1534) and by the attempts of his daughter Mary to restore Roman Catholicism (1553). The decades between the 1530's and the 1580's or thereabouts were marked by religious strife, and again the field of church music was affected. Anglican and Catholic music existed side by side, but eventually the Anglican rose supreme and developed its own repertoire. This chapter, then, will be concerned with the music of three separate religious groups: the Lutherans, the Calvinists, and the Anglicans.

Lutheran Music

LUTHER's first concern, insofar as the musical portion of his reforms comes into account, was to modify only those portions of the Catholic liturgy which conflicted with evangelical teachings. The churches in the larger cities (in the German areas which eventually adopted Luther's reforms) had capable choirs as well as schools in which children were taught singing and the rudiments of Latin, and here a high regard for the traditional music was maintained. For such churches Luther advocated the retention of the Latin Mass but suggested some alterations and "improvements." The Offices too—Matins and Vespers primarily—were to be retained; changes appropriate to the new teachings were specified, and a number of new texts and melodies supplied. As a first step, the *Credo* and the *Agnus Dei* were omitted from the Ordinary of the Mass. Numerous Masses by Catholic composers exist which were thus shortened for use in the Protestant church. The Proper of the Mass was modified by the exclusion of the Latin Introit, Gradual, Offertory, and Communion, which were gradually replaced by hymns in German.

For smaller communities and rural areas, where musical training did not exist, Luther offered other modifications. Recognizing the various levels of education and musical skill represented by his adherents, Luther offered these modifications only as suggestions; considerable latitude was allowed. For example, German prose texts or songs could be substituted for any of the Latin portions of the Mass; songs could in general replace any prose item—whether in Latin or German; and appropriate songs could be added at various points in the service.

The songs which thus found their way into the service were of many

A Lutheran hymn, *Wir gläuben all an einen Gott*. From a songbook printed at Wittenberg, 1544.

kinds. Some were Catholic hymns with texts translated (many by Luther himself) but with melodies left intact. Others, with translated texts, were melodically modified or given new melodies. Some were fourteenth- or fifteenth-century German religious songs which had never been part of the liturgy. Others were songs—secular or sacred—with texts modified to suit evangelical teachings. And finally, a number were new, written and composed specifically for the Lutheran service.

These religious songs were of several types. Some consisted of text and melody only and were distributed mostly in single sheets. Others were set in four-part harmony, but did not yet include the rhythmic structure characteristic of the later chorale. Still others were polyphonic settings, similar to the motets and secular songs of the time. The first collection of the first type, published as early as 1524 at Wittenberg, contained eight texts and four melodies; this was followed by other collections published at Erfurt, Strassburg, Leipzig, and elsewhere. Each new publication included more texts and melodies, and by the 1570's over two hundred songs were available.

Luther took an active part in the preparation of the new repertoire. He provided many of the texts—including translations and original poems —and it is likely that he composed the melodies of *Ein' feste Burg* ("A Mighty Fortress") and others of the fifty-odd songs that form the body of the original repertoire. He was well qualified to do this; he is known to have played several instruments and to have been a competent singer, and he composed at least one four-voice motet. And his writings are filled with discerning observations about the music of his contemporaries (apparently he esteemed Josquin most highly) and the effects of music on the listener. But he also called upon professional musicians to help in the enormous task of providing a repertoire for the new church.

The musician most active in this task was Johann Walter (1496–1570), who was a singer in the choir of the Elector of Saxony when he was called to Wittenberg in 1525. His first assignment was to work on the formation of Luther's German Mass (published in 1526). An earlier work, his *Geystliche gesangk Buchleyn* (1524), contains two dozen polyphonic settings of Luther's texts,[1] about fifteen by other German writers, and five settings of Latin texts; they are set for three to five voices.

The two styles seen in this publication call attention to the performance practices of the early Lutheran church. About half of the settings are written in free counterpoint with occasional imitative passages; the melody, treated as a *cantus firmus,* is given to the tenor. The remainder are written chordally, usually one note to each syllable, each line of the text coming to a cadence and marked off from the next line by a pause; here again the melody is placed in the tenor. The polyphonic settings were sung by members of the choir schools and lay singing societies the establishment of which Luther had urged. The chordal settings, on the other hand, were designed for the congregation at large; the tenor melody was sung by the (untrained) populace, presumably accompanied by organ or instruments. Both types of performance exemplified the basic Lutheran tenet that each member of the congregation participate in the service according to his talents.

Luther had encouraged the use of the organ in his services, but as in the vocal field, no appropriate repertoire yet existed. The organ was at first limited to playing preludes and postludes, giving intonations for the choir, and accompanying the congregation. On festive occasions the custom arose of alternating the playing and singing; that is, the organ introduced the hymn and, after each stanza was sung, repeated it with embellishments. Here is to be seen the origin of the chorale prelude and the chorale variations, both of which occupied Lutheran organists beyond the time of Bach.

It is likely that instruments were used, primarily at the courts and in the larger churches and especially on festival days, but direct evidence is lacking. It is significant that the cantor of the first Lutheran church in Magdeburg, Martin Agricola (1486–1556), wrote an important treatise, *Musica instrumentalis deudsch,* published in 1529 at Wittenberg by George Rhaw, who also published many of Luther's writings. Agricola's treatise, based to some extent on Sebastian Virdung's *Musica getutscht* (1511), was among the first to give instructions for playing all instruments.

Walter's *Buchleyn* of 1524 was revised and enlarged four times; the last edition of 1551 was expanded to include seventy-four German and forty-

---

1 One setting is given in *HAM*, No. 111a, *Aus tiefer Not.*

A Lutheran Communion in the Church of the Minorites in Augsburg. Engraving by Bernard Picart, 1732.

seven Latin settings. As the first Lutheran collection and one which had enjoyed the support of the great Reformer himself, it served as a model for many later sets. A collection of 123 polyphonic song settings, *Newe deudsche geistliche Gesenge . . .* , published by Rhaw in 1544 and designed "for the common schools," is typical. More than a dozen composers are represented here,[2] some of them Catholic. The compositions in general are in contrapuntal style; the melody is placed in the tenor and treated in *cantus firmus* fashion. In some cases bits of imitative writing

EXAMPLE 67

Bruck, Chorale

Kommt her zu mir, spricht Got-tes Sohn, All' die ihr seid be-schwe-ret nun

2 See *Denkmäler deutscher Tonkunst*, Vol. 34, for a reprint of the work.

introduce each phrase, but passages in chordal style also occur.[3] In the settings by Sixtus Dietrich (*c.* 1492–1548) and in many by Arnoldus de Bruck (*c.* 1470–*c.* 1554) chordal style dominates and the form of the Lutheran chorale comes somewhat closer (see EXAMPLE 67).

Calvinist Music

IN THE first decades of the sixteenth century Ulrich Zwingli (1484–1531), a Swiss priest, developed a strong opposition to Catholic teachings on the ground that they interfered with individual freedom. His views gradually won acceptance in parts of Switzerland, and various communities broke away from the Roman church. The Zwinglian doctrine differed widely from the Lutheran, both in theology and in attitudes toward church music. Adherents of Zwingli forcibly removed art works from the churches, destroyed organs and other instruments, and virtually abandoned music, feeling that music in general promoted self-indulgence and that all church music reflected the Catholic tradition.

Five years after Zwingli's death Jean Calvin (1509–1564), a French theologian, was invited to align himself with the followers of Zwingli at Geneva. The reforms and austerity Calvin preached brought him temporary banishment from the city, but in 1541 he returned and subordinated the state government to a government by the church. Under his leadership, ecclesiastical discipline was enforced, the Bible became the source of all law, and sobriety and self-discipline became guides for all conduct. Calvin held that the Psalms were the only texts suitable for singing in church and translated a number of Psalms into French for this purpose. He permitted Psalms to be sung to Lutheran melodies but confined them to single-line unaccompanied performance. Singing in parts was permitted only in the home or at civic festivities.

In 1539, during his years of exile from Geneva, Calvin published a Psalter containing eighteen Psalms translated into French (some by himself, the others adapted from translations by Clément Marot, a French court poet); the melodies were supplied by Louis Bourgeois (*c.* 1510–*c.* 1561). In subsequent years the rest of the Psalms were translated (after Marot's death in 1544 the translations were done by Theodore de Bèze), and Bourgeois composed additional melodies even while revising some of the older ones. The Genevan Psalter was completed in 1562; in its final form it contained about a hundred of Bourgeois's melodies, with the rest by a variety of minor composers. Bourgeois also prepared harmonized settings in four parts for some of the Psalms; these are in chordal style throughout, with one note to each syllable.[4]

The four-part settings of the Psalms by Claude Goudimel (*c.* 1505–1572) were destined to carry the melodies of the Genevan Psalter into other parts of Europe and into many of the Reformed (that is, Calvinist) churches (see EXAMPLE 68). Goudimel, a Catholic to about 1560, had com-

---

3 Hymns by Stoltzer and Senfl, given in *HAM,* Nos. 108, *Christ ist . . .* , and 110, *Da Jakob . . .* , illustrate the style.

4 See *HAM,* No. 132, *Qui au . . .* , for an example.

Example 68

Goudimel, *Psalm LXXXIX*

posed Masses, motets, and other sacred works before he became a Hugue-
not, as the French Calvinists were called. In the 1550's he had set a number of Marot's and Bèze's Psalm texts in motet style for three to six voices.
At that time both Catholics and Protestants engaged in psalm-singing;
later the Catholics were forbidden to do so. After Goudimel's conversion
he again turned to the Psalms and composed two complete versions. One
is in note-against-note style, each syllable set to one note, with the melody
usually in the tenor. The other version is somewhat more florid, containing short melismata, and the melody is usually in the soprano. The first
of these harmonized settings of the Psalter, published in 1565, established
the configuration of the Protestant hymn. The Psalms in their Marot-Bèze

translated versions had been set in metrical stanzas, usually in duple meter, and Bourgeois had employed the same melody for each stanza. Goudimel retained the form of the stanza and melody in his harmonizations; thus his Psalms were short musical settings to which several stanzas were sung.

The popularity of Goudimel's work was immense. In the French version it was reprinted many times until well into the nineteenth century. It was translated into German in 1573 and adopted by other churches influenced by Calvinism. The Separatists or Puritans, while they were refugees in Holland, used the Ainsworth Psalter of 1612, which contains many of Goudimel's settings. But Goudimel's Psalter also paved the way for many other and similar psalters. An independent polyphonic setting of the Genevan melodies was published by Claude Le Jeune in 1564, antedating Goudimel's version by one year.[5]

Catholic composers also brought out collections of psalm tunes, many of them written under the influence of the Genevan Psalter. In 1540, a collection of melodies, most of them folk or popular songs, to which Psalm texts had been set was published at Antwerp. Called *Souterliedekens* ("little psalm songs"), it became enormously popular and was reprinted many times in the following seventy-five years, presumably for use in the home rather than in the church. Clemens non Papa undertook to make a three-voice setting of the collection, and his polyphonic *Souterliedekens* were published in 1556–1557. He employed various combinations of voices, ranging from three high to three low voices, thus making the set useful in all manner of social groupings. The settings are mainly in chordal style, with the borrowed melody most often in the middle voice. In keeping with his style elsewhere, he composed a variety of expressive melodies to surround the borrowed one, and a pleasant work results. Clemens' settings, like both the harmonized and contrapuntal settings of Goudimel, were not designed for use in the service—Catholic in his case—but for secular occasions.

The Chorale

Toward the middle of the sixteenth century the use of the *cantus firmus* as a structural device declined. As a consequence the tenor voice, which had been the carrier of the principal melody, lost its pre-eminent role. This development, seen most strikingly in the Catholic music of the time, also played a part in the transformation of Protestant psalm settings. In many of Goudimel's harmonizations the melody had been placed in the soprano; in other works contemporary with his, the position of the melody had been somewhat variable. In a work by the German composer, Lucas Osiander (1534–1604), *Fünfftzig geistliche Lieder und Psalmen,* published in 1586, the tendency to shift the melody into the soprano part became fixed.

5 Settings of a rhymed version of Psalm 35 by Goudimel and Le Jeune, respectively, are given in *HAM,* No. 126, *Deba contre. . . .*

Religious songs of the general type found in the collection by Osiander represent a Lutheran branch of Protestant music as distinct from the Calvinist branch. The songs soon came to be known in Germany as chorales. In the century and a half from Osiander to Bach the characteristics of the Lutheran chorale changed, but its essential elements were constant. Its text was usually a poem expressing a religious thought or paraphrasing a Psalm; it consisted of several rhymed stanzas. Four-part note-against-note style was most common, with the melody to which the text was set placed in the upper voice. At an early stage the chorale was somewhat unmetrical, while toward the end of its development metrical rhythm prevailed (see Example 69). It was sung in unison by the congre-

Example 69

Metrical types in the chorale

gation; organ accompaniment, rare in the early decades of the Lutheran church, was established definitely in the first years of the seventeenth century.

It is likely that the straightforward, unadorned settings of religious texts, as illustrated in the chorales of Osiander and others, marked a temporary decline of art music among Lutherans, but they represented only one facet of music in the Lutheran church. Hymn-singing became the chief musical activity of the congregation and the lay choir declined in importance—except in the larger churches, where a few Latin texts were retained in the liturgy and where contrapuntal settings of both Latin and German texts, in motet style, continued to be sung, sometimes by professional choirs.

Such contrapuntal settings were composed well into the seventeenth century. Among the composers represented in the development of this literature was Johann Eccard (1553–1611). Eccard, born in Thuringia, studied with Lasso, then became professionally active at Königsberg and Berlin. Several collections of sacred songs, some for four voices and some for five, reveal him to have been an accomplished composer in the modified Franco-Flemish style that had become the common property of Catholic and Protestant composers alike. Hans Leo Hassler (1564–1612) is of greater importance, perhaps, for his efforts to transmit the Venetian style to German Protestant music. A pupil of Andrea Gabrieli and one of the foremost organists of the time, Hassler was associated with the cities of Nuremberg, Ulm, and Dresden and composed in the secular and sacred fields, both Catholic and Protestant, with equal facility. Like Goudimel, he composed settings of Psalm texts in both contrapuntal (1607) and chordal (1608) styles. His early works are often polychoral in the Venetian manner, rivaling the compositions of Giovanni Gabrieli in size and elaborateness.

Anglican Music

THE REFORMATION in England took a course quite different from that on the Continent. Henry VIII, a staunch Catholic, had petitioned the Pope to have his marriage annulled; the Pope refused the petition. Parliament, acting for Henry, then passed an act—in 1534—removing England from the Pope's control and placing the King at the head of a new English Catholic church. Henry wished to maintain Roman Catholic doctrines, but the strength of Protestant ideas in England made this impossible. The period from about 1534 to 1558 was a time of turmoil, un-

A page from Merbecke's *Booke of Common Praier Noted,* 1550.

certainty, and religious confusion. The position of the Lutherans and Calvinists in England was precarious until the death of Henry VIII (1547), improved under the brief reign of Edward VI (died 1553), and declined again with the advent of Mary. Not until Elizabeth ascended the throne in 1558 was the religious controversy finally settled in favor of a church that inclined somewhat to Calvinist teachings. Even then a high church party remained, one that sought to emphasize the Catholic heritage of the Anglican church.

It is difficult to draw a sharp line between English Catholic and Protestant music in the period after about 1540. Many composers remained Catholic even though they wrote sacred music to English texts. Some Latin texts were retained in the English service even after a definite turn to a Protestant form of worship took place. English sometimes replaced Latin in motets. And finally, whether set to Latin or English words, one sacred piece in contrapuntal style was in general similar to another.

Several steps led to the establishment of distinctive English liturgical forms. In 1544 Archbishop Cranmer had prepared the official version of the English Litany, in which the traditional chant was employed but was set one note to each syllable. Other liturgical items were sometimes set for several voices, but in chordal style rather than contrapuntal. It was generally understood that in the interest of achieving textual clarity in multi-voice settings, note-against-note style would prevail, conforming to the syllabic setting of the chants themselves. An official book of Common Prayer was first issued in 1549 (without music), following which John Merbeck (or Merbecke, c. 1510–c. 1585) published his *Booke of Common Praier Noted* (that is, set to music). Basing his monophonic setting on the traditional chant but including many melodies of his own composition, Merbeck devised a rhythmic style which is partly metrical and partly free or unmetrical. The normal accentuation of the English texts served as a point of departure in determining the metrical flow.

The Anglican services (of Communion, Vespers, and so on) stemmed originally from the corresponding Catholic Mass and Offices. At an early stage (1543) the Communion service seems to have included musical settings of the six sung items of the Ordinary of the Mass. By 1559 only the *Kyrie* and *Credo* were set regularly and the *Sanctus* was set occasionally. The principal canticles for the morning and evening service were the *Te Deum, Magnificat,* and *Nunc dimittis*. These and similar texts were often set in a motetlike style which included both contrapuntal and chordal writing. These new English settings, however, differed stylistically from motets; they were more syllabic, rhythmically simpler, and they had shorter, harmonically conceived phrases. The term "anthem" (probably derived from "antiphon") was often applied to such a setting of an English text; thus an anthem is essentially the English equivalent of a Latin motet. A "full anthem" was for choir throughout, while a "verse anthem" contained passages for solo voice or voices, usually instrumentally accompanied.

The English Psalter, with metrical translations made in large part by Thomas Sternhold and John Hopkins, was in general similar to the

Genevan Psalter and greatly influenced by it. After a number of preliminary editions published by English Protestants in exile at Geneva, the single-line *Whole Booke of Psalms* was published at London in 1562. A year later a setting in chordal style for four voices was published, and the definitive form of the English Psalter was attained. In Scotland the influence of the Genevan Psalter was stronger; John Knox chose for his services many of the melodies favored by Calvin himself.

Taverner. John Taverner (c. 1495–1545) stands at the beginning of the transitional period. He was appointed organist and master of the choristers at Cardinals' College, Oxford, in 1526 and during the following four years composed the Catholic music for which he is remembered today. Eight Masses and a number of motets have survived, all set to Latin texts. About 1530 his religious views changed and he became a paid persecutor of the Catholics.

Tye. Appointed organist at Ely Cathedral in 1540 and ordained as a priest in 1560, Christopher Tye (c. 1499–c. 1572) composed for both the Catholic and Anglican liturgies. His surviving music includes four Masses and several motets (in Latin) and almost two dozen anthems and services (in English). The style in the Latin works reflects that of the Flemish school of the mid-sixteenth century, which often included a high degree of melismatic writing. Tye's anthems, on the other hand, contain many chordal passages in the midst of their basically contrapuntal texture. This mixture of styles, it may be noted, did not entirely conform to the Royal Injunction of 1548, which prescribed the content and style of the anthem. According to this injunction, the style was to be syllabic throughout, concerned only with Our Lord and not with the saints, and of course the text was to be in English.[6]

Tallis. For over forty years, Thomas Tallis (c. 1505–c. 1585) was a member of the Chapel Royal. In partnership with William Byrd, he obtained a monopoly for printing music; the monopoly, granted in 1575, was held by Byrd alone after Tallis's death. In spite of his position as organist of a Protestant royal chapel, Tallis composed several dozen Latin motets, Masses, and other Catholic works, revealing a masterful contrapuntal technique. Involved works in canon for six or more voices, a motet for eight choirs of five voices each, Masses in which the *cantus firmus* technique is employed—such compositions are filled with lyric beauty and real melodiousness in spite of their technical complexity.[7] His English works are somewhat different. In keeping with the practice of the time, Tallis set his anthems (about seventeen have survived) in a style that is generally chordal; the flowing counterpoint that animates his Latin works is noticeably absent in those set to English texts. Yet Tallis seems not to have been hampered by a style that was basically foreign to him.

6 Reese, *Music in the Renaissance*, p. 796.
7 A *responsorium* by Tallis is given in *HAM*, No. 127, *Audivi*. . . .

Byrd. As a composer of secular vocal music and music for the virginal, William Byrd takes one of the highest places in the history of English music. His sacred compositions, on both Latin and English texts, add to his stature and make him one of the most versatile composers of the entire Renaissance period. During his long life (1543–1623) he remained a devout Catholic, but he was professionally active as organist of Lincoln Cathedral and the Chapel Royal.

Among Byrd's Latin works are several books of motets, three Masses, and many smaller compositions. One of the Masses, set for three voices, is graceful and serene. Another, for four voices, is more elaborate in scope and more striking in effect. The third, for five voices, is a vigorous and brilliant work throughout. In all three Masses (without *cantus firmus*) Byrd's technical mastery never obscures the expressiveness of the melodies. It is rare in the Renaissance period that a single voice part, taken out of its polyphonic context, shows intrinsic melodic beauty; yet in Byrd's Masses this is repeatedly the case (see Example 70).

E x a m p l e   70

Byrd, *Mass for Three Voices*

The motets of 1575, 1589, and 1591 and the miscellaneous works contained in the *Gradualia* of 1605 and 1607 are considerably more varied. Although imitative textures predominate,[8] strict canons are found in several of the motets, notably in *Diliges Dominum* of 1575 and *Quomodo cantabimus* of 1583, both for eight voices. In several cases examples of word painting and other style elements from the secular madrigal occur. Settings employing a *cantus firmus* are decidedly in the minority, perhaps indicating that in England, as on the Continent, this structural principle was on the way toward obsolescence.

Of Byrd's sacred music set to English texts, several anthems and four services have been preserved. The anthems exhibit all the variety of texture found in his motets. Among the full anthems, the six-voice *Sing Joyfully unto God* is dramatic and brilliant; another, the three-voice *From Depth of Sin,* is brooding and filled with pathos throughout. Byrd's verse anthems include a variety of accompaniments. *Teach me, O Lord,* for example, contains passages for solo voice and organ alternating with passages for full choir unaccompanied. His *Christ Rising Again* [9] includes

8 See the motet *Non vos relinquam* in *HAM,* No. 150.
9 Given in *HAM,* No. 151.

an introduction for viols alone, passages for a solo voice accompanied by a quartet of viols, and other passages for full choir with solo voice set in the manner of an obbligato. As in the motets, examples of word painting are occasionally found.

Byrd's four services differ considerably from one another. The first, a Short Service (comparable to the Catholic *Missa brevis*), containing texts for both the morning and evening services, is in chordal style and seems to conform to Archbishop Cranmer's injunction to set texts in note-against-note style. The second and third contain only texts for the evening service; in the second Byrd introduces the principle of the verse anthem, for passages in the *Magnificat* and *Nunc dimittis* are set for solo voice with organ accompaniment. The fourth, the Great Service for five voices, is one of Byrd's finest works. Here, as in the first of the four compositions, texts for both morning and evening services are included, but in the Great Service the settings are both elaborate and lengthy. Chordal passages and passages in involved imitative counterpoint are equally characteristic and are set with great rhythmic freedom. Occasionally a vocal part is divided into two, so that the basic five-voice setting is augmented to eight.

Many other composers of the time contributed to the formation of a body of Tudor church music. Several of the madrigal composers to be discussed in Chapter 11 wrote anthems and services also: Thomas Morley, Thomas Weelkes, John Bull, Thomas Tompkins, and Orlando Gibbons are among the many excellent musicians represented. Although Tompkins (*c.* 1571–1656) composed far into the seventeenth century, Gibbons (1583–1625) may be considered the last important composer of the contrapuntal style in England. He was associated entirely with the Anglican church, and his forty anthems are among the finest works of the late Renaissance in England. Full and rich sonorities are characteristic of

EXAMPLE 71

Gibbons, Motet

Gibbons whether the style is chordal or contrapuntal. He often carried imitative writing to a high level of consistency (see EXAMPLE 71), and a syllabic style is most often in evidence.

In much of the music from Tye to Gibbons, several stylistic elements that are specifically English may be observed. Chief among them is the "cross relation" or "false relation"—that is, the use of two forms of the same tone (F and F♯, for example) either simultaneously within the same chord or in different voices in adjoining chords. The cross relation resulted from the employment in one voice of the unaltered form of the mode and in the other voice, the mode altered by *musica ficta*. It gives evidence of the strength of the conservative attitude in English composers. The cross relation is a linear (melodic) phenomenon and arises in a modal context; at the time English composers featured the device, composers on the Continent were moving from linear to harmonic considerations and from modal to tonal thinking.

English music in general often revealed a direct and light-hearted melodic style that recaptured the nature of English folk music. Simple scalewise patterns, small leaps, and well-rounded melodic contours occur most often, and the music is always eminently singable. The melodies are placed in a strongly rhythmic context that develops vigor and momentum and is filled with syncopations, polyrhythms, and brief changes of meter. The result is a kind of music with varied sonorities and contrasts of expression that reflects the animation characterizing life in Elizabethan England.

The Renaissance:
Secular Music

I N   T H E   discussion in Chapters 7–9 of the developments in the field of sacred music, the contributions of important groups of Franco-Flemish composers were described. The strength of the Italian influences on those composers—particularly on Obrecht, Isaac, and Josquin—was also mentioned. During the late fifteenth and sixteenth centuries both influences increased in significance, especially in the secular field. The diverse nature of Italian influences on Renaissance secular music will be discussed in the first part of this chapter.

Woodcut by Hans Nell, from title page of Orlando di Lasso's *Patrocinium Musices,* 1589.

Until about 1450 the chief creative impulse still came from north of the Alps. While the *caccia* and *ballata* of the period of Landini continued to flourish in Italy in the early fifteenth century, French models still shaped that music. The forms of the *rondeau* and *virelai* seemed attractive to the Italian composers of the time (indeed, the *ballata* is simply the Italian counterpart of the *virelai*), and occasionally French poems are found set to music by Italian composers. The composers were seldom of more than local renown, and few biographical items about them are yet available.[1]

Frottola

TOWARD the middle of the fifteenth century in Italy a reversal of that influence began. The practice became general, especially in the courts and in the homes of the nobility, of reciting poems over an improvised instrumental accompaniment. In the palaces of the Medici in Florence and the d'Este in Ferrara all the arts flourished, and one may assume that the recitation of poetry to music was included. When Isabella d'Este married Francesco Gonzaga, the marquis of Mantua, the Mantuan court became a center of the new activity. And there, toward the end of the century, a new kind of vocal setting originated. The *frottola,* as the new form was called, became one of the means of transmitting to the rest of Europe the essentially Italian love for melody, feeling for chordal structure, and taste for clear, vigorous, but simple expression.

The *frottola* texts deal with amorous subjects for the most part, but these were often treated with humor and satire. Although written and performed in aristocratic circles, the poems often show a deliberate attempt to be folklike, unassuming, and even naive. They are generally strophic, each strophe consisting of six lines, usually followed by a four-line refrain.

The musical setting of a typical *frottola* is for three or four voices and in chordal texture. The form is similar to that of the old Italian *ballata,* the main musical interest centering on the refrain (see EXAMPLE 72). Generally only the top voice, which carried the principal melody, was to be sung; the others were given to instruments. The bass line, in which leaps of fourths and fifths to root tones of triads are characteristic, provides a kind of harmonic foundation; inner voices, not melodically inspired, serve primarily to fill out the harmonies. The upper melody, of small range, typically moves stepwise and contains repeated tones, especially at cadences; it was often set in standardized rhythmic patterns, of which the dactyl (long-short-short) is the most common.

Few names of late fifteenth-century *frottola* composers are known. Bartolomeo Tromboncino, Marchetto Cara, and Filippo da Luprano may be mentioned, but a host of Italian composers in a dozen Italian cities contributed to the repertoire. Their importance lies mainly in having standardized a chordal style in which Flemish counterpoint played no

1 See Reese, *Music in the Renaissance*, pp. 29–33, for details.

EXAMPLE 72

Anon., *Frottola*

TRANSLATION:
The love, my lady, that I bear you will I gladly reveal.

part, and in establishing a lighthearted mode of expression which was
warm and human rather than profound.[2]

A few other forms related to the *frottola* may be mentioned. The *strambotto,* with an eight-line strophe but without a refrain, is often of a more
serious nature than the *frottola*. The *canzone* is freer in form, but its
lines are generally seven or eleven syllables in length. The text, often of a
higher literary quality than the text of a *frottola,* consists of any number
of strophes, and the music is repeated from strophe to strophe. The
sonetto adheres to the familiar fourteen-line poetic form. Unaccompanied
vocal performance in the *sonetto,* as in the *strambotto* and the *canzone,*
was probably more common than in the *frottola* itself.

The *canto carnascialesco* originated in Florence about 1450 and was
performed out of doors during the carnival season. The form is essentially
a Florentine version of the *frottola* and the Franco-Flemish chanson, but
modified in accord with its different function. Subtleties of form and expression are out of place in a piece designed to be sung above crowd noises
in a torchlight procession; hence the *canto carnascialesco* is generally in
chordal style with a humorous tone. During the years of Savonarola's
virtual domination of Florence (1494–1498) and the temporary eclipse of
the Medici, the carnivals were not held. After the return of the Medici

2 Two *frottole* are in *HAM,* Nos. 95a *Non val aqua,* and 95b *In te Domine;* others
will be found in *GMB,* Nos. 69, *Benche amor . . . ,* 70, *Ite caldi . . . ,* 71, *El Grillo,*
and 72, *Non è tempo. . . .*

the old gaiety was restored only in part, and the *canto carnascialesco* in the sixteenth century became a dignified piece of no special distinction.[3]

The *lauda* may be discussed here if only because of its musical similarity to the *frottola;* its function was religious rather than secular. *Laude* as monophonic songs in praise of the Virgin had existed well back into Medieval times. Polyphonic settings date from at least the fourteenth century, and by the mid-fifteenth *laude* for two, three, and four voices were composed in quantity. Many of them exhibit the same chordal style and unpretentious tone found in the *frottola;* indeed composers of the latter frequently wrote *laude* also, and on occasion set a *lauda* text to the music of a *frottola*.

Finally, the *villanella* (which an earlier Italian generation had called *villanesca*) may be mentioned. Also derived from the *frottola* and containing the same general style traits, it appeared first at Naples. It exaggerated the lofty tone and sentimental expression of the madrigal; in a sense it parodied or satirized the madrigal's characteristic features. Its texts were in dialect or in a mixture of languages, and eventually it merged with the more refined *canzonetta*.

Madrigal

ABOUT the second quarter of the sixteenth century a reaction against the frivolous tone of *frottola* texts set in. Under the leadership of Cardinal Pietro Bembo (1470–1547) a host of minor Italian poets produced short lyric poems of dignified character designed to be set to music. Bembo himself supplied models; the form was free, consisting only of a single stanza or strophe containing lines of seven or eleven syllables in any desired rhyme scheme. The length of line, reminiscent of the old *canzone,* became a standardized feature. The single strophe was usually ten lines long, but both shorter and longer strophes were also used. Such poems, then, were set to music—usually for four or five voices; the madrigal, one of the most influential of all secular musical forms, was the result.[4]

Among the earliest madrigal composers was the Flemish Philippe Verdelot (?–1550), a choir singer at St. Mark's in Venice and later choirmaster at St. John's in Florence. Verdelot's madrigals, about one hundred in number, may have been the first works in this form.[5] Contemporary with him was an Italian, Costanzo Festa (see page 144), associated primarily with the Papal chapel in Rome. Jacob Arcadelt (*c.* 1505–*c.* 1560), born in Flanders but active principally in Rome, composed some two hundred madrigals. Adrian Willaert (see pages 153–54), also Flemish by birth but an Italian resident from 1522 and *maestro di cappella* at St. Mark's in Venice from 1527, was almost as productive. These four men ushered in

---

3 An example is given in *HAM*, No. 96, *Per scriptores*.

4 The sixteenth-century madrigal, a relatively free setting of various types of poetic texts, has little connection with the similarly named form of Landini and his school in the fourteenth. Landini's madrigal was a setting of a poem several strophes in length, with each strophe adhering to a rather fixed rhyme scheme. See Einstein, *The Italian Madrigal,* for complete details.

5 One is reprinted in *GMB*, No. 98, *Madonna*. . . .

the first period of madrigal writing and set standards for later generations to follow.

An essential feature of the early madrigal is a four-voice texture that is primarily chordal. The top line carries the principal melody, while the lines of the inner voices have a lesser degree of melodic integrity. The mixture of eleven- and seven-syllable lines was adhered to rather generally.[6] Of their performance Einstein says, "Nothing hinders the lower voices from being degraded to the role of instrumental accompaniment; the century was openminded in such matters." [7] In spite of this, the inner voices proved attractive to performers and made the madrigal into "singers' music." A few bits of imitation interspersed in the homophonic texture provide moments of variety. Phrases in general end together and pauses often separate them, so that the form can "breathe"; but lest the madrigal disintegrate into a series of fragments, this feature often gives way to passages in which phrase endings overlap in motet style.

The early madrigal, 1540–1580. Toward the 1540's the madrigal began to develop a closer relationship to its text and a higher degree of expressive quality. With Willaert and his pupil, Cipriano de Rore (1516–1565), a five-voice setting became standardized. De Rore, also Flemish by birth, was active principally in Ferrara and Parma, and for a short time served as Willaert's successor in Venice. In De Rore's madrigals, as in Willaert's later ones, contrapuntal textures often replaced chordal writing, although the latter was still used for expressive purposes.

Willaert, apparently dissatisfied with the conventional tone of madrigal texts of his time, turned to the lyric poetry of Petrarch (1304–1374), one of the most important figures in Italian literature and one of the first of the humanists. Petrarch's Italian poems include some of the most elegant and refined love poems in the literature. Following Willaert's example, other madrigal composers turned to Petrarch over and over again; virtually every one of the poet's *canzoni* and sonnets was set to music, often dozens of times.

A tendency to illustrate musically the meaning of textual details is marked in Willaert's madrigals of the 1540's. Word painting found an increasingly prominent place, for example; a mood of depression was suggested by the use of low tones, and agitation, by rapid rhythmic motion. This tendency to utilize the descriptive potential of music took on great dimensions in the following decades; the madrigal in effect became a piece of descriptive music.

Willaert and De Rore, together with other madrigalists of the time, went far to bring about a renewed interest in contrapuntal writing. Passages with overlapping phrases had not often occurred in the earlier madrigal; now such passages became common and the texture of the

6 Especially in a madrigal by Arcadelt in *HAM,* No. 130, *Voi ve* . . . ; in another by the same composer in *GMB,* No. 100, *Voi mi* . . . ; and to a lesser extent in one by Festa, *HAM,* No. 129, *Quando ritrova.*

7 "Die mehrstimmige weltliche Musik von 1450–1600," in Adler, *Handbuch der Musikgeschichte,* I, p. 363.

madrigal came close to that of the motet. Occasionally the five-voice group was divided into two semi-groups that sang in alternation in the manner of a *concertato* (in the original meaning of the term, which implied competing groups; see EXAMPLE 73). This device, however, found its fullest

EXAMPLE 73

De Rore, *Anchor che col partire*

employment later in the century. Imitation was used more frequently than in the earlier period, and considerable use of syncopation in the melodies made the dissonances in the imitative passages even more pungent. Further, the faint beginning of the chromaticism that was to mark madrigals of the later period is occasionally found in the works of Willaert and De Rore (see EXAMPLE 74).[8]

EXAMPLE 74

De Rore, *O sonno*

8 See also De Rore's madrigal, *De la belle contrade*, in *HAM*, No. 131, on the words *sola mi lasci* in the soprano; and elsewhere as well.

Chromaticism is also found in the madrigals of Nicolò Vicentino (1511–1572), another pupil of Willaert and active principally in Ferrara and Rome. Vicentino attempted to restore the three ancient Greek genera diatonic, chromatic, and enharmonic—to the modal music of his time. His understanding of the genera, incomplete as it was, led him to devise a system in which the octave was divided into thirty-one microtones, in order to permit a reconstruction of the enharmonic genus. His theories were elaborated in a book, *L'antica musica ridotta alla moderna prattica* (1555), and he invented a type of harpsichord with six keyboards, upon which the Greek genera could be reproduced and illustrated. Vicentino's madrigals (Book V, 1572) abound with chromatic devices of the kind later exploited by Gesualdo. Tones such as D♭, D♯, and A♯ are common, as are cadences built upon those and other rarely used tones.

Finally, the madrigals of the middle years of the century differed in notation and rhythm from those of the 1530's. The basic time unit had been the minim (modern half-note); quarter-notes had found employment principally in melismas or in ornamented cadences. Now, in the late 1540's, quarter-notes became much more common. They were given separate text syllables (as in EXAMPLE 73) and were often surrounded by eighth-notes; in effect they became new time units. This greater degree of rhythmic animation and use of syncopation accompanying the new use of quarter-notes are so marked that the madrigals make a different visual impression than earlier works in which the minim is the basic unit. Because of this, such works were called "black-note madrigals" or "chromatic madrigals" (in the sense that black notes are "colored"). It should be mentioned that this term is not related to the "chromaticism" of the Baroque period and later.

Several of the giants among late sixteenth-century composers wrote madrigals too, but in some cases their madrigals are not among their most significant works. Such a composer was Palestrina (*c.* 1525–1594), who composed about 140 madrigals. The majority of these compositions are conservative in tone, somewhat reminiscent of works of the 1530's and not in general widely different from Palestrina's sacred works. In fact, more than a third of the total are called "sacred madrigals."

Orlando di Lasso (1532–1594) is another case in point. Though without peer in the field of sacred music and scarcely matched in his chansons, Lasso remained rather conservative in his many madrigals. The devices in the music of De Rore are found again in Lasso's. Among them are a discreet use of melodic chromaticism, which became even less common in his later works; a sensitive approach to his texts, with only occasional moments of descriptive writing; and a style compounded largely of chordal writing interspersed with passages in counterpoint. The harmonic freedom found on occasion in Lasso's madrigals (and in Lasso one may begin to use the word "harmony" in the sense of tonal harmony) approaches the freedom of his motets. Passages occur which can be described only as containing transient modulations by circle of fifths, for example, from E through A, D, G, C to F or B♭. Passages of this kind are found more frequently in the motets, however; wherever they occur, they indicate that

Lasso was well aware of the trend that led eventually to the breakdown of modal integrity and to the establishment of major and minor tonalities within the tonal system.

With Philippe de Monte (1521–1603) and Giaches de Wert (1535–1596) the line of important Flemish composers of madrigals comes virtually to an end. Monte, after a dozen or more years in Italy, became *maestro di cappella* in Vienna, where he remained for over thirty years. Wert, on the other hand, spent almost his entire professional life at the courts of Mantua and Ferrara.

Monte composed over a thousand madrigals. A high level of seriousness and musical quality characterized his work, and in a sense he summarized the technical developments within the middle-period madrigal. He used chordal writing when text emphasis made it desirable, but in general his textures are contrapuntal and imitative. The five-voice setting remained the standard for Monte, although he did not hesitate to write for six or more parts. Wert, on the other hand, was more forward-looking in his attitude toward harmony, descriptive writing, and texture. He was a contemporary of the radical composers who led the madrigal to its next stage of development, and on occasion he made use of the devices which became characteristic in the following decades.

Meanwhile, a number of Italian composers were also contributing to the madrigal literature. Wert's successor at Mantua, Giovanni Gastoldi (*c.* 1556–1622), was one such composer. But Gastoldi is better known as a composer of *balletti,* which may be characterized as light, dancelike offshoots of the madrigal. The typical *balletto,* unlike the madrigal, consisted of two sections in chordal style, each of which was repeated; it included a refrain on the text "fa-la-la" or a similar set of nonsense syllables. Rhythmic patterns derived from dance music tend to be stereotyped, thus one *balletto* sounds much like another.[9]

Andrea Gabrieli (*c.* 1520–1586) reputedly studied with Willaert. He traveled and worked in Germany for some years, but he was associated primarily with St. Mark's in Venice. As chorister (1536), second organist (1566), and first organist (1585), he contributed vitally to the formation of a Venetian school of composition. His nephew, Giovanni Gabrieli (*c.* 1557–1612), who studied with him, also lived in Germany for several years and then returned to St. Mark's as second organist (1585–1612). Essential features of the Venetian style are extreme brilliance, writing for eight or more voices with the voices divided into two groups, and the use of a kind of choral recitative. Andrea's use of these features in his madrigals was somewhat tentative; only in his later works did he rise to the full possibilities of the Venetian style.

It remained for Giovanni Gabrieli to develop polychoral writing to a high point. Writing for an eight-voice double chorus, he made use of a variety of sonorous effects. Gabrieli's use of choral recitative, with rapid *parlando* effects over a static harmony, inevitably brought with it a decline in the amount of contrapuntal writing and a greater concern with

9 An example is given in *HAM,* No. 158, *L'Acceso.*

E X A M P L E 75

Giovanni Gabrieli, *Quand'io ero Giovinetto*

TRANSLATION:
Of every halter, of every halter and bond . . .

harmonic color. And it is just in the employment of such features that Giovanni Gabrieli moved to the threshold of a new style period (see EXAMPLE 75). Before that period began, however, the madrigal underwent yet another set of changes that were to make it a musical expression of pathos and drama.

The late madrigal, 1580–1600. The hyperexpressive madrigal owes its development primarily to Luca Marenzio (1553 1599). Marenzio, born near Brescia, served at various courts and visited in Rome, Ferrara, and Florence. His seventeen books of madrigals, published between 1580 and 1599, contain some of the most expressive, varied, and important works in the madrigal literature. The majority of the madrigals are for five voices, although several works for four and six voices also exist. Beyond this, it is difficult to generalize about characteristic features of Marenzio's style. In virtually every madrigal Marenzio achieves the closest possible relationship between text and music, using a great variety of means. Imitative counterpoint, chordal textures, and chordal recitative are all used to enhance the meaning and clarity of a text phrase. On occasion a short motive is used to reiterate one phrase of the text.[10] In some works five-part imitative writing with a sixth part in free counterpoint is characteristic; in others the writing is homophonic throughout, with the chief melody confined to the top voice. There are six-voice works that begin with the top four voices, change to the bottom four, and continue with all six.[11]

In detailed word painting, in associating a word or phrase with music that gives a graphic picture of it, Marenzio was unsurpassed. In setting the word "eyes," for example, he regularly used a pair of half-notes in a context of quarter-notes; the "openness" of the eyes is thus suggested. According to Reese, "The noble six-part apostrophe to Rome, *Cedan l'antiche tue chiare vittorie,* represents the arches of the great city by means of an ascending and descending curve in several voices. . . . In *Rideau gia per le piagge,* the idea of the words in *al tempo novo* and *novo tempo* is represented literally by a change of meter." [12] In contrast to such graphic notational effects are those in which a musical fragment reflects the sense of the text. A leaping melody to suggest joy, an undulating figure to picture singing, a melodic rise and fall by minor seconds to imply sighing, a diminished triad to depict grief—such examples of word painting abound. These devices, however, were not used to excess, nor were they used naively. Marenzio's concern with the musical expression of the *entire* text is everywhere evident, and the devices of word painting were only incidental to expressing the whole. This aspect of his style remained influential for several generations.

10 See *HAM,* No. 155, on the phrase *tal che m'avviso;* and *MoM,* No. 27, on the word *perchè.*

11 Several of these devices are found in Einstein, *The Italian Madrigal,* II, pp. 651–52; and III, p. 252.

12 *Music in the Renaissance,* p. 422.

In a harmonic sense, too, Marenzio employed the full resources of the art of this time; indeed, he increased those resources. Chromatic fragments in the melody and chromatic intervals had long been admitted to the vocabulary of the madrigalists (De Rore, for example), as had expressive dissonance. Likewise, triads on tones not found in the modes had become customary. Diminished triads as well as triads on G♯, D♭, A♭, and other nondiatonic tones are found even more frequently, making Marenzio's harmonic means far richer than those of his predecessors. In the process of using such triads the integrity of the modes declined considerably, of course, and tonal harmony came appreciably closer. But since the new triads were used as individual sound-complexes and did not relate to tonal centers, it is not possible to ascribe to Marenzio the use of tonal harmony.

Carlo Gesualdo (*c.* 1560–1613), Prince of Venosa, spent some years at the court of Ferrara but lived principally in Naples, his birthplace. His life was filled with tragedy (the well-known story of his murder of his wife and her lover need not be retold here). He became an accomplished lutenist, and he composed a number of madrigals unmatched in harmonic boldness and pathetic expression. There is little word painting in Gesualdo; his effects were achieved primarily through the use of extreme chromaticism.

In textures that range from block chords to six-voice polyphony, Gesualdo sometimes employed fragments of chromatic melody.[13] But his effects were achieved most often through the juxtaposition of triads related only chromatically: an F-major triad set before a triad on F♯, a chord on C♯ followed by the first inversion of an A-minor triad. Or again, as in EXAMPLE 76*a,* chords on G, B, and G minor are set close together. To these are added sharp dissonances created by passing tones or suspensions (as in the second measure of EXAMPLE 76*b,* where G, A, and B♭ momentarily sound together). In other passages cross relations add their bit to the basic chromatic style.

In Gesualdo's madrigals are seen, to an extreme degree, the preoccupation with pathos that characterized the late sixteenth-century madrigal in Italy. Texts by Petrarch were still being chosen by composers; in addition, texts by Ariosto, by Gesualdo's contemporary, Tasso, and by a number of minor poets were set to music. With increasing frequency, strophes concerned with death, anguish, lamentation, and the like became favorite texts for madrigal composition. Wert and his school had begun this development, and Gesualdo brought it to its completion. Gesualdo, like Gabrieli, stood at the turning point of a new style; it remained for other composers, notably Monteverdi, to carry the madrigal into the seventeenth century and there to change its style and bring it to another peak of development.

---

13 See *HAM,* No. 161, *Io pur . . . ,* throughout, but especially the last dozen measures; see also *GMB,* No. 167, *Dolcissima . . . ,* and *TEM,* No. 33, *Moro lasso.* In 1961 Stravinsky honored the memory of Gesualdo in a composition embodying some of his music.

EXAMPLE 76

Gesualdo, *Arditta zanzaretta*

Chanson

ONE IMPORTANT guiding principle of French culture through the cen
turies has been that its art must be understandable in logical or intellectual terms. Instrumental music seldom satisfied this requirement, and
French composers as a group are not notable for their contributions to
the instrumental field. Vocal or choral music, however, being supplied
with a text, can appeal to the mind, and ever since early Gothic times
music with a text has been most favored by French composers. Whether
in organum, the monophonic songs of the troubadours, the *ars nova,* or
the later opera, the French musical spirit has felt most at home in the
broad field of texted music.

The mutual interdependence of music and text reached a high level
in the sixteenth-century French chanson. The chanson appeared as early
as the fourteenth century, often in a rhythmically complicated style. In
the fifteenth century, notably in the works of Matteo da Perugia, its
rhythm was simplified and its melodic attractiveness enhanced; imitative
counterpoint and dominant-tonic final cadences became characteristic.
In this form the chanson was taken over by Dufay and Binchois (see pages
109 and 113); the works referred to earlier were primarily three-voice
compositions, predominantly contrapuntal, which showed close relationships to the old *formes fixes.* The chansons of Josquin (see page 124) and
Isaac, on the other hand, approached a new type that dominated French
music in the years about 1520 to 1610. In these works contrapuntal textures often gave way to chordal writing in short passages. Settings for five
or more voices were common, and something of the folklike spirit found
in Italian secular music became characteristic. Indeed, the chanson of
this type corresponds roughly to the Italian madrigal of Verdelot and
Willaert.

The madrigal had been designed primarily for courtly circles; it played
an important role in the entertainment of the nobility in Italy, its folklike tone reflecting a kind of patronizing attitude. The chanson, on the
other hand, represented a genuine popular spirit. Although it was cultivated at the courts, it came into enormous demand on all levels of
French society. The short lyric poems of Clément Marot (1496–1544) and
his imitators provided composers with a body of verse free of all pretense
that required no sophistication for its enjoyment. The text could be sentimental, humorous, or erotic, but it was always appealing to the general
audience.

To such short poems a host of French and Flemish composers applied
themselves; the new chanson came into being about the 1520's. Claudin
de Sermisy (*c.* 1490–1562), who spent most of his life in Paris, is one of
the first composers of what is often called the "Parisian chanson." In this
type the writing is usually for four voices in predominantly chordal style,
with the melody in the upper voice. The piece usually begins with a
dactylic motive (long-short-short), and the harmonic structure approaches
modern tonality (see EXAMPLE 77). Pierre Attaingnant, one of the earliest

EXAMPLE 77

Sermisy, Chanson

Pour - tant si je suis bru - net - te, a - my

ne pre - nez et moy, au - tant

of French printers to employ movable type, published almost two thousand chansons in a twenty-year period beginning in 1528. Sermisy's chansons are well represented in the earliest of Attaingnant's publications, and many of them were reprinted after the composer's death. At a time when dozens of worthy composers were writing innumerable chansons, it speaks for the high quality of Sermisy's works that they were reprinted at all.

The quality in his and other chansons of the time lies in the light and deft style of the music, the simplicity of its texture, and the skillful setting in a form that brought out the structure of the text. Phrases are usually separated by rests in all the parts (see EXAMPLE 77), and the first phrase often returns, with new text, as the last phrase of the chanson. Thus a closed, symmetrical form is characteristic. Repeated tones in all parts give a lilting rhythm to the music, and occasional syncopations lend an air of rhythmic flexibility.

It is possible that Clément Janequin (c. 1485–c. 1560) even exceeded Sermisy in popularity. Janequin was known especially for a descriptive type called "program chanson," in which various extramusical sounds and events are suggested.[14] Here the chordal style is replaced by a rapidly moving, rhythmically diverse style in which short phrases appear in several voices in turn. Titles such as "The War," "Song of the Birds," "The Lark," "Cries of Paris," and "The Fall of Boulogne" indicate the nature of Janequin's program chansons. The works are often filled with nonsense syllables which, set in short notes and repeated many times over, provide rhythmic animation and a truly humorous tone. Janequin composed many chansons in other styles as well; his works in chordal style rival Sermisy's in grace, elegance, and wit.

14 See *HAM*, No. 107, *L'Alouette*, for an example.

Contrapuntal chanson. Even during the time when the chordal chanson reigned supreme, roughly from 1520 to 1560, another type of chanson continued to flourish. Resulting from the application of Flemish contrapuntal techniques to French verse, it represents a continuation of the chanson type composed by Josquin. The contrapuntal chanson was not confined to France; numerous collections were published by Tielman Susato of Antwerp, Pierre Phalèse of Louvain, and others, and the chief composers represented in them are of Flemish birth.

Many of these composers were also active in writing Italian madrigals. Among them was Willaert, who favored older techniques such as the use of canon; he placed the main melody in the tenor, often treating the tenor as a *cantus firmus*. Arcadelt is represented by well over a hundred chansons. He wrote in a mixture of contrapuntal and chordal styles, although the rhythmic clarity and vivacity of the latter did not suffer. Lasso generally wrote contrapuntally, but the lightness and rhythmic clarity of his chansons remain outstanding features (see EXAMPLE 78).

The chansons of Nicolas Gombert (*c.* 1490–1556), Thomas Crequillon (?–1557), and Jacobus Clemens (*c.* 1510–*c.* 1556, called Clemens non Papa) rise above many hundreds of chansons by other French and Flemish composers of the time. Gombert's chansons resemble the type seen in EXAMPLE 78. Canonic writing, imitation in pairs of voices, and all the other contrapuntal devices inherited from a long line of Flemish com-

A chanson performance, with voice, flute, and lute. Sixteenth-century Flemish painting.

EXAMPLE 78

Lasso, Chanson

posers of church music also come to life in the chansons. In the chansons of Crequillon, Clemens, and others of their group, a tendency to write for five voices became relatively fixed; after about 1550 the five-voice chanson became virtually standard, and thus another of Josquin's style elements found roots in the French chanson.

Many of the secular polyphonic songs of the early and middle sixteenth century contained a short section—often no more than a phrase in length—set in triple meter and thus in contrast to the prevailing duple. Chanson, madrigal, and even *canto carnascialesco* occasionally illustrated this characteristic (see EXAMPLE 79).[15] While this sectionalization is of only passing importance in the vocal works themselves, it becomes a significant element in the creation of the forms of independent instrumental music in Italy later in the century.

The present account of the contrapuntal chanson mentions only a few of the principal composers involved in its development. Dozens of minor masters contributed to the literature, among them such men as Guillaume Costeley (1531–1606),[16] Pierre Certon (*c.* 1510–1572), Claude Goudimel (*c.* 1505–1572) and many others. The influence of the Italian madrigal is to be seen in numerous chansons by these men; a greater concern with text details and a wider range of expression became typical. But there was no less interest in closed forms, occasional phrase repetition, and melodiousness in chansons of this type.

15 For an example of this treatment in a madrigal, see *HAM,* No. 130, *Voi ve* . . . , and *GMB,* No. 98, *Madonna* . . . ; in a *canto carnascialesco,* see *HAM,* No. 96, *Per scriptores.*

16 See *HAM,* No. 147, *Allon* . . . , for a Costeley chanson in mixed chordal and contrapuntal style.

EXAMPLE 79

Lupi, *O attroppoz*

Measured chanson. Even while the free, contrapuntal chanson was being developed to its high level, yet another type of chanson had a brief period in the sun. Under the influence of the expanding humanistic movement, a number of French poets wrote verse which, while designed to be set to music, attempted to restore the style of classic Greek and Latin verse. Pierre de Ronsard (1525–*c.* 1585) became associated with Jean-Antoine de Baïf (1532–1589) and a group known as the *Pléiade* in the formation of a body of poetry called *vers mesuré.* A poem of this type, written as a reaction to rhymed verse with its regularly recurring accents, was based on the classical system of quantity, whereby the succession of long and short vowels determined the poetic meter.

Composers friendly to the tenets of the *Pléiade* and of the *Académie de poésie et de musique,* which was established in 1570 under Baïf's direction, set *vers mesurés* to music. The resulting works, which may be called measured chansons, were in chordal style; they were theoretically to include only long and short tones in proportionate lengths of two to one. The principal composers of this type seldom restricted themselves to the rigidity demanded by Baïf, however. Short melismas, running figures in one or another voice, and similar liberties gave their chansons a degree of melodiousness and rhythmic vitality. Claude Le Jeune (1528–1600) and Jacques Mauduit (1557–1627) were chief among the composers of measured chansons (see EXAMPLE 80).[17] The main virtue of this type is that it brought modern harmonic feeling another step closer; in developing a style which consists essentially of a harmonized melody, these chanson composers paved the way for the monodic revolution of the seventeenth century. There the chanson, appropriately modified, appeared under such names as *vaux de ville, air,* and *air de cour.*

17 See *HAM,* No. 138, *D'une coline,* for another chanson by Le Jeune.

EXAMPLE 80

Le Jeune, *O rôze reyne*

cet- te bou - che plei - ne tou - jours et d'o-deur rar'   et   de dou -   ceur

cet- te bou-che plei - ne tou - jours et d'o-deur rar'   et   de dou -   ceur

English Vocal Music

THE MUSICAL leadership that England had shown in the time of Dunstable disappeared in the second half of the fifteenth century. English composers were content—as far as present-day knowledge goes—to write rather bland music and seemed to remain largely untouched by the developments found in the Burgundian and Franco-Flemish schools. One new item may be mentioned, however: the carol, a polyphonic piece which, although secular in its usage, often contained a religious or quasi-religious text. Usually set for two or three voices in a style reminiscent of the old *conductus,* the carol found employment in popular entertainments. Since it was joyful in character, it was also used on religious occasions (Christmas and Easter) and seasonal festivals (May Day and the like). Toward the end of the fifteenth century it was sometimes treated contrapuntally, finding its way then to higher social levels.[18]

Madrigal types. For two generations, beginning about the 1440's, political conditions in England had been turbulent. The conflicts between various noble houses gave rise to the Wars of the Roses, which ended in 1485 when the first of a line of Tudors (Henry VII) gained the English throne. Under his successor, Henry VIII (1491–1547, king from 1509), England emerged as a political and commercial power and became receptive to the culture of the Italian Renaissance. Italian music began to be a valued article of importation, and by the 1560's, early in the reign of Elizabeth, Italian madrigals circulated in large numbers. The publication of a volume of madrigals in translation (*Musica transalpina,* 1588) was soon followed by a second (*Italian Madrigals Englished,* 1590), and within a few years several more anthologies of Italian secular music (containing works by Marenzio and Gastoldi principally), translated into English, were published. The way was open first, for English madrigals which were derived from the Italian, and second, for works which were

18 See Greene, *The Early English Carol,* for details.

original in every sense. The latter gave rise to one of the finest flowerings of English music.

The earliest English madrigals, published in the 1590's, were preceded not only by the carols mentioned above but also by a number of part-songs. These three- or four-part secular works, with texts apparently derived from the popular verse of the day, resembled the fifteenth-century Flemish chansons in their use of free counterpoint and their generally ingratiating style.[19] Composers such as Robert Fayrfax (1464–1521), Henry VIII himself, Thomas Whythorne (c. 1528–?), and William Byrd (1543–1623) contributed to the type, which in the hands of Whythorne and Byrd often was set for five or six voices.

The part-songs of Byrd first appeared in his *Psalmes, Sonets, and Songs of Sadnes and Pietie* of 1588. Texts are supplied for all five voices, but the preface makes clear that the works may be sung by one voice with instrumental accompaniment. Two later secular publications by Byrd, in 1589 and 1611, are similar to the first, except that the works contained in them are for three to six voices.[20] Byrd successfully resisted the blandishments of the popular Italian style and continued to write rather contrapuntally and in a serious vein. Only occasionally, as if to demonstrate his versatility, did he compose in the Italian manner, notably in the publication of 1611.

Thomas Morley (1557–1602), one of the founders of the English repertoire, issued his first publication in 1593. The work contained compositions for three voices, set in a light and ingratiating style, called "canzonets." The texture, compounded of short motives which pass from voice to voice, gives the appearance of being contrapuntal. Actually, however, it is basically a chordal, harmonic style with its chords rhythmically diffused (see EXAMPLE 81).

Morley is best known for the works he wrote in the style of Gastoldi, namely the "ballets." Influenced by his Italian models, he wrote in a dancelike, fleet, and piquant style, incorporating a "fa-la-la" refrain. Such works as *Sing we and chaunt it* and *Now is the month of Maying*, which were included in his *First Booke of Ballets to five Voyces* of 1595, have not lost their popularity; they perfectly represent the style. Morley's ballets often became longer, more contrapuntal, and even more brilliant than Gastoldi's. Brief changes of meter, found often in Morley, became characteristic in later ballets such as those by Thomas Weelkes (c. 1575–1623).[21]

The madrigal proper differed from its Italian counterpart in one important respect. Whereas the Italian madrigal texts were drawn from the works of established poets of great stature (Petrarch, Ariosto, and Tasso, for example), the English were by popular poets of the day; few of the English texts can qualify as great literature. As a consequence, the

---

19 See *HAM*, Nos. 85, *Tappster* . . . , 86a, *A dew* . . . , and 86b, *I have been* . . . , for three early examples in which the style is more chordal.

20 A madrigal from the 1589 set is printed in *GMB*, No. 145, *The nightingale.* . . .

21 Morley's *My Bonny Lass* is reprinted in *HAM*, No. 159, and a ballet by Weelkes is in *HAM*, No. 170, *Hark.* . .

EXAMPLE 81

Morley, *Clorinda False*

English madrigal enjoyed great popularity among the middle class that attained size and influence under the Tudor monarchs. Further, it was sung by the people themselves, and not by professional groups as in Italy. Thus it was of necessity more direct, immediately appealing, and forthright than the Italian madrigal. Involved counterpoint, musical symbolism, and subtle word painting found little place in the English version. In the absence of those features came a clear and usually diatonic melody in the top voice, a strong harmonic feeling, and rhythmic vitality.

These qualities are seen in the madrigals of Thomas Weelkes. His first set, published in 1597, contained works for three to six voices; a second set, of 1598, for five voices, was followed in 1600 by *Madrigals of five and six parts apt for the viols and voices*. The set of 1600 shows a certain closeness to the style of Marenzio, for here Weelkes departs on occasion from the tightly knit style of Morley and writes expansively and at considerable length. In addition, the works display powerful dramatic utterance and an imaginative feeling for textual implications. A plurality of meters is sometimes found in Weelkes: the chief melody, following exactly the rhythm of the text, implies "measures" of various lengths (3/4, 5/4, 2/4) over a predominantly duple-meter set of lower voices. This device, common enough in the best sacred music of the day, brings a degree of rhythmic complexity that the Italian madrigal seldom contained.

John Wilbye (1574–1638), Orlando Gibbons (1583–1625), and perhaps a dozen additional composers contributed to the madrigal literature before its popularity declined sharply about 1613. The madrigals of Gibbons have a highly expressive, even sentimental style and are characterized by sensitive treatment of the text. Seldom were the freshness of Morley or the harmonic strength of Weelkes exceeded, unless in the works of Wilbye. Later works in the form—that is, those published after 1600—did not keep abreast of developments in the Italian madrigal. The English version, having found its scope and subject matter early in its brief career, was content to remain essentially on that level. But while it flourished, roughly from 1590 to 1610, it made a significant contribution to music, one that may be enjoyed today, since the madrigal is still represented in the current concert repertoire.

English ayre. The English ayre, as a category distinct from the madrigal, rose to supremacy only a few years after it and continued in favor for about a generation. The ayre has certain resemblances to the madrigal; indeed, the terms were often used interchangeably in the period about 1590. An essential difference, however, is that the ayre was specifically designed as a solo song, usually with lute accompaniment, for which a substitute set of lower parts was provided, while the madrigal, as we have seen, was conceived as a polyphonic vocal piece, the lower voices of which could be played by instruments (or combined to provide for lute accompaniment).

John Dowland (1562–1626), one of the most eminent lutenists of the Elizabethan period, was largely responsible for the vogue of the ayre. He was active in Ireland (his native country), France, Italy, Germany, and Denmark at various times but always returned to England. Dowland's *First Booke of Songes or Ayres of Foure Partes, with Tableture for the Lute,* published in 1597, gives evidence of the ayre's double function. The ayre was cast in either strophic or through-composed form; short phrases predominated, and repetition of one or more sections was typical. Florid writing was rare, the texts being set primarily in syllabic style.[22]

Dowland himself referred to his melancholy temperament; his ayres largely reflect moods of sadness, depression, and woe. Other composers of ayres—among them Morley, Danyel, and Thomas Campion—wrote lighthearted, frivolous, and dainty works. The variety of expressive types rivaled that in the madrigal and made the ayre equally popular. But in the decades after the death of Elizabeth (1603) and the gradual ascendancy of the Puritans, the elegant ayre declined in favor. A collection published in 1622 marked the virtual end of its development.

German Vocal Music

THE THIRTEENTH-CENTURY German and Austrian *minnesingers* had left a repertoire of secular monophonic songs which were closely related to the songs of the French troubadours. The influence of France on German musical matters continued through the fifteenth century, even into the field of polyphonic song. The few German manuscripts of the time, notably the *Lochamer* and *Glogauer Liederbücher,* contain a variety of works which testify to the strength of that influence. French or Flemish works appear with texts translated into German, and eminent Flemish

---

22 Ayres by Dowland and John Danyel are given in *HAM,* Nos. 162, *Stay* . . . , and 163, *What if.* . . .

composers are represented in the manuscripts, along with minor and anonymous composers who must be presumed to be Germans. Many instrumental arrangements and vocal forms appear, the latter set mainly for two or three voices. The songs which can be identified as German are related to the monophonic, courtly songs of the minnesingers in that their texts (usually concerned with noble love) and their forms (often *Barform*, that is, *aab*) are in general similar to those of the earlier period.[23]

About 1500, however, the German polyphonic song seems to have freed itself from the minnesinger tradition. Texts began to resemble the texts of the French chanson; love songs, peasant songs, soldiers' songs, and even what may be called political songs appeared. Some, those connected with the court, were aristocratic in style; others, which have been preserved in the German song repertoire, were folklike in spirit. The majority are set for four voices, of which probably only the top voice was sung and the others were performed instrumentally. The songs in general are through-composed; imitative counterpoint is found in the majority of them, and the principal melody is most often in the tenor.[24] The most important composers in this connection are Heinrich Finck (1445–1527), a German who served in a variety of posts in Poland, Austria, as well as in his native country; Paul Hofhaimer (1449–1537), the most eminent organist of his time and active mainly in Innsbruck; and the great Flemish composer, Heinrich Isaac (*c*. 1450–1517).

Isaac, a truly international composer, had written Italian *canti* and French chansons, each in the appropriate style. Now, in his German polyphonic songs, he employed the full range of appropriate stylistic elements: simple chord-like settings (his famous *Isbruk, ich muss dich lassen* is an example), songs with original folklike melodies set in the tenor, and others freely composed in imitative counterpoint.

Toward the middle of the sixteenth century a new style emerged. The traditional and well-known melodies still appeared in recognizable fashion in the tenor, but the other voices became melodic as well; this led to the polyphonic *Gesellschaftslied* ("social song"). Ludwig Senfl (*c*. 1490– *c*. 1542) was one of the most prolific and significant composers of this new style. A pupil of Isaac, he was associated primarily with Augsburg and Munich, but gradually came under the influence of the French chanson. His melodies became graceful, the texture often nonimitative, and an appealing air typical. These characteristics are also to be seen in the German songs of Lasso, who contributed so greatly to virtually every category of vocal music.

Finally, near the beginning of the seventeenth century, foreign influences on German song increased. Songs *alla madrigalesca* and *alla villanesca* were freely composed and the use of *cantus firmus* declined. Hans Leo Hassler (1564–1612), one of the greatest masters of the period, be-

23 *GMB*, Nos. 44, *Aus fahr* . . . . , 45, *Der Wald* . . . , and 46, *Wach auff* . . . . , gives three examples of the type.

24 A song by Finck in *GMB*, No. 87, *O schönes* . . . . , illustrates the general style. See also *GMB*, No. 85, *Ach Elslein* . . . . , for a somewhat different style in a song by Senfl.

came a leader on the path toward the Baroque chorale and the solo
song with *basso continuo.*

Instrumental Music

INFORMATION about the use of musical instruments in the Middle
Ages is relatively scanty. A variety of pictorial and literary evidence indicates that instruments were employed on many levels of society, but
the number of surviving musical manuscripts is not large enough to
allow a detailed study to be made. The extramusical evidence in general
leads to the conclusion that instruments were at first most widely used
to accompany vocal performances and the dance. Specific literary references to music, together with indications in the few available manuscripts, make it possible to say that virtually any instrument of the proper
range was suitable for accompaniments.[25]

Medieval instrumentalists were on a lower social level than the troubadours and minstrels, who were primarily singers even though they combined vocal with instrumental performance. In order to elevate their
status, instrumentalists founded religious brotherhoods and organizations
(known as "guilds"), the earliest of which was established in Vienna in
1288. In the fourteenth century the heads of the guilds were commonly
appointed by the king or other authority. Each guild had its own laws,
and some of them prospered to such an extent that they controlled their
own hospitals, living establishments, chapels, and inns. In Paris, for example, they occupied quarters in the Rue des Jongleurs, where they were
available when their services were needed.

In Germany the larger municipalities employed *Stadtpfeiffer* (town
trumpeters). These groups of four to twelve instrumentalists played concerts at designated hours from the tower of the town hall, and provided
music for funerals, weddings, and public functions; they are the predecessors of today's municipal bands. The instruments in common use included the *Zink* or *cornetto* (equipped with holes like a flute, but supplied
with a cup mouthpiece) and the primitive forms of trumpet and trombone. Among the string instruments were the rebec, probably of Oriental
origin; the *Fidel* or *vielle* (later supplanted by the viol); the *tromba
marina,* an instrument of bass range with one or two strings; and the
hurdy-gurdy, also called "peasant lyre" or *lyra rustica.*

Keyboard instruments (organ and the various predecessors of the
harpsichord) were also known; some of the earliest manuscripts of pure
instrumental music are for the organ. The lute was the principal instrument used for accompaniments, but it also played a leading role as a
solo instrument in the fifteenth to the seventeenth centuries.

It seems likely that the lute, of Arabic origin, had been introduced into
Europe as early as the tenth century. Medieval paintings of the lute show
a gourd-shaped back, a peg-box bent back at an angle from the finger-

25 See Reese, *Music in the Middle Ages,* pp. 324–70, for descriptions of the instruments in use from the twelfth to the fifteenth centuries, and any standard book on
instruments for further details.

board, and a series of frets (narrow metal or ivory bars set into the finger-board) marking the position of the half-steps. Each string except the highest was actually a double string (called a "course"), so that the six-stringed lute had eleven strings. One typical tuning (counting from the bottom) was A, d, g, b, e', a'.

The instrumental music of the Renaissance period may be divided into three large categories according to origins or function: (1) arrangements or imitations of vocal music, either sacred or secular, with or without a *cantus firmus;* (2) purely improvisational music written for a specified instrument or ensemble; and (3) music composed or arranged for dancing —perhaps the oldest group.

Much of the music that employed lute or keyboard instruments was written not in staff notation but in a special form called "tablature." In lute tablature, for example, a staff was used, but each line of the staff represented a string. A system of symbols (numerals in the Italian tabla-tures, letters in the French) was employed to indicate the number of the fret each finger was to occupy. The metrical value of each note or chord was indicated by a row of stems or note symbols placed above the top line of the system.

Many of the early collections of lute music contained instructions for reading tablatures and for setting music in tablature notation. Among

Woman playing a clavichord. Six-teenth-century Flemish painting.

such books were Arnold Schlick's *Tabulaturen etlicher . . . lidlein uff die orgeln und lauten* ("Tablatures of some . . . little songs for organ and lute"), published in 1512, an *Intabolatura de lauto* published by Petrucci in several volumes beginning in 1507, and a similar work published by Attaingnant at Paris in 1529. In addition to the instructional material, the books contained a variety of works for lute—both arranged and original.

Forms derived from vocal music. The earliest manuscripts of instrumental music of the first category (arrangements and imitations of vocal music) date from about 1450. The *Fundamentum organisandi*, by Conrad Paumann (c. 1410–1473), is essentially a manual for writing counterpoint for the organ, but it also contains some elaborations of songs. The *Buxheimer Orgelbuch*, about 1460, contains almost two hundred transcriptions of chansons and similar works (see EXAMPLE 82). The *Tabulaturen*

E X A M P L E 82

Transcription of Binchois's chanson, *Je loe amours*

F R O M *Das Buxheimer Orgelbuch*, Part 2. Reprinted by permission of Bärenreiter-Verlag, Cassel and Basel.

by Arnold Schlick, mentioned above in reference to lute music, include a number of keyboard elaborations of plainsongs composed in a style that is a mixture of chordal and imitative writing.[26] Many of the pieces in the Paumann collection have the *cantus firmus* in the lower voice, below an embellished melody. Other pieces in the set are improvisational in the style of a toccata (see below, page 203) and contain running passages and

26 See *HAM*, No. 81, *Mit ganczem* . . . , for an example from Paumann, and No. 101, *Maria zart*, for an organ hymn by Schlick. Another Paumann song transcription is given in *GMB*, No. 48, *Elend.* . . .

arpeggios. This figural technique became common in the sixteenth century and led to a German keyboard school called "colorists," from their disposition to embellish ("color") the melodies.

Other collections of arrangements for keyboard instruments, with titles such as *intavolature* ("settings in tablature"), include *ricercari, canzoni,* and a variety of other forms. The collections became increasingly numerous toward the end of the sixteenth century. In these sets no essential difference between organ and clavichord or harpsichord seems to have been attempted.

The existence of ensembles of wind and string instruments (sometimes both) is attested to by paintings and literary references long before any ensemble music makes its appearance. Small groups of instrumentalists performed at banquets, court festivities, entertainments, and other gatherings in the late fifteenth century, at least in Italy, Germany, and England. A few instrumental pieces are contained in the *Glogauer Liederbuch* and other German manuscripts of the time.[27] Early instruction books for viols and other instruments date back to 1511 in Germany (one is the well-known treatise by Sebastian Virdung, *Musica getutscht*—"Music Germanized") and to the 1540's in Italy. Arrangements of chansons, similar to those for lute and keyboard instruments, also exist from the first decade of the sixteenth century. A large and significant body of ensemble music is not found, however, until the years after about 1560; from the 1580's music for instrumental ensembles is available in generous amounts.

The genesis of these arrangements of vocal music for lute, keyboard instruments, and ensembles is fairly clear. The practice of playing the lower voices of vocal compositions had arisen as early as the fourteenth century. Apparently the only criterion in choosing the instruments was their range; considerations of tone quality seem to have played a minor role. Movements of Masses, motets, and chansons were among the principal works so performed, and generally the main melodies were somewhat embellished for instrumental use.[28]

The terminology for the instrumental arrangements of vocal forms without *cantus firmus* is very vague. Apparently the principal terms were *canzona da sonar* (that is, "sounded" or played instead of sung) and *ricercare.*[29] The term *canzona,* derived from "chanson," usually implies a moderate amount of contrapuntal work in a form similar in its general style to the chanson. The *ricercare,* at the highest point of its develop-

27 See *HAM,* No. 83, and *GMB,* No. 50, *Das yeger Horn,* for two examples of short pieces for three instruments; and *GMB,* No. 49, *Der pfoben* . . . , for a short dance tune set for four, all dated before 1500.

28 A lute arrangement of a vocal chanson by Josquin is given in *GMB,* No. 63. *GMB,* No. 62, contains an instrumental version of the chanson on which the lute piece is based.

29 A few large ensemble works called *sonate* are found in sixteenth-century publications; two notable examples are included in Giovanni Gabrieli's *Sacrae symphoniae* of 1597. One of these, the famous *Sonata pian e forte,* for antiphonal groups, is among the first ensemble works to indicate dynamic levels (given in *HAM,* No. 173, as well as in *GMB,* No. 148). An elaboration of the term "sonata" properly belongs in an account of the seventeenth century and will be found in a later chapter.

ment, was a form in which a theme was manipulated contrapuntally; it was treated in augmentation, inversion, and the like and varied rhythmically. At first written in imitation of vocal melodies, the various lines soon became more florid and rhythmically more concise.[30]

The *canzoni* were of several types. One, essentially an embellished version of a vocal motet, contained generally florid writing; this type soon disappeared. A second type, in all respects similar to the *ricercare*, was written in continuous form and contrapuntal style throughout. A third type, called "patch canzona" or "sectional canzona" by various writers, justifies those names in all particulars. Typically it consisted of a number of sections, ranging from two to eight or more, marked by contrasts in texture and separated by well-defined cadences. The piece often began with a dactylic motive, and often one or more sections were in a contrasting meter as well (triple in the midst of the prevailing duple); thus the continuing relationship to the French chanson is shown.[31]

Two sets of keyboard tablatures by a father and son, Marco Antonio and Girolamo Cavazzoni, appearing in 1523 and 1542 respectively, contain transcriptions of a number of vocal forms—French chansons, motets, and the like—as well as a few original works. The *ricercari* of the younger Cavazzoni introduce a real polyphonic texture to keyboard music and go far to establish the stylistic elements which the *ricercare* was to maintain for over a century. The *canzoni francesi*, likewise, contain more contrapuntal writing than similar transcriptions by older composers.[32] The few surviving French collections before the middle of the century contain mainly transcriptions of chansons similar to the German and Italian works of the time.

Composers of *ricercari* and *canzoni francesi* in Italy after about 1550 seem to have followed Cavazzoni's example. Several collections by Andrea Gabrieli, published posthumously (1587 to 1605), led the way toward a tightening of the *ricercare* form; the number of motives treated contrapuntally was reduced from half a dozen or more to one or two. As a consequence, the seventeenth-century fugue, an outgrowth of the *ricercare*, came appreciably closer. Indeed, a *ricercare* from about 1550 by the Spanish composer, Antonio de Cabezon, is called *fuga al contrario* ("fugue in contrary motion").[33] The *canzona*, too, began to show stylistic individuality; at the hands of many composers it took on a sectional form, often with contrasting meters (in the manner of the chanson), and moved gradually toward a more lyric style.

Ensemble *canzoni* for several instruments can be traced back to the early sixteenth century.[34] Original *canzoni* (that is, not arrangements of

30 Examples of lute *ricercari* are given in *HAM*, No. 99, and *GMB*, No. 63b. An early keyboard *ricercare* by Willaert is given in *HAM*, No. 115.

31 See *HAM*, Nos. 175 and 136 for *canzoni* by Maschera and Andrea Gabrieli, respectively, which illustrate the second and third types discussed here.

32 See *HAM*, No. 116, for a *ricercare* by Cavazzoni, and No. 118, *Falte d'argens*, for a *canzona* by the same composer.

33 Reprinted in *GMB*, No. 113.

34 See examples by Obrecht in *HAM*, No. 78, *Tsaat* . . . , by Josquin and Senfl in *GMB*, Nos. 62b, *La Bernadina*, and 86, *Fortuna*, respectively.

pre-existing vocal works) were not long delayed. Among the first works in this form were *Canzoni da sonar* by Nicolò Vicentino, published in 1572, and a set by Florentio Maschera in 1584. The phrase *da sonar* is significant here. It recalls that much music of the time could be either played or sung, and that now music was being designed specifically for instrumental performance. Many other composers wrote in the new form, notably Giovanni Gabrieli, whose *Sacrae symphoniae* of 1597 represent one of the highest points achieved in sixteenth century ensemble music.

A remarkable collection is Gabrieli's *Canzoni e sonate* of 1615. Some of the pieces in the set are *ricercari* arranged for orchestra, and others are original compositions. Echo effects, repetitions of sections, and a concern with instrumental idioms mark these works. They represent a progressive trend which was to characterize generally the instrumental music of the first half of the seventeenth century.

A small amount of English keyboard music in the form of arrangements of chansons and motets also exists, notably in *The Mulliner Book,* which dates from sometime after the middle of the sixteenth century. A more important branch of the literature consists of the English "fancies" (de-

Musicians performing on treble and bass viols. Seventeenth-century woodcut.

rived from "fantasias") for groups of instruments. A large number of these compositions exist, the earliest dating from about the 1550's and the last from the 1680's. The typical fancy of the sixteenth century is a motetlike piece with instrumental figurations, roughly analogous to the

E X A M P L E 83

Alfonso Ferrabosco II, Fancy

Italian *ricercare*. The fancy was cultivated by the finest Tudor composers from Byrd to Gibbons, including John Bull (*c.* 1562–1628), Weelkes, Tallis, Alfonso Ferrabosco II (*c.* 1575–1628) and many others. Written for consorts of two to six instruments, in mixed chordal and imitative style, the fancies contain some of the most effective contrapuntal writing and harmonic touches of the period (see EXAMPLE 83). Many are long movements constructed without breaks; others, consisting of contrasting sections, are externally similar to the *canzona*.

Forms employing cantus firmi. The tradition of performing instrumental pieces between sections of a hymn or other vocal composition was established as early as the end of the fifteenth century. The instrumental inserts took several forms: improvisations, short *ricercari* called "versos," and pieces based on a *cantus firmus* derived from the hymn melody. The *Hymni* of Cavazzoni (1542), for example, include interludes with *cantus firmi* in long notes in the tenor and imitations in the other voices. A related type is found in the special group of English fancies called *In nomine;* well over two hundred works in this form exist in two British manuscripts alone. The name is derived from the fact that these pieces employ as *cantus firmus* a section of the *Benedictus* that begins "In nomine" from Taverner's *Missa Gloria tibi Trinitas*.[35] Some of the works are written for organ, others for instrumental ensemble. A similar type is found in the organ works of John Redford (?–1547), one of the most eminent of British organists. Redford concerned himself almost entirely with organ music; some fifty works survive, most of them of the type called "organ hymns" by some writers and "fantasies on plainsongs" by others.[36] In some of these works a true organ style is in the process of formation, while in others the familiar devices of motet transcription are found.

Improvisational forms. The improvisational forms constitute the second category into which Renaissance instrumental music may be divided. Preludes to church services or to secular performances were often required in the sixteenth century. The instrumental forms (mostly for the organ) which developed out of this need succeeded in illustrating the virtuosic attainments of the performer. Pieces of this type, first called "preambel" or "priamel" (from the Latin *præambulum*), were later known as "intonations" or *intonazioni;* they may have served to give the opening pitch to the unaccompanied choir. Significant early examples of the type are those by Hans Judenkunig for the lute (1529) and Leonhard Kleber for the organ (about 1524). The short *Intonazioni d'organo* (1593) by Giovanni Gabrieli are more advanced, in that they generally begin with a chord sequence which gives way to rapid passage work and fast scale figures and usually end with cadential patterns embellished with trills.

35 See Bukofzer, *Studies in Medieval and Renaissance Music*. An *In nomine* setting by Thomas Tompkins is given in *HAM*, No. 176.
36 See *HAM*, No. 120, *Veni redemptor* and *Lucem tuam*, for two examples of Redford's music.

Out of this type of *intonazione* Gabrieli evolved the longer but still improvisational *toccata*. Girolamo Diruta (*c.* 1550–?), a famous organist and theorist of the time, also added to the early literature. Claudio Merulo (1533–1604), however, is the principal exponent of the sixteenth-century toccata. His works were based on polyphonic textures (in distinction to Gabrieli's), but they retained the rapid passage work and exciting air. The toccata in Merulo's hands became a virtuosic display piece.[37] This combination of brilliant passage work and improvisational polyphonic writing led to other forms of organ music in the Baroque period.

Forms derived from dance music. The third large class of Renaissance instrumental music consists of music written for the dance or derived from dance forms. The social dances of the Middle Ages, notably the *ductia* and *estampie,* apparently had lived on into the Renaissance period with changed names. In general, two dances with different meters and tempi, but with melodic similarity, were combined into a "primary pair," which later served as the nucleus of the seventeenth-century dance suite. One dance, usually slow or stately and in duple meter, was combined with a faster dance in triple. The names and characters of the two components differed in different countries. Italy favored the *passamezzo* and *saltarello* or the *paduana* and *gagliarda;* the latter pair (with the *paduana* variously spelled as "pavanne," "paven," or "pavin" and the *gagliarda* as "gailliarde" or "galliard") became popular in other countries as well. In Germany the pair was often called simply *Tanz* and *Nachtanz* or *Hupfauff* (dance and afterdance or "jump up"). Eventually various national dances were added to the pair or at times substituted for it. Among the French, for example, the *basse danse* and *tourdion* were often used, but here both dances were in triple meter. In England the jig and hornpipe, both in fast tempo, became popular.

The earliest surviving collections of original lute music, notably one by Petrucci printed in 1509, include dances of various types. Among them are the *pavana, saltarello,* and the *gagliarda.*[38] Sets of three dances often occurred: a *piva,* also in fast triple meter, followed by the *pavana* and *saltarello.* Standardization of sets was not achieved by the Italians, however. Not until the seventeenth century, and then in France, was a regular sequence of dance pieces adopted, leading to the important form of the dance suite.

Collections of dance music for the lute appeared in several countries, but the composers are not often given in the sources. It is possible that the compilers or publishers themselves composed the pieces. Among the composers who are known are Hans Newsiedler (1508–1563) in Germany, Francesco di Milano (1497–1543) in Italy, and Miguel de Fuenllana (*c.* 1550) in Spain; the English composer John Dowland, who flourished at the end of the century, has already been mentioned.

37 Several short preambles by German composers are given in *HAM,* No. 84. A longer prelude by Gabrieli is printed in *HAM,* No. 135; and two toccatas by Merulo will be found in *HAM,* No. 153, and *GMB,* No. 149.

38 A *saltarello* is given in *GMB,* No. 95; No. 181 is a *gagliarda.*

"The Dancing Party," engraving by Master MZ.

Dance music for keyboard instruments did not appear in quantity until late in the sixteenth century. Much of it originated in England. The pavane,[39] passamezzo, galliard, allemande, and many other dance types were treated with variation techniques. Sometimes a pair (pavane-galliard) was treated as a unit, and since both members of the pair are melodically related, a kind of double variation results.

Most of the sixteenth-century dance music surviving in England seems to be not for the organ but for the virginal, the name given to the rectangular version of an instrument with strings that were plucked, like those of the harpsichord. Music for the virginal is known to have been cultivated at the English court from at least the end of the fifteenth century, but the earliest surviving manuscripts date from after the middle of the sixteenth. The *Fitzwilliam Virginal Book* contains music, mostly in the form of sets of variations, written from the 1560's to the end of the century; *Lady Nevell's Book,* of 1591, is devoted entirely to the music of William Byrd; and several other collections, produced well into the seventeenth century, exist as well.

One of the forms favored by English composers for the virginal was the set of variations on a dance, an air, or a folksong. In a set such as the one attributed to John Munday (or Mundy, ?–1630),[40] each variation is given a distinctive figure or texture. Passages in sixths or tenths in one

39 See *GMB,* No. 147, for John Bull's *Spanish Paven.*
40 Given in *HAM,* No. 177, *Goe from my window.*

variation, scale passages in another, imitative counterpoint in a third—such devices became standard. Works in this form by William Byrd, Orlando Gibbons, and many others constitute a special contribution of English composers to the repertoire of sixteenth-century music. In other sets of dance music for the virginal, the form of each piece was expanded from two sections to three (each repeated), and at times a variation took the place of the expected repetition.

Dance music for instrumental ensembles was also cultivated. Works of this type are similar to the keyboard dance pieces of the time. Italian sources are scant. Surviving examples of English dance music for ensembles seldom go beyond the usual pairing of pavane and galliard; such pairings are found occasionally in works for six instruments by Byrd, Weelkes, and many others. These and similar pieces, for groups of instruments in which viols are prominent, appeared in collections often called "consort lessons." One well-known work of this kind is Dowland's *Lachrimae* of 1605; it includes his *Seaven Passionate Pavans,* based on his song *Flow, my teares,* which is treated with paraphrase and quasi-variation techniques in the several parts.

French, Flemish, and German contributions to this field are, like the English, mostly single dances or dance pairs. Settings are for three to five instruments (probably viols, although specific instruments are not named). Collections published by Attaingnant at Paris (between 1530 and about 1560), by Susato at Antwerp and Phalèse at Louvain (about 1550 to 1570) constitute the bulk of this music.[41] Chordal style, clear phrase structures, and rhythmic vitality characterize these pieces of dance music for ensembles. Dances for larger orchestral ensembles became integral parts of the *ballet de cour* which, beginning in the late sixteenth century in France, flourished mainly in the seventeenth.

A summary of sixteenth-century developments in the field of instrumental music shows that a majority of the compositions are small in scope. The style of writing strongly resembles that of vocal writing, and independent instrumental idioms are seldom found (except possibly in some of the keyboard works). Of the many categories represented in the instrumental field, two were of great influence on composers of the following century: the embryonic set (usually a pair) of dances and the ensemble *canzone.* Among the keyboard works, the unified *ricercare,* the Italian toccata, and the variation set of the English school were of lasting importance. Together with the ensemble works, they carried within them the seeds of the instrumental literature of the seventeenth century.

41 Examples are given in *HAM*, No. 137, and *GMB*, Nos. 119 and 134.

Emergence of Baroque Style

The last decades of the sixteenth century brought the Renaissance style to its highest level of expressive power and technical consistency. The works of Lasso, Palestrina, Byrd, and others represent the end of a development, begun in the time of Obrecht, to which many composers in half a dozen different countries had contributed. But even while the Renaissance style was reaching its culmination another style was in the process of being formulated. A new aesthetic philosophy, a new harmonic concept, and a variety of new textures and forms challenged the dominant practice. The Renaissance style was not immediately abolished, however. Continuing to function parallel to the new style, it was distinguished by the names *stilo antico* (antique style), *stilo grave* (strict style), or *prima prattica* (first practice), especially in the field of church music.

Detail from title page of Michael Praetorius' *Theatrum Instrumentorum*, Wolfenbüttel, 1620.

Early Developments

THREE developments, taking place almost simultaneously in the late sixteenth century, were of prime importance in undermining the dominant style. First, during the time of Palestrina the complexity and "artificiality" of Flemish-derived counterpoint had alienated many Italian composers. The extent to which polyphony dominated church music had begun to concern Church officials; as we have seen, the Council of Trent worked on the problem, and for a time the very justification for polyphonic music was seriously questioned. The intellectual aspects of the style were basically foreign to the Italian musical temperament, and the age-old battle between the obscure, contrived style of the north (as many Italians thought of it) and the clear, direct style of the south entered into a new phase. Anti-Flemish and anti-contrapuntal were almost synonymous terms. As a consequence of this attitude toward counterpoint, a new way of setting words to music had to be developed.

Second, Renaissance music had been characterized primarily by restraint and intimacy. In the basically contrapuntal texture of its music, the several voices had been more or less of equal importance. As we have seen, four- and five-part madrigals were frequently performed with the top part sung and the others performed instrumentally (on lute, keyboard, or string instruments), but in this practice the instruments were considered simply as substitutes for the voices and were not employed for their specific sonorous qualities.

Late in the Renaissance period the element of color became increasingly important to musical performance. Instruments began to be valued for their particular sonorities and to be employed more widely than ever before. A growing use of instruments, an increase in the writing of music for instruments and voices, a rise in number of musical amateurs, a new interest in secular matters—all these contributed to a new concern for pure melody. Inevitably, the concept of solo song with instrumental accompaniment was developed to a high level. To this concept came a desire for excitement and brilliance in performance; the vocal part was embellished and made more difficult to sing, and a degree of virtuosity was required of the soloist. The consequence was a further abandonment of the strict contrapuntal style, in which the several voices had been of more or less equal importance, and the substitution of a style in which a single melody rode supreme over an accompaniment.

Third, the humanistic movement in fifteenth-century Italy had been set in motion by men who were primarily members of the laity (although a few were ecclesiastical dignitaries). Their interest lay in secular literature rather than in the writings of such Church fathers as St. Augustine and Thomas Aquinas, and they "rediscovered" the works of Homer, Plato, Cicero, and other Greek and Latin writers. Later in the sixteenth century this interest was extended to the music of ancient times, which was understood to have been secular also. But whereas the literary documents were numerous, available, and thoroughly comprehensible, the musical sources were not. The few fragments of Greek music then known were virtually undecipherable and the theoretical works full of contradictions. It seemed clear to the humanists of the time, however, that Greek music had been combined with poetry and that a restoration of that music was desirable.

This desire was not confined to Italy. For example, the *Académie de poésie et de musique,* founded by Jean-Antoine de Baïf (1532–1589), dedicated itself to the problem. Baïf wrote poems in French, but in classical poetic meters, later set to music by Le Jeune and Mauduit, among others. In Germanic countries several composers—Senfl, Hofhaimer, and Tritonius among them—set the Odes of Horace in a four-voice chordal style and in the rhythms of Latin prosody, for use in educational institutions. These French, German, and Austrian attempts to effect a rebirth of the music of antiquity were soon abandoned or modified, even though the interest in ancient culture was maintained. Not until the last years of the sixteenth century did another series of speculations and experiments succeed in altering the relationship between word and music, approaching the ideal that generations of cultured men had been striving for. This activity was centered around a group of Florentine noblemen, poets, and musicians, and embraces the years about 1580 to 1600.

Monodic Style

THE MEN who constituted the group known as the Florentine Camerata, who met first at the home of Count Giovanni Bardi and later at that of Count Jacopo Corsi, had various interests. They were united, however, in their professed antagonism to counterpoint and in their desire to restore the musical style of the Greeks. Further, they were among the more articulate men of their time in these matters and produced a body of writings which unequivocally stated their purposes.

Guiding principles. A series of *Discourses on Ancient Music and Good Singing* (about 1580), long attributed to Bardi but written probably by Vincenzo Galilei (*c.* 1520–1591), is one of the principal manifestos of the group. The author, after defining music in Plato's terms, pleaded with the composer "not to spoil the verse, not imitating the musicians of today who think nothing of spoiling it to pursue their ideas or cutting it to bits to make nonsense of the words. . . . In composing, then, you will make it your chief aim to arrange the verse well and to declaim the words as intelligibly as you can . . . you will consider it self-evident that just as the soul is nobler than the body, so the words are nobler than the counterpoint." And in discussing the new rhythmic type that he visualized, he suggested that it will be "neither too slow nor too fast, but will imitate the speech of a man magnificent and serious." [1] One of the essential elements of the new principle, it may be stressed, was that the text should be intelligible; thus arose the Camerata's opposition to the contrapuntal settings of texts.

1 Both excerpts are given in *SRMH*, pp. 294–96.

Galilei, father of the great astronomer, was the first successful composer in the new style and probably one of the most capable men in the Camerata. In addition to furthering Bardi's technical ideas, he gave thought to the content of the music as well. His *Dialogo . . . della musica antica e moderna . . .* (Dialogue . . . about Ancient and Modern Music, 1581) contains penetrating criticisms of the aesthetics of contrapuntal music. He asserted that the continual sweetness of the consonances and the slight harshness of the various dissonances "are, as I have said, the greatest impediment to moving the mind to any passion. For the mind, being chiefly taken up and, so to speak, bound by the snares of the pleasure thus produced, is not given time to understand, let alone consider, the badly uttered words. . . . Passion and moral character must be simple and natural, or at least appear so, and their sole aim must be to arouse their counterparts in others." And in this connection, "the last thing the moderns think of is the expression of the words with the passion that these require. . . ." [2] Finally, Galilei recommended that musicians attend the theater to learn how actors delineate character and express emotion, observing that actors speak high or low, fast or slow, according to the conception they are expressing.

In these quotations, then, the principles of monodic style are implied. The music must be subordinate to the text and the musical rhythm must imitate the speech rhythm. The melodic line should be a kind of musical declamation or recitation (*stilo recitativo*) that mirrors the natural inflections of the speaking voice. And the music in general must express or heighten the emotion aroused by the text—even to the extent that the singer should imitate the grimaces and gestures which come naturally to the actor.

Galilei's setting of a scene from Dante's *Inferno,* sung to the accompaniment of four viols, was probably the first work in the new style; it has, however, been lost. This was followed by his similar treatment of the Lamentations of Jeremiah (both works date from about 1582). Apparently the new style made slow headway. It was not until 1597, when the composer Jacopo Peri (1561–1633) and the poet Ottavio Rinuccini (1562–1621) collaborated in the creation of *Dafne,* that the first large composition in the style was created. It is particularly unfortunate that this work has also been lost, for *Dafne* was the first composition that can be called an opera (see below, page 212).

Another work by Peri and Rinuccini has been preserved, however: the opera *Euridice,* performed in 1600 at the wedding of Henry IV of France and Maria de Medici. Rinuccini's text was also set to music by Giulio Caccini (1546–1618) and published in the same year. A more elaborate work by Emilio del Cavalieri (c. 1550–1602), entitled *Rappresentazione di anima e di corpo* and composed in 1600, was long considered to be the first oratorio. Since no stylistic differentiation between opera and oratorio had yet been developed, however, the work might more fittingly be called a sacred opera. These works brought the declamatory manner, its new type of accompaniment (the *basso continuo;* see below), and the chief

2 *SRMH,* pp. 312–15.

technical feature of that accompaniment (the figured bass) to full expression.

All of these compositions adhere to the precepts of Bardi and Galilei. The melodic line follows to a considerable extent the natural inflections and cadences of the reciting voice, and the vocal rhythms duplicate the textual rhythms. The melody pauses between phrases, sinking at ends of sentences; it proceeds with shorter note values in moments of tension or excitement, and with longer ones in moments of repose or relaxation (see EXAMPLE 84). In brief, the melodic line can transmit to the listener all the emotions implied by the text.

EXAMPLE 84

Peri, *Euridice*

Basso continuo. The type of accompaniment chosen to support these monodic melodies consists of chords and chord progressions; only by this means could the opposition to polyphony be brought to a focus. It is true that chordal progressions as such were not among the innovations of the Camerata, for works elsewhere in the sixteenth century had contained them (see EXAMPLE 77). Such other progressions, however, were limited to triads and chords of the sixth; they were essentially the result of simultaneous motion in all the parts. Dissonances appeared only as passing notes on weak beats or as suspensions and were resolved by regular stepwise progression to the nearest upper or lower consonance. Thus the harmony that resulted had no functional purpose; it consisted of a combination of intervals, and its melodic progressions were determined by the church modes.

In the monodic works, the melody and bass alone were composed; the chords implied by the interaction of these two polarities were left to be improvised. A type of musical shorthand for notating the chords was employed, to assure that the accompanist did not depart too far from the composer's harmonic intention. This system had appeared late in the sixteenth century but in connection with the large polychoral works that were often accompanied by the organ. A bass part, made up of whatever was the lowest voice at the moment, was written out for the organist; sharps or flats written above certain notes indicated that the corresponding chords were to have major or minor thirds, respectively.

Adriano Banchieri, for example, had separately written out the bass and treble parts of his works for double chorus, *Concerti ecclesiastici* of

1595, presumably to permit the organist to improvise an accompaniment. This device was called, among other terms, a *basso seguente*. In the seventeenth century, in works which employed the new monodic style, the *basso seguente* was elaborated. Figures were used to designate essential intervals above the bass and thus to imply triads, seventh chords, and the like (see EXAMPLE 85). Various other symbols, such as sharps, flats, and

EXAMPLE 85

Caccini, Figured-bass passage

crosses, also played their parts in the process. The *Cento concerti ecclesiastici* by Ludovico da Viadana (1564–1645), published in 1602, were among the first works to employ the symbols consistently. In its final form the device came to be known simply as "figured bass," "thorough bass," or *basso continuo*.

The realization of the bass line's symbols was entrusted to a keyboard or other harmony instrument—theorbo, archlute, organ, and early forms of the harpsichord. To enhance the sonorities of the instrument used for the purpose, a melody instrument of bass range doubled the bass notes. Bass viol, viol da gamba, bassoon, and trombone were thus employed at times; later, cello and bass came to specialize in that work. Thus, a line of figured-bass notes, a harmony instrument to supply the chords, and a melody instrument to reinforce the bass—all are implied in the term *basso continuo*. For over a hundred and fifty years the *continuo*, as it was familiarly referred to, remained a potent stylistic element, becoming the principal distinguishing feature of Baroque music. It was employed in virtually all fields of music, and as late as 1765 theorists recommended that composers use the *continuo*—even though they gave instructions for creating unfigured basses.[3]

The chords that now resulted were quite different from the "chords" of Renaissance music. Chromatic, augmented, and diminished intervals had appeared in the madrigals of Marenzio and others, for example, but those works were written in polyphonic style and the nondiatonic intervals were most often used (in one voice) to create passing notes or suspensions, or (in several voices) to establish cross relations. In the new monodic style, however, the dissonant intervals were embodied in the chords themselves. A variety of dissonant chords was now made possible—thanks to the flexibility of figured-bass notation—and the body of harmony was greatly enriched. But the resulting chord progressions did not yet imply a sense of

3 See Arnold, *The Art of Accompaniment from a Thorough-Bass*, pp. 66–67.

direction. Cadences, which are analogous to punctuation, could be built on virtually any scale step, but the concepts of cadences and chord relationships were still in an embryonic stage. The unifying force of a tonal center was not yet felt; one cannot here speak of the system of tonality as opposed to that of modality. At best one can refer to the period of monodic reforms as one which employed pretonal harmony. Awareness of tonality and tonal centers was to be the accomplishment of later generations.

New Musical Forms

The opera. Soon after its inception the monodic style was made to serve another of the purposes of the Florentine Camerata—namely that of setting a dramatic work to music in (they thought) the manner of the Greeks. As we have seen, the result was the invention of opera; the titles of the earliest operas have been given. It is not only the monodic style that made opera possible, however, but also the simultaneous development of suitable musical forms with dramatic content.

The liturgical dramas of the eleventh to thirteenth centuries and the mystery plays of the fourteenth to sixteenth had contained musical inserts, as had the secular plays and school dramas. Some masques (see Chapter 13) contained dramatic action, and some ballets had librettos and vocal parts. A special genus was formed by the madrigal comedies, in which a dramatic scene was enacted by a chain of madrigals.[4] The immediate forerunners of the opera, however, were the *intermedio* and the pastorale. The *intermedio,* placed between acts of serious plays, contained dances, songs, and instrumental pieces. Its character was humorous, however, and its standards were rather low. This form, consequently, was not suited to the Camerata's purposes.

The pastorale, however, was suited to those purposes in every respect. It placed shepherds and shepherdesses upon the stage, usually in idyllic settings representing the countryside. Its form was dramatic, its poetic content lyric; the action seldom went beyond mild flirtations and similar pastoral pursuits. "The attraction of the pastorale consisted, therefore, not in the plot but in the scenes and moods, the sensuous charm of the language, and the delicately voluptuous imagery, at which the Italian Renaissance poets excelled."[5] It was the form of the pastorale that Rinuccini used in his poems *Dafne* and *Euridice,* and Peri's musical settings of those poems, along with Caccini's very similar setting of *Euridice,* became the first operas.

In Peri's version of *Euridice,* the poem is divided into a prologue and ten scenes, but there is not yet an overture. The accompanying "orchestra" consists of four instruments playing the bass and realizing the continuo. The musical numbers include recitatives, solo songs in metrical rhythm, instrumental interludes, a few unison choruses in simple declamatory

4 Outstanding examples of the madrigal comedy are Alessandro Striggio's *Il cicalamento delle donne al bucato* ("The Cackling of Women at the Washtub") of 1567, and Orazio Vecchi's *L'Amfiparnasso* ("The Two-fold Parnassus") of 1594.

5 Grout, *A Short History of Opera,* p. 34.

An early opera at Florence, possibly Gagliano's *Dafne*. Engraving by Giulio Parigi, 1608.

style, and other choruses set in note-against-note fashion. Florid embellishments sometimes animate the unison choral melodies; counterpoint is very rare.[6]

The new form—not yet called "opera," but designated as "pastoral fable," "drama in music," or something similar—had the appeal of novelty. But it lacked variety and offered little possibility of expressing a wide range of emotion. Moreover, it was confined to the courtly circles in which it had been introduced. The development of the opera into a dramatic, widely expressive form was the work of Claudio Monteverdi, who was not associated with the Florentine group. Details of that development will be discussed below (see Chapter 13).

The name eventually given to the new form is an outgrowth of its table of contents, so to say. The form may contain a short piece or work in recitative style, a number of short works for chorus, and so on. A "work" in this sense is an *opus,* and its plural is *opera.* Thus to a series of works which in turn constituted a larger composition, the descriptive term *opera in musica* was applied; later this was shortened simply to *opera.*

The monody. The monodic style was not confined to opera; it was soon made use of in other forms which may be grouped under the term "monodies." Caccini's collection, which he proudly entitled *Le nuove musiche* (1602, but probably written across the years since 1591), was the first of many similar sets in which the style was exploited. The monodies repre-

6 See *HAM*, Nos. 182, "*Funeste . . . ,*" 183, "*A questi . . . ,*" and 184, "*Sfogava . . . ,*" for examples of the style.

sent a type of vocal chamber music, and as such they could not depend upon stage action and theatrical excitement for their effect (see EXAMPLE 86). Very quickly they adopted a higher plan of organization than the

EXAMPLE 86

Caccini, *Le nuove musiche*, aria 7

TRANSLATION:
The immortal glory and splendor of love: arm yourself with a bundle of golden shafts, here is my heart, here is my heart.

opera recitatives, which were bound to the single line of verse, and became something more than strings of unmetrical phrases.

In many monodies of the time the melodies went far beyond the limits of recitation. They freed themselves from the rhythms of the text, tending toward lyricism, fluency and grace, distinct form and phrasing, and intimate expressive content. Melodies of this type appeared in a form often called "canzonetta." In other monodies the melodic expression reflected the prose text to which it was set, hence it inclined toward the recitative component of the new style. And although the melodic and recitative aspects of monodic style were recognized as being distinct in function and expressive possibility, the complete separation of the two (as "aria" and "recitative," respectively) required much of the seventeenth century and the development of a suitable form, the chamber cantata (see Chapter 14), to accomplish.

The chief organizing principle in the monodies was perhaps that of the strophic bass. Here the same bass line appeared under each stanza of the text, while the melody was suitably varied from stanza to stanza. The melodic line seldom attained the status of the variation set, nor did the bass often embody the striking contour or distinctive shape of the true *basso ostinato*.

Other principles played their parts also. In some monodies, notably those with sacred texts, bits of contrapuntal imitation between melody and bass are found; here the relationship between the parts was tightened and the bass therefore approached melodic expression. In others, short sections of text and music returned periodically in the manner of a refrain, *R*; a form which may be diagrammed *aRbRc* resulted. Finally, instead of a regularly recurring bass, as in the strophic type, or a fundamental bass which existed only as a support for chord structures, a "striding" bass, moving with strength and some melodic integrity through the phrase, was introduced.

It is likely that the various types of bass line represent attempts to bring unity and a closed form to the monody. The typical motet or madrigal of the sixteenth century had been unsymmetrical, of course, in that a musical section appearing at the beginning did not reappear at the end (even though immediate repetition of sections within or at the end of the form did occur); hence the form was continuous or "open." On the other hand, a monody built upon a bass melody which was recapitulated at the end of the piece could be felt to be symmetrical, hence in a "closed" form.

Progress along this line was not made uniformly on all fronts, however. For example, Caccini's *Le nuove musiche* of 1602 resembles, in a formal sense, the works of an earlier period. The ten arias are cast in the form of strophic variations. The twelve continuo madrigals, on the other hand, do not employ the recurring bass phrase; they may be called "through-composed," quite in the manner of the fifteenth and sixteenth centuries. Other works of the time, notably the above-mentioned *Cento concerti ecclesiastici* of Viadana, also published in 1602, contain many examples of symmetrical form.

Independent Instrumental Music

THE FOREGOING discussions indicate the extent to which monodic style elements can be found in vocal forms. The opera, monody, and other forms owed their very existence to this style. It may fairly be said that this development was not entirely what the Florentine composers had intended; the new forms were by-products of the reform. It is more than interesting that another set of by-products also grew out of those reforms —this time in a direction exactly opposite to the Camerata's intentions.

Galilei, Peri, and their colleagues hoped to raise the word to a dominant position, to make the text master of the music. They had developed melody to such a point that it was eminently capable of reflecting the content of the text. It was expressive and dramatic, no longer bound by restrictions of mode, range, rhythm, or contour. Thereby they developed melody to such a point that it could be significant and expressive even without the text. In short, they created the possibility of writing instrumental music not in imitation of or in support of vocal lines but independent and potentially idiomatic.

Canzona and sonata. In Chapter 11 the transformation of the vocal chanson into the organ canzona was discussed. In the years after about 1571 the latter form was transformed further; the ensemble canzona appeared and the field of chamber music for instruments came into existence. The earliest examples, as we have seen, were similar to the motet or chanson in style. Imitative textures were much in evidence, and many ensemble canzonas of the time strongly resemble textless motets.

The development of the canzona progressed along two divergent paths. One path led to the unification of the sections ("points of imitation") which were analogous to those of the motet, so that an unbroken or non-contrasting form resulted. The other led to an important form called "sonata," [7] in which the sections were made independent and their contrasts increased, gradually resulting in a separation of the sections to form a series of movements. The sonata made considerable use of monodic style elements. The polarity of melody and bass was strongly in evidence, the top voice tending to be melodically expressive while the bass was figured. Further, a diversity of note values, ranging from a sixteenth- to a half-note, made possible a greater range of rhythmic motion.

Both the canzona and the sonata employed the principle of alternation; the fourteen *canzoni da sonar* of Giovanni Gabrieli (1597) are typical. Works of this type were often composed of short sections; slow tempo alternated with fast, duple meter with triple, and chordal textures with monodic or contrapuntal. One may say, in fact, that the principle of alternation became extremely important to early seventeenth-century composers. In addition to the above aspects, alternations of dynamics (loud-soft) and quality or content (rhythmic-lyric) are found. And yet other manifestations of the principle played significant parts in later instrumental developments—notably the alternation of mass (concertino-ripieno, as in the concerto forms), and theme (as in the rondo forms). One recognizes here certain characteristics of the Venetian polychoral style. Many composers in the years after 1600 adopted the principle of alternation, thereby adding considerable color and variety to their compositions.

Attempts to write idiomatically for instruments—especially to develop a true violin style—are copiously reflected in the early sonata literature.

7 This form must not be confused with the sonata of Haydn's period and later. The term sonata (from *suonare*, to sound) was set in opposition to the term cantata (from *cantare*, to sing) and hence indicated merely a work for instruments. Earlier composers, about 1572, had sought to differentiate between a work designed for instruments (*canzona da sonar*), one which could be sung and played (*da sonare e cantare*), and one sung or played (*da sonare o cantare*). By the early 1600's that distinction was no longer necessary, for they were all played.

Ensemble music in the early 17th c. Engraving by Abraham Bosse, "The Five Senses—Hearing."

Indeed, idiomatic instrumental writing constitutes an essential element of seventeenth-century music. The prevailing instrumentation was that for the *sonata a tre:* two viols (later, violins) and bass, with of course the continuo keyboard instrument. Composers such as Salomone Rossi (1587–1628) and Biagio Marini (*c.* 1595–1665) were among the first to realize that string instruments required a different type of writing than voices. For example, various types of figuration, broken chords, and rapid scale passages are as appropriate to the one as they are unsuited to the other. The *sonate a tre* of Rossi (1607) include sets of variations in which suitable string-instrument patterns are exploited. Marini's *Affetti musicali* (1617) go even further in establishing the violin idiom. These are only beginnings, however; we shall see later that it remained for Arcangelo Corelli to crystallize violin style in his compositions of the 1680's and later.

The Baroque Period

THE VARIOUS elements grouped under the term "monodic style" greatly changed the look and sound of music. New vocal forms arose, namely the monody and opera, and vocal music itself took on new dramatic, expressive, and affective qualities. Monodic style devices, when applied to instrumental forms, made independent instrumental music possible. The integrity of the modal system was broken down, and long steps were taken toward the establishment of major and minor tonality. But the old contrapuntal style was not abolished entirely. From the 1600's the two styles existed side by side, the old confined largely to sacred music, the new making itself felt in the many branches of secular musical composition.

Parallel developments took place in the fields of art and architecture; art historians writing in the late eighteenth century, too close to properly evaluate those developments, stigmatized them with a derogatory name. The term "baroque," derived from the Portuguese *barocca* and referring to something misshapen, irregular, or grotesque, was applied to the seventeenth-century examples of the new style. Music historians in the nineteenth century borrowed the term, and thus the Baroque period received its name. The period extends roughly from 1600 to about the death of Bach in 1750. It begins with the developments described in the present chapter, and its most prominent technical element is the figured bass or continuo.

The earliest Baroque composers had two styles to choose from; composers of the Medieval and Renaissance periods had rarely been faced with such a choice. The stylistic unity that had been the principal characteristic of earlier periods of music history now, after about 1600, became impossible. Earlier musicians "took style for granted, whereas it became a problem for baroque composers. The baroque era is the era of style-consciousness." [8]

8 Bukofzer, *Music in the Baroque Era*, p. 4.

৩১ 13 ৫৯

The Baroque Period: Opera

Wɪᴛʜɪɴ a few decades of its inception at Florence about 1600, the opera began its triumphal march across the stages of Europe. It first attracted the attention of composers in various Italian cities; an individual style that developed at Rome was succeeded by another style at Venice, one that was influential well into the eighteenth century. About 1660 composers in France created another kind of opera that offered great competition to the Italian styles for almost a century. About the same time yet another operatic type emerged in England, but it eventually gave way to the Italian type. At German and Austrian courts Italian opera was successfully produced after about 1650; later works composed by local or imported musicians departed to some extent from Italian (principally Venetian) models, and a distinctive Austrian style emerged. Finally, in the period about 1690–1720, a new operatic style arose that was to dominate virtually all operatic production (except perhaps at Paris) beyond

Detail from a drawing for an opera setting by Ludovico Burnacinia. [ᴛʜᴇ ᴍᴇᴛʀᴏᴘᴏʟɪᴛᴀɴ ᴍᴜsᴇᴜᴍ ᴏғ ᴀʀᴛ, ᴇʟɪsʜᴀ ᴡʜɪᴛᴛᴇʟsᴇʏ ᴄᴏʟʟᴇᴄᴛɪᴏɴ, 1953]

the middle of the eighteenth century. Until recently this style has been identified with Naples and called the Neapolitan style. Recent research has pointed out, however, that cities other than Naples shared in its development and that it was the result of a general change of taste not confined to a particular geographical area. The new style stands opposite the Baroque operatic style that emerged at Rome and Venice earlier in the seventeenth century; hence it might appropriately be called "pre-Classical style" or even, by analogy with other developments to be described in Chapter 16, "Rococo style."

Early Works of Monteverdi

THE HISTORY of this complex series of developments began with Claudio Monteverdi (1567–1643) at Mantua about 1607. Monteverdi, serving as chapelmaster to the Duke of Mantua, was the earliest Baroque composer fully to realize the dramatic possibilities inherent in the monodic style developed by the Florentine Camerata. In his fortieth year, after having composed five books of madrigals and a variety of other works, he turned to the new field of opera, and as his first work in that field he produced one of the masterpieces of the literature. *Orfeo* (1607) went far beyond the Peri and Caccini versions of *Euridice* in dramatic tension, variety, and musical interest.

Monteverdi was not concerned, as were the Florentines, with merely illustrating a new musical style. Adopting the elements of monody, declamation, figured bass, and all the rest, he wrote recitatives that are models of expressed pathos and fervor.[1] But he also made use of musical forms which the Florentines, with purists' singleness of mind, had discarded. Strophic songs with instrumental *ritornelli,* independent orchestral sections that return at various places in the opera, colorful instrumental accompaniments to the vocal parts, dramatic motives in the recitatives that add to the declamatory effect, a toccata used as an overture—such elements are characteristic of *Orfeo.* The work is a unified musical drama with a planned structure, and this the Florentine operas seldom were.

In his madrigals Monteverdi had employed the striking harmony, unprepared and unresolved dissonances, and other devices that had marked the form in the late sixteenth century. Now, in *Orfeo,* he went even further in the direction of a wide-ranging, poignant, and dramatic harmony. His recitatives contain juxtaposed E-major and G-minor triads in alternation, for example. One phrase ending in D major is followed by another beginning in C minor; a dissonant F♮ is set above an A-major triad. Similar uses of harmony, most often in connection with texts expressing extreme emotions, are found in the famous "Lasciatemi morire," the only surviving portion of his opera, *Ariadne* (1608).[2] In the purely instrumental portions of *Orfeo,* of which there are more than a dozen, dissonances of another type occur. They are found in imitative textures,

1 Examples are given in *HAM,* No. 187, "Ma che . . . ," and *GMB,* No. 176, "Rosa. . . ."

2 The aria is given in *GMB,* No. 177.

where Monteverdi permits an imitative voice to follow its model rather closely and thus to produce vertical clashes which are not harmonically conceived.

Opera at Rome

IMPORTANT developments in the opera at Rome were confined largely to the years between 1620 and about 1650. Since the principal supporters of Roman opera were members of the clergy, librettos with religious over-tones—no matter how faint—were favored over those based on purely secular subjects. Operas of the Roman school contained dramatic recita-tives, polyphonic elements in the choruses, and arias moving in the direc-tion of closed forms. Allegorical figures (Beauty, Fortitude, and the like), found in earlier operas, were introduced into the librettos, and the operas, often based on sacred subjects similar to those found in oratorios, served a moralizing purpose.

One important work of this type was *Sant' Alessio* ("Saint Alexis"), with music by Stefano Landi (*c.* 1590–*c.* 1655) and libretto by Giulio Rospig-liosi, a Roman nobleman and poet who later became Pope Clement IX. *Sant' Alessio* contained most of the features characteristic of the short-lived Roman school. The presence of choruses, at the ends of acts and elsewhere, testified to the strength of the choral tradition in Rome. The fact that the inner life of St. Alexis was treated in Landi's opera suggested to later composers that human conflicts and human emotions could provide sub-ject matter for opera.

Landi and other Roman composers, notably Luigi Rossi (1597–1653), especially concerned themselves with musical forms within the opera.[3] The vocal line for example, began to be separated into two types: one, characterized by repeated notes and a quasi-speech rhythm, became the recitative; the other, with melodic contours and clearly defined phrase structures, was the prototype of the aria. In the instrumental portions of *Sant' Alessio,* Landi placed the main stress on string instruments, relegat-ing the winds and percussion to a less prominent place, and thereby gave a tentative example of what the opera orchestra would become.[4]

A completely different operatic type, the *opera buffa* or comic opera, is also to be credited to the Roman school. The founder of this type was Rospigliosi, who wrote as his first comic opera libretto a work called *Chi soffre, speri* ("He Who Suffers May Hope"). Composed by Virgilio Maz-zochi (1597–1646) and Marco Marazzoli (?–1662) in 1639, the work con-tains fast-moving recitatives with many repeated notes and few melodic inflections: the style later called *parlando* ("speaking"). This type of rec-itative, familiar from its applications as late as Mozart and Rossini, was always performed in what was later called *recitativo secco* (dry recitative), that is, accompanied by harpsichord and bass, as opposed to a later recita-tive type called *accompagnato* (accompanied), in which the orchestra pro-

3 A trio from Rossi's *Orfeo* is given in *GMB,* No. 199, "Dormite. . . ."

4 A *sinfonia* and a duet, "Poca voglia . . . ," from *Sant' Alessio* are given in *HAM,* Nos. 208 and 209.

vided the accompaniment. *Chi soffre, speri* was followed by another collaboration of Rospigliosi and Marazzoli, this time with Antonio Abbatini
(*c.* 1595–1680), called *Dal mal il bene* ("Good from Evil"), produced in
1653. Here all the essential features of the later *opera buffa* are present:
type characters (bumbling servants, lovers separated through a misunder-
standing, elderly guardians, and the like), ensemble numbers for the
principal actors, a light and comic touch in the music, and unpretentious
and melodious writing throughout.[5]

Opera at Venice

THE OPENING of a public opera house, the Teatro San Cassiano, at
Venice in 1637 marks one of the most important events in the long history
of opera. At Florence, Mantua, and Rome opera had been an entertainment for the nobility, confined to a small circle of auditors and designed
for the sophisticated tastes of the few who made up the aristocratic audience. From 1637, however, opera gradually became a public entertainment. It was supported by three groups of the populace: the court and the
nobility (who occupied the boxes), the wealthy Venetian merchants, and
the lower middle class. Opera now became a "property" to be exploited
commercially, and its new status was reflected in a gradually changing
subject matter and style. Since the first purveyors of opera at Venice were
Romans, the Roman style, with emphasis on elaborateness rather than
dramatic truth, had at first prevailed. A profusion of scenes within each
act, overwhelming scenic effects, many theatrical machines (which made
possible sudden appearances, disappearances, supernatural effects, spectacles, and the like) and the full use of imagination on the part of author,
designer, and producer marked these early Venetian operas. The reappearance of Monteverdi on the operatic scene, however, soon gave a new direction to Venetian opera.

Later works of Monteverdi. In 1613, having served at the Mantuan
court for over twenty years, Monteverdi moved to Venice as chapelmaster
at St. Mark's. In that position he wrote quantities of church music, several
additional books of madrigals, and incidental music for a few plays. When
public opera became a reality in Venice, after 1637, he came out of virtual
retirement and composed two more operas (in addition to two which have
been lost): *Il ritorno d'Ulisse* ("The Return of Ulysses"), produced in
1641, and *L'incoronazione di Poppea* ("The Coronation of Poppea"), in
1642. Monteverdi was then in his middle 70's. Thirty-four years had intervened between *Orfeo* and *Il ritorno d'Ulisse,* and the works of the 1640's
differed in many details from the earlier operas.

Chief among the differences was the more complex organization of the
recitatives. Bits of lyric melody were set between sections of the *secco* recitative, and the recitative and its bass line were unified through the use of

5 An aria from Abbatini's portion of *Dal mal il bene* is given in *GMB,* No. 204,
"E che farete. . . ."

the same melodic motives, sometimes used in imitation. At times the recitative was abandoned altogether and short melodic sections were substituted; these included incipient arias in two or three parts, strophic variations with coloratura embellishments, sections resembling passacaglias, and even *concertato* ensembles. Choruses and instrumental pieces declined in importance, and the orchestra was smaller than in earlier operas. All this was done in the interest of intensifying the drama and suggesting the emotions felt by the characters. The characters were so drawn that they became real people on the stage; the vocal parts suggested passion or comedy or pathos, as the drama required, and laid bare the inmost feelings of the characters. The power to delineate character, rare among later operatic composers, was possessed by Monteverdi in full measure. It is this power, plus his technical surety and vivid imagination, that raise him to his high place among the great composers of all time.[6]

Cavalli and Cesti. The development of Venetian opera after the death of Monteverdi may be divided into three phases. From about 1640 to 1660 strongly dramatic recitatives and an overture in chordal style, called *sinfonia,* became characteristic. Examples are found in the works of Cavalli and Cesti. The second phase, from about 1660 to 1680, was marked by the introduction of fugal overtures and by the increasing clarification of the two- or three-part incipient aria still attached to the recitative. Pallavicino's operas are representative of this group. In the third phase, from about 1680 to 1700, the polyphony in the overture and in the *ritornelli* of the arias became more involved, and the aria was separated from the recitative; the latter lost in dramatic power even as the aria gained in lyric strength. These elements are seen in the operas of Legrenzi and Pollarolo.

Returning now to the works of the first phase, we find that Venetian opera through the 1660's was dominated by Pier Francesco Cavalli (1602–1676) and Marc' Antonio Cesti (1623–1669). Cavalli, organist at St. Mark's under Monteverdi, composed over forty operas, many of which were performed repeatedly in other cities.[7] They were characterized by a new type of melody that appeared almost simultaneously in cantata and opera and that was to dominate virtually all vocal music for a century or more. The *bel canto* style, as it was called, is a purely musical creation subservient neither to the rhythm nor to the sense of the text to which it is set. A typical *bel canto* melody, usually in triple meter, flows smoothly and with restraint, avoiding sharp melodic contrasts; the affective intervals (diminished fifths, major sevenths, and the like) are usually absent (see EXAMPLE 87). To the degree that *bel canto* was employed, the domination of the text over the music decreased, for the melody followed musical laws rather than the laws of declamation. Thus scarcely two generations after the Florentine reforms had raised the word above the music, and about the

6 A duet from *L'incoronazione di Poppea* is given in *GMB,* No. 178, "Pur ti miro. . . ."

7 An opera by Cavalli was revived at La Scala in Milan in 1961. It was given under his real name, Coletti-Bruni, however.

A scene from Cesti's *Il pomo d'oro,* showing elaborate set by Burnacini. Engraving by Matthaeus Küsel.

same time that Monteverdi achieved a balance between word and music, the opera became predominantly a musical form and a theatrical spectacle at the expense of dramatic truth.

In Cavalli's operas, of which *Giasone* ("Jason," 1649) and *Serse* ("Xerxes," 1654) were most widely performed, the lyric passages which had been interspersed in the recitative were eliminated; a gradual separation of the recitative and aria took place, the latter often in *bel canto* style. This separation became standard practice in later operas, but a mixed type, later called "arioso," was also retained as a separate category. The arioso was held to be most suited for impassioned, affective texts.[8] The climaxes of Cavalli's operas were carried by duets, often over a *basso ostinato.* The music was most expressive in solemn scenes, especially those concerned with death.

EXAMPLE 87

Cesti, *Il pomo d'oro*

[8] A recitative and aria from Cavalli's *Xerxes* are given in *HAM*, No. 206, "Ecco . . ."; another such pair, from his *Ormindo*, are in *GMB*, No. 200, "Io moro."

THE METROPOLITAN MUSEUM OF ART, DICK FUND, 1953

Audience at the performance of *Il pomo d'oro* in Vienna, 1668. Engraving by Francesco Geffels.

Cesti was principally active as a singer and composer in Rome, Florence, and Vienna, but his success as an operatic composer came primarily in Venice. Only a few of his hundred or more operas have been preserved; *La Dori* (1661) and *Il pomo d'oro* ("The Golden Apple," 1667) are among the best known. Cesti employed the full range of operatic forms and styles in these works. In some the separation of recitative and aria is well marked and the latter expanded beyond previous dimensions; this has the effect of giving his operas a predominantly melodious or lyric tone, rather than a dramatic one. His love scenes are tender, often elegiac, although he sometimes employed folklike melodies and humorous elements. In other works a fusion of the types took place, and an animated, terse passage resulted.[9] Arias of various types occurred, and they varied also in the types of accompaniment given them. While arias with *basso continuo* accompaniment were in the majority, many included accompaniments (called *accompagnato* or *stromentato*) in which the orchestral parts were fully written out.

Later composers. The popularity of opera, evident in the middle years of the seventeenth century, increased enormously as the century neared its end. Dozens of composers at Venice and elsewhere contributed hundreds of operas, many of which were performed a few times and then forgotten. Male sopranos, called *castrati,* were employed. This practice, an

9 See a passage from *Il pomo d'oro* in *HAM*, No. 221, "Di bellezza . . . ," and an example of another type, from *L'Argia,* in *GMB*, No. 203, "Alma mia. . . ."

importation from the Orient, led to the creation of a style that exploited the vocal characteristics of the *castrati*. Possessing great endurance, lung power, and a range greater than a normal (female) soprano, the *castrati* had spectacular and virtuosic music written for them. Coloratura scales and arpeggios, dazzling trills, and sustained high tones became typical in soprano roles, and the exciting vocal aspects of other operatic parts increased proportionately.

Another trend, begun in the time of Cavalli, took on greater dimensions in the later operas of the Venetian school: the decline of the chorus. Cavalli had inclined toward a type of solo opera, in which ensemble and chorus were of relatively little importance. A large increase in the number of opera houses in Venice brought one company into commercial competition with another. It became increasingly necessary to reduce costs, and the opera chorus was the principal victim of the urge to economize. No expense was spared, however, in securing the finest available solo singers. With the decline of the chorus and the increasingly dominant role of the soloists, a change came in the texture of Venetian operas. Possibly in an effort to conform to the taste of the large public upon which their success depended, composers tended toward a simple, melodious style. The dramatic recitative declined in importance, and the aria became the dominant form, more and more frequently with orchestral accompaniment.

Toward the 1680's the trend toward simplicity was slowed somewhat. In the operas of Giovanni Legrenzi (1626–1690), for example, vocal ensembles were often carefully worked out in contrapuntal textures; the stereotyped bass lines of arias adopted instrumental idioms from the concerto, or else they took on some of the smooth elegance of the *bel canto* style.[10] A mixture of heroic and comic elements is also characteristic of Legrenzi's style. Concertolike basses, often consisting of series of eighth-notes moving stepwise, were sometimes used in the operas of Carlo Pallavicino (1630–1688), another important Venetian composer of the time. The melodic types employed in the operas of these men differed considerably, however. Legrenzi's inclined toward the dignified or pompous and often developed out of "mottos" of three or four tones. Pallavicino's melodies often resembled folk songs in their clear rhythms, lightly undulating contours, and short phrases.[11]

Opera in France

OF ALL the countries of Europe, France proved most resistant to the blandishments of Italian opera. France possessed a long tradition of ballets, extending back to 1581 when the famous *Ballet comique de la reine* was produced. In the decades after 1640 Corneille and, later, Racine had raised classical tragedy to new heights; a form of drama adulterated

10 An aria which shows the *bel canto* influence is given in *GMB*, No. 231, "Ti lascio. . . ." Bukofzer calls attention to the omission of two sharps in the key signature of this aria.

11 A *sinfonia* from Pallavicino's *Il Diocletiano*, given in *GMB*, No. 224, shows a relationship to the concerto.

by song seemed unnecessary. Further, the French language was felt to be unsuited to the requirements of operatic recitative. Finally, the French temperament found Italian operatic recitative too extravagant and emotional for its taste. Italian singers had been imported to the French court as a political measure about 1645, however, and the court was acquainted with the expressiveness of Italian opera. An anti-Italian faction at the court sought to keep the works performed there—notably Cavalli's *Egisto* and Rossi's *Orfeo*—from leading to the permanent establishment of an Italian opera company. Thus when opera finally became established at the French court, after another twenty years, it took on a characteristic French tone.

The ballet provided the basic framework within which the indigenous French opera was created. It was first of all a court entertainment; the king and his courtiers danced in it. In addition to a variety of lavishly staged, instrumentally accompanied dances, it sometimes contained solo songs and stately choruses. In about 1650 the ballet acquired a coherent dramatic plot and became something more than a series of tableaux. Much of the dance and choral music for those ballets has been lost, but a large number of *airs de cour,* namely, strophic songs for solo voice, have survived. The musical accompaniment to the ballet was provided by a string orchestra, the famous "Twenty-four Violins of the King," which under Louis XIII became the first permanent orchestra to require several performers on each part. The presence of written-out inner voices made the continuo virtually unnecessary; this characteristic Baroque device was not used generally in France until after the middle of the century. An important feature of the *ballet de cour* was its overture. This was a piece in two sections, slow and fast, respectively, with the stately, slow first section based on repetitions of dotted rhythms and chains of suspensions and sequences.

Lully. Jean Baptiste Lully (1632–1687), born in Florence, came to Paris in 1646 and about 1652 entered the service of Louis XIV, then fourteen years old. As a singer, dancer, and violinist Lully quickly rose in the royal favor. By 1661 he had become composer to the King; through a combination of subservience to those in power and arrogance and intrigue toward his rivals, he made himself the most powerful musician in France. At first he represented the Italian faction at court and provided ballet music in which the airs and recitatives were in the Italian style but the danced portions were typically French. In the ballets, notably *Alcidiane* (1658) and *Serse* (1660), the form known as the French overture became standardized. Here the slow first part was stately and filled with dotted rhythms, as in the earlier *ballets de cour,* but the fast second part was written in triple meter and in fugal texture, sometimes containing a short coda in slow tempo in the style of the beginning. In this form the overture was adopted by other composers, sometimes for use in other kinds of works (opera, oratorio, and orchestral dance suite), and remained in use until the end of the Baroque period.

In 1664 Lully began a period of collaboration with Molière. Jointly the two men produced a number of comedy ballets, of which *Le Bourgeois gentilhomme* (1670) is perhaps the best known. In these works Lully departed from the Italian style in all particulars. The recitative reproduced the accents, inflections, and cadences of the French language. Large choruses and extended orchestral numbers were frequently used, lending an imposing air to the ballets; solo ensembles, often in contrapuntal style, completed the total effect. Thus all the ingredients of opera were at hand.

About 1669 the composer Robert Cambert (*c.* 1628–1677) and the poet Robert Perrin became the first directors of a newly established Royal Academy of Music. Under the auspices of the Academy they produced *Pomone* (1671), a work which can be called the first French opera.[12] Since the new form seemed to offer promise of success, Lully virtually abandoned his ballet activity and seized control of the Academy. From 1672, secure in his position as musical dictator of France, he concentrated on composing in the operatic form and produced fifteen operas in which French characteristics became fixed.

The essence of Lully's operatic production was that it brought together all the forms and styles that had found favor in France during the preceding decades. The librettos, most of them written by Philippe Quinault, whom Lully favored after he had discarded Molière, were modeled upon the tragedies of Racine. They were concerned with love, glory, duty, and the interactions between them. A prologue and five acts became traditional; the whole was dignified, conservative, and directed toward the small aristocratic audience of which Louis XIV was the center.

The musical elements were those which had been developed earlier. The two-part overture was derived from the comedy ballet, but refined and lengthened.[13] The recitative, likewise taken from the ballet, closely reflected the accents and inflections of French as delivered by the best actors of the day. To achieve this, Lully often shifted meters (e.g., from duple to triple) across short sections to accommodate the declamation; he also often inserted brief melodic phrases where the prose rhythm or text declamation required (see EXAMPLE 88). Recitative and aria were often undifferentiated or flowed into one another, as in the earlier Italian tradition.[14] The arias in general were shorter, less extravagant in their contours and ornaments, and often in small two-part form (*aabb*). Larger forms were rare, and arias with recapitulation even rarer, but he sometimes wrote through-composed arias with *ritornelli*. The choruses and instrumental pieces were derived from the corresponding sections of the ballets. The choruses, however, owed much to Italian models, such as those in Carissimi's oratorios, in their rhythmic solidity and traces of choral declamation. They were both sung and danced, as they often had been in the ballets. The form of the chaconne (essentially variations on a four- or eight-measure chordal phrase) was favored by Lully; many of his

12 The overture to *Pomone* is given in *HAM*, No. 223. A scene from the same work is in *GMB*, No. 222, "Ah, ma soeur. . . ."

13 The overture to Lully's *Alceste* is given in *HAM*, No. 224.

14 Two examples, from Lully's *Alceste* and *Persée*, respectively, are given in *HAM*, No. 225, "Le Ciel . . . ," and *GMB*, No. 232, "Mont! venez. . . ."

E X A M P L E 88

Lully, *Atys*

SANGARITE: Ah! de-meu-rez, A- tys, mes soup-çons sont pas-sés; vous m'ay-mez, je le croy, j'en veux ê - tre cer-taine;— je le sou-hai-te as- sez, pour le croi - re sans peine.

TRANSLATION:
Ah, stay, Atys, my suspicions have vanished; you love
me, I believe, I wish to be certain; I wish it enough to
believe it without difficulty.

most imposing choruses and instrumental pieces are large chaconnes employing sarabande patterns.[15] The opening section of the chaconne sometimes returns periodically, thus giving the whole the effect of a rondo. The music is pompous, spectacular, and often richly orchestrated, with woodwind and brass instruments added to the five-part string orchestra. Lully's harmonic scheme was rather conservative and seldom employed the tonal logic, the modulatory freedom, and the harmonic drive to cadences that characterized the majority of Baroque music of the following generation.

In the decades after Lully's death a change of taste gradually occurred, parallel to the slow decline of the massive, formalistic, and severe Baroque style and the emergence of the light and ingratiating Rococo (see Chapter 16). Lully's operas began to be looked upon as remnants of an outworn tradition. Italian operatic elements were often inserted into performances of them; the stark melodic lines were modified by means of graceful and elaborate ornaments. A number of minor composers contributed to the development of a new form, the opera ballet, which they intended for public rather than royal consumption. These composers dispensed with dramatic plot entirely and presented a variety of exotic, humorous, but always lavish ballets interspersed with singing. Chief among the composers was André Campra (1660–1744), whose Italian heritage was reflected in his use of concerto-style elements within arias [16] and his use of harmonic devices typical of the pre-Classic opera of the time (see below, page 240).

Rameau. Jean-Philippe Rameau (1683–1764), the foremost organist of France and the eminent author of the important *Traité de l'harmonie* of 1722, turned to serious opera composition about 1733. His *Hippolyte et Aricie* of that year marked the beginning of a new phase of French operatic history, even though it adhered to Lullyian models. Rameau was acclaimed for the harmonic clarity he brought into his music and for the quality of his instrumental writing; at the same time he was considered a traitor to French music and an adherent of the Italian style. His later works included the opera ballet, *Les Indes galantes* (1735), *Castor et Pollux* (1737), his masterwork, and *Dardanus* (1739). These works caused the adherents of the Lully tradition to change their minds; Rameau was then looked upon as one of the greatest dramatic composers in French history. Bringing to the arias and recitatives all the rich resources of late Baroque harmony—including much use of secondary and diminished-seventh chords and wide-ranging modulations—he wrought an affective air and a kind of dramatic intensity that French music had earlier lacked.[17]

Rameau's operatic choruses, like Lully's were brilliant, mostly chordal and sonorous; but they were often contrapuntal as well, and they were more numerous than Lully's. In his *Traité de l'harmonie* Rameau had

15 An instrumental chaconne from Lully's *Roland* is given in *GMB*, No. 233.
16 See *GMB*, No. 261, "Quelle audace . . . ," for a scene from Campra's opera ballet, *Les Fêtes Vénitiennes* (1710).
17 See two examples of Rameau's style in *GMB*, Nos. 297a, "Ma voix . . . ," and 297b, "Mars. . . ."

A performance of Lully's *Alceste* in the Marble Court at Versailles, 1674. Etching by Jean Le Pautre.

expressed his theory of a fundamental bass (not to be confused with *basso continuo*) that consists of the root tones of all chords, whether inverted or not, and relates one chord to another in a logical, musical manner. The surety of Rameau's harmonic touch was made evident in his choral writing, for the choruses moved forward with logically connected harmonies.

The imaginative use of a large orchestra, the fondness for descriptive *sinfonie*,[18] and a great variety of dance forms gave the instrumental portions of Rameau's operas a special appeal. The dances ranged from unassuming gavottes to massive chaconnes, and each dance had its share of subtle instrumental touches, of rhythmic variety, and of grace.[19] The overtures, too, went beyond Lully's in their forms and varieties of texture; occasionally, as in *Zoroastre* (1749), Rameau employed a form that is related to the Neapolitan overture in its fast-slow-fast structure and its outspokenly homophonic texture. His orchestra was larger than Lully's: in addition to strings and the ubiquitous continuo, he sometimes used flutes, oboes, bassoons, trumpets, and tympani.

Opera in England

The masque. In the discussion of English secular music of the late sixteenth century (see Chapter 11), it was pointed out that the lute-accompanied solo song (called "ayre") enjoyed popularity until about the 1620's. The ayre then became an ingredient of the form called "masque," and thus it had an indirect bearing on the evolution of English opera. The masque, early in the sixteenth century, was a form similar to the French *ballet de cour*. A court entertainment, it relied upon elaborately staged dances and spectacular scenery for its effects. It included the semblance of a dramatic plot, solo songs of the ayre type but with orchestral accompaniment, and dialogue. The latter was at first (about 1600) spoken and later (after 1617) set in quasi-Italian recitative style.

Ben Jonson (1572–1637), dramatist and friend of Shakespeare, was also active as a writer of masques, some of them for James I. It is likely that the composers who set to music the masques of Jonson and others were of relatively minor rank; to judge from the small amount of music that has survived, the songs were unpretentious in scope, often resembling folksongs. By the 1630's settings in recitative style were fairly numerous. Surviving masques by Henry Lawes (1596–1662) and his brother William (1602–1645) indicate that English composers of the time applied the free rhythmic aspects of Italian recitative to the English language without approaching the emotional concentration or the expressiveness of the older version. By the 1640's the masque began to decline. Its slight dramatic content was swallowed up by elaborate staging, and its text came under attack by the emerging Puritans, who gained political power on the beheading of Charles I in 1649.

For a number of years the Puritan opposition to the theater put a

---

18 An illustration of the descriptive style in a soliloquy from *La Temple de la gloire* is given in *HAM*, No. 276, "Ramage. . . ."

19 See *HAM*, No. 277, and *GMB*, No. 296, for the styles of Rameau's dances.

virtual halt to public performances of all forms of dramatic music. In 1652, however, a work disguised as a "representation of scenes and a story sung in recitative," with music by a number of composers including Henry Lawes and Matthew Locke (*c.* 1630–1677), was successfully performed in London. This work, *The Siege of Rhodes,* with text by William D'Avenant, was composed of recitatives and arias throughout and hence may be called the first English opera. But it had no immediate successors; even after the restoration of the monarchy in 1660 the court remained cool to the new form, perhaps because the opera represented an Italian tradition and the court under Charles II was influenced by French culture rather than Italian.

The masque, however, was revived after 1660. Locke emerged as the outstanding composer of the time, contributing a number of masques and other forms of dramatic music to the Restoration stage. The work of John Blow (*c.* 1648–1708) was perhaps of greater importance to English music, for Blow's *Venus and Adonis,* composed about 1685, was in all essentials an opera, even though it was still called a masque in the traditional fashion. In the music of Locke, and to a greater extent in that of Blow, a distinct English idiom came into being. The emotionally rich recitative of Monteverdi's generation was brought into contact with a harmonic system that was well on the road toward the fully developed system of major and minor tonalities. Augmented and diminished intervals in the melody over a basically diatonic harmony gave rise to many transitory modulations; dissonances, cross relations, and a free rhythmic scheme resulted in the impression that the melodies and their underlying harmonies were somewhat at odds. The music of Blow represents a fusion of French and Italian style elements. His *Venus and Adonis,* for example, begins with a modified version of a French overture and contains instrumental portions that strongly resemble those found in Lully's operas. Recitatives, airs, and choruses, however, are filled with the concentrated emotional expressiveness typical of Italian works.

Purcell. A fusion of French and Italian styles similar to that found in Blow's music is also present in the music of Blow's great pupil, Henry Purcell (*c.* 1659–1695). Purcell was a chorister in the Chapel Royal until 1673 and numbered Cooke, Blow, and Pelham Humfrey among his teachers. At the age of twenty he succeeded Blow as organist of Westminster Abbey and later also served as organist of the Chapel Royal and composer to the court. He was a prolific composer of church music; in addition, he composed excellent chamber music, masques, sets of incidental music for plays, one opera, *Dido and Aeneas* (1689), and a variety of other works.

Purcell in a sense summarized a century of Continental and English musical developments and in many ways went even beyond them. The recitatives in his dramatic works, either completely separated from the arias or else containing melodic phrases in arioso fashion, are eloquent and declamatory in the best Italian tradition, but they are also sensitive to the special requirements of English prosody. *Dido and Aeneas,* as well as *The Indian Queen* and other works, contains many passages in which every textual accent is properly accounted for. One of the most intense and famous of Purcell's arias, Dido's farewell from *Dido and Aeneas,* is in the form of a passacaglia over a chromatically descending bass line. The freedom with which the irregular phrases of the melody overlap the regular five-measure phrases of the bass constitutes one of Purcell's masterstrokes.[20]

Purcell employed the chorus in a variety of ways and wrote for it in several styles. In *Dido and Aeneas* the chorus participates in the action; in *The Indian Queen* it functions as an element around which a spectacle is built, as in the operas of Lully; in masques, such as *The Fairy Queen,* it is purely ornamental. The choral writing is sometimes contrapuntal, at other times chordal, dancelike,[21] or even in *concertato* style. But it is always imposing and sonorous. The orchestral writing is similarly varied. French overtures and sets of dances abound in his dramatic works, and the aria accompaniments range from those with simple continuo harmonization to those with all the pulsating rhythm and brilliant figurations of the Italian concerto style.

The presence of Italian style elements—including small *da capo* arias—in Purcell's later works testifies to the decline of the French influence at the court and the growing popularity of everything Italian. Purcell, building on the work of John Blow, had gone far to develop a genuinely English operatic style, a style derived partly from French and Italian elements yet containing many typically English idioms. His early death, at the age of about thirty-six, halted this development; in the early eighteenth century the domination of Italian opera in England became complete. Handel, who first came to England in 1710, continued and strengthened the Italian tradition for several decades. Even Handel, however, could not long cope with English taste, which soon changed again. The enormous success of a satirical ballad opera, *The Beggar's Opera,* written by John Gay with music arranged by John Christopher Pepusch[22] and performed in 1728, accelerated the decline of Italian opera in England. A large number of tuneful ballad operas by minor English composers were written in the eighteenth and nineteenth centuries, but significant operatic developments are not to be looked for.

Opera in Austria and Germany

As EARLY as the middle of the seventeenth century the Viennese court had revealed its fondness for and given lavish support to opera, primarily of the Venetian type. Monteverdi's and Cavalli's works were performed there, and beginning with Antonio Bertali (1605–*c.* 1669), a number of Italian composers wrote and produced operas for the entertainment of

---

20 The aria is given in *HAM,* No. 255, "Thy hand, Belinda."

21 An aria and chorus from *King Arthur* are given in *GMB,* No. 247, "I call. . . ."

22 Several songs from *The Beggar's Opera,* given in *HAM,* No. 264, "My love . . . ," "Hither . . ."; and *GMB,* No. 281, "A maid . . . ," "O ponder well . . . ," illustrate the light-hearted, satirical tone of this work.

the court. Antonio Draghi (1635–1700) may be mentioned as one of the most prolific composers, in whose works the Venetian style was kept alive if not carried forward. While Johann Joseph Fux (1660–1741), chapel-master at the Viennese court, is known principally as a contrapuntalist and author of the treatise *Gradus ad Parnassum* (1725), upon which generations of counterpoint instructors have based their teaching, he was also the composer of eighteen respected operas. Fux's works brought the Viennese fondness for contrapuntal textures to expression. Large *da capo* arias with contrapuntal orchestral accompaniments, sometimes in fugal style, were numerous.[23] Choruses set within solo or ensemble scenes provided means for rounding off the forms, and a lavish use of wind instruments in the orchestra lent an air of variety to the music. Associated with Fux were Antonio Caldara (1670–1736) and Francesco Conti (1681–1732). Caldara composed eighty-seven operas and large quantities of church music, but few of the operas have been published. Conti brought elements of the pre-Classical style (see below, page 240) to Vienna, introducing there the operatic aria with lute accompaniment. After almost a century the Viennese operatic establishment at the Austrian court declined in 1740 with the death of Charles VI, the crowning of Maria Theresa, and the beginning of the War of the Austrian Succession.

The first German opera was composed by Heinrich Schütz (1585–1672) in 1627. Schütz, one of the most important of seventeenth-century composers, was a pupil of Giovanni Gabrieli in Venice and was among the composers who introduced the recitative style and *basso continuo* to Germany. His opera, *Dafne,* was based on a translation of Rinuccini's libretto; both it and a ballet, *Orpheus und Eurydice* (1638), have been lost. In any event, Schütz's work had few immediate successors, for political conditions during and following the devastating Thirty Years' War (1618–1648) were not conducive to vital operatic activity. When operatic production was firmly established in Germany, toward the century's end, it was largely in the hands of Italians.

Agostino Steffani (1654–1728), Italian by birth, is associated with Germany both by reason of his training in Munich and of his long professional activity there (intermittently from 1675) and in Hanover (after 1688). In his eighteen operas, of which *Marco Aurelio,* produced at Munich in 1680, was the first, a fusion of many styles came to expression. His overtures were modeled upon those of Lully, whose music he had studied on a long visit to Paris, but within the typical fugal second section Steffani introduced alternations of instrumental groups in the manner of the Italian concerto grosso. Many of his arias, which were most often in the *da capo* form (see page 241) developed by the Neapolitans,[24] were built on recurring bass passages similar to those found in Venetian operas of the 1660's. Recitatives were separated from arias in the usual way, but the arias were set in contrapuntal style and the orchestral ac-

23 An aria from Fux's *La costanza e fortezza* is given in *GMB,* No. 272, "Saprei morir. . . ."

24 An aria from *Enrico detto il leone,* of 1689, is given in *HAM,* No. 244, "Un balen."

companiment was far richer than that in Italian works. It is this fusion of national style elements, with great dignity and musical craftsmanship, that differentiates Steffani's operas from those of the south. His works prepared the way for the operas of Handel and to some extent served as Handel's models.

Short-lived contributions to the creation of a native German opera were made by a number of composers at various German cities in the early eighteenth century. At Weissenfels, for example, Johann Philipp Krieger (1649–1725) produced a number of works distinguished by short strophic songs set in a pleasantly melodious style.[25] Johann Sigismund Cousser (or Kusser, 1660–1727) was active at the court of Brunswick for several years before moving to Hamburg. A pupil of Lully, he favored the French style in his instrumental music, and many of the short arias in his operas were cast in French dance meters. He also composed larger *da capo* arias in the style of Steffani, with rich instrumental accompaniments. After 1694 Cousser became influential in strengthening the Hamburg opera. His work at Brunswick and nearby Wolfenbüttel was later continued by Georg Kaspar Schürmann (*c.* 1672–1751); the latter, however, wrote in a more dignified and restrained fashion and developed a harmonic vocabulary akin to Bach's.[26]

The most significant developments took place at the public opera house founded in Hamburg in 1678. Beginning with an opera on the subject of Adam and Eve by Johann Theile (1646–1724), and continuing for a while with similar religious subjects, the Hamburg repertoire soon became secularized entirely. Works by Italian composers were translated or otherwise adapted, and a few French and Italian operas were sung in the original languages. The mainstay of the repertoire, however, was a series of operas in German by Johann Wolfgang Franck (*c.* 1644–1710) and other less significant composers.

The high point of the Hamburg opera was reached during the period of activity, almost forty years (1696–1734), of Reinhard Keiser. Keiser (1674–1739) composed well over a hundred operas, of which about two dozen have survived. These are sufficient to reveal the existence of a wide-ranging talent employed in virtually all the operatic types then available. Instrumental pieces within the operas, as well as the choruses and ballets, reflect the influence of Lully and Steffani. Keiser's orchestral writing is distinguished by imagination and consummate skill in handling the instruments; he made considerable use of Italian concerto elements, such as running passages in the bass.[27] Arias are of various types, of which the *da capo* type is the least often represented; Keiser preferred either a dramatic arioso type or a lyric, rhythmically attractive song in quasi-popular vein.[28]

25 Two operatic songs are given in *GMB*, Nos. 236a, "Wer's Jagen," and 236b, "Freien ist. . . ."

26 An aria from Schürmann's *Ludovicus Pius* is given in *GMB*, No. 293, "Wohnt nach. . . ."

27 See the duet from Keiser's *Adonis* in *HAM*, No. 267, "Fahret wohl."

28 A duet of this type is given in *GMB*, No. 269, "Kleine Vöglein"; a brief *da capo* aria is seen in *GMB*, No. 268, "Holder Zephyr."

The outline of the first act of Keiser's *Croesus* (1711, revised in 1730) is given here to show the form of a typical opera of the time.

Sinfonia (fast-slow-fast)

A C T   I
  Chorus, *da capo*
  Recitative and aria (CROESUS)
  Aria, recitative, aria, and recitative (ELMIRA)
  Aria (ORSANES)
  Recitative (ORSANES and ELMIRA)
  Aria (HOLINACUS)
  Aria (ELMIRA)
  Recitative (HOLINACUS and ELMIRA) and aria (ELMIRA)
  Recitative (ELMIRA) and aria (NERILL)
  Recitative (ELMIRA and ELCIUS) and duet (ELMIRA and NERILL)
  Recitative (ELCIUS) and duet (ORSANES and ELCIUS)
  Duet (ELMIRA and CLERIDA)
  Trio (ELIATES, CLERIDA, and ORSANES)
  Aria (ELMIRA), interrupted by recitative (ELCIUS) between first and second
    stanzas
  Recitatives (VARIOUS CHARACTERS)
  Recitative and aria (ELCIUS)
  Recitative (CROESUS)
  Recitative (HOLINACUS and CROESUS)
  Recitative (ORSANES) and aria *da capo* (CLERIDA)
  Recitative and aria (ELCIUS)
  Dances. Entrance of the HARLEQUINS
  Aria (CYRUS) and recitative (CYRUS and CROESUS)
  Chorus
  Ballet
  Recitative (CROESUS and OTHERS)
  Ritornello (orchestra) and aria (CYRUS). Ritornello *da capo*
  Ritornello (orchestra) and recitative (CAPTAIN and OTHERS). Ritornello
    da capo

Keiser's librettos often included songs in the Low German dialect of Hamburg, and arias in Italian often stood next to those in German. The operas ranged from serious portrayals of historical or mythological subjects to trivial treatments of local or topical events. Indeed, the gradual decline and eventual extinction of the Hamburg opera may be related to the decline in aesthetic quality of Keiser's operas. Parallel to the change in subject matter was the change in style from the dignified, massive, and contrapuntal Baroque to the light and merely tuneful works of the Rococo period (see below, Chapter 16). A number of operas written by Georg Philipp Telemann (1681–1767), one of the most prolific composers of the time, during the years of his residence in Hamburg (1721 to 1767) reveal that the trend to write in a lighter style continued. With those works, as well as the later ones of Keiser, the activity of a distinctive Hamburg school ceased in 1738.

The Operas of Handel

GEORGE FRIDERIC HANDEL (1685–1759), in spite of German birth and long residence in England, is to be considered a representative of Italian opera and a follower of Alessandro Scarlatti (see page 241). Born and educated in Halle, in central Germany, he was an accomplished violinist and harpsichordist while still in his teens and mastered the arts of composition before he was twenty. At the age of eighteen he abandoned his study of law and moved to Hamburg, where he was engaged as violinist in the orchestra of the Hamburg Opera, then led by Reinhard Keiser. He wrote and produced several operas in Hamburg, then (from 1706) spent several years in Italy. Returning to Germany in 1710, he became Steffani's successor as chapelmaster to the Elector of Hanover. Later in the same year he made his first visit to England. He returned there in 1712, and when, in 1714, the Elector ascended the English throne as George I, Handel remained in England. Except for a few brief visits to Germany, Italy, and elsewhere, he lived in England for forty-seven years.

For much of this time Handel served as impresario and producer as well as composer of his operas, and of course he conducted them from the harpsichord. His activities as producer were often accompanied by difficulties not of his own making, for Handel found himself caught between the German and anti-German factions at court. For example, about 1720 he was unwittingly placed in competition with Giovanni Bononcini, an eminent Italian composer who had been invited to London by members of the anti-German party. Again, in 1734, Handel's rivals sought to persuade Hasse (see page 243), then in London, to set up a rival operatic establishment, but Hasse declined. Such political intrigues, plus the larger public's lack of interest in opera in general, made Handel's career a precarious one; he was alternately well off and close to poverty, but his artistic integrity did not waver. By 1741 Handel was reconciled to abandoning the operatic stage, and from that year he devoted himself to the composition of the oratorios on which his fame so largely rests today.

Handel's first opera, *Almira,* was written for Hamburg in 1705, either in imitation of or under the influence of Keiser's style. Its libretto contains both German and Italian texts, and the music includes a French overture, a succession of arias in the best Italian tradition, and a variety of numbers in the songful, popular style represented in Keiser's works. With this opera Handel demonstrated his complete understanding of the techniques and problems of composing for the stage. His successful Italian visit confirmed him in that understanding and gave him opportunities to perfect his craft, but his operatic style was virtually established by his twentieth year. The operas *Rodrigo* (Florence, 1708) and the very successful *Agrippina* (Venice, 1709) immediately brought him an enviable European reputation, and he was looked upon as the equal of any composer then active. His English period began with the production of *Rinaldo* in 1711, included such masterpieces as *Ottone* (1723), *Giulio Cesare* (1724) and *Serse* (1738), and ended with *Deidamia* (1741).

Handel's accomplishment lay in infusing conventional musical ideas with new life. His arias in *bel canto* style were masterpieces of phrasing and proportion. Those in coloratura style, often set in large forms with recapitulation (*da capo* arias), were exciting and dramatic and not merely technically brilliant. Passages with running bass melodies and incisive, rhythmically alive figures in the upper parts lent sweeping power to the arias or ensembles in which they appeared. And the type of melody that became almost a Handelian trademark took on a new expressiveness. The short phrases of the melody are separated by pauses bridged by a continuous accompaniment that leads inexorably to the cadences. It is usually in a stately sarabande rhythm and characterized by emotional intensity (see EXAMPLE 89).

E X A M P L E 89

Handel, *Rinaldo*

Operatic convention of Handel's time required that an aria devote itself to a single mood or emotion or trait of character; the concept of contrasting moods within a single piece was foreign to virtually all Baroque music. Thus it was the succession of contemplative arias, not the single aria, that reflected the totality of a characterization. Handel was in full accord with this convention and lavished all his skill and musical imagination on the many arias that constitute the bulk of his operatic composition. The ensembles, many of which are large compositions in a variety of contrapuntal textures, brought in elements of dramatic conflict between characters. The choruses, relatively few in number and serving primarily an ornamental function, seldom reach the level of his masterful oratorio choruses and contribute little to the dramatic progress of the operas. The function of carrying forward the plot and approaching the solution of what few dramatic problems the opera contained was given to the recitatives. The latter range from the *secco,* continuo-accompanied section to the large and complex *scena.* The *scena,* which typically includes arioso and aria fragments interspersed with affective recitative sections, was brought into musical unity by its concentration on one phase of a dramatic problem.

The instrumental portions of Handel's operas are as varied as the vocal numbers. French overtures predominate, but often a few dances are added at the end of the second part.[29] Passages in concerto style often serve as

29 See, for example, the overture to *Rinaldo,* given in *GMB,* No. 278.

ritornellos within the larger arias. A variety of dances, ceremonial pieces, and processionals in both Italian and French styles add a festive air. Many of the instrumental pieces as well as the vocal numbers appear in several different operas and even among Handel's chamber-music works and concertos. This self-borrowing was compounded by Handel's occasional practice of borrowing pieces of other composers' music for insertion in his own. Plagiarism is not involved here, in view of the Baroque attitude toward "ownership" of musical ideas. Copyright was unknown, of course, and composers felt at liberty to borrow, to improve, or to modify any music that would serve their own needs at the moment. Under pressure of time, Handel frequently resorted to the practice—using his own works more often than others'—and usually adapted the borrowings so skillfully to their new environment that they became in effect new compositions.

The Pre-Classical Opera

FOR MORE than a century music historians have referred to a Neapolitan school of opera, of which Alessandro Scarlatti was considered the founder. The term has been generally accepted, even though developments in many cities other than Naples contributed to the style and though north Italian and German composers were among its most prominent representatives. In the light of recent research [30] the term requires modification.

The style to which the term "Neapolitan opera" referred is now seen to be part of the general transition that accompanied the decline of the Baroque period and the gradual emergence of the Classical; as such it was roughly contemporary with the sub-period called Rococo (see Chapter 16). And Alessandro Scarlatti is thus to be considered one of the last representatives of the declining Baroque operatic style, but one in whose works elements of the new pre-Classical style are to be seen.

The Baroque opera associated largely with Venice had found a firm foothold in Naples soon after its rise to a dominant position about the middle of the seventeenth century. Alessandro Stradella (1642–1682), composing operas for Venice, Turin, and presumably Naples, used vigorously moving bass lines much in the manner of Pallavicino. His melodies were of a wide-ranging, graceful type with subtle phrase extensions.

In the works of Francesco Provenzale (1627–1704), the first important opera composer born in Naples, the chief elements of Venetian style were still present; but they were accompanied by a new melodic expressiveness and a rich, somewhat chromatic harmony. Provenzale went far to establish the system of tonality in the opera. Modal inflections and what has been called pre-tonal harmony (that is, chords and chord sequences existing independently and not related to a common tonality) found little place in his music. The essence of the tonal system is, of course, the presence of a tonal center created by chords grouped around a common

30 See Helmuth Hucke, "Die neapolitanische Tradition in der Oper," and Edward O. D. Downes, "The Neapolitan Tradition in Opera," both in *Report of the Eighth Congress*, International Musicological Society, New York, 1961, pp. 253–77 and 277–84, respectively.

keynote and serving to reinforce it. Seventh chords, diminished-seventh chords, and series of sixth chords were used centrifugally by Provenzale and became potent means both to establish keys and to modulate from them.[31] A tonal center thus established could serve as a harmonic rallying point within an aria, making possible an expanded, extended, and harmonically unified form.

Scarlatti. Alessandro Scarlatti (1660–1725) composed over one hundred operas; the majority were for Naples, but about twenty-five were first performed in Rome, Venice, or elsewhere. Scarlatti brought many elements of the Venetian style into his works, among them the separation of recitative and aria, a detail found earlier in some of Cesti's works. The *secco* recitative, accompanied only by the continuo, carried forward the details of the dramatic plot and in effect became the means of expounding the dramatic element.[32] The aria, on the other hand, concerned itself with the character's emotional reaction to the drama or his reflections about it; it was musical rather than dramatic, often impeding instead of furthering the progress of the plot. It became customary, in the years after about 1710, to compose the aria in a large three-part form, with the third part like the first; the end of the second part carried the designation, *da capo* ("from the beginning"), thus the third part was not written out. Here arose the famous *da capo* aria, which became a formula in virtually all Italian opera (as well as in many oratorios and cantatas) for more than a century. Scarlatti also made use of strophic forms, duets, and small ensembles. His music is often passionate, combining melodic ingenuity with dramatic power.

A new type of opera overture, also credited to Scarlatti, appeared in his operas about 1700. This was the *sinfonia,* a short three-part composition with sections in fast, slow, and fast tempos, respectively. The new "Neapolitan overture," as it is generally called, was in homophonic texture; this marked its greatest departure from the Venetian opera overture and the successor to the latter, the French or Lully overture (see above, page 227), in which polyphonic texture was more common. Scarlatti's Neapolitan overture brought to opera the harmonically supported melody, clear phrase structure, instrumental figurations, and driving rhythm of the concerto grosso. It prepared the way for the independent orchestral *sinfonia* of the 1730's, out of which the Classical symphony developed.[33]

In the later operas of Scarlatti, notably *Tigrane* (1717) and *La Griselda* (1721), the arias also were often set in concerto style. Instrumentally conceived melodies, characterized by concise rhythmic figures, running passages in the bass, and rapid harmonic changes, dominated. The *secco* recitative often was replaced by an orchestrally accompanied recitative; here a rich antiphonal interplay between voice and orchestra became the rule, and the musical interest of the recitative was heightened.

---

31 An example of Provenzale's style is given in *HAM*, No. 222, "Lasciatemi morir." An aria by Stradella is found in *HAM*, No. 241, "Tra cruce. . . ."

32 A recitative from Scarlatti's *La Griselda* is given in *GMB*, No. 259, "Figlio. . . ."

33 The overture to Scarlatti's *La Griselda* is given in *HAM*, No. 259.

Opera seria. During the course of the seventeenth century the typical opera libretto had lost its dramatically unified plot. Unmotivated episodes, comic situations unrelated to the action, florid and unrealistic declamation, supernatural "solutions" to dramatic problems, a variety of mechanical spectacles and devices—such elements had tended to obscure whatever inherent virtues the drama possessed. A movement to purify the opera and to restore a semblance of dramatic truth to its libretto was set in motion by Apostolo Zeno (1668–1750), court poet in Vienna, and continued by his successor, Pietro Metastasio (1698–1782). Zeno, influenced by seventeenth-century French dramatists, notably Racine, established new standards of literary excellence for opera librettos; Metastasio carried the implications of his drama to the point where a tragic ending was inevitable. Comic episodes were consequently not employed in the dramatic works of Metastasio, and when his works were made into operas —as they were repeatedly by dozens of composers well into the time of Mozart—they brought a high degree of pathos, expressiveness, and seriousness to the operatic stage. Thus arose the *opera seria,* or serious opera. The characters were typed, however, and the plots were schematic, lacking psychological development. The arias employed the affects of Baroque music, and they were so spread through the work that structural symmetry rather than dramatic intensity resulted. As evidence of the appeal of Metastasio's dramas to a variety of composers, one need mention only Pergolesi's *Olimpiade* (1735), Hasse's *Didone abbandonata* (1742), and Gluck's and Mozart's settings of *La clemenza di Tito* (1752 and 1791, respectively).

Opera buffa. The years about 1700 also marked the emergence of a vital and lasting tradition of *opera buffa.* This comic opera type, introduced by Mazzochi in Rome in 1639, now came into prominence as one result of the Metastasian reform, which had removed comic scenes from serious opera. Whereas the *opera seria* found its chief support among courtly circles (in Italy as well as elsewhere), *opera buffa* became an entertainment for the middle class. Mythological and historical subjects, of little appeal to the wider public, were replaced by topical plots; parodies of *opera seria* became common subjects. A melodious and unpretentious musical style was most usual. The *recitativo secco* was employed for comic effects, and a special type called *parlando,* consisting of a rapid, dialogue-like interplay of bits of recitative between the two or three main characters, became a feature of the style. Most importantly, all the parts were sung by normal singers: the *castrati* found no place in *opera buffa.*

Among the many musicians who contributed to the development of the *opera buffa* in the first half of the eighteenth century, Giovanni Battista Pergolesi (1710–1736) was outstanding. His comic operas included the well-known *La serva padrona* ("The Maid Mistress," 1733) as well as *Livietta e Tracollo* (1734) and *Lo fratre 'nnamorato* ("The Brothers in Love," 1732). The first two of these works are properly called intermezzos; originally such works were performed during the intermissions of a three-act serious opera and hence are themselves likely to be in two acts. A distinctive feature of the *opera buffa* was the ensemble finale, in which a full quartet of voices (including the bass, which was seldom used in the *opera seria*) engaged in a quick crossfire of short phrases set in highly humorous fashion. Pergolesi mastered the art of giving full weight to the text without affecting the melodiousness and easy flow of the music.[34] The melodies themselves, often formed out of short motives, were influenced by Italian popular song; their unpretentiousness and the naturalness of their style made them ideal vehicles for the lighthearted plots.

A number of composers earlier than Pergolesi outlived him and continued the development of the pre-Classical opera, both the comic and serious types. Leonardo Vinci (1690–1730) and Leonardo Leo (1694–1744) were especially notable in this connection. Nicola Porpora (1686–1768), born at Naples, was active principally in Venice, Vienna (where he was Haydn's teacher), London, and Dresden. Known primarily as a teacher of singers, Porpora wrote almost fifty operas, of which less than a dozen were composed for Naples. He carried the *aria di bravura* (a brilliant, cadenzalike piece filled with spectacular vocal effects) to its highest peak and provided the most eminent *castrati*, many of whom were his pupils, with exciting arias worthy of their special talents.

Hasse. The pre-Classical style reached its culmination in the works of Johann Adolph Hasse (1699–1783), born near Hamburg. A pupil of Scarlatti and Porpora, Hasse achieved great success as the composer of about eighty operas. He worked in London, Vienna, Warsaw, and several Italian cities, but he is associated primarily with Dresden, where over a dozen of his operas were produced between 1737 and about 1760. Many of his librettos were by Metastasio; in composing them he utilized all the resources of the pre-Classical style and revealed a consummate ability to write for the human voice. The gracefulness and elegance of his melodies were unmatched by any of his contemporaries—even by Karl Heinrich Graun (1704–1759), a composer of Italian operas for Frederick the Great of Prussia, and one of the most highly esteemed masters of his craft. Hasse concerned himself, to a larger extent than other composers of the time, with subtleties of the drama. He had no hesitancy in departing from operatic conventions—such as the one which required that a large *da capo* aria follow each recitative—if the action demanded it. Particularly in accompanied recitatives [35] Hasse succeeded in writing with depth of expression. Although his arias have often been held to be somewhat superficial, the beauty of their melodic line cannot be denied.

The last great representatives of pre-Classical opera, Niccolò Jommelli and Tommaso Traëtta, will be discussed in Chapter 17, in relation to the reform opera usually attributed to Gluck.

34 A duet from *La serva padrona* is given in *HAM*, No. 287, "Lo conosco." The aria in *HAM*, No. 286, "Le virtuose," from *Il maestro di musica,* while there attributed to Pergolesi, is probably not by him; it nevertheless illustrates the delightful comic style typical of *opera buffa.*

35 The recitative given in *HAM*, No. 281, "Ma giúnge . . . ," although from one of Hasse's many oratorios, illustrates the style.

The Baroque Period: Other Vocal Music

I<small>N SPITE</small> of the fact that the opera was the dominant secular vocal form of the Baroque period, and that virtually every major composer placed the opera at the center of his creative interests, a number of other and smaller forms continued to flourish. The madrigal, transformed mainly into a solo genre in keeping with the demands of monodic style, existed to about 1650, primarily in Italy. A new form, eventually called

"The Oratorio." Satirical engraving by William Hogarth. [T<small>HE</small> M<small>ETROPOLITAN</small> M<small>USEUM OF ART, DICK FUND,</small> 1932]

the chamber cantata, came into being also in Italy and remained influential for over a century in other countries as well.

The period also gave rise to new forms and styles in the field of sacred music. The differences between Catholic and Protestant church music became ever more marked; a large number of compositions now called *concertati* brought these differences to clear expression and laid the groundwork for the important Protestant church cantata. Finally, a compound form that began in the Catholic church was taken over largely by Protestant composers and culminated in the oratorios of Handel and the Passions of Bach.

The present chapter, then, will be concerned with such unlike composers as Monteverdi, Schütz, Purcell, Handel, and Bach. It will begin with Italian developments early in the seventeenth century and will end with the activities of Germans in the mid-eighteenth century, but it will move back and forth in time and geography as each form or stylistic development is discussed in turn.

Continuo Madrigal

THE EXPRESSION of extreme emotions and the concentration on pathos had reached a high point about 1595 in the madrigals of Gesualdo (see page 183), whose technical means included an extreme use of dissonance and a preoccupation with chromatic melodic lines. But Gesualdo kept within the framework of contrapuntal part-writing and contributed only slightly to the evolution of the monody or the new harmonic concepts. The application of monodic style to the field of the madrigal and the composition of masterpieces in that style was accomplished by Claudio Monteverdi, whose contributions to the opera have already been discussed (see pages 220–22).

Monteverdi's first four books of madrigals, all published before 1603, reveal a composer abreast of new developments in the hyperexpressive madrigal but in no sense going beyond them.[1] In the fifth book (1605), however, Monteverdi introduced madrigals over a continuo accompaniment (obligatory for the last six madrigals of the set, but optional for the others). Paralleling this innovation, in which composers other than Monteverdi took part (notably Salomone Rossi), came a decided change in texture. The new treatment of dissonance, which Monteverdi called the "second practice" as opposed to the old Renaissance modal and contrapuntal "first practice," was based on the combination of a polyphonic melodic element (in two or more parts) and a harmonic framework. The polyphony of the Renaissance madrigal had been self-sufficient; the new madrigal was dependent on the harmonic progressions of the *basso continuo*. Upper voices and bass consequently became the most important parts—the former to establish the chief melody and the latter to provide a harmonic foundation. Inner voices engaged in motivic interplay with the outer voices and could enter or leave the tonal fabric whenever the

---

1 See *HAM*, No. 188, *Ohimè* . . . , for an example from Book IV.

composer desired. Thus the composer was no longer bound to a texture consisting of four or five independent parts; a light and varied free texture became most usual (see EXAMPLE 90).

EXAMPLE 90
Monteverdi, *T'amo, mia vita*

Continuo

Many of the later continuo madrigals of Monteverdi and his contemporaries also contained parts for instruments. This type has since become known as a *concertato* madrigal (from *concertare*, to compete or dispute), for in a sense the two tonal groups—one vocal and the other instrumental—competed with each other. The *concertato* madrigal often contained an introductory, purely instrumental *sinfonia* and a number of short instrumental interludes, called *ritornelli*, which returned periodically. The instruments no longer merely doubled or supported the vocal lines; rather, they were supplied with short, rhythmic motives often derived from the vocal lines themselves. Further, the same kind of broken, rhythmically animated melodic lines often appeared in the vocal parts as well, and instruments and voices engaged in a dialoguelike play with melodic or rhythmic motives. It is in this sense that the term *concertato* is appropriate.

Monteverdi's late works contain instrumental effects which, although found earlier in the instrumental literature, had not been used generally in the vocal field. Among such effects were the pizzicato and string tremolo. In combining them with a rapid syllabic recitative and dramatic or abrupt harmonic contrasts, Monteverdi created a *stile concitato* (agitated style) which served generations of later composers in all manner of dramatic situations. The *concertato* madrigal, with its choral and instrumental sections, became one of the two sources out of which the later

Baroque cantata developed. The other source, the chamber cantata, will be discussed below.

Monodic Chamber Cantata

THE OPERA was, as we have seen, a direct result of applying the monodic style to a suitable dramatic poem; as such, it was one of the important innovations brought about by the first generation of seventeenth-century Italian composers. Of parallel importance was another form which emerged simultaneously with the opera and which had many stylistic points in common with it: the chamber cantata, for solo voice or voices and continuo.

The monody itself was the starting point for the new form. The recitative principle, one of the components of monodic style, found employment in the monody, of course, but it was not used exclusively. The melody often took on a lyric shape and a definite phrase structure; it developed a degree of expressiveness and often embodied many of the affective intervals found in the most advanced operas of the time. A favorite technical device was the strophic variation, in which successive stanzas of the text were set above a recurring bass pattern but with the melody varied from stanza to stanza. The text of the monody was usually based on the idealized adventures of mythological figures, who were placed in pastoral settings.

In a set of monodies by Giovanni Berti (1624), entitled *Cantade ed arie,* an embryonic stage of the cantata may be seen. One of the pieces consists of a number of strophic variations over an animated bass line moving in quarter-notes; the piece begins and ends with a short phrase for continuo alone, and the same phrase, which serves as a *ritornello,* intervenes between each of the variations (see EXAMPLE 91). The kind of striding bass seen in the Berti composition eventually displaced the standardized bass patterns used earlier, namely certain traditional melodies, the passacaglia, and the *basso ostinato.* Further, it often engaged in tentative imitation of the melodic phrases above it; the eventual readmission of counterpoint to Baroque musical textures was a logical consequence.

A number of composers prominent in other fields were also active in the field of the emerging cantata. Luigi Rossi, known for his operas, and Giacomo Carissimi (1605–1674), one of the masters of the early oratorio, composed many cantatas in which the form was expanded.[2] As in operas of the time, passages in recitative style were separated from purely lyric passages; the short sections or movements—recitative, aria, and arioso— were often separated from each other by interspersed *ritornelli.* A short aria, recurring periodically, unified the work, and the name "rondo cantata" for the whole seemed justified to later historians. The new *bel canto* principle, introduced about this time (1650) in both the cantata and the opera, gave to the cantata a greater degree of formal flexibility

[2] A short cantata by Rossi, but in *da capo* form, is given in *HAM,* No. 203, *Io lo vedo.*

EXAMPLE 91

Berti, *Cantade ed arie*

FROM *Handbuch der Musikgeschichte*, by Guido Adler.
Reprinted by permission of Verlag Hans Schneider, Tutzing,
Germany.

and lyric charm; it also resulted in the decline of the standardized use of strophic variations over a *basso ostinato*. In many of Carissimi's cantatas the *ostinato* was dispensed with; the bass became a true counterpoint to the melody, and a degree of coloratura ornamentation characterized the melodic line.

Later in the seventeenth century the cantata became one of the most important forms of vocal composition, attracting composers in Venice, Naples, and in northern countries. Marc' Antonio Cesti, for example, composed many cantatas distinguished by a varied and expressive melodic line.[3] Legrenzi made increased use of counterpoint between melody and bass, and occasionally expanded the accompaniments from simple continuo to several instruments used in *concertato* fashion. And in the cantatas of Alessandro Stradella a high degree of expressive dissonance pointed the way to the fully developed, chromatically inflected harmony of the late Baroque period.

The undisputed master of the chamber cantata was Alessandro Scarlatti, to whom more than six hundred cantatas are ascribed. Only a few

3 One is reprinted in Adler, *Handbuch der Musikgeschichte,* I, pp. 439–42.

of those works have been published,[4] and a comprehensive study of his contributions has not yet been completed. The available works reveal that two contrasting arias, each preceded by an expository recitative, provided the essentials of the form, and that the arias were usually cast in the large *da capo* pattern. Wide-ranging modulations, a chromatically inflected melodic line, and experimental harmonies placed Scarlatti's cantatas among the most forward-looking works of the time (see EXAMPLE 92). Indeed, in the hands of composers such as Handel, Durante, and

EXAMPLE 92

Alessandro Scarlatti, *Lascia al fine*

Se di cu - re mo-le-ste in fra le spi - ne di ge - lo - so ti- mo-re in mar'de

Basso continuo

fie - le d'un i - dol trop-po in'-gra - to tragl' in - gan- ni mor- ta - li

Marcello, the cantata became a form in which experiments could be made, new harmonic combinations introduced, and vocal effects measured. To this extent, the cantata of the early eighteenth century was considerably in advance of the opera, in which the taste of the larger public had perforce to be considered.

The cantata illustrates one highly characteristic aspect of Baroque music: the transfer of melodic idioms from instrumental music to vocal. At the beginning of the seventeenth century instrumental melodies had been composed largely in imitation of vocal ones; stepwise progressions, narrow range, and "singable" intervals had been most common. Toward the end of the century and well into the eighteenth century, this tendency was reversed; vocal melodies took on many of the characteristics of instrumental melodies, for mixtures of long and short tones, wider range, arpeggiated figures, and larger leaps became usual. In addition, many cantata arias adopted the rhythms and forms of instrumental dance music. Scarlatti's arias, for example, were often cast in the form of minuet, sarabande, or siciliano. This tendency to exchange idioms became marked in other vocal forms also, of course, and in time led to the instrumentally

---

4 Two cantatas are given in *HAM*, No. 258, *Matilde* . . . , and *GMB*, No. 260, *Lascia.* . . .

conceived vocal melodies that are in general typical of Bach's music (see below).

Two additional characteristics of the cantata may be noted. The tendency to employ obbligato instruments in addition to the continuo instruments became almost a requirement; this detail was derived from the *concerto grosso* (see Chapter 15). Many of Scarlatti's cantatas are for solo voice and small groups of instruments, and toward the end of the Baroque

The orchestra in a cantata performance of Bach's time. Engraving from J. G. Walter's musical dictionary, 1732.

period a bare continuo accompaniment was most unusual. In addition, the arias became more homophonic, the bass line simpler, and emphasis was put on vocal virtuosity with a consequent increase of coloratura effects. The other characteristic, even earlier, was to depart from the solo-voice concept and add a second voice (rarely a third) to the cantata. This type, unlike the solo cantata, did not deteriorate into superficiality because of the necessity of treating the two voices individually. In this form, as a chamber duet, the cantata enjoyed a favored position in the seventeenth and eighteenth centuries. Virtually all the composers who wrote solo cantatas also wrote duets—Monteverdi, Carissimi, and Cesti among them. A variety of textures, interplay of melodic motives, and sustained lyricism characterized the duet, and it reached a high level of symmetry, consistency of style, and formal perfection. Steffani, Handel, and Bach all excelled in this form.[5]

The Italian chamber cantata was carried to other countries also. Marc-Antoine Charpentier (1634–1704), André Campra (1660–1744), and Louis-Nicolas Clérambault (1676–1749) were among the successful cantata composers in France. Charpentier, hailed as the representative of Italian style in France, was a pupil of Carissimi and developed in his cantatas a flowing, lyric style in the best *bel canto* tradition. Campra and Clérambault, profiting from Lully's development of French recitative in his operas, employed a similar type of recitative in their cantatas. The arias in general, however, are Italian in style, with accompaniments influenced by the trio sonata (see page 294).

Continuo Song

GERMAN secular music of the seventeenth century was also affected by the Italian style, but the development did not follow a direct line. Rather it was the result of a conflict between the influence of Italian monody, *bel canto,* and virtuosic stylization on the one hand, and the performance of simple folklike melodies on the other. In the first decades of the century, German composers seemed somewhat reluctant to employ the innovations of the Florentine Camerata. Hans Leo Hassler (1564–1612), Melchior Franck (c. 1579–1639), and many others, for example, composed songs for voices and instruments.[6] The dancelike spirit and freshness of the Italian manner are recaptured in these songs, but a part for continuo is not usually included, nor do the songs employ the rich chromatic style of Italian music of the time.

Not until the 1620's did elements of the monodic style, including the recitative and continuo, take hold in German music. In the vocal works of Johann Hermann Schein (1586–1630), the continuo was firmly established. Schein's *Musica boscareccia* (1621–1628) consisted of sets of

---

5 An early example of a duet related to the cantata type, by Giovanni Capello, is given in *GMB,* No. 180, *Abraham.* A true chamber duet by Steffani is found in *GMB,* No. 242, *Occhi.* . . .

6 A six-part song by Hassler is found in *GMB,* No. 152, *Ach, süsse Seel';* a song by Demantius in *GMB,* No. 154, *Es ist nit.* . . .

strophic songs in which optional methods of performance—solo songs or duets, with or without instrumental accompaniment—were provided for.[7] The texture combines chordal and imitative passages; the sections, compounded of rhythmic motives and usually dancelike in spirit, are often separated by pauses.

The song with continuo accompaniment flourished widely in Germany between about 1640 and 1670. Outstanding composers included Heinrich Albert (1604–1651), Andreas Hammerschmidt (1612–1675), and Adam Krieger (1634–1666). The transition from simple, appealing songs, sometimes in dance rhythms and with unassuming melodic charm (see EXAMPLE 93), to elaborate songs in *bel canto* style can be seen in the works

EXAMPLE 93

Albert, Continuo song

of these composers.[8] The strophic form, with *ritornelli* between stanzas, continued to be widely used. A characteristic combination of lyric melody, rhythmically alive accompaniment, and an air of humor give Krieger's songs particular charm. The fact that the songs were sometimes called arias testifies to the influence of the opera on the smaller forms.

The instrumentally accompanied songs served an important social function in seventeenth-century Germany. They provided material for the *Musizieren*—informal music-making—that has traditionally been an important element of German life. Groups of humble amateur musicians, recovering from the devastating effects of the Thirty Years' War (1618–1648), performed the songs for self-entertainment and as a means of re-

7 Two songs by Schein are given in *GMB*, No. 187, *Viel schöner . . .* and *Gleich wie. . . .*

8 Examples of the songs of Albert, Hammerschmidt, and Krieger are given in *GMB*, Nos. 193, *Der Mensch . . .* , *Du vormals . . .* , *Wir sehn . . .* ; 194, *Nirgend hin . . .* ; and 209, *Rheinwein, O schöne . . .* , respectively. Other songs are found in *HAM*, Nos. 205, *Auf, mein Geist*, and 228, *Adonis Tod*.

storing a modicum of normal social life. The songs thus entered firmly into the cultural tradition of the country and laid a foundation for the art songs of the nineteenth century.

Toward the end of the century and beyond, Italian influences became stronger and the continuo song approached the style and organization of the chamber cantata. Operatic recitatives, *da capo* arias, and the *concertato* elements of the Baroque madrigal sometimes appeared. These elements are seen in arias by Johann Theile (1646–1724), Philipp Erlebach (1657–1714), and many other composers active in the period about 1670 to 1730. Instrumental *ritornelli* became more elaborate, the vocal line often took on a high degree of embellishment, and the mood became outspokenly dramatic.[9] Works of this kind usually appeared in sets or collections, often supplied with fanciful titles. Johann Staden's *Venuskräntzlein* ("Wreath of Venus") and Erlebach's *Harmonische Freude musikalischer Freunde* ("Harmonious Joys of Musical Friends") are examples. To this type belongs one of the most influential collections of the early eighteenth century, namely *Die singende Muse un der Pleisse* ("The Singing Muse of the [River] Pleisse," 1736 and 1745), by Sperontes, a pseudonym for Johann Scholze (1705–1750). Sperontes' work, as well as a similar collection by Telemann published in 1734, stands virtually at the end of the Baroque period. Elements of Rococo style (see below) had begun to enter the continuo song. A new sophisticated naiveté, a deliberate attempt at musical simplicity, and a decline of the continuo mark the songs of the following period.[10]

Baroque Mass

THE INSTRUMENTALLY accompanied secular vocal music written in Italy shortly before and after 1600 had been characterized by a new kind of texture described above under the term *concertato*. Early in the seventeenth century the *concertato* style also gained a commanding position in the field of church music—without, however, driving the *stile antico* completely out of favor. Masses which purported to be in the style of Palestrina continued to be written, for example. Since the latter were in the old style, and thus were in a sense opposed to the new (which included the use of instruments), it became customary to disregard the fact that Renaissance works too had often required instrumental support and to think of them as being for voices alone. Soon the term *a cappella* (in chapel style) was applied indiscriminately to all vocal works in which instrumental parts were not specifically included—and a historical misconception of lasting strength was born. While composers such as Felice and Giovanni Anerio, Gregorio Allegri, and many others continued to write in a modified Renaissance idiom, works in the new *concertato* style soon overwhelmed those to which the *a cappella* designation was given.

9 See examples by Theile (1667) and Erlebach (1710) in *GMB*, Nos. 210, *Durchkläre dich . . .* , and 262, *Fortuna;* and one by Erlebach in *HAM*, No. 254, *Himmel. . . .*

10 Examples from the collections by Sperontes and Telemann are given in *GMB*, Nos. 289, *Liebste . . .* , and 299, *Die vergessene. . . .*

An account of the Mass in the Baroque period must deal largely with the gradual domination of the *concertato* principle.

The Mass in general, whether accompanied or not, at first remained close to the choral idiom, especially in Rome. Felice Anerio (*c.* 1560–1614) wrote works very much in the style of Palestrina, although later composers adopted the polychoral manner of Venice. Paolo Agostino (1593–1629) and Orazio Benevoli (1605–1672) were among the leaders of a massive, spectacular school of composition. A famous Mass by Benevoli, written for the consecration of the Salzburg Cathedral in 1628, employed eight choirs, entire families of string and wind instruments, and continuos—fifty-three separate parts in all.[11] In works such as this the choirs were spatially separated: some in the choir loft, others under the dome, and so on. In this way composers of the time sought to come to terms with the architecture of their churches.

While spectacular Masses of the Roman school employed instruments and departed in other ways from the *stile antico,* they were not truly representative of the *concertato* style. And while true *concertato* Masses were written elsewhere in Italy, they have not yet been thoroughly studied; little can be said about them. In Austria, however, as well as in the Catholic sections of Germany, the presence of the *concertato* Mass is well documented. The earlier composers, especially Johann Stadlmeyer (1560–1648), Christoph Strauss (*c.* 1580–1631), and Giovanni Valentini (?–1649), all connected with the Hapsburg Imperial court, are significant in this connection. They wrote partly in *concertato* and partly in a purely vocal style; the strict division between vocal and instrumental parts was not yet definite. Only some fanfarelike inserts are purely symphonic. Elements of the Renaissance parody Mass are also found. A stylistic distinction between chorus (*tutti*) and solo was made, and a *sinfonia* preceded the *Kyrie.* Not until after the middle of the century, for example in Masses by Antonio Bertali (1605–1669) and Joseph Schmelzer (*c.* 1623–1680), did a more unified, quasi-contrapuntal, or outspokenly chordal style become usual. To Bertali has been attributed the introduction of the long and elaborately fugal "Amen" at the close of the *Credo* and *Gloria.* To what extent this gives evidence of the domination of the music over the liturgy is a matter for speculation.

The Mass in the second half of the century—in Munich and Salzburg as well as Vienna—gradually came under the influence of the opera; indeed, the majority of composers of sacred music were also active in the secular field. Schmelzer, Johann Kerll (1627–1693), and Heinrich Biber (1644–1704) were prominent among them. A further elaboration of the solo passages—running figures in the accompaniment and ornamentation in the vocal line—became typical. Contrasts between the solo and choral passages became more pronounced (see EXAMPLE 94), and the longer Mass movements (*Credo* and *Gloria*) were often divided into shorter sections set variously or alternately for solo, ensemble, or chorus. The use of the

11 See Adler, *Handbuch der Musikgeschichte,* I, p. 511, for a description of a similar Mass by Mazzochi.

EXAMPLE 94

Schmeltzer, *Missa nuptialis*

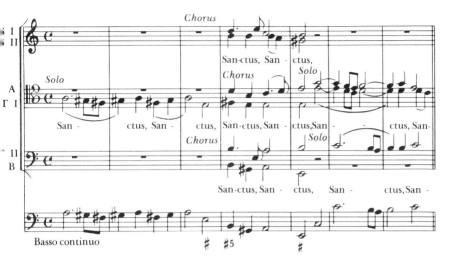

solo quartet became typical. Thematic material itself also approached secular models; coloratura as well as *bel canto* melodies in the solo passages and dramatic chordal writing in the choruses resembled their operatic counterparts. Johann Joseph Fux (1660–1741), one of the last adherents of strict contrapuntal writing,[12] attempted to adapt Palestrinian textures to Baroque harmony. But he also on occasion employed the Roman-Venetian-Neapolitan amalgamation and composed accompanied Masses on the model of his Viennese predecessors, Schmelzer and Kerll.

Concertato and Motet

THE MOTET in the seventeenth century underwent a series of changes that led first to its considerable expansion and then to its complete transformation into a new form. Early in the century the *concertato* principle was applied to the motet. A work by Ludovico Grossi da Viadana (1564–1645), published in 1602 under the name *Cento concerti ecclesiastici* ("One Hundred Ecclesiastical Concerts"), in a sense bridged the gap between the Renaissance motet and its emerging Baroque counterpart. The *Cento concerti* included some text settings for one voice, others for two, three, and four voices; thus a selection could be made when a full quartet of singers was not available. And while the work included an obligatory continuo, it did not employ other aspects of the *concertato* style.

Viadana's work was imitated by other composers, mostly of the Roman school, in whose works the monodic style and *concertato* textures took firm root. Still other composers not associated with Rome, notably Monteverdi and Alessandro Grandi in Venice and Marco da Gagliano in Flor-

12 The *Qui tollis* from Fux's famous *Missa canonica* is given in *GMB*, No. 271.

ence, composed *concertato* motets; here the interplay of voices and instruments resulted in a brilliant and colorful style. As late as the first decades of the eighteenth century such motets were still being composed in many Italian cities, in Paris, Vienna, and elsewhere.

In France the *concertato* motet often became an adjunct to the Low Mass (spoken or chanted, in contrast to the High Mass, which was sung), which Louis XIV preferred. The Low Mass was elaborated and expanded through the addition of imposing motets for voices and instruments. Lully, Charpentier, and Michel-Richard de Lalande (1657–1726) all contributed to the literature. Lully, in typically Baroque fashion, made his motets into large-scale works of several movements, complete with soloists, chorus (sometimes double chorus), and the full orchestra of his time. Contrapuntal, dramatic, and sonorous, the motets brought the lavish resources of the theater into the chapel. Charpentier's motets, almost as massive as Lully's, were melodious rather than spectacular, and Lalande's were distinguished by mellifluous counterpoint, dramatic expressiveness, and a high degree of elegance and ornamentation.

English Church Music

TOWARD the middle of the seventeenth century, as a consequence of the migration of Italian composers to all parts of Europe, the *concertato* style became widely known. It was applied to many sacred and secular works in a variety of forms. In the Catholic south such compositions bore names which referred to their liturgical use, such as "offertory," "litany," "vespers," and even "motet." In the Protestant north the works were most often called "cantata." Many of the subsequent developments in the field of the cantata (or *Konzert*, as it continued to be called for some decades) took place within the field of Protestant church music, even though the Catholic version held the interest of composers well into the eighteenth century. In England, finally, the Continental variants were assimilated, and a distinctive English contribution to music was achieved.

Humfrey and Blow. The strength of the Renaissance choral tradition, exemplified by the anthems and services of William Byrd and Orlando Gibbons (see Chapter 10), may have contributed to a rather slow acceptance of the continuo and the *concertato* style in English church music. Byrd's works were sung at the Chapel Royal for several decades after his death in 1623, and until about the 1640's English composers were in general content to write anthems in imitation of his style. Verse anthems, with texts taken from the Book of Psalms and in a harmonic style that seldom went beyond that of the early masters, were in the majority.

From about 1639 Italian style devices began to make themselves felt. Walter Porter (c. 1595–1659), one of the early composers of anthems, had been a pupil of Monteverdi, and William Childs (1606–1697) acknowledged the Italian influence in his music. A set of works by Childs, for a small vocal ensemble and continuo, was among the first English compositions of its kind. Continuing with the works of Christopher Gibbons

(1615–1676), the son of Orlando, Matthew Locke (*c.* 1630–1677), and a number of minor composers, the new type of anthem survived the period of the Commonwealth (1649–1660), when psalm-singing was favored over more elaborate forms of musical activity, and rose to full stature with the restoration of the monarchy in the person of Charles II. And after 1660 the accompanied anthem, with *concertato* texture and alternations of solo and choral sections, was developed primarily by Pelham Humfrey (1647–1674), John Blow (*c.* 1648–1708), and their great pupil, Henry Purcell (*c.* 1659–1695).

The music of the Restoration period had little of the intensity, drama, and excitement expressed in Italian music of the time. Reflecting a society which found life pleasant, it was designed to be graceful and entertaining in the style of the French music favored by Charles II. To a certain extent church music was expected to resemble its secular counterpart, specifically, to contain dance rhythms for the special delectation of the King. But Humfrey had mastered the Italian style of musical declamation in spite of his study in France, and the advanced harmonic factor of that style lay close to his heart. And sensitive to matters of prosody, he set the words of his anthems and sacred songs with full regard for their meaning as well as their accentuation.[13] Blow brought much of the emotional tension of Italian music into his dozen or more anthems, and he did not hesitate to write in a contrapuntal style on occasion. In the anthems of both Humfrey and Blow many of the devices typical of Italian *concertati* are found; the ground bass (*basso ostinato*) is an example. Likewise in those of other composers, alternations of solo and choral sections, independent instrumental passages, and a texture that is chordal or homophonic all relate the English anthem of the Restoration period to its Italian prototype.

Purcell. In about his tenth year Henry Purcell was made a chorister of the Chapel Royal, where he received instruction from both Humfrey and Blow. At eighteen he became composer to the King's string orchestra, and at twenty, organist of Westminster Abbey. Three years later he was also appointed organist of the Chapel Royal, and a year later, when he was twenty-four, he became composer to the court—keeping his other posts meanwhile. He died at the age of thirty-six, yet even during his lifetime he was recognized as one of England's greatest composers. His collected works embrace some thirty volumes, including among the sacred works anthems, services, odes, and miscellaneous pieces.

The services contain the regular canticles of the Anglican liturgy, such as the *Te Deum* and *Jubilate* for the morning service, the *Magnificat* and *Nunc dimittis* for the evening. Anthem texts, of various kinds, were drawn mainly from the Book of Psalms. Sacred songs and elegies were not parts of the liturgy but could be performed at private devotions. Odes and welcome songs were for secular, courtly occasions or for feasts (that of St. Cecilia, for example).

Purcell's anthems are among his early works and date from about his

13 A verse anthem by Humfrey is given in *HAM*, No. 242, *O Lord, my God*.

twentieth to his twenty-sixth year. The decline in the popularity of the full anthem, noted above, continued to the end of the century, and the majority of Purcell's are verse anthems. The few full anthems inclined toward the texture of Byrd's works: sonorous polyphony for five to eight voices was most characteristic. The long contrapuntal lines of the Elizabethan period, however, found little place in Purcell's music. Instead his melodies were shorter, at times angular, and somewhat declamatory. Purcell's harmonies, too, showed the results of a half-century of harmonic development in Italian music. Dissonances were no longer chance encounters of melodic lines but parts of a chordal approach, serving to increase the general harmonic tension.

The verse anthems profit from Purcell's familiarity with the music of Humfrey. The same sensitivity to text setting is present, and an even greater awareness of the effect of melodic contour on text meaning. Wide leaps, unusual skips, rhythmic effects in the melody—all such devices increase the descriptive aspects of the texts, and Purcell made full use of them. The external form of the verse anthem greatly resembles that of sacred cantatas elsewhere: recitative and aria sections, overture, *sinfonia, ritornello,* and choral passages in both declamatory and polyphonic styles are found in great variety. Often a high degree of unity between sections is achieved, in that instrumental sections are thematically related to choral or vocal passages. Purcell made clear distinctions between solo and choral idioms. The solo or ensemble sections require a degree of virtuosity, while the choral parts depend upon masses of sound, block chords, or simple but effective counterpoint.[14]

In the verse anthems, and to an even greater extent in the elaborate ceremonial odes, tonal harmony came a large step closer. A few chromatic lines, many cross relations (often present in the works of Humfrey and Blow as well), and occasional modal inflections are still present. But in general the harmonic structure of the works gives evidence of circle-of-fifth progressions, tonic-dominant relationships, tonal centers, and vertical spacing of dissonances.

It was once customary to refer to Purcell's harmonic "crudities" and to compare them unfavorably to the completely tonal, late-Baroque harmonies of Handel, who came to England thirteen years after Purcell's death. That view misunderstood the true historical position of the English master (see EXAMPLE 95). English composers of the seventeenth century were faced with a variety of imported styles and textures. Italian madrigalisms and Renaissance polyphony were still alive in the first decades of the century; the monodic style and the *concertato* principle were well established by the 1650's; and by the final portion of the century, the rhythmic vigor of Lully's music and the ornamented elegance of other French compositions were known. Purcell dealt with this stylistic variety in an individual fashion. Absorbing Italian melodiousness, Lully's rhythmic figures, and the technical novelties of the century, he forged them into a higher

---

14 The final chorus, "Alleluia," from *My Heart Is Inditing,* given in *GMB,* No. 246, illustrates a typical combination of passages in parallel motion, short fragments used sequentially, and chordal declamation.

EXAMPLE 95

Purcell, Anthem: *Be Merciful Unto Me*

unity to which the solid polyphony and sonority of Byrd's music were fundamental. Rather than being a harbinger of late Baroque style, and thus a minor predecessor of Handel, Purcell stands as one who clarified and brought into focus a mélange of English stylistic elements in the middle Baroque period. And for this achievement he holds one of the most honored places in the history of English music.

German Protestant Music

PROTESTANT Germany in the seventeenth century included most of the central and northern regions of the country, as well as a long strip running roughly southwest into Württemberg. Most of these regions adhered to the Lutheran faith, but Calvinist areas existed along the Rhine and such minorities were active even within the Lutheran areas. A distinct difference in attitude toward church music distinguished the two denominations, a difference that greatly influenced the developing Protestant forms of music within Germany and left its mark even on the music of Bach toward the 1730's.

The Calvinist tradition, suspicious of the emotional strength and appeal of music in general, confined itself largely to simple songs, offshoots of the German Psalter, which could be sung by everyone As the reformed Calvinist church emphasized the Christian influence in everyday life, a particular emotional aspect called "pietism" was emphasized. Pietism permeated the thoughts of some Lutheran theologians and laymen as well as of Calvinists, and adherents of Pietism, coming to activity about 1670, followed the Calvinist tradition. The orthodox Lutherans, on the other hand, saw music as a means of glorifying God and favored any kind of vocal or instrumental work serving that function. Two types of music were felt to be especially appropriate by the Lutheran church: freely composed art music, which served subjectively to prepare the listener for the reception of the Divine word, and music based on the Lutheran chorale, which brought the sense of the Scriptures directly to the listener. It follows naturally that the great majority of German Protestant composers adhered to the Lutheran point of view, for only in that view was a full development of music encouraged.

Lutheran composers in Germany, like their Catholic contemporaries in Bavaria, Austria, and elsewhere, had first to come to grips with the new elements brought to music by the Italians. Much of the seventeenth century was taken up with the problem of absorbing the *concertato* principle as well as other outgrowths of the monodic style. The Venetian polychoral style in all its splendor was known and imitated in Germany; works by Hassler, Melchior Franck, and many others specified the use of instruments in the Venetian manner. Other composers, notably Johann Hermann Schein (1586–1630) and Johann Staden (1581–1634), composed monodies and similar works for voices and continuo. Even in the earliest German works in this style, however, a well worked-out instrumental accompaniment was the rule. One receives the impression that German composers, used to the full sonorities of the sixteenth century, found unadorned monodies too sparse for their tastes. In all these works, whether they were derived from Venetian or Florentine models, texts from the Psalms or the Gospels (in either Latin or German) were the most usual. The works bore a variety of titles such as *symphonia, cantio sacra, harmonia;* only later did the term *geistliches Konzert* (sacred concert) become fairly standard. An important theoretical work, *Syntagma musicum,* by Michael Praetorius (1571–1621), contains in its Part III (1619) an account of ways to combine instruments and voices and suggests ways in which a motet (by Lasso, for example) could advantageously be elaborated through the addition of instrumental prologue and interludes, ornamentation, and the like. The integrity of Renaissance style, it is clear, fell victim to the urge to find uses for the new style.

Schütz. Heinrich Schütz (1585–1672), whose many works tower high over those of his contemporaries, was completely successful in amalgamating *concertato* elements with the old style. Born in Hesse and active as a choirboy in Kassel, he journeyed to Venice and studied with Giovanni Gabrieli from 1609 to 1612. In 1617 he was appointed chapelmaster to the Elector of Saxony in Dresden and remained in the employ of the court for fifty-five years. The Thirty Years' War (1618–1648) greatly disturbed the course of music in Dresden, and he made repeated visits to Italy and spent six years—interrupted by returns to Germany—as court conductor at Copenhagen. Schütz achieved in his music the fusion of Venetian and Florentine styles and, more importantly, set a standard for German Protestant music that influenced composers for over a century. Although raised as a Calvinist, he was a Lutheran by conviction. He adhered to the tradition of freely composed art music, however, and made virtually no use of Lutheran chorale melodies. Further, he confined himself almost entirely to the fields of vocal and choral music (his composition of the first German opera was mentioned in Chapter 12); as far as is known, he wrote no independent instrumental music.

Schütz's compositions fall into several categories. One early work was a set of madrigals (old style), in which the dramatic, affective style of Gesualdo and Monteverdi was reborn. In the massive *Psalms of David* (1619), many of them for several choruses and continuo (with additional instruments not always specified), Schütz brought to the polychoral style of Gabrieli the intensity, drama, and word painting characteristic of his madrigals. The *Cantiones sacrae* of 1625, on Latin texts, are in quite another category. These are four-voice motets (the continuo is virtually unnecessary) on liturgical texts, but again the intensity typical of the late works of Monteverdi is suggested. Severe, dissonant, and pictorial, they represent a rare side of Schütz's art.

The three parts of the *Symphoniae sacrae* (1629, 1647, and 1650) are again of quite different character. Part I brings the *concertato* style to full expression. Set for three voices and specified instruments, often with instrumental introductions and *ritornelli,* the *Symphoniae* express Schütz's debt to Monteverdi, whose last two books of madrigals they resemble. Part II consists of smaller *concertati,* thus reflecting the dissolution of the Dresden Chapel as a consequence of the War. Part III, finally, is again for large combinations, including single or double choruses, solo passages, and instrumental ensembles.[15] Again marking a radical shift of style is a set of *Kleine geistliche Konzerte* ("small sacred concerts"), published in 1636–1639, between the first two parts of the *Symphoniae.* Like Part II of the latter, the *Konzerte* reflect the breakdown of Schütz's vocal forces at Dresden; they are for one or a few voices, with continuo alone. Here the

15 One of the most moving of these pieces, *Saul, was verfolgst du mich?* ("Saul, Why Persecutest Thou Me?"), is given in *HAM*, No. 202.

composer modeled his style on Florentine monodies but succeeded in avoiding the stiffness and aridity of the models.[16]

In spite of his lifelong championship of Italian styles, Schütz expressed his concern that younger composers had lost the art of writing good counterpoint. In his *Geistliche Chormusik* of 1648 he wrote in a deliberately archaic style that is nevertheless infused with the harmonies of his own day. Some works in the set require instrumental accompaniment, while others are designed for *a cappella* performance (see EXAMPLE 96).

EXAMPLE 96

Schütz, *Unser Wandel*

Here is an unlikely amalgam of Rennaissance and Baroque styles; only the controlled intensity and technical skill of the composer kept the work from being a historical curiosity. At the time (1648) Schütz was in his sixties, but he had lost none of his creative energy. Another category of works, composed when he was approaching or had passed his eightieth year, will be discussed below (see page 268).

Other composers. The other type of Lutheran music, that in which a chorale was employed, emerged fully as early as the freely composed type to which Schütz directed his attention. One of the earliest seventeenth-century examples was the chorale motet. In works of this kind the chorale melody, roughly analogous to a Gregorian chant melody, was employed as a *cantus firmus.* It could be used in chordlike homophony, with the other parts written in the same note values; it could be accompanied by freely composed and independent vocal lines; it could permeate the other parts through the use of imitative texture, and thus give rise to real poly-

16 An example is given in *GMB*, No. 190, *Was hast du. . . .*

phonic treatment; and often it moved freely from voice to voice in the interest of greater flexibility of expression. This development lasted to the middle of the seventeenth century. Chorale motets were written by many composers of the time, notably Praetorius in his *Musae Sioniae* (1605–1610), Hassler in *Psalmen und Christliche Gesäng* (1607), and Scheidt in his *Cantiones sacrae* (1620).[17] The approach to the form was not standardized, however. Schein, for example, in his *Geistliche Konzerte* of 1626 sometimes so disguised the *cantus firmus* with motivic work that the chorale melody can be recognized only with difficulty; and Scheidt introduced a kind of treatment in which each verse of the chorale text was set to a different melody or in a different texture. By the 1650's the chorale motet fell out of favor as a liturgical form and became an occasional piece for funerals, weddings, or civic festivities.

The chorale *concertato* enjoyed a longer life; transformed into the chorale cantata, it remained an important form well into the eighteenth century. Early in the seventeenth century its development in Germany paralleled that of the Italian *concertato*—except, of course, that the German version employed a chorale text (and usually a chorale melody) instead of a psalm. Many of the chorale *concertati* of Praetorius (in his *Polyhymnia* of 1619), Scheidt (in his *Geistliche Konzerte* of 1631–1640), and others employed the brilliant polychoral style of Venice along with rich vocal ornamentation, instrumental *sinfoniae,* and *ritornelli.* In other works fewer vocal forces were called upon, and a form analogous either to the Italian monody or the chamber cantata, for two or three voices and continuo, appeared.[18] Toward the 1660's, finally, elements of the polychoral, monodic, and few-voiced *concertati* began mutually to influence one another. The monodic *concertato,* for example, sometimes appeared with some sections for one voice, others for several, and perhaps a four-part setting of a chorale at the end. Andreas Hammerschmidt (1612–1675), Franz Tunder (1614–1667), and Matthias Weckmann (1619–1674) were chief among the composers who wrote in the traditional style.

The final step in the transformation of the chorale *concertato* took place about 1700. Operatic style, which had affected the development of the dramatic *concertato,* now became marked in the chorale *concertato* as well. A form of several movements—including choruses, arias, sometimes recitatives, and even instrumental pieces—became typical. Textures ranged from simple recitative over a continuo to elaborate six-voice fugues; chorale settings in four-part homophonic style, sometimes set in variation form, were also common. For this stage the name "chorale cantata" is appropriate. Cantatas of this type differ from those composed on the Schütz model only in that they are based on a chorale. The chorale cantatas of Diedrich Buxtehude (1637–1707), Johann Philipp Krieger (1649–1725), Johann Pachelbel (1653–1706), and Johann Kuhnau (1660–1722) are among the outstanding examples of the type.

17 A smaller motet by Eccard, given in *GMB*, No. 159, *Wach auf . . .* , illustrates one aspect of the style.

18 An example by Schein is given in *GMB,* No. 188, *Gelobet. . . .*

Meanwhile, through the last decades of the century, the chorale itself had undergone many changes. Under the influence of Pietistic musical thought, measures of irregular length virtually disappeared from the majority of chorales; a regular duple meter having a quarter-note as the basic unit became most usual, and rhythmic irregularities (such as a triple-meter measure in the midst of duple) were smoothed out. Sometimes, as in the influential collection published by Freylinghausen in Halle in 1704, chorale tunes based on dance rhythms appeared. Melodies became sweetly sentimental and more directly appealing to the untutored churchgoers of the day.

Cantata texts of a new kind also came into vogue. Erdmann Neumeister, a Lutheran pastor at Hamburg, wrote a series of poems that paraphrased Scriptural passages and interpreted the central thought in a moral, pleading, or hortatory tone. These were then set to music in the new cantata style. *Sinfonia,* recitative, aria, chorus, chorale, and similar single-movement forms were combined under a common title (usually taken from the first line of the chorale) and unified by the edifying tone of Neumeister's texts. The so-called reform texts of Neumeister and his followers were of great influence on Lutheran composers to the very end of the Baroque period. The presence of stylistic elements derived from the opera was not questioned by the most orthodox of Lutheran churchmen, for in the Lutheran view all "artificial" music served to glorify God and a distinction between sacred and secular fields was no part of that view. Further developments in the chorale cantata, which occurred primarily at the hands of Bach, will be discussed below.

The Oratorio

THE ORATORIO was the musical result of a devotional movement among laymen in Rome in the years after about 1560. Under the leadership of St. Filippo Neri, a group of men met in the oratory (prayer hall) of a Roman church for devotional services. Sermons, meditations, and prayers were followed by the singing of hymns and similar works in the vernacular, and the musical portion of the services soon assumed large dimensions. Polyphonic *laude* by Palestrina and other composers were gradually replaced by works in monodic style such as Cavalieri's *Rappresentazione di anima e di corpo* ("Representation [of Dialogues] Between Soul and Body," 1600). The development of a more dramatic form soon brought forth the figure of a narrator *(testo),* whose text included scriptural passages, explanatory narrative, and the like, and whose vocal part was usually written in recitative style. However, in a work by Giovanni Francesco Anerio *(c.* 1567–1620), *Teatro armonico spirituale* (1619), the *testo* is sung by a six-part chorus set in *concertato* texture.

In the years up to about 1640 the music designed for the oratory services gained in social stature. The Jesuits in Rome supported it, partly to combat the growing popularity of the opera. It also gained in technical organization; the requirement of a *testo,* a chorus, and an instrumental group

became standardized, and the form began to be called "oratorio" in reference to the type of hall in which it was usually sung. Since it was designed
for the populace at large, it was supplied with text in Italian, but another
type, for the aristocracy and the clergy, was written in Latin. The chief
difference between the oratorio of either type and the opera lay in the
fact that the oratorio often required a *testo* and stressed the chorus,
whereas the opera did neither.

The principal composer of the Latin oratorio was Giacomo Carissimi
(1605–1674). His fifteen works in this form brought to dramatic expression episodes in the lives of Biblical figures. Typical in this regard are
David and Jonathan, The Judgment of Solomon, Job, Abraham and Isaac,
and his masterpiece, *Jephtha.* In placing the chorus in the center of the
dramatic action Carissimi set a pattern for the great majority of all later
oratorios. Chordal texture, simple triadic harmonization, relentless driving rhythm, and variety in vocal color (for example, solo and ensemble
passages as well as passages for double chorus are found) gave Carissimi's
oratorios an elemental strength that even Handel admired half a century
later (see Example 97). The recitative avoided the dry, *parlando* style of
the contemporary Venetian opera and contained bits of lyric melody, expressive rhythmic figures, and the like.[19] Arias and arioso passages inclined
toward the *bel canto* style, which was soon to become characteristic in the
oratorio as it had in the opera and the cantata.

Italian composers in the last third of the seventeenth century, primarily
active in Bologna and Modena, favored the *oratorio volgare,* in which the
text was in the vernacular. Here the element of drama rose to supreme
importance. To heighten the dramatic conflicts implied in the texts, many
composers minimized the expository function of the narrator and removed
the chorus from its central place in the action. Instead they emphasized
the purely melodic aspects, concentrating on virtuosic or *bel canto* arias,
sung by *castrati,* and clearly separating recitative and aria. This kind of
oratorio stands opposite the oratorio of the Carissimi type, based on a
Latin text, in which the chorus remained of prime importance. The names
of Giovanni Battista Vitali (*c.* 1644–1692), Giovanni Legrenzi (1626–
1690), and Alessandro Stradella (1642–1682) are prominent among the
many oratorio composers outside Rome. Most of their works have remained in manuscript, but on the basis of the few available reprints [20] one
can call attention to the further inroads of operatic style on the oratorio.
Stradella, for example, employed the same kind of affective, chromatically
embellished harmony that is found in his operas and composed instrumental parts in a colorful, varied texture far removed from the sacred
style found in earlier works. In the fourteen oratorios of Alessandro Scarlatti the stylistic unification of opera and oratorio was fully accomplished.
Two types are found. One still reveals the influence of Stradella in its
rich instrumental detail. The other is quite operatic in character: the *da*

19 A portion of Carissimi's *Jephtha* is given in *GMB,* No. 198, "Cum vidisset . . .";
a selection from his *Jonas* is in *HAM,* No. 207, "Miserunt. . . ."
20 An aria from Stradella's *Suzanna* is given in *GMB,* No. 230, "Da chi spero. . . ."

EXAMPLE 97

Carissimi, *Baltazar*

capo aria appears; recitatives are often accompanied by instrumental ensembles rather than by a continuo alone; and a lyric, ingratiating melodic style, which did not distinguish between sacred and secular text, is typical.

The oratorio failed to gain a real foothold in France. Among the few major composers to write in the form was Marc-Antoine Charpentier

(1634–1704), a pupil of Carissimi. He modeled his works on those of his teacher, with Latin text in some cases and with French in others,[21] restoring the chorus to a place of central importance. But he went beyond Carissimi in the richness of his orchestration and felt no need to confine himself to simple harmonies, as Carissimi had done to make his works directly appealing to masses of people; he wrote, rather, in an affective, modulatory style.[22] Charpentier's efforts to establish the oratorio in France went for nought, however. Partaking of both the church and the theater but firmly identified with neither, the oratorio was an ambiguous form that failed to make a rational appeal to Frenchmen. Almost a century went by before other significant French oratorios were written.

In Vienna, on the other hand, the oratorio became well established, but primarily at the court. Various Austrian emperors were themselves active as composers. A *Sacrifice of Abraham* by Leopold I, written in German and performed in 1660, is often called an oratorio, but it is actually representative of the *sepolchro,* a special type of Austrian composition.[23] The *sepolchro* was a short narrative work of sacred character, performed on Good Friday with costumes and scenery, before the sepulcher in the church. Many works in this form were composed by Italians attached to the court; they served as substitutes for opera, which could not be performed during the Lenten season, and provided a form out of which a true Austrian oratorio could be created. About 1700 the composition of the *sepolchro* type ceased and the oratorio on the Italian model took its place. Virtually all the Viennese court composers—notably Antonio Draghi, Antonio Caldara, and Johann Joseph Fux—wrote oratorios that were scarcely distinguishable from their operas.

Protestant Germany was perhaps better prepared to accept the emerging oratorio in the mid-seventeenth century than any other country. In Nuremberg, for example, it had long been customary to combine a public reading of portions of the Bible with interspersed short vocal or choral pieces as well as chorales. Cantatas based on sacred texts and written in monodic style were performed throughout Germany; Schütz's contributions to that literature (the *Geistliche Konzerte*) have been discussed. And finally, the portions of the Gospels dealing with the Betrayal and Crucifixion of Christ were set to music; the texts for the Evangelist (or narrator) and other individuals were set in recitative style, and those for the disciples, the crowd, and other groups were set for chorus. This type of setting, called a Passion, was modeled upon earlier settings, such as a twelfth-century plainsong version, in which the various textual sections were divided among several chanters, and a fifteenth-century motetlike version, in which the parts for the Evangelist, the Apostles, and all the other characters in the sacred drama were set for choral groups. The

---

21 See *HAM,* No. 226, for a selection from Charpentier's *La Reniement de St. Pierre* ("The Denial of St. Peter"), in Latin despite its French title.

22 See H. Wiley Hitchcock, "The Latin Oratorios of Marc-Antoine Charpentier," in *Musical Quarterly,* XLI (1955), pp. 41–65.

23 An aria from another of Leopold's eight oratorios, *Die Erlösung des menschlichen Geschlechtes* "The Redemption of Humanity") is given in *GMB,* No. 225, "Jesus tot."

seventeenth-century Passion, especially as it developed in Protestant Germany, may be thought of as a special kind of oratorio, for its technical components, musical style, and religious content are like those of the true oratorio in all essential respects.

The oratorios of Schütz, like the other classes of his works discussed above (see page 261), represent a fusion of different styles. The earliest work of the set, the *Easter Oratorio* (1623), is reputedly a free adaptation of a sixteenth-century polyphonic Passion by Scandello, and contains a kind of recitative in which modal and operatic elements are combined in highly expressive fashion. Schütz's setting of *The Seven Last Words of Christ* (1645) and the *Christmas Oratorio* (1664) shows the influence of the Italian oratorio of the time. Here, in settings which include recitatives, vocal ensembles, choruses, and instrumental numbers, he wrote dramatically, simply, or poignantly according to the expressive quality of his texts.[24] In his three Passions, those setting the texts of Matthew, Luke, and John, respectively (1666), Schütz reverted to an archaic style. Not even a continuo accompanies the recitatives, which are set in the

EXAMPLE 98

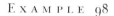

Schütz, *St. John Passion*

EVANGELIST

Da nun Je - sus den Es - sig ge - nom - men hat - te, sprach er:

JESUS   EVANGELIST

Es ist voll - bracht. Und nei - get das Haupt und ver - schied.

S

O hilf Chri - ste, Got - tes Sohn

A

O hilf Chri - ste, O hilf Chri - ste, Got - tes Sohn

T

O hilf Chri - ste, Chri - ste, Got - tes

B

O hilf Chri - ste, Got - tes Sohn_____

24 The opening chorus and a section taken from the final portion of the *Seven Last Words* are given in *HAM*, No. 201, "Da Jesus . . . ," "Und um die. . . ." Other selections from the same work are found in *GMB*, No. 191, Sinfonia, "Und es war. . . ."

style of a modified plainsong, and the choruses are designed for *a cappella* performance (see EXAMPLE 98).[25]

Schütz occupies a unique position in music history. For much of his long life he was an outspoken champion of the new style coming out of Italy. Drama, energy, and utmost expressiveness mark most of his music; he, as much as anyone, provided models for what Baroque sacred music could be. Yet the mystic, ascetic aspects of his character could not be denied. In his eighties he departed from the style he had mastered decades earlier and reverted to a form of expression that would have been quite suited to the consciousness of Renaissance man. The result was a set of works that were strangely anachronistic, works which revealed a man dedicated to expressing only universal Biblical truths. None of his contemporaries or successors was influenced by his Passions; no one could follow where he had led.

The Culmination of Baroque Vocal Style

IN HAMBURG, toward the 1700's, a free approach to the Scriptures and other religious texts became customary. The contributions of Erdmann Neumeister in writing texts for what has been called the "reform cantata" have been mentioned. Other poets, following the lead of a town official, Heinrich Brockes, essayed a similar approach to texts suitable for oratorio and Passion. Even the sanctity of the Scriptures gave way to an interest in transforming favorite Biblical prose episodes into sentimental, allegorical poems. Many composers, taking advantage of the new textual freedom, adopted the operatic style when they set these poems as oratorios. Keiser, Mattheson, Telemann,[26] and Handel did so in composing Brockes's texts on the Passion, but here at least the Evangelist was restored to the list of characters. The poetic freedom declined after a generation or two, under the influence of reforms undertaken by Metastasio in Vienna, and more Biblical sections were included. But the elements of operatic style became a permanent part of the oratorio and colored the style of virtually all church music for over a century.

Handel. When Handel left Germany to take up permanent residence in England in 1712, he had already written two oratorios, *Il trionfo del tempo* (1707) and *La Resurrezione* (1708). Those works, both composed during his Italian visits, revealed Handel's ability to master every style that interested him. The Italian oratorio of the time was essentially a solo vocal medium rather than a choral one, and the textures of the *concerto grosso* found their way into oratorio and opera alike. Handel's compositions reflected these elements; choruses in *Il trionfo* were simple in scope and served only an ornamental function at the ends of acts.

In 1717, while serving as chapelmaster to the Duke of Chandos, Handel

---

25 An extended section of the *St. Matthew Passion* is given in *GMB*, No. 192, "Aber am ersten. . . ."

26 Examples of the styles of Karl Heinrich Graun and Telemann are given in *GMB*, No. 308, "Christus hat . . . ," and *HAM*, No. 272, "Das Lamm . . . ," respectively.

briefly abandoned his chief interest, the composition of operas. He turned to other fields, composing his first English oratorio, *Esther* (first version, 1720), and a number of other works, notably the so-called Chandos anthems (1719). Within a few years he resumed his operatic composition and remained active in that field to about 1740, when the difficulties he had periodically experienced in connection with his operatic ventures (see page 238) increased. The last two decades of his life were devoted to the composition of oratorios; between *Esther* (1720) and *The Triumph of Time and Truth* (1757, a revision of his first oratorio, composed fifty years earlier) lie some two dozen works.

Handel's indebtedness to other composers, noted in connection with his operas, is also evident in the oratorios. His concept of placing the chorus at the center of the dramatic action was probably derived from Carissimi. Various choral textures he employed can be traced to the music of Venice, of Vienna, of Hamburg. Formal schemes such as the *da capo* and instrumental treatment such as seen in the *concerto grosso* were common property of a host of Italian composers. And the massive choral idiom itself was part of the Purcell tradition. In Handel's works, however, all these diverse elements were refined and synthesized to such an extent that a unique Handelian style resulted, unified by the purity of the *bel canto* melodic line of which Handel was one of the greatest masters.

A few of Handel's oratorios are essentially nondramatic and their texts based on allegorical poems: *The Occasional Oratorio* and *L'Allegro* are examples. Others resemble operas in their choice of subject matter (mythological or Biblical heroes) and dramatic treatment: *Hercules, Susanna,* and *Semele* represent this type. The majority, however, deal with Old Testament figures who represent their people in a monumental, almost impersonal manner. At the same time, Handel so treated the Biblical figures and events that they became symbols for contemporary problems—hence their immediate appeal to the general public. *Belshazzar, Saul, Joshua,* and *Judas Maccabaeus* are typical of this treatment. *Messiah* is unique, for it is essentially a reflective work of pure devotion and its text has few of the characteristics of drama.

Any discussion of Handel's oratorios must recognize the powerful role played by the chorus. Dramatic episodes, moments of contemplation, points upon which subsequent action hinges—virtually all were given to the chorus. The variety of means Handel employed to achieve this role resulted in the creation of a new choral idiom. Whether set as choral recitatives, as dances, in *concertato* style, or in polychoral style, the choruses bring to expression a wealth of imagination and technical resource unmatched in the field. The choral movements are surrounded by an array of solos and ensembles and supported by a rich, throbbing orchestral accompaniment that is equally varied. Ornamental virtuosic passages alternate with expressive *bel canto* melodies.[27] The counterpoint is flexible and dramatic rather than strict or severe. Thematic motives

---

27 An aria from the revised version of *The Triumph of Time and Truth* is given in *GMB*, No. 280, "Guardian Angels. . . ."

Handel [RIGHT] among his players and singers at an oratorio performance. Contemporary drawing, artist unknown.

are employed in part only; imitations are short—even in fugues—and the polyphonic writing often gives way to chordal texture. Finally, the driving rhythmic force that is one of Handel's finest characteristics is everywhere present.

Handel's switch from opera to oratorio was symbolic of his turning from the nobility to the people. Where his operas were designed for and supported by the aristocracy, the oratorios were written for a wider public. Perhaps for this reason, the oratorios are more direct in their appeal—and more lasting in their effect—than any comparable group of Baroque works. A few of his contemporaries, notably Keiser, Mattheson,[28] and Telemann, rose above a host of minor composers, but even their oratorios have been

28 A recitative from a Mattheson oratorio is given in *GMB*, No. 267, "Und der Engel. . . ."

forgotten. Handel's works, however, have remained part of the European musical tradition and are respected today—even those that are not often performed.

Bach. In the music of Johann Sebastian Bach the various styles and forms of the Baroque period were synthesized. The mystical element that had lain behind much German music since the time of Martin Luther and had emerged so strongly in the music of Schütz came to expression in more personal form in Bach's. Bach marks at once the highest point of Baroque creativity and its end.

Bach (1685–1750) was born at Eisenach in the shadow of the Wartburg, the castle that had sheltered Luther in 1521. Except for a few years spent under the tutelage of his brother, Johann Christoph, and a short period as a choirboy in Lüneburg, he was largely self-taught. He copied manuscripts of other composers, studying and mastering their styles. His curiosity in musical matters was insatiable, and he remained a student throughout his lifetime. He was employed successively as organist to the Duke of Weimar (1708), chapelmaster to the prince of Anhalt at Cöthen (1717), and cantor at St. Thomas's Church in Leipzig (1723–1750). He looked upon composition as his reason for being, and whether his music was for organ or other instruments, ensemble, solo voice, or chorus, he remained true to a religious spirit that never faltered. Born into a family that had furnished Thuringia with composers and performers for two centuries, he became the most outstanding member of his family and one of the greatest composers of all time.

Among Bach's most notable achievements is his group of cantatas, numbering more than 150 extant works. Perhaps three dozen are secular cantatas or cantatas set for solo voice and instruments. The vast majority of the rest are sacred cantatas, consisting usually of six to ten or more movements. Bach's half-dozen earliest works in this form, dating from about 1705–1708, are similar to the chorale *concertati* of the 1690's. Solos, vocal ensemble numbers, and choruses alternate with instrumental sections, and the pronounced instrumental idiom that became so typical of Bach's vocal lines is already present.

In the years about 1711 to 1717, during his stay at Weimar, Bach adopted the structure and spirit of Neumeister's reform cantatas (see page 264) and several of his texts. In the cantatas of these years the deeply reverent tone and the mystical, symbolic nature of Bach's mature style came to expression. Occasionally, as in the Cantata No. 21, *Ich hatte viel Bekümmernis* ("My Heart Was Greatly Troubled"), or in No. 106, *Gottes Zeit ist die allerbeste Zeit* ("God's Time Is the Best Time"), the sectional form of the *concertato* is still in evidence; abrupt contrasts of tempo and texture are characteristic. The recitatives, arias, and *sinfonie* which loom large in these Weimar cantatas call attention to Bach's complete assimilation of all the forms and expressive devices of his time. Chorales are employed in only two-thirds of these cantatas; Bach was still in the process of synthesizing his style, and he had not yet come to the point of concentrating on one form to the exclusion of others.

Among his duties when he moved to Leipzig was the task of providing a cantata for every Sunday and high feast day of the year: some sixty occasions annually. He reputedly composed five complete sets, totaling about 300 works, of which about half have been preserved. The chorale cantatas, in which all verses of the chorale text are set in a variety of forms, are by far the most numerous. The dozen solo cantatas of the Leipzig period were written in a virtuosic style and in a few cases conclude with a chorale setting. The chorale cantatas, on the other hand, usually begin with a large choral setting of the first verse and end with a simple four-part chorale setting; the middle verses, often employing the melody of the chorale, are set in a variety of arias, duets, and choruses, often cast in the form of variations.

These cantatas, written primarily in the years after 1725, disclose the full extent to which Bach created new forms by combining a variety of older style elements in new fashions. Arias are in the style of an instru-

St. Thomas's Church in Leipzig, where Bach was cantor from 1723 to 1750.

mental concerto; fugal passages are woven into a chorus basically in *con-certato* style; instrumental idioms interpenetrate vocal, which is to say that Bach created a melodic idiom suitable either to the voice or instruments (see EXAMPLE 99). Forms of the early Baroque, such as a set of

EXAMPLE 99

Bach, Cantata No. 5, *Wo soll ich fliehen hin?*

chorale variations or a motetlike movement employing a double *cantus firmus*, are brought to new life under the influence of Bach's unbelievable contrapuntal skill. And through this astounding array of forms and styles and textures flows the spirit of Bach's concern with the liturgy, the spirit of his dedication to the glorification of God. The terms secular and sacred cease to have any meaning in Bach's work, for all of it is fashioned out of the same material, designed to the same end, and infused with his unique spiritual expressiveness.

Four other large choral works belong to the Leipzig period: the *St. John* and *St. Matthew Passions*, the *Magnificat*, and the Mass in B Minor. The *St. Matthew Passion* (1729) represents the most intense point of development in this form. The theatrical, sensational, and sentimental moments that had often characterized the Passions of other Baroque composers are not found in Bach's *St. Matthew*. Here is a work in which poignancy, contemplation, dramatic power, and reverence are combined. The massive double chorus which begins the work is supported by a double orchestra and augmented by a choir intoning the melody of a chorale. Other choruses vary greatly in texture and size; one, the shout on the single word "Barabbas!", is only one measure in length. A variety of expressive arias, an eloquent recitative for the Biblical text given to the Evangelist, and a number of chorales—some of which are used several times with different harmonizations, in keeping with the changing moods of the text—combine to create a work which cannot be compared with any other Passion setting, or with any other oratorio, for that matter.

The Mass in B Minor was written in part for the Catholic court of Dresden; Bach hoped thereby to be named court composer, a title which he later achieved. It is a work, therefore, which is unsuited to the Protestant liturgy, but its size and scope make it equally unsuited to the Catholic. It remains an ideal work that transcends the requirements of either church and brings to a focus Bach's universal religiosity. The operatic style elements that had marred other Baroque Mass settings find no place here; a polyphonic texture dominates. The first *Kyrie* is set as a fugue; other sections are in canonic or imitative style, and in the *Credo* a Gregorian melody is accompanied by what must be called German Protestant counterpoint, to symbolize a union of faiths. Three duets, six arias, and sixteen choruses constitute the work; the emphasis on the choruses, some set in *da capo* form, contributes to the massiveness of the whole. The result is a work that in scope and grandeur rises far above any other setting of the Mass text.

❧ 15 ❧

The Baroque Period: Instrumental Music

O NE OF the most significant aspects of the Baroque period was the emergence of independent instrumental music. It is true that a considerable amount of instrumental music existed before 1600; the principal forms and styles of that music were outlined in Chapter 11. In addition to instrumental arrangements of vocal forms and music for the dance, a few original compositions were written. But the latter were rudimentary and important only as starting points for later developments, and the main activity of major composers was directed toward sacred or secular vocal music rather than instrumental music. The relatively few instrumental ensemble pieces produced by composers of the Venetian school in the decades before 1600 were harbingers of what was to come. In the early seventeenth century, a variety of musical forms specifically designed for keyboard, for instrumental ensemble, or for orchestra were developed. They quickly cast off their dependence upon vocal models; melodic and figural idioms suited to the instruments concerned became essential elements of the new instrumental style. In this sense they may be called independent.

Two principles that had been applied somewhat tentatively in music before 1600 became of considerable importance after that date. Several of the emerging instrumental forms were based on the principle of variation: a melody, phrase, or entire composition was repeated a number of times, each time with one or more of its components altered or varied. The principle of improvisation likewise became a point of departure, especially in compositions for the organ, and gave rise to a number of works which are essentially written-out improvisations. In addition, the rudimentary dance music of the sixteenth century and the instrumental pieces based on the chorale and the canzona were employed in the seventeenth in new ways to provide material out of which the independent instrumental music could evolve.

The present chapter, then, will first discuss briefly developments in the field of lute music and review the state of keyboard forms in sixteenth-century Italy, tracing those forms to their culmination in the late Baroque period. It will then follow the course of music for small ensembles from the Italian *canzona da sonar* (mentioned on pages 198–200) to the trio sonata, which became the principal Baroque chamber-music form of western Europe. And finally it will outline the development of orchestral music in its two principal manifestations: the dance suite and the concerto.

Lute Music

THE ACCOUNT of the lute and its music, given on pages 195–97, may be reviewed briefly to provide a background for seventeenth-century developments. Composers for the lute employed tablature notation, in which the lines represented the strings of the instruments and various symbols, letters, or numerals represented the position of the fingers on the strings as well as the relative lengths of the notes to be played.[1] Tablature notation remained in use until well into the eighteenth century. Sixteenth-century lute music included a variety of *ricercari, fantasie,* and *praeambulae,*[2] but the forms which most greatly influenced the seventeenth century were the various dances and sets of dance pieces.

In the seventeenth century, and especially in France, the lute came to be greatly favored by the aristocracy. It played an important role in the *ballet de cour,* where it accompanied the *air de cour* and took part in lute ensembles. The most accomplished composer of the time was Denis Gaultier (*c.* 1603–1672), member of a family of lute virtuosi. Gaultier worked primarily in the field of dance music and his works were refined and stylized to a degree far beyond those of other lutenists. An essential

---

1 Illustrations and transcriptions of pieces notated in tablature are given in Adler, *Handbuch der Musikgeschichte,* pp. 398–407.

2 See examples in *GMB,* Nos. 93, 94, 115, 138, and 150.

ingredient of Gaultier's style was elaborate ornamentation of all the melodic parts, including various kinds of trills, tremolos, and grace notes. Variation, too, was copiously employed; often a varied repetition took the place of the exact repetition of each part of the dance. Gaultier's dances often appeared in suites of which allemande, courante, and sarabande formed the core, with other dances optional.

An essential feature of much Baroque lute music was its free-voiced style, that is, a style opposed to the strict three- or four-voice writing of a typical keyboard work. A four-note chord could be followed by a few single notes in different registers or ranges, these by a three-note chord, and so on (see EXAMPLE 100a). Yet the existence of a full harmonic structure below the melody was implied in the lute writing, as it were (see EXAMPLE 100b). This feature of lute style was found also in harpsichord music of the time.[3]

3 Other examples of lute music may be found in *GMB*, Nos. 215, 216, and in *HAM*, Nos. 211 and 233.

"The Lute Player." Painting attributed to Caravaggio.

GALLERIE DEL PIEMONTE, TURIN

EXAMPLE 100

Gaultier, *Pavane*

Organ Music

Italy. We have seen that the most influential organ forms in sixteenth-century Italy were at first the keyboard equivalents of French chansons and Latin motets. As mentioned above (see page 199), Marco Antonio Cavazzoni (*c.* 1490–*c.* 1570) set a new line of development in motion in 1523 by transcribing pre-existing vocal chansons. The transcriptions were then "colored" by adding runs and flourishes to the erstwhile vocal lines, and the new form was called *canzona.* His son, Girolamo (*c.* 1520–1560), in 1542 produced a set of organ works called *ricercari,* similar in form and texture to motets, but with sections longer and more definitely separated than the corresponding portions of a motet.[4] The younger Cavazzoni also composed original canzonas (that is, not transcriptions of vocal works), in a contrapuntal texture and a form comprising several short sections in contrasting meter.[5] About 1572, the canzona was taken over by composers of instrumental ensemble and keyboard music and, under the name *canzona da sonar,* became the prototype of the sonata in the seventeenth century. The *ricercare,* on the other hand, remained primarily a keyboard piece (although ensemble *ricercari* exist also); the principal ancestor of the fugue, it appeared in a variety of types.

Girolamo Frescobaldi (1583–1643), organist at St. Peter's in Rome and the most eminent organ virtuoso of his time, contributed to two different forms of the *ricercare,* the polythematic and the monothematic. In the first type he employed a different theme for each section, which consisted of a short fugal exposition such as those in earlier *ricercari* by Giovanni Gabrieli and Merulo in Italy, by Cabezon in Spain, and by a host of minor composers elsewhere. The first theme sometimes reappeared in other sections in augmentation and diminution, however. In the second type he

---

4 A somewhat later *ricercare,* by Willaert, is given in *GMB,* No. 105.

5 A later canzona, by Giovanni Trabaci and in a style similar to Cavazzoni's, is given in *HAM,* No. 191. See also *MoM,* No. 26.

used one theme throughout the various sections, the theme appearing in rhythmic transformations (changed note values and meter) over melodic variants or combined with new countersubjects. This type was called *variation ricercare* and eventually developed into the fugue of the later Baroque period.

The principle of improvisation appeared primarily in the *toccata* and the prelude (or *praeambulum*) for organ. The toccata was a rhapsodic form, stressing a brilliant, virtuosic tone (see page 203). Two books of toccatas by Claudio Merulo (1533–1604), published in 1604,[6] set a standard for Italian organists in the following decades. Frescobaldi also composed toccatas, but his works went far beyond Merulo's in their wide-ranging harmonies, dramatic contrasts, and emotional tension.[7] Indeed, the toccata in general became a vehicle in which organ idioms were established and exploited; to the end of the Baroque period it remained a virtuosic display piece.

The death of Frescobaldi (1643) marked the beginning of a temporary decline of Italian keyboard music. For a time the majority of Italian instrumental composers concerned themselves primarily with music for small ensembles. But in the last decades of the seventeenth century Bernardo Pasquini (1637–1710), organist at Rome and eminent teacher, rose above the numerous minor keyboard composers active in Italy and composed brilliant toccatas and other keyboard works. His canzonas still show the influence of Frescobaldi's variation technique, but his *ricercari* are full fledged fugues. He also wrote a few keyboard sonatas, in which the form and style of the ensemble sonata (see below, page 290) were transferred to the keyboard. It must be stressed, especially in connection with these works, that a true distinction between organ and harpsichord styles was not made until late in the Baroque period.

Holland. Jan Pieterszoon Sweelinck (1562–1621), eminent organist of Amsterdam, brought to a close a long line of Dutch musical masters that had lasted for over two centuries. He was a composer of the transitional period; many of his choral works were written in Renaissance style without continuo, whereas his instrumental works in general are typically Baroque. His toccatas were rhapsodic and brilliant in the Italian manner, and some of them (called "fantasies in the manner of an echo")[8] recall the antiphonal devices of the Venetian school.

Sweelinck's true fantasies, however, are related to the *ricercare* type and are fugues in all but name. A typical fantasy is based on a single subject presented in a number of expositions and heard alternately on tonic and dominant scale steps. A number of different countersubjects may appear during the course of the fantasy, contributing rhythmic vitality and leading to rhythmic climaxes in which running figures and stretto devices dominate (see EXAMPLE 101).[9] Clarity of form is also present; a typical

6 See *GMB*, No. 149, for an example.
7 An example is given in *HAM*, No. 193. See also *MoM*, No. 34.
8 See *HAM*, No. 181, for an example.
9 The entire fantasy is found in *GMB*, No. 158.

EXAMPLE 101

Sweelinck, *Fantasia chromatica*

procedure was to compose a large three-part form in which augmentations of the subject occupied the second part and diminutions the third. The fantasies of Sweelinck greatly influenced the styles of his pupils, notably Samuel Scheidt (1587–1654), and a direct tradition runs from Sweelinck to Bach himself.

The principle of variation employed by Italian instrumentalists in the late sixteenth century and by composers for the virginal in Elizabethan England (discussed above, page 204) found its first great Germanic representative in Sweelinck. Italian and English composers employed the variation principle primarily as a means of lengthening their compositions, and variation served a musical purpose entirely. In Sweelinck's works, on the other hand, variation was applied to chorale melodies as an act of piety and in a sense symbolizes the interpenetration of secular and sacred worlds. The chorale melody, treated as a *cantus firmus* for the most part, was repeated several times in different voices; each time a distinctive figuration or web of motives in the other parts surrounded the chorale, and a set of variations resulted. Chorale variations, as such sets became known, remained an important type of organ music through the entire middle Baroque period.

Germany. In his chorale variations (notably in the *Tabulatura nova* of 1624), Samuel Scheidt adopted the rhythmic characteristics found in Sweelinck but went beyond them. Where Sweelinck had most often employed one rhythmic pattern throughout an entire variation, Scheidt often invented a different but related pattern for each phrase of the chorale melody (see EXAMPLE 102). Thus Scheidt's works in this form gained im-

EXAMPLE 102

Scheidt, Variations on *Warum betrübst du dich?*

measurably in richness and rhythmic variety.[10] In keeping with the custom of the time, one stanza of the chorale was often sung by the congregation or the choir, the next played at the organ, and so on through the entire chorale. The variation set thus provided the composer-organist with a means to express an act of devotion, since any elaboration of the chorale was considered to glorify God.

A host of north German organists of the middle seventeenth century followed the path marked out by Sweelinck and Scheidt. Among the more notable were Franz Tunder (1614–1667), in Lübeck; Matthias Weckmann (1619–1674), primarily in Hamburg; and the long-lived Jan Reinken (1623–1722), also in Hamburg. A greater amount of rhythmic freedom marked the chorale variations of these men, along with an interest in freely elaborating the chorale melody itself. A tendency arose to write only a single variation, in which the chorale melody could be used as a *cantus firmus* in a number of ways or ornamented as a melody in a contrapuntal context; thus arose the chorale prelude. Johann Nikolaus Hanff (1630–1711), organist in Eutin and Hamburg, was one of the foremost composers in this form, in which virtually all German Protestant com-

10 Examples are given in *GMB*, No. 185, and *HAM*, No. 196.

posers wrote.[11] Organ composers in south Germany were strongly influenced by the styles of Italian organists; employed mainly in Catholic churches, they contributed little to the evolution of forms employing the chorale.

Another form to emerge in the middle years of the seventeenth century was the *chorale fantasy*. As early as the *Tabulatura nova* of 1624 Scheidt had used a chorale melody as the basis for a fantasy on the Sweelinck model. Essentially similar to a chorale motet, it consisted of a series of fugal expositions, each one taking for its subject a single line of the chorale. Later composers, however, notably Tunder and Reinken, stressed virtuosic elements in the chorale fantasy. Elaborate ornamentation of the chorale, running passages, broken chords—all set to provide a brilliant effect—became characteristic. And to the extent that the chorale prelude and chorale fantasy flourished, the chorale variations lost some of their strictness, becoming subjective treatments of chorale melodies and preparing the way for the related form of chorale partita.

The dominant position enjoyed by the German Protestant organ school in the middle seventeenth century continued well into the eighteenth. Diedrich Buxtehude (1637–1707), of Swedish birth but active in Lübeck from 1668 as Tunder's successor, Johann Pachelbel (1653–1706), organist in Erfurt and Nuremberg, Friedrich Zachow (1663–1712), Handel's teacher in Halle, Georg Böhm (1661–1733), in Lüneburg, and Johann Gottfried Walther (1684–1748), in Weimar—these men were prominent among the dozens of capable and industrious organists of the time. Many of them were notable for their influence on Johann Sebastian Bach, and all contributed to the solidification of the textures and forms of organ music.

The various kinds of chorale treatment which had occupied composers through the 1670's were expanded still further in the following fifty years, after which they rose to their highest level of artistic development at the hands of Bach. Four types of manipulation, based on those used earlier in the period, rose to prominence and led to the chorale prelude, chorale fugue, chorale partita, and chorale fantasy. Pachelbel and, later, Walther excelled in the composition of all four types.

The *chorale prelude* was the most influential in view of later developments. It contained sections in imitative or fugal style placed just before and between the *cantus firmus* lines of the chorale verses. The subjects were derived from the chorale itself, and even though the prelude employed a polyphonic texture composed of short motives and rhythmic figures, the melody stood out clearly. This was perhaps made necessary by the function of the chorale prelude, that is, to serve as an introduction for congregational singing. The chorale preludes of Buxtehude and Pachelbel stand next to Bach's in technical variety and expressive worth.

When fugal treatment dominated, the form was called *chorale fugue*.

11 Steps in the evolution of the chorale prelude from the single variation of Scheidt to a fully developed example by Bach may be traced in *HAM*, No. 190, a–d. See also *GMB*, No. 243, for a chorale prelude by Pachelbel.

In this form the fugue theme was derived from the first line of the chorale, and subsequent lines were usually treated in imitative fashion and embedded in the contrapuntal texture. A similarity in general style to the chorale motet was still marked, but organ idioms in the counterpoints and a wide-ranging harmony made the chorale fugue into a thoroughly modern form.

The *chorale partita,* derived from the chorale variations of Scheidt, was favored by virtually all the organ composers of the time. Pachelbel, Böhm, and Walther wrote outstanding works in this form. Here, perhaps more than in any other form employing the chorale, the individuality of the respective composers was revealed. Pachelbel, a virtuoso at heart, wrote more brilliantly than many of his contemporaries. Böhm brought to the chorale partita the elegance and grace of the French keyboard style. Buxtehude at times employed the rhythmic patterns of the dance suite (see below) in his partitas; the chorale in such cases was set successively in the style of an allemande, courante, and sarabande. Walther, finally, wrote in a solid contrapuntal style and exploited the full sonorities of the organ.[12]

The *chorale fantasy,* favored especially by Buxtehude, moved further in the direction of a brilliant display piece and often became similar to the toccata. The chorale was often simply a point of departure; Buxtehude habitually used only fragments of the melody to develop a brilliant and rhapsodic rather than hymnlike tone.

Organ compositions not using the chorale flourished also. Fugal devices, emerging out of the *ricercare* of Frescobaldi and his school and carried forward by Sweelinck in his fantasies, were solidified and regularized in the middle of the Baroque period, and the four- or five-voice fugue was the result. In Buxtehude's works the fugue was often the second section of an extended movement called "prelude" or "preamble," an outgrowth of the Italian toccata. The first section in such cases was usually brilliant, composed of broken chords, running passages, or other types of virtuosic figuration. Eventually, in the early eighteenth century, the two sections were actually separated, and the pair of "prelude and fugue" rose to a high level of workmanship.[13] The toccata proper, building upon the brilliance introduced into the form by Frescobaldi and Sweelinck, paralleled its relative, the chorale fantasy, in virtuosic effects and dazzling technical display.

Harpsichord Music

THE EVOLUTION of a harpsichord literature, as opposed to that for the organ, was not accomplished until after the middle of the Baroque period. Composers of several countries contributed to it, drawing on a variety of formal types. The variation principle was of prime importance

12 See *GMB*, No. 291, for an example.

13 See *GMB*, Nos. 249 and 265, for such pairs by Buxtehude and Fischer; and *HAM*, Nos. 215, 234, and 237, for similar works by Tunder, Buxtehude again, and Johann Christoph Bach.

in the early years of the period, and elements of the ensemble dance suite (see below), of vocal works, and of organ compositions became ingredients of the new literature. Variation sets based on dances, as found in the compositions for the virginal in England before and after 1600 (see pages 204–05), were written for the harpsichord in the seventeenth century by Italian and German composers. Fancies for the virginal continued to be written. In addition, composers for the harpsichord adopted stylistic elements found in the music of their French contemporaries, notably the suite form with dance movements and with many of the French *agréments* or melodic ornaments. Matthew Locke, John Blow, and Henry Purcell were the most prominent English composers in this area.

France. The dance suite (also called *ordre* or *partita*) for harpsichord became one of the most important items of the emerging literature. The harpsichord suite was at first not cast in a regular order; a number of allemandes, two or three courantes, and the like were common. Only later did it adopt the regular sequence of allemande, courante, sarabande, with an occasional gigue. The broken style of lute music was taken over by the harpsichordists and refined and standardized. The ornaments of lute music were modified or discarded, and a number of new *agréments* were applied to the melodic line to give it unprecedented delicacy and rhythmic animation (see EXAMPLE 103). In many cases fragmentary voices

E X A M P L E   103

Chambonnières, Sarabande

entered the composite texture on subdivisions of the main beats, adding up to a succession of short notes that contributed greatly to the rhythmic vitality of the whole (see EXAMPLE 104).

Jacques Champion de Chambonnières (*c.* 1602–1672), chamber musician to Louis XIV, was the first eminent composer among the French harpsichordists, and an esteemed teacher as well. His pupils included Louis Couperin (*c.* 1626–1661), the first of a long line of Couperins prominent in French music into the nineteenth century, and Jean Henri d'Anglebert (*c.* 1628–1691), who succeeded Chambonnières at the royal court. In the works of these men the characteristic style of French harpsichord music was established. The dance suite was regularized to include allemande, courante, sarabande, sometimes gigue, and possibly other movements as well. But variations (called *doubles*) of single movements, especially courantes, often appeared in place of one or another of the more usual movements. Couperin at times inclined toward a more solid texture by including fugal and even canonic sections in his dances. Striking modulations and a thicker texture, often including four real parts, became characteristic, especially in the works of d'Anglebert. About the 1650's, the French harpsichord style became important as an article of export, to be widely imitated by composers in other countries.[14]

Germany. The emergence of a significant German literature for harpsichord was delayed until about 1650; the first major composer in the field was Johann Jakob Froberger (1616–1667). After a boyhood spent in Vi-

EXAMPLE 104

Froberger, Allemande

enna as a choirboy and, later, as court organist, Froberger lived in Italy for several years, where he studied with Frescobaldi. He returned to Vienna in 1641 to a position as organist, but he also made extended concert tours to France and England. His solid German training was enhanced by familiarity with the styles of Italian, French, and English composers, and he became acquainted with the major lutenists and harpsichordists of his time. But rather than assimilating those various foreign influences and blending them into a neutral, quasi-universal style, Froberger was able to master them all and to write distinctively in a variety of styles.

The fragmentary or sectional form that had marked the keyboard canzonas of Frescobaldi and his school (see above, page 280) disappeared in those of Froberger; in its place came a flowing, continuous web of polyphony such as in the fantasies of Sweelinck. The organ toccatas, also, went beyond Frescobaldi's in rhythmic momentum, touches of chromaticism, and dazzling passage work.[15] The virtuosic effect of these works, and the employment of the full idiomatic resources, gave Bach cause to admire them half a century later.

Froberger's harpsichord compositions reveal the influence of French composers, notably of Chambonnières.[16] Occasionally, as in the *Lamento*

14 Examples of the style of the French harpsichordists may be found in *GMB*, No. 218, and *HAM*, Nos. 212, 229, and 232.

15 An example is given in *HAM*, No. 217.

16 A suite by Froberger is given in *GMB*, No. 205. The fourth movement, a gigue, was not present in the original but was inserted in a posthumous edition.

on the death of Ferdinand IV, he touched upon the field of program music; the *Lamento,* the first movement of a suite, ends with an ascending scale representing the ascent of the emperor's soul.[17]

German developments later in the seventeenth century were marked by a growing separation of harpsichord and organ idioms. This development had been anticipated by south German (Catholic) composers, who wrote primarily for the harpsichord because the organ played a minor part in the Catholic service, generally confined to toccatas and versets (the chorale was not employed, of course). The north German organists continued to concern themselves primarily with chorale forms, with single movements such as toccatas and fantasies, and with preludes and fugues. The harpsichordists—or the organists whenever they composed for the harpsichord—completed the evolution of the suite and regularly added the gigue as a last movement. Further, they made use of the form of the Lully overture (see above, page 227) when they added an introductory movement to the suite. And on occasion they adopted the form of the *sonata da chiesa* (to be discussed below), writing works formally identical with trio sonatas of the *chiesa* type.

Johann Kuhnau (1660–1722), Bach's predecessor as cantor of St. Thomas's Church in Leipzig, is remembered for his *Klavierübung* ("Keyboard Practice," Part II, 1692) and his *Frische Klavier-Früchte* ("Fresh Keyboard Fruits," 1696). It was in these collections that the *sonata da chiesa* form was first used for harpsichord. The alternation of chordal and contrapuntal textures in the sonatas, along with fully developed fugues in some of them, was a new departure and marked the clear separation of German and French keyboard styles. In 1700 Kuhnau published a set of *Biblische Historien* (the full title is "Musical Representations of Various Biblical Stories") in which program music took a firm hold in the harpsichord literature. Here Kuhnau superimposed a series of musical descriptions upon the form of the keyboard sonata. The conflict between David and Goliath, the wedding of Jacob, the illness of Hezekiah—these and other stories are represented.[18] The sonatas contain dance movements, chorale preludes, fugal movements, and complete descriptive titles of the various episodes.

The majority of the organ composers mentioned above also wrote suites for the harpsichord. Buxtehude, Pachelbel, Böhm, and Johann Caspar Ferdinand Fischer (*c.* 1665–1746) are in this group, and to them may be added a later generation including Johann Mattheson (1681–1764), Georg Philipp Telemann (1681–1767), and Gottlieb Muffat (1690–1770). In the harpsichord suites of these men the influence of the French harpsichordists—introduced into Germany by Froberger—was still to be reckoned with.[19] While the four movements of the French suite (often called *ouverture*) had long since been standardized, other movements were occasionally introduced into the German version, which sometimes carried the name *partita.* Variations (*doubles*), and other dances (hornpipe,

17 The *Lamento* is given in *HAM,* No. 216.
18 *The Mortally Ill Hezekiah* is given in *HAM,* No. 261.
19 Suites by Fischer and Pachelbel are given in *HAM,* Nos. 248 and 250.

bourrée, and minuet were popular) were added to the suite. Finally, non-dance movements often found their way into the suite also: slow lyric movements, fast movements in contrapuntal style, Lully-type overtures, or other elaborate forms of prelude. With these additions a closer relationship to the *sonata da chiesa* is seen; the late Baroque harpsichord suite thus became something of an amalgam, a repository for a number of Baroque forms.

Ensemble Music

THE FORMS out of which the independent ensemble music of the Baroque period developed were the *canzoni* of 1523 by Marco Antonio Cavazzoni (see page 199) and the pairs of dances written for the lute, keyboard, and other instruments as far back as the fifteenth century (see page 203). Two separate lines of development will be followed here: the one leading from the canzona to the sonata and then to the *sonata da chiesa*, or church sonata, and the other in the keyboard field leading first to the suite and then to the form called *sonata da camera* (chamber sonata) in Italy. About 1667, roughly in the middle of the Baroque, a merger of the two types took place, to result in the fully developed trio sonata of the late Baroque period.

Canzona to sonata da chiesa. Beginning with ensemble *canzone da sonar* by Nicolò Vicentino (see page 200), a number of similar works designed for combinations of string and wind instruments were published. Works by Merulo, Banchieri, and Giovanni Gabrieli head the list of compositions in which elements of the *canzona da sonar* were standardized. Usually beginning with a dactylic motive (long-short-short), the canzona consisted of short sections in either imitative or chordal style. At least one of the internal sections was likely to be in triple meter, as opposed to the duple meter of the remaining sections.[20] The number of instrumental parts ranged from four to eight or more; Gabrieli's posthumous *Canzoni et sonate* of 1615 contain canzonas with twenty-two parts.

The phrase *da sonar* ("to be played") points to the fact that the works were designed solely for instruments, and not for instruments and voices. In these *da sonar* compositions, instrumental idioms gradually began to emerge; that is to say, their melodies no longer merely "singable," took into account the mechanics, sonorities, and technical characteristics of the instruments for which they were designed.

Shortly after the turn of the seventeenth century, ensemble canzonas were written in the new style, which included a part for *basso continuo.* One of the first works in this style was a *canzona francese* by Ludovico Grossi da Viadana, published in 1602 as an appendix to his *Cento concerti ecclesiastici* and written for four instruments and continuo. In the following decades a large number of canzonas were written for a variety

---

20 The organ canzonas of Frescobaldi often exhibited similar characteristics. See *HAM,* No. 194.

Ensemble concert at the time of Bach. Engraving.

of small ensembles, from one instrument and bass (plus the ubiquitous harmony instrument whose function was to realize the figured bass) to eight or more instruments and bass. But the larger ensembles soon declined in favor and left the field; the remaining ensembles, those for one or two instruments and bass, proved the most popular and the longest lasting. Biagio Marini (1595–1665) and Tarquinio Merula (*c.* 1600–*c.* 1655) were among the many composers who contributed to the literature of the *canzona a tre*.[21]

About 1610 the separation of the canzona literature into two distinct types began to be marked (see page 216) and eventually resulted in the establishment of two different forms. The naming of the forms, however, did not follow suit, for the term "canzona" persisted in both types for several decades. One type, which resembled the *ricercare,* remained the province of more conservative composers. It became a piece in imitative texture, relatively homogeneous as to note lengths, and usually cast in one uninterrupted section; its relationship to the *ricercare* is thus evident

21 A canzona by Merula, from 1637, is given in *GMB,* No. 184; another by the same composer is in *HAM,* No. 210.

although it was generally lighter in texture and style. In this form the canzona became an important item through the seventeenth century in English ensemble music, where it was called "fancy."

Early composers of fancies for ensembles of viols included Alfonso Ferrabosco II (c. 1575–1628), whose Italian father had done much to bring Italian music to the court of Elizabeth, and John Coperario (originally "Cooper," c. 1575–1626). Continuous in the manner of the *ricercare*, their works are consistently imitative and approach fugal writing on occasion. Similar fancies were composed by Matthew Locke, Christopher Gibbons, John Jenkins (1592–1678), and many others.[22] In about 1680 Purcell wrote a set of fancies in the same general style, among the last of their kind to be composed.

The characteristics of the other canzona type included sectional form (six to ten sections were common), chordal or homophonic style, and instrumental (as opposed to quasi-vocal) writing, and a variety of note lengths from very long to very short. To this type the name "sonata" was eventually given. Suggestions of lyricism and a greater range marked the uppermost melody, which soon came to dominate the other voices and the bass. A line of composers from Marini, Salomone Rossi (1587–c. 1630), and Frescobaldi to Giovanni Legrenzi (1626–1690) wrote works in this form.[23] A variety of names was applied to the new form, however; the terms canzona, sonata, symphonia, fantasia, and others were used indiscriminately near the beginning of the century. Not until after the 1650's did a degree of order prevail in this matter.

The sonatas for two or three instruments and continuo by Legrenzi in Venice, as well as those by Marco Uccellini (c. 1605–c. 1667) in Modena and by others, are marked by a reduction in the number of sections to four and an expansion and separation of the sections. The term "sections" must therefore be abandoned and "movements" substituted. Legrenzi's eighteen sonatas of 1655 include four movements, alternately fast and slow, in each sonata; at least one of the internal movements is in triple meter, and the remaining duple-meter movements are predominantly in contrapuntal texture. It was the practice of the church of San Petronio at Bologna to enrich its services through the use of instrumental music. Maurizio Cazzati (c. 1620–1677), chapelmaster of the church, and Giovanni Battista Vitali (c. 1644–1692), up to 1674 a member of the Bolognese orchestra, were among the most eminent composers of the early Bolognese school. Building upon the style elements of Uccellini and Legrenzi, Vitali composed many sonatas for the church, called *sonate da chiesa*, or church sonatas. The usual fast imitative movements in duple meter and slow lyric movements in triple were filled with idiomatic violin figures and great rhythmic drive.[24]

In the work of Arcangelo Corelli (1653–1713), almost a century of development in the sonata was clarified and the form itself became vir-

22 A fancy by Locke is given in *HAM*, No. 230; one by Purcell, in *HAM*, No. 256.
23 See sonatas by Marini in *GMB*, Nos. 182, 183; by Fontana in *HAM*, No. 198; by Cazzati in *HAM*, No. 219; by Legrenzi in *HAM*, No. 220.
24 A *sonata da chiesa* by Vitali is given in *HAM*, No. 245.

tually standardized. Corelli was an accomplished violinist when, in his twenties, he moved from Bologna to Rome. There he became one of the most honored of violinists and composers, as well as a distinguished teacher. His widely imitated system of teaching formed the basis of modern violin playing, and in his compositions he perfected most of the violin idioms in use today. Corelli's *sonate da chiesa* for trio include twelve each in Opus 1 (1681) and Opus 3 (1689); six similar works, but for one violin and continuo, in Opus 5 (1700); and eight *sonate da chiesa* written for the instrumental group of the *concerto grosso* (see page 296) in Opus 6 (1712).

The majority of Corelli's *sonate da chiesa* have four movements in slow-fast-slow-fast tempo sequence. First movements are either chordal or contrapuntal in style, and often contain broad melodies designed to be embellished with improvised ornamentation. Second movements are imitative, sometimes strictly or freely fugal, with the bass often taking part in the imitations. Third movements, slow and in triple meter, are instrumental equivalents of the *bel canto* style. Fourth movements are rhythmically alive, sometimes contrapuntal and sometimes not, but always light and gay.[25] In these works, as well as in others contemporary with them, certain harmonic practices which had been used experimentally or tentatively in earlier decades now became standardized, and fully developed tonality was the result. Passages based on circle-of-fifth modulations or on series of seventh chords evolving out of sets of suspensions marked the style of Corelli (see EXAMPLE 105). A similar style is seen in the *sonate da chiesa* of Giovanni Battista Bassani (c. 1657–1716), active

EXAMPLE 105

Corelli, Harmonic devices

[a]

[b]

---

[25] Two movements of Corelli's solo sonata, Op. 5, No. 3, are given in *HAM*, No. 252. Other sonatas of the Corelli type, by Tommaso Vitali, are found in *HAM*, No. 263, and *GMB*, No. 241.

in several Italian cities; in those of Evaristo dall' Abaco (1675–1742), primarily in Munich; and in many other composers. The style was regularly transmitted to sonatas for one violin (with bass and continuo) by Francesco Geminiani (1687–1762), a pupil of Corelli and author of the earliest known violin method (published anonymously at London in 1730); by Pietro Locatelli (1695–1764), also a Corelli pupil but active principally in Amsterdam; and again by many others.

The Italian instrumental style, carried abroad even during Vitali's lifetime, found a firm foothold in England and Germany and, to a lesser extent, in France. In England the *sonata da chiesa* was cultivated notably by Henry Purcell. Purcell's two sets of trio sonatas (twelve in 1685 and ten in 1697) are modeled upon those of Vitali and do not yet exhibit the comparatively regular form of Corelli's. They range from one to six movements in length, the majority containing five movements. Contrapuntal textures dominate in the two sets; strict imitations, fugal expositions, and even a canon in double augmentation are found. A number of sonatas also contain movements cast in dance rhythms, however; this characteristic points to the merger of the *sonata da chiesa* with the *sonata da camera*.

The church sonata was imported to Germany, possibly through the efforts of Italian composers like Carlo Farina (about 1660), who held positions at the German courts. Works in this form were composed by Johann Kaspar Kerll (1627–1693) in Munich and Johann Heinrich Schmelzer (*c.* 1623–1680) in Vienna. In Salzburg, Heinrich Franz Biber (1644–1704) was active. Sixteen of his sonatas and a number of other works have survived. Biber was one of the most important German violinists of the Baroque period. He is known primarily for advancing the technical possibilities of the violin, and he was among the first to use *scordatura* ("mistunings") to facilitate the playing of certain chords and double stops.

The *sonata da chiesa* became known in France, but it had relatively little influence there. Later in the period it was occasionally employed by François Couperin, whose contributions will be discussed in the following chapter.

Dance suite and sonata da camera. The nucleus of the suite was the pair of dances, contrasting in tempo and meter but related melodically (see page 203). The pair was expanded into a larger compound form by composers for the lute and harpsichord, as described in the foregoing pages. Almost simultaneously, it was also composed for instrumental ensembles, both orchestral and chamber. As in the case of early organ and harpsichord music, however, a stylistic distinction between works for the two instrumental media cannot at first be made. Many of the works to be discussed below could be performed by either group, and only later did the two fields separate. At that point, roughly in the 1670's, two terms became significant: *suite,* applied to the orchestral version, and *sonata da camera,* to the chamber-music set.

Perhaps the earliest type of suite resulted from the application of the variation principle to the pair of dances. The developments in England, leading to such works as John Dowland's *Lachrimae,* for lute ensemble, have been described (see page 205). In Germany the variation principle was applied somewhat differently. Since the second dance of the pair was essentially a rhythmic variant of the first, it seemed logical to add a third and fourth dance to the pair and to extend the variation principle across the resulting suite. Hans Leo Hassler (1564–1612) had worked tentatively in this direction in his collection, *Lustgarten,* of 1601. Paul Peuerl (*c.* 1570–1624) did so more consistently and created a true variation suite. Peuerl's collection of *Newe Padouan, Intrada, Däntz, unnd Galliarda* (1611) consists of a number of suites, each of which is a true set of variations. One melody is common to each dance set but appropriately modified to conform to the rhythmic patterns of the successive movements (see EXAMPLE 106). The same method of suite construction was followed

E X A M P L E 106

Peuerl, Suite

by other German and Austrian composers of the time, notably Johann Hermann Schein (1586–1630) in his twenty suites called *Banchetto musicale* (1617). In a set of *Paduan, Galliarda, Couranta* of 1621, by Samuel Scheidt (1587–1654), the variation principle is applied less strictly; and in this set the *basso continuo* makes its appearance in German ensemble music. From this point forward the variation suite was treated ever more freely, but the use of the continuo, a degree of imitation between bass and melody, and a thematic relationship between at least two of the movements remained features of the style.

The dance suite in seventeenth-century France was developed primarily by lutenists and harpsichordists, as has been noted above. Dances appearing in the ballets and operas of the time were probably performed outside the opera house on occasion, but the independently composed small-ensemble suite played little part in the evolution of French music. In Italy, on the other hand, sets of dances for instruments appeared among Monteverdi's works as early as 1607. Here we find six or seven unrelated dances, each one supplied with a text. Somewhat later, in 1637, Giovanni Battista Buonamente (?–1643) published several books containing pieces entitled *Sonata, Sinfonia, Brando, Galliarda, Corrente.* The Italian dance sets in general were standardized neither in number nor in sequence of movements. Suites involving movements based on dance rhythms were composed for the favorite ensemble instrumentation (two violins, bass, and continuo) by many Italian composers in the years after about 1660, but the most successful were again by Corelli. A name for the type, *sonata da camera* ("chamber sonata"), had existed earlier—notably in Tarquino Merula's *Canzoni, overo Sonate concertante per chiesa e camera* of 1637; the separation of sonatas for church and chamber seems to have been achieved in Corelli's time.[26]

The *sonate da camera* of Corelli were published between 1685 and 1712; twenty-four (Opus 2, Nos. 1–12, and Opus 4, Nos. 1–12) are for trio, six (Opus 5, Nos. 7–12) for solo violin and bass, and four (in Opus 6) for orchestra. Most usually a sonata consists of a prelude and two to four dances, the latter often identified as *Allemanda, Sarabanda, Giga, Tempo di Gavotta,* etc. The prelude, generally in slow tempo, is often in contrapuntal texture, while the dance movements are rhythmically alive in homophonic or broken-chord style. The animated bass parts share in the imitations where the texture permits and require a degree of technical proficiency not far behind that required of the violins.[27]

At the turn of the eighteenth century the *sonata da chiesa* and *sonata da camera* existed side by side with their respective characteristics relatively intact. The *chiesa* type was most often in contrapuntal style; it included four movements alternately in slow and fast tempo, of which the third brought lyric expression to the fore. The *camera,* on the other hand, stressed homophonic style and dance rhythms and typically contained from two to six movements in no particular order. Early in the new century, however, the two types began mutually to influence each other. Contrapuntal textures appeared in the *sonata da camera,* dance-like rhythms in the fast movements of the *sonata da chiesa,* and both types regularly comprised four movements. The term "trio sonata" was adopted by many German and Italian composers to call attention to the merger of the two types, and the terms *chiesa* and *camera* gradually fell into disuse.

Evaristo dall' Abaco was among the most industrious composers of the new type (as he had also been of the old), but virtually every instrumental composer wrote for trio in the new composite style and the trio sonata

26 The translation of *camera* into "chamber" should not be taken literally, for sonatas of this type were also performed at large public occasions. Hence the term "court sonata" has been suggested. See Newman, *The Sonata in the Baroque Era* for details.

27 Examples of the Corelli style are found in *GMB*, No. 240, and *HAM*, No. 253.

flourished in all of western Europe. Tommaso Albinoni (1671–1750), Francesco Bonporti (1672–1749), George Frideric Handel (1685–1759), Johann Sebastian Bach (1685–1750), and many others are represented in the surviving literature. The four-movement form remained a standard, along with a variety of textures including chordal, contrapuntal, and homophonic.

About the time that the merger of the two sonata types became effective, the new form was adopted by composers of sonatas for violin and continuo (see page 292). Their works in general resemble the trio sonatas in form, texture, and content; but a degree of virtuosity marks the violin part, and a brilliant tone is most characteristic. Similar sonatas for flute and continuo, oboe and continuo, and the like came into prominence also, especially among composers of French ancestry or those influenced by France. Jean-Baptiste Loeillet (1680–1730), a Belgian composer active in London, popularized the transverse flute in England through his many flute sonatas, but he also composed for other instruments.

Orchestral Music

THE LINE between chamber music (with one player on a part) and orchestral music (with several players each on at least the string parts) is not always possible to draw in the field of the *sonata da camera* and the suite, as indicated above. In other fields of ensemble music, however, the problem does not exist. French compositions derived from the *ballet de cour* and Italian works in a new form called *concerto grosso* were entirely orchestral, for even at the beginning of their development the requirement of more than one player on a part was made clear.

In France the *ballet de cour* had provided an orchestral repertoire as early as the 1640's. The ballets were performed by the "Twenty-four Violins of the King" (Louis XIII), a five-part string orchestra with four to six players on each part. The dance movements of these ballets were arranged in sets of several movements, usually all in two-part form and all in the same key. They were customarily preceded by a two-part introduction called an *ouverture,* the first part of which, in a slow and stately tempo and based on dotted rhythms, was connected to a fast second part that often began in imitative style. Lully adopted this overture type for his ballets (from 1653) and operas (after 1673), and the slow-fast "Lully overture" became a model for French and German composers for almost a century. In Lully's works, however, the second part was fugal rather than merely imitative. The first movement itself quickly became the longest and weightiest movement of the orchestral suite, and the suite as a whole often was called "overture" in deference to this fact.

Corelli. When Corelli transferred the forms of the *sonata da chiesa* and *da camera* to the orchestra, as he did in his Opus 6 (published in 1712 or 1714, but probably written as early as 1682), he set in motion a line of development that was to culminate in the mid-eighteenth century in the concerto for one instrument and orchestra. The full title of

Corelli's Opus 6 may be roughly translated as follows: "Concerti grossi with two violins and cello in the concertino, and two other violins, viola, and bass in the concerto grosso, whose parts may be doubled at will." Implied here is a dualism between a smaller group (concertino) and a larger (concerto grosso), a dualism that has remained characteristic of the concerto to the present day.

Music containing two tonal groups had existed in earlier centuries, of course. Antiphonal chant was of this type; the polychoral works of the Venetian school, as well as the continuo madrigal and other *concertato* works of the early Baroque period had exemplified the principle of alternation and hence were dualistic. In the evolving concerto grosso, however, another element was added, namely a distinctive concerto style. It is this that distinguishes the late Baroque concerto from earlier examples of dualistic music.

Concerto style was characterized first of all by a texture that has been called "continuo-homophony." [28] This texture, found most often in fast movements, distinguished all forms of later Baroque music. It embodied the principle of a polarity between the melody and the bass, which moved in stereotyped but vigorous figures in a fast harmonic rhythm and a firmly established key. The tonal system, with its related chords on every step of the diatonic scale and its movement away from and toward a single tonal center, had been evolving gradually since the early Renaissance, more quickly in the early Baroque. Now it became firmly established. Certain harmonic patterns appeared in the concerto, as they had in Corelli's *sonate da chiesa* and *da camera*: circle-of-fifth progressions, series of suspensions, series of chords of the sixth (see EXAMPLE 107). The weight of the harmonic accompaniment thus derived exerted an ever increasing influence on the formation of the melodies, which grew out of the harmonic progressions instead of being independently conceived. Continuo

EXAMPLE 107

Corelli, Harmonic patterns

28 Bukofzer, *Music in the Baroque Era*, pp. 221–22.

homophony represents a balance between the *basso continuo,* with its short-lived chordal progressions, and the true homophony of the early Classical period, in which chordal progressions moved logically and inexorably to relatively far-distant cadence points.

In Corelli's *concerti grossi* of Opus 6, the main elements of continuo homophony were firmly established. Violinistic idioms, too, became basic to the figuration, as they had in the sonatas of both types. The melodic content of the concerto consisted largely of a few phrases heard alternately in the tutti and the soli, thus continuing the tradition of loud-soft alternation that had played an important part in the music of the Venetian school. The first eight concertos of the twelve in Opus 6 are of the *chiesa* type and contain five or more movements—some of them quite short and in contrapuntal style; the last four of the set exhibit more formal regularity, for each includes a prelude and six dance movements in the style of the *sonata da camera.*

Many movements of Corelli's concertos are primarily in contrapuntal style. Fugal passages had been common in the *sonate da chiesa,* and they are found again in the first eight concertos of Opus 6. Tightly woven contrapuntal lines, full of suspensions and poignant dissonances, are characteristic of the slow movements; here again the relationship to the church sonata is close. Elsewhere, notably in the dance movements of the *concerti*

da camera and the fast movements of the *concerti da chiesa,* the new concerto style, based on continuo homophony, dominates. And in most such
movements the first violin is featured more than the second.

Torelli. Even while Corelli was perfecting his style in Rome, Giuseppe
Torelli (1658–1709) in Bologna was making far-reaching changes in the
form and content of the concerto. Torelli's early works, to about 1690,
were in general built on the Corelli model, in that they continued the
form of the church and chamber sonata. In his Opus 5, however, published in 1692, he wrote a series of works that are called concertos but
do not distinguish between tutti and soloists. This is not at all incompatible with the idea of the concerto; it must be stressed that the concerto
was more a matter of style than of instrumentation. This type of work
has been called a "concerto for orchestra," and at Torelli's hands it was
soon standardized as a three-movement form in fast-slow-fast tempos.

In Torelli's concertos of Opus 6, a brisk running passage was often
given to a solo violin. In a later set of works, those of Opus 8 (published
in 1709, but written probably in 1700), the occasional solo passages became prominent elements of the form (see EXAMPLE 108) and Torelli gave

EXAMPLE 108

Torelli, Concerto, Op. 8, No. 8

sections to the tutti and the solo violin alternately. The material of the
tutti was usually an incisive or vigorous melody with strong rhythmic
distinction; most importantly, the same material appeared, usually in
different keys, at each return. The solo parts generally consisted of figurations set idiomatically for the violin that added a brilliant tone to the
concerto as a whole.[29] The structural principle involved here—a series of
ritornelli for orchestra, set in different keys and separated by virtuosic
passages for the solo violin—became influential for the remainder of the
Baroque period. Until about 1750 hundreds of concertos were written on
the model introduced by Torelli.

While the concerto grosso and the orchestral concerto continued to
flourish, it was the solo concerto that attracted the greatest amount of
attention and became the dominant orchestral form of the late Baroque
period. There is some uncertainty about who should be credited with the
origin of the form. Torelli's solo concertos of Opus 8 were presumably

29 Examples are given in *GMB,* No. 257, and *HAM,* No. 246.

Concert given in Rome in 1729 in celebration of the birth of the Dauphin, son of Louis XV. Painting by Panini.

written about 1700. But violin concertos had been published by Tommaso Albinoni at Venice in 1700, and a host of composers entered the field in the first decade of the eighteenth century.

The pupils of Corelli, notably Geminiani and Locatelli, carried the concerto idea still further than Torelli. Both were virtuoso violinists and added to the brilliance of the solo part in their concertos, as they had done in their violin sonatas. Geminiani wrote rather conservatively, favoring fugal fast movements in his *concerti grossi*. Locatelli, on the other hand, inclined toward a style that fully exploited the technical possibilities of the solo violin. His concertos are brilliant beyond any other works of the time; like Biber, he employed *scordatura* (mistuning of the violin) on occasion to make possible a greater variety of double stops.

Vivaldi. The most prolific and most important master of the concerto in the early eighteenth century, however, was Antonio Vivaldi (*c.* 1669–1741). Vivaldi was born in Venice. He studied with his father and with Legrenzi and became a priest in 1703. From that year to 1740 he was employed as teacher, composer, and musical director of the conservatory attached to the Ospedale della Pietà, an orphanage for girls. During his tenure at Venice he traveled widely, spent about three years in the service of a German prince at Mantua, and passed his last year at Vienna, where he died, but he is associated primarily with Venice. Although Vivaldi composed almost four dozen operas and much church music, he is remembered principally for his enormous quantity of instrumental music. Dozens of trio sonatas or solo sonatas, about fifty *concerti grossi,* and about 450 other concertos for various solo instruments have survived. Most of Vivaldi's works have been published only in recent years, and a full evaluation of his work is yet to be undertaken.[30]

The high quality and great variety of Vivaldi's compositions may be partly explained by the nature of the position he occupied for almost forty years. The girls and young women of the Pietà were well trained in music. The excellent orchestra, composed of some forty students, was famous for the quality of its performances, and hundreds of Vivaldi's concertos were written for it. Over two hundred concertos are for solo violin and orchestra; another one hundred or so are for cello, oboe, bassoon, and the like (even for piccolo); and a number of the remainder are for various combinations of strings—three violins, four violins (one of which was transcribed by Bach as a concerto for four harpsichords), two violins and two cellos, and many other groupings—or strings and winds. It is obvious that the distinction between concerto grosso and solo concerto is not easily drawn, for some of the works labeled concerto grosso are quite similar to the solo (more properly, "ensemble") concertos, even though they employ three or more concertizing instruments.

Few generalizations can accurately encompass so large a mass of material. One can say only that the formal plan of the concertos is an im-

30 The most thorough study is by Marc Pincherle, *Antonio Vivaldi et la musique instrumentale.*

portant element of Vivaldi's style. The alternation of orchestral *ritornelli* with brilliant passage work for the soloist had appeared in the concertos of Torelli. In Vivaldi's works the place of the *ritornello* was enlarged. It provided the chief thematic material of the movement, often appearing as many as five times, with its middle appearances usually in keys other than the tonic. The solo material often expanded the melodic idea presented in the *ritornello* and elaborated it with brilliant figuration, but occasionally the solo instrument was given a thematic idea of its own—a contrast that was influential in shaping other instrumental forms in the later eighteenth century. The great majority of Vivaldi's concertos are in the three-movement form—fast-slow-fast—standardized by Torelli. And invariably the tutti themes of the fast movements, striking in contour and rhythm, are written idiomatically for the string instruments that make up the body of the concerto accompaniment (see EXAMPLE 109).[31]

Vivaldi's accomplishments in the field of the concerto were of little influence on French composers. In Germany, on the other hand, the concerto was looked upon with considerable favor. Bach, as has been noted, arranged several of the Italian master's works in order to study and perform them. A number of German composers imitated them, many writing more contrapuntally than Vivaldi. Others among the Germans inclined toward the melodious, ingratiating style that marked the decline of Baroque style and the rise of the Rococo. Among the former were the theorist Johann Heinichen (1683–1729); the composer Christoph Graupner (1683–1760), who was offered (and refused) the post of cantor at St. Thomas's Church in Leipzig, resulting in Bach's selection; the violinist Johann Georg Pisendel (1687–1759); and the eminent composer Johann Friedrich Fasch (1688–1758). Composers in whose concertos the emerging *style galant* was carried further will be discussed below.

Handel. The concertos of George Frideric Handel are in another category. They include about fifty items, some of them consisting of only a single movement. The concerto grosso rather than the solo concerto is the dominant form, and the works are modeled more closely on those of Corelli than on those of Vivaldi. A set of six *concerti grossi* (Opus 3, about 1720 but published in 1734) is scored for the usual two violins and cello in the concertino and an orchestra for the tutti (doubling is optional, as in Corelli's Opus 6), but parts for pairs of oboes, flutes, and bassoons are included also. These works are sometimes called "oboe concertos" to distinguish them from the concertos of Opus 6, in which no wind instruments are used. The unstandardized form of two to six movements is employed, and contrapuntal textures—including double fugues and canons—are most often evident.

Handel's major instrumental work is probably the set of twelve concertos written about 1739 and published in the following year as Opus 6. At a time when virtually every composer of concertos had adopted the

---

31 A typical concerto first movement by Vivaldi is given in *HAM*, No. 270; a slow movement in *GMB*, No. 276.

EXAMPLE 109

Vivaldi, Concerto grosso Op. 9, No. 4

three-movement form and the tight structure of Vivaldi, Handel was content to resort to the style and forms, although not the dimensions, of Corelli. The concertos range from four to six movements. They are scored for two violins in the concertino and string orchestra and continuo in the tutti, but Handel dealt freely with his soloists. In some cases the distinction between soli and tutti disappears completely; the result is the texture of the orchestral concerto. In other cases the principal figurations are given to one solo violin, while the other is reabsorbed into the orchestral tutti; here the concept of the solo concerto is approached. Individual movements range from simple chordal patterns (as in the introduction to No. 9) to large fugues (No. 4), and the variety of moods in the set is equally great. Phrases are usually four or eight measures in length, and in all textures and all moods are primarily melodious. Violinistic idioms appear in the solo figurations, of course, but Handel seldom wrote melodies that are not eminently singable. In this vocal-mindedness, which is quite different from the instrumental-mindedness of, say, Vivaldi and Bach, Handel revealed himself as a composer whose main concern was with the human voice.

The creation of the concerto for organ and orchestra may be attributed to Handel. It was customary in his day to perform a concerto in connection with opera and oratorio performances. Handel, as one of the foremost organists of the time, took the opportunity to combine his skills as a composer and organist and wrote a set of six concertos for organ during the years about 1735 to 1738, published in 1738 as Opus 4. Two other sets, each containing six concertos, were published in 1740 (without opus number) and in 1761 (Opus 7), respectively. Some movements of the later sets are arrangements of movements from Opus 6 or from other compositions. In keeping with the English practice of using small organs without pedals in the theater, these works are for manuals alone. They are improvisational in spirit and marked by the absence of contrapuntal textures. It is likely that the organ parts do no more than provide skeletons of what actually took place in Handel's performances. They need to be filled out and appropriately ornamented today.

Handel's orchestral compositions also include two well-known suites, each containing many movements. The two works, *The Water Music* and *The Music to the Royal Fireworks,* were designed for outdoor performance, hence are written for a larger orchestra than his other compositions.

Bach

SEVERAL different Baroque instrumental forms were brought to the peak of their development by Johann Sebastian Bach. Whether writing for organ, for harpsichord, for instrumental ensemble, or for orchestra, Bach clearly saw the technical problems and expressive possibilities of the form under consideration. He brought into focus, refined, and synthesized the diverse stylistic elements of Baroque music and created an individual style that is the result of fabulous technical competence, soaring musical imagination, and the utmost emotional sensitivity. Bach wrote at a time when with a few exceptions, notably Rameau and Handel, other composers had adopted the light, ingratiating, and merely entertaining style that paralleled the art and architecture of the Rococo. Bach perfected the concerto and the many Baroque organ and harpsichord forms at a time when those forms were well on the way to obsolescence elsewhere. In maintaining the integrity and profundity of Baroque style for two or more decades after its virtual abandonment by composers at large, Bach was considered old-fashioned and all but forgotten by the generation which came after him.

In keeping with professional requirements in the Baroque period, Bach was a practical musician. His compositions reflect the needs of whatever position he occupied at the time of writing. After two short periods of employment in Arnstadt and Mühlhausen (1703–1708), Bach moved to his first major position, as organist at the court of Weimar (1708–1717); there he composed the majority of his organ works. Moving to Cöthen in 1717 as chapelmaster and director of chamber music, he occupied himself with orchestral and smaller ensemble compositions, but he also composed a number of keyboard works that served instructional purposes. In 1723 Bach became cantor of St. Thomas's School in Leipzig and musical director of the town's principal churches, St. Thomas and St. Nicholas; here the majority of his choral compositions were written. The many cantatas and other choral compositions of the Leipzig period have been discussed (see Chapter 14), and the present chapter will be confined to a discussion of the instrumental compositions.

The organ works. Bach's compositions in this field include about forty preludes and fifty fugues (about thirty of them paired as "preludes and fugues" and the rest single movements); almost two dozen compositions such as toccatas, fantasias, trio sonatas, and smaller works; and some two hundred settings of chorales, many of which appeared in sets. While their exact chronology is difficult to determine, it is fairly certain that the majority of the preludes, fugues, and toccatas originated in Weimar. The chief elements which set the Weimar works above those of Bach's contemporaries (and indeed above the works he himself wrote before 1708) are their dramatic tone and concise thematic contours (see EXAMPLE 110),

EXAMPLE 110

Bach, Fugue themes

elements that came to Bach by way of the Italian masters. Two of the fugues are based on themes by Corelli and Legrenzi, and Bach's six organ concertos are in fact arrangements of concertos by other composers, notably Vivaldi. The clarity of form and the expressiveness ranging from deepest pathos to jubilation that mark these works clearly show the Italian influence. The two great toccatas in C major and D minor, S. 564 and 565,[32] reflect the keyboard virtuosity for which Bach was known. And the well-known Prelude and Fugue in D major, S. 532, reveals how completely

32 These and the following references are to Schmieder, *Thematisch-systematisches Verzeichnis der musikalischen Werke von J. S. Bach.*

Bach had mastered the rhythmic aspects of early harpsichord music and adapted it to the requirements of organ polyphony (see EXAMPLE 111 and compare EXAMPLE 104). The harmonic course of Bach's fugues is sure,

EXAMPLE 111

Bach, Prelude and Fugue, S. 532

firmly establishing a tonality, and the fugues contain episodes which circumscribe the key. The harmonic progressions Bach employed were often similar to those established by the *ritornelli* (for example, I-V-VI-

Johann Sebastian Bach at the organ. Lithograph by Edouard J. C. Hamman, *c.* 1865.

IV-V-I) in typical concertos by Italian masters, and alternations of full organ and solo stops give further evidence of the interpenetration of concerto elements and contrapuntal style. Yet even while Bach was successfully introducing elements of concerto style in these works, he brought the rhapsodic and imaginative tradition of north German organists to its highest level of expression. Such works as the Fantasy and Fugue in G minor, S. 542, the Prelude and Fugue in D major, S. 532, and the somewhat later Prelude and Fugue in E♭, S. 552, reveal how Bach freed himself from patterns and formulas, composing freely and dramatically.

The harpsichord works. One of Bach's outstanding characteristics was the orderly and systematic way in which he approached the art of composition. This is seen strikingly in the many sets of pieces he composed for the harpsichord or the clavichord (both of which are included in the German term, *Klavier*). He was active as a teacher through much of his career, especially at Cöthen and Leipzig, and many of his compositions were designed as instructional pieces. When writing a set of such pieces (often using works composed earlier for other purposes), Bach kept in mind the needs of variety. Thus in the *Klavierbüchlein* compiled for his eldest son, Wilhelm Friedemann (1710–1784), about 1720, he included chorale preludes, two- and three-part inventions, nine easy preludes and eleven more difficult ones (which later appeared in *Das wohltemperierte Klavier* ["The Well-Tempered Clavier"], Part I), fugues, and stylized dance pieces—all in a variety of keys, textures, and styles. The systematic approach is seen in the famous *Air with Thirty Variations* (the so-called Goldberg Variations, S. 988, of about 1742). Here the variations are arranged in sets of three; the third in each set is a canon, progressing from canon at the unison to canon at the ninth. Only at the end of the work does a break in the system occur; the thirtieth variation is a quodlibet, a free composition in which two popular songs are used as contrapuntal material.

Probably the best known of Bach's keyboard works is the monumental set of forty-eight preludes and forty-eight fugues that constitute the two parts of *The Well-Tempered Clavier* (Part I in Cöthen, 1722; Part II completed in Leipzig, 1744). Each part contains twenty-four preludes and fugues arranged in chromatic order (C major, C minor, C♯ major, C♯ minor, D major, etc.). Virtually each prelude represents a distinct type of figuration, texture, form, or technical problem, and the fugues summarize the various possibilities of fugal writing, including inversion, augmentation and diminution of theme, and the like. The variety and strength of the fugue themes, noticeable in the organ works, here reach their highest level (see EXAMPLE 112). The preludes are cast in a variety of forms. Some resemble movements of church sonatas, others are brilliant toccatalike pieces, and yet others are keyboard versions of vocal or ensemble forms such as the trio-sonata slow movement. The preludes of the second part often employ the Baroque binary form as well. The systematic ordering of a number of types, styles, and forms is in keeping with Bach's purpose in writing the sets, for the title of the (incomplete) autograph reads:

EXAMPLE 112

Bach, *The Well-Tempered Clavier*

". . . The Well-Tempered Clavier . . . assembled and completed for the use and welfare of young musicians eager to learn. . . ."

Other sets of Bach's keyboard works reveal a similar intention. Of the six partitas, S. 825–830, for example, four are based on the standard form of introductory movement, allemande, courante, sarabande, optional movement, and gigue. But the introductory movements include a *sinfonia,* a Lully overture, a fantasy, a *praeambulum,* and a toccata; the optional movements are either minuet, passepied, rondeau, burlesca and scherzo, or gavotte. Similarly, there is considerable inner variety in two sets of suites, S. 806–811 and 812–817, familiarly known as the *English Suites* and *French Suites* without any formal justification. The so-called *English Suites* all contain the usual movements and the introductory movement is in each case a prelude; it is the optional dances that provide the inner variety. These are paired: one suite contains a pair of minuets and another a pair of passepieds, two have bourrées, and two have gavottes. The *French Suites* show similar variety—even to the extent of containing (in No. 6) a group of four dances (gavotte, polonaise, bourrée, and minuet) between sarabande and gigue.

The significant thing here is that these works, along with the majority of Bach's other works, represent a thorough amalgamation of different national style elements. Italian melodic flow in the *correnti* is clearly distinguished from the ornamental and elegant melodic patterns of the French *courantes*. Bach distinguished between the Italian *giga* and the French *gigue*—one often in $12/8$ meter, the other usually in $6/8$. Regional dances—loure, passepied, polonaise, gavotte—stand next to or substitute for the more usual formal types. Italian drive and fervor are combined with French grace, and both find their way into German contrapuntal textures. Another prime example of this synthesis is seen in Part II of the *Klavierübung*, which contains an "Overture in the French Style," S. 831, and a "Concerto in the Italian Manner," S. 971. The transfer of the idiom of the concerto to the solo harpsichord brought to completion the process at work in the various sets of suites: the final amalgamation not only of Italian and French characteristics, but of organ and keyboard styles as well.

Other instrumental works. The compositions in this category include first of all three sonatas and three partitas for solo violin, S. 1001–1006, and six suites for solo cello, S. 1007–1012, all composed at Cöthen about 1720. Polyphonic writing for a solo string instrument had been attempted before Bach's time, notably by Heinrich Biber (see page 292). In Bach's works the polyphony reaches new heights of expressiveness; the fugue from the third violin sonata and the monumental chaconne that ends the second partita are noteworthy in this respect. Bach's use of double and triple stops (see EXAMPLES 113*a* and 113*b*) and his ability to suggest the

EXAMPLE 113

Bach, Solo sonatas and suites

presence of two or more simultaneous lines through his choice of arpeggiated contours that exploit the natural resonance of the instrument (EXAMPLES 113*c* and 113*d*) everywhere convey the effect of several instruments playing together. Yet the *tour de force* represented here did not exhaust Bach's ingenuity, for even in these works he provided models in various styles. The first partita, for example, represents the English style, the second the French, and the third the Italian. Similarly in the cello suites, models of various dances are at hand. The optional group of the first two suites consists of a pair of minuets; that of the third and fourth suites, bourrées; and of the fifth and sixth, gavottes. Wherever possible, it seems, Bach took pains to tie up the loose ends of the Baroque period by composing masterworks in virtually every form that the period had developed.

The small ensemble works of Bach include about two dozen items, most of them sonatas for violin and harpsichord. They are usually cast in the standard four-movement form (slow-fast-slow-fast) and are similar to trio sonatas in texture, for the right hand of the keyboard part generally serves in place of the other melody instrument of the trio. It was Bach's practice in many cases to write out the keyboard part completely, thus dispensing with the figured bass and the supporting bass instrument. To the extent that Bach eliminated the continuo he approached the practice of Rococo composers who began their activity about the 1730's.

In the orchestral field Bach is represented by the six so-called Brandenburg Concertos, S. 1046–1051, four Overtures or Suites, S. 1066–1069, and about six other concertos for various combinations. Still other concertos found among Bach's works are arrangements of works that appeared originally in other forms.

The Brandenburg Concertos, composed about 1721 at Cöthen, are outstanding even in their varieties of form and instrumentation. Two of the six (Nos. 3 and 6) are concertos for orchestra and require no soloists; three (Nos. 1, 2, and 5) are *concerti grossi;* and one (No. 4) is in effect a concerto for solo violin and orchestra. Although the standard three-movement form (fast-slow-fast) appears in the majority of cases, No. 1 contains an additional finale consisting of minuet and polacca, each with a trio, and No. 3 has no middle slow movement. Yet even within compositions that outwardly adhere to the Italian models, Bach combined, synthesized, and brought to a higher level a variety of stylistic elements. The basic style of the concertos is that of continuo homophony, with concise rhythmic motives, running figures, and inexorable forward movement toward the cadences. Within this style, however, are dance movements allied to the French suite (finale of No. 1), canonic slow movements (andante of No. 2), fugues (finales of Nos. 4 and 5), and a movement based consistently on imitation (first movement of No. 6). The writing for the solo instruments is virtuosic at times, notably throughout No. 2 and in the harpsichord part of No. 5, and Bach exploited all the possibilities of instrumental color. The formal divisions within the several movements are carefully calculated, so that the polarity of soli versus tutti gives way to a sonorous texture. Among Bach's earliest orchestral works, the Brandenburg Concertos represent the culmination of Baroque concerto composition.

Of the four orchestral suites, two were presumably written at Cöthen about 1721 and two at Leipzig after 1727. The instrumentation is varied in the four works, and they are even richer in orchestral color than the Brandenburg Concertos. Each suite begins with a massive French overture in three-part form (it will be remembered that Bach usually added a third section in slow tempo to the two-part, slow-fast form of the Lully overture). The overture is followed by four to seven movements, most of them stylized dances. Here again Bach's customary fusion of style elements is eloquently presented. Imitative and fugal elements in bourrées and sarabandes, dancelike passages in the fugal sections of the overtures—these are typical. In addition, many of the dances are composed in pairs, with the second of the pair called *double* or *alternativement* and consisting of a variation of the first dance, in the French manner. Finally, soli-tutti contrasts are worked into the fugal textures of the first movements in several cases. As in the Brandenburg Concertos, virtuosity marks the instrumental writing, and the third suite resembles a concerto for flute, so prominent is that instrument. Very few suites of this type were written after the 1750's; it is fitting that virtually the last works in the form should be among the most expressive and brilliant.

Bach's last years at Leipzig were marked by two unique compositions: *Das musikalische Opfer* ("The Musical Offering"), S. 1079, written in 1747, and *Die Kunst der Fuge* ("The Art of the Fugue"), S. 1080, begun about 1749 and left incomplete at his death in 1750. The first resulted from Bach's visit to the court of Frederick the Great at Potsdam in 1747. The King gave Bach a theme upon which to improvise, and after returning to Leipzig Bach elaborated this theme into a large ensemble composition of five parts, for two to six instruments. A *ricercare* for three instruments begins the work, and another *ricercare* for six ends it. The second part consists of five canons in which the "royal theme" is carried by one instrument while two other instruments engage in canonic imitations of new counterthemes. In the fourth part, also consisting of five canons, the royal theme is itself treated in canon by two to four instruments. The middle portion of the work consists of a four-movement trio sonata in which the royal theme is employed as part of the melodic material. The canons in the second and fourth parts revive old practices of the Renaissance: canons in contrary motion, canons by augmentation, crab canon, and canon in quadruple counterpoint are among the types represented. The whole, designed as a "musical offering" to the King, is symmetrical in over-all design. But there is also a cumulative pace: the canons of the fourth part are longer and more elaborate than those of the second, and the six-part *ricercare* that ends the work rises to a higher level of intensity than the first *ricercare*, forming a suitable climax. The work is a monument to Bach's contrapuntal genius.[33]

Bach's last work, *The Art of the Fugue*, is a cycle consisting of nineteen fugues, the last of which is unfinished. The method of performance is not indicated, although it is written in open score and thus is presumably designed for instruments. Yet it also lies within the range of two hands at a keyboard and is therefore suitable for performance at the organ. One theme and the modifications of it are basic to the work, although other themes appear in systematic order—one of them on the notes (in German) B-A-C-H, which are B♭, A, C, and B♮. Single, double, and triple fugues, mirror fugues (in which one complete fugue is mirrored by another that is the exact inversion of the first), and canonic fugues constitute the cycle. And the whole concludes with a gigantic quadruple fugue, of which a little more than half was completed.

---

33 For details, see David, *Bach's Musical Offering*, New York, G. Schirmer & Co., 1945.

Externally, *The Art of the Fugue* is a stupendous work, a summary of all the fugal arts developed in the past. Some sections of the work are profound, others are light and gay—and perhaps equally profound; yet the whole is more than a collection of fugues. Considerable uncertainty exists about the true ordering of the nineteen fugues, and half a dozen editors have attempted to solve the problem. In one edition, done by Wolfgang Graeser in 1927, the ordering is so arranged that the fugues in which the cycle's main theme appears are placed in logical order at the beginning and end of the work; the fugues which anticipate the appearance of the B-A-C-H theme are placed before those in which that theme is gradually reabsorbed into the tonal fabric, and the fugue on B-A-C-H then forms the midpoint of the work. At least one commentator on Graeser's edition sees *The Art of the Fugue* as an esoteric work symbolizing the incarnation of the human spirit.[34] In this view, the B-A-C-H theme is the symbol of the human ego.

Seen in retrospect, the entire body of Bach's vocal and instrumental works forms a unique whole. The outstanding characteristic of Bach's style as a composer was his ability to combine the diverse elements of various national styles and weld them into a whole. An inconceivably high level of technical competence marks his music, but the technical aspects are lost sight of under the influence of the spirituality, sincerity, and fervor that it expresses. An age-old conflict between vertical (harmonic) and horizontal (melodic) elements was solved in his creation of a style that consists of melodies harmonically conceived and harmonies contrapuntally controlled. The polarity between sacred and secular likewise disappears in Bach's music. All of it is dedicated to the glory of God, whether its texts are scriptural or profane, whether its forms are associated with the church or the concert hall. Considered old-fashioned in its day, forgotten for almost a century after his death, Bach's music is filled with such vitality, musical quality, technical worth, and beauty that it can be considered among the priceless possessions of Western civilization.

34 See Ulrich, *Chamber Music*, pp. 138–42, for details.

Emergence of Classical Style

A PROGRESSION of major changes in style has marked the course of music history for many centuries. Each new style, as we have seen, had its tentative beginnings at a time when the old style had reached its peak. As the new style approached its mature shape, the old style fell out of favor or declined in effectiveness. Thus the change from Renaissance to Baroque style can be rather clearly marked about the year 1600, and an equally clear change from Romantic to contemporary style can be seen shortly after the year 1900.

At the end of the Baroque period, marked by the death of Bach in 1750, a major successor to Baroque style was not immediately apparent. Three decades earlier, however, a competing style had emerged that ran parallel to the Baroque during the years in which Bach and Handel were

"Quartet at Schloss Strüth." Engraving by Edward Ade. [CULVER PICTURES]

composing their most monumental works and then continued on its course for another thirty years after the death of Bach. Not until about 1780 was it transformed into a major style, the Classical, which is best represented by the works of Haydn, Mozart, and Beethoven.

Several terms are commonly used to describe various aspects of the new style that prevailed from about 1720 to 1780. It emerged at a time when French architecture was ornamented and decorated to excess with elaborate stone carvings, plaster encrustations, and other elements designed to obscure the clean, structural lines of a building. Hence the term "rococo," derived from the French *rocaille* and referring to the artificial rockwork itself, is often applied to the music of the time. Since much of the music was composed for the entertainment of the aristocracy and of the fashionable world in general, the style in which it was written became known in France as the *style galant*. A later version of the style, transported to north Germany and there modified in the direction of increased feeling and sentiment, is referred to as the *empfindsamer Stil* ("sensitive style"). But the period in general is most conveniently known as the Rococo, for the term "Rococo style" may be applied to those Italian and other works which are neither in the *style galant* of France nor the *empfindsamer Stil* of north Germany.

In essence, the Rococo period represents a reaction to the formalism, rigidity, and seriousness that had become characteristic of the Baroque. The formalism was, in the minds of many musicians, equated with rules emanating from authority, and the reaction to it paralleled the revolt that was taking place in all fields against the authority of the king, the clergy, and even the authority imposed by tradition. The revolution in philosophical and scientific thought that had begun in the seventeenth century in the ideas of Bacon, Descartes, Newton, Spinoza, and Locke, among others, now inspired the men of the eighteenth and strengthened them in their search for intellectual freedom. Superstition, veneration or fear of the past, and blind faith in the power of the church were dethroned; a belief in science and faith in natural reason took their places. In the development of this new idea of "enlightenment," as it came to be called, the work of Montesquieu (1689–1755), Voltaire (1694–1778), and Rousseau (1712–1778) was of prime importance. And in 1715 the death of Louis XIV, who as King of France had exercised absolute authority in all areas of the arts for over fifty years, made possible a rapid expansion of the stylistic elements that underlie the art, architecture, and music of the Rococo period.

The *Style Galant*

THE NEW style as it developed in France, principally at Versailles and Paris, consisted of several new elements. Perhaps the most striking was the tone or emotional content of the music. Simply stated, the music was designed to be entertaining. Seriousness, profundity, or structural intricacy were characteristics to be avoided at all costs. Polyphonic textures in general found no place in this music, for polyphony was a "learned" style and therefore serious. A single melody was placed uppermost in the composition and supplied with the most transparent harmonic accompaniment. The melody most typically consisted of a series of short motives, repeated several times and cast in four- or eight-measure phrases. And to satisfy the Rococo taste for embellishment, the melody was generously supplied with a variety of trills, mordents, and the like (see EXAMPLE 114). Grace and

EXAMPLE 114

Couperin, *Soeur Monique*

elegance animate the music; an edifying or inspiring tone, such as was typical of much Baroque music, is not to be looked for.

The formulation of the *style galant* was quickly followed by its rapid rise to a dominant position in France and in the German courts that imitated Versailles. As a consequence, the elements of Baroque style were virtually abandoned by many fashionable composers. Contrapuntal texture and polyphonic writing in general were not suited to a style that sought to be entertaining and elegant. *Basso continuo* was abandoned, and inner parts were written out in full. The strong rhythmic drive of continuo homophony, as developed primarily in the concerto grosso, was out of place in the dainty miniatures that carried the *style galant*. The long phrases and well-spaced cadences that gave Baroque music its unbroken lines were inappropriate to music that employed a fragile harmonic foundation. The unity established in Baroque music by a single melodic or rhythmic figure representing a single mood or affection was felt to be undesirable in a style that depended upon variety to achieve its diverting effect. Finally, the abstract patterns of tone that constitute the greater part of Baroque instrumental music were held to be unsatisfactory by a generation of listeners who, under the influence of the newly found rationalism, demanded *meaning* in their music. And meaning was given to music in the *style galant* by providing titles for the compositions, in other words, by making it program music.

The earliest generation of French composers of the Rococo concerned themselves largely with the harpsichord (*clavecin*). Their model was Francois Couperin (1668–1733), the most illustrious of a long line of Couperins who had been active as composers and keyboard performers in Paris for almost two centuries. A virtuoso organist, one of the finest harpsichordists of the day, and music master to the royal family of Louis XIV, Couperin was also a highly esteemed composer. A number of his

A salon performance. Engraving by Duclos, after a painting by St. Aubin, *c.* 1750.

early works, both sacred and secular choral compositions and sets of pieces for organ, are largely in Baroque style, and a valuable instruction book, *L'art de toucher le clavecin,* published in 1716, was of great influence on a whole generation of Baroque composers including Bach and his German contemporaries. Between 1713 and 1730, however, he published four volumes of *Pièces de clavecin* that place him among the composers of the *style galant.* The more than two hundred pieces, while arranged in suites in Baroque fashion, bear descriptive titles, and although the *basso continuo* technique is dominant, the melodies are cast in short periodic phrases that reflect elegance rather than vigor.

Couperin in effect sought a compromise between Italian and French music. He composed a number of trio sonatas that testify to his admiration for Corelli; both *sonate da chiesa* and *sonate da camera* are represented, filled with the graceful, embellished melodies that are among the finest characteristics of French music of the time. A few titles among his ensemble works—trio sonatas as well as a set for *clavecin* and various other instruments—testify to the direction of Couperin's interests: *L'Apothéose de Corelli* ("The Apotheosis of Corelli"), *Apothéose de Lully* ("The Apotheosis of Lully"), and *Les Goûts-réunis* ("The Styles United").

Couperin's many suites or *ordres* departed widely from the Baroque suites of his predecessors. Dance terms as titles of movements (allemande and courante, for example) were often abolished and names of allegorical persons substituted. To each *ordre* Couperin gave a fanciful title such as *Les petits moulins à vent* ("The Little Windmills") and *Les barricades mystérieuses* ("The Mysterious Barricades"). Although the external form (two-part, with each part repeated) and characteristic metrical patterns of the dances were retained, the melodic line was so elaborately orna-mented that the direct and straightforward tone of the erstwhile dance gave way to moods of grace and delicacy. Couperin's concern with perfec-tion of small detail is everywhere apparent.[1] Occasionally in the *ordres* Couperin employed the form of the *rondeau,* comprising a recurring re-frain separated by *couplets,* in the form *ABACADA.* The tendency to employ repetition of short phrases became characteristic of the French composers of Couperin's generation and later of the *style galant* in gen-eral.

Many French composers adopted the *style galant,* but few approached Couperin in refinement of melodic ideas and elegance of expression. Jean François Dandrieu (1682–1738) and Louis-Claude Daquin (1694–1772) were among the many whose keyboard music appealed to the public of their own time. Not even Jean-Philippe Rameau, whose *clavecin* music is in the *galant* tradition, could compete with Couperin.

The keyboard music and the relatively small amount of instrumental ensemble music composed in the *style galant* in France had the virtues of being graceful, entertaining, and tasteful. The forms in which it was com-posed were seldom more elaborate than the two-part forms common to Baroque suites, although many composers, like Couperin, had written successfully in the form of the rondeau. By its very nature, however, the music in the *style galant* was prevented from progressing toward either a more complex form or a richer and more varied expressive content. Those two ingredients, necessary to lift music beyond the level of mini-aturization and entertainment, were provided by Italian and German composers.

Development of Sonata-Form

THE MOST far-reaching event in the history of Rococo music was the development of the simple two-part dance form of the Baroque, through a gradual enlargement and refinement, to the sonata-form of the Classical period. This development had actually begun earlier, primarily in the pre-Classical opera overture. The end result was a form that remained in a dominant position in the field of instrumental music for almost two hundred years, one that all instrumental composers from Haydn to Stra-vinsky employed repeatedly. It is a marvel of structural flexibility, capable of the greatest conceivable variety of expressive content.

Pre-Classical opera overture. The first steps toward sonata-form were taken in the opera overture introduced by Alessandro Scarlatti. By the

---

1 See examples of Couperin's style in *HAM,* No. 265 and *GMB,* No. 264. A piece for *clavecin* is given in *MoM,* No. 40.

beginning of the eighteenth century, it was generally cast in a form consisting of three movements arranged in fast-slow-fast tempo sequence. The first movement (and often the third) employed a two-part form, with both parts customarily repeated in performance. The first part, in two sections, A and B, began in the tonic key and modulated to the dominant, or to the relative major if the tonic was a minor key. The second part, again with two sections A and B, reversed the harmonic progression by beginning in the dominant (or relative major) and moving back to the tonic. This form, which was virtually identical with the form of the typical dance movement (allemande, courante, etc.) of the orchestral suite, may be diagrammed as follows:

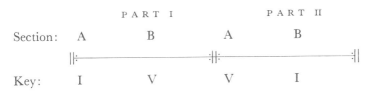

The melodic content of the movement consisted usually of a stereotyped running figure or broken-chord passage, carried by sequence repetition or other standardized device from tonic to dominant and back. The B section often provided a small degree of contrast to the A section by being set for fewer instruments, having a greater degree of rhythmic repose, or appearing in the minor dominant instead of the major. In the second part of the movement, the A section was frequently modified; instead of being a simple transposition of the A section of the first part, it frequently was based on a figure derived from that section. The opera overtures of even the most outstanding pre-Classical composers, such as Alessandro Scarlatti, Nicola Porpora, and Leonardo Leo, seldom went beyond the simple form described here.

Keyboard sonata. The overture form at this level of development was soon transferred to the keyboard, primarily by Domenico Scarlatti (1685–1757), son of the eminent opera composer. The younger Scarlatti spent almost forty years in Lisbon and Madrid in the service of the Portuguese princess who in 1746 became Queen Maria Barbara of Spain. He composed about six hundred pieces, which he called "exercises" but which are generally referred to as sonatas. These one-movement pieces exploited all the technical possibilities of the harpsichord idiom. Large leaps, passages in thirds and sixths, broken chords, repeated notes, and hand crossings appear in profusion in textures derived from the free-voiced style of earlier keyboard composers (see pages 278 and 285).

The form of the sonata gained considerably at Scarlatti's hands in the incisive shape given to the A section, which may henceforth be called a first theme. A distinctive rhythmic figure, a well-defined melodic contour, a striking broken-chord device—such elements are characteristic (see EXAMPLE 115). The B section is treated more freely; it often contains a

EXAMPLE 115

Domenico Scarlatti, Sonata themes

brilliant running figure, a technical display, or something similar. The vivid imagination, technical skill, and keyboard virtuosity of Scarlatti are everywhere mirrored in these attractive and exciting works.

Sinfonia. Returning now to the field of instrumental ensemble music, we must mention another set of developments introduced by Italian composers. Of prime importance to those developments is the fact that the pre-Classical overture was often performed as a three-movement concert piece, and that original compositions in the same form were also composed. The term *sinfonia,* which had earlier referred to an instrumental piece set within an opera or oratorio (the *sinfonia* or "Pastoral Symphony" in the first part of Handel's *Messiah* is a well-known example), was now given to this concert version of the opera overture. It is significant, too, that the trio sonata, which in the late Baroque period had been standardized as a four-movement form (see page 294), was in this period often composed in the same three-movement fast-slow-fast sequence that was characteristic of the *sinfonia* and of the Vivaldi concerto, or else in a two-movement form.

Of the host of composers who worked in the new form of the sonata, the short-lived Giovanni Battista Pergolesi (1710–1736) and the Milanese organist Giovanni Battista Sammartini (1701–1775) may be singled out. In the majority of the twelve trio sonatas attributed to Pergolesi, two further steps on the road to sonata-form were taken. In his two-part movements, the B section of the first part, no longer merely a figuration over dominant harmony, began to have melodic and rhythmic distinction and thus came appreciably closer to the status of a true second theme.

And in the second part, the concept of recapitulation of the first theme
made one of its early appearances. After the first theme (A section) on
the dominant, Pergolesi customarily referred back to phrases of the first
theme on the tonic before the part ended with the B section, also on the
tonic. In general the following diagram, a modification of the one given
on page 317, became characteristic:

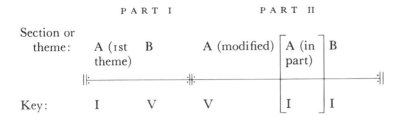

A similar form now became common in the first movements of many
sinfonie of the time. Sammartini was among the most prolific of the many
Italian composers who worked in this form; twenty-four *sinfonie*, composed from 1734 onward, are among his published works, along with a
number of trio sonatas, *concerti grossi*, and miscellaneous pieces. In the
first movements of his *sinfonie* a form which may be diagrammed exactly
like Pergolesi's is to be found.[2] The B section, however, does not yet
exhibit thematic integrity; in most cases it is a broken-chord pattern, a
series of repeated tones, or a similar conventional device. The complete
recapitulation of the A and B sections, both on tonic harmony, is a regular
feature, however.

The embryonic sonata-form was sometimes employed as a last movement also. Even in keyboard sonatas that outwardly adhere to the old
Baroque four-movement form (slow-fast-slow-fast), this practice took hold.
Examples are seen in the six sonatas for harpsichord published by Giovanni Platti (1690–1763), an Italian composer long active in Würzburg.[3]
In these works, however, as well as in Sammartini's and those of many
other composers, a main characteristic that was to distinguish sonata-form
later in the eighteenth century was not yet present: the contrast of mood
between the lyric quality of the second theme and the dramatic quality
of the first.

The *Empfindsamer Stil*

ALMOST from the moment of its inception, the music of the *style galant*
in France attracted composers in Germany. François Couperin, one of the
earliest composers in the style, became a model for German musicians as
well as the later French. A number of Bach's contemporaries imitated
Couperin's style, notably Georg Philipp Telemann (1681–1767), who was
among the most prolific composers of all time. Telemann became adept

---

2 The first movement of a *sinfonia* by Sammartini is given in *HAM*, No. 283.
3 The finale from Platti's sonata, Op. 1, No. 2, is given in *HAM*, No. 284.

The orchestra of C. P. E. Bach accompanying Frederick the Great in a flute concerto. Engraving by P. Haas.

in many different styles: Baroque, Italian Rococo, *style galant,* and, later, the north German "sensitive style" are all represented in his hundreds of suites, trio sonatas, concertos, cantatas, and operas.

C. P. E. Bach. In the works of composers associated with the court of Frederick the Great at Berlin and Potsdam, the French *style galant* was modified to conform to the expressive needs of the north German temperament. This version, as has been noted, is customarily called the *empfindsamer Stil* ("sensitive style"). The most prominent composers of the group were Carl Philipp Emanuel Bach (1714–1788), the second of Johann Sebastian's surviving children, and the Graun brothers, Johann Gottlieb (1703–1771) and Karl Heinrich (1704–1759). Although the composers of the north German school were active in many fields of composition, they excelled in writing harpsichord sonatas. The several sets of sonatas by Bach, for example, are among the most important compositions of the time.

Bach composed almost seventy sonatas, in addition to numerous rondos, fantasias, and smaller pieces for the harpsichord. The sonatas are deeply expressive; the various moods are conveyed by cantabile melodies that owe much to the *bel canto* style of Italian opera. It is likely that Bach's melodic types were influenced by the operatic productions of Hasse, one of the finest representatives of Italian opera in Germany.

The chief characteristic of Bach's version of the *empfindsamer Stil* is that it expressed a wider range of emotions than the *style galant*. This is true not only of his sonatas for harpsichord but also of his symphonies, concertos, chamber-music works, and his many Passions and cantatas. Whereas the French style was primarily graceful and elegant, the German approached sentiment, nostalgia, rough vigor, and boisterousness in addition to elegance. Bach rose above his colleagues in quality of imagination, range of harmony, and even romantic feeling. Neither the stereotyped affections of Baroque music nor the surface ornamentation of the *style galant* found much place in Bach's music. In place of these elements came a resourceful play of material that expressed contrasting emotions in close juxtaposition, made full use of the technical resources of the harpsichord, and appeared in a free style influenced by the broken style of the earlier harpsichordists (see EXAMPLE 116).

EXAMPLE 116

C. P. E. Bach, Sonata No. 5

Bach favored a three-movement form, fast-slow-fast, analogous to the emerging *sinfonia*. First movements resemble those of the Italian orchestral and chamber-music works discussed above, with a few notable exceptions. In Bach's works the A section of the second part became far more than a mere transposition of the first A section and went beyond the transitional type of passage that some Italian composers favored. A vigorous manipulation of thematic fragments drawn from the first A section was common, and the concept of a development section (which in the 1770's became virtually standard) drew appreciably closer. As a consequence of these, however, Bach felt it unnecessary to continue the second part with a recapitulation of the A (first theme) material. Many of his sonatas contain recapitulations that begin either with the B material or with phrases that had preceded the B section in the first part. The B section itself began to assume a more lyric, cantabile character, no longer composed of scale patterns, broken chords, and the like. And often, whenever the nature of the A section permitted, Bach derived the B theme from fragments of the A, thus imparting a considerable degree of unity to the form. By doing this, however, he lessened the amount of thematic contrast between sections; this thematic contrast was to become the outstanding characteristic of later Classical sonata-form.

In yet another respect Bach was among the leading composers of the time—namely in his efforts to bring sonata-form to the concerto. The first movement of a typical concerto, it will be recalled, had included a tutti theme that returned often (hence was called *ritornello*) in various keys during the course of the movement and that alternated with other thematic material and figurations presented by the soloist. Toward the 1750's it became customary, in Bach's concertos as well as those by other composers of the time, to reduce the number of *ritornelli* to two or three, principally on tonic and dominant, and to place them at the beginning, middle, and end of the movement. Later, the first body of solo material was anticipated or presented in the first tutti (eventually giving rise to the double exposition of the Classical concerto). Finally, the middle *ritornello* on the dominant became a transition to the recapitulation. Further developments in the concerto, including differentiation between first and second themes, were delayed for another generation or more. The concertos of Bach in Germany, Giuseppe Tartini (1692–1770) in Italy, and Georg Christoph Wagenseil (1715–1777) and Georg Matthias Monn (1717–1750) in Austria were among those in which various steps in this development are to be seen.

Changes in texture. The changes in musical texture brought about by Bach and other members of the north German school ran parallel to innovations in the forms of instrumental music. Those composers, as noted above, were interested in a wider range of expression than their French contemporaries, and expressive contrasts were set relatively close together in their music. The unified, homogeneous kind of texture—either polyphony or continuo homophony—characteristic of late Baroque music was, of course, unsuited to music in which sublime, merry, ponderous, light-hearted, and other moods followed in close succession. Baroque textures, therefore, were abandoned, and in their place came a series of textures in which chordal patterns, running figures, unsupported melodies, and other devices alternated according to the expressive requirements of the composer. One of the problems faced by musicians of the time was to reconcile this kaleidoscopic array of expressive types with the requirements of musical unity. The long lines of Baroque music had not been forgotten, but the wish to retain long melodic sweeps was difficult to reconcile with the desire to provide expressive variety. A lasting solution to the problem was seldom achieved in the period under discussion. The balancing of variety and unity was accomplished by the Viennese masters of the following generation.

Parallel to the variety of texture—or perhaps a consequence of it—came a marked change in the relative weight of the outer and inner voices. In music of the early eighteenth century a polarity between melody and bass was most usual; the melody in general expressed the mood of the music and the bass merely supported the melody. This is understandable in view of the fact that the idiom came to the instrumental field by way of the Italian opera, which reigned supreme in music (except perhaps in Paris) for half a century. Under the dominating melody lay the figured bass, which enabled the improvising performer at the keyboard to provide the required harmonic support; between these two poles the inner voices did little more than fill out the harmonies. In the new music of the mid-eighteenth century, on the other hand, the inner voices were raised to the level of real accompaniments, sometimes by means of parallel thirds and sixths, sometimes with a judicious selection of chord tones that created small countermelodies, and sometimes with rhythmic figures derived from those tones. Motives derived from the melody often appeared in the inner voices, to give rise to the illusion of polyphony, and unison passages in all the voices were employed to enhance sonority and achieve dramatic contrasts (see EXAMPLE 117).

EXAMPLE 117

C. P. E. Bach, Rondo

The end result of the new practices was to free the bass from its old function of providing merely a continuous harmonic support. The bass could now become melodic and carry forward the play of motives begun in the inner voices. It could be absent from the texture through extended passages, and it could divest itself of the figures and other harmonic symbols with which it had been supplied for a century and a half. In a word, the need for figured bass, for *basso continuo,* was no longer felt, and composers in general abandoned the device. The realization of figured basses, which had been the principal function of keyboard performers since about 1600, now ceased to be a vital activity. It remained of theoretical importance, however, and was used (and is still used) as a teaching device. A new era of fully written-out music, free in texture and varied in emotional content, was at hand.

New performing media. The harpsichord was the principal representative of the instruments to which the continuo had been entrusted. Now that it no longer had that function, composers began to concentrate on other ways of employing it. It was no longer needed in the orchestra (although Haydn conducted from the instrument as late as the time of his London visits about 1792–1794—purely for traditional reasons) or the trio sonata. Thereupon it began to acquire a larger repertoire of solo sonatas, it became the solo instrument in concertos of the new type, and it entered into a new relationship with one or two string instruments in the field of chamber music. The harpsichord sonatas of Carl Philipp Emanuel Bach have been discussed as representatives of the many works written by Italian and other German composers for the solo harpsichord. Giovanni Platti, mentioned above, Baldassare Galuppi (1706–1785), and Gottlieb Muffat (1690–1770), among many others, also cultivated the type, but relatively few sonatas of the period have been published.

In the field of chamber music, the virtual abandonment of the figured bass had far-reaching results. The three- or four-movement trio sonata, which had employed two violins, cello or bass, and continuo with harpsichord, quickly declined. In its place emerged the form of harpsichord sonata accompanied by a violin, a cello, or both. Here the respective roles of the string and keyboard instruments showed a complete reversal of Baroque practices, for now the harpsichord carried all the musical material and the string instruments were reduced to doubling the corresponding voices of the keyboard part.[4] As late as the 1790's, when the piano had long since replaced the harpsichord, the tradition was remembered, for Beethoven's two sonatas for cello and piano, Op. 5, were originally published as "sonatas for pianoforte with cello accompaniment." In the course of a few decades the string instruments gradually achieved more independence and soon became equal partners of the keyboard instrument. Thus the important combinations of sonata for violin and piano, or cello and piano, and trio for violin, cello, and piano (called "piano trio") came into being.

The three string instruments that had constituted the "trio" of the trio sonata required additional harmonic support, now that the keyboard instrument had been withdrawn from the ensemble. About 1740, probably in Vienna, a viola was added to the two violins and cello, and the modern string quartet resulted. It is likely that the string quartet had existed informally even earlier, in the sense that works for four-part string orchestra had sometimes been performed with only one player on a part.

The music written for string quartet was not yet on a level comparable to that of the *sinfonia.* Much of it was cast in the form of the divertimento, which originated about the beginning of the Rococo period. The divertimento was in effect an offshoot of both the Baroque suite and the pre-Classical *sinfonia.* It sometimes appeared as a two-movement form (one movement was usually a minuet), but it could also contain as many

4 A somewhat later example (about 1780) of a sonata for piano accompanied by violin, by Johann Edelmann, is given in *HAM,* No. 304.

A typical setting for a Rococo concert: the reception room at Nymphenburg in Munich.

as six or eight movements. No regular sequence of movements seems to have been attempted. Marches, minuets and other dance forms, fast movements in embryonic sonata-form, lyric slow movements in *ABA* form, concerto movements—all these are found. Italian composers in general favored two-movement forms, while the north Germans most often wrote three movements and the Austrians and south Germans inclined toward the longer sets. The terms "serenade" and "cassation" often appear in connection with "divertimento," and much of the time the terms are virtually interchangeable.

The content of the pieces was appropriate to the name. The music was diverting and entertaining and sought to serve no other function. It was employed in a variety of ways: as dinner music; as what is now called "background music" at social festivities; as music for serenading. It was composed for a variety of instrumental combinations, including string quartet, wind group, mandolin plus other instruments, and small orchestra. A clear distinction between the media was not always apparent; the final separation of chamber music from orchestral music was not made until early in the Classical period, but its beginning is to be found in the enjoyable, unassuming music of the divertimento class.

The Mannheim School

AMONG the most important centers at which the new instrumental ensemble forms were cultivated were those in Vienna and Mannheim. The
Mannheim school, attached to the Electoral court of that city, rose to
prominence through the work of a Bohemian violinist and composer,
Johann Stamitz (1717–1757). In his fourteen years as violinist and concertmaster of the Electoral orchestra, Stamitz brought his ensemble to a
position of world renown. The orchestral discipline he imposed upon
his musicians led to a quality of performance unmatched elsewhere, and
his activity as a teacher assured the continuation of Mannheim traditions
for decades after his death. Among his colleagues and successors the
names of Franz Richter (1709–1789), Ignaz Holzbauer (1711–1783), Christian Cannabich (1731–1798), and Karl Stamitz (1745–1801) may be singled
out. But Stamitz owes his permanent place in music history to his development of a new style of composition.

The symphony in the years about 1745 had been generally standardized as a three-movement work (for an exception, see below, page 328).
Embryonic sonata-form appeared regularly in the first movement and
often in the last, and a degree of contrast between first and second themes
(that is, the A and B sections of the first part of the form) was to be
found rather regularly. But transitions between themes and between
sections were scarcely more than routine passage work that carried the
harmony from tonic to dominant or vice versa, as required.

In his more than seventy symphonies Stamitz led the way to a tighter
and more logical organization. In particular, he gave new weight to
transitions between themes and to the section after the double bar (section A of Part II), which may from this point on be called the development section. Stamitz set a pattern for all to follow by deriving transitional material from the themes themselves. Further, by employing
sequence repetitions of bass passages, motives derived from themes, and
similar devices, he went far in the direction of thematic manipulation
instead of thematic statement and restatement.[5] He seems to have been
animated by a desire to eliminate nonessential and stereotyped material
(see EXAMPLE 118).

Stamitz also worked to give the B section of sonata-form movements
true musical integrity and symphonic breadth. While many other composers had provided a degree of contrast in that section, few had introduced melodic materials clearly enough individualized to justify the term
"second theme." In Stamitz's work the term is fully justified, and the
Classical sonata-form came appreciably closer. Stamitz's second theme,
in contrast to his dramatic, striking, or incisive first theme, is often filled
with cantabile expressiveness, bringing a lyric note into the symphony.

In the structure of his first themes, too, Stamitz revealed a fertile imagination, and they served as models for other members of the Mannheim

5 The first movement of Stamitz's Symphony in D, Op. 5, No. 2, is given in *HAM*,
No. 294.

EXAMPLE 118

Stamitz, *Sinfonia*, Op. 3, No. 1

(sustained tones in oboes and horns omitted)

school. Themes based on an ascending series of tones of the triad became common; known as "Mannheim rockets" when played at fast tempo, they were widely copied and appeared in the works of Mozart and Beethoven decades later.[6] Another device, later called the "Mannheim sigh," was an accented suspension or appoggiatura placed in a prominent melodic position. This device, derived from operatic melodies, was used generally throughout Germany and Austria and continued to find a

6 See, for example, the finale of Mozart's D-minor piano concerto, K. 466; the finale of his G-minor symphony, K. 550; and the first movement of Beethoven's piano trio, Op. 1, No. 1.

place in music of the later Classical period.[7] In connection with these devices, and with the closely juxtaposed thematic and textural contrasts that became striking features of large quantities of Rococo music, the Mannheim composers introduced abrupt dynamic changes at short intervals. In a typical passage, a phrase containing two or three chords played at a *forte* level was followed by a contrasting phrase played at a *piano* level or less, after which the *forte* passage returned.

A new approach to tonal nuance, introduced by Stamitz and widely employed by his followers, became another outstanding stylistic device. Dynamic variation had been an ingredient of music for centuries, of course. Baroque ensemble music had typically employed alternations of loud and soft on phrase repetitions; such alternations, typically referred to as "terrace dynamics," had provided composers with one means of achieving contrast. In sonatas and other pieces for violin, gradual increases and decreases of tonal volume had long been employed; Francesco Geminiani published a number of works dealing with violin instruction in the decades after 1730 in which the problems of crescendo and decrescendo had received considerable attention. The Italian opera orchestra, too, had been familiar with swellings of tone, and composers there had used them with striking dramatic effect. Operas employing this device were widely performed throughout Europe in the first years of Stamitz's activity at Mannheim. Stamitz, however, had developed his orchestra to such a high level of precision that he was able to execute crescendos and diminuendos with accuracy; the carefully controlled crescendo became known as the "Mannheim crescendo." In any case, the expressive crescendo, now applied to symphonic performance, became another feature for which the Mannheim composers were renowned.

The three-movement structure of the symphony, finally, was expanded to four by Stamitz. Somewhat earlier, Georg Matthias Monn in Vienna had added a minuet to one of his symphonies.[8] This innovation, achieved about 1740, seems not to have been adopted by other Viennese composers, but from about 1745 Stamitz regularly employed a four-movement form consisting of fast-slow-minuet-fast. Even at Mannheim the minuet was not regularly included by other members of the school. It remained for Haydn, about 1765, to rediscover the virtues of the expanded form and to include a minuet in the symphony (and in the string quartet) as a matter of course.

Other Composers

AS WE have seen, several of the innovations in form and style formerly attributed entirely to composers of the Mannheim school are now known to have been employed by composers at Vienna, Berlin, and elsewhere. Another example may be seen in the work of Niccolò Jommelli (1714–1774). This outstanding opera composer, after a successful career in

7 The main theme of Mozart's G-minor symphony, K. 550, first movement, is based on a "Mannheim sigh."

8 The finale of this symphony is given in *HAM*, No. 295.

Naples, Venice, and Rome, became active at Stuttgart in 1753. Some of his operas, however, had been produced at Mannheim as early as 1750, and the solid symphonic accompaniments on which they were based were known to Mannheim composers. Melodic phrases rich in striking motives were a part of Jommelli's style, and it has been noted that similar motive-aden phrases became a part of the Mannheim vocabulary as well. Visitors to Mannheim—including Mozart, who spent several months there in the winter of 1777–1778—were undeniably impressed by the performance standards of the Electoral orchestra, however, and they spread the fame of the school. In the process, significant Viennese composers such as Monn, Georg Christoph Wagenseil (1717–1777), and Josef Starzer (1726–1787) may have been overlooked.

Monn's work in creating a four-movement symphony has been mentioned. He in effect marked a transition from the Baroque to the Rococo. Stylistic devices such as bass lines carried forward in diatonic, stepwise fashion, passages based on sequence repetition of phrases—these testify to the influence of the past upon him. Wagenseil, on the other hand, inclined toward the new style in every detail. A typical Wagenseil theme is a two- or four-measure phrase containing motives that provide him with material for use in transitions and in development sections.

At other centers, notably Paris and London, the leading composers may be counted as disciples of the Mannheimers. The most prominent of these include Johann Schobert (1720–1767), active in Paris from about 1760; Johann Edelmann (1749–1794), in Paris from the 1770's; and Johann Christian Bach (1735–1782), the youngest surviving son of Johann Sebastian, active in London from 1762. In each case, Mannheim characteristics were individually modified. Schobert inclined toward moody and dramatic utterance; a direct line runs from Schobert through Mozart to Beethoven. Bach wrote in an unfailingly melodious style, favoring two-movement instrumental compositions in the Italian tradition. It may be not without significance that he spent eight years in Milan before moving to London.

It must be stressed that not all composers employed the Italian-German-Austrian fusion that eventually resulted in the style of the Classical period. The *style galant* remained an ingredient of French opera, and *galant* elements emerged in the music of certain Italian composers. Chief among the latter was Luigi Boccherini (1743–1805), eminent cellist and prolific composer primarily in the field of chamber music. As a concertizing cellist Boccherini was especially successful in Paris, where his earliest publications appeared. Later he lived and worked in Madrid. In Boccherini's almost three hundred chamber-music works one finds a unique blend of Italian lyricism and French elegance. His charming melodies are profusely ornamented, but they are also motivic in structure. The voices below the melody are often set in imitative texture. His music avoids drama and tension, and its unfailingly lyric quality prevents it from achieving great expressive variety (see EXAMPLE 119).

It is perhaps this last point that represents both the strength and the weakness of Rococo music in general. Many talented composers were

EXAMPLE 119

Boccherini, Quartet, Op. 33, No. 1

active in the period; they wrote engagingly, melodiously, and gracefully. Many industrious composers were also active, doing much to lay the basis for the significant thematic manipulation upon which the future of sonata-form depended. But few of them were equally gifted in both directions. The problem of manipulating themes so that expressive music resulted was solved by only a relatively small number of Rococo composers. A new relationship between the way of expressing musical ideas (namely, form) and the quality of the ideas themselves (content) was in the process of being developed, and finding it was beyond most composers of the period. It remained for other more gifted musicians to achieve a satisfactory relationship between form and content in the period beginning roughly in the 1770's, at the point where the Rococo period begins to fade and give way to the Classical.

The position of Vienna as a musical center in the late eighteenth century was unique. Vienna represented the cultural center of the flourishing Austrian empire; geographically it lay at the crossroads of Europe. Music from Italy and north Germany was heard there, as well as music from the east and the west. Folk music from Hungary, Croatia, and Turkey mingled with folk music from the Tyrol, Bohemia, and south Germany. The musical products of the French and German courts were welcomed as eagerly as the products of Italian and French opera houses. Mannheim, Berlin, Paris, and London were all represented musically. Out of this variety of kinds and styles of music, a new style emerged at Vienna that was to dominate Europe for several generations and to influence all music for more than a century.

The Classical Period: Opera

As the eighteenth century passed its midpoint, the Italian type of serious opera began to lose its dominant position. Characteristics that had first helped to raise it to that position now became virtually rigid formulas, for it had become simply a vehicle in which accomplished singers displayed their vocal agility, in the process departing widely from the composer's intentions. The conventional *da capo* aria, for example, was usually sung with its recapitulation elaborately embellished by the singer, and contributed little or nothing to the unfolding of whatever dramatic plot the libretto possessed. The recitatives, which did present the drama, were usually relegated to a subordinate position. They were most often of the *secco* type, in which the orchestra played no part; the harpsichord alone supported the declamatory vocal line with a few chords. Since

Perspective view of the mechanism of a theater. Engraving by Patour, Paris, 1766.
[THE METROPOLITAN MUSEUM OF ART]

ensembles were rarely used the composer was generally limited to setting arias for one voice and orchestra; this seriously hampered the exceptional composer who wanted to infuse his scores with dramatic life. The basic harmonic simplicity and the homophonic texture of the pre-Classical opera of the period from 1710 to 1740 were reflections of the simplicity and mere tunefulness of other forms of *galant* music. Toward the 1750's, as we have seen in Chapter 16, *galant* music became somewhat more expressive and significant, and a parallel to this deepening of mood and thickening of texture can be seen in the opera as well.

The defects of opera were widely recognized. Perhaps the best-known document dealing with the state of opera in the early eighteenth century is a satire called *Il teatro alla moda* ("The Fashionable Theater"), written by Benedetto Marcello, himself an eminent composer, about 1720. The work purports to be a series of instructions to those connected with the opera—poet, singer, composer, and all the rest. The author of the libretto, says Marcello, "will write the whole opera without formulating any plot, simply composing it line by line. . . . He will absolutely never allow the singer to make his exit without the customary *canzonetta*, especially when by vicissitude of the drama, the latter must go out to die, commit suicide, drink poison, etc." The composer must "see to it that the arias, to the very end of the opera, are alternately a lively one and a pathetic one, without regard to the words, the modes, or the proprieties of the scene. . . . If the modern composer should give lessons to some virtuosa of the opera house, let him have a care to charge her to enunciate badly, and with the object to teach her a great number of divisions and graces, so that not a single word will be understood, and by this means the music will stand out better and be appreciated." In similar fashion, he advises the singer to bow to his friends during the performance, to embellish his part at will, to use the highest tones of which he is capable, to ignore the composer, and to monopolize even those scenes of which he is not a part.[1]

It is true that while many composers and listeners were perfectly satisfied with the Italian opera of their time, other composers recognized its imperfections and sought to restore a balance between music and drama. The orchestrally accompanied recitative as cultivated by Hasse, for example (see Chapter 13), had been given a greater degree of musical interest, raising the dramatic tension of the whole, although Hasse remained within the framework of pre-Classical opera. The simple and direct appeal of *opera buffa* (see below, page 340) probably contributed to an awareness that serious opera had become overly elaborate and dramatically questionable. Developments in the *sinfonia* and in orchestral writing generally made it obvious that the opera orchestra was not being employed to the fullest extent of its possibilities. Rousseau's appeal for a return to naturalness may be taken as evidence that the times de-

---

1 An extended portion of *Il teatro alla moda* is reprinted in *SRMH*, pp. 518–31. The complete work in English translation may be found in *The Musical Quarterly*, XXXIV (1949), pp. 371–403, and XXXV (1949), pp. 85–105.

manded a change. In the century and a half of its existence, opera had been modified or reformed several times. Now, at the midpoint of the eighteenth century, it was ripe for another series of reforms.

The Reform of Opera

THE ESSENTIAL characteristic of the new kind of serious opera that arose in the period after 1760 is that renewed weight was given to the dramatic element; in a sense, the form began again to justify its earlier name of "drama in music." While this achievement is often credited solely to Gluck, many composers took part in it, notably Niccolò Jommelli and Tommaso Traëtta.

Jommelli (1714–1774), born in Naples, began his career in 1737 with operas of the conventional type. In 1749, moving to Vienna, he developed a friendship with Metastasio; this, perhaps, kept him from abandoning the older type of opera completely. The influence of Hasse was equally strong, however, particularly in regard to the flexible, orchestrally accompanied recitative.

In 1753 Jommelli was appointed chapelmaster to the Duke of Württemberg in Stuttgart, where he remained for fifteen years. Here Jommelli found himself in a center of French culture; the works of Lully and Rameau were well known, and Jommelli profited from the examples set by the older French masters. In his operas of this period, the recitatives are expressive and varied in style, well suited to carrying forward the dramatic implications of the librettos. Choruses, which had been important elements in the French opera and had been used to further the dramatic action, appeared in his works to an increasing degree. In fact, large scene complexes, consisting of many disparate elements welded together into a dramatic unity, became features of his Stuttgart operas. As an example, the ninth scene of Act I of *Fetonte,* the first work he composed for that city, has the following plan:

> *March,* orchestra (*andante*), two phrases, six and ten measures; both phrases repeated
>
> Chorus with orchestra (*andante*), nine measures; recitative, sung by ORCANE, sixteen measures; then Chorus *da capo*
>
> Recitative, sung by ORCANE and EPEFO
>
> Aria, sung by CLIMENE, six measures (*grave*), four measures (*allegro*), six measures (*grave*), twenty-eight measures (*andante*), three measures (*adagio*), forty-nine measures (*allegro*)

Jommelli's arias, too, were designed to present details of the dramatic action rather than to comment or reflect on that action (Climene's aria, outlined above, is of this type). The traditional *da capo* aria, which so often impeded the progress of the drama by presenting a full recapitulation of the reflective text of the first part of the aria, was also modified. In the Stuttgart operas much stress is laid on the middle part of the aria, and the recapitulation contains only a portion of the first part; this is the so-called *dal segno* aria. The following diagram will clarify the distinction between the two types:

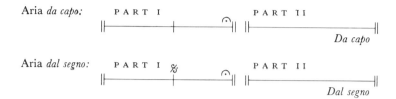

Aria *da capo:*

Aria *dal segno:*

Finally, ensembles began to play a larger part in the serious opera, as they had long done in the comic opera.

German influences, especially in the area of orchestral writing, also worked on Jommelli. Hasse at Dresden had led the way in composing orchestral parts that were varied in texture and colorful in effect, and the early German symphonists had begun to show the possibilities of fully developed inner voices in their orchestral scores. Jommelli went beyond his operatic models in employing a richer harmonic scheme, in applying principles of thematic development in orchestral accompaniments, and on occasion in composing as overtures small pieces of mood music that effectively foreshadowed the emotional tone of the operas to which they were attached. The overture sometimes embodied themes that were to appear in the opera itself, and thus a tighter connection between the two was assured.

Tommaso Traëtta (1727–1779), after a number of operatic successes in Naples and other Italian cities, spent seven years (1758–1765) at the court of Parma. Thereafter his career took him to Venice, St. Petersburg, London, and back to Venice. Parma, in northern Italy, was another seat of French culture; Traëtta heard and conducted Rameau's operas there, and his works reflect many of the French influences found in Jommelli's operas. Traëtta recaptured the dramatic ideals of Rameau (some of whose texts he modified and set to music); choral operas containing elaborate ballets are one result. He also employed large ensemble scenes, attesting to his familiarity with the *opera buffa*. Orchestrally accompanied and emotionally varied recitatives are notable features of his style, as are the *dal segno* arias that advance the dramatic action rather than inhibit it.

Thus both Jommelli and Traëtta made notable changes in the serious opera of their time. Choruses, ballets, ensemble scenes, dramatic recitatives, rich orchestral passages—such elements were regularly employed. But neither composer departed completely from the old type of libretto. Jommelli remained attached to the work of his friend Metastasio. Both composers wrote melodic lines of the kind to delight the virtuoso singers and provided opportunities for cadenzas, freely improvised ornaments, and other vocal embellishments. Their choruses remained largely homophonic and harmonically simple. In short, the operas of these composers mark a way station on the path to reform. It remained for a German composer, Italian trained but long a resident of Austria and France, to complete the journey and to reform the opera in the direction of dramatic truth.

Gluck

CHRISTOPH WILLIBALD VON GLUCK (1714–1787) was born in Bavaria near the Bohemian Forest. After some training in nearby towns and in Prague, he spent the years from 1737 to 1745 in Milan, where he studied with Sammartini and composed his first opera. For several years he traveled widely, visiting Paris, London, Copenhagen, and other opera centers. About 1750 he settled in Vienna, where he continued his activities as a composer and conductor and wrote a number of successful operas. From 1773 to 1779 he lived in Paris, after which he returned to Vienna, where he died in 1787.

In the first twenty years of his career, during which he wrote about twenty operas, Gluck distinguished himself as a capable composer in the general style of Hasse. The majority of the operas of this period were set to texts by Metastasio; *Artaserse* (Milan, 1741), *Ipermestra* (Venice, 1744), and *La clemenza di Tito* (Naples, 1752) are representative. The solid orchestral writing he learned from Sammartini—similar to the instrumental style found in Jommelli's works—is characteristic, but there is little indication in these works that Gluck was to lead opera in a new direction. Although serious purpose, vigorous rhythms, and restrained melodic lines raise them above many other Italian works of the time, these operas are not essentially different from the latter in purpose or dramatic intensity.

In 1754 Gluck was appointed composer of theater and chamber music to the Viennese court, where his duties brought him into contact with the *opéra comique* (see below, page 343). Such works were popular in Vienna, and he was made responsible for preparing, arranging, and conducting the performances. In the years after 1755, with the encouragement of Count Giacomo Durazzo, superintendent of the Royal Theater, Gluck began to add more and more of his own music to the French works, until in 1764 a completely original *opéra comique* resulted: *La rencontre imprévue* ("The Unexpected Meeting"). He also worked in the field of the tragic ballet, his most outstanding work of this type being *Don Juan* (1761). Through this concern with two different aspects of French culture, *opéra comique* and ballet, Gluck revised his style considerably. The influence of the text on the music grew stronger, melodic lines became more restrained, darker emotions were touched upon, and simplicity of utterance took the place of elaborate or spectacular expression. The music seemed designed to reinforce the dramatic tension of the opera text and of the dances in the ballet.

At this point in his career Gluck was aided by Ranieri da Calzabigi (1714–1795), Italian poet, amateur musician, and government official. Calzabigi became the central figure in a revolt against Italian opera in general and Metastasio's texts in particular. He wrote a libretto for Gluck based on the Orpheus myth, and the collaboration resulted in the first of the reform operas, *Orfeo ed Euridice,* produced at Vienna in 1762.

The aesthetic purpose of Calzabigi and Gluck in writing *Orfeo* was to bring the substance and form of Greek tragedy to the opera. This, it will be recalled, had been the purpose of the Florentine Camerata (see Chapter 13), and it also underlay the French operas of Lully. In the Calzabigi version of the Orpheus legend, however, the action is confined to a few large tableaux and to the expression of a few emotional states. The distinction between the recitative as vehicle of the drama and the aria as vehicle of the music tends to disappear, for the music permeates every bit of the dramatic action. The chorus, too, plays a different role than before; at times it is reflective, at times it participates in the action. And the whole is characterized by a simplicity of mood approaching austerity. No vocal extravagances are permitted to mar the reposeful tone of the various scenes; the drama becomes effective through the sheer economy of the vocal writing (see EXAMPLE 120). Yet a few characteristics of the old opera type are still present: the title role (Orpheus) is

EXAMPLE 120

Gluck, *Orfeo ed Euridice,* Act II

TRANSLATION:
Thousand torments, threatening shadows, I too bear
in my heart.

given to a male alto, various allegorical figures are introduced, and the overture is thematically independent of the opera. In the subsequent collaborations of Gluck and Calzabigi described below, some of these old-fashioned touches, such as the *recitativo secco,* were removed.

Alceste, produced in Vienna in 1767, is a larger and more elaborate work than *Orfeo* in many respects. The chorus plays a more important role, and from the opening choruses of mourning to the closing chorus of jubilation, the opera is sonorous and truly monumental. The various scenes are tightly constructed with recitatives, arias, ensembles, and choruses welded into wholes. There is less of the air of restraint and economy that had characterized *Orfeo.* Gluck's purpose comes to eloquent expression both in the opera itself and in the preface published with the score in 1769. This famous document, one of the milestones on the path of operatic evolution, expresses Gluck's intention ". . . to restrict music to its true office of serving poetry by means of expression and by following the situations of the story, without interrupting the action or stifling it with a useless superfluity of ornaments." [2]

The third collaboration between Gluck and Calzabigi was *Paride ed Elena,* produced at Vienna in 1770. While both *Orfeo* and *Alceste* had been enthusiastically received and had inspired several imitations (Traëtta's *Iphigénie en Tauride* is a notable example), *Paride* was not a success. Gluck's collaboration with Calzabigi ceased and the poet left Vienna in the following year.

At this point, probably inspired by his success in composing French *opéras comiques* for the Austrian court, Gluck turned his attention to Paris. A suitable libretto based on Racine's *Iphigénie en Aulide* was prepared by François du Roullet, who was attached to the French embassy staff in Vienna. Gluck began to compose the work in 1772, and in 1774, through the urgings of Du Roullet and the intervention of Queen Marie Antoinette, *Iphigénie en Aulide* was produced at the Paris Opéra.[3] Gluck had gone to Paris a year earlier to supervise the production; he remained six years. The success of *Iphigénie* prompted him to revise *Orfeo* for a Paris production in the same year, and this was followed by a revision of *Alceste* in 1776. In 1777 Gluck wrote *Armide,* on a libretto by Quinault, and in 1779 he composed his masterwork, *Iphigénie en Tauride,* arranged from Euripides' tragedy by Guillard.

The two *Iphigénies* and *Armide,* taken together, represent first of all a fusion of French and Italian operatic types. Varied ensembles (quartets, solos or duets with chorus, and the like); short airs of a few measures only, set between passages of arioso or accompanied recitative; considerable fluidity and speed in the dramatic action; a chaconne in *Armide,* on the model of those of Lully and Rameau; an idyllic tone where appropriate to the respective texts; many dramatic choruses similar to those in Rameau—these are all characteristics derived from the French opera. On the other hand, *Iphigénie en Tauride* contains several purely lyric

2 The preface is reprinted in *SRMH,* pp. 673–75.
3 Du Roullet's letter to a director of the Opera is given in *SRMH,* pp. 676–80.

A performance of Gluck's *Armide,* Paris, *c.* 1777. Eighteenth-century drawing.

passages (even a *da capo* aria) on the Italian model, and borrowings from Gluck's earlier Italian operas are incorporated into the score.

The revisions of *Orfeo* and *Alceste* reveal further evidence of the fusion of French and Italian styles. The title role of Orpheus, given to a *castrato* in Vienna, was rewritten for tenor in the Paris version, and several ballets were added to the score. *Alceste* was extensively rewritten. The figure of Apollo, whom Calzabigi had introduced into the Viennese (that is, Italian) version, was replaced by that of Hercules, borrowed from Lully's opera. Certain scenes were rearranged to form a more logical sequence, some were omitted as unsuited to French taste, and a number of dances were added.

With *Iphigénie en Tauride,* a new international operatic type was at hand. The chorus had returned to hold an important place in the unfolding of the drama. The old polarity of drama (in the *recitativo secco*) and music (in the arias) was gone. In its place came a new kind of dramatic musical expression, far richer than the entertaining or spectacular expression of the Rococo opera. The music had not become slavishly subordinate to the drama; by simplifying the drama and removing all irrelevancies, the composer was able to write music which was itself dramatic. Many devices that had been found dramatically effective and moving in other operatic types were incorporated: the large-scale declamatory style of the French lyric tragedy, the terseness and concentration of the new symphonic style, the purely sensuous appeal of beautiful melody, and the uncomplicated structure of comic opera. Through his amalgamation of many style elements, and through his ability to combine them so that drama and music were balanced and inseparable, Gluck achieved an operatic reform.

Serious Opera after Gluck

GLUCK's reform operas were in general successful both in Vienna and Paris. The strength of the Italian tradition, however, was such that the reforms were not unanimously adopted. Even after the success of *Iphigénie en Aulide* and the revised versions of *Orfeo* and *Alceste* (1774–1776), a portion of the Parisian operatic public sought a champion of Italian opera to oppose Gluck. Niccolò Piccinni (1728–1800) had come to Paris after a successful career in Naples and Rome, where he had composed both *opere serie* and *buffe*. In the hope of demonstrating the superiority of Italian music over the French, the proponents of the Italian asked Piccinni and Gluck to set the same text in their respective styles, choosing Quinault's *Roland*. When Gluck became aware of the purpose of the proposal, he turned to another of Quinault's librettos instead; the opera *Armide* (1777), mentioned above, was the result. Piccinni completed his version of *Roland* in 1778, and rather than upholding the integrity of the Italian style, he adopted many of the style elements of Gluck. He continued writing French operas until 1785 with estimable success; among his most important works are settings of *Iphigénie en Tauride* (1781) and *Didon* (1783).

Gluck's ideals were kept alive, even though somewhat transformed, for another generation by a series of Italian composers who, like Piccinni, came to Paris as representatives of Italian art and succumbed to the French operatic style. Antonio Sacchini (1730–1786) composed some fifty operas for Naples, Rome, and Venice before moving to London about 1772. In 1781 he was invited to Paris, where he arranged a few of his earlier operas for French production and composed others. His most successful work was *Oedipe à Colone* (1786), a work which was performed until the 1840's. The noble dramatic tone, reticence, and expressiveness found in Gluck were maintained by Sacchini.

Antonio Salieri (1750–1825), court composer at Vienna from 1774 to 1790, came under Gluck's influence in 1774. At Gluck's recommendation he composed several operas for Paris, of which *Les Danaïdes* (1784) and *Tarare* (1787) were the most successful. Salieri made the music subordinate to the drama, thus carrying out the implication of the reform operas. He returned to Vienna about 1785, where he later numbered Beethoven, Schubert, and Liszt among his pupils.

Gluck's help was also extended to French composers. Étienne-Nicolas Méhul (1763–1817) came to Paris from Ardennes in 1778 to seek instruction in composition. Gluck awakened his interest in the musical stage, and in the fields of both *opéra sérieux* and *opéra comique* (see below, page 343) Méhul worked industriously for over thirty years. With a sense of economy and restraint similar to Gluck's, he brought a heartfelt melodiousness into his major works. Many of them are related to the *opéra comique* type (with spoken dialogue) in all respects but subject matter. His best works of this type are *Euphrosine et Coradin* (1790), *Joseph* (1807), and *Les Amazones* (1811).

Two other Italian composers, Luigi Cherubini (1760–1842) and Gasparo Spontini (1774–1851), settled in Paris after Gluck's death. The influence of the reform operas on them was neither as direct nor as long-lasting as it was on the earlier generation of Italian composers in Paris. Cherubini's first success in the French capital was *Lodoïska* (1791); this was followed by *Médée* (1797) and his most important work, *Les deux journées* (1800, performed at London and in Germany as *The Water Carrier* and *Der Wasserträger*).

Cherubini composed on a large scale and brought moods of excitement and suspense to the opera. He frequently employed the device of the "rescue" (of the hero, who was placed in a dangerous situation and saved from harm at the last minute). The device itself and the suspense it engendered were particularly appreciated by a public that had recently lived through the terrors of the Revolution. Another feature, found especially in *Les deux journées,* is the admixture of sentiment, compassion, and humane feeling in the music given to the exemplary or noble characters, as opposed to the "villains." This characteristic touch, along with an occasional dark, moody, or stormy atmosphere, leads directly to the Romantic opera of the period after about 1825; in fact, Cherubini's music was highly esteemed by Beethoven. *Les deux journées* and *Faniska* (1807) were both performed in Vienna, and a similarity in style between *Faniska* and Beethoven's works of that time is to be noted.

Spontini arrived in Paris about 1803. His importance in the French capital rests almost entirely on two works, *La Vestale* (1807) and *Fernand Cortez* (1809). Spontini synthesized all the dramatic and spectacular elements the stage had to offer, but he employed them with restraint and good taste. His works may be considered as forerunners of the sensational grand opera of the 1830's. Rescues, turbulent crowd scenes, and various stage effects (lightning flashes are typical) are set opposite expressive ensembles, sentimental solo passages, and static but effective choruses. Spontini enjoyed the patronage of Napoleon and the Empress Josephine, who did much to have his revolutionary works accepted. In 1820 he was named musical director of the court at Berlin; there he was influential in German musical life, primarily as a conductor, for over twenty years.

Opera Buffa

ITALIAN composers of serious opera remained largely unaffected by the reforms of Gluck. *Opere serie* continued to be written, and although they differed to some extent in form and content from earlier works, the differences were largely derived from the form of the *opera buffa,* or comic opera, which became the most important item of Italian music through the remainder of the eighteenth century and beyond.

The *opera buffa,* as indicated in Chapter 13, had grown out of the intermezzo, a light-hearted or farcical piece in two acts sung during the intermissions of a three-act serious opera. The form was characterized by the use of *recitativo secco,* with the dialogue carried on in repeated notes sung at a rapid tempo. The bass voice was employed in the intermezzo (*castrati* found no place in that form), and the full quartet of voices made possible a number of ensembles in which all characters joined.

A trend toward a new, greatly expanded type of comic opera was set in motion by Carlo Goldoni (1707–1793), a Venetian poet and dramatist. Goldoni's comedies were solid in plot and structure. They substituted subtle humor and honest sentiment for the farcical and coarse humor that had characterized the earlier type and brought dignified language and an air of refinement to the musical theater. One of the first composers to set Goldoni's librettos to music, beginning in 1749, was Baldassare Galuppi (1706–1785). After a career which took him from Venice to London and St. Petersburg, Galuppi returned to Venice in 1748 and became second chapelmaster at the Cathedral of San Marco. He composed over a hundred operas, in addition to large quantities of sacred choral music; and he became the subject of a well-known poem by Robert Browning, "A Toccata of Galuppi's."

Composers in other Italian cities also made use of Goldoni's texts and of similar texts written on the Goldoni model. Niccolò Piccinni, before his move to Paris and his encounter with Gluck, was one of the most successful composers in the new style. With almost 140 operas to his credit, he is remembered primarily for the *La buona figliuola* ("The Good Girl," Rome, 1760), on Goldoni's text; the work was performed and enjoyed throughout Europe. Florian Gassmann (1729–1774) composed fourteen comic operas for Vienna; his most successful works were two on Goldoni's texts: *L'amore artigiano* ("Love Among the Artisans," 1767) and *La contessina* ("The Little Countess," 1770).

In the works of Giovanni Paisiello (1740–1816) and Domenico Cimarosa (1749–1801), the *opera buffa* reached a new high level. Paisiello began his career in Naples, where he studied with Durante and composed about fifty comic operas in twelve years. From 1776 to 1784 he was at St. Petersburg as opera composer to Empress Catherine II, where his masterpiece, *Il barbiere di Siviglia* ("The Barber of Seville," 1782), was written. He then returned to Naples, became active in the fields of sacred and instrumental music, and brought the total of his operas to about one hundred. Cimarosa, like Paisiello, is associated primarily with Naples, but he succeeded his fellow townsman at St. Petersburg from 1787 to 1791 and spent the two following years at Vienna as imperial chapelmaster. Cimarosa composed fluently and easily; he wrote about seventy-five operas, most of them in the comic vein, and a considerable amount of instrumental and sacred and secular choral music. His most famous work is *Il matrimonio segreto* ("The Secret Marriage"), produced at Vienna in 1792.

A number of stylistic and formal elements distinguish the *opera buffa* from the *opera seria.* Chief among these elements is the ensemble, particularly the ensemble finale. In some cases the final scene was merely one in which the main characters appeared and presented an appropriate closing sentiment in ensemble style. In an attempt to carry the action through to the very end of the opera, later composers—notably Nicola Logroscino (1698–c. 1765)—devised a large through-composed piece in which the singers acted out their respective roles in concert. This plan suffered, however, from having neither unity nor dramatic impact. In the comic operas of Galuppi an ensemble consisting of short sections, each concerned with one character and one bit of action, was attempted; this type was later called the "chain finale." Piccinni in turn gave a higher level of organization to the finale by employing a recurring theme that unified the whole and gave rise to the "rondo finale." There the matter rested until the time of Mozart.

The content of the librettos continued to show both literary and dramatic advances over the earlier type. Parody of serious opera continued to be a favorite device. In addition, plots revolved around domestic situations (Pergolesi's *La serva padrona* had provided a notable example a generation earlier), mistaken identity, love affairs among the high-born as well as the lowly, and similar matters. Subtle comedy rather than farce had long since become the guiding principle; sentiment and the milder passions brought variety to the librettos. The composers mentioned here, notably Piccinni and Paisiello, exhibited great resourcefulness in adapting the forms to fit the comic or dramatic situations. Apt characterization and clever delineation of individual character traits through appropriate music became features of the new *opera buffa,* especially of the type favored by Paisiello.

The texture and other inner details of the *opera buffa* were at times influenced by developments in the serious opera; indeed, the major composers of the time wrote with equal ease in both fields. The growth of the orchestra and the enriching of orchestral texture through motivic manipulation, both characteristic of the *opera seria,* contributed to the increasing sonority of the *opera buffa* as well. Before about 1760 the orchestra had consisted mainly of string instruments. After that date woodwinds and brass instruments were employed in increasing numbers, until an orchestra of virtually symphonic dimensions was usual. Piccinni and Paisiello again are distinguished for their use of striking melodic or rhythmic motives that, when employed throughout a scene in a variety of orchestral contexts, greatly enhanced its appeal. Gassmann, in common with other members of the Viennese school and under the influence of the emerging symphony, developed a more diversified orchestral texture through the use of instrumental doublings, bits of imitation, and recurrence of motives often employed in sequence.

The melodic line remained, of course, the most immediately apparent aspect of the music, and it is here that the major composers revealed their deftness and comic sense. The melodies range from the sentimental to the truly comic. In the latter, many repeated notes, large leaps, sudden turns of phrase, abrupt pauses, irregular phrase lengths, and similar devices contributed to the element of the unexpected, upon which this type of humor is generally based. In the more lyric type of melody, a gently undulating contour, an assimilation of the tones of the tonic triad, and a simple and direct expression were found most appealing (see EXAMPLE 121). Cimarosa excelled in a limpid and spontaneous

EXAMPLE 121

Paisiello, *Il barbiere di Siviglia*

TRANSLATION:
Praise heaven, for at last my Argo has opened the shutter.

melodic flow; lively moods are appropriately expressed in fast-moving and witty music, and sentimental moods are correspondingly graceful or lyric. Finally, both types of recitative (*secco* and *accompagnato*) continued in use. The first was usually in the *parlando* or "patter" style. The second found considerable employment in scenes where parody and exaggeration were called for. The melodic aspects of the Italian *opera buffa*, together with the formal, textural, and comic aspects, became favorite articles of export to all the countries of Europe and continued in vogue until well into the nineteenth century.

Opéra Comique

THE FRENCH comic opera, whose beginnings may be placed about 1750, had two roots, one French and the other Italian, running back to the seventeenth century. The so-called *ballets comiques,* compounded of dances, simple songs, and spoken dialogue, had been performed at Paris through the early 1600's and had risen to their highest level of development at the court of Louis XIV in the time of Lully and Molière, about 1670. About that time an Italian theater in Paris, which had for a decade presented the ancient and improvised *commedia dell' arte* (in Italian), moved gradually in the direction of a popularized comic ballet by adding dances, songs, and dialogues in French to their improvised plays.

At the beginning of the eighteenth century, French comic plays interspersed with music became the stock-in-trade of itinerant groups of actors who performed for a few weeks annually at the fairs held outside Paris. The music necessarily was of the simplest sort, since the actors were not trained musicians. For the most part it consisted of short popular tunes in strophic form, to which the performers adapted new texts; the songs were called *vaudevilles* (probably derived from *vaux de Vire,* the valley of the Vire, where the songs presumably originated). A practical reason for the interpolation of songs existed also. The Académie Royale de Musique held a monopoly on operas and the Comédie Française on spoken plays; the mixture of speech and song apparently was considered satisfactory to the officials of both royal institutions, since it encroached upon neither one directly.

In the course of the next few decades the quality of the works improved. A competing institution called the New Italian Theater had been established shortly after the death of Louis XIV, however, and in the 1740's came under the influence of Charles-Simon Favart (1710–1792). The latter, a dramatist, sought to remove the improvisational tone which had marked the earlier comedies and encouraged the composition of new songs in place of the old *vaudevilles.* Eventually the two theaters merged and took the name of Opéra Comique. The opposition offered by the Royal Academy had long since been withdrawn, and comic opera now enjoyed a formal name, a theater, and a degree of patronage.

The way had been prepared for the new *opéra comique* even earlier, however. Pergolesi's *La serva padrona* had been performed in Paris in 1746 without noticeable success, but by 1752 the cultural climate had changed markedly and a second performance of Pergolesi's little masterpiece was enormously successful. The performance of 1752 provoked another of the public disagreements that occur frequently in French cultural history: the relative merits of Italian music in general and Italian opera in particular, as opposed to French music, were loudly debated. Even the royal family took sides. Louis XV became a champion of French music; Queen Marie—possibly because her father, Stanislaus I of Poland, was an admirer of Rousseau—publicly espoused the cause of the Italian *buffa.* The whole episode, which antedated the Gluck-Piccinni controversy by twenty-five years, is known to music history as the "war of the buffoons."

Jean-Jacques Rousseau (1712–1778), philosopher and self-trained musician, became an ardent spokesman for the Italian camp. His hostility to French music was made evident in his musical writings in the French

Encyclopédie (1751–1772), in his *Dictionnaire de musique* (1767), and more pungently in a pamphlet, *Lettre sur la musique française* (1753).[4] In the *Lettre* Rousseau criticized severely a number of aspects of French music: among other things, it had no melody, it was unsingable, the language itself was unsuited to vocal setting, and the plots of its operas were sterile and unnatural. His pleas for the employment of reason and for a return to nature found application in his music. A few months before the publication of his famous letter he had produced his *Devin du village* ("The Village Soothsayer," Paris, 1753), a comic opera Italian in its form (including sung recitatives) but French in its text. Melodies were related in feeling to the *vaudevilles* of earlier decades, and the opera was laid in a rural setting. Insofar as the setting was a "natural" one and not mythological, the opera served to support Rousseau's plea for a return to nature. The success of the work, along with the success of many Italian comic operas later than Pergolesi's, prepared the public to accept a new type of comic opera entirely French in form, conception, and feeling.

Among the earliest composers of the new French *opéra comique* was an Italian, Egidio Duni (1709–1775). After a career that took him to several Italian cities (including Parma, where French influence continued strong) and to England and the Netherlands, Duni settled in Paris about 1756. There he composed some twenty French comic operas. Contemporary with him was an eminent chess player and composer, François Danican-Philidor (1726–1795), the last of a line of French musicians extending back for five generations. Philidor became enormously popular in Paris; many of his more than twenty operas (1756–1788) were performed repeatedly. The third member of this generation of comic opera composers in France was Pierre-Alexandre Monsigny (1729–1817). Largely self-trained in music, Monsigny composed about a dozen comic operas with ever-increasing success between 1759 and 1777. To these names must be added the name of Gluck, who at Vienna had concerned himself with the *opéra comique* in the years from 1755 to 1764.

Several features continued to distinguish the *opéra comique* from other types of opera, serious as well as comic. Most notable was the spoken dialogue instead of recitative; the other types, of course, employed either *recitativo secco* (with harpsichord and bass accompaniment) or *recitativo accompagnato* (with orchestra). The elaborate ensemble finale as established in the *opera buffa* found little place in the *opéra comique*. In its place stood a final song in strophic form with a refrain, and in a melodic style similar to that of a *vaudeville*. Duets and trios were frequent, but the major part of the singing was done in the form of the "ariette," a term that was applied to an original tune as opposed to a *vaudeville*. The new *opéra comique* embraced a wide variety of subjects. It included true comedy or even farce, sentimental episodes, fantasy, exotic material such as Oriental and Medieval tales, and mildly serious plots dealing with oppressed peasantry and noble lords.

4 An extended portion of Rousseau's pamphlet is given in *SRMH*, pp. 636–54.

In the works of Duni, Philidor, and Monsigny the *opéra comique* continued to grow in subtlety, scope, and refinement. The influence of the *vaudeville* was gradually diminished, the ariettes gained in melodic appeal, and well-balanced phrase structures became characteristic. A wide variety of forms—including small *da capo* arias, rondos, and the like—marked both the solo songs and the small ensembles; the latter were cultivated especially by Philidor. Quartets and larger ensembles were occasionally introduced in such works as his *Tom Jones* (1765) and *Le Sorcier* ("The Sorcerer," 1764). Monsigny's arias inclined primarily toward a melodious and sentimental style that effectively contrasted with the style of the programmatic pieces distributed throughout his works.

André Ernest Grétry (1741–1813), born in Belgium and educated in Italy, where he composed some sacred and instrumental works, became a resident of Paris in 1767. There, between 1768 and 1803, he composed about fifty operas. Both serious and comic types are represented in his works, and both types are distinguished by elegance, melodic charm, and fine craftsmanship in all details (see EXAMPLE 122). Indeed, the line be-

EXAMPLE 122

Grétry, *Richard Coeur-de-Lion*

TRANSLATION:
O Richard, my King! The universe has abandoned thee,
there is none but me on earth who is interested in thee.

tween *opéra comique* and *opéra sérieux* tended to disappear with certain composers, among them Monsigny and Grétry. Sentiment, dramatic tension, finely wrought detail, a minimum of comic scenes, and spoken dialogue are characteristic of the comic opera; the same elements with sung recitative characterize the serious type. Thus a division between types could be made primarily on whether the recitative was spoken or sung, and not on whether the plot was comic or serious. And it was this detail that determined whether a work was to be performed at the Opéra Comique or at the Académie Nationale de Musique (which is the full name of the famous Paris Opera).

The "rescue plot," which was mentioned in connection with the serious operas of Cherubini (see page 340), became an ingredient of the *opéra comique* as well. A notable example is seen in Grétry's masterpiece, *Richard Coeur-de-Lion* ("Richard the Lion-Hearted," 1784). Other types of setting, including fairy tales, exotic stories, and the like, continued to grow in favor at the expense of comic plots; the end result was a merger of comic and serious opera in all respects save that of recitative performance. This step is seen in several works by Étienne-Nicolas Méhul, mentioned above in connection with Gluck (see page 339). Of his more than thirty operas, about twenty-five have spoken text between musical numbers, and several of those, notably *Euphrosine et Coradin* (1790) and *Stratonice* (1792), are on serious subjects. From the time of Méhul the implication that an *opéra comique* must be on a comic subject has no validity.

Méhul tended toward flexible and imaginative orchestral writing, in the course of which he sometimes associated melodic motives with main characters in the opera. The repetition of such motives in a colorful instrumental context gradually led the way to the use of "leading motives," which became striking ingredients in the music of Wagner and other Romantic composers.

Other National Types

COUNTRIES other than Italy and France also took steps during the eighteenth century to create a native comic opera. In England, for example, a reaction to the dominant Italian opera took place about 1725. The result was the *ballad opera,* of which the best-known example is *The Beggar's Opera* (1728) with text by John Gay and music arranged by John Christopher Pepusch. The ballad opera in its earliest form was similar to the French plays with interspersed *vaudevilles.* It brought together farce, political satire, and entertaining music consisting of a number of popular folk ballads sung at intervals during the play. In later developments, up to the end of the century, new songs in ballad style began to replace the familiar tunes, and occasionally the plot took on a more serious or adventurous tone. The ballad opera, which offered serious competition to Handel when it first appeared in London, did not lead to a more highly developed form, however; it remained primarily an eighteenth-century product.

A scene from Gay's *The Beggar's Opera*. Painting by Hogarth.

The Spanish version of comic opera had an origin like that of the Italian *intermezzo*. It was customary to perform a short sketch (called *entremés*) interspersed with songs between the acts of a *zarzuela* (the Spanish version of Baroque serious opera) or dramatic play. The final song of the *entremés* was called a *tonadilla*. During the course of the eighteenth century the *tonadilla* itself was often expanded to include two or three musical numbers held together by spoken dialogue; it was supplied with a dance or two, and the whole was orchestrally accompanied. Eventually the *tonadilla* in its expanded form was separated from the *entremés* and appeared as a musical entity. By 1800 it had come under the influence of the Italian *opera buffa:* recitative, aria, and even Italian words were supplied to the dialogue, and the form soon lost its identity.

The Singspiel. The circumstances which led to the formation of a national comic opera in Germany were similar to those in France. Comedies performed by traveling groups of actors in eighteenth-century Germany were occasionally embellished with simple folklike songs inserted at appropriate places. Shortly before the middle of the century an English ballad opera, *The Devil to Pay*, was translated into German as *Der Teufel ist los* and performed at Berlin. There is no record of new music having been composed for this performance, but in 1752, a second version of the same work, with text arranged by Christian Weisse (1726–1804) and new music by a little-known violinist named J. C. Standfuss, became popular. A similar development took place in Austria, where the *Stegreifkomödie* (literally, "improvised comedy") was on occasion supplied with popular tunes or folksongs. The term *Singspiel* ("song-play") was later applied to such works.

In north Germany a productive collaboration between Weisse and Johann Adam Hiller (1728–1804) began in 1766. Weisse's librettos were often translations or adaptations of French *opéra-comique* texts. Hiller, a well-trained composer, maintained the traditional folklike air in his songs. He also sought to distinguish between his two classes of characters by composing more elaborate Italian-influenced arias for the gentry and aristocrats who appeared in the plays, reserving the simpler songs for people of lower station. The Italian influence, marked by coloratura arias in *da capo* form, ensembles in *buffa* style, and the like, remained a characteristic of Hiller's *Singspiele* to the 1780's. His major work, *Die Jagd* ("The Hunt," 1770), was popular for a generation and may be considered a forerunner of the later German Romantic opera.

The *Singspiel* was enthusiastically received in virtually all parts of Germany. Other works on the Hiller model were written by dozens of composers in the next several decades. The more prominent names include Johann Zumsteeg (1760–1802) at Stuttgart, even better known as a composer of ballads; Christian Neefe (1748–1798) at Bonn, who became Beethoven's teacher; and Georg Benda (1722–1795) at Gotha, known as one of the originators of the *melodrama,* a form that enjoyed considerable vogue.

The melodrama in a musical context consists of spoken words supplied with a musical accompaniment; the words and phrases of the text are either spoken simultaneously with the accompaniment or divided into short passages separated by musical fragments. Benda customarily employed the second of these styles; his *Ariadne auf Naxos,* produced at Gotha in 1775, is perhaps the best-known example.[5] Others before him had employed a similar device. Rousseau's *Pygmalion* was given in melodramatic style in 1772 at Weimar (with music by Anton Schweitzer) and at Vienna (with music by Franz Asplmayr), for example. But Benda was perhaps more consistent in his use of this novel device, and his dozen works in this form were most influential. The principle of melodrama was employed by Mozart in *Zaide,* by Beethoven in *Fidelio,* by many Romantic composers including Liszt, and later by Richard Strauss in his setting of Tennyson's *Enoch Arden* (1890), by Prokofiev in his *Peter and the Wolf* (1936), and by Stravinsky in *The Flood* (1962).

In Austria the *Singspiel* was strongly influenced by the *opera buffa* rather than by the *opéra comique,* as in Germany. The establishment of the national *Singspiel* in the Burgtheater in Vienna in 1778 provided the stimulus for creating a large and vital repertoire of *Singspiele.* The line of composers began with Ignaz Umlauf (1746–1796), whose *Die Berg-*

5 A passage from *Ariadne* is given in Adler, *HBM,* II, p. 752.

knappen ("The Miners," 1778) was followed by six other highly popular works, and it continued with Karl Ditters von Dittersdorf (1739–1799), eminent violinist and the composer of almost thirty stage works. In those works the transformation of the German *Singspiel* into a distinctive Viennese comic opera was completed. Sparkling gaiety, unexpected turns

EXAMPLE 123

Dittersdorf, *Doktor und Apotheker*

TRANSLATION:
Lovers need no witness, they are sufficient; and when tired of speech they're silent.

of phrase, unmotivated modulations, and a variety of orchestral effects lent an unfailing air of good humor to his works. Folklike melodic elements were retained, but they were surrounded by a number of devices borrowed from the Italian opera. Dittersdorf employed the ensemble finale quite in the manner of the *opera buffa;* a range of forms from small rondos to fully developed *da capo* arias with coloratura effects was characteristic. The melodies, however, remained typically Viennese in their lilting charm, piquant rhythms, and native simplicity (see EXAMPLE 123).

Mozart

WOLFGANG AMADEUS MOZART, one of the greatest composers of all time, completed sixteen works for the musical stage. They encompass several types and, in two or three cases, represent the culmination of the types. Both Italian and German operas are included, ranging from student works to profound masterpieces. Built upon existing models for the most part, they bring to expression the musical mastery and depth of insight that raise Mozart far above other composers of opera. Mozart is an example of the rare composer who is truly versatile, equally at home in dramatic, instrumental, and sacred choral music. And he is perhaps the extreme example of the child prodigy whose early promise is realized in maturity.

Mozart was born in Salzburg in 1756. His father, Leopold, an excellent composer and violinist, was the author of an important violin method (1756) that was translated into several languages and widely used for many decades. The boy showed musical aptitude from the age of four. His progress on the harpsichord and violin, as well as in improvisation, sightreading, and composition, was rapid. In 1762, together with his talented sister Anna ("Nannerl"), he was taken to Munich and Vienna for a year in order to exhibit his musical prowess to a wider public. His performances, many of them for the nobility, excited wide admiration. Other trips of longer duration and wider scope followed; by Mozart's twenty-fifth year, when he moved permanently to Vienna, he had been away from home almost eleven years.

From the point of view of Mozart's musical development, the significance of the many trips was that he was able to hear a wide variety of music. The works of Johann Schobert in Paris and Johann Christian Bach in London; the current Italian operas of all types in Vienna, Milan, and Rome; the symphonies and concertos of the Mannheim school; the various local versions of the *style galant* and the Rococo style in general —all these Mozart heard, remembered, and assimilated or discarded. Elements of the most diverse styles found a place in his works from time to time, but they were modified or transformed to meet his personal requirements. In a sense, Mozart's style is the result of everything he heard and experienced throughout his lifetime, brought into order and refined by his immaculate sense of taste.

Mozart's career in the last decade of his life was centered in Vienna. Making his permanent home there in 1781, he undertook several short trips to Linz, Prague, Berlin, and elsewhere, and he periodically returned to his old home in Salzburg. He led an active life, filling commissions, giving many concerts of his own works, supervising the production of one or another opera in other cities. His income was uncertain, however, and he looked vainly for a permanent position commensurate with his ability. Management of his personal finances was not one of Mozart's strong points, nor of his wife's (he had married a cousin of Carl Maria von Weber in 1782); he lived in a world of poverty and unpaid debts, brightened only occasionally by the success of a new work. He died in 1791, at the age of thirty-five, and lies in an unmarked pauper's grave.

Early works. The first eight of Mozart's sixteen works for the stage were composed between 1768 and 1775, that is, between his twelfth and nineteenth years. Although they represent several different types, they may be grouped here because they reflect a Mozart who was learning his craft and finding his way in the problems of combining music and drama. With one exception they are all in Italian. Two works are in the style of *opera buffa: La finta semplice* ("The Pretended Simpleton," Salzburg, 1769), and *La finta giardiniera* ("The Pretended Gardener," Munich, 1775). Two are cast as *opere serie: Mitridate, rè di Ponto* ("Mithridates, King of Ponto," Milan, 1770) and *Lucio Silla* (Milan, 1772). One work, *Bastien und Bastienne* (Vienna, 1768), is a German *Singspiel.* Two are of the type known as "serenata," which was a small work with only a few characters, usually performed for a particular occasion such as a wedding or other celebration; these are *Ascanio in Alba* (Milan, 1771) and *Il sogno di Scipione* ("The Dream of Scipione," Salzburg, 1772). A festival opera, *Il rè pastore* ("The Shepherd King," Salzburg, 1775), completes the list.

In few respects are these works at all distinctive, except insofar as they reveal the young Mozart's ability to adapt himself to different operatic styles. The two serious operas are good imitations of the prevailing Italian type; they show little attempt at originality. An occasional moment in the works reveals what Mozart would become, however: an aria in *Mitridate,* for example, or the duet in Act I of *La finta giardiniera.* In general throughout the group, the music is appropriate to the type of opera being composed; more one cannot say.

Later Italian operas. Of the remaining eight works, five are in Italian and on a completely different plane from the earlier Italian works by Mozart; they were all written between 1781 and 1791. The set includes two serious operas, *Idomeneo, rè di Creta* ("Idomeneo, King of Crete," Munich, 1781) and *La clemenza di Tito* ("The Clemency of Titus," Prague, 1791); two comic operas, *Le nozze di Figaro* ("The Marriage of Figaro," Vienna, 1786) and *Così fan tutte* ("Thus Do They All," Vienna, 1790); at the midpoint of the group is *Don Giovanni* (Prague, 1787), a work that is technically allied to the *opera buffa* but whose tragic and dramatic moments loom too large to be dispelled by the comedy which surrounds them.

The serious opera of 1781, *Idomeneo,* is the first work in which Mozart revealed what his mature method would be. Externally, the opera is of the conventional type. It contains a full complement of accompanied recitatives and arias, including some old-fashioned coloraturas with space for improvised cadenzas. Several choral scenes in the general style of Gluck indicate not that Mozart was an adherent of the Gluck reform principles but merely that he found a chorus appropriate at that moment. The orchestral writing is lavish in detail and truly symphonic in scope; this was to be expected of a composer who up to this time had written about forty symphonies and some twenty concertos. Finally, the words of the text are set with full regard for their meaning and implication, so that a close union of text and music exists.

One other detail sets *Idomeneo*—and virtually all of Mozart's later operas—apart from the works of other composers, however. Its characters are flesh-and-blood human beings, no longer merely examples of conventional types. Mozart showed keen insight into the characteristics, the motivations, the general psychological constitution of the people who appear in his operas. It was not enough for him to set to music the various situations required by his plots; he took pains to draw psychologically true portraits of Idomeneo, Ilia, and all of his characters. He achieved this miracle through his employment of subtle harmonic changes and melodic turns of phrase to suggest two or more contrasting moods simultaneously. The result was to raise *Idomeneo* to a high place among eighteenth-century serious operas.

Mozart's last serious Italian opera, *La clemenza di Tito,* followed ten years after *Idomeneo;* it was written for the coronation of Leopold II at Prague in 1791. In keeping with the solemnity of the occasion and perhaps as a result of the rather unimaginative libretto (adapted from one of Metastasio's), the music is a bit reserved and even impersonal. It was written in about two and a half weeks at a time when Mozart was ill, when his interests were centered on other works (he was composing *Die Zauberflöte* and the *Requiem Mass* at the time), and when he was more concerned about his future than usual. It does not represent Mozart at his best; perhaps for this reason the work was coldly received at its first performance.

The eighteenth-century *opera buffa* culminated in Mozart's *Le nozze de Figaro* and *Così fan tutte,* of 1786 and 1790, respectively. Both works were written on librettos by Lorenzo da Ponte, official poet of the Italian Theater in Vienna. The first of the operas remains one of the finest examples of the blending of comedy and seriousness, of surface charm and underlying profundity, of spontaneous wit and heartfelt emotion. To an even greater extent than in *Idomeneo,* Mozart here reveals the inmost problems and feeling of his characters, who are real people; operatic stereotypes and characters representing abstract qualities find little place in his works. The various loves of the Count for Susanna, of Susanna for Figaro, and of Cherubino for the Countess; the intrigues, intercepted messages, and revelation of Figaro's parentage—all these are in the best comic opera tradition. But Mozart created a touching human document out of what might have been yet another *opera buffa.* The characters are individualized through the kind of music given to them, and one of the magical details of *Figaro* is the fact that this individualization is carried on even within the frequently contrapuntal ensembles (which predominate throughout the opera), in spite of the musical unity and structural logic that prevail in them (see EXAMPLE 124). Nowhere in the eighteenth

EXAMPLE 124

Mozart, *Le nozze de Figaro*, Act I

TRANSLATION:
Susanna: "There's no way to make it worse now, Ah no, ah no."
Basilio: "That's the way everyone does it."
The Count: "O, you pattern of all virtue."

century did the ensemble finale reach a higher level than in *Figaro*. Instead of a section in which many characters are brought together in a mood of growing excitement, it became a piece in several sections (almost to be called movements) each of which carries the dramatic action forward, completes the psychological portrait of the characters involved, and achieves symphonic dimensions through development of motives, key relationships, and general thematic integrity. All of this happens, finally, in a delightful melodic context, in the light of the pure lyricism which is Mozart's unique trademark.

Don Giovanni, also on a libretto by Da Ponte, is outwardly an *opera buffa*. It was the result of a commission from Prague, where *Figaro* had been an enormous success. The opera deals essentially with the concept

Setting by Schinkel for a scene from Act II of Mozart's *Die Zauberflöte,* Berlin, 1800.

of sensual love, the principle of divine retribution, and the conflict between them. That conflict animates the overture and comes to expression throughout the opera, resulting in several striking and awe-inspiring scenes. Elsewhere *Don Giovanni* has its full share of melodies, some of them the most eloquent Mozart ever wrote.

In this work Mozart rose to his highest stature as a psychologist and dramatist. The figure of Don Giovanni is shown in all its tragedy; the scene in which divine judgment is invoked against him is shattering in its intensity and emotional force. The comic characters provide entertaining moments, but they perform against the dark background of the play and throw the drama into still greater relief. *Don Giovanni,* another of Mozart's masterpieces, is an example of the *opera buffa* type that contains characters who would be more at home in *opera seria*. In this case the serious, universal, and tragic aspects of the score outweigh the comic ones, and a work of great impact results.

German operas. Mozart's stage works with German text include (in addition to the *Bastien und Bastienne* of 1768, mentioned above) three works: *Die Entführung aus dem Serail* ("The Abduction from the Harem," Vienna, 1782), *Der Schauspieldirektor* ("The Impresario," Vienna, 1786), and *Die Zauberflöte* ("The Magic Flute," Vienna, 1791). To these may be added a minor work left unfinished: *Zaide* (1779). *Zaide,* in the form of a *Singspiel,* is a sentimental work set in a harem; it is distinguished by a few serious moments and the use of melodrama. The latter device followed the model of Georg Benda (see above, page 349), about whose work Mozart wrote enthusiastically. Three years after abandoning *Zaide* Mozart composed another *Singspiel* with a similar setting; this work, *Die Entführung,* is one of his masterpieces.

The *Singspiel,* which had begun as a little play with added songs, had by the last decades of the century become a full-fledged dramatic work with a full complement of highly developed musical numbers. This is seen especially in *Die Entführung,* in which virtually every aria and ensemble grows out of the dramatic situation. Each character is individualized through the kind of music he is given to sing, and the contribution of each one to the drama is fully realized. The ensembles, too, carry the dramatic action forward in exemplary fashion. The orchestral writing, including the use of Turkish color through cymbals, triangle, and piccolo in the overture and elsewhere, and the magical fusion of the Italian vocal style with the warmth of German song (see EXAMPLE 125)—these combine to give *Die Entführung* its lasting quality. It far overshadows another work in German, *Der Schauspieldirektor,* a one-act comedy with an overture and four musical numbers.

Mozart's last work for the musical stage was *Die Zauberflöte,* written

EXAMPLE 125

Mozart, *Die Entführung,* Act I

Herz, Klopft mein lie - be - vol - - - - les Herz!

TRANSLATION:
O how fearsome and inflamed pounds my love-filled
heart.

for one of Vienna's suburban theaters; its first performance, late in 1791,
took place barely two months before his death. The subject matter of *Die
Zauberflöte*, unique in Mozart's works, has given rise to much discussion.
Compounded of magic, fairy-tale elements, supernatural effects, and
Masonic symbolism, its text was written by Emanuel Schikaneder, the
manager of the theater for which the work was composed. According to
some commentators, the author and composer changed the course of the
opera halfway through, converting the magic tale into a "glorification
of Freemasonry." Other commentators find the plot consistent in all respects and a superb symbolic representation of "rebellion, consolation,
and hope." [6]

The music of *Die Zauberflöte* is characterized first of all by variety of
form and content. The overture is a sonata-form with a slow introduction
and contains fugal developments of the principal theme. The two acts
of the work contain arias filled with ornate coloratura passages, choruses,
folklike songs in strophic form, and elaborate ensembles. Accompanied
recitatives appear also, but they are dramatically inspired, include lyric

6 The two opposing views are represented by Grout, *A Short History of Opera*, I,
pp. 293-95, and Einstein, *Mozart*, pp. 463-65.

phrases of the arioso type (see EXAMPLE 126), and play major parts in de-
lineating the characters of those who sing them. The Masonic symbolism,
first appearing in the series of three chords with which the overture

EXAMPLE 126

Mozart, *Die Zauberflöte*, Act I

TRANSLATION:
The gates and the columns reveal that wisdom, labor,
and arts tarry here, where activity is enthroned and
sloth finds no place.

begins, is found primarily in the second act. An unusual feature for Mozart is the reappearance of similar musical structures (remembrance motives and even entire phrases, for example) at appropriate moments in the opera. This feature, plus the carefully organized scheme of tonalities, helps to bring about the feeling of musical unity.

There is little evidence that Mozart sought to reform or even to modify the opera of his day. Whether *opera seria, opera buffa,* or *Singspiel,* his operas are superior to other works of the eighteenth century simply because Mozart was a finer composer, a keener psychologist, and a more imaginative dramatist than virtually any operatic composer before him. Obviously, the superior quality of his music cannot be demonstrated verbally. One can do no more than point to the moving or humorous or sentimental melodic lines, to the variety of phrase structures, to the harmonic richness, and to the sense of form that is evident everywhere. Yet all of these elements are placed in the service of the libretto; they illuminate, explain, and justify the various dramatic actions and motivations. The result is a set of operas that are musically superb, dramatically gripping, and psychologically true.

⊷ 18 ⊶

The Classical Period:
Other Vocal Music

Mᴜᴄʜ of the music of the later eighteenth century was stylistically indebted to the Italian opera; that fact has been stressed in earlier chapters.
The *sinfonia,* the embryonic sonata-form, and a light and diverting type of
musical content were in large part the contributions of the pre-Classical
school of opera. Stylistic impulses not derived from the Italians, however,
also played important roles in the emerging Classical period. Many contradictory trends and incompatible ideas were refined to create the Classical idiom. Such observations, customarily made in connection with instrumental music, can be made about the period's sacred music with equal

Etching by P. Ransom, Paris, 1778. [ᴛʜᴇ ᴍᴇᴛʀᴏᴘᴏʟɪᴛᴀɴ ᴍᴜsᴇᴜᴍ ᴏꜰ ᴀʀᴛ, ʀᴏɢᴇʀs
ꜰᴜɴᴅ, 1952]

justification. In the present chapter the influence of those diversified factors on Catholic church music will be discussed—even though that influence was at times nebulous and at other times negative.

The Mass

TWO TENDENCIES seen at the beginning of the eighteenth century were still vital near its end: the first was to employ secular style elements in sacred compositions, and the second, to compose sacred works on the basis of musical logic (rather than textual necessity) and what might be called instrumental thinking. The principal form in which these tendencies came to expression was the Mass—*Missa brevis* as well as *Missa solemnis*—although motets and other sacred forms were not immune. So thoroughly did they permeate the entire body of sacred music, in the period after about 1750, that this music is often reputed to represent an aesthetic aberration of the most extreme type. Such is not entirely the case.

The keynote of the period at first was stylistic multiplicity. Many Masses of the time still contained a rich array of early and late Baroque style elements. They were orchestrally accompanied, with instruments often employed soloistically in obbligatos. The dividing line between solo pieces and choruses often broke down; vocal soloists were sometimes given extended passages within a single choral movement. And in keeping with the Venetian-Roman tradition, polychoral textures were frequently introduced.

Other Masses were equally rich in Rococo stylistic devices. Often one Mass section (embracing a sentence or paragraph of the text) was given to a soloist, another to the chorus, and yet another to a duet or trio of singers; solo sections were cast in the form of recitative and two-part aria. The attitude toward the text was typically sentimental, expressed in a variety of lyric and coloratura tunes. Finally, the orchestral texture contained short, incisive motives treated imitatively and sequentially—quite in the fashion made familiar by the *sinfonia* of the time.

Masses of both types had an important element in common, however: an easygoing approach to the sense of the liturgy and toward the inviolability of the sacred Office. The dignified treatment typical of the early Baroque Mass, in which the underlying sentiment of each textual section was reflected in the music composed for it, was abandoned. In its place came the feeling that the laws of musical construction—regarding the balance of phrases, location of cadence points, and contour of melodies, for example—had to determine the expressive content of a composed Mass, that reason and logic had to play their parts in the setting of the Mass text, even if liturgical requirements were unsatisfied thereby. And finally, the tradition was observed that certain sections of the text—notably the end of both the *Gloria* and the *Credo*—were to be set in fugal style.

The Mass in Naples. Although Neapolitan composers in the early eighteenth century are perhaps best known for their operas, they were also active in the field of sacred music. A thorough investigation of much of that music has not yet been undertaken. The relatively few available works show that in general composers in Naples wrote in a rather conservative manner. Early in the eighteenth century the influence of the opera on the Mass became strong, and what has been called a "cantata-Mass" emerged. Arias at times took on the symmetrical form of their operatic counterparts and eventually assumed the shape of the *da capo* aria. Instrumental ritornellos appeared between sections of the liturgical text. Phrases were often cast in lengths of two, four, or eight measures, and repetition to round out the musical form was common. A variety of dramatic and sentimental effects such as vocal sighs, coloratura passages, and orchestral tremolos became typical. The last traces of modal writing disappeared, and in point of style a Mass movement differed scarcely at all from its operatic equivalent. The orchestra, finally, was made more flexible and colorful. Writing in blocks of tone for a family of instruments gave way to writing for a single instrument; a solo oboe, for example, replaced the woodwind choir in accompanied solos. And as a

An appropriate setting for the Rococo Mass: church at Freising in Bavaria.

harbinger of the future, string instruments were given the leading roles in the orchestra.

In these developments Alessandro Scarlatti played a leading part, as he had in the opera and the cantata. Of the many Masses attributed to him, few have been adequately examined and fewer published. Francesco Durante (1684–1755), who worked primarily as a teacher but who left a large number of sacred compositions, has been similarly neglected. Leonardo Leo (1694–1744), another eminent Neapolitan musician, was also active in both sacred and secular fields, but his music too has remained largely in manuscript.

The Mass in Germany and Austria. The influence of the operatic style on sacred music was strongly felt in the German-speaking countries. The principal centers of German Catholic church music in the period about 1750 were Dresden, Vienna, and Salzburg. Composers active in those cities reflected their personal backgrounds and heritages, of course, in spite of the weight of the Italian tradition. Johann Adolph Hasse, at Dresden from 1739 to 1763, serves as a prime example. A pupil of Alessandro Scarlatti, Hasse brought many operatic devices to expression in his ten Masses. Choral parts as well as solo arias are filled with gay tunes that often become sentimental. Profound, doctrinal, and glorifying texts alike are set in the same operatic-dramatic style. Often such Masses could have passed as secular cantatas—except for their texts. On the other hand, Hasse often attempted to unify each Mass movement by using a single rhythmic figure or melodic motive, and on occasion by employing a similar motive in several movements. His orchestral writing in the Masses, too, showed a greater degree of motivic manipulation and approached the later symphonic texture in its freedom from stereotyped accompanying patterns (see EXAMPLE 127).

Johann Joseph Fux (1660–1741), chapelmaster at St. Stephen's Cathedral, was among the principal Viennese composers of the time. His treatise on counterpoint, the famous *Gradus ad Parnassum*, published in 1725, helped generations of composers to understand the principles of the art, and homage is still paid to Fux's methods whenever "species counterpoint" is taught. He was called the Palestrina of his time, in spite of the fact that his contrapuntal method is only indirectly derived from the style of that late-Renaissance master, and understandably enough, a considerable amount of his sacred music is written in polyphonic style. His chief work in this category is a *Missa canonica* of 1716, for four voices unaccompanied, one of more than fifty Masses Fux composed. It contains elaborate canons in every movement; sometimes two separate canons progress simultaneously. For example, the *Crucifixus* begins with a canon at the second between bass and tenor, with the tenor part an inversion of the bass; at the same time the alto and soprano parts, on another theme, are in canon at the fourth. It is likely that the contrapuntal Masses of Fux were designed as study pieces, as examples of the solutions of contrapuntal problems. Others of Fux's Masses are thoroughly modern; they are instrumentally accompanied and bring to expression free

EXAMPLE 127

Hasse, Requiem Mass

melodic lines, a wealth of harmonic subtlety, and the spirit of the opera.

In the Masses of Antonio Caldara (1670–1736), who served as Fux's assistant chapelmaster for almost two decades, the same stylistic variety is seen. Caldara, evidently under the influence of Fux and of Viennese traditions generally, composed some of his thirty Masses in a contrapuntal and even a canonic style. One work in particular is an elaborate canonic Mass in which contrary and retrograde motion, inversions of themes, and all the other practices of a skilled contrapuntist are employed. The Mass contains a sixteen-voice setting of the *Crucifixus* built on the Venetian pattern of Benevoli; early Baroque display and thoroughly modern harmonies occur in the midst of great polyphonic complexity.

Others of Caldara's Masses, in fact the majority of them, are in the pre-Classical tradition in all major respects. Solos, ensembles, and choruses written in the typical style are found in these works, but passages for one or two solo singers within a choral movement are encountered as well. Caldara's favorite form seems to have been the cantata-Mass on the Venetian model, with florid two-part arias, many *concertato* instrumental obbligatos, and little recitative. The use of the solo instruments above the continuo accompaniment adds both expressive interest and tonal variety to the movements in which the obbligatos occur.

The few available works by Salzburg composers show that in that center, too, a variety of influences was at hand. At first allied to the Venetian school with its sonority and antiphonal writing, Salzburg church composers such as Carl Heinrich Biber (1681–1749), the son of the famous Baroque violinist, later used ingratiating and melodious Rococo elements. The infusion of operatic dramatic recitative is seen in the works of Johann Eberlin (1702–1762), and the approach of the *sinfonia* to sacred forms appears in the music of Anton Adlgasser (1729–1777), Mozart's predecessor as cathedral organist at Salzburg. Michael Haydn (1737–1806), a younger brother of the great Franz Joseph, virtually completed the evolution of the Salzburg school during and after Mozart's lifetime. Distinguished as much by his use of Gregorian materials and ecclesiastical modes as by his modern thematic devices, Haydn marked in his own way a transition from Baroque to Classical styles.

Thus an array of styles (contrapuntal Roman, massive Venetian, expressive Italian, melodious Viennese), a range of attitudes from conservative to forward-looking, a preoccupation with symphonically conceived accompaniments, a melodic variety that included folklike tunes as well as lyric ariosos and florid recitatives—this geographical and stylistic mixture was basic to the Viennese choral tradition about 1750. A unified Classical style eventually grew out of that mixture, but not until some forty years had elapsed and Haydn and Mozart had reached their artistic maturity. Such was the background out of which they composed their Masses. Out of such variety did they—almost alone in their period—bring about a unified style in their sacred compositions and achieve a new balance between text and music.

Haydn and Mozart

FRANZ JOSEPH HAYDN (1732–1809) was in many respects a product of the Viennese tradition. From his eighth to his sixteenth year, as a choir boy at St. Stephen's Cathedral, and for another decade thereafter, Haydn lived and worked in Vienna. He played with strolling bands of musicians and composed serenades for them. He heard all the music Vienna had to offer, and from that music his own style gradually developed. Haydn was largely his own teacher, never averse to experimenting with new materials and discarding what did not meet his musical requirements. The Viennese tradition formed a major ingredient in his early instrumental works; it came to expression in other categories of his music also, particularly in his Masses.

Haydn's early Masses. Haydn is known to have composed fourteen Masses. Twelve have been known since his time, one was recovered as late as 1957, and the remaining one (the second of the fourteen) has been lost. Of the set of thirteen extant Masses, seven were written across a period of more than thirty years, 1750 to 1782; yet they have much in common. They all reflect the optimism and affirmation of life that animated the music of the second half of the century. Haydn was a reverent Catholic, but reverence did not imply or demand a withdrawal from the world, as it seemed to among many men of the Romantic period. He could set the *Dona nobis pacem* of the *Agnus Dei* in a lively, almost rollicking style—and he did so repeatedly—secure in his faith that the prayer would be answered. He could compose a festive cantata-Mass of great length—the St. Cecilia Mass of about 1772—out of the feeling that the Church's most fundamental liturgy deserved brilliant treatment. Dramatic arias, florid ariosos, and imposing choruses never, in his mind, detracted from the sanctity of the text (see EXAMPLE 128).

Haydn's treatment of textual details in the seven Masses reveals the shift in religious outlook that had come about in the mid-eighteenth century. Perhaps under the influence of the Enlightenment, the musical setting of the Mass text was approached logically. For example, it had been the custom previously, in composing the *Gloria* and *Credo*, to begin with the second phrase of the respective texts. The *Gloria in excelsis Deo* was customarily intoned by the priest; the composer therefore began with the following phrase, *et in terra pax*. Likewise, the music of the *Credo* customarily began with the phrase, *patrem omnipotentem*, after the first phrase, *Credo in unum Deum*, had been intoned. Indeed, Haydn's first few Masses followed the old practice. But in a form that was logically and musically conceived, it seemed pointless not to begin where the text did. From about 1772 the full text was usually composed and the traditionally intoned beginning was disregarded by the composer. More-

Franz Joseph
Haydn, 1732–
1809. Portrait by
Charles Maucourt.

EXAMPLE 128

Haydn, *Missa Sanctae Caeciliae, Credo*

EXAMPLE 129

Haydn, *Missa Brevis, Credo*

over, Haydn—along with other composers of the time—did not hesitate to repeat the word *credo* out of context to round out a phrase, to carry forward a motivic texture, or to provide textual material for a musical cadence. Even more characteristic was the tendency to employ different phrases of the text simultaneously, especially in Masses of the *Missa brevis* type (see EXAMPLE 129). These are small points, but liturgically important ones.

Mozart's Masses. It will become apparent later that the styles of Haydn and Mozart evolved differently, that Haydn deepened and refined his Viennese musical heritage, while Mozart assimilated and perfected every new stylistic manner that came to his attention, regardless of its origin. This eclecticism of Mozart's stands clearly revealed in his settings of the Mass. He completed fifteen works in that category; they range from K. 49 to K. 337 and were composed between 1768 and 1780. Thus all of them are closely contemporary with Haydn's first seven Masses.

The majority of Mozart's Masses were written in connection with his official duties as concertmaster and, later, organist to the Archbishop Colloredo of Salzburg. The Archbishop apparently had no patience with long Masses, so that the majority of Mozart's are of the *Missa brevis* type. The works written to about 1774 give evidence that the old Baroque traditions had been modified considerably at Salzburg and that the tuneful and brilliant manner of the Rococo style was acceptable in the Church. Contrapuntal texture appears in these Masses at the traditional places, and short solo passages often emerge out of the choral tutti to give variety to the choral textures. Many of the Masses, however, contain orchestral accompaniments that recall the *concertato* style of the earlier period. Mozart's orchestra at Salzburg was limited in size, but he took full advantage of its quality by writing brilliantly for it.

In another group of Mozart's Masses, those of the *Missa solemnis* type or the few written for special occasions, the influence of Hasse is apparent. Hasse, who spent several years in Vienna, had himself written Masses that embraced the style of the opera, as we have seen. The result of the youthful Mozart's acquaintance with the elderly German master may be surmised in the C-minor Mass, K. 139, of 1772. This work is in many respects a cantata-Mass with operatic pathos in the arias and considerable manipulation of thematic fragments in the orchestral accompaniment. In the C-major Mass of the following year, K. 167, the cantata form is somewhat modified, in that soloists are not called for.

The operatic style was not the only influence that pervaded Mozart's Masses, however. Equally important is the revelation of a gradual approach to instrumental forms. Many of Mozart's settings of the *Gloria* and *Credo* were cast as rondos or in sonata-form; in all such cases, the traditional closing fugue serves as a coda. Even when instrumental forms were not employed, the texture of the *sinfonia* was brought close. The character of the themes, the use of contrasting motives and harmonic sections, and the appearance of instrumental figurations strongly suggest

EXAMPLE 130

Mozart, Mass in C minor, K. 139

that instrumental thinking had become a habit for the young composer (see EXAMPLE 130).

Mozart often treated the text of his Masses with great freedom. He freely introduced textual repetitions, quite unmotivated from a liturgical standpoint, if the musical structure required them. Yet it is just here that his great contribution to the Mass is seen: in devising forms that enhanced the expressive content or meaning of the text, he raised the composed Mass to a far higher aesthetic level than it had enjoyed earlier in his period.

A perfunctory tone is found occasionally in the seven Masses Mozart composed between 1776 and 1780. The Archbishop had strong ideas about the manner in which music for his court was to sound, and Mozart's independent spirit rebelled against what he felt to be unwarranted restrictions. It seems likely that the composition of Masses in virtually a prescribed style lost its attractiveness for Mozart after about ten years; at any rate, he became strongly interested in writing for the dramatic stage. He felt impelled to leave the Archbishop's service in 1782; the move could not have displeased him, for it relieved him of duties which had become truly irksome and removed him from his native city, which offered little artistic stimulation.

When Vienna became Mozart's permanent home in 1781, he had no professional reason for writing Masses. Yet one additional work resulted, a work in quite a different category than the other Masses—the unfinished C-minor Mass, K. 427, of which the *Credo* is fragmentary and the *Agnus Dei* is missing completely. He composed the work during a period when he had become preoccupied with the music of Bach. Once again Mozart came under the spell of a style that was foreign to him yet succeeded in transforming it to meet his own artistic needs.

The C-minor Mass reflects the power and earnestness of the Baroque and has its great moments of pure polyphony. Its closeness to the form of a cantata-Mass, however, in its several florid arias and sectional form in the *Gloria* and *Credo,* is equally undeniable. It was written for Salzburg (but not for the Archbishop, it must be said), and it employs the restricted instrumentation typical of that city; yet it is not in the tradition of Salzburg's music.

The Mass contains movements of the greatest brilliance, in particular the *Laudamus te* for mezzo-soprano solo; of ethereal beauty, such as the soprano solo, *Et incarnatus est;* of foreboding and mystical power, in the *Qui tollis.* Elsewhere there are involved fugal movements, ensembles filled with melodies of ravishing beauty, and light—even gay—passages for one or another of the solo voices. And yet the C-minor Mass is unified by Mozart's personal approach to the text. This is truly a work in which he solves the problems brought about by the stylistic disunity of the time; all the conflicting elements are brought together. The polarities of sacred and secular, of homophony and polyphony, of liturgy and musical logic —all are reconciled, resulting in a style that is Classical in every sense.

Mozart's Requiem Mass. One type of Mass has so far not been brought into these pages: the *Missa pro defunctis,* or Mass for the Dead, commonly referred to as the Requiem Mass. In this form of the Mass the *Gloria* and *Credo,* being joyful, are omitted and three texts from the Proper plus the Sequence *Dies irae* are incorporated. Thus the several movements of the Requiem Mass are as follows: Introit (*Requiem aeternam*), *Kyrie,* Sequence (*Dies irae*), Offertory (*Pie Jesu*), *Sanctus, Benedictus, Agnus Dei,* and Communion (*Lux aeterna*). The early Requiem Mass was considered to be essentially a prayer for the repose of departed souls; consequently, the *Dies irae* (Day of wrath) played a minor part. In Requiem Masses by Palestrina and Lasso, for example, the Sequence was not set to music by the composer but left to be chanted by the priest. The mid-seventeenth century saw the introduction of orchestrally accompanied Requiems, and at first the Sequence in those Masses kept its restrained or chanted character.

With the rise of the pre-Classical opera, however, composers began to exploit the dramatic possibilities of the *Dies irae.* The terrors of the Last Judgment seemed ready-made for their operatic talents, and an agitated and fearful style in the Sequence became usual. After about 1730, in the works of Jommelli and Hasse, Italian dramatic feeling and vocal extravagance took over completely; the Sequence became a sensational rather than a reposeful section, in spite of the fact that such treatment contradicted the essential spirit of the *Missa pro defunctis.* In other respects the Requiem did not become as profane as the regular Mass, perhaps because its subject was too close to the hearts of composers.

Mozart was commissioned to write a Requiem Mass a few months before his death in 1791. Just as he had transcended the liturgy in his unfinished C-minor Mass of 1783, so now he brought Requiem text and music to a higher level of interpenetration. He freed himself from all models and avoided the snares of the operatic style. He reduced the orchestra in size and color (the upper woodwinds find no employment here) and established a somber tone. Above all, he created a work in which the metaphysical problems presented by the text are solved musically, in closed forms, with great variety of texture, and with the utmost restraint and economy.

The terrors of the Last Judgment are not pictured in Mozart's Requiem; instead a cool yet friendly attitude toward death comes to expression, an attitude that is said to reflect the composer's close association with the Masonic order. It is significant that the work was composed during the time that Mozart was also working on *Die Zauberflöte;* the Masonic implications of that work have been discussed. An objective, almost Baroque mood pervades the whole. The spirits of Bach and Handel —and suggestions of Handelian themes—animate the *Kyrie* and that part of the Sequence that begins *Rex tremendae.* Divine calm and a sublime air of resignation are wonderfully expressed elsewhere. Mozart died before the Requiem was completed; whatever weaknesses appear in its later portions may be attributed to Franz Süssmayr, the composer's pupil and friend; though Süssmayr employed Mozart's sketches, he completed the work according to his own specifications—to satisfy the Count Walsegg, who had commissioned the Requiem with the idea of passing it off as his own.

Haydn's late works. When Joseph II ascended the Austrian throne after the death of his mother, Maria Theresa, in 1780, he sought to reform the Empire overnight. A redefinition of the place of the Church was among his objectives; tolerance toward Protestants, reorganization of Church government, and simplification of the liturgy were included in his program. For a decade the content and scope of the music of the Church were in question, and conditions for writing in the sacred forms were not of the best. It is likely that the gap in Haydn's composition of Masses (he wrote none between 1782 and 1796) reflects the uncertain official attitudes toward church music.

Joseph died in 1790 with the reforms unfinished, and during the short reign of his successor, Leopold II, the Church regained its prestige. In a new burst of enthusiasm for sacred music many composers turned again to the Mass. Their enthusiasm was indistinguishable from their feeling for secular music, however. The idealism and optimism that had marked earlier decades came to expression with renewed force. In their attempts to bring those attitudes to realization in sacred forms, composers often overlooked the requirements of the liturgy entirely and allowed themselves to be influenced solely by musical considerations.

Not even Haydn was able—or willing—to restore the liturgy to its erstwhile place as a framework to which the music must be adapted. The six Masses he composed between 1796 and 1802 reveal how musical form and phrasing triumphed over the rhetoric of the text. Themes are similar to those found in his instrumental music and developed symphonically. Sonata-form movements often appear, together with slow introductions, as in the "London" symphonies. The orchestral accompaniment is often independent of the choral parts and no longer finds its principal employment in supporting the voices.

Simultaneously, however, the vocal parts become more polyphonic than before, and the counterpoint is no longer confined to the traditional places. The opera-inspired recitative and solo aria virtually disappear, and a quartet of soloists is periodically lifted out of the choral tutti to provide another and more intimate dimension to the musical structure. It is in this detail that the final sublimation of pre-Classical style influences can be observed. In Haydn's late Masses, as in Mozart's Requiem Mass, the polarity of dramatic solo and expository tutti is largely dissolved. A polyphonic ensemble emerging from the unified, sonorous choral group is the result (see EXAMPLE 131).

The smaller forms of sacred music occupied both Haydn and Mozart during their lifetimes. Litanies, vesper services, motets, single movements of Masses, and various other forms are represented. These miscellaneous works are, in general, stylistically similar to whatever larger composition is contemporary with them. Among the sacred works of Haydn, but in a category separate from all the others, is the set of choruses entitled *The Seven Last Words of the Redeemer on the Cross.*

EXAMPLE 131

Haydn, Mass in D

The history of this composition is an unusual one. The work was composed originally as a set of slow movements for orchestra, as the result of a commission received from the Cadiz Cathedral in 1785. Subsequently Haydn arranged it for string quartet and published it as Opus 51. Still later, about 1794, Haydn arranged it for yet another medium after having heard a version arranged by an obscure musician in Bavaria; he added a set of choral parts, the texts consisting of paraphrases or commentaries on the words of Christ on the Cross.

The several movements are large rondos, for the most part. A *sinfonia* appears in the middle of the work, and a movement entitled "Earthquake," set in presto tempo, ends it. Yet the work as a whole, containing a portion of the Passion text and constituting in effect a choral cantata, was named "oratorio" by Haydn, in keeping with the current practice of so designating any large musical setting of a reverent text. Three other works of Haydn are oratorios in the usual sense, however. The first, *The Return of Tobias* (1775), has been completely overshadowed by the two great compositions of his last productive decade—*The Creation* and *The Seasons,* written about 1798 to 1801.

Conditions for composing oratorios were not propitious during the last decades of the eighteenth century. The religious attitude of the time was largely directed against mysticism and even against dogma. Forward-looking minds attempted to restore the dignity of the oratorio by inveighing against the operatic elements that infected the form. Others questioned the very justification for the oratorio, writing polemics against Handel. The Old Testament no longer furnished literary source material, and the New Testament was interpreted from a vague, moralizing standpoint. As a result, only an empty oratorio tradition remained. Very few works rose above the level of mediocrity—*The Resurrection and Ascension of Jesus* by Carl Philipp Emanuel Bach and *The Death of Jesus* by Karl Heinrich Graun being among the notable exceptions—even though some minor composers attempted to revitalize the form and write in the Handelian manner. Haydn's *Creation* was the first oratorio since Handel's that successfully solved the problems of content and treatment in the modern manner.

Haydn's musical setting brings to expression the natural, idyllic, and deceptively simple tone that reflects the literature of the period and that the times demanded—in spite of the fact that the text employs portions of the Book of Genesis and of Milton's *Paradise Lost*. Further, the theme of the Creation itself was foreign to the old oratorio and hence marked a step in the modern direction.

On the other hand, the work contains many factors of Handel's style. Haydn had attended a great Handel festival in London in 1791; one may be sure that he had not forgotten his impressions of that style. His reliance upon the Biblical text, his restoration of the part of the *testo* or narrator (in *The Creation* given to three different archangels), and his use of a rich choral writing and of a hymn of thanksgiving that follows the Divine acts—these are all typical Handelian style elements. *The Creation* is freely constructed; evidence of instrumental thinking is less evident here than in the late Masses. Indeed, one has the impression that textual considerations were uppermost in Haydn's mind—as they were in Handel's—and that the tendency to raise musical laws above textual requirements was reversed.

The Creation quickly became an epoch-making work, one of the best-known and most widely performed oratorios of the entire nineteenth century. Its dignity and serious import, achieved without damage to charm, transparent texture, or melodiousness, quickly reduced the Italian type of oratorio to a secondary position; Haydn's own *Return of Tobias,* just such a work, lost stature quickly. The subject of the Creation appealed to many other composers in the nineteenth century, and the style of Haydn's work influenced many who came after him.

Beethoven

THE NATURE and scope of the music of Ludwig van Beethoven (1770–1827) are such that a discussion of his works logically constitutes a separate chapter in the history of the art. The great bulk of that music is for instruments, and it is as an instrumental composer that he made his unique contributions to music. His works for voices and instruments are, with two or three exceptions, somewhat removed from the main path of his development, so that the principal items in this field may appropriately be discussed here. They include several sets of incidental music for various plays, some of which contain a few choruses: *The Ruins of Athens,* Op. 113, and *King Stephen,* Op. 117, both composed in 1811, are representative. A few cantatas, some early in his career and some late, may be mentioned; the best known title of this group is *The Glorious Moment,* composed in 1814. A Choral Fantasy, Op. 80, for piano solo, chorus, and orchestra, and the choral movement of the Ninth Symphony will be discussed in a later chapter, since they are primarily instrumental works. There remain, then, two Masses.

Beethoven, as one of the first independent or professionally unattached composers, had neither a church position nor access to a choral group. As a consequence, the quantity of his church music is small; the two Masses—one in C major, Op. 86, of 1807, and the other in D major, Op. 123, of 1823—are its principal items. Although Beethoven made little outward show of his Catholic faith and was never a regular attendant at church services, the reverent attitude that was one of his outstanding personal characteristics marked him as a truly religious man. He brought a profound philosophy to expression in his two Masses—in a personal, subjective way, it is true, yet one that is a reflection of Christianity's highest aims.

The C-major Mass reveals the influence of Haydn in many respects. The fusing of solo, ensemble, and chorus into one vocal whole is even more apparent here than in Haydn's late Masses. The orchestral texture is similar to that of Beethoven's first two symphonies and the early piano concertos: sonorous, motivic in style, and varied in expressive power. Beethoven's intention to express musically the inner significance of the text is beautifully realized in large portions of the work, but less apparent elsewhere. The size of the C-major Mass and the free handling of its text make the work unsuited to liturgical use. Beethoven himself spoke of having it performed in concert and declared himself not averse to publication with a German translation of the text. That fact in itself suggests how far the Mass had departed from tradition and had approached the secular concert world.

It is clear that in Beethoven's mind the two worlds of secular and sacred no longer needed to be separate. Religious attributes such as reverence, humility, faith, and moral purpose became ingredients of his secular music—his later string quartets and the Ninth Symphony are eloquent examples. Music became for Beethoven a religion, literally (compare *religare*, to bind anew): a relinking of divine and human. In the D-major Mass (*Missa solemnis*), completed in 1823, the distinction between sacred and secular disappears completely.

In a technical sense the *Missa solemnis* has much in common with its predecessor, but here everything is on a grander and more moving scale. In sheer size, profundity, and general conception it is akin to Bach's Mass in B Minor, and it remains one of the most revealing and significant of Beethoven's compositions. It is difficult to isolate or separate the elements of solo or ensemble, chorus, and orchestral accompaniment, for all are welded into one plastic, flowing texture. Thematic and expressive interest shifts from one plane of sound to another; instruments and voices are organically united. A glowing, homogeneous, and expressive sound results.

Beethoven's free treatment and individual conception of the text come to view repeatedly, in detail as well as in large sections. A recapitulation of the phrase *gloria in excelsis Deo* at the very end of the second movement, even after the elaborately contrapuntal *amen,* is contrary to liturgical usage, but it provides a wonderfully conceived musical moment. Beethoven often emphasized key words for the sake of stressing ideas contained in the text: the words *credo* and *non* in the second movement, the word *dona* in the *Agnus Dei,* and many others. More revealing, perhaps, are the proportions of the final section of the *Credo.* The paragraph of doctrinal statements from *et in spiritum sanctum* to the end of the *Credo* requires scarcely one minute, whereas the single last phrase of that movement, *et vitam venturi saeculi,* is then repeated and set in a triumphant, optimistic passage more than seven minutes in length, truly suggestive of the "life of the world to come." Never before had the setting of a Mass text so clearly revealed the inmost hopes and beliefs of its composer in such intimate detail.

Still more revealing of Beethoven's thought processes, perhaps, is the famous section in the *Agnus Dei,* namely the *Dona nobis pacem* bearing the composer's superscription, "Prayer for inner and external peace." With the same type of abrupt emotional contrast seen in his instrumental works, Beethoven interrupts the prayer with a martial passage for trumpets and tympani introducing short recitatives that realistically picture the terrors of war (see EXAMPLE 132). Then, as a peaceful mood is

EXAMPLE 132

Beethoven, *Missa solemnis*

restored, the *Dona nobis pacem* is treated in fugal style to a theme re-
calling Handel's *Messiah:* "And He shall reign forever."

 Throughout the D-major Mass, such details and such treatment reveal
how Beethoven went behind the liturgy, so to speak, and made the Mass
text into an expression of his own personal attitude toward the Divinity.
He seemed more concerned with ethical than with dogmatic problems; a
similar ethical purpose animates the choral finale of the Ninth Symphony. It is in this sense that Beethoven showed himself to be more
reverent and more truly religious than many a lesser composer who followed tradition and set the Mass text in accord with liturgical requirements. As an expression of deep faith and as a work that brings to profound solution the musical problems that beset a composer of sacred
music in the Classical period, the *Missa solemnis* of Beethoven is one of
the monuments of the human spirit.

৩৩ 19 ৫৫

The Classical Period: Instrumental Music

T HE TWO previous chapters, which dealt with different areas of Classical music, may have shown how great a variety of expressive types the period produced. Serious and glorifying moods are found in the sacred music; broad humor and keen musical characterization come to expression in the operas; joyful and richly ornamented passages fill the pages of both. In the present chapter still other aspects of the style will be encountered. Profound and delicate moods are expressed side by side; melodies pour out spontaneously as though inspired, yet the structures are carefully planned and give evidence of musical calculation and a high standard of conscious workmanship.

All these elements, however diverse they may be, are consistent with the central problem of the period: the reconciliation of personal freedom

"How to Play the Harpsichord." Eighteenth-century engraving. [BETTMANN ARCHIVE]

and universal law, the relationship of the individual to a world of order and system. Subjective feeling and objective reality found a meeting place in the Classical period, and the balance between free expression and self-imposed discipline is reflected in its music. Of the many composers who worked in the last third of the eighteenth century, none exemplified this idea more eloquently or pursued it more successfully than Haydn and Mozart.

These two composers, a generation apart in age, illustrate two different approaches to the problem of their time. Their musical styles reflect different backgrounds, training, and kinds of musical talent. Yet their mutual relationship was such that one cannot be discussed without reference to the other. The influence of Haydn on the younger Mozart was considerable; when Mozart reached maturity and Haydn was in his fifties, the influence was reversed. An account of Haydn's works to about the 1780's is a necessary prelude to a discussion of Mozart's music, but the style of Haydn from about 1785 is in many respects a direct reflection of his encounter with Mozart. These facts will dictate the arrangement of the present chapter, which will open and close with the older composer and discuss the younger in between.

Haydn, 1755–1782

FRANZ JOSEPH HAYDN (1732–1809) was born in Rohrau, an Austrian village on the Hungarian border. In 1740 he was taken to Vienna, where he sang for eight years as a choirboy in St. Stephen's Cathedral. When his voice broke in about 1748, he was discharged from the choir and thrown upon his own resources. He spent the next ten years educating himself, taking a few lessons from the eminent Niccolò Porpora in exchange for accompaniments and earning a precarious living as a teacher. After two short-lived positions with minor Austrian noblemen, he entered the service of the fabulously wealthy Esterházy family in 1761 as second chapelmaster. He became first chapelmaster in 1766 and remained in the employ of several Princes Esterházy until 1790, for a total of almost thirty years. When he retired in that year he was made a pensioner of the family until his death.

At Esterháza, the magnificent family palace on the Hungarian plains far from Vienna, Haydn was responsible for the orchestral and chamber music and, after 1766, for the stage and chapel music. He conducted and composed music of all types for the many concerts given for the entertainment of the Prince and his guests. Except for a few trips to Vienna and frequent visits from other musicians, he was virtually removed from the larger world of music. Forced to become original, he experimented and composed ceaselessly. During his years with the Esterházys he composed about ninety symphonies, almost seventy string quartets, a large number of operatic and other vocal works, quantities of keyboard compositions, and hundreds of pieces in smaller forms. Gradually his fame as a composer grew, and his music was favorably known in Germany, France, England, and Spain.

Painting of an opera performance in the theater at Esterháza, with Haydn directing from the harpsichord.

In 1791–1792 and again in 1794–1795 he visited London and took part in series of concerts arranged by Johann Salomon, a German impresario resident in England. For those visits he composed his last twelve great symphonies as well as another dozen quartets and smaller works. After his return to Vienna he wrote the two oratorios discussed in the previous chapter. He died in 1809 during a French occupation of the Austrian capital.

The fields of the symphony, divertimento, concerto, keyboard music, and chamber music are copiously represented in Haydn's works. Many of his compositions, especially the smaller ones, are occasional pieces that throw little light on the development of his style, but other works parallel to a great extent those in the two principal categories of symphony and string quartet. The account in the present chapter, therefore, will be confined to the developments in the two latter fields.

Early works. The line between orchestral and chamber music was not clearly drawn in the middle of the eighteenth century. This fact became apparent in reviewing Haydn's first twelve published string quartets: six each in Opus 1 and Opus 2, written about 1755–1756 when he was a house guest (there is no record of his having been paid) of Count Joseph von Fürnberg at the latter's country home. At least one of the quartets was designed as a symphony, another was a sextet in its original form, and all twelve were designated as cassations in the earliest catalogues. The form, indeed, is that of the cassation or divertimento; all but one of the works contain five movements, of which the second and fourth are minuets. The content is no more advanced than other Rococo instrumental music of the time; it gives evidence of the direct line connecting early Haydn with his Viennese forebears and contemporaries. Six quartets of Opus 3 (about 1765), each containing four movements, stand on a higher level than the works of a decade earlier. And the six of Opus 9 (about 1769) mark a step forward in melodic interest and variety. The four-movement form including a minuet became virtually standard after 1765.

Parallel to these twenty-four quartets are about forty symphonies, written between 1759 and about 1769. The first two were written during the course of Haydn's employment at the residences of Count Ferdinand Morzin in Vienna and in Bohemia; the others date from his first eight years at Esterháza. Beginning with the third symphony (1761), Haydn's lifelong desire to improve his works became evident. Three elements may be singled out: a greater amount of contrapuntal writing, extending as far as fugal and canonic imitation; the enrichment of orchestration through the more frequent use of wind instruments in the slow movements; and the addition of brilliance through the use of solo passages and, in a few cases, of a true *concertato* texture (solos for two violins and cello over a *concerto grosso* type of accompaniment).

The sonata-form of the first movements was often tightened through the use of motives from which both first and second themes emerged; the economy implied here became one of Haydn's lifelong traits. Further, the manipulation of those motives sometimes began even in the first part (exposition) of the movement, so that the development section proper became virtually unnecessary. Haydn seemed uncertain about the role of the minuet in the early symphonies. It appeared in about half of the works up to No. 20 (probably written in 1764); not until after that date, more than twenty years after the minuet had occasionally appeared in symphonies by other Viennese composers and some of the Mannheimers, did it find a regular place in Haydn's symphonies. In the earlier symphonies the trio of the minuet was usually in the key of the minuet itself (and the key of the symphony as a whole); thereafter it appeared primarily in a related key, most commonly the subdominant or dominant, tonic minor or (when the symphony was in a minor key) relative major. In general, the minuets retained much of the folklike spirit common to most of Haydn's early works and seldom developed the kind of sophisticated, "learned" (that is, contrapuntal), or highly organized texture that Haydn was at pains to establish in other movements.

The period 1770–1782. A growing dissatisfaction with surface charm and superficial expression of the Rococo style had been apparent in Haydn's works of the late 1760's. This feeling was apparently shared by writers and poets also, for a movement known as *Sturm und Drang* ("storm and stress") came to the fore in German literature of the time.

Just as Carl Philipp Emanuel Bach, a decade earlier, had turned away
from the light gracefulness of the French Rococo and had contributed to
the formation of the *empfindsamer Stil,* so Haydn sought to bring deeper
emotions and subjective expression to his music. In fact, the music of
Bach may have stimulated Haydn to deepen his style. He was well acquainted with Bach's sonatas, having studied them and modeled some
of his own keyboard works on them.

As always, the new style began with experiments, seen first in the six
quartets of Opus 17 (1771) and the six of Opus 20 (1772). The earlier
set reveals a new element of instrumental brilliance; first-violin parts
especially rise to a virtuosic level and require technical attainments of
the highest order. In both sets attempts are made to vary the texture
by giving the lower instruments thematic material instead of confining
them to routine harmonic accompaniments. In the quartets of Opus 20
the complete independence of the lower instruments is achieved. Thematic statements are given to the cello (for example, in Opus 20, No. 2);
parts frequently cross; and on occasion the viola or second violin provides
the bass while the cello rises above the inner parts (see EXAMPLE 133).

EXAMPLE 133

Haydn, Quartet, Op. 20, No. 2

Having achieved a texture in which four equal instruments are represented, Haydn was able to increase the quality and quantity of his contrapuntal writing; the finales of three of the quartets are four-voiced
fugues. It is likely that Haydn realized the consequences of this development, that the expressive nature of his style would suffer from the continued use of "learned" counterpoint and fugal style. For nearly ten
years he wrote no more string quartets, carrying forward his experiments
in the orchestral field instead. In the period from 1770 to 1782, Haydn
composed about thirty symphonies (Nos. 43 to about 73) that contain
ample evidence of his experimental approach to problems of form, texture, and mood. In his search for a new expressive content he sometimes
employed remote keys. The symphony No. 44, for example, is in E minor;
No. 45, the famous "Farewell" Symphony, is in F♯ minor and contains a

minuet in F♯ major; No. 46 is in B major; and No. 52 is in C minor. In none of his later symphonies were such remote keys exceeded, though Nos. 78 and 95 are also in C minor. Haydn also experimented with themes in the works of this group. Many exhibit striking contours and rhythmic diversity, and many consist of short fragments that are almost motivic in their effect (see EXAMPLE 134).

E X A M P L E 134

Haydn, Middle period, symphonic themes

With his attention focused on the invention of new types of themes, Haydn seems to have been less interested in thematic manipulation in the earlier symphonies. Development sections of many of the sonata-form movements return to the level of mere transitions or else rely on formalized patterns of melodic sequence and harmonic modulation. This tendency was reversed about 1775, however; from that date on the manipulation of themes became of prime importance. But the processes were not regularized, for new melodic ideas sometimes appear in the development sections, and recapitulations are often freely introduced with unexpected modulations. Other experiments in the form of the symphony also took place. Slow epilogues at the ends of fast finales, connections between one movement and another, and even the brief quotation in one movement of a theme from a previous movement—these are among the experimental devices. Finally, movements in the form of theme and variations appear in these works more frequently than before. This might suggest that Haydn's interest in thematic elaboration and expansion rather than in thematic statement and restatement was increasing.

The "new manner" of 1782. Six string quartets, Opus 33, written about 1781, brought Haydn's process of thematic manipulation to its culmination. It is obvious that he was aware of the extent of his innovation, for the quartets were published with a note explaining that they were "written in an entirely new manner." The chief features of the new manner are a type of melody consisting of several motives capable of being isolated and used in other contexts and a process of employing the motives in a variety of textures and as a basis for new motives and new melodies. The motives in a sense serve as building blocks out of which entire movements are constructed.

The new type of theme is illustrated in EXAMPLE 135. In each case, the motives shown by brackets are employed in two ways: first they appear

EXAMPLE 135

Haydn, Quartet themes

sequentially in the theme phrases themselves, and then they are lifted out of context and become the material out of which transitions and passages in the development section are generated. Further, a motive in the first theme is sometimes used to construct the second theme as well (the first bracketed motive in EXAMPLE 135a is so employed). The process is seen in a most concentrated fashion in Haydn's Opus 33, No. 2. The upbeat of the theme, bracketed in EXAMPLE 136a, is expanded, in measures 5 and 6, from a fourth to an octave. The octave interval, then, becomes the basis for further development in measures 7 and 8. In a passage in the development section (EXAMPLE 136b) other motives from the theme give rise to short melodic lines used contrapuntally; and the motive marked "x" is compressed from a fourth to a second ("y") and appears in the inner voices in inverted position ("z"). The result is a texture in which the four voices are mutually independent and in which polyphony is used in a free and flexible way.

Other movements of the quartets are in general similar to the corresponding movements of earlier works. Three-part forms (*ABA*) in the slow movements and rondo forms in the finales are typical. The minuets are

EXAMPLE 136

Haydn, Quartet, Op. 33, No. 2

labeled "scherzo," but without being essentially different from conventional minuets. In only one of the six (No. 5) is the movement appreciably faster and livelier than in the others. It remained for Beethoven not only to adopt Haydn's term but also to invest the internal fast movement (usually placed after the slow movement) with the humorous character implied in the term "scherzo."

The new type of development introduced in the quartets of Opus 33 was immediately applied in the symphonies that followed. Beginning with No. 73, written about 1781, and to an increasing extent in the later symphonies, themes in the sonata-form movements show ample evidence of motivic construction (see EXAMPLE 137). At the same time, however,

EXAMPLE 137

Haydn, Last period, symphonic themes

Mozart's influence, which had occasionally appeared in Haydn's works for piano, began to be an important element in the larger instrumental works as well. Before proceeding with this account of Haydn's music, therefore, we will review the chief elements of Mozart's style.

Mozart

TWENTY-FOUR years younger than Haydn, Mozart was born in Salzburg in 1756. The summary of his life, given in Chapter 17 (see page 351), need not be repeated here; a few details may be added, however, to emphasize the difference between Mozart's life and Haydn's. The many journeys Mozart made as a child and young man began with a visit of a year's duration to Munich and Vienna in 1762. This was followed by a tour that included extended stays in Paris and London, with long stopovers in many Dutch, German, and Swiss cities, lasting for three and a half years from June, 1763, to November, 1766. Three separate trips to Italy were undertaken between 1770 and 1773. A relatively quiet period

GIRAUDON

The young Mozart entertaining the guests of the Prince of Conti, 1766. Painting by Ollivier.

in Salzburg followed, from Mozart's seventeenth to twenty-first years, but then another twenty-month visit to Mannheim and Paris took place.

These journeys bear a significant relationship to Mozart's stylistic development. He was given an unparalleled opportunity to hear a wide variety of music. Possessing probably the keenest ear and most fabulous musical memory of any musician, he was able to abstract from any new style the elements that served his purpose. In his first twenty years his music was a reflection of what he had heard or studied most recently. Whether he was writing a Neapolitan *sinfonia,* a Viennese divertimento, or a Mannheim concerto, Mozart refined the stylistic elements and incorporated them into his own style. At times he imitated Haydn directly, adopting the older composer's harmonic scheme, thematic outline, and even phrase structure, as in the quartets K. 168–170, for example. From the early 1780's, however, his style was fixed. Everything he composed bore his individual touch, and external influences are difficult to trace. His mature style is the result of a synthesis, on the highest level, of all that musical Europe had to offer.

The succession of influences that helped to determine the style of Mozart took approximately the following sequence: Johann Christian Bach, to about 1764; Vienna in general, to about 1768; Italy, specifically the operatic style, to about 1773; and Haydn from 1773 onward. Mixed with these, or modified by them, were a number of lesser influences, some lasting for only a work or two, some affecting the basic influences, and some appearing as faint recollections at a much later time. The music of Johann Schobert (1720–1767), a German composer living in Paris, may be responsible for several moody, dramatic, almost romantic elements in Mozart's music, for example. The Mannheim style cast its shadow over many portions of Mozart's output, but always in the company of deeper style elements. An acquaintance with the music of Johann Sebastian Bach, which he began to study about 1782, developed into an abiding affection for polyphonic textures.

Mozart employed a greater variety of significant instrumental media than did Haydn. In addition to almost fifty symphonies and twenty-six string quartets, he wrote a number of piano sonatas and works for piano with one, two, or three string instruments, ranging from the earliest violin sonatas, K. 6 to K. 9, written about 1763, to the last piano trio, K. 564, of 1788. These violin sonatas, piano trios, and piano quartets, as well as many miscellaneous works, are in general stylistically similar to the string quartets and symphonies written at about the same time. Similarly, each of the several quintets for strings (with two violas) and the famous quintet for clarinet and strings, extending from K. 174 (1773) to K. 614 (1791) has its individual character but also reflects the stylistic qualities of the contemporary symphonies; the same is true of the large number of divertimentos for various instruments. The twenty-one concertos for piano and orchestra (from K. 175 of 1773 to K. 595 of 1791) not only equal the symphonies but sometimes transcend them. The following account, therefore, will focus on the symphonies, piano concertos, and string quartets.

Early works. Mozart had already written nine symphonies by 1768, his twelfth year. The earliest of them, composed on the first long journey to Paris and London in 1763–1767, bear the strong imprint of the style of Johann Christian Bach, then in the English capital. Melodic grace, nervous energy, a three-movement form, clear articulations, and quick alternations of *forte* and *piano* in the first few measures of themes—these were elements of Bach's style at the time, and they are echoed in Mozart's. A number of four-movement symphonies written for Vienna about 1768, on the other hand, are somewhat more formal in tone than the earlier truly diverting works and characterized by a fuller orchestral texture.

Mozart composed almost thirty symphonies between 1770 and 1773, most of them for his three visits to Italy or in anticipation of a fourth trip. The majority of them reflect the purpose of Italian symphonies of the time and also reveal how deftly Mozart captured that purpose and made it his own. The symphony was primarily a piece designed to open or close a program, to frame the "important" works—solos, arias, concertos—that occupied the middle portion of the program. As such, it was meant to be entertaining; profundity would have been out of place. It sought to express the ideals of the Italian *buffo* style: melodiousness, a degree of bustle and speed to keep interest alive, and only enough dramatic emphasis to raise it above the purely formal. If the majority of Mozart's early symphonies meet these specifications, they only give evidence of his ability to do what was expected of him.

Mozart's first ten string quartets—all written for the Italian journeys—are much like the symphonies in scope and general musical content. They are little more than pleasantly melodious in homophonic textures and well balanced in form, though they show a degree of ingenuity in the voice-leading of the inner parts. Yet a few details reveal that the fifteen- or sixteen-year-old Mozart would soon progress far beyond the bounds of the Italian *buffo* style. An occasional chromatic inflection in both harmony and melody, an occasional flash of deep feeling in a conventional slow movement, and the generally lyric tone of many themes give a preview of what Mozart would soon become.

The change to a more significant style came with dramatic suddenness. It may be dated late in 1773, and it is seen first in six string quartets, K. 168–K. 173, and in three symphonies, K. 200, K. 183, and K. 201.[1] Several factors may account for the change, chief among them the fact that Mozart spent the summer of 1773 in Vienna, where he became acquainted with Haydn's quartets of Opus 17 and Opus 20. He had known the music of Haydn from afar, so to say, but of the earlier Rococo Haydn, whose works could not have taught Mozart a great deal. The quartets, however, were among the first results of Haydn's *Sturm und Drang* experimentation; the brilliance of the one set and the imaginative voice-leading and contrapuntal textures of the other were revelations to the impressionable young Mozart. The influence was direct and immediate. A fugue theme in F minor, found in Haydn's Opus 20, No. 5, reappears in Mozart's K. 168, changed from duple to triple meter. A few of the finales in Opus 20 are fugues, as they are in two of Mozart's six quartets. Haydn's sets both include minuets; Mozart, who had not written minuets in his earlier quartets, did so in this set. The tone of several of Haydn's slow movements is broad, lyric, and somewhat sentimental, and Mozart attempted a similar kind of expression in his.

Such relatively external relationships are not found in the three symphonies (K. 200, K. 183, and K. 201) of 1773–1774, however. The Haydn influence here is more in the direction of emotional tone and dramatic content; subjective feeling and personal expression come to the fore. It is possible that Mozart knew Haydn's symphonies Nos. 39, 44, and 49, written about 1768–1773, for the passionate tone that first appeared in them marks Mozart's first symphony in a minor key, K. 183, in G minor. The personal emotion, even of underlying grief, portrayed in that work is among the early examples of a mood that was to be reflected in many of Mozart's later works. The minuets in the three symphonies of the group go far beyond Haydn's, in a sense. Suppressed fury comes to expression, but the control that is so characteristic of the later Mozart is

---

1 In the revised edition (by Einstein) of the Köchel Index (1937) these symphonies are numbered K. 173*a*, K. 183, and K. 186*a*. The revised numbers reveal the relative closeness in time of the symphonies to the quartets.

also evident. With the six quartets and three symphonies of 1773–1774 the Rococo spirit is left behind.

Having encountered a new style and modified his own, Mozart needed time to absorb it and fully realize its implications. A four-year period ensued during which he wrote no significant symphonies, and a ten-year period in which he composed no string quartets. True, he had no Italian journeys in mind that would have required works of either class, and he received no commissions to compose symphonies or quartets during the four years spent primarily in Salzburg.

A long visit to Mannheim and Paris, from 1777 to 1779, provided a commission to write a symphony, resulting in 1778 in the "Paris" symphony, K. 297. The work was composed for one of the largest and best orchestras in Europe. The Mannheim style (see page 326) prevailed in Paris, and Mozart, familiar with the style, wrote accordingly. The familiar Mannheim devices—unison passages for strings, brilliant writing for wind instruments, and long crescendos—are present, but as usual Mozart transcended the style. He composed a three-movement work that is full of skillful contrapuntal writing. Two other symphonies were written in Salzburg after the return from Mannheim and Paris; these are in four movements on the general model of Viennese symphonies.

The early concertos. The majority of Mozart's twenty-one concertos for one piano and orchestra were designed mainly for his own use. Four of them (K. 175, 238, 246, and 271) were written between 1773 and 1778, while he was still a resident of Salzburg. Mozart had been affected by the charm and *galanterie* of Johann Christian Bach's concertos while on his visit to London, about 1766, and a year or two before that time he had converted several of Bach's sonatas into piano concertos. Even his earliest original concertos, however, reveal how quickly he went beyond Bach's surface charm and brought deeper emotions to his music. The chief contribution of Mozart to the piano concerto—the new relationship between solo piano and orchestra—is scarcely more than hinted at in these works, except perhaps in K. 271, the so-called "Jeunehomme" concerto. Nor was it fully realized in the first three concertos Mozart wrote for Vienna about 1782–1783 (K. 414, 413, and 415). It came appreciably closer in the *Sinfonia concertante* for violin, viola, and orchestra, K. 364, written about 1779. But not until well into his Vienna period, when he composed a full dozen concertos between 1784 and 1786, did that relationship become an essential ingredient of his style. Those works will be discussed below.

The quartets. In 1781 Mozart left Salzburg and took up residence in Vienna. There he married and, except for a few short visits to Prague, Berlin, and neighboring cities, lived for the ten years that remained to him. It was probably in the winter of 1781 that he met Haydn. The acquaintance developed into warm mutual friendship and esteem, and Haydn's influence on Mozart, previously exerted at a distance, now became tangible and direct.

The first result of Haydn's influence was a series of six string quartets, written at intervals from late 1782 to early 1785: K. 387, 421, 428, 458, 464, and 465. Published in 1785, the set was dedicated to Haydn with the phrase, "the fruit of a long and laborious work." The quartets are Mozart's response to Haydn's "new manner" of the quartets of Opus 33. The manuscripts reveal how even a Mozart had difficulty in fully absorbing Haydn's new principle of thematic development; they are among the few of Mozart's that show passages struck out, modified, erased, and altered. Yet none of the "laborious work" is apparent in the finished quartets.

If in earlier compositions Mozart had been content to model some aspects of his style on that of Haydn, he now used the latter as a point of departure and transcended it. The principle of thematic development is basic to Mozart's quartets, as is the new texture of four independent and equal instruments. Mozart's thematic statements in first movements are less motivic than Haydn's, however; essentially lyric in character, they depend upon sequence repetition of phrases for their expansion (see EXAMPLE 138). Transitions often consist of variants of the phrases of the

EXAMPLE 138

Mozart, Quartet themes

main theme, and other melodic variants appear in the development sections. It is these variants of themes, then, that are developed in Haydn's manner.

Other movements in these quartets are of various types; they include sets of variations, deceptively simple slow movements, reserved and aristocratic minuets, and, in one case, a fugal finale. Indeed, the variety of forms and expressive content is so great that the six quartets cannot be thought of as a set (as one could think of earlier works), but only as individual compositions. The moods of the quartets are equally diverse. Grace

and elegance in the G-major, K. 387, pessimism and resignation in the
D-minor, K. 421, good humor and untroubled expression in the B-flat,
K. 428—such contrasts of mood characterize the six.

One element of Mozart's style, not derived from Haydn, that makes
a striking impression in the quartets is melodic chromaticism (see Ex-
AMPLE 138a). Darker moods and moments of pessimism had occurred
earlier in Mozart's career, of course, and they were usually carried by
short passages based on the chromatic scale. In the last decade of Mozart's
life, however, the chromatic element became more pronounced; much
of the dark tone and passionate feeling in his latest works are expressed
in such passages. In addition, chromatic lines four or five tones in length
often appear in passages that are in themselves optimistic or cheery in
tone. The result is Mozart's unique combination of light and dark in the
same phrase (see EXAMPLE 139 and the last measure of EXAMPLE 138a).

EXAMPLE 139

Mozart, Melodic chromaticism in the "Haydn" quartets

The chromaticism is often deftly concealed, in that a diatonic tone or
two are inserted between the chromatic tones, but the mood of inner
tension is felt nevertheless. The famous introduction to the first movement of the C-major quartet, K. 465, provides perhaps the most extreme
example of this type of melodic chromaticism in all of Mozart's works,
for here it is coupled with extreme dissonance (see EXAMPLE 139c).

Mozart composed four additional quartets, one (K. 499) about 1788
and three (K. 575, 589, and 590) in 1789–1790. The last three, dedicated
to Frederick William II of Prussia, bring in an element of virtuosity; the
king was a good cellist, and in deference to his royal patron Mozart provided richer cello parts than usual. Themes are given to the cello and
first violin in equal proportions, while the inner voices share in the generally enhanced melodic content of the various movements. The result is
a set of quartets unequalled in lyric quality, grace, and perfect proportion.

The late symphonies. The five symphonies composed between 1783 and
1788 mark the culmination of Mozart's symphonic writing. The first of

the five, K. 425, written at Linz, begins with a slow introduction, in the manner of many Haydn symphonies. Haydn had often prefaced a first movement with an introductory section in slow tempo, most often in a formal, almost stylized mood that served primarily as an ornamental façade for the musical structure that followed. Mozart knew several such works of Haydn and adapted the device to his own "Linz" symphony—the first in which he did so—but again without imitating the older man. The introduction to the symphony, as well as those in the later K. 504 and 543 (as also in the C-major quartet, K. 465), is no mere architectural ornament. In each it is a piece of heartfelt music; each has its own content and each contrasts effectively with the fast movement that follows.[2]

Three years elapsed before Mozart returned to the symphonic form. The D-major symphony, K. 504, known as the "Prague," was written late in 1786. It contains a slow introduction but no minuet. This does not represent a return to the light or trivial Italian type (as opposed to the four-movement Viennese type), however, but rather a work which in Mozart's estimation did not require a minuet. Mozart had long since mastered the principle of thematic development. He applied it here, in the first and last movements, to unassuming thematic material with profound effect. Concentrated contrapuntal textures abound in the first movement; tension and energy are everywhere present. The use of chromatic inflections gives an especially poignant tone to the Andante (see EXAMPLE 140); the finale is a wonderful blend of joy and sorrow.

EXAMPLE 140

Mozart, Symphony, K. 504

Mozart's last three symphonies, K. 543 in E♭, K. 550 in G minor, and K. 551 in C, were written in the incredibly short space of about two months in the summer of 1788. There was no external reason for writing them; no concerts of his music were projected for Vienna, and no trips were being planned. Perhaps they were composed to fill an inner need, to bring to completion the final synthesis of all stylistic elements that had marked Mozart's career since the beginning. In these works all the influences that had played upon him disappear; the result is a style uniquely Mozart's. One cannot point to an Italian or a Rococo or a

2 The "Linz" symphony is No. 36 in the Complete Edition of Mozart's works. The work which follows, No. 37, K. 444, is falsely attributed to him. It is actually by Michael Haydn, Joseph's younger brother; only the slow introduction is by Mozart.

galant or a Haydnesque element in isolation, for while such elements are present, all are perfectly fused. Even more remarkable is the fact that the three symphonies are individual works of art in spite of their stylistic unity.

The first of the three, with an eloquent slow introduction, is a blend of cheerfulness and resignation. The four movements are filled with many details that conceal Mozart's technical command of the medium. Subtle phrase elisions and extensions, more motivic development than usual, extreme harmonic freedom in the last movement, a new soloistic approach to the wind instruments—such details lift the E♭ symphony far above the works that preceded it.

The G-minor symphony is vastly more than the graceful, enjoyable work it is often held to be. It suggests stormy, restless, and anguished moods. Twisting chromatic lines in three of the movements do much to express the pathos that is everywhere apparent. All but the slow movement are in minor; never before had Mozart (or Haydn) concentrated so intensely on the minor mood. The harmonic progressions in the last movement and the fierce, almost brutal energy expressed there far exceed anything that the Classical period had heard to this time.

The C-major symphony, called the "Jupiter," is completely unlike the other two and unlike virtually any other work of Mozart's. Its underlying tone is one of optimism or courage, and its texture is a unique blend of homophony and polyphony. Songful melodies, stereotyped accompanying

EXAMPLE 141

Mozart, Symphony, K. 551, finale

(Horns, Trumpets, and Tympani omitted)

figures, a variety of contrapuntal devices, and—in the finale—a sonata-form movement with fugal passages are all absorbed into a unified whole that breathes creative joy in every measure. The fusion of lyric and polyphonic devices, especially in the last movement, represents a *tour de force* even for Mozart (see EXAMPLE 141). The end of his last symphony, in which a stretto composed of *galant* themes set in invertible counter-point, serves as a symbol of Classical style, a style in which all the ex-traneous and contradictory elements of the late eighteenth century are brought under control, unified, and perfected.

The late concertos. Mozart's last piano concertos—twelve written be-tween 1784 and 1786 and one each in 1788 and 1791—are unique in the literature. Each has its individual character, its special emotional tone, and its own form. Taken together, they contain some of his finest writing for orchestra; even the last symphonies do not rise above them in expres-sive variety and musical quality. They represent an achievement not found in the concertos of earlier composers and scarcely evident even in Mozart's own earlier works in the form: here for the first time the orchestra is raised to a truly symphonic level and the solo part stands both opposed to and connected with the orchestral part. In these works Mozart provides at once conflict and unity.

Part of this accomplishment results from Mozart's expansion of sonata-form. In general, the first movements exhibit a form similar to that of the symphony, but with several notable exceptions. (1) A second exposi-tion, in which both piano and orchestra take part, may introduce new thematic material not present in the orchestral (first) exposition. (2) Tran-sitions between themes and codettas at section endings may be more ex-tended than in a symphony and based on repetitions of motives heard earlier (thus the character of a *ritornello,* found in the old *concerto grosso* and solo concerto of the Baroque period, is preserved). (3) A cadenza intervenes at the end of the recapitulation, in which the soloist freely elaborates and improvises on thematic material. In many cases Mozart composed cadenzas for other performers to use. (4) A coda, for orchestra alone, may again be based on earlier thematic material, thus strengthen-ing the feeling of a *ritornello.*

The abundant amount of thematic material makes possible antiphonal effects between piano and orchestra, enables the orchestra to develop themes in a symphonic manner under an obbligato passage in the solo piano, and permits themes to be combined contrapuntally in the two separate tonal entities—piano and orchestra, respectively. In such ways the orchestral part is far removed from mere accompaniment, and the piano stands as an equal partner of the orchestra without losing its identity as a solo instrument.

The chromaticism that is so significant elsewhere in Mozart's melodic writing also comes to expression in the piano concertos. Passionate, gloomy, or dramatic moods are often concentrated and strengthened by the use of chromatic passages. In slow movements generally, Mozart de-parted widely from the *galant* type of expression. The level of profundity expressed there equals or even exceeds that of his other instrumental works. It is usually accomplished by simplifying the melodic line, removing excess ornamentation, and allowing the magic of simple melody and simple harmony to carry its emotional message. From Mozart onward, the concerto became a medium for expressing significant and heartfelt music; its other function, of being merely a brilliant display piece, lost ground with serious composers. A direct line leads from the piano concertos of Mozart to those of Beethoven.

Haydn, 1782–1802

THE MEETING of Haydn and Mozart, late in 1781, was as significant for the older composer as for the younger. In his fiftieth year Haydn proved himself to be receptive and adaptable. His stature as a widely respected and experienced composer notwithstanding, he was willing and able to learn from Mozart, scarcely half his age. The influence of Mozart is to be seen in the almost thirty symphonies and more than thirty string quartets Haydn was yet to write, bringing about an increased lyricism, a greater harmonic freedom, and a renewal of his experimental approach to musical form.

The late symphonies. In the roughly fourteen years between his meeting with Mozart and his return from the second London visit, Haydn's symphonic style reached new levels of expressiveness. About a dozen of the late symphonies were written for Esterháza (he was active there until 1790), six were written for a concert organization in Paris, and the last twelve were composed in or for London. One of the noteworthy facts about the three groups is that the slow introductions, which appear in a majority of the symphonies, are no longer of the formal, façadelike type that had characterized Haydn's symphonies up to about No. 73. Haydn wholeheartedly adopted Mozart's type of introduction, in which eloquent melodies, harmonic freedom, and touches of pathos prepare the mood—or contrast with the mood—of the first movement to follow. Most often a phrase near the end of the introduction anticipates the theme of the following first movement, so that thematic connection between the two is assured. Of the twelve London symphonies on which Haydn's fame so largely rests today, only No. 95 is without a slow introduction; the remaining eleven contain introductions unequaled in their harmonic variety and expressive scope.

In his earlier works Haydn had often concentrated his attention on the first theme or theme groups. In the post-1782 symphonies, on the other hand, he repeatedly adopted Mozart's practice of giving equal weight to the contrasting second theme. In addition to lending greater variety to the structure of the exposition, this made development sections unpredictable. One cannot generalize about Haydn's practice in these sections—except to point out that the composer's imagination and skill were always equal to the task he set for himself. In the years after the "new manner" of 1782, he became increasingly skillful in the art of creating new melodies out of the motives that had gone before. As a consequence, each development section establishes its own unique pattern.

The development principle itself was employed ever more extensively. Successive phrases of the first theme group are sometimes derived from the first phrase, as are the transitions between themes. Recapitulations are seldom exact but rather modified under the influence of the principle. And in one noteworthy respect the proportions of the sonata-form movements were radically changed: the coda of the movement often becomes in effect a second development section (sometimes called "terminal development").

Melodic chromaticism, of the kind so effectively employed by Mozart, also became an element of Haydn's style for a brief period to about 1790. Less important to Haydn than to Mozart, however, it was not used extensively in the London period, suggesting that after Mozart's death Haydn reverted to his innate, essentially diatonic style.

In spite of the influence of Mozart, and in spite of increasing age, Haydn never lost the optimism, humor, and straightforward expression that had marked his work since the 1750's. The humor is revealed in a number of unexpected modulations, false recapitulations, and sudden turns of phrase, but also, especially in last movements, in a buoyant, good-natured melodic style whose effervescence carries the listener along in joyous fashion.

Profound and wonderfully expressive lyric moments abound in the slow movements; one does Haydn a great injustice if one overlooks this point. Many of his adagios and andantes are cast in the form of theme and variations, and sometimes two themes are employed and varied in alternation, after which an extended coda closes the movement. However serious or profound, the slow movements are seldom gloomy or morbid; Haydn's optimism is never long absent. Minuets, in turn, often reveal Haydn's interest in contrapuntal treatment of themes, and frequently true canons result. Such treatment, of course, contrasts greatly with the formal, stylized, dancelike patterns that had characterized the older type of minuet since the 1750's.

In last movements, especially in the rondo, Haydn often introduced innovations in form, as Mozart had done. The conventional rondo consisted of a regular alternation of two or more thematic sections harmonically contrasted, as seen in the following diagram:

Theme:	A	B	A	C	A	B	A
Harmony:	I	V or III	I	VI or III	I	I	I

In the late symphonies, as well as in many of the late quartets, a form that has been called "sonata-rondo" emerged. It differed from the conventional rondo in containing more elaborate transitions, in substituting a type of development section for the middle ("C") part, and in remaining in the tonic key for the final return of the "B" section. And it differed from true sonata-form by bringing back the final "A" section in the form of a coda. The sonata-rondo often took the following form:

A transition	B codetta	A	pseudodevelopment	A trans.	B codetta	A coda
I	V	I	various keys	I	I	I I

The late quartets. Following the six quartets of Opus 33 (1781), Haydn composed about eighteen more during his remaining years with the Esterházy family (to 1790) and fourteen during and after the London visits (1791 to 1799). As in the symphonies, the influence of Mozart is clearly evident. Perhaps the most obvious new element is an enhanced lyricism in melodies of all types (see EXAMPLE 142). The bucolic, folklike

EXAMPLE 142

Haydn, Late period, quartet themes

tone of many of Haydn's earlier melodies is here refined and sublimated, giving way to a combination of elegance and deep feeling.

Slow introductions, which had become almost standard in the symphonies, are noticeably absent in the quartets. Very few of Haydn's seventy-six works in this form,[3] principally those of Opus 71 and Opus 74, contain introductions to first movements. This may suggest that in Haydn's mind a quartet was not merely a reduced symphony (as it had often been considered in the 1740's) and that he felt an introduction would interfere with the intimate tone characteristic of the form.

In respect to structure and thematic treatment, the last quartets are much like the symphonies. The same expanded use of the development principle occurs, as well as the same type of expanded coda. In many of the quartets, Haydn's general practice of basing an entire movement on one main idea and derivations of that idea prevails, while others reflect Mozart's practice of employing contrasting second themes.

3 The number of quartets is often given as eighty-three; that number, however, includes the quartet arrangements of the seven orchestral movements known collectively as *The Seven Last Words of Christ on the Cross* (see p. 372).

The expansion of Haydn's harmonic practices may be seen in many of the late quartets, as it may in the London symphonies. In several cases the trio of a minuet is in the mediant or submediant key instead of the more usual subdominant, dominant, or relative minor; in Opus 74, for example, an A-major minuet has a trio in C major, and another in the same set moves from F in the minuet to D♭ in the trio. The use of mediant and submediant modulations became a striking feature of Beethoven's style and of the early Romantic style in general. Here, as in many other respects, Haydn anticipated a detail that was to become general decades later. And in a few quartets, even more distant harmonic relationships occur: Opus 76, No. 5, in D major, contains a sublime largo in F♯ major; and Opus 76, No. 6, in E♭, contains a slow movement that begins and ends in B major. The latter movement is marked "fantasia," almost as if Haydn meant to justify his harmonic boldness.

The Orchestra of Haydn and Mozart

THE REFERENCES to the opera orchestra in earlier chapters may have shown that it was greatly expanded in the period from about 1730 to 1790. A parallel expansion took place in the symphony orchestra; its direction and scope may be seen in the gradually increasing size of the group for which Haydn and Mozart wrote. A summary of their practice is appropriate here.

In roughly the first fifty of Haydn's 104 symphonies, an orchestra consisting of two oboes, two horns, and strings was basic. In about ten of them one flute was added, in another symphony, two, and in two of the symphonies a pair of flutes replaced the oboes. Through much of the eighteenth century the flute had been considered a solo instrument, most useful in chamber music and concertos; when it appeared in *sinfonie* it was often given a part more important than that of the tutti instruments. Not until about 1780 (Symphony No. 70) is the presence of one or two flutes regularly to be expected in Haydn's orchestra.

As part of the tradition arising out of the old continuo practice, the bassoon was seldom specified in the orchestra but was expected to add sonority to the bass part, which was regularly played by the cellos and basses in octaves. To about 1780 the bassoon remained unmentioned except in six of Haydn's symphonies; after that date one or two bassoon parts were regularly written into the score.

Tympani parts, most often confined to tonic and dominant tones, were usually improvised, so there was little need to indicate them in the score. Haydn did so in only about ten of his first seventy symphonies, and in the remaining thirty-odd works they are required about half the time. Trumpet parts, likewise, were seldom specified, but trumpets were expected to be available in occasional tutti passages, especially in fast movements. Often the trumpet parts were written separately and not included in the score. A pair of trumpets is specifically called for in only about seven of Haydn's first seventy-five symphonies, but this does not necessarily mean that they were not used along with the tympani.

the like took the place of the doublings or sustained tones that had been allotted to the winds in earlier works. The art of orchestration, and the beginning of a real appreciation of orchestral color as a factor of musical expressiveness, may be said to have begun in the late 1780's in these works of Haydn and Mozart.

The Ideals of Classicism

WE HAVE seen that periodically in the course of music history a reaction to the existing order has resulted in a considerable modification of the existing style. Invariably a number of composers have taken part in both the reaction and the formulation of the new style. Inevitably, individual approaches to the problem of the time lead to individual solutions in such number that a time of sterile experiment, of stylistic multiplicity, of artistic chaos results. Gradually the musical excesses die out; some of the experimental lines are seen to lead nowhere, and others mature and form the basis for a new style. The time in which order and balance are restored is generally called the classical phase of the period.

Seen from this point of view, the roles of Haydn and Mozart can be better appreciated. During the last decades of the Baroque period there occurred the expected reactions to Baroque formalism and stylized expression, described in the previous chapters. The emergence of the pre-Classical opera style and of the French *style galant* represents two of the reactions; the various styles of Berlin, Mannheim, Vienna, and other areas were in a sense local modifications of them. The operatic reform associated with the name of Gluck is yet another reaction. And against all these, the "learned" contrapuntal style of the Baroque refused to die out completely.

Parallel to the developments in the field of music, or perhaps in part responsible for them, were the new ideas and ideals mentioned at the beginning of this chapter. The relationship between personal freedom and universal law was brought into question, and a new one sought. Although it is unlikely that either Haydn or Mozart was actively concerned with the philosophical currents of his time, neither one could escape them. Caught up in the social currents, in the changing forms of institutions, both men reflected the changes and responded in an artistic fashion. The result was the Classical style.

Specifically, a reconciliation between the poles of lyric melody and polyphonic texture was achieved by both masters; countless passages in the later instrumental works of Haydn and Mozart give eloquent testimony. This polarity was in effect the reflection of the basic difference between Italian and German styles; Mozart, with his Germanic training and his temperament directed toward Italian grace and melodiousness, was in an advantageous position to achieve the synthesis, and Haydn became his peer.

A relationship of a different kind was achieved first by Haydn: the relationship between heart and mind, between inspired creation and conscious manipulation of musical material. Haydn's receptivity to an expressively significant musical idea was coupled with the intellectual discipline needed to employ the idea in the most artistic fashion. The result is best seen in his introduction of the "new manner" of thematic development. In this case Mozart proved an apt pupil and quickly developed a competence that equaled that of the older composer.

The problem of individual freedom in a world of order was solved musically by both masters, and in equal measure. In musical terms, this is the age-old problem of content versus form, of the relationship between the thing expressed (content) and the manner of expressing it (form). The appearance of fully developed sonata-form and of the so-called sonata-rondo, as seen in the works of Haydn and Mozart, are manifestations of this relationship. For it was in the freedom with which they applied basic formal principles, or the manner in which the principles were adjusted to their musical material, that the two men reached the heights of Classical style.

This point is often overlooked or misunderstood. All too often, sonata-form is thought of as a rigid pattern into which musical material is forced; and all too often the flexibility of the form in the hands of great composers is overlooked. Even a casual examination of a few works in this form by Haydn and Mozart will reveal that no single pattern exists. Every work discloses appropriate modifications of the exposition, development, and recapitulation, dictated by the nature of the thematic material and the composer's expressive purpose. There are sonata-form movements based on a single motive, others in which new ideas are brought into the development section and old ones are not, and still others with either incomplete recapitulations or greatly modified ones.

It seems to have been the special faculty of minor composers to misunderstand this free and flexible approach to musical form in general. A composition by a minor composer is generally predictable: it follows the "rules." In the music of the masters, the rules (if there are any) are constantly modified by the expressive requirements of the moment. This is the point at which form and content, heart and mind, freedom and universal law, are perfectly balanced, representing Classicism at its finest. The musical content itself was selected with principles of moderation, beauty, and good taste uppermost. Classical music, as we have seen, is not necessarily the music of powdered wigs and knee breeches—although the period had its full share of graceful, courtly, and elegant music. It is also the music of boisterous humor, of passionate feeling, of equanimity; and as we shall see in the equally Classical works of Beethoven, it is also the music of elemental power, of universal feeling, of sublime beauty. The two requirements of Classical music—that its form be appropriate to its content, and that it be balanced and proportioned in all details—are fully met by the music of Haydn and Mozart, to the immeasurable benefit of all who hear it.

The Classical Period:
Beethoven

THE CHANGING relationship of the individual to society, which had taken a characteristic turn in the second half of the eighteenth century, reached a new stage in the early nineteenth. Haydn's generation had come to an understanding with the spirit of the time—a time when the artist was considered no more than a servant; Beethoven rebelled against such a status. Among musicians, he stood alone in surmounting whatever impediments lay in his path. Through sheer strength of character and personal integrity he mastered the social forces that might have broken him. Exerting his will to the utmost, he conquered both his musical material and his personal afflictions. In the process he created a new kind of music, a kind which opened up new vistas of the human soul.

Beethoven is identified most closely with instrumental music. A number of songs, a few cantatas and other choral works, one opera, two Masses, and a few miscellaneous vocal compositions exist, but with two or three exceptions they are not among his most important or even char-

Engraving of Beethoven, presumed to be by Lÿser. [THE METROPOLITAN MUSEUM OF ART, CROSBY BROWN COLLECTION, 1901]

acteristic works. It is in his extensive instrumental music that Beethoven's significance lies. A consideration of the various styles of the works for orchestra, for chamber-music groups, and for piano, then, will occupy the present chapter.

Beethoven's Life

LUDWIG VAN BEETHOVEN was born in the Rhine city of Bonn in 1770. His grandfather, of Flemish ancestry, had been a singer in the Electoral chapel since 1733 and in 1761 was made chapelmaster; available accounts indicate that he was a man of integrity and upright character. Beethoven's father, also a singer in the Electoral chapel, was of lesser stature in all respects. Harsh and unpredictable in his behavior, he was scarcely fitted to nurture the future composer's talent. Beethoven was placed with a succession of mediocre teachers during his formative years, but from about 1781 he studied under Christian Neefe, an excellent musician and court organist. A year later the boy was able to serve as organist in Neefe's absence; he remained a member of the Electoral establishment as accompanist, organist, and viola player for about ten years. During this period his mother died, his father became virtually incompetent from alcoholism, and the care of his two younger brothers fell upon him. In spite of a wretched home life, scanty education, and considerable professional responsibility, Beethoven became active as a composer. He also made several fast friends among the nobility of Bonn.

Beethoven's musical training was irregular and sparse. During a visit to Vienna in 1787 he had met Mozart, but apparently no lessons resulted from the meeting. In 1792 he was enabled to go to Vienna to study with Haydn, but Haydn's teaching proved a disappointment to Beethoven; he sought out an eminent contrapuntalist, Johann Albrechtsberger, and studied with him for about a year. He also received some instruction from Salieri, at that time chapelmaster to the Imperial court. In the main, however, Beethoven was self-taught; even his formal schooling had ended in about his eleventh year. Yet he succeeded in mastering the techniques of composition, became one of the most accomplished pianists of his day, and through intensive reading became familiar with the major works of literature.

In Vienna he began his career as a pianist, becoming well known in aristocratic circles especially for the quality of his improvisations, and earned a living as a teacher. From about 1795 his published compositions attracted favorable attention; soon every new work was eagerly anticipated by the Viennese public, and his reputation as one of the foremost composers of the time rose rapidly. He was at home with members of the Imperial court circles and numbered many aristocrats as his friends and occasionally as his patrons. In general, however, he subsisted on fees, royalties, and commissions—the first major composer to do so.

About 1800 Beethoven became aware of a deterioration in his hearing, and by 1802 he realized that total deafness was in prospect for him. A period of extreme mental anguish and despair resulted, and for a time he contemplated suicide. His strength of will surmounted the affliction, but the deafness increased and by 1820 had become almost total. His public performances as a pianist continued to about 1808, however; thereafter composing was virtually his sole occupation.

In 1815 his brother Caspar Karl died and left the care of his son, Karl, to the composer and to the boy's mother jointly. Beethoven despised his sister-in-law and considered her unfit to act as her own son's guardian. He succeeded in having young Karl, then nine years old, placed under his sole guardianship. The boy's mother sought to have her son restored to her charge; a series of court hearings, lasting almost four years, resulted in her victory. A year later, however, in 1820, a higher court reversed the lower, and the boy was given into his uncle's care. Almost five years were filled with the unpleasant affair, during which Beethoven's productivity as a composer suffered immeasurably; only half a dozen works were written. Ironically enough, Karl became a constant source of disappointment and anxiety to his uncle and saddened the composer's life.

Beethoven's last seven years were marked by his increasing fame as a composer, by continued absorption in his work, and by growing social isolation. His deafness made normal social contacts difficult and frustrating for him, and he avoided them whenever possible. He was heartened by the success of virtually every new work he composed, most of which were published shortly after their completion, and he enjoyed the visits of the many musical and other notables who called on him. His health had deteriorated steadily since about 1818, and from 1826 his decline was rapid. He died in 1827, mourned as the greatest composer of his age. From that year to the present the estimation of Beethoven as one of the supreme masters of all time has grown steadily.

Beethoven's Works

THE PRESENCE of three distinct styles in Beethoven's music has been recognized for more than a century,[1] although there is no agreement on the exact dates of each style period. The problem of dating the periods arises in part from the fact that the style changes appeared rather gradually, some being apparent in certain works and not in other, contemporary pieces, and it is complicated by Beethoven's habit of working on a composition for a long time, revising it frequently and publishing it after later works had already been issued. In general, however, the dates 1802 and 1816–1817 may be taken as marking the internal style changes. Those dates, it will be noticed, coincide closely with the turning points in Beethoven's personal life: the year 1802 marks his realization of impending deafness and his return to normal mental health, while 1816 represents the period of intense litigation with his sister-in-law and his gradual return to full activity as a composer.

1 The earliest systematic account was probably that of Wilhelm von Lenz, *Beethoven et ses trois styles,* published in St. Petersburg in 1852.

The chief purpose of this chapter is to indicate the scope and variety of Beethoven's style characteristics. For this reason, it will be desirable to discuss style in terms of specific works rather than groups of works. First, therefore, a brief description of the principal instrumental works will be given in systematic order; the detailed style elements will then be discussed in the second half of the chapter.

First-period works. When Beethoven moved to Vienna in 1792 he brought with him several compositions he had written in Bonn. Some of these works were subsequently revised and published posthumously; many of the compositions with opus numbers higher than 135 are among them. The group includes two cantatas, music to a ballet, three piano quartets, and a variety of smaller pieces. The piano quartets are noteworthy in being among the first of their type; they were composed in 1785, the year in which Mozart wrote his two piano quartets, K. 478 and K. 493, and thus these five works introduced an important new performing medium to the field of chamber music.

Beethoven chose to disregard all the works written in Bonn when he began his career as a professional composer in Vienna. He wrote a new Opus 1, consisting of three trios for violin, cello, and piano, about 1795. Chamber music engaged Beethoven's attention through all of his career; not only his first numbered work but also his last (Opus 135 of 1826) was

Ludwig van Beethoven, 1770–1827. From a portrait by J. C. Stieler.

in that field. In the works of the first period [2] the models of Haydn and Mozart lie close at hand. Four-movement forms predominate, but the true scherzo most often replaces the minuet. The textures are clear, almost transparent, and the works are well proportioned. In addition, however, they reveal two characteristics that Beethoven was to employ throughout his career. One is the use of motives rather than themes as principal structural material; the other is the interest in sudden and far-reaching modulations.

Haydn's practice after his Opus 33 quartets, it will be recalled, was to compose his themes in such a way that motives could be abstracted from them. Beethoven reversed the process: motives became the basic element, and out of them his themes were constructed. The technique begins at the very outset of Opus 1, No. 1. A motive of the kind called a "Mannheim rocket" is employed to form the phrases of the first theme (see EXAMPLE 144); it appears in transitions, development section, and coda. Other examples of the process will be given below.

E X A M P L E   144

Beethoven, Trio, Op. 1, No. 1

2 Piano Trios: Op. 1, No. 1, Eb major; No. 2, G major; No. 3, C minor (1793–1795). Op. 11, Bb major (1798).

Quintet for piano and winds: Op. 16, Eb major (1796); arranged by Beethoven as a piano quartet (1796).

Septet, Op. 20, Eb major (1800).

Sonatas for violin and piano: Op. 12, No. 1, D major; No. 2, A major; No. 3, Eb major (1797). Op. 23, A minor (1801). Op. 24, F major (1801).

Sonatas for cello and piano: Op. 5, No. 1, F major; No. 2, G minor (1796).

String trios: Op. 3, Eb major (1792). Serenade, Op. 8, D major (1796). Op. 9, No. 1, G major; No. 2, D major; No. 3, C minor (1798). Serenade, Op. 25, D major, for flute, violin, and viola (1797).

String quartets: Op. 18, No. 1, F major; No. 2, G major; No. 3, D major, No. 4, C minor; No. 5, A major; No. 6, Bb major (1798–1800).

String quintet: Op. 29, C major (1801).

The sudden modulations often found in Beethoven's first-period works represent one factor in his attempt to widen harmonic resources generally. A typical case occurs in Opus 1, No. 3; a passage in the finale ends in F major (the movement itself is in C minor), the tone F is carried across two measures, and without transition moves to D♭ major (see EXAMPLE 145). Similar passages occur in later works.

E X A M P L E   145

Beethoven, Trio, Op. 1, No. 3

The six string quartets of Opus 18 reveal how quickly Beethoven had mastered the quartet style developed by Haydn and Mozart. The four instruments take equal part in forming the texture; themes are equally distributed among them, and imitations and other contrapuntal devices are employed frequently. Motivic development is characteristic here, as it is in the other works of the first period. But despite these common characteristics, each quartet has such individuality that it cannot be considered one of a set. Rough energy in one, elegance in another, deep feeling in a third—such descriptions call attention to the variety of expressive types found even in Beethoven's first-period works.

No fewer than seventeen of Beethoven's thirty-two sonatas for piano were composed between 1795 and 1801.[3] The majority carry all the earmarks of first-period style; the three latest ones—Opus 27, No. 1, Opus 27, No. 2 (the "Moonlight"), and Opus 28—are on the border of the second period and suggest what is to come in later works. Beethoven, as

3 Piano sonatas: Op. 2, No. 1, F minor; No. 2, A major; No. 3, C major (1795). Op. 7, E♭ major (1796). Op. 10, No. 1, C minor; No. 2, F major; No. 3, D major (1796–1798). Op. 13, C minor (1798). Op. 14, No. 1, E major; No. 2, G major (1795–1799). Op. 22, B♭ major (1800). Op. 26, A♭ major (1801). Op. 27, No. 1, E♭ major; No. 2, C♯ minor (1801). Op. 28, D major (1801).

one of the foremost pianists of his day, composed many of the piano sonatas for his own use. It is evident that he felt particularly attached to the form, for some of his most eloquent movements as well as the majority of his experiments are contained in the sonatas. Forms and textures are more varied here than in other kinds of works. The sonatas are about evenly divided between three- and four-movement forms; in one case a slow introduction precedes the first movement, in another the first movement contains two tempos, and in yet another two slow movements occur. These details give evidence of Beethoven's willingness to adapt the forms of his works to his expressive requirements. The contents of the movements are equally diverse. In two or three cases an internal movement has the form of minuet and trio, but its content is serious, with none of the usual dancelike rhythmic elements or even the humorous tone of the scherzo. These movements provide hints of the profound, mysterious treatment that marks certain scherzos later in the second period.

The orchestral works of the first period include Beethoven's first two symphonies and first three piano concertos.[4] The first symphony bears a relationship to the works of Haydn and Mozart, but its originality probably outweighs its similarity to the earlier style. The slow introduction, beginning with a dominant seventh chord of F that resolves immediately to that key, brings to the fore a device that Beethoven was to employ on many occasions. The introduction, with harmonic sections on F and G, is in retrospect seen to be an extended and ornamented cadence whose function is to prepare the tonality of the first movement proper, thus:

$$\begin{array}{c|c} \text{Adagio} & \text{Allegro} \\ \text{IV--V} & \text{I} \end{array}$$

In other respects, too, the symphony bears Beethoven's individual stamp. Boisterousness, rough vigor, and broad humor characterize the first and last movements, and a deft and light tone distinguishes the scherzo.

The second symphony differs in many respects from the first. It is probably the largest symphony written up to that time, and its content and energy are commensurate with its size. A lengthy slow introduction in three harmonic sections leads to a fast sonata-form movement containing three groups of themes rather than single themes. The slow movement is also in sonata-form and is laid out in unusually broad fashion. After a brisk scherzo, the finale is similarly extended by means of theme groups. Transitions, developments, and codas in the various movements are proportional in size to the thematic sections themselves, and this gives the symphony its length. In only a few later works did Beethoven extend a composition in this manner; with a few notable exceptions he worked in the direction of thematic economy.

4 Symphonies: No. 1, Op. 21, C major (1799–1800); No. 2, Op. 36, D major (1802). Piano concertos: No. 2, Op. 19, B♭ major (1795, revised in 1798); No. 1, C major, Op. 15 (1797); No. 3, Op. 37, C minor (1800).

Second-period works. The mental depression that consumed Beethoven about 1802 and the deafness that grew ever more severe are not reflected in his music of the second period. Rather it is his reaction or response to his personal problem that comes to expression. If the works of the first period reveal a composer who brought boisterousness and unrestrained energy to the Classical style, those of the second period reveal one who expanded that style and touched expressive regions that Haydn and Mozart had not known or had avoided. The forcefulness of the first period was now brought under control and concentrated. At times, in the midst of the most sublime slow movements, it was held in abeyance, particularly in the middle movements of the three great concertos of 1805–1809. New elements were present also, among them an air of utmost simplicity, a sense of extreme contrast, and a rough humor. These characteristics are seen in the third to the eighth symphonies, the violin concerto, and the two piano concertos.[5] Various sets of incidental music and a few overtures, notably those designed for Beethoven's only opera, *Fidelio,* are on the same emotional level as the symphonies.

The symphonies are completely individual in content and expressive effect. The third symphony contains a great amount of thematic material, most of it in the form of motives or short phrases; the material undergoes the most concentrated kind of development, and every fragment is fully accounted for. The first movement of the fifth, by contrast, is based entirely on one motive and its variants; it is shorter and even more concentrated than the corresponding movement of the "Eroica." The sixth symphony is broad, expansive, and leisurely, while the fourth breathes lyricism and joy from beginning to end. The seventh and eighth likewise have individual characteristics—tremendous drive and concentration in the one, equal drive combined with subtle humor in the other.

Slow movements in the symphonies are equally diverse. A profound funeral march in the third contrasts with a lyric and elegant tune in the fourth. The descriptive "Scene at the Brook" in the sixth stands opposite a broadly humorous movement in the eighth. Similar variety is seen in the third movements. All but one are essentially scherzos in tempo and form, but their moods vary from gay and humorous to somber and foreboding. One scherzo has a trio in duple meter; in another the trio is played twice; and in two cases the trio is connected to the following movement. The finales are still more individual in mood and form.

No brief listing of a few details of these symphonies can hope to suggest the range of expression they contain. The chief technical devices Beethoven employed in these and other works will be discussed later in this chapter. While one may gain from that discussion some insight into

5 Symphonies: No. 3, Op. 55, E♭ major ("Eroica," 1803); No. 4, Op. 60, B♭ major (1806); No. 5, Op. 67, C minor (1805–1807); No. 6, Op. 68, F major ("Pastoral," 1807–1808); No. 7, Op. 92, A major (1812); No. 8, Op. 93, F major (1812).

Concertos: for piano, No. 4, Op. 58, G major (1806); No. 5, Op. 73, E♭ major ("Emperor," 1809). For violin, Op. 61, D major (1806). For violin, cello, and piano, Op. 56, C major (1805).

the methods whereby Beethoven achieved his effects, the essential nature
of the music will not—cannot—be revealed. Beethoven, almost more than
any other composer, defies classification. His music is unpredictable; the
most sublime effects are created by the simplest means, and standardized
melodic or rhythmic patterns take on new life and reveal new beauties
at his hands.

The same is true of the ten piano sonatas [6] of the second period. As in
those of the first period, the forms and contents are extremely varied.
They include four two-movement sonatas; one of these begins with a
slow introduction, and another has a slow introduction to the second
movement. One sonata is in four movements, containing, in addition to
the minuet, a movement in duple meter marked "scherzo." The five remaining works have three movements; in one case Beethoven utilizes
two different tempos in the first movement. This extreme flexibility of
form is not matched in the other kinds of works that Beethoven wrote.
The conviction grows that the sonatas represent an intimate, experimental category for him, one in which his great skill in improvisation is
crystallized and perpetuated.

6 Piano sonatas: Op. 31, No. 1, G major; No. 2, D minor; No. 3, Eb major (1802).
Op. 53, C major ("Waldstein," 1804). Op. 54, F major (1804). Op. 57, F minor ("Appas-
sionata," 1804). Op. 78, F♯ major (1809). Op. 79, G major (1809). Op. 81a, Eb major
("Les Adieux," 1809). Op. 90, E minor (1814).

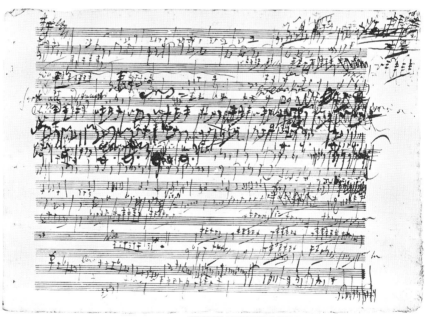

Beginning of scherzo, from autograph score of Beethoven's "Archduke" trio,
Op. 97.

The chamber-music works of the second period are more numerous than the symphonies or the piano sonatas.[7] The five string quartets, in spite of the formal regularity, exhibit the greatest diversity in content. The moods range from utmost sadness through sublimity to wild exuberance. Humor and virtuosity are present, as well as moods of great seriousness. Certain stylistic details, to be examined below, are common to all the works, yet the emotional tone differs so much from movement to movement that the technical similarities between one work and the next are often overlooked.

The piano trios of the second period are similarly varied in content. Opus 70, No. 1, contains a concentrated first movement based entirely on two contrasting phrases, both of which appear within the first nine measures of the movement (see EXAMPLE 146). The usual harmonic con-

EXAMPLE 146

Beethoven, Trio, Op. 70, No. 1

trast and sonata-form sections are found here, but they are all concerned with motives drawn from these two phrases. This type of utmost concentration on small thematic bits was to become an essential style element in later works as well.

Third-period works. The events of 1815–1817, centered around the litigation with his sister-in-law, contributed to a marked decline in Beethoven's productivity. A few songs, one piano sonata, two cello sonatas, and an arrangement or two were the only works completed during the two-year period. About 1818 Beethoven returned to greater activity, but in the interim his style had changed again. With deafness almost total, with normal social contacts virtually stopped, with no need to concern himself with the world around him, Beethoven turned inward. Introspection, a growing absorption with the manipulation of thematic material,

7 String quartets: Op. 59, No. 1, F major; No. 2, E minor; No. 3, C major (1806) Op. 74, E♭ major (1809). Op. 95, F minor (1810).
Violin sonatas: Op. 30, No. 1, A major; No. 2, C minor; No. 3, G major (1802).
Cello sonata: Op. 69, A major (1808).
Piano trios: Op. 70, No. 1, D major ("Ghost"); No. 2, E♭ major (1808). Op. 97, B♭ major ("Archduke," 1811).

and a new regard for the flexibility of musical form—such attitudes in part characterize the third-period style. Contrasts were enhanced to an extreme degree, the use of counterpoint was increased, all unessential details were cast out, and moods of sublime repose as well as furious activity came to expression.

The emotional content of the third-period works was also altered. The subjective emotions of joy, sadness, or pensiveness gave way to the spiritualized equivalents of those moods; and an ethical purpose, which had been apparent in several earlier works, animates many of the later ones as well. As befits their changed content, the third-period works are comparatively less numerous.[8]

The expansion of form introduced in the "Eroica" symphony is transcended in the ninth. Each of the themes in the first movement consists of several short phrases, and additional material appears in the transitions, and in the coda. The whole is firmly unified by the intensive development of all its themes. The first part of the scherzo consists of a full-scale sonata-form, and yet it is concerned almost entirely with manipulations of a one-measure motive. The Adagio is an eloquent movement based on a set of variations twice interrupted by a contrasting theme and its variation. The moods presented in these three movements range from dark and foreboding in the first movement to diabolically energetic in the scherzo to divinely resigned in the Adagio.

The finale is unique in all of musical literature. Its essential parts are a recitative for baritone solo on Beethoven's words, "*O Freunde, nicht diese Töne! Sondern lasst uns angenehmere anstimmen, und freudenvollere*" ("O friends, no more these tones; rather let us sing more joyful ones"); and a complex set of variations for chorus, quartet of soloists, and orchestra on stanzas taken from Schiller's *An die Freude* ("Ode to Joy"). Beethoven selected stanzas having to do with the ethical ideal he sought to express in the symphony: joy will be attained when universal brotherhood is achieved under Divine guidance. All the power of Beethoven's imagination was addressed to the expression of this ideal. The movement contains passages with symbolic meaning: contrasting themes, each concerned with one element of the ideal, are combined contrapuntally to express the union of Divine guidance and human joy. Once before, in the Choral Fantasy, Opus 80 (about 1808) had Beethoven combined chorus with orchestra in this fashion; there, however, the textual sentiment is concerned with harmony in daily life. That work in a sense served as a preliminary study for the finale of the ninth symphony; a few melodic turns in the choral parts anticipate the melodic outlines of portions of the later work.

---

8 Piano sonatas: Op. 101, A major (1816). Op. 106, B♭ major ("Hammerklavier," 1818). Op. 109, E major (1820). Op. 110, A♭ major (1821). Op. 111, C minor (1822).

Cello sonatas: Op. 102, No. 1, C major; No. 2, D major (1815).

Symphony: No. 9, Op. 125, D minor (1817–1823).

String quartets: Op. 127, E♭ major (1824). Op. 132, A minor (1825). Op. 130, B♭ major (1825). Op. 133, B♭ major ("Great Fugue," originally the finale of Op. 130, 1825). Op. 131, C♯ minor (1826). Op. 135, F major (1826).

The freedom of form seen in the earlier piano sonatas is increased in the sonatas of the third period. Each of the five works has its own formal scheme. A monumental first movement is coupled with an arietta with variations in Opus 111. Cyclical form (made evident by the return of a first-movement theme in the third movement) characterizes Opus 101. The finale of Opus 109 is a set of variations in slow tempo, and Opus 110 ends with a fugue prefaced by a slow introduction. The content of these sonatas cannot be described briefly; their range of expression, the subtleties of feeling, and the overwhelming power they exhibit are not subject to verbalization.

The last quartets, finally, bring to a culmination Beethoven's creative activity. Concentration on thematic economy here reaches its ultimate: three quartets and the Fugue, Opus 130–133, are all based on the development of one four-note motive (see EXAMPLE 153*a*, page 421).[9] With this concentration, however, comes an expansion of form, for Opus 132, Opus 130, and Opus 131 contain five, six, and seven movements, respectively. The moods of the nineteen movements of this vast cycle include rollicking humor, bucolic pleasantry, profound meditation, sublime beauty, and superhuman forcefulness. They reveal areas of the soul which no other composer had explored and result in a kind of music beyond which no composer was able to go. Later composers were forced to begin anew in a new style.

Characteristics of Beethoven's Style

WHILE it is true that the three style periods reveal individual characteristics, it is equally true that they are united by a common approach to the problems of musical expression. Certain methods of composition are seen in Beethoven's first works as well as his last; other methods became prominent in one composition or one decade, only to be held in abeyance; and a few details appear once or twice, never to return. In an attempt to present a systematic account of the principal style elements, each element will be discussed out of context in the pages that follow.

Melody. Lyric melody, of the kind seen so copiously in Mozart and Schubert, played a comparatively smaller part in Beethoven's work. In its place are hundreds of short, incisive motives out of which themes and transitions are constructed. To observe the expansion of a motive into a theme or into several themes is to gain an insight into Beethoven's unique approach to composition. The key word, perhaps, is manipulation; his many sketchbooks and the manuscripts themselves reveal how often Beethoven discarded a dozen ways of forming his material until the result satisfied him.

Motives, as indicated above, appear in the earliest piano trios. They are also found throughout the string quartets and the symphonies (see EXAMPLE 147). Often the motive is expanded into a theme by simple

9 See Ulrich, *Chamber Music*, pp. 274–80, for details.

EXAMPLE 147

Beethoven, Motives

sequence repetition, as in the first quartet and the fifth symphony. Sometimes the rhythm of the motive becomes the element out of which additional motives are derived, as in the seventh symphony. And occasionally
a small detail of the motive is itself abstracted from its context to give
rise to still other motives or themes. The old Gothic device of hocketing
(see page 91) is even used in transitions, as seen in EXAMPLE 148. In at
least two cases a single motive is the element out of which all the thematic
material of a work is derived, namely the first movements of the fifth

EXAMPLE 148

Beethoven, Quartet, Op. 131

and seventh symphonies. Wherever one turns in Beethoven's music one finds evidence of his overwhelming ability to construct the most profound and forceful passages out of small scraps of musical material.

Harmony. The miracle of Beethoven's harmony is that the most far-reaching effects are achieved with the simplest and most familiar chords. Chromaticism finds little place in Beethoven's music, nor does a complex of altered chords. Tonic-dominant relationships, modulations to keys a third above or below the tonic, accented suspensions, and a few striking dissonant devices are the limits beyond which Beethoven seldom ventured. Key relationships between consecutive movements may often seem of an unusual nature: B major in an E♭ concerto (Opus 73), for example, or F♯ minor in a B♭ sonata (Opus 106). Such relationships, however, are no more than enharmonic equivalents of a tonic-submediant relationship: E♭ to C♭ in Opus 73, and B♭ to G♭ minor in Opus 106.

Beethoven established his tonalities without ambiguity—and often at considerable length. The introduction of the first symphony has been mentioned (see page 410) as one example of an extended IV-V-I cadence designed to establish the key firmly. The two chords with which the "Eroica" symphony begins provide an example of another kind. Three cadenzalike flourishes occur at the beginning of the "Emperor" concerto, on E♭, A♭, and B♭, respectively; they serve to introduce a I-IV-V progression before the main body of the movement begins. The slow introduction of the seventh symphony consists of harmonic sections beginning on A, C, and F, respectively; here the harmonic scheme is one in which the tonic (A) is surrounded by mediant (C) and submediant (F) keys. Finally, the eighth symphony is an opposite example in which, for humorous reasons, harmonic ambiguity is deliberately sought; the entire symphony represents a struggle between F and non-F.

Rhythm. Beethoven was probably the first major composer who consistently manipulated rhythm as an expressive element. The manipulation takes several forms. Many passages are based on running figures or on the reiteration of rhythmic motives, to result in inexorable forward motion with scarcely a moment's relaxation. The finales of the E-minor quartet, Opus 59, No. 2, of the G-major violin sonata, Opus 30, No. 3, and of the seventh symphony are outstanding examples of this type. Many scherzos, notably those in the E♭ quartet, Opus 74, and the F-major quartet, Opus 135, are similarly constructed.

Syncopation was used by Beethoven to a greater extent than by any earlier composer. From the first period to the last this element remained a potent means of creating a conflict between the foreground rhythm (of the syncopations) and the background rhythm (formed by the strong beats themselves). An early example is found in the quartet, Opus 18, No. 6 (see EXAMPLE 149); one of the latest is in the scherzo of Beethoven's last quartet, Opus 135.

Sometimes coupled with syncopations, but often occurring in other contexts, are many accents on weak beats or fractional beats. A variety

EXAMPLE 149

Beethoven, Quartet, Op. 18, No. 6

of *forzandi* and *sforzati* appear, most often in transitional passages, where the momentary rhythmic conflict enhances the solid rhythm of the passage which follows. Outstanding examples are numerous in Beethoven's pages; a few may be selected at random to illustrate the device (see EXAMPLE 150).

Texture. From the very beginning of his career at Vienna, Beethoven exhibited full command over a variety of textures. Even in his earliest ensemble works he was able to move from homophonic to imitative and even to fugal textures at will. The slow movements of the C-minor quar-

EXAMPLE 150

Beethoven, Use of *forzandi*

tet, Opus 18, No. 4, and of the first symphony illustrate how polyphonic passages were embedded into sonata-form movements that were themselves in mixed texture. The early piano sonatas, following the pattern of Mozart's, are generally in a free or broken style. The sonatas are most often characterized by two- or three-voice writing augmented by appropriate doublings or a purely harmonic part.

The second and third periods saw a gradual increase in the use of true polyphonic textures. The element of imitation was employed to an increasing extent, fugato passages became more numerous, and movements written entirely in fugue occurred often. Among the outstanding examples are the finales of the quartet, Opus 59, No. 3; the cello sonata, Opus 102, No. 2; the piano sonata, Opus 106; and the first movement of the quartet, Opus 131. It need scarcely be mentioned that a Beethoven fugue resembles a Bach fugue only remotely. In the former the episodes lead far afield, fugal expositions are free, and the clear divisions between these two formal elements are sometimes obscured by Beethoven's penchant for developing the thematic material.

One other element of texture came to expression increasingly often in Beethoven's later works, namely, recitativelike passages, sometimes accompanied and sometimes not. The eloquent recitatives in the first movement of the piano sonata, Opus 31, No. 2, the brief oboe passage in the first movement of the fifth symphony, the two recitatives (one orchestral, the other vocal) in the finale of the ninth symphony—such passages may serve as examples. Outstanding recitatives are also in the quartets, notably in the fifth movement of Opus 130, the third movement of Opus 131, and the fourth movement of Opus 132.

Contrasts. The heightened dramatic effects produced by Beethoven's music are in large part the result of the extreme contrasts he often employed. Contrast in Beethoven takes several forms. One type is achieved by the use of extreme dynamic changes; the piano sonatas are especially rich in passages in which a sudden *fortissimo,* structurally unmotivated, follows a soft passage purely for dramatic reasons (see EXAMPLE 151). This device had appeared in chamber music as early as the finale of Opus 1, No. 1, and was to remain one of Beethoven's most effective tools. The-

EXAMPLE 151

Beethoven, Sonata, Op. 57

matic contrasts within movements tended to remain at what may be called normal levels; changes from dramatic to lyric were seldom extreme.

Contrasts between movements, on the other hand, became almost abrupt and violent in the works roughly from Opus 73 onward. The last two movements of the "Emperor" concerto and those of the "Archduke" trio, Opus 97 (see EXAMPLE 152), are good examples of these extreme contrasts.

EXAMPLE 152

Beethoven, Trio, Op. 97

Form. The expansion of form that marked Beethoven's work from about 1800 on was accompanied by changes in the proportions of the forms. The presence of theme groups in place of single themes in certain sonata-form movements has been mentioned. With this came a tendency to raise the codetta of the exposition section to thematic level, with the result that the sonata-form acquired three themes instead of two. This tendency, in turn, led to longer development sections, for the additional thematic material was also subjected to the manipulative process. The erstwhile coda of a sonata-form movement, too, was often expanded, a process begun by Haydn and carried to its logical development by Beethoven, with the result that the coda sometimes equaled or exceeded the development section in length.[10]

To an increasing degree, the divisions between sections of the form tended to be minimized also. A typical transition between, say, a first and second theme was so written that it grew out of first-theme material and anticipated or merged with that of the second. Sectional forms, such as rondos and three-part arias, were also provided with transitional material to such an extent that smoothly flowing forms became typical in all movements. The traditional repetition tended to become increasingly rare in the sonata-form movements of the second and third periods. In approximately forty examples of that type in the chamber music, sonatas, and symphonies from Opus 59 to Opus 135, the exposition is repeated in about twelve cases only.

Cyclical forms are comparatively rare in early Beethoven, but they become somewhat more common in his later works. One of the best-known examples occurs in the fifth symphony; the scherzo and finale are connected and a section of the scherzo reappears in the finale. The last movement of the ninth symphony contains a short section in which themes from the three previous movements are briefly quoted. The outstanding example of cyclical form, however, is found in the three quartets and fugue of Opus 130 through Opus 133. A four-note motive (see Example 153*a*) serves as a source for dozens of themes in those four works. And on the largest possible scale, those four tones are suggested in the keys of the first four movements of Opus 131 (see EXAMPLE 153*b*).

EXAMPLE 153

Beethoven, Quartets

Occasionally Beethoven employed two or more tempos in the same movement. As early a work as the second string quartet, Opus 18, No. 2, has an adagio movement with a middle section in allegro. The sonatas are especially rich in use of this device, notably Opus 31, No. 2, Opus 101, and Opus 109, and the last quartets also contain examples of it. The presence of two or more tempos within the same movement necessarily

10 The following table is revealing:

	EXPOSITION	DEVELOPMENT	RECAPITULATION	CODA
Trio, Op. 97, finale	72 meas.	80 meas.	101 meas.	157 meas.
Sym. No. 8, finale	91 meas.	70 meas.	105 meas.	236 meas.
Sym. No. 9, first movement	163 meas.	152 meas.	112 meas.	120 meas.

increases the thematic contrast of the movement. In Beethoven's hands, however, the contrasting tempo is often the result of notation rather than absolute speed change. The first movement of the quartet, Opus 130, for example, contains many changes from adagio to allegro. Yet one eighth-note of the adagio measure is roughly equivalent to one quarter-note of the allegro, so that the flow of beats is essentially unimpeded. There remains only a sharp contrast in texture and mood, and it is upon this that Beethoven's expressive intention is centered (see EXAMPLE 154).

EXAMPLE 154

Beethoven, Quartet, Op. 130

Orchestration. The advances made especially by Mozart in the art of writing for orchestral instruments were continued by Beethoven. The orchestra in Beethoven's first-period works regularly contained two clarinets (see page 400) in addition to the pairs of winds customarily employed by Haydn and Mozart in their last works. In the "Eroica" symphony a third horn was added; in later symphonies piccolo, contrabassoon, trombones, and a few percussion instruments (also a fourth horn in the ninth symphony) were sometimes called for. Further than this Beethoven did not go. In each case the additional instruments were included because of the composer's expressive requirements (for example, a marchlike section in the finale of the ninth symphony makes the contrabassoon and percussion instruments desirable), and not out of any desire to add color for its own sake.

Beethoven's methods of thematic development increased the flexibility of his orchestral textures. When a phrase comprises sequential repetitions of a short motive, it seems obvious to spread the repetitions of the motive among several wind instruments; Beethoven did so on numerous occasions. Thematic statements are given to the woodwinds in ever-increasing amounts. The tympani, finally, which had previously done little more than support tonic and dominant harmonies in tutti passages, now come into their own. Exposed rhythmic motives are heard prominently in the fourth and ninth symphonies as well as in the violin concerto.

With the increasing independence of wind instruments, the use of winds for thematic statements, and the consideration of instrumental colors and ranges in planning orchestral texture, modern orchestration came appreciably closer. Although Beethoven was too much of a Classicist to think of orchestral color apart from formal structure and function, he prepared the ground upon which composers later in the century could construct the flexible orchestration of the Romantic period.

Moods and ethical purposes. The great majority of Classical instrumental works are essentially abstract patterns of tone. While they have form and emotional content, they do not have "meaning" in the usual sense; that is to say, they are not illustrative, they do not represent anything outside music, and they do not have symbolic connotations. Beethoven's music is primarily of this kind, of course. In a few cases, however, a symbol, representation, or ethical purpose may be surmised. Beethoven himself gave a few clues that strengthen such surmises, and occasionally the work in question, by nature of its origin, almost requires an explanation in extramusical terms.

A case in point is the slow movement, labeled *marcia funebre,* of the "Eroica" symphony. In the final measures of that movement, the main theme is fragmented and dissolved. It does no violence to the music if one sees this passage as a symbol of the physical dissolution that follows death and burial. In a wonderfully eloquent manner Beethoven illustrates the concept, "to dust thou shalt return."

In a group of four unrelated works another concept is illustrated. Beethoven overcame his destiny and fought successfully against the social forces of his time. He was the victor in a conflict between a single human being and overwhelming impersonal forces. A symbol of that struggle appears in the finale of the "Eroica" symphony, in the slow movement of the fourth piano concerto, in the Overture to *Coriolanus,* Opus 62, and in the Great Fugue, Opus 133. In each case, but in four different ways, extreme contrast of thematic elements is expressed: bass and melody of the theme in the "Eroica"; tutti and solo themes in the concerto; first and second themes in the sonata-form overture; and theme and counter-theme in the Fugue. In each case the second element of the contrast is weaker, simpler, or more lyric than the first. And in each case, finally, the movement is so constructed that during the course of the thematic conflict the weaker theme emerges triumphant and the apparently unassailable strong element is dissolved or transformed. It may be mentioned that the two elements of the theme of the "Eroica" finale were used by Beethoven as the last section of his music for the ballet, *Prometheus.* And Prometheus, in Greek legend, was the figure who freed humanity from the tyranny of the gods.

It must be stressed that in these examples and in other similar ones, Beethoven had not entered the field of program music, that is, music whose form and content are dictated by the nature of the extramusical object or idea being described. The symbolism in Beethoven is incidental to the form, not the reason for it. At no time in these works did Beethoven allow his musical logic to falter. Musical laws and musical requirements are fully met, and in this sense the works are as Classical as any of Haydn's and Mozart's. In going beyond those requirements, as it were, and in combining objective expression with subjective symbols, Beethoven revealed yet another aspect of his genius.

Romantic tendencies. The Classical style, which had found its greatest representative in Beethoven, could not be carried farther than he had carried it. The composers who came after him measured themselves against his tremendous accomplishments—and went in other directions. A new style, that of the Romantic period, came into being during Beethoven's lifetime. Among its characteristics were an interest in new means of expression and a search for new kinds of content. Beethoven, too, was interested in new expressive types and new contents, but in contrast to the Romanticists, he found them within his own imagination.

As parts of the general musical culture of his day, remnants of earlier styles were still available, and Beethoven seized upon them and made them his own. Fugal textures represent one such remnant; we have seen that the amount of fugal writing increased greatly in his later works. An overture in C major, Opus 124, *Die Weihe des Hauses* ("The Consecration of the House"), resembles the French overture type that Beethoven had learned to admire in the works of Handel. And the slow movement of the A-minor quartet, Opus 132, bears the superscript, "Holy song of thanksgiving . . . in the Lydian mode." These cases represent some of the results of Beethoven's turn to the past in search of new expressive means. Other results exist as well. Beethoven's use of cyclical form principles has been mentioned. As his expressive purposes changed he sometimes found it necessary to increase the length of single movements as well as of entire works; outstanding examples are the third and ninth symphonies and the quartets of Opus 130 and 131. Conversely, however, he also found shorter forms adequate for his purpose; an important group of his late works for piano are single-movement pieces called "bagatelles." Although the bagatelles were published in sets (as Opus 119 and 126), each piece is an independent work of brief duration, and in many cases the term "bagatelle" ("trifle") is scarcely justified.

In summary, then, Beethoven was sometimes drawn to older styles, elements of which he incorporated in his works. Movements and entire works were sometimes longer or shorter than normal in the Classical period. Cyclical form makes its appearance occasionally. And a psychological or ethical purpose can sometimes be surmised. These are all characteristics that composers of the Romantic period adopted, that became basic to Romantic style. For this reason Beethoven is often considered to be a forerunner of the Romantic period, and his contributions to Romantic style are stressed. We shall see in the following chapter, however, that Romanticism had other roots than Beethoven, and that it followed a path quite opposite to his.

Emergence of Romantic Styles

THE FIRST quarter of the nineteenth century, dominated by the figure of Beethoven, witnessed the activities of many other instrumental composers who carried the traditions and idioms of the Classical period to the threshold of the Romantic. Of French, German, or Italian birth, they revealed in their music the international diffusion of the Classical style. Among them was the long-lived François Gossec (1734–1829), of Belgian birth but active in Paris for almost sixty-five years. Gossec became one of the founders of French instrumental music and composed about thirty symphonies and a dozen quartets distinguished by formal clarity and elegance. Muzio Clementi (1752–1832), born in Italy but associated primarily with England, was a composer, pianist, publisher, and piano manufacturer. His many symphonies were built on the model of Haydn's, and in more than a hundred piano sonatas (some with violin or cello

Drawing from title page of an early edition of Schubert's *Der Erlkönig.* [COURTESY MUSIC DIVISION, NEW YORK PUBLIC LIBRARY]

accompaniment) he revealed excellent craftsmanship and a warm, lyric style.

Another Italian, but one primarily associated with Paris, was Giovanni Battista Viotti (1755–1824). Viotti became one of the foremost violinists of the generation before Paganini's and composed primarily in the fields of chamber music and the concerto. High performing standards distinguished his playing, and an excellent sense of form marked his concertos. He was among the composers who applied fully-developed sonata form to the first movements of concertos and who raised the orchestral accompaniments to symphonic levels. Ignaz Pleyel (1757–1831), also active in Paris, was an Austrian pianist. A pupil and protégé of Haydn's, Pleyel composed many symphonies and quartets in the general style of his teacher. He founded a piano factory in Paris that is still operating, and gradually retired from the field of composition.

Johann Dussek (1760–1812), born in Bohemia, became an outstanding pianist and an excellent composer, primarily of chamber music and piano sonatas. Many of his works exhibit fine contrapuntal writing and advanced harmonies. Another Bohemian, Adalbert Gyrowetz (1763–1850), came to Vienna shortly after Beethoven and eventually became director of the Vienna opera. In the public mind he was often linked with Beethoven, and his symphonies and quartets were highly esteemed in their day.

Johann Hummel (1778–1837), born in Hungary but active principally in Vienna and Weimar, became one of the finest pianists of the time. A pupil of both Mozart and Haydn, he was an excellent composer whose works were favorably compared to Beethoven's. Ludwig Spohr (1784–1859), eminent German violinist and conductor (see page 448), composed over a dozen violin concertos and large quantities of chamber music. In many of Spohr's works Romantic traits are in evidence; he wrote programmatic symphonies and experimented with musical color.

None of these composers remotely approached the power and scope of Beethoven's second-period works, and the third period was worlds removed from their comprehension and experience. Highly gifted, industrious, and well qualified in a technical sense, these minor contemporaries of Beethoven represent the sterling professional composers against whom the great masters are measured. The new impulses that were to give rise to the Romantic movement found little reflection in their works (except in the case of Spohr), however, and after Romanticism became the dominant aesthetic fact of the nineteenth century, they and much of their music soon disappeared from view.

The Romantic Spirit

THE SERIES of style changes marking the course of much music history represent the alternation of two creative attitudes. One attitude represents the conservative aspect of creativity; it is characterized by an interest in the status quo and its marks are balance and control. The other favors a more radical kind of expression; it seeks out the new, the curious, and the adventurous. The first approach, on its highest level, gives rise to classicism, with its balance, proportion, and restraint. The second leads to romanticism, characterized by restless seeking and impulsive reaction.

Many times in the past, individual composers have permitted the romantic inclination to dominate their creative activity to a greater or lesser degree, and musical periods essentially romantic in their outlook have occurred. Moreover, the elements of novelty and emotion have at times marked the music of men who were essentially classical by temperament: such composers as Lasso, Bach, and Mozart are examples. Beethoven, too, as we have seen, widened his expressive scope in several works. In these cases, however, the balancing tendency was close by, and an extreme manifestation of romanticism is not to be looked for.

The early nineteenth century, for a number of complex reasons that are not yet thoroughly understood, witnessed an extreme concentration of the romantic spirit. First in German literature and then in music, romantic tendencies emerged and became dominant. As a parallel to the ideal of political unification that arose even before the Napoleonic wars, poets and philosophers sought a union of all the arts. Lyric poetry stressed its kinship to melody; paintings had literary significance; and music acquired poetic or philosophical meaning. In addition, an interest in novelty led to a search for new types of subject matter. Antiquity, folklore, history, and exotic cultures were examined as possible sources of inspiration. The artists, writers, and musicians of the time grew enthusiastic about the new worlds which opened to them; and out of that enthusiasm grew friendship, sentiment, deep feeling, and love—all expressed artistically.

A feeling of closeness to the world of the past, to everything that was strange or removed from immediate experience, could scarcely be expressed objectively. The men of the time felt a need to identify themselves with the new, the unusual, and the exotic elements they were discovering. This identification took the form of subjective expression, in which the individual sought to express—in artistic forms—his personal reaction to whatever stimulated him. With enthusiasm as the basic state of soul and subjectivity as the basic viewpoint, traditional forms seemed meaningless or at least unnecessary. The balance, control, and proportion that had marked the Classical period in all the arts were modified or discarded in favor of freedom, impulsiveness, and individuality of utterance.

In this series of developments, which in music encompassed the period from about 1825 to about 1900, individual differences among composers and styles still existed, of course; in fact, they became more pronounced. The stylistic unity that had existed in earlier periods was not paralleled in the period after 1825. Training, tradition, and temperament worked with varying degrees of strength upon virtually every major musician of the time, and stylistic multiplicity was the result, perhaps a manifestation of the strength of the subjective impulse. A number of different approaches to the problems of the time may be seen in composers as far apart stylistically as Chopin and Berlioz or Hugo Wolf and Richard Strauss. Yet in spite of such divergent styles, and in spite of many seemingly contradictory elements in the music of the time, the period was unified by its all-embracing purposes—namely, a striving for unattainable unity in life, a search for new subject matters, and an urge toward freedom of expression. The time during which these warm, personal, and variously proportioned manifestations of the creative spirit dominated virtually all music is called the Romantic period. The Romantic movement, as indicated above, was at first fostered by a number of German writers and poets. Among the earliest were August Wilhelm Schlegel (1767–1845), known for his translation of Shakespeare and for restoring to public attention the famous twelfth-century epic, *Das Nibelungenlied* ("The Song of the Nibelungs"), and Johann Paul Richter (1763–1825), better known as Jean Paul.

Wilhelm Wackenroder (1773–1798); Ludwig Tieck (1773–1853), one of the first of the Romantic poets; Friedrich von Hardenberg, known as Novalis (1772–1801), the finest lyric poet of his time; and the dramatist, Heinrich von Kleist (1774–1811)—these men brought legends and the remote worlds of Medieval life into their works, and expressed an enthusiasm for all things artistic. Their influence on other writers and on musicians was pervasive and enduring.

Ernst Theodor Hoffmann (1776–1822), who adopted the name Amadeus out of veneration for Mozart and who is usually referred to as E. T. A. Hoffmann, combined the careers of writer and composer in successful fashion. The power of Hoffmann's imagination was outstanding, even among his contemporaries. His stories combine fantasy, tender lyricism, and realistic horror, a variety of subject matter that found its way into the works of other writers and established the tone of much of the literature of the time. (Several of Hoffmann's stories form the basis for Offenbach's opera of 1881, *The Tales of Hoffmann*.) His music, however, exhibited little of the imagination that was so vividly displayed in his literary works. In almost a dozen operas (see page 448), a few choral works, and several instrumental compositions he seldom rose above the level of good proportion, clear textures, and routine melodic lines. His influence on the emerging Romantic period cannot be denied, however, and he must be considered one of the important figures in the transition to Romanticism.[1]

Weber

CARL MARIA VON WEBER (1786–1826) was of incomparably higher stature than Hoffmann as a composer of the transitional period. While he is best known for his operas, which will be discussed in the next chapter, his instrumental works are significant for the influence they were to have on composers of the Romantic period.

Weber, the son of a musician who directed a traveling theatrical troupe, studied with a host of teachers in whatever town he found himself. He

---

1 Selections from the literary works of several of the writers mentioned here are given in *SRMH*: Wackenroder, pp. 750–63; Jean Paul, pp. 743–49 and 764–74; Hoffmann, pp. 775–97.

began composing at an early age; his first works were published when he was twelve. In spite of much traveling and sporadic, interrupted instruction, he became a piano virtuoso of the highest quality.

The dramatic genius Weber illustrated in his operas is combined with his feeling for brilliance in the instrumental works. Four piano sonatas, several sets of variations, and some miscellaneous pieces including the well-known *Invitation to the Dance* constitute the bulk of his solo piano compositions. Two piano concertos, the favorite F-minor *Konzertstück* for piano and orchestra, three clarinet concertos and one each for bassoon and horn are among the principal orchestral works. Weber's compositions for piano are full of novel pianistic effects that reflect the virtuosity of which he was capable. He employed the full range of the instrument, introduced rapid passages in thirds and sixths for both hands, favored wide leaps in the melodic line, and at times approached orchestral sonorities (see EXAMPLE 155). Coupled with these effects were wide-ranging

E X A M P L E   155

Weber. *Rondo brillante,* Op. 62

melodies, in each case idiomatically written. It is one of Weber's virtues that he thoroughly understood the nature and capabilities of each instrument and was able to adapt his melodic style to the technical requirements of the instrument for which he was writing at the time. The clarinet concertos, for example, give the impression of having been written by a master performer on that instrument, as does the bassoon concerto. Yet Weber did not play any wind instrument.

The influence of Beethoven is marked in many of Weber's instrumental works. This is seen, for example, in key relationships, especially in the second piano concerto, which was written after Weber had become acquainted with Beethoven's "Emperor." And in the bassoon concerto, one of the themes of the first movement is taken in its entirety from Beethoven's first cello sonata. Yet in spite of this proximity to Beethoven and his awareness of that master's style, there is little similarity in workmanship. Motive development hardly plays a part in Weber's music; a succession of melodies strikingly contrasted with each other form the bulk of the material. This provides a dramatic, ever-changing musical sound of the kind that adds luster and excitement to Weber's operatic works.

One aspect of Weber's instrumental works that points toward the forthcoming Romantic period may be mentioned: an interest in tone color as a separate musical entity, which may be surmised from his activity in writing for solo wind instruments and orchestra. In addition to the woodwind concertos mentioned above, Weber composed orchestral pieces calling for viola, flute, cello, horn, and harmonium, respectively, on solo parts. Another Romantic aspect is seen in the programmatic content of the *Konzertstück* for piano and orchestra: two lovers, separated by wars, are reunited after periods of foreboding and romantic melancholy. It is primarily in the operatic works, however, that the full impulse toward Romanticism appears; in those works Weber's stature as a herald of Romanticism is fully revealed.

Schubert

THE TRANSITIONAL steps toward Romanticism are seen in most concentrated fashion in the music of Franz Schubert, the only one of the Viennese masters who was a native of Vienna. Elements that came to characterize Romantic music—harmonic boldness, extremes in point of size, subjective expression, and fascination with instrumental tone color —were fully exploited in his works, but within forms most of which the Classical masters had perfected. Thus, neither a faithful adherent to his Classical heritage nor an enthusiastic exponent of every novel musical device, Schubert holds a unique place in the history of nineteenth-century music.

Schubert was born in 1797 in a suburb of Vienna. He received his first musical instruction at the age of eight from his father, a schoolmaster, and learned to play the violin, piano, and organ. With an excellent voice as a boy, he was a member of the Imperial Court choir for about five years, until his voice changed. Membership in the choir included thorough instruction in musical theory (Salieri was among his teachers), and Schubert was an apt pupil. By 1813, when he left the choir, he had composed an opera, several choral works, a symphony, a number of overtures, some string quartets, and half a dozen songs.

In 1813 he entered a seminary for teachers, and the following year he became an elementary teacher in his father's school. Except for a one-year interval, he remained there for four years, composing assiduously all the while. His first masterpiece, the song *Gretchen am Spinnrade* ("Gretchen at the Spinning Wheel"), set to a text from Goethe's *Faust,* was written in 1814; he had composed about thirty songs up to this time. From about

Schubert and his friends at the home of Joseph von Spaun. Sepia drawing by Moritz von Schwind, 1868

1818, Vienna at large became his home. He shared lodgings with one or another of his friends, moving from place to place at frequent intervals. In the summer of 1818, and again in 1824, he was employed as music teacher to the family of Count Johann Esterházy at Zelesz, in Hungary. With these exceptions Schubert had no regular employment in the ten years that remained to him. He earned a precarious living, subsisting largely on teaching fees and on small fees from his music publishers. The first works to be published were some twenty songs in 1821. His songs and a few piano pieces were performed in public and greatly esteemed, but only a few of his larger works, performed privately at the homes of his friends, were known. Schubert gave only one concert of his own works, early in 1828; the program included the E♭ Trio, Opus 100, a string quartet movement, and a few songs. The concert was an artistic and financial success, but it did not lead to a permanent improvement in Schubert's economic position. He had been ill through much of 1827, and in the following year his health declined rapidly. An attack of typhus ended his life late in 1828, in his thirty-first year.

In the approximately seventeen years during which Schubert composed, he wrote almost a thousand works. The list includes over six hundred songs, many short single-movement pieces, a number of incomplete compositions, and many sketches, but it also includes many longer works that range from three or four movements each to sets containing thirty-six or more dances. Operas and *Singspiele,* sets of incidental music, and a variety of sacred and secular choral works are included in the larger vocal compositions. The instrumental works include symphonies, overtures, some thirty-five chamber-music compositions, many piano sonatas, literally hundreds of pieces of piano music, a large quantity of music for piano duet, and miscellaneous compositions.

Piano music. Among Schubert's works for piano are many single movements in dance forms: roughly fifty minuets, ninety écossaises, one hundred Deutsche, 125 Ländler, and 150 waltzes. In addition, there are several works in forms that Schubert called impromptus, *moments musicaux,* and the like. Schubert's early dance music (the first set of minuets was written in 1813) is often in an improvisational style; his later works (the last set of waltzes was composed in 1827) are highly stylized, harmonically subtle compositions of fine proportions. The presence of so large a group of works calls attention to the favorite place of the piano in Schubert's mind. In these miniatures he revealed the full scope of his flexibility, harmonic subtlety, and melodic inventiveness.

The larger works for piano include almost two dozen sonatas, ranging from student compositions to outstanding masterpieces. In spite of his undoubted competence as a pianist, he sometimes wrote awkwardly in a texture that failed to take full advantage of piano sonority. Many overly extended passages occur in the earlier sonatas, but in the later works harmonic variety overcomes the feeling of repetitiousness. The eleven impromptus written in 1827–1828 bring to the fore a new type of "mood music." Each piece presents a different mood in concentrated fashion and in brief compass. In view of the preoccupation of the Romantic period with single-movement forms, each dedicated to the expression of a single mood, the impromptus may well have been of influence on composers such as Chopin, Mendelssohn, and Schumann.

Chamber music. Of Schubert's fifteen string quartets, about a dozen reveal a tendency to experiment. The majority of them were written for the family quartet (in which Schubert played viola) and show the influence of Haydn and Mozart as well as attempts to go beyond Classical style. A wide range of keys, thematic material repeated rather than developed, and considerable variety of texture mark these works. The last three quartets, however, along with five other chamber-music works, must be listed among Schubert's masterpieces.[2] The fact that two of the works

2 The works are given here with their customary opus numbers, although these do not reflect the dates of origin. The numbers in parentheses throughout this chapter refer to the listing in Deutsch, *Schubert Thematic Catalogue.*

1819: Quintet for violin, viola, cello, bass, and piano ("The Trout"), A major, Op. 114 (D. 667)
1824: Octet for string quartet, bass, clarinet, bassoon, and horn, F major, Op. 166 (D. 803)
——: Quartet No. 13, A minor, Op. 29 (D. 804)
——: Quartet No. 14 ("Death and the Maiden"), D minor, Op. posth. (D. 810)
1826: Quartet No. 13, G major, Op. 161 (D. 887)
1827: Piano Trio, B♭ major, Op. 99 (D. 898)
——: Piano Trio, E♭ major, Op. 100 (D. 929)
1828: Quintet, string quartet and cello, C major, Op. 163 (D. 956)

contain sets of variations based on songs by Schubert is reflected in the names by which these works are generally known.

No summary paragraph can do justice to the variety of moods and expressive types contained in these eight compositions. The style characteristics which they have in common with Schubert's other instrumental works will be discussed later in this chapter. In addition, however, each work has its own unique style. A light melodiousness characterizes the "Trout" quintet from beginning to end. The D-minor string quartet, on the other hand, is the embodiment of restless energy and driving rhythm. The C-major string quintet brings Schubert's innate lyricism to expression in wonderfully eloquent and dramatic fashion. Each of these works represents another facet of Schubert's boundless melodic genius and his harmonic resourcefulness.

Orchestral music. Eight or nine concert overtures and an equal number of symphonies[3] comprise Schubert's principal works for orchestra. The overtures in general follow the plan introduced by Beethoven—that is, the basic structure of sonata-form is adhered to. If the overture is connected with a stage work, as are the various overtures to Beethoven's *Fidelio,* the themes are usually derived from melodies found in the stage work itself. This type of overture stands opposite another type introduced by Rossini, in which operatic tunes supply the themes of the exposition and recapitulation, while another theme or theme group appears in place of a development section. The majority of Schubert's overtures are modeled on Beethoven's type; two, however, are called "overtures in the Italian style" and are directly influenced by Rossini's works.

The first four and the sixth of Schubert's symphonies[4] contain large quantities of thematic material spun out repetitiously and a considerable amount of harmonic experimenting; they have little of the scope, symphonic breadth, and solid workmanship typical of other symphonies of the time and are of interest only in revealing the rather tentative touch Schubert exhibited as a boy and young man. The fifth of the set, however, is a concise work with Classical refinement evident on every page. Mozart served as Schubert's model here; lyric grace and well-proportioned phrases are everywhere apparent.

The famous "Unfinished" symphony, called No. 8, brings a new Schubert to the fore. Sustained lyricism even in the midst of dramatic tension,

3 The number of symphonies is variously given, depending on whether one does or does not count a symphony in E (D. 729), of which only a portion of the first movement was orchestrated and the rest sketched out.

4 1813: No. 1, D major (D. 82)
    1814: No. 2, Bb major (D. 125)
    1815: No. 3, D major (E. 200)
    1816: No. 4, C minor, "Tragic" (D. 417)
    ——: No. 5, Bb major (D. 485)
    1817: No. 6, C major (D. 589)
    1821: Unnumbered sketch, E major (D. 729)
    1822: "No. 8," B minor, "Unfinished" (D. 759)
    1828: "No. 7," C major (D. 944)

qualities of moodiness and resignation, a great leap forward in the handling of orchestral colors—these characterize this two-movement masterpiece. The qualities that permit Schubert to be considered a harbinger of the Romantic period are abundantly revealed in this symphony, yet ironically it remained unknown for decades after Schubert's death and was not performed until 1865.

Schubert's last symphony, the monumental C-major of 1828, contains all the power, rhythmic drive, and intensity one usually associates with Beethoven; yet it has none of Beethoven's concentration, nor does it show the type of thematic manipulation characteristic of the older composer's work. Schubert's thematic material is of the simplest kind—most of it based on melodic fragments that outline a rising or falling third or an ascending triad. The themes are repeated rather than developed, but always with changed harmonies and changed orchestral colors; the reiteration of a few rhythmic patterns gives the work tremendous vitality. Much of the thematic material of the introduction is prominently employed in the first movement, and trombones take a greater part in the unfolding of the music than in any previous symphony. Similar devices became characteristic of symphonies by later Romantic composers.

Stage and choral music. Schubert composed about a dozen operas and *Singspiele,* some of them only sketched and several left incomplete; they will be discussed in Chapter 22. His choral works include six Latin Masses, one Mass set to a German text, and over a hundred miscellaneous compositions, some on sacred texts and others on secular. Many of these works were doubtlessly occasional pieces that did not call forth his best efforts, and they have long since disappeared from the repertoire. In others Schubert exhibited the same sensitivity to the moods of his texts that marked his song composition. Passages in the last two Masses (in A♭, D. 678, and in E♭, D. 950) reveal that he rose to the levels demanded by the sacred texts and wrote profoundly and effectively. And some of the pieces for mixed voices and piano, melodious and richly sonorous in the best choral tradition, are filled with honest sentiment.

Style characteristics. Perhaps the outstanding characteristic of Schubert's music is its melodiousness. Out of the simplest diatonic materials he was able to fashion a melodic type that is uniquely his and yet defies analysis. One may point out that a typical Schubert melody contains a recurring element (a melodic or rhythmic figure), that it clearly outlines the harmony, that it is basically diatonic, and so on (see EXAMPLE 156). Yet such observations cannot capture the intrinsic beauty, charm, or poignancy of the melodies themselves. An essential part of their magic is the context in which they appear, which is usually the result of Schubert's harmonic practices and inventive accompaniments.

The device of moving from the tonic to a key a third above or below the tonic, often seen in Beethoven, became a potent means for Schubert to enrich his harmonic scheme. In Schubert the shift may be made

EXAMPLE 156

Schubert, Melodic lines

directly, or within a phrase, or after a brief chromatic passage that serves in place of a modulation.[5] The late chamber-music works contain several examples of a similar relationship of tonic to a third above or below, but in consecutive movements. The A-major "Trout" quintet, for example, has a slow movement in F; the A-minor string quartet has a slow movement in C; the slow movement of the G-major quartet is in B minor; and so on.

More than this is involved, however, for shifts of tonality embracing a second also occur. The slow movement of the "Trout" quintet provides

---

[5] Examples of the three manners may be seen, respectively, in the "Trout" quintet, first movement, at the double bar; in the A-minor string quartet finale, measures 72–79, seen in EXAMPLE 156*b;* and in the C-major quintet, first movement, measures 58–60, immediately before the passage shown in EXAMPLE 156*e.*

A page from autograph of Schubert's *Rondo brillant* for violin and piano, D. 895.

examples of both of Schubert's chief harmonic practices. It contains three thematic sections in F major, F♯ minor, and D major, respectively; in the second half of the movement these sections are repeated note-for-note in A♭ major, A minor, and F major. This movement in a sense epitomizes Schubert's harmonic manner: abrupt changes from major to minor or the reverse; subtle modulations within phrases; and direct changes of tonality of a second or third in either direction. The following diagram will illustrate the scheme of this movement.

Theme:	I	II	III	I	II	III
Key:	F major	F♯ minor	D major	A♭ major	A minor	F major
Measures:	23	12	25	23	12	26

Possibly the greatest expansion of Schubert's harmonic scheme is seen in the finale of the E♭ piano trio, D. 929. The movement is in sonata-form with three contrasting themes in E♭, C minor, and B minor, respectively. The tonalities entered or touched upon in the course of this 748-measure movement are seen in the following diagram. With so color-

SECTION	MEAS. NO.	THEME	KEY	SECTION	MEAS. NO.	THEME	KEY
Exposi-	1	I	E♭ major				E♭ minor
tion	73	II	C minor				B minor
	121	II	B♭ major		↓	↓	E♭ minor
	163	II	C minor	Recapitu-	441	I	E♭ major
	193	I	B♭ major	lation	519	II	F minor
	275	III	B minor		551	II	E♭ major
Develop-	315	I,	B minor		593	II	F minor
ment		II,	D minor	Coda	623	I	E♭ major
		and	B minor		693	III	E♭ minor and major
		III	F major				

Movement ends in measure 748

ful and wide-ranging a harmonic scheme, Schubert apparently felt no need to develop the thematic material in addition. In most cases literal transpositions of the respective sections occur, and variety is provided by the almost kaleidoscopic array of harmonic color.

Rhythmic motives rather than melodic motives play a prominent part in Schubert's later works. Virtually every movement in the last symphonies, sonatas, and chamber-music works introduces one or more rhythmic motives that, recurring through extended passages, provide much of the unity of the movement even as they propel the music forward. EXAMPLE 157 illustrates a selection of such motives. A major difference between

E X A M P L E   157

Schubert, Rhythmic motives

Beethoven's and Schubert's treatment of rhythmic motives is that for the former the motive is a point of departure leading to other related motives; for the latter it is a fixed element providing the needed stability.

Sonata-form is basic to Schubert's instrumental works, as is the four-movement sonata that the Classical composers used most frequently. In first movements he typically repeats the first-theme group before introducing the second, with the repetition generally more elaborate than the first statement. The repetition, however, seldom occurs in the recapitulation. That section, in turn, often begins with the second-theme group (in the early works on the subdominant instead of the tonic), the first theme then being reserved for the coda of the movement. The development sections are usually extended, giving Schubert full opportunity to express his sense for harmonic color contrasts; consequently, transposed repetitions of thematic sections rather than true developments are to be looked for. Slow movements exhibit considerable formal variety: sonata-form, rondo, variations, and three-part (*ABA*) form are most usual, and a form such as that in the "Trout" quintet (see above, page 436) must be considered an exception. Scherzos with greatly contrasting trios (sometimes in slow tempo or in duple meter) are more common than minuets. Finales, like first movements, are most often in extended sonata-form with elaborate codas.

The texture of Schubert's works is related to the use (or nonuse) of counterpoint and to his method of orchestration. His style is primarily melodic, to which homophonic texture is most suited, but the homophony is modified by small countermelodies, subtle imitations, and harmonic voices that take on melodic character to such an extent that they virtually become counterpoints (see EXAMPLE 158). The often repeated assertion

EXAMPLE 158

Schubert, Symphony, D. 944

that Schubert was deficient in contrapuntal techniques is not borne out by the facts. One has only to point to the many polyphonic, even fugal passages in his Masses, to the felicitous use of countermelodies everywhere in his works, and even to such devices as the canon in the scherzo of the E♭ piano trio. In general, however, Schubert's style is too spontaneous and direct to permit the kind of calculation and planned manipulation that extensive counterpoint requires.

In methods of orchestration, Schubert revealed a keen sense for tone color and balance even in his early works. Themes are often given to woodwind instruments accompanied by strings instead of the reverse. Woodwinds supply atmosphere, mood, and color to many passages, as in the introduction to the fifth symphony, and they often alternate with the strings in tossing bits of thematic material back and forth. The lower strings are employed for their mood values, notably at the beginning of the "Unfinished" symphony. Finally, trombones come strongly into prominence in both of his last two symphonies; they are used not only in climactic tutti passages, but also in thematic statements, to which they lend dignity and serious import. In all these respects Schubert showed himself sensitive to the element of instrumental color (quite separately from melodic content) and, together with Weber he led the way to the concern for tone color that characterizes much of the music of the Romantic period.

The Art Song

SCHUBERT'S accomplishments in the special category called art song mark one of the most significant events in the period with which this chapter is concerned. On the one hand he brought to a close a long tradition of song writing that extended back at least to the sixteenth century; on the other, he created a new type of song that influenced composers for a hundred years after his time. The art song is one of the purest and most concentrated symbols of the Romantic period, but it also represents a late flowering of Classical ideals of proportion, balance, and refinement. Because of this dual role it deserves a separate section here, one that will trace developments in the form from the Baroque period to Schubert's own time.

The Baroque song. In the Baroque period it is difficult to distinguish a clear and separate category of song corresponding to the type brought to its first perfection by Schubert. Solo songs existed throughout the seventeenth century, but many of them were arrangements, for one voice and instruments, of polyphonic songs of the chanson type. Others were operatic airs separated from the stage and supplied with simpler accompaniments for chamber and concert use. Still others were essentially dance tunes to which texts had been applied. Somewhat later, songs in the general style of folksongs were composed.

At first many of the songs, whose composers remembered the airs written by John Dowland and his school at the beginning of the seventeenth century, were set with lute accompaniment; that instrument remained in favor to about 1650. Other songs were accompanied by continuo, quite in the style of other categories of Baroque music. Improvised keyboard parts over a figured bass were the essential ingredients of this type of accompaniment, of course, and the harpsichord, to which the keyboard part was generally assigned, provided little more than a harmonic support for the voice. As the Rococo period approached, in the eighteenth century, the continuo began to fall out of fashion and was replaced by obbligato accompaniments, in which the upper line doubled the voice part and the harmony was laid out in simple triadic figures.

The songs showed various types of treatment. Elements derived from folksong—namely, restricted range, modal inflections, simple phrase structure, and strophic form—were characteristic of many songs. In others, a declamatory style resembling that found in operas and cantatas of the time was employed; in these cases, the song was almost necessarily through-composed—that is, each stanza of the text was given its own music. A third type was that derived from dance songs: recurring rhythmic patterns suggesting the forms of pavane, galliard, and other dances were common.

Many countries took part in the development of Baroque song. In England and France, each of which had developed its own lute-accompanied type, the operatic air gradually became dominant; by the beginning of the eighteenth century the separate song literature declined in importance. In Germany a number of composers developed individual styles and contributed to the formation of a large repertoire. Hammerschmidt, Albert, and Krieger may be taken as representative of the dozens of capable men who worked in this field.

Andreas Hammerschmidt (1612–1675) active in Zittau in Saxony, combined the simplicity of folksong with the free style of the cantata and wrote with keen regard for the declamation of the text. Heinrich Albert (1604–1651), a pupil and cousin of Heinrich Schütz but active in Königsberg, favored an aria in which the free-flowing melodies of each stanza were separated by short *ritornelli*. In the arias of Adam Krieger (1634–1666) of Dresden, the *ritornelli* are often expanded and the melodic line achieves great expressiveness. The arias of Philipp Heinrich Erlebach (1657–1714), active at Rudolstadt, show the growing influence of operatic style; his songs, often in large *ABA* form, are sometimes embellished by florid, highly expressive melodic lines.[6] The solo song occupies a relatively small place in the works of Bach and Handel.

Rococo and Classical song. Interest in song was renewed after 1736 by a collection called *Die singende Muse an der Pleisse* ("The Singing Muse on the [River] Pleisse"), published at Leipzig and containing instrumental dance pieces to which texts had been added. After about 1750 the composition of songs was centered in Berlin at the court of Frederick the Great. Although Carl Philipp Emanuel Bach and Karl Heinrich Graun composed songs (many of the former's being miniature masterpieces), the important work was done by the following generation, of whom Johann Friedrich Reichardt (1752–1814) was the leader. Reichardt, following the path taken by Johann Abraham Schulz (1741–1800), brought the qualities of folksong into his works, which are characterized by simplicity, straightforward expression, and direct appeal. He was also among the first to bring fully written-out accompaniments to his songs, thus dispensing with the continuo almost entirely. In the work of his contemporary, Carl Friedrich Zelter (1758–1832), friend of Goethe and the young Mendelssohn, greater rhythmic variety and subtlety of phrase structure is to be found.

6 The styles of Albert, Krieger, and Erlebach are illustrated in *HAM,* Nos. 205, *Auf, mein Geist;* 228, *Adonis Tod;* and 254, *Himmel . . . ,* respectively.

South German and Austrian song took a forward step in its development in the period after about 1760, when the *Singspiel* became firmly
established. One of the leaders in this development was Johann Adam
Hiller (1728–1804), associated with Leipzig, who sought to enlarge the
folklike song by giving it dramatic character, occasionally modifying the
strophic form by providing more variety in successive stanzas. In the work
of Johann Zumsteeg (1760–1802) in Stuttgart, a long narrative song called
"ballad" was established. Here attempts were made to match text sentiment and melodic contours in imaginative fashion, but the perfection of
the ballad form, which plays a small part in Schubert's songs, was the
work of Carl Loewe (1796–1869), active in Stettin later in the century.

The song occupies a relatively minor place in the work of the three
great masters of the Classical period. The songs of Haydn are folklike
and in strophic form; influenced by the opera of the time, however, they
sometimes become free and dramatic with embellished melodies, irregular
phrase structures, and the like. Although the majority of Haydn's accompaniments double the voice part, some of them reveal the growing independence of voice and piano that was to culminate in the songs of Schubert. Mozart, with about three dozen songs to his credit, showed a greater
sensitivity than Haydn to the moods of the texts. Irregular phrase structure at times, contrasts of lyric and dramatic moods, and variety in the
piano accompaniments characterize his songs. In a few of Beethoven's
eighty-odd songs, a transformation from a social entertainment to a
vehicle of deep feeling is to be seen. The majority are in simple strophic
form; others, notably the famous *Adelaide,* reveal the influence of the
operatic cavatina, and the song cycle, *An die ferne Geliebte* ("To the
Distant Beloved"), contains imaginative harmonic and formal touches
prophetic of Schubert.

Schubert's songs. The essence of Schubert's songs is that they express
the mood of their texts directly and thus do not require that the concepts
or verbal images on which the texts are based be musically described.
The lyric poems he used illustrate the basic elements of subjective expression, namely that the poet was speaking for himself, not acting as a universal spokesman, and that his audience consisted of a restricted number
of sensitive listeners rather than the world at large. Thus the two criteria
of a Schubert song, expressive content and intimacy, are determined.

Several types are found among Schubert's works. The majority of the
early songs are cast in strophic form; *Ungeduld* ("Impatience") and the
famous *Horch, horch, die Lerch* ("Hark, Hark, the Lark") are of this type.
The strophic songs of Reichardt and Zumsteeg probably served as his
models, but he was more imaginative in his choice of phrase structures
than the older composers. Further, modifications of strophic form occur
to such an extent that one may almost speak of a separate type here;
Wohin? ("Whither?") and *Der Wegweiser* ("The Signpost") represent the
modified strophic form. Through-composed songs dominate from about
1816 on, and the majority of Schubert's most expressive works are cast in
this form; *Der Erlkönig* ("The Erlking") and *Die Allmacht* ("The

Omnipotence") are among the best-known examples. To avoid the danger of diffuseness in a setting where virtually each phrase has its own contour and musical characteristics, Schubert usually introduced a motive in the accompaniment that pervades and unifies the entire song. A number of songs show the influence of the operatic *scena,* in that sections in contrasting tempo, mood, and meter are brought together into one song. *Der Wanderer* ("The Wanderer") and *Tod und das Mädchen* ("Death and the Maiden") are outstanding songs of this type, embodying great contrast in small dimensions. Another type is based on declamation, with the melodic rhythm derived from the text instead of from musical laws themselves. The most intensely dramatic songs are often of this type, *Der Doppelgänger* ("The Double") and *Die Stadt* ("The Town") chief among them.

The varied relationships between voice and piano accompaniment are among the marvels of Schubert's songs. In some the piano merely accompanies and all the aesthetic weight of the song is carried by the melody, which is likely to be simple and folklike in style; in a sense the accompaniment is unessential, as it is in a true folksong. In others the aesthetic weight is shared equally by voice and piano; in this type the melody's function is to express the feeling inherent in the text, while the accompaniment suggests the mood or atmosphere out of which the poet writes. Still other songs, usually those of the declamatory type, are weighted in favor of the accompaniment; they comprise miniature dramas of great intensity and expressiveness.

The wealth of accompanying figures Schubert devised is equaled only by the variety of his melodic types. Some figures reflect the imagery of one element of the poem: the whirring of a spinning wheel, the glistening of a trout in the sunlit water, the rustling of leaves, the sound of the postman's horn—these are among Schubert's happiest inspirations. In other figures moods are expressed: utter loneliness, superstitious fear, buoyant energy, and the like (see EXAMPLE 159). Harmonic devices play a large part in this descriptive quality, and abrupt modulations or harmonic ambiguity become strong factors in establishing moods. Contrasts of mood between stanzas of through-composed songs are achieved harmonically for the most part, so that the transitions (as well as the preludes and

EXAMPLE 159

Schubert, Songs

Du bist die Ruh' ("Thou art Repose")

[b]

Der Doppelgänger ("The Double")

[c]

Still ist die Nacht, es ru - hen die Gas-sen,

TRANSLATION:
Still is the night,
the streets are deserted.

postludes that often occur) are not merely formal elements but also essential expressive ones.

The great majority of the texts Schubert set were written as single pieces, sometimes only a page or two in length, by various authors and reflect Schubert's wide reading in the large field of German lyric poetry. In two cases, however, he set to music an entire series by the same author and thus employed the form of the song cycle. The first cycle, consisting of fourteen poems by Wilhelm Müller, is called *Die Schöne Müllerin* ("The Maid of the Mill") and was composed in 1823. Four years later he turned to the same author and set a series of twenty-four poems, *Die Winterreise* ("The Winter's Journey"). A third set of fourteen songs, published posthumously and called *Schwanengesang* ("Swan Song"), presumably because it contains Schubert's last song (No. 14 of the cycle), is technically not a song cycle, for it contains poems by three authors: Rellstab, Heine, and Seidl.

Schubert was fortunately placed, historically speaking. He began to compose at a time when the whole wealth of German lyric poetry lay close at hand. Poems by Goethe, Schiller, and Klopstock on one level of merit, and on another level those by Schubert's friends Mayrhofer and others, testify to the composer's ability to select poems suitable for musical setting, regardless of their qualities as literature. Earlier generations of song composers had favored lighthearted or sweetly sentimental content; in Schubert's songs, moods of seriousness and darkness become more common, especially in the later songs. The fact that many of his choices reflect the moods of pathos, melancholy, and fantasy are perhaps to be taken as evidence that the spirit of the approaching Romantic period weighed upon him. And the fact that his songs are economically written, restrained, and balanced between form and content gives rise to the apparent contradiction that Schubert is most Classical in just the area in which he is most Romantic.

❦ 22 ❧

The Romantic Period:
Opera, 1810–1850

THE ENORMOUS number of operas of many kinds composed in the years after about 1790 makes it difficult to achieve a just critical evaluation and historical perspective, especially since public acclaim (and place in the repertoire) does not always coincide with artistic value. The central problem in opera is the relationship between drama and music. Mozart achieved a synthesis of these elements, based on the aesthetic principles of Classicism. Minor composers after Mozart, writing industriously in the old manner, generally failed to relate drama and music properly. Their unsuccessful attempts at synthesis demonstrated to Romantic composers the need for other methods.

Several trends in Romantic thinking, mentioned in Chapter 21, influenced the style of opera in the first half of the nineteenth century. In

Lithograph of Donizetti rehearsing his singers, artist unknown. [BETTMANN ARCHIVE]

searching for new means of expression, composers became conscious of a national artistic heritage, and the first strong signs of nationalism in opera appeared. The study of folk poetry, national legends and remote history opened new vistas for composers of opera. An interest in the literature of other nations further widened their horizons. Philosophers spoke of pictures as poems, of architecture as frozen music, and a fusion of the arts was attempted, resulting finally in Wagner's concept of the *Gesamtkunstwerk* (collective or united work of art; see Chapter 26).

During and after the Napoleonic era, benevolent despotisms in several countries had led to oppression, and the arts—especially music—became means of escape from the harsh realities of life. Supernatural and irrational elements were introduced into the opera, and current events were treated with lighthearted parody. Hope for miracles, for salvation and deliverance, permeated the texts and music of the new operas. These general thoughts and feelings were projected in three ways: through a dissolution of the old closed operatic numbers (arias, recitatives, ensembles, etc.) and the development of new forms, the evolution of new melodic and harmonic devices, and the introduction of a new ideal of sound in the orchestra.

Opera in Germany

Development of Romantic opera. The Romantic opera did not come into being suddenly; it was the result of a process extending over several decades. Several operas of the early 1800's contain stylistic elements pointing to the new form, notably Beethoven's only opera, *Fidelio* (1805). *Fidelio* is similar in subject matter to the French "horror and rescue" operas (see page 340): an innocent man is cast into prison by his political enemy; his wife, disguised as the jailer's assistant, liberates him, and thus faith in justice and humanity are restored. Although the composer insisted that the poetic element be expressed in traditional musical forms, one feels the presence of the unreal and of other manifestations of the Romantic spirit; this is especially strong in the dungeon scenes of Act II.

The original libretto of *Fidelio* was written by Jean Bouilly, also the author of the libretto for Cherubini's *Les deux journées* (see page 340), a work that represented Beethoven's operatic ideal. It had been set to music three times by composers before Beethoven: once in French by Pierre Gaveaux, under the title *Léonore, ou L'Amour conjugal,* and twice in Italian by Simon Mayr and Ferdinando Paër, respectively. The first performance of Beethoven's version in 1805 (in Sonnleithner's translation of Bouilly's libretto) was unsuccessful, as was a revision in 1806. Some years later Beethoven and Georg Treitschke undertook a major revision of both music and text, which resulted in the definitive version, first performed in 1814.

The existence of four different overtures for the opera (*Leonore Nos. 1, 2, 3* and *Fidelio,* respectively) and the many sketches for the vocal numbers (eighteen for the famous Florestan aria alone) testify to the place of this work in Beethoven's heart. In the first act, the tradition of the

Viennese *Singspiel* was observed, for spoken passages intervene between vocal numbers. Even there, however, Beethoven's genius is at work, especially in a celebrated canon for vocal quartet. Many numbers, notably Pizarro's demoniac aria and the prisoners' chorus, give evidence of the composer's profundity and dramatic power (see EXAMPLE 160). The prison scene itself (Act II), beginning with Florestan's aria and continuing with the eerie melodrama and the episode of the attempted murder, contrasts greatly with the exuberant choral finale. Beethoven's only opera is unique in its ethical power, dramatic strength, and spiritual depth.

The transition from the Viennese *Singspiel* to Romantic opera is seen in the stage works of Franz Schubert. Three operas, one of them a magic fantasy, five *Singspiele,* and a few fragments reveal the lyric gifts and dramatic limitations of the master of the German *Lied.* Many of his arias resemble art songs in their melodic beauty but contain little of the dramatic intensity required of operatic music. Although various stylistic elements—bold melodrama and remembrance motives, for example—add to their interest, Schubert's operas were unsuccessful and contributed

A scene from Beethoven's *Fidelio.* Engraving by Vincent Raimund Gruner, *c.* 1820.

EXAMPLE 160

Beethoven, *Fidelio*

TRANSLATION:
Oh, God! What a moment.

little to the development of the form. Several instrumental excerpts from the stage works, however, have remained gems of the concert repertoire— notably the overture and ballet music from *Rosamunde* (1823).

The celebrated literary figure, E. T. A. Hoffmann (see page 428), who also composed and painted, takes a more important historical place than Schubert. Hoffmann's best known opera, *Undine* (1816), reveals Romantic traits in its folklike melodies and supernatural scenes. Although his music is characterized by technical deficiencies, his influence—especially as a music critic and writer on aesthetics—was considerable.

Ludwig Spohr (1784–1859), eminent composer of symphonies, concertos, and oratorios, and perhaps the foremost German violinist and conductor of his time, also composed eleven operas. Two of them, *Faust* (1816) and *Jessonda* (1823), were eminently successful and the latter remained in the German repertoire for half a century. Spohr exhibited an unusual mixture of conservative and radical tendencies, both in his personality and in his musical tastes. He was, for example, unable to find aesthetic values in

Beethoven's compositions beyond the first-period style, yet he was among the earliest champions of Wagner. This mixture is reflected in his operas; while he composed in Classical operatic forms, he employed dramatic recitation, chromaticism, declamatory style, and motive techniques in a highly Romantic manner. He must be considered one of the important predecessors of Wagner.

Weber. Carl Maria von Weber (1786–1826), one of the most influential figures of the entire Romantic movement (see pages 428–30), established in his dramatic works a nationalistic style that equaled the Italian and French styles in significance. He began his operatic career in conventional fashion, composing four rather unimportant *Singspiele* and one (unfinished) opera.

In 1817 a friend, Friedrich Kind, prepared for him a libretto based on a ghost story, *Der Freischütz* ("The Freeshooter"). The resulting work was produced at Berlin in 1821 and immediately opened a new chapter in the history of opera. The text caught the imagination of the entire German nation, and the music brought to full expression all the Romantic elements contained in the text. The forested German landscape, peopled with peasants and hunters, formed the background. Supernatural elements were present in the form of Samiel (Satan), who sought to ensnare the innocent Max. Devoted sentimental love was reflected by Max's bride, Agathe, and a lighter humorous type was represented by Ännchen. The defeat of the villain and the triumph of Good symbolized the victory of the German people. Weber found the appropriate musical styles to express this mixture of elements, and the opera enjoyed an immediate success.

Der Freischütz is filled with outstanding musical numbers. The famous overture contains a synopsis of the entire drama, even though it is in a loose sonata-form with slow introduction; the introduction depicts the forest (see EXAMPLE 161*a*) and the appearance of Satan (161*b*). Other numbers, still divided by spoken dialogue, include several choruses of hunters, peasants, and bridesmaids as well as Ännchen's arias in a folk-like idiom. The arias of Agathe and Max express a sensitive, emotional element, and the chorus provides a dramatic climax in the famous "wolf's glen" scene. This unsurpassed episode is filled with apparitions

EXAMPLE 161

Weber, *Der Freischütz*

and demons and, rising to a high level of excitement, provided later composers with a model of Romantic treatment.

In his next opera, *Euryanthe* (1823), Weber approached the Romantic ideal even more closely. The overture is again a masterpiece, and several vocal numbers and choruses reach an equally high level. Weber here approached Wagner in his harmonic vocabulary and skillful use of motives. Through-composed passages are substituted for the spoken dialogues that had marked *Der Freischütz*. Orchestral colors, too, already remarkable in the earlier work, here take on a new glow and brilliance. The unreality of a ghost scene has seldom been realized more successfully in a musical context than in the second act of *Euryanthe*. In spite of its outstanding musical quality, however, the opera did not achieve lasting success; dramatic weaknesses of the libretto may be held responsible.

Weber's last stage work, *Oberon*, was written to an English libretto and produced in London in 1826. Here the composer reverted to the earlier technique, for large sections of the piece are spoken; his contribution consists primarily of the overture and several vocal numbers, notably the famous aria, "Ocean, thou Mighty Monster." It was Weber's intention to tighten the libretto and rearrange and amplify the music after the first London performance; but, overworked and ill, he died in his fortieth year before the revision could be undertaken. His great historical contribution consists of having blended elements of the *Singspiel,* French opera, and Italian opera and, with the admixture of Romantic subject matter and treatment, raised them to a higher unity. His musical techniques and his dramatic ideas were brought to culmination by Richard Wagner.

Heinrich Marschner (1795–1861) may be called Weber's successor, although his creative power did not approach that of the short-lived older composer. Among his operas, *Der Vampyr* (1828) and *Hans Heiling* (1833) were immediately and overwhelmingly successful, and the latter was performed in German theaters for a century. Marschner stressed supernatural elements and wrote spectacularly at times, but at other times he introduced humor and a folklike idiom into his music. His orchestral writing is generally dark in color, to fit his ghostly scenes, and he was a master of the orchestral idiom. In *Hans Heiling* the overture is placed after a scenic prologue; this innovation, it may be noted, is reflected in Mendelssohn's oratorio *Elijah,* in which the overture is heard after the opening recitative (Mendelssohn, who was acquainted with Marschner, had briefly considered composing the *Heiling* libretto in 1826). It may also be pointed out that certain figures and situations in Marschner's operas are found again in some of Wagner's early works.

Early operas of Wagner. The early operas of the creator of the *Musik-drama* may be discussed here, since they were written under the influence of Weber and Marschner. Richard Wagner (1813–1883), after studying philosophy and music, began his career as a theatrical conductor. In this capacity he became familiar with a large repertoire of standard and contemporary operas. His first work in the field, *Die Feen* ("The Fairies"), composed in 1834 but not produced until 1888, is a typically Romantic pageant without noteworthy personal characteristics. His second opera, *Das Liebesverbot* ("The Ban on Love"), based on Shakespeare's *Measure for Measure,* was performed only once, at Magdeburg in 1836. It is a light work in which Wagner leaned strongly on Italian and French operas; it contains the conventional arias and ensembles, coloratura passages and cadenzas, and even traces of Meyerbeer's style (see page 460).

Wagner's third opera, *Rienzi* (1842), which may be called a grand opera (see page 459), was also modeled on Meyerbeer's works. *Rienzi* was hugely successful at its first performance and is still given in many German theaters; the success of this work and of his next opera *Der fliegende Holländer* ("The Flying Dutchman," 1843), brought Wagner a position as musical director of the court of Saxony at Dresden. The overture, some ensembles, and a few arias from *Rienzi* are excellent, but they are not strong enough to support the diffuse libretto—the only Wagner opera based on a historical subject.

In *Der fliegende Holländer,* Wagner was well on the way to a new style and a new philosophy. The opera is based on a Medieval legend about a seafarer who is condemned to sail for eternity, but ultimately redeemed by true love. Wagner himself wrote the libretto, in which symbolism plays a dominant role; the raging sea becomes a symbol of the hero's emotions, for example. *Der fliegende Holländer* is the last of Wagner's works to contain separate musical numbers, and these are unified by recurring motives. Senta's famous ballad, in which she expresses a premonition of her encounter with the Dutchman, contains a motive that is heard later in the work, and other remembrance motives are also employed. Wagner's harmonic and orchestral language became highly individualized here; we shall follow that development in Chapter 26.

Comic opera. Paralleling the course of Romantic opera, the comic opera in Germany developed along separate lines. It may be characterized as a blend of the *Singspiel* and the *opéra comique.* Directed primarily to the German middle class, which sought to be moved by sentiment and humor and had no wish to reach great emotional depth, it features melodic simplicity and shows no influence of Weber and Wagner. The most important representative of the German comic opera was Albert Lortzing (1801–1851), whose works, almost unknown in English-speaking countries, are still performed in Germany almost as frequently as Mozart's. In his professional career as singer and actor, Lortzing traveled widely and became acquainted with every phase of the German theater. Most of his librettos, which he wrote himself, deal with simple love stories and comedies; his characters, modeled somewhat on the ancient stock types, are effective nevertheless. He preferred small arias and strophic songs, which are amiable and witty and always well constructed. His ensembles in particular reveal a fine talent for composition and dramatic effect.

Lortzing's most successful works include *Zar und Zimmermann* ("Czar and Carpenter," 1837), based on the adventures of Peter the Great when he was in Holland to learn the ship-building craft, *Der Wildschütz* ("The Poacher," 1842), and *Der Waffenschmied* ("The Armorer," 1846). Hilarious scenes in the two last-mentioned works have retained their appeal to the present day. In 1845 Lortzing turned to the Romantic field and composed *Undine,* a work that fails to reach any emotional depth, despite its descriptive devices and remembrance motives.

A few other comic operas have retained places in the German repertoire to the present day. Otto Nicolai (1810–1849) recaptured the real spirit of mirth in his successful *Die lustigen Weiber von Windsor* ("The Merry Wives of Windsor," 1849). The ensembles of this work are masterly, the arias are full of exquisite detail, and the overture is a perennial favorite. The opera can be favorably compared with Verdi's *Falstaff,* based on the same subject. Friedrich von Flotow (1812–1883), taking the French *opéra comique* as his model, is represented by *Alessandro Stradella* (1844), a romanticized biography of the Baroque composer, and *Martha* (1847), which is notable especially for one inserted number, "The Last Rose of Summer."

In the second half of the century only a few composers could escape the influence of Wagner's style. Two among them contributed to the field of comic opera. Hermann Götz (1840–1876) composed in a conventional style in *Der Widerspenstigen Zähmung* ("The Taming of the Shrew," 1874). Peter Cornelius (1824–1874) in *Der Barbier von Bagdad* (1858) created a masterpiece full of humor, exotic touches, and tender lyricism. A decline in the comic opera genre is marked in the period after about 1870. Few notable works were composed until Richard Strauss raised the type to new heights early in the twentieth century.

Opera in Italy

THE TWO types of opera, serious and comic, which had been clearly and distinctively established in Italy since the middle of the eighteenth century, found continued employment to the threshold of the new period. Many composers wrote in the pre-Classical style (see Chapter 17), and others repeated the clichés of the *opera buffa*. The latter, however, employed a few new elements on occasion: small, characteristic rhythmic motives alternating between the vocal and orchestral parts, more variety in the orchestration, and more frequent use of ensembles. Gluck's operatic reforms had relatively little influence on Italian composers, possibly because the lighter musical type prevailed in that country.

Simon Mayr (1763–1845), of Bavarian origin but active principally in Italy, cultivated both the serious and comic operatic types and laid the groundwork for a new style. Among his sixty-one works for the stage are two-act comic operas, one-act farces, and also many serious works in an idiom that, while based on pre-Classical techniques, was much more individual. In the latter works Mayr included choruses and lengthy instrumental pieces in the style of the French operas. His influence, especially in regard to new instrumental writing, more progressive harmony (including the use of altered chords), and dramatic effects, is seen in the work of many French, Italian, and German composers. Prominent among them are Peter Winter (1754–1825) in Munich and Saverio Mercadante (1795–1870), active in Naples, Rome, Bologna, and several other cities. The latter, nicknamed the "Italian Beethoven," composed about sixty operas, all of them forgotten today.

Ferdinando Paër (1771–1839), born in Parma, was celebrated during his lifetime in Vienna, Dresden, Paris, and Warsaw. Paër composed primarily in the lighter vein. Many of his later operas (he composed forty-three in all) were strongly influenced by Mozart. He was briefly associated with Rossini at the Italian Theater in Paris, and the latter became his artistic successor.

A scene from
Rossini's
*Il barbiere di
Siviglia.* Mural
painting by
Moritz
von Schwind
in the old Vienna
Staatsoper, 1865.

Rossini. Gioacchino Rossini (1792–1868) is unsurpassed as a master of the early Romantic Italian *opera buffa.* His career began auspiciously before his twentieth year, and in 1813 he enjoyed his first major success with *Tancredi,* produced in Venice. His best known work is the eternal masterpiece *Il barbiere di Siviglia* ("The Barber of Seville"), produced at Rome in 1816.

After the great success of Paisiello's opera of that title (see page 341), Rossini at first hesitated to set the same libretto to music; indeed, the initial reception given his work was not too encouraging. But Paisiello's *Barber* was written with the typical vocabulary of *opera buffa,* while Rossini entered more closely into the spirit of Beaumarchais's play, its wit, elegance, and irony. He was unable, however, to fill the libretto with real tenderness, serious overtones, or psychological characterization, as a greater genius—Mozart—had done before him in similar librettos. But the character of the ubiquitous Figaro, who dominates the opera, became somewhat similar to Rossini's own: vital, humorous, full of mockery, and fond of intrigues. Rosina's haughtiness and the Count's aggressiveness, serving as foils to Figaro's machinations, contribute strong elements of contrast that extend to the minor figures as well. Many numbers in *The Barber* are unsurpassed in ingenuity and effect; among them are Rosina's first aria, the thunder scene, Basilio's glorification of calumny, and Figaro's sparkling "factotum scene."

Among Rossini's other comic operas, *Cenerentola* ("Cinderella," 1817) and *L'Italiana in Algeri* ("The Italian in Algiers," 1813), an exotic comedy of errors, have been retained in the repertoire. *Le Comte Ory* ("Count Ory," 1828) has recently been revived with much success; but the serious operas—even the best ones such as *Mosè in Egitto* ("Moses in Egypt," 1818) and *Semiramide* (1823)—have been all but forgotten. At the end

EXAMPLE 162

Rossini, *Il barbiere di Siviglia*

FIGARO: Là sen - za fal - lo mi tro - ve - rà   IL CONTE: Ho ben ca - pi - to.

TRANSLATION:
"You can't mistake it, I will be there."
"Yes, I will find it."

Woodcut illustration for an early edition of *The Bride of Lammermoor* by Sir Walter Scott, the source for Donizetti's *Lucia di Lammermoor*.

of his creative period Rossini composed one grand opera for Paris, *Guillaume Tell* ("William Tell," 1829; see page 459). Then, at the age of thirty-seven, for reasons never satisfactorily explained, he retired from the theater. In his last thirty-nine years he composed no major works.

Rossini's ingenuity in creating melodies that could capture the imagination of his audiences is a major factor of his importance. His humor does not have the psychological subtlety of Mozart's, but it is more forceful and ironic than the humor found in the conventional *opera buffa*. He is a master of formal clarity and brilliant vocal coloratura style; his exquisite treatment of the orchestra never permits the voices to be overshadowed. His harmonies in general are simple and conventional, but they include a few striking modulations (see EXAMPLE 162). In his overtures, several of which are still in the concert repertoire, he employed a loose sonata-form; his arias and ensembles contain strettos and the famous "Rossini crescendo," which combines a gradual dynamic increase with great rhythmic momentum. Finally, he eliminated *secco recitativo* and indicated specific ornamentation in his scores. Not without reason was he called, in reference to his birthplace, the "Swan of Pesaro."

Donizetti and Bellini. Gaetano Donizetti (1797–1848) was the last master of the typical *opera buffa*. As a pupil of Simon Mayr he adopted

EXAMPLE 163

Donizetti, *Lucia di Lammermoor*

TRANSLATION:
Let words of love enchant me.
Let trouble now flee away.

the older composer's style, but Rossini's idiom appears in his works as well. The clarity and careful writing found in Rossini's scores, however, are missing from Donizetti's; rich melodies, sometimes sentimental and sometimes robust, dominate. Aria forms are conventional and usually end with dazzling coloratura cadenzas; the chorus is used only to decorate the stage and add tonal volume.

Of Donizetti's seventy operas, those written between about 1830 and 1842 were the most successful. He cultivated both types, serious and comic, and both are represented in the three works that survive in the repertoire. The tragic *Lucia di Lammermoor* (1835) contains the famous sextet and the "Mad Scene," which has been a testing ground for coloratura sopranos for well over a century (see EXAMPLE 163). A *buffo* opera, *Don Pasquale* (1843), and a light French comedy, *La Fille du régiment* ("The Daughter of the Regiment," 1840), are still enjoyable. It is interesting to note that Richard Wagner spent two years (1840–1842) in Paris as a musical journalist and publisher's assistant, and that among his routine tasks he prepared piano scores of several of Donizetti's operas.

The meteorlike career of Vincenzo Bellini (1801–1835) occurred during the period of Donizetti's greatest successes, and for a short time the triumvirate of Rossini, Donizetti, and Bellini added new luster to the production of Italian opera. In his short life Bellini composed eleven operas, most of them serious in tone. The influence of both Rossini and Donizetti may be traced in his works, but Bellini had an individual style. He preferred dark subjects, employed symbolism, and even approached psychoanalytical problems (as in *La sonnambula* ["The Sleepwalker"] of 1831); the influence of early German Romanticism upon him may be surmised.

Bellini's operatic love scenes are tender and elegiac in spirit, but coloratura effects still predominate; the melody, accompanied by a homophonic orchestral texture, is the sole carrier of emotion. Bellini, like Donizetti, cultivated the "scene and aria," in which the latter is introduced by a lengthy instrumental prelude and an extended accompanied recitative. His harmony is somewhat more elaborate than Donizetti's, and his writing in general reveals an elegance that the older composer sometimes lacks. A serious opera, *Norma* (1831), is still performed today and is thoroughly representative of his style (see EXAMPLE 164).

EXAMPLE 164

Bellini, *Norma*

NORMA: Ah be - llo a me - ri - tor - no, _____ del fi - do a - mor pri -

mie - ro; e con - tro il mon-do in tie - ro, di - fe - sa - a —
te - sa - ró. Ah bel- lo a me ——— ri - tor - no

TRANSLATION:
Ah, the beauty and merit of first faithful love, and
against the whole world . . .

In the first phases of the long operatic career of Giuseppe Verdi, which extended from 1839 to 1893, the styles of Donizetti and Bellini are reflected. But after about 1850 Verdi's development took another direction, which will be discussed in Chapter 26.

Opera in France

THE CHARACTERISTICS of French Romantic opera can be traced back to certain elements in the operas of Cherubini and Spontini (see Chapter 17). The highly emotional scenes and intensified expressive power in the music of those composers are found again in the operas of the new period. Whereas the older composers in essence adhered to the principles of the Classical opera and of Gluck's successors, the newer composers sought a new direction. The *opéra sérieux* and *opéra comique* developed independently, and not until about the middle of the century did a union of the two types take place. The single musical numbers (arias, ensembles, instrumental pieces, and the like) remained independent and separate in both types; only the ways of connecting them were changed. And operatic composers of the time were strongly influenced by French Romantic writers, especially by the novelists.

Grand opera. The vogue of French grand opera, which lasted for about two decades, was closely related to political and socio-economic developments. After the collapse of the Napoleonic era and the eventual restoration of a stable Europe, increasing industrialization and the extension of colonialism and trade resulted in the emergence of a new, wealthy middle class that formed a new audience for opera, demanding lavish entertainment. It seemed a requirement that operatic texts be colorful and filled with action. Subjects were chosen from relatively recent history, and the vogue of classical antiquity passed. The action was expected to lead to climaxes with pageants, mass ensembles, and ballets. Violence and passion, also reflected in French literature of the time, became rampant in the operas as well. Librettos containing issues related to contemporary developments, such as political independence and religious freedom, were received with acclamation, and scenic and dramatic effects played upon the emotions.

The operas consisted mainly of large choral sections, multivoiced ensembles, and extended and ornate arias, but short, simple instrumental melodies also became part of the style. Orchestral resources were increased and employed with skill. The orchestration of grand opera was not without influence on Wagner and other later Romantic composers.[1]

Grand opera is usually associated with the name of Giacomo Meyerbeer, who is justifiably considered the earliest master of the form. Two outstanding works antedate his spectacular successes, however: Auber's *La Muette de Portici* ("The Mute of Portici," also known as "Masaniello") and Rossini's *Guillaume Tell* ("William Tell"). Daniel François Auber (1782–1871), primarily a representative of the *opéra comique* (see below), composed *La Muette* in 1828, successfully anticipating the grandiose style. Its libretto is concerned with an historical event: the revolution in Naples against the Spanish rulers in 1647, led by Masaniello, a fisherman; the mute girl in the title role is a symbol of the powerless, exploited population. The climax of the opera is a catastrophic eruption of Mount Vesuvius (though that had actually taken place sixteen years before the revolution with which the opera is concerned). The performance of the opera in Brussels in 1830 provoked riots that led to the separation of Belgium from the Kingdom of the Netherlands and her establishment as an independent kingdom. Yet there is nothing in Auber's musical style in this opera to warrant such drastic consequences. A few melodious and rhythmically attractive numbers emerge from mass ensembles; nothing more.

Rossini's single essay in grand opera, *Guillaume Tell*, written for Paris in 1829, is musically more valuable than Auber's work. Its subject, a dramatization of events in the life of the legendary Swiss hero, offered manifold possibilities to the composer—the pastoral character of peasant

---

1 For details, see William Crosten, *French Grand Opera: An Art and a Business,* New York, King's Crown Press, 1948.

scenes contrasts with the elaborateness of the large ensembles and ballets —but only the overture and a few exquisite vocal numbers have remained in the repertoire.

Meyerbeer and Halévy. The most important composer of grand opera had a somewhat checkered career. Born in Berlin in 1791 of Jewish parentage, his name was originally Jacob Liebmann Beer. At the wish of a wealthy relative whose heir he became, he affixed the name "Meyer" to his family name, and he adopted "Giacomo," the Italian form of Jacob. In 1815, at Salieri's suggestion, he went to Italy, where he wrote a series of successful operas on the models of Mayr and Rossini. In 1831 his career in Paris began with the first of his grand operas, and his works to about 1850 enjoyed great acclaim. Meanwhile, in 1842, he became musical director of the Prussian court at Berlin, but periodically he returned to Paris and composed additional works for the Paris opera. He died there in 1864.

Meyerbeer has been criticized for his desire to achieve effects even at the cost of musical quality, but it cannot be denied that he mastered dramatic technique, showing an innate sense for the theater and a great gift for writing for both solo voices and chorus. Some of his melodies reveal rare beauty, and several of his operas remained in the repertoire for half a century. Those works were later displaced because of the change to a taste that desired less elaborate display and superficial brilliance. Recently some of his operas have been revived; we can now evaluate his importance and style more objectively, especially his control of the factors of motivic technique and orchestral sound. It must be admitted, however, that the librettos, most of them written by Eugène Scribe, seem antiquated and even preposterous at times.

The first of Meyerbeer's Parisian operas was *Robert le Diable* ("Robert the Devil," 1831), concerned with a Medieval duke possessed by Satan. This was followed by a work on a higher musical level, *Les Huguenots* (1836), which is a spectacular story of the events leading to the massacre of St. Bartholomew's Day (in Paris, 1572), combined with a tragic love story. Meyerbeer's advanced harmony and personalized treatment of the orchestra add color and sonority. Another grand opera, *Le Prophète* (1849), dealing with the life of John of Leyden, a leader of the Anabaptist movement in the sixteenth century, was also highly acclaimed.

Meyerbeer's last opera, *L'Africaine,* produced in Paris in 1865 a year after the composer's death and sung most often in Italian (with the title *L'Africana*), reveals a continuation of his creative ability and a greater consistency of style. Although the story, concerned with a tragic romance between the explorer Vasco da Gama and a native princess, is full of absurdities, the musical numbers contain melodic beauty and refined harmonies. Vasco's famous aria, "O paradiso," is especially noteworthy (see EXAMPLE 165). Meyerbeer, although belittled and attacked by Wagner, influenced both Wagner (in *Rienzi*) and Verdi (in *Aïda*).

Only one of the more than thirty operas by Jacques Halévy (1799–1862)

EXAMPLE 165

Meyerbeer, *L'Africana*

TRANSLATION:
This is to die twice, to lose together, to lose together
life and immortality.

has remained in the repertoire. *La Juive* ("The Jewess," 1835) reveals all
the positive and negative characteristics of the grand opera type: magnificent pageantry, sumptuous ballets, an air of emotional excitement,
coupled with melodrama and superficiality. Grand opera remained at a
high level of popularity during much of the time Halévy was active
(roughly 1835 to 1854) but declined rapidly after the middle of the
century. Some of its features were retained in later operatic types, however, notably the elaborate ballets and ensembles. Even some of Verdi's
works, adapted for the Parisian stage, could not escape the influence of
the genre.

Berlioz. The dramatic works of Berlioz cannot be fully dissociated from
grand opera. His most important score, *Les Troyens* ("The Trojans"), is
a huge, epic drama that contains striking elements of pageantry; ballets,
large choral scenes, and a hunt scene are outstanding. Berlioz' style does

not reflect Meyerbeer's virtuosity, nor does it contain the latter's coloratura and other brilliant effects; it reflects, rather, the expression of drama
in Gluck's sense, however Romantic its spirit. The opera is based on the
fall of Troy and the voyage of Aeneas to Carthage, and it ends with a
prophecy of a new (Roman) empire. Berlioz himself wrote the libretto,
using Virgil as his source. *Les Troyens* was not performed in its entirety
during the composer's lifetime, although Part I was given at Paris in 1863;
Part II was first performed at Karlsruhe, Germany, in 1890. The work as
a whole was performed at Cologne in 1898, at Rouen in 1920, and at
Glasgow in 1935; those performances established its historical importance,
but its artistic value as a whole is still open to question. Some critics find
it lengthy, dull, and undramatic, while others hail it as the greatest French
opera of the nineteenth century.

Two other operas by Berlioz offer no problems. *Benvenuto Cellini*
(1838), a comic opera based on the life of the famous Renaissance sculptor,
contains excellent vocal ensembles as well as two celebrated overtures, *Le
Carnaval romain* and *Benvenuto Cellini*. *Béatrice et Bénédict* (1862, based
on Shakespeare's *Much Ado About Nothing*), is a delicate and lyric work
full of exquisite music but not too effective in a dramatic sense. These
works did not establish a new style, and Berlioz had only one follower:
Félicien David (1810–1876), who introduced Oriental elements into his
music, notably in his opera *Lalla Rookh* (1862).

Opéra comique. As indicated in Chapter 17, the *opéra comique* was
established in the eighteenth century and distinguished from *opéra
sérieux* mainly by virtue of its spoken dialogue. A new type of Romantic
opéra comique was introduced in Paris, shortly after the turn of the
century, by Nicolò Isouard (1775–1818), an Italian (Maltese) composer
who settled in Paris in 1799. His talent lay in his ability to write singable
melodies and graceful ensembles, and of his many operas, widely performed in France and Germany, *Cendrillon* ("Cinderella," 1810) became
the best known.

Isouard was overshadowed by François Adrien Boieldieu (1775–1834),
the chief representative of the new type. While Boieldieu's music was
elegant, transparent, and based on piquant harmonies (see EXAMPLE 166),
it had little dramatic power or brilliance. His operas were typically Romantic in subject matter; *La Dame blanche* ("The White Lady," 1825),
for example, is an adventurous ghost story, with touches of folk material
in its music. This opera remained in the European repertoire for more
than a century and is sometimes performed even today.

Daniel François Auber (1782–1871), mentioned in connection with
grand opera (see page 459), achieved great importance in the musical life
of Paris as chief conductor at the court of Napoleon III. He composed
about fifty works for the stage, most of them *opéras comiques;* his best
works contain tuneful arias and charming ensembles, while some of his
later works reveal a decline of his creative imagination, especially in
rhythm. Auber was influenced by Italian composers to some extent, and

E X A M P L E 166

Boieldieu, *La Dame blanche*

TRANSLATION:
Everywhere protecting ladies and taking pity on their sex, she informs the better halves when husbands are unfaithful.

REFRAIN: The white lady watches you, hears you . . .

many of his operas contain brilliant coloratura passages. Two of his engaging works, *Fra Diavolo* (1830) and *Le Domino noir* ("The Black Domino," 1837), are still popular.

Ferdinand Hérold (1791–1833), with some thirty operas to his credit, enjoyed only two lasting successes: *Zampa* (1831), especially popular in Germany, where its overture became a staple of the orchestral repertoire, and *Le Pré aux clercs* ("The Field of Honor," 1832), which was performed more than a thousand times in Paris. The Italian influence noted in Auber's works is even more prominent in those of Hérold; some of the latter's early operas were composed in direct imitation of Rossini's style. In the works of Adolphe Adam (1803–1856), a light ingratiating style approaching that of the operetta is seen. Two of his fifty-three operas, *Le Postillon de Longjumeau* (1836) and *Si j'étais roi* ("If I Were King," 1852), have kept his name alive on the stages of France and Germany to the present day.

After the revolution of 1848 and the founding of the Second Republic in France, the *opéra comique* lost its stylistic identity. The light and superficial style introduced by Adam was continued in one group of operas, which soon became identified as light operas or operettas. A semiserious and sentimental style prevailed in another group; gradually transformed into a style of realism, it led to the formation of a new operatic type called *drame lyrique,* or lyric opera. These developments will be discussed in Chapter 26.

The Romantic Period: Abstract Music

B ᴇᴇᴛʜᴏᴠᴇɴ cast a long shadow over the Romantic period. Composers were forced to come to terms with his monumental accomplishments. It was not within their power to exceed him, nor could they follow where he had led. Each one, however, felt comfortable with one aspect of Beethoven's genius and sought to identify himself with it. Thus Mendelssohn, in accord with his temperament, became an exponent of idealism and restraint. Berlioz primarily saw Beethoven's symbolism and soaring imagination and utilized these elements in the field of descriptive music. Toward the midpoint of the period, Wagner responded to the finale of the Ninth Symphony by declaring that instrumental music had reached its limits and henceforth needed to be combined with voices. Schumann, with typical Romantic enthusiasm, represented various aspects at various times. And Brahms, in characteristic fashion, combined the restrained and logical approach with noble idealism and set himself in firm opposition to the descriptive school represented by Liszt. To this mixture of aesthetic purposes and musical elements, one ingredient not part of

Woodcut by Fernand Simeon.

Beethoven's music was added: the expression of national aspirations, brought to a focus through the use of national legends and folk materials.

Out of this mass of somewhat contradictory factors, three tendencies or schools appeared: the abstract, later identified with the so-called neo-Classical school headed by Brahms; the descriptive, best represented by Berlioz early in the period and by Richard Strauss at its end; and the nationalistic, which was furthered primarily by composers outside the dominant musical countries. The three schools shared the same musical materials, of course, and to some extent employed similar methods the nationalists were largely composers of descriptive music, for example). Yet their individual approaches to that material and their basic aesthetic positions differed so greatly that not one Romantic style but several styles resulted. The various styles are united by an abiding concern with lyricism and instrumental color. Among the composers who adhered largely to the abstract tendency, Chopin, Mendelssohn, Schumann, and Brahms are the most significant.

Chopin

IN THE music of Frédéric Chopin (1810–1849), one of the most truly original composers of all time, a feeling for refinement and intimacy is everywhere apparent. Chopin, of mixed French and Polish ancestry, was born near Warsaw. A student in composition at the Warsaw conservatory, he was largely self-taught as a pianist. His talent was of the highest order; some early compositions were performed and published in his seventh year, and he made his first concert appearance at the age of eight. He later became one of the most accomplished performers of the time, but he had no interest in displaying his virtuosic skill. Every effort was directed toward achieving tonal control, expressiveness, and perfection of detail. He played often in Warsaw and once in Vienna during his formative years. His first major concert tour, begun late in 1830, was planned to include Vienna, Paris, and London. His success in Vienna was considerable, but in Paris he was so warmly received that he canceled his London plans and remained a resident of the French capital for the rest of his life, from 1831 to 1849.

Endowed with a pleasing personality, refined manner, and capacity for friendship, Chopin quickly became a favorite of the Parisian aristocrats. He played at innumerable salons (confining himself to his own music), took an active part in the strenuous social life of the time, and earned a comfortable living by teaching piano—at high fees—to the sons and daughters of his wealthy patrons. His style of playing was not compatible with the requirements of large-scale public performance, and after 1838 he virtually retired from the concert stage. His private performances continued, however, and his music became an object of admiration to every leading musician of the time. His activity as a composer, which had begun even before he left Poland in 1830, also continued, but at roughly half the rate that had marked the years 1830 to 1838. Despite his ever-weakening physical condition, he made a long visit to England in 1848 where

BETTMANN ARCHIVE

Chopin playing for the Prince Radziwill. Painting by Siemisadszki.

he performed at a number of private entertainments and made one or two public appearances. Physical exertion became increasingly difficult during that visit and almost impossible in the following year, when he was again in Paris. He died in October, 1849, in his thirty-ninth year, a victim of tuberculosis.

Compositions. About two hundred works for piano alone, two piano concertos, and a few dozen miscellaneous pieces represent Chopin's accomplishments as a composer. The great majority of the piano works are single-movement pieces, arranged in sets upon publication but not otherwise connected. Mazurkas, études, nocturnes, preludes, waltzes, polonaises, and a few other forms are represented. Three sonatas are included among the piano works; they and the two concertos are among his few successful works in compound form.

Style characteristics. The uniqueness of Chopin's music results from his ways of combining texture, harmony, melodic types, and emotional content. The melodic types range from a suave, expressive, and gently undulating *cantabile* to a widely spaced, highly embellished, and fast-moving line. Polyphony occupies a minor place in Chopin's style; his basic texture is homophonic to the extreme. The supporting chords, however, are employed in a variety of ways (see EXAMPLE 167). They are (a) spread across an octave or more to form rhythmic patterns; (b) used as solid blocks of tone in both hands; (c) divided between strong and weak beats in the left hand alone; (d) used as chord structures in the middle or upper voices; and they appear in many other ways and combinations as well. Chopin's harmony ranges from simple diatonic progressions to com-

EXAMPLE 167

Chopin, Harmonic types

plex passages in which altered chords, sharp dissonances, and the like are connected chromatically. He was among the first composers to employ the damper pedal extensively, and he achieved many new sonorities by blending consecutive chords through the use of the pedal. Harmonic inflections or transient modulations to keys a half-step removed (from C minor to Db major, for example), chromatic embellishments over pedal points—these and many other devices produced a fluid, colorful harmonic style that influenced Liszt and prepared the way for the fully developed chromatic harmony of the later Romantic period. Yet all this was done in a refined and delicate manner.

Chopin's national heritage came to expression in about sixty mazurkas and over a dozen polonaises. In these two old Polish dance forms, one reminiscent of folk festivals and the other long associated with court ceremonials, Chopin paid homage to the intense feeling of nationalism that arose in the wake of the political events (1772–1795) that had dismembered Poland and destroyed her identity as a nation. Chopin did not often employ folk tunes or idioms, as became the fashion among later nationalist composers; he suggested or expressed moods of nostalgia, pathos, and—in the mazurkas—some of the simpler aspects of Polish life. As a consequence, Chopin has long been revered as a Polish nationalist composer; yet he in no sense inclined to programmatic expression or deserted the field of abstract music.

In devoting himself to the piano and in concentrating on single-movement forms, Chopin was able to develop his unique gifts to the fullest. He was not interested in the kind of musical manipulation that leads to tightly developed forms; indeed, the various movements of the three piano sonatas and the two piano concertos (as well as of a cello sonata and a piano trio) are not distinguished by logical organization or continuity of ideas. In the single-movement works, each devoted to one or two moods, he revealed the full scope of his fertile imagination. The moods embrace all varieties from gay (but seldom humorous) to melancholy. Yet they are all expressed with polish and complete consistency of style

Mendelssohn

THE FORMAL perfection and lyricism of Mozart were to a large extent recaptured by Felix Mendelssohn—modified, of course, by Mendelssohn's temperament and interpreted from a Romantic viewpoint. Mendelssohn (1809–1847), born in Hamburg into a wealthy and cultured family, enjoyed every advantage that social position and refinement carried. The family moved to Berlin in 1812, and the Mendelssohn home became a center of cultural activity. The talent he showed as a child was wisely nurtured, and he grew up to be an accomplished linguist, painter, and writer, as well as one of the foremost pianists, conductors, and organists of the time.

He made his first appearance as a pianist in his ninth year, and a large number of compositions dating from his eleventh year marked his industry as a composer. He traveled widely from early childhood, visiting Austria, Switzerland, and Italy in 1830–1832, and making ten separate trips to England between 1829 and 1847. He was on friendly terms with the leading musicians and poets of the time, including Goethe; his general culture and personal charm gave him access to the highest circles of each country he visited.

One of the important events of his youth was arranging for and conducting a performance of Bach's *St. Matthew Passion* in Berlin in 1829—the first performance since the composer's death in 1750. Bach's music had been out of the repertoire for generations, and only a few musicians knew some of his major works. In restoring the *Passion* to public notice, Mendelssohn set in motion an appreciation of Bach and a revival of his music that has lasted to the present.

From about his twenty-sixth year Mendelssohn became most closely associated with Leipzig, first as conductor of the famous Gewandhaus Orchestra (in 1835) and later as founder and director of the Leipzig Conservatory (1843), where Schumann was among the teachers. In addition, he became attached to the Prussian court at Berlin as Royal director of music, remained active as a guest conductor in England and at many German festivals, and continued his career as a piano virtuoso. He composed industriously in spite of this varied activity, often working beyond his capacity. His administrative and musical responsibilities were discharged with the highest efficiency, and his standards never faltered; he did much to make the profession of music an accepted and respected field of activity. Inevitably, the constant activity and strain seriously affected his health. He died in 1847, at the age of thirty-eight, mourned by all of musical Europe.

Compositions. A large number of Mendelssohn's youthful compositions —those written before his thirteenth year—remained unpublished, and the works written between 1822 (his Opus 1 was a piano quartet) and 1825 (up to a string octet, Opus 20) are not representative of his mature style. From about 1825, however, his style suddenly attained its finished form; the compositions of his sixteenth year are as representative of the mature composer as are any of the later works.

The principal published items in the orchestral field are five symphonies, a violin concerto, two piano concertos, two or three overtures, and the incidental music for Shakespeare's *A Midsummer Night's Dream.* The latter work reveals the extent to which Mendelssohn's style became fixed early in his career. While the famous overture was composed in 1826, the other numbers (nocturne, scherzo, wedding march, and so on) were not written until 1842; yet no major difference in style is perceptible. The symphonies include the "Reformation," written about 1832, the "Italian," completed in 1833, and the "Scotch," finished in 1842; these works were published in reverse order as Nos. 5, 4, and 3, respectively.

The major chamber-music works are the octet for strings, mentioned above, seven string quartets written at intervals between 1829 and 1847, and two piano trios, composed in 1839 and 1845 respectively. Among the keyboard works are about fifty short pieces called "Songs Without Words," three sonatas, a large number of miscellaneous single-movement pieces (fantasies, scherzos, caprices, and the like), all for piano, and six organ sonatas and a few other organ pieces.

The vocal works include about three dozen sacred choral compositions —hymns, psalms, motets, and anthems among them. Some fifty unaccompanied part-songs on secular texts, about eighty songs for voice and piano, and a dozen vocal duets are also numbered in this group. By far the most significant of the choral works, however, are two oratorios: *St. Paul,* composed in 1836, and *Elijah,* completed in 1846. A third oratorio, *Christus,* remained unfinished.

Style characteristics. Unlike many other Romantic composers, Mendelssohn felt perfectly at home in the larger forms. His compositional technique in both homophonic and polyphonic styles enabled him to expand his material, to sustain moods across long time intervals, and to organize his forms in logical manner. Contrasts of harmony and texture are well defined in the sonata-form movements, and the formal divisions are clearly outlined. One ingredient of sonata-form is lacking, however: the striking emotional contrast that made the development section a battlefield of conflicting forces. The essence of the sonata-form, as Beethoven had so eloquently demonstrated, lay in just this contrast between lyric and dramatic moods, between two sets of conflicting musical ideas. Mendelssohn's talent reached into all areas of music save the dramatic; his few attempts at opera composition were not successful. Thus, the crucial section of the larger forms, the development section, is not greatly differentiated from the exposition and recapitulation. The result is a succession of charming melodies, well proportioned and elegantly presented, that proceed without conflict.

In other respects, however, Mendelssohn was a complete master of form. Phrases are invariably clear in structure, even in the many cases where phrase elision or overlapping takes place. They are not often capable of symphonic development; rather, they give evidence that Mendelssohn was primarily a lyricist. Several of his practices were of considerable influence on composers later in the century. His use of cyclical form, for example, impressed Schumann, Liszt, and many others, and the expansion of the principle eventually led to the symphonic poem of the 1850's. In the "Scotch" symphony, the slow introduction is thematically connected with the first movement and again employed in the form of an epilogue; further, the four movements are designed to be connected in performance. The two string quartets, Opus 12 and 13, written about 1827–1829, show the use of material from one movement in another. The violin concerto presents two outstanding innovations. The double exposition, a tradition since the time of Mozart, is done away with in the interest of directness; the work begins with the first theme in the solo instrument after the briefest of introductions. And the cadenza of the first movement is not only written out by the composer (instead of improvised afresh by each performer) but made into an integral formal element by being placed at the transition between development and recapitulation. The traditional position of the cadenza, just before the coda of the movement, often had had the effect of an anticlimax.

Another of Mendelssohn's unique contributions was a light, dainty content, usually called fairylike or elfin, that is found in movements played in fast tempo and very softly. It is characterized by rapidly moving melodic lines, repeated notes or rhythmic figures, delicate dynamics, and the thinnest of textures (see EXAMPLE 168); its mood is lively and

EXAMPLE 168

Mendelssohn, Trio, Op. 49

vivacious throughout. This type appears most often as a scherzo in the larger works in compound forms. Outstanding examples are found in the octet for strings, Opus 20, the F-minor quartet, Opus 44, No. 2, and the D-minor piano trio, Opus 49. It is also found in the sonata-form overture to *A Midsummer Night's Dream* and in many solo piano works, and passages of this type are often incorporated into compositions basically in another style.

Mendelssohn's contributions to the form of the scherzo as well as to its content call attention to the relative instability of that movement in works of the sonata type. It will be recalled that the minuet took its regular place in the *sinfonia* in the period after about 1760, and that it was also employed in many chamber-music works—notably in string quartets—by Haydn and Mozart. By the beginning of the nineteenth century the minuet had fallen out of favor and the Beethoven-type scherzo was substituted. Changes in the form itself then came with ever-increasing frequency. The trio of the scherzo was written in duple meter or in slow tempo; sometimes two different trios were employed, to make the form into an *ABACA* type. In Mendelssohn, then, we see further modifications of the type, for his scherzos, sometimes in ⅜ meter, are in sonata-form throughout, dispensing with the trio entirely. Later in the century the scherzo was sometimes eliminated altogether; in the symphonies and certain chamber-music works of Brahms, for example, a movement called intermezzo, containing no dance characteristics, took its place.

Mendelssohn's role in restoring Bach's music to public notice has been mentioned; his interest in Bach left its mark on his own music in many details. The most obvious, perhaps, is his use of Lutheran chorales in the larger works. The finale of the "Reformation" symphony, for example, based largely on "A Mighty Fortress Is Our God," is in effect an

A performance in the concert hall of the new Gewandhaus in Leipzig. Nine-teenth-century engraving.

extended chorale prelude. The hybrid second symphony, *Hymn of Praise,* consists of a three-movement *sinfonia* followed by a large choral move-ment in several sections, much of which is based on the chorale "Now Thank We All Our God." The C-minor piano trio, Opus 66, the D-major cello sonata, Opus 58, and other works contain movements in which a chorale is embedded. The use of chorales in the two oratorios, *St. Paul* and *Elijah,* provides further evidence of Mendelssohn's interest in this source.

Fugal writing, another aspect of Bach's style that Mendelssohn adopted, appears to a limited extent in virtually all categories of his works. Preludes and fugues exist among the keyboard compositions, especially those for the organ. There are fugues among the string quartets, notably in the set assembled under Opus 81, and fugal passages provide some of the finest moments in his choral music.

Mendelssohn's interest in the style of Bach was one aspect of the search for strikingly new means of expression which, as we have seen, typified Romanticism. The search also led him to the tentative use of what may be called nationalistic material employed for its exotic color value; old traditional Italian dances such as the tarantella and saltarello, incorpo-rated into the finale of the "Italian" symphony, provided new melodic and rhythmic idioms.

Descriptive intentions are sometimes ascribed to Mendelssohn because of the titles he gave to his concert overtures, notably *Fingal's Cave* and *Calm Sea and Prosperous Voyage.* He is not to be grouped with composers of program music, however, for these works are not actually descriptive. They are abstract forms that do no more than bear titles suggesting the source of the composer's inspiration.

Mendelssohn's style is perhaps seen to best advantage in his famous oratorio, *Elijah*. Completed in 1846, it is characterized by great formal variety; its numbers range from arias and an accompanied chorale to elaborate and extended movements that include fugal writing, sonorous choral passages and striking orchestral accompaniment. Elegance and lyricism imbue even the most dramatic moments of the oratorio, and the different textures and melodic types provide a degree of variety not always present in the instrumental works. The element of profundity enters neither the instrumental works (least of all the piano compositions) nor the oratorios, but sincerity, deep feeling, and melodiousness are found; they do much to raise *Elijah* to the favorite place it has enjoyed among singers and listeners for over a century.

Schumann

THE INFLUENCE of literature on musicians, seen in most Romantic composers, is particularly evident in the career of Robert Schumann. He was born in Zwickau, Saxony, in 1810. His father was a bookseller and publisher, and from early childhood Schumann was permitted to browse in his father's shop. An interest in Romantic literature, especially in the writings of Jean Paul and E. T. A. Hoffmann, remained strong throughout his lifetime.

Schumann received piano lessons as a child and attempted several compositions without having had any training. In his eighteenth to his twentieth years he attended the universities of Leipzig and Heidelberg (one year at each), presumably to study law in accord with his mother's wish. His interest had become centered upon a musical career, however, and he neglected his work. He began serious piano study in Leipzig with Friedrich Wieck, who eventually became his father-in-law, and studied composition as well. His career as a budding virtuoso came to an end in 1832, however, when in using a mechanical device of his own invention he permanently lamed a finger. Although he was able to play in private and to continue the practice of improvisation which had fascinated him since childhood, he was unable to perform in public, and instead he devoted himself to composition and musical journalism.

In 1834 Schumann and several associates founded a periodical, *Die Neue Zeitschrift für Musik,* and until 1844 he served as editor. Its purpose was to combat the current shallow musical taste and exhibitionism, called "philistinism" in Schumann's journalistic writings. To fight the philistines, Schumann created a *Davidsbund* ("Band of David"), the imaginary members of which peopled his mind and signed his articles. "Florestan" represented the sturdy, forthright, and vigorous aspect of Schumann's personality; "Eusebius" was the reflective, moody, and introspective dreamer; others of the *Davidsbündler* were slightly disguised personifications of his friends. The periodical eventually became influential, and Schumann may be credited with having exerted a beneficial influence on the musical culture of his time. One of his first articles was an early appreciation of Chopin, and one of his last heralded the approach of a new young genius—Johannes Brahms.[1]

In 1840, after a long courtship and despite the violent objections of his old piano teacher, Schumann married Clara Wieck, whom he had known since his student days and who had meanwhile become an outstanding pianist. She introduced much of his music on concert tours that took her to all parts of Germany and as far afield as Russia and England. The year 1840 marked an important turning point in Schumann's activity as a composer; before then he had confined himself almost entirely to piano music, but after that date he turned to songs, chamber music, orchestral works, and choral forms. He also continued his work in journalism and made many appearances as a conductor. His teaching career was less successful; in 1843 he was invited by Mendelssohn to join the faculty of the newly established Conservatory in Leipzig to teach piano and composition, but he found himself not suited to teaching and left after a year.

Schumann lived in Dresden from 1845 to 1850, then moved to Düsseldorf as musical director of the city. But signs of mental illness, which had concerned him fifteen years earlier, soon became stronger, and he was compelled to leave the Düsseldorf position in 1853. Early in 1854 he attempted suicide, and from that time onward was confined to an asylum near Bonn. Gradually he suffered a complete mental collapse, and in mid-1856 he died. A constant source of strength to Clara Schumann during the last two years of her husband's life was the young Brahms.

Compositions. The piano music to which Schumann devoted the ten years between 1830 and 1840 embraces all but six of the opus numbers from 1 to 32; the six exceptions are solo songs or part-songs. This unusual concentration on one medium resulted in about eight sets of single-movement pieces, three sonatas, and about two dozen miscellaneous compositions. Five years of composing in other media went by before he returned to solo-piano composition; then, between 1845 and about 1854, he composed another half-dozen sets of pieces and about twenty short single movements. The sets, including such well-known works as *Carnaval* (1834–1835), *Études Symphoniques* (1834), *Fantasiestücke* (1837), *Album für die Jugend* ("Album for Youth," 1848), range from three to as many as forty-three individual pieces. Among them are simple pieces less than a page in length and extended compositions of several minutes' duration, and their content is as varied as their dimensions.

During the intervening five-year period Schumann first devoted himself largely to the composition of songs. About 130 songs were written in 1840, and another hundred or more from 1841 to 1852. The majority of

---

[1] These essays, together with other selections from the *Zeitschrift*, are given in *SRMH*, pp. 827–45.

these songs were written in sets of three to twenty-eight items. Sometimes a set is given entirely to the poems of one author (Eichendorff, Chamisso, and Heine are thus represented), but more often various authors are grouped under a common opus number or title. In addition to solo songs, Schumann composed over a hundred songs for two or more voices and piano; the majority of these were written in the years about 1849–1851.

The preoccupation with songs during the year 1840 gave way in 1842 to a concentration on chamber music. Five of Schumann's eight major works were written in that year: three string quartets, a piano quartet, and a piano quintet. The combination of string quartet and piano, as represented in the latter work, had not been attempted by earlier composers; Schumann's piano quintet, Opus 44, was the first in that significant category of chamber-music works. Three piano trios followed these five works at intervals from 1847 to 1851.

The orchestral field is represented by four symphonies (1841 to 1851), a number of overtures, the well-known piano concerto (1841, revised in 1845), a cello concerto, and a few miscellaneous works. A single opera, Genoveva (1847–1850), music to a play, Manfred (1849), and more than a dozen works for chorus and orchestra conclude the list.

Style characteristics. Schumann's personality and character are reflected in virtually every work he composed; the objectivity that permits a composer to remain outside his music, so to say, was neither among his gifts nor his intentions. As a person he was warm-hearted, idealistic, sentimental, and impulsive. In the years of his mental decline the impulsiveness often became exaggerated, but the idealism did not decrease. Just as there was no exhibitionism, arrogance, or affectation in his personality, so are there no reflections of those qualities in his music. Schumann remained a poetic, imaginative, and sensitive artist in both his private and his professional life.

The musical equivalents of Schumann's personal characteristics are everywhere apparent in his music. His interest in children, for example, is reflected in the set of piano pieces *Kinderscenen* ("Scenes from Childhood"), in the *Album für die Jugend,* and in a set of twenty-eight songs composed in 1849. Many of these works are miniatures, composed simply and melodiously and representing Schumann at his best. His idealism is perhaps best seen in the piano concerto, where he had every opportunity to write with virtuosic effect; instead, he chose to cast it in a dignified and noble fashion.

It was Schumann's practice, in the great majority of his single-movement piano pieces, to devise a melodic line, a rhythmic figure, or a texture as the musical element around which the entire piece was to be constructed. A syncopated pattern, a series of broken octaves, a triplet figure, an arpeggiated chord series—these and many other distinctive elements give each piece its unity and special mood or character. Variety is achieved in these small forms by the use of a somewhat contrasting second part and occasionally by the use of a small three-part form. The pieces are perfectly proportioned and well worked out in detail; yet they give the impression of being free and spontaneous, almost in the style of improvisations.

In some of the larger forms Schumann employed the same methods of construction that marked the smaller ones, that is, reiteration of motives or figures on the one hand, and contrasts of material across short time spans on the other. These practices led to two opposite results: some such forms are tightly unified by the continuous use of the same material throughout (see EXAMPLE 169); others tend to fall into a number of con-

E X A M P L E   169

Schumann, Rhythmic motives

trasting sections, so that the feeling of unity is endangered. In still other larger forms, however, Schumann contributed a new element to formal design: the entire development, suitably transposed, was repeated after the recapitulation and made to serve in place of the coda; the result was a compound-binary version of sonata-form, thus:

EXPOSITION   DEVELOPMENT I   RECAPITULATION   DEVELOPMENT II

A   B   A^1 B^2

The nature and extent of the contrasts in the first method of construction were closely connected with one aspect of Schumann's personality. Two members of his imaginary *Davidsbund,* Florestan and Eusebius, came to play ever larger parts in his life, and their presence was reflected in his music. As we have seen, Florestan represented vigor, animation, and strength, while Eusebius was quiet, meditative, and withdrawn; they are depicted in respective sections of the *Carnaval* set, Opus 9 (see EXAMPLE 170). These two characters personified the two aspects of Schumann's creative personality that often contrast at close range in Schumann's larger works. An intimate, dreamlike passage is suddenly interrupted by a few sharply accented measures, as in the first movement of the D-minor piano trio; or a roughly exuberant movement gives way to a lyric passage for only a few measures, as in the finale of the A-minor string quartet. Such abrupt contrasts, which became more numerous as Schumann neared the end of his career, give evidence that the other aspect of his creative personality had momentarily become dominant. Further, they suggest

EXAMPLE 170

Schumann, *Carnaval*, Op. 9

that the impulsive quality of much of Schumann's music is related to the conflict of personalities that marked his life.

The songs of Schumann, like the smaller piano pieces, contain some of his happiest inspirations. Strictly strophic songs are rare, but songs in which a modified strophic form appears are numerous. Often the middle strophe of the text is set in a contrasting key or otherwise altered. Through-composed songs are in the majority, however, and they exhibit a close relationship between text and music. To an even greater extent than in Schubert, the piano part plays a crucial role in suggesting the mood of the song. Many of Schumann's most eloquent melodies are found in the numerous introductions and postludes. The variety of moods contained in the songs reflects the whole range of Romantic poetry. Delicate masterpieces such as *Mondnacht* ("Night of Moon") stand opposite passionate outpourings such as *Ich grolle nicht* ("I Resent Not"). Cheerfully sentimental songs, *Sonntags am Rhein* ("Sunday on the Rhine"), for example, contrast with stirring patriotic songs, of which *Die beiden Grenadiere* ("The Two Grenadiers") is the best known. As in the piano pieces, the mood of each song is set by a distinctive rhythmic figure, lyric fragment, or textural type. The refined spinning-out of that detail works magically to suggest the atmosphere of the text.

One outstanding stylistic element in Schumann's instrumental music is his rhythmic subtlety, employed primarily in veiled or dreamy passages. Syncopations, accented weak beats, empty beats, and what may be called a counterpoint of rhythms—these devices are combined in imaginative ways to bring about the temporary clouding-over of the rhythmic pulse. Sometimes an entire movement is constructed on the basis of such devices, such as the slow movement of the D-minor trio (see EXAMPLE 171);

EXAMPLE 171

Schumann, Trio, Op. 63

at other times a short passage of this sort is introduced in an otherwise clear rhythmic texture, and the momentary presence of Eusebius is felt.

Cyclical form principles appear at times in the songs and in the piano pieces. For example, the postlude to the last song in the *Frauenliebe* cycle, Opus 42, contains material with which the first song begins, and certain of the themes of the *Waldscenen* ("Woodland Scenes") show subtle relationships to each other. In the D-minor symphony, Opus 120, however, cyclical form is employed in concentrated fashion, and a work that is unique in the nineteenth century results. In addition to the usual four movements, the symphony contains a slow introduction to the first movement and an extended transitional passage in slow tempo between the scherzo and the finale. Schumann directed that all movements be connected in performance (as did Mendelssohn in his "Scotch" symphony); in recognition of this detail, he originally called the work a "symphonic fantasy." More than mere mechanical connection is involved here, however, for the several movements are thematically related to an extreme degree. Two motives appear in the introduction (see EXAMPLE 172*a* and 172*b*); they are themselves related, and they contain the material out of

EXAMPLE 172

Schumann, Symphony No. 4, Op. 120

which a large part of the thematic and transitional material of the symphony is derived. The first and second themes of the first movement, as well as the main theme of the finale and the transition leading to it, are all based on EXAMPLE 172*b*. Conversely, themes in the second movement and scherzo are derived from 172*a*. Since the motives are themselves related, a concentrated, highly unified work results.

Schumann in effect transformed the four-movement symphony into a continuous, multisectioned work having a single set of themes. In so doing he unwittingly laid the groundwork for the programmatic symphonic poem. Liszt employed a form closely analogous to that of Schumann's fourth symphony after about 1850; details will appear in a later chapter. Schumann's contact with the programmatic tendency is slight, however. His many mood pieces for piano bear identifying names in most cases, it is true, but attempts at musical descriptions of objects outside music find little or no place in his work. Schumann represents Romanticism in its purest form. Enthusiasm, novelty, subjectivity, and eloquent lyricism —these are the essential elements out of which his music is compounded.

Brahms

THE FIRST three decades of the Romantic period saw many composers stimulated by and preoccupied with things outside music. The influence of literature on music grew stronger; some composers sought inspiration in legend, folklore, and mythology. Program music came into fashion, and a composition was expected to have "meaning" derived from its program. As a result, the forms inherited from the Classical period were modified almost to the point of extinction, and the position of abstract music threatened to decline.

Johannes Brahms consciously and deliberately set himself against these trends and espoused a kind of music that was organized according to musical laws only. He became the major exponent of the trend towards restoration of Classical restraint and balance and objective writing. Brahms was born in Hamburg in 1833, the son of a bass player. He began to study piano at an early age, and in his fourteenth year he was able to give a public recital. Up to about 1853 he made a precarious living by playing in the taverns of Hamburg, but his main interest, even in his formative years, was in composition. He was fortunate in having a competent local musician, Eduard Marxsen, as a teacher and later expressed his gratitude for the excellent instruction he had obtained by dedicating his second piano concerto to him.

In 1853, during the course of a tour with Eduard Remenyi, a Hungarian violinist, Brahms met Liszt, Joachim, and Schumann. It was after this meeting that Schumann wrote the prophetic article about the young Brahms. The latter felt the responsibility keenly; he composed carefully and slowly and developed a ruthless sense of self-criticism that remained characteristic throughout his career. For about ten years after 1853 he continued to live in Hamburg, but he also occupied a minor position as a conductor at Detmold and traveled about Germany as a pianist. In

1863 he conducted the concerts of the Vienna Singakademie but left the position after a year. Vienna became his permanent home, however, and in spite of continued travel he always returned there. Except for a brief period (1872–1875) as musical director of the Gesellschaft der Musikfreunde, he supported himself as a professional pianist, conductor, and composer.

Brahms' life was externally uneventful. He composed industriously, and as his reputation as a composer steadily grew, he was in demand as a conductor of his own works. Twice offered an honorary degree by Cambridge University, he refused out of fear of the Channel crossing. Breslau University's offer of a degree was accepted in 1879, however, and for the occasion Brahms composed the *Academic Festival* overture. He continued composing to 1896, the last works being *Vier ernste Gesänge* ("Four Serious Songs") and a set of eleven chorale preludes for the organ. He died in 1897, at the age of sixty-four.

Brahms enjoyed many warm friendships, particularly with Joseph Joachim and Clara Schumann; but his sensitive nature, masked by external gruffness, often led him to misunderstand and alienate his friends. He lived an essentially lonely life and took no part in the action of various partisans of his music, who sought to establish him as the leader of an anti-Wagner party. His music was often attacked for its conservative, abstract nature, and violent diatribes against him were written. He re-

Brahms at the
piano. Caricature
by Von Beckerath.

mained outwardly untouched by all such matters, however, and composed in his chosen style out of inner conviction. His sense of self-criticism was matched by his thoughtful approach to composition. There is little evidence of impulsiveness in his work. His music is the result of imagination coupled with flawless technique and colored by moderation and good taste. As a consequence, there are probably fewer unsuccessful or unsatisfactory works in Brahms than in any other major composer.

Compositions. By his twenty-first year (1854) Brahms had completed about a dozen of the opus numbers he deemed worthy of publication. The earliest of those works (Opus 1, 2, and 5) are the three piano sonatas that Schumann admired sufficiently to recommend to a publisher; there are also some piano ballades and sets of variations—all written before about 1856. After a five-year lapse, Brahms turned to the piano again to write the well-known sets of variations on themes by Handel and Paganini. Then followed a fifteen-year gap, after which ten intermezzos, caprices, and rhapsodies were completed about 1878–1879. And after another gap of twelve years, the remainder of the single-movement pieces for piano were written.

The field of chamber music, by contrast, was cultivated with great regularity from about 1853 to 1894. Twenty-four works are in this group, including three sonatas for violin, two for cello, and two for clarinet (all with piano); five piano trios (one with clarinet), three piano quartets and one piano quintet; three string quartets, three string quintets (one with clarinet), and two sextets. The first piano trio, Opus 8, from about 1853, was rewritten about 1890. The two versions reveal the changes in temperament Brahms had undergone, but they also demonstrate the basic consistency of his style across the forty-year interval.

The orchestral works form an early and a late group. Brahms' first piano concerto and two serenades for small orchestra were composed before 1858. Fifteen years later he turned again to the orchestral field to compose the *Variations on a Theme by Haydn.* During much of that interval he had been working on his first symphony (Clara Schumann had seen an early version of the first movement in 1862), but the work was not completed until 1876. The rest of the orchestral works—three additional symphonies, the violin concerto, two overtures, the second piano concerto, and the double concerto for violin and cello—were all composed in the ten-year period between 1877 and 1887.

Brahms' major choral works fall relatively early in his career. The famous *Deutsches Requiem* was begun in 1857 and completed in 1868. The cantata *Rinaldo* was finished in the latter year, after which three additional major works were composed: the Rhapsody for Alto and Men's Chorus, the *Schicksalslied* ("Song of Destiny"), and the *Triumphlied* ("Song of Triumph")—all between 1869 and 1871. The last two large choral works, *Nänie* and *Gesang der Parzen* ("Song of the Fates") were written about 1880–1882. The majority of the smaller compositions for unaccompanied chorus as well as the vocal duets and quartets with piano accompaniment—about two hundred items in all—fall in the period

1858–1875 and reflect Brahms' activity as conductor of three different singing societies.

One major category remains, namely the songs with piano accompaniment. More than two hundred songs are spread rather uniformly across Brahms' forty-odd years of composing. Three sets were composed before 1853, the last in 1896. Only two or three of the more than thirty sets of songs contain texts by one author. The great majority of the sets are short, ranging from four to six songs. They are not song cycles of the kind Schubert and Schumann composed; the relationship of the songs to each other must be found in their mood content.

Brahms was not among the most prolific composers of the time. His method of working slowly and carefully and his habit of destroying or rewriting whatever did not measure up to his high standard are probably responsible. The result is a body of music that can be grasped as a whole. The outstanding impression is of a style that is consistent throughout in spite of a great variety of mood content. The stylistic factors that distinguish Brahms' music are perceptible in his earliest works as well as in his latest.

Style characteristics. The forms that the Classical composers had brought to perfection were the forms to which Brahms dedicated himself. Sonata-form found its last great exponent in him; almost alone among the Romanticists, he understood that the essential problem of sonata-form was dramatic conflict. Thus the form in his hands became again a balanced three-part structure in which the development section was the scene of the interplay of contrasting materials. With only one or two exceptions, the large instrumental works begin with this form. Yet even from the outset of his career Brahms showed originality and keen judgment in modifying the form to suit the needs of his thematic material.

Some of Brahms' most significant and expressive music is found in the variation forms. Early in his career sets of variations for piano had shown his mastery of the technique, and his first thoroughly successful work for orchestra was the set of variations on a Haydn theme. Sets of variations had appeared in many of the multimovement works as well—as early as the string sextet, Opus 18, and as late as the clarinet quintet, Opus 115. Brahms generally avoided the style of figural variation, in which ornamentation of the melody is the principal device, and wrote instead in the character-variation style, in which one element of the theme is abstracted to form the basis of each variation. Thus, in the "Haydn" variations, the theme ends with a five-times-reiterated chord; the sequence of five tones is developed to constitute the first variation. Similarly, the theme begins with a three-note pattern on the tones D-E♭-D; that figure is developed in the second variation. Later variations are constructed in like fashion.

Scherzos are in general found only in the sonatas and chamber-music works; among the orchestral compositions of the late group, only the second piano concerto contains a true scherzo. Elsewhere, in place of that movement Brahms devised a form that takes on the character of an intermezzo. Not based on dance rhythms, it is usually a sectional form with thematic connections between the various parts; and it contains moods that contrast greatly with the moods of the other movements. These intermezzos, in the first three symphonies, provide the most intimate and relaxed moments in the respective works. It may be surmised that, given his tendency toward moderation and proportion, Brahms felt that with the intensity and rhythmic drive of the other symphonic movements, any added intensity and drive in a scherzo would be out of place. He therefore composed slower, gentler movements.

Brahms was sufficiently aware of the virtues of the cyclical-form principle as a unifying device not to avoid it entirely. Slow introductions are generally thematically related to the movements that follow; this practice, derived from Schubert, is of course a tentative application of the cyclical principle. He did not often go much further; the few exceptions that come to mind are found in the *Deutsches Requiem,* the third string quartet, Opus 67, the third symphony, and the clarinet quintet. In each of these cases the work closes with a thematic reminiscence of the opening theme of the work. A degree of external symmetry is thus achieved without violating the integrity of the individual movements.

Themes and melodic types in Brahms' music are of the most diverse kind; yet they have many elements in common. Whether lyric or dramatic in character, they usually contain a short recurring element—a melodic turn, an interval, a rhythmic pattern—that unifies the melody no matter how greatly it is extended. Brahms' very first chamber-music composition shows the device to perfection (see EXAMPLE 173). Here two

EXAMPLE 173

Brahms. Piano Trio, Op. 8

recurring elements, a chord tone preceded by an upbeat and a short ascending diatonic pattern (marked *a* and *b* in the example), give organization and unity to the long melody.

Brahms' melodies are very often cast in irregular lengths. While four- and eight-measure phrases do occur, phrases of five, seven, or any number of measures are equally common. Often the irregular length is the result of an insert—an additional measure embodied in the phrase to provide emphasis or climax. Or it may result from an extension at the end of the phrase. Further, his melodies often have no true endings; that is to say, they are absorbed into the contrapuntal textures in such a way that one cannot with certainty determine where the phrase has ended.

Rhythmic practices are of an imaginative and individual kind. Possibly influenced to some extent by Schumann, Brahms often wrote phrases that are unmetrical within themselves even though placed in metrical contexts (see EXAMPLE 174). At other times a phrase is placed above a

EXAMPLE 174

Brahms, String Quartet, Op. 51, No. 1

EXAMPLE 175

Brahms, Symphony No. 1, Op. 68

syncopated accompaniment in such a way that the expected strong beats are momentarily obscured in the interest of creating rhythmic conflict (see EXAMPLE 175). Another common practice leads to a counterpoint of rhythms. For example, a regularly recurring rhythmic figure in one hand of a piano part may be set in opposition to a line of syncopations in the other (see EXAMPLE 176*a*). Again, a figure may be divided between two or more voices (176*b*); or it may appear in close imitation in various voices (176*c*). Passages of this kind, alternating with passages in which the rhythms are clear and straightforward, do much to give his music its tremendous vitality and fascination.

EXAMPLE 176

Brahms, Rhythmic types

A page from autograph score of Brahms' Piano Concerto, Op. 83.

Brahms' use of these rhythmic constructions, which are the result of thought and calculation, is in keeping with his general approach to the process of composing. To a greater extent than any other musician of the period, he placed his intellect at the service of his craft. Many of his most effective passages come about through conscious manipulation. For example, a melody in the first five measures of the allegretto of the first symphony is simply inverted to form the next five measures. The chords (in the woodwind instruments) that accompany the first theme of the fourth symphony generate a contour identical with that of the theme itself. A tenor countermelody in the second movement of the *Requiem* is set in notes twice as long as those of the soprano phrase directly above it but in the same contour. Such passages, which can be found virtually anywhere in Brahms' larger works, are the result of contrivance, in the best sense of the word. They reveal his concern with the smallest detail and his intention to make his works organic entities. As a consequence, there are few rootless and "inspired" excursions in his music; there are even fewer passages that are not firmly related to the context in which they appear.

The choral works are constructed according to the same principles, with the same care and the same logic, as the instrumental compositions. What has been said about Brahms' melodic types, his rhythmic practices, and his methods of thematic development apply in equal measure to the *Requiem* and the *Schicksalslied,* for example. In addition, however, these works are so composed that the moods of the respective texts are observed and honored. As a consequence, changes of emotional tone and degrees of contrast are often even greater than in the instrumental works. The dark orchestral accompaniment at times supports the voices, at times establishes moods, and at times transcends the textual content. The *Requiem* was one of the works that first brought Brahms to fame, and it remains one of the most expressive and eloquent compositions in the entire choral field.

In his songs Brahms took Schubert as a model. Although the piano part in general is appropriate to the text it supports, it seldom attempts to establish a mood. Thus the tendency to raise the piano accompaniment to a dominant place in the art song was temporarily halted. Many of the songs are cast in modified strophic form, with the accompaniment appropriately altered in successive strophes, and many are through-composed. Only a few are of the declamatory type that Schubert and Schumann favored. In his selection of texts Brahms seems to have indulged his Romantic temperament to a large extent, for many of the texts deal with love's problems and are melancholy in tone.

The stylistic traits discussed in the foregoing pages are in general applicable to all of Brahms' works, although perhaps in differing degrees and in different periods. Lyric melodies, for example, are common in the early works and are evidence of the Romantic exuberance with which he approached his task. Toward the 1870's he became somewhat more restrained and composed with greater economy. Thereupon the broad and expansive lyricism became somewhat less dominant, and the melodic type based on recurring elements is found more often. Similarly, while rhythmic complexity is found even in his earliest works, it becomes more common and is regularly to be expected in compositions after the middle period of his career.

These differences of degree are not to be taken as representing a change of style. Early in his career Brahms turned his attention toward the music of his great predecessors and sought to revitalize the old forms and preserve the old aesthetic attitudes. He remained steadfast in that purpose, which is reflected in his musical style, and therefore he felt neither a need nor a desire to modify his way of writing.

In spite of his veneration of the past, Brahms could not deny his Romantic environment. New standards of orchestral sonority and color, harmonic practices that had arisen primarily from the works of Schubert, Schumann and Chopin, and other Romantic elements became parts of Brahms' style. Together with his interest in smaller forms, in folksongs, and in the expression of the darker emotions, they testify to his active presence within the Romantic period. It is chiefly in his espousal of the objective, Classical approach to composition and in his refusal to let himself be diverted by Romantic literature in his expression of emotional states that he stands outside and above his own period.

৩৯ 24 ৫৩

The Romantic Period: Program Music

THE PREVIOUS chapter was devoted to composers who wrote primarily in the field of abstract music—music that is based on musical laws only, has no external meaning, and seeks to be understood on its own terms. In the sense that the principle of abstract music was a heritage from the Classical period, the composers who adhered to it may be considered to represent a conservative tendency.

Parallel to those composers was another group who abandoned their Classical heritage by seeking new forms, new types of content, or new modes of expression. These composers may be considered experimental or radical in their outlook. As typical Romanticists, they often sought musical inspiration in the fields of literature, mythology, or history. Their

Cartoon of Berlioz conducting, by Andreas Geiger, after a cartoon by Grandville, 1846. [REPRODUCED FROM *An Illustrated History of Music,* BY MARC PINCHERLE, PUBLISHED BY REYNAL & CO.]

music, as a consequence, was often cast in forms or idioms that were unfamiliar to listeners of the time. Many such listeners, especially in France, required some explanation or interpretation of the new music, preferably couched in poetic or narrative terms. It became fashionable, therefore, for composers to indicate the source of their inspiration by giving the work an appropriate title and sometimes by furnishing a detailed explanation or "program" in addition.

Several French composers cannot easily be classified. César Franck adopted certain of the technical procedures of the programmatic school though he seldom composed descriptive music; Camille Saint-Saëns wrote in both fields with equal facility; and Gabriel Fauré composed in traditional forms with a highly individualized harmonic idiom that bore little relationship to the idiom of either group. The music of these composers will be discussed in this chapter even though its relationship to program music is tenuous at best.

Thus during the Romantic period program music, abstract music, and a mixture of the two flourished side by side. It should be emphasized, however, that the program in works of the first type was often written after the music had been composed and the two were joined only to satisfy the listener. Further, it was understood to apply to the music only in general terms, and was not to be taken literally. Franz Liszt, one of the most important musicians of this group, was quite explicit on this point: "It is not without value . . . for the composer to give in a brief sketch the spirit of his work and, without a lengthy explanation, to recount the idea which is basic to his composition." [1] Thus, the attempts of many writers and listeners to find in the music exact illustrations of extramusical objects or events are doomed to failure.

Program music had existed long before the Romantic period, of course. Ancient liturgical music contained many symbolical representations of items or ideas connected with the Divine service. Renaissance composers in their "word painting" sought to suggest musical equivalents of thoughts expressed in their texts. Baroque and Classical composers had worked in like fashion, employing the concept of program music on occasions when it suited their expressive purposes.

In the Romantic period, however, those who used it did so rather generally and in concentrated fashion. The principal composers who represent this trend were either French or associated with French culture; the names of Berlioz and Liszt loom largest, and Franck and Saint-Saëns, among many others, were stylistically indebted to them.

Berlioz

HECTOR BERLIOZ (1803–1869) the son of a physician, began the study of medicine in Paris in 1821 but soon abandoned that field in favor of music. His early training had been sparse; he had acquired some proficiency on the flute and guitar and some familiarity with the piano, but

1 Liszt, *Gesammelte Schriften,* I, page 130.

little more. In Paris, nevertheless, he entered the Conservatoire, where he studied with Antonin Reicha and Jean-François Le Sueur. Even as a student his musical ideas were grandiose; in 1825 he arranged to have his early Mass performed with an orchestra of about 150 players.

About 1828 he became infatuated with an Irish actress, Harriet Smithson, who at first ignored him and later (in 1833) married him. In 1830, after two failures to win the Prix de Rome, he was awarded the coveted prize which carried with it the opportunity of living in Rome for two years. He returned to Paris late in 1832, and in 1835 was appointed as music critic to the influential *Journal des Débats*. He kept that post for almost thirty years, until about 1864, and became widely known for his discerning writings as well as for his unconventional compositions, which emerged at regular intervals up to about 1860.

Meanwhile he traveled widely as a conductor of his own works, touring much of Germany and visiting England, Austria, Italy, and Russia. He made several trips to Weimar, where Liszt championed his music, and in general he seems to have been better received in Germany than in France. He died in 1869, at the age of sixty-six.

Compositions. The compositions that reveal the full extent of Berlioz' genius and the nature of his musical innovations are primarily in the orchestral field. The earliest is the *Symphonie fantastique,* composed in 1828–1830, at the height of his infatuation with Harriet Smithson. A sequel to that work, entitled *Lélio,* for orchestra and chorus, has been forgotten. The next major work, for orchestra and viola obbligato, was *Harold en Italie* (1834), based on Byron's *Childe Harold* and composed for Paganini, who, however, never played the solo part. Following this came a work that Berlioz called a "dramatic symphony," *Roméo et Juliette* (1839). It is in three large parts, each divided into several sections, some for orchestra (one of which is the famous "Queen Mab" scherzo), some for chorus or solo voices. The text was arranged by Berlioz himself from Shakespeare's play.

Among the more orthodox choral works are the enormous Requiem Mass (1837) for tenor, chorus, orchestra, and band; *La Damnation de Faust* (1846), for solo voices, chorus, and orchestra, cast somewhat in the form of a cantata or even a concert opera; a *Te Deum* (1849), requiring even larger forces (three choirs) than the Requiem Mass; and a small, intimate oratorio, *L'Enfance du Christ* (1854). Three operas, which were discussed in Chapter 22, several overtures, and a variety of miscellaneous works conclude the list.

Style characteristics. Berlioz' chief contributions to Romantic music are a new ideal of orchestral sound coupled with orchestral virtuosity and a structural device, named by him *idée fixe* (which may be translated roughly in musical terms as "recurring melody"), that served to unify whatever large work in which it was used. The *idée fixe* made its first appearance in the *Symphonie fantastique;* according to Berlioz' program for this work, the *idée fixe* is a symbol for the beloved one who haunts the dreams of a young musician; the latter has taken opium because of unrequited love. The five movements of the symphony are explained as representing various visions and imaginary experiences the hero undergoes during the course of his dreams. The *idée fixe,* heard either in its full length or appropriately modified or shortened in the several movements, serves to tie together the widely contrasting contents of the work (see EXAMPLE 177).

EXAMPLE 177

Berlioz, *Symphonie fantastique*

The same device is used in *Harold en Italie.* Here it is given to the solo viola; that instrument is placed "in the midst of poetic memories left by my wanderings in the Abruzzi, to serve as a kind of melancholy dreamer in the manner of Byron's 'Childe Harold'." Berlioz' program here is confined to the titles of the four movements: "Harold in the Mountains," "March of the Pilgrims," "Serenade," and "Orgy of the Brigands." It was clearly Berlioz' intention that these two symphonies be listened to as music, independently of the programs. The forms bear relationships to Classical forms: themes (other than the *idée fixe,* which runs its course largely apart from the main themes of the respective movements) are expanded, manipulated, and often recapitulated in the general manner of sonata-form and other abstract forms.

The real element of novelty in these compositions, then, is their orchestral sound, and in this area Berlioz revealed complete mastery. English horn, E♭ clarinet, harp, and tympani were given prominent parts to a degree unknown earlier. In addition, instruments were combined in new ways, employed in unusual ranges, and given unusual functions. The *Symphonie fantastique* provides numerous examples: the end of the third movement ("Scenes in the Country"), for instance, is scored for English

horn and four tympani, while the beginning of the fourth movement
("March to the Gallows") contains a passage for horns and bassoons in
the low register and two tympani, with cellos and basses (the latter in
a fourfold division) playing pizzicato. Even in passages that are conven-
tionally scored, rapid changes of dynamics, sudden changes of texture,
and an unusual balance of tone produce a new sound. A single two-meas-
ure passage in the introduction of the *Symphonie fantastique* is marked
as follows: |mf > pp <|ff ppp. Virtually every page in this work con-
tains examples of Berlioz' flexible and imaginative scoring. Other works
provide even more colorful sound. The addition of four brass bands separated spatially from the orchestra in the Requiem Mass, the use of three
choirs in the *Te Deum*—such factors create overwhelming, almost un-
bearable tension through sheer dynamic range.

Berlioz' melodies, not eloquent in themselves, owe much of their effectiveness to their rhythmic shape and to the way they are often expanded
into phrases of unusual length (see EXAMPLE 178). The harmonies under-

EXAMPLE 178

Berlioz, *Roméo et Juliette*

lying the long melodic periods give adequate support, but they are not
distinguished by subtlety or even great resourcefulness. These negative
characteristics, however, are virtually lost sight of under the spell of
Berlioz' rhythmic drive and exciting contrasts. Whether in the overtures, the symphonies, or elsewhere, the climaxes are overwhelming.
Rhythmic figures are repeated at ever higher dynamic levels, and the
orchestral sound is unfailingly brilliant; the result is a kind of music in
which a new concept of sound is substituted for the Classical concepts
of form and structural logic. Berlioz cannot be compared to other composers—either his predecessors or his contemporaries. He envisaged a
gigantic tonal world and sought to make it audible through the means
available to him. His use of existing forms and his occasional difficulty
in mastering them give evidence only that his imagination was in advance
of his technique.

Liszt

THE PROCESS of creating a new form suited to the aesthetic philosophy of program music was completed by Franz Liszt (1811–1886). Born in Hungary, Liszt was a precocious pianist. He was taken to Vienna in his tenth year and studied piano with Carl Czerny and composition with Salieri. In 1823 Liszt went to Paris to enter the Conservatoire, but he was refused admission because of his youthfulness. He continued the study of composition privately and, without instruction, developed a fabulous pianistic skill. From his sixteenth year he supported himself as a concert pianist. An encounter with Paganini in 1831 inspired him to achieve unheard-of feats at the keyboard, and he developed a quality of virtuosity that has probably not been equaled to the present day.

His large-scale concert tours began in 1839 and covered literally all of Europe, from England to Russia and from Portugal to Turkey, with

Liszt conducting a choral festival in Budapest, 1865. Wood engraving after a drawing by J. Reve.

phenomenal success. In spite of his devotion to the highest ideals he performed many transcriptions of dubious value: operatic arias, songs of Schubert, symphonic movements, and the like. The tours lasted until 1848, when Liszt virtually retired from the concert stage to become conductor at the court of Weimar. He showed great generosity to other musicians and gave strong support to the cause of contemporary music up to 1859, when he left Weimar to take up residence in Rome. There, in 1865, he became a secular priest and later was made an abbé.

In 1870 he returned to Weimar to conduct the Beethoven centennial festival, and from that year to his death in 1886 he lived in Weimar, Rome, and Budapest alternately. Honored as one of the greatest musicians of the time, venerated for his selfless devotion to the furthering of other men's music, and sought out as a teacher, Liszt remained professionally occupied to the very end of his life.

The principal works of Liszt may be grouped in four categories: (1) original compositions for piano; (2) arrangements and transcriptions for piano of songs, orchestral works, and symphonies; (3) orchestral works, including two piano concertos, about a dozen symphonic poems, and two symphonies; and (4) a large number of other compositions, including two oratorios and many choral works, songs, and the like.

The original piano compositions reflect the tremendous virtuosity of which Liszt was capable. Employing the full range of the keyboard, they require complete independence of the fingers and control of every other technical element. Hand crossings, tremolos in inner parts below a legato melody in the upper part, extended passages in thirds, sixths, and octaves, wide-ranging arpeggios, heavy chordal passages—these are some of the technical devices Liszt brings into play (see EXAMPLE 179).

A typical example of Liszt's procedures is found in the set called *Études d'exécution transcendante* ("studies of transcendental execution"). Based on a set of studies composed in 1827 as Opus 1, they were twice revised and expanded before reaching their final form in 1851. Each of the twelve studies elaborates one or two technical devices, usually in free form in the manner of an improvisation. The individual pieces are more than technical studies, however; each one has mood qualities and poetic content, and ten of the twelve are given descriptive titles. The latter include *Paysage* ("Landscape"), *Feux follets* ("Will-o'-the-wisps"), *Wilde Jagd* ("Wild Hunt"), and *Ricordanza* ("Remembrance"); the mixture of French, German, and Italian in the titles casts a revealing light on the international aspect of Liszt's life and thinking. Finally, the set also includes an extended piece called *Mazeppa;* inspired by a poem of Victor Hugo, it eventually became the sixth of Liszt's symphonic poems.

Other piano works include three sets of pieces called *Années de pèlerinage* ("Years of Pilgrimage"); the individual pieces in the sets are based on or inspired by folk songs, poems, landscapes, and the like. The virtuosic devices found in the *Études* are also present in the *Années* sets, and the air of unfailing brilliance that surrounds Liszt's other piano music is present here in full measure. A large number of pieces based on national melodies, including the nineteen *Hungarian Rhapsodies,* are free in

EXAMPLE 179

Liszt, *Étude transcendante,* No. 6 ("Vision")

form; each usually contains several sections of a czardas, often in contrasting tempos, in which the various tunes are brilliantly elaborated with all manner of virtuosic devices.

In his many transcriptions of songs and operatic arias, Liszt gave his gifts of improvisation free play. These works, together with Liszt's original compositions, virtually exhausted the technical possibilities of the piano. The earlier works are overelaborate and often superficial in musical content; they represent the spectacular side of Liszt's nature. Later works, notably the *Legend, St. Francis of Assisi,* the Variations on a theme by

Bach, and a few works from the 1880's, show Liszt in a dark and serious mood and bring to full expression the sensitive, subtle, chromatic harmony that was of lasting influence on later composers.

A major innovation was introduced by Liszt in a number of his orchestral works, in his B-minor piano sonata, and to a lesser extent in his two piano concertos—namely, the principle of theme transformation. Works constructed under this principle are usually in sectional form (although in a few cases the device is used in compositions with several movements); the sections are linked together by one theme, which is appropriately modified or transformed to conform to the tempo, mood, and texture of the respective sections.

Liszt's principle is in a sense an expansion of the cyclical-form principle and is related to Berlioz' principle of the *idée fixe*. It comes to clearest expression in the twelve orchestral compositions for which he invented the name *symphonische Dichtung* ("symphonic poem"). The symphonic poem, in a typical case, is a new form whose genesis is seen in the D-minor symphony of Schumann (see page 479). Its several sections, in contrasting tempo and mood, suggest that the various movements of a symphony have been compressed, connected, and given thematic material in common. Transitions between the principal sections also occur, as well as passages which serve as introduction and sometimes epilogue. Thus one may expect to find from five to eight or more sections, each with a characteristic mood or texture and each with its individual transformation of the theme that is the main element of unity in the composition.

The twelve symphonic poems were composed between 1848 and 1857. Many of them, first orchestrated by Joachim Raff, were enlarged, rewritten, or otherwise altered before attaining their final form at Liszt's hand. Several were originally designed for some other function and only later achieved the status of symphonic poems. *Les Préludes,* perhaps the best-known work of the set, is typical; in its first version it was the introduction to a composition for chorus and piano entitled *Les quatre élémens* ("The Four Elements"), and only later was it enlarged, at which time the present title and a fragment of a poem by Lamartine were fitted to it. Similarly, *Hamlet* was originally designed as a musical prologue to Shakespeare's play, and *Tasso* was meant to serve the same function for a play by Goethe. These facts go far to strengthen the statement that the symphonic poem of Liszt was programmatic in a general sense only and did not contain musical descriptions of specific objects or ideas.

In the best-known of Liszt's two symphonies, *Eine Faust Symphonie,* the form of the symphonic poem as well as the device of theme transformation are applied. The "Faust" theme of the first movement is eloquently transformed in the second movement, entitled "Gretchen"; the third movement, "Mephistopheles," contains its own themes as well as caricatures of the "Faust" theme from the first movement and an idealized form of the "Gretchen" theme (see EXAMPLE 180). Thus the three movements are essentially three symphonic poems united under a common title and by common thematic material.

EXAMPLE 180

Liszt, *Eine Faust Symphonie*

Liszt relied heavily on the use of melodic and harmonic sequences in the majority of his works, and chromatic harmony became ever more frequent. EXAMPLE 181 shows both elements. Diatonic harmony was equally characteristic of Liszt, however, and the mixture of the two harmonic styles in works of all categories is regularly to be expected.

A direct line leads from Liszt to Wagner, who expanded the use of chromatic harmony into a system and developed the device of theme transformation into the *leitmotif* (leading motive). The creation of the symphonic poem, too, was an event of crucial importance to the history of music. A long line of composers from Franck and Smetana to Respighi and beyond employed the form, sometimes revealing an attempt to be more realistic and illustrative than Liszt had been.

In summary, Liszt occupied a most important position in the history of Romantic music. The founder of modern piano style, he introduced a number of new idioms and technical devices that became the stock-in-trade of later composers. His methods of theme transformation and his refined concept of program music influenced a large part of the later

EXAMPLE 181

Liszt, Fantasie and Fugue, *Ad nos*

orchestral literature. And in developing the symphonic poem, he devised a new form suited to the aesthetics of the nineteenth century, succeeding where Berlioz, who attempted to graft that aesthetic concept onto the form of the symphony, had failed.

In supporting and encouraging a host of his contemporaries and in making possible performances of their works, Liszt became one of the most influential figures in the development of the music of his day. His activities as a pianist were responsible for raising the general level of piano technique to a height previously unknown, and his work as a teacher aided a whole generation of pianists in attaining a high degree of musical and technical proficiency. At times his music was bombastic, merely spectacular, and even trivial, yet his sensitivity, powerful imagination, and resourcefulness in expressing deep feeling were equally evident. In his many-sided nature, in his support of every contemporary musical development, and in the mixture of sentiment and clear thinking that came to expression in his life, he represents yet another aspect of the complex Romantic musician.

Other Composers

THE STYLE represented in the orchestral field by Liszt and in the operatic field by Wagner (see Chapter 26) exerted great influence on many other composers in the last third of the Romantic period. Even those who sought to adhere to Classical forms and abstract music found themselves unable to remain aloof from the techniques and principles of the new music, and the resulting stylistic character and musical purposes became somewhat ambiguous. Perhaps the foremost of these composers was César Franck.

Franck. César Franck was born in 1822 in Liége. His excellent piano playing as a child attracted favorable attention in Belgium, and his father planned for him a career as a virtuoso. In 1835 the family moved to Paris, and young Franck entered the Conservatoire. With the exception of one year, he remained in Paris for the rest of his life.

Franck quickly became established as a pianist, organist, and teacher, and he continued the composing that had occupied him since early youth. About 1841, however, he discarded all the compositions written up to that time and wrote three piano trios which he called Opus 1. His career as a composer may thus be said to have begun in his twentieth year. In 1851, after having held a minor post as organist at one of the smaller Parisian churches, he became organist at the church of St. Jean–St. François; two years later he moved to the church of St. Clotilde as choirmaster, and in 1858 he became organist there. He remained at St. Clotilde until his death in 1890.

Franck's professional life was uneventful in the extreme: he conducted his church services, he composed, and he taught. When he was appointed teacher of organ at the Paris Conservatoire in 1872 he virtually turned his classes into composition classes, to the annoyance of the regular teachers of composition. He gathered around himself a loyal band of disciples who, in turn, influenced the course of French music well into the twentieth century. He was not taken seriously as a composer—except by his students—until the very end of his life. The few performances of his works, given in the years about 1879–1889, were generally received indifferently by the public as well as by the majority of his professional colleagues. His first success as a composer came with the performance of his string quartet in the spring of 1890, when Franck was in his sixty-eighth year. Six months later he died.

In the almost fifty years between the writing of the three piano trios, Opus 1, and the end of his life, Franck composed fewer than ninety works. They include operas, sacred and secular choral music, orchestral and chamber-music compositions, pieces for piano and for organ, and a few songs and miscellaneous works. Less than a dozen of his compositions have survived, and all of these were written during his last twelve years. Probably no composer in recent times has achieved so high a reputation on the basis of so small a quantity of music: one work for piano and orchestra, one symphony, one violin sonata, one piano quintet, one string quartet, two or three keyboard compositions, and two choral works.

Franck's approach to musical form was virtually unique in his time. Temperamentally allied to forms inherited from the Classical period, but thoroughly familiar with the ideas and practices of Berlioz and Liszt, Franck attempted a synthesis of these incompatible elements. Several of his larger works—the symphony and the three chamber-music compositions—are cast in separate movements; the string quartet even contains a scherzo with trio and recapitulation. Certain movements resemble sonata-form in their basic outlines. Yet the process at work within these movements is not theme development but theme transformation in the Lisztian manner. Further, the movements generally are marked off into sections of contrasting texture and mood, again analogous to the methods of Liszt. In addition, the cyclical principle is strongly in evidence, in that the principal thematic material from one movement often appears in another.

The melodic lines of Franck's late compositions are uniquely his own. Phrases are predominantly regular in construction—two, four, or eight measures in length—and one phrase is generally balanced by another of equal length, so that regular periods result. Melodic phrases themselves are most often tied to a single tone to which they regularly return (see

César Franck at the organ of the Church of St. Clotilde in Paris.

EXAMPLE 182). These melodies, then, are repeated sequentially in extended series of chromatic modulations. Indeed, the basic element of

EXAMPLE 182

Franck, Typical themes

Franck's harmonic style is constant mediant and submediant modulation. The restless, almost improvisational nature of his harmonies is supposedly the result of Franck's long service as a church organist, an activity in which modulation and improvisation play significant roles; his competence in his position was legendary.

The chromatic wandering typical of Franck's style seldom led to phrase extension, however; very rarely is a phrase harmonically or sequentially extended beyond its normal length. The result is a series of short sections of rich harmonic color, with cadences every two, four or eight measures; there is none of the continuity or long line generally associated with larger forms. Franck's music is episodic; its climaxes are most usually achieved by thickening of texture or by the addition of more voices or instruments, and not by rhythmic drive or cumulative pace.

It should perhaps be mentioned that Franck is included in this chapter, devoted largely to the music of Berlioz and Liszt, because of his adoption of certain of Liszt's technical devices, not because of his espousal of the program-music ideal. It is true that Franck attempted the symphonic poem on several occasions; in fact, he and Liszt independently based their first works of this kind on the same poem—namely *Ce qu'on entend sur la montagne* ("What One Hears Upon the Mountain") by Victor Hugo. One of Franck's symphonic poems, *Le Chasseur maudit* ("The Cursed Hunter"), is occasionally performed, but it is not truly representative of his style. Franck's chief interest was on the side of abstract music. The relationship to Liszt is seen more closely in Franck's use of theme transformation, sectional forms, sequential writing, and chromatic harmony.

Apart from his music, Franck exerted considerable influence as a teacher. In his time, French composers and the public generally were enamored of the opera, and the quality of French instrumental and church music had reached its lowest point. Franck directed the attention of a score of his pupils to the virtues of writing good instrumental music and gave them the necessary techniques. He stressed the value of counterpoint at a time when it had virtually disappeared from French music. By teaching and by example he exerted a beneficial influence on French music that lasted for several generations. One of Franck's foremost students, Henri Duparc (1848–1933), distinguished himself primarily as a composer of songs. The bulk of his work was completed by 1884, when Duparc retired from professional activity because of ill health. Another, Ernest Chausson (1855–1899), brought a sonorous Wagnerianism into the symphonic field, combined with subtle chromatic harmony and elegant workmanship. A third, Gabriel Pierné (1863–1937), became active as a conductor; his many works have virtually disappeared from the repertoire. Franck's most ardent disciple, Vincent d'Indy (1851–1931), became one of the most important French musicians of his time.

D'Indy. D'Indy, who spent eight years with Franck as a student of composition and organ, became infatuated with the music of Wagner. At the same time, he remained a loyal follower of Franck's precepts and employed contrapuntal textures in traditional forms. The result was a series of works that are complex in structure, large in size, and varied in content. Only a few of his many works are still performed, notably his second symphony (1903) and a work for orchestra with piano obbligato called *Symphony on a French Mountain Air* (1886).

D'Indy's influence was especially strong in the field of teaching. Along with others of Franck's pupils and a number of musicians not members of the Franck school, he became a leader in a rebirth of French musical education. One result of the joint effort was the establishment of the famous Schola Cantorum, established in 1894. Founded primarily to revive interest in Gregorian chant and Renaissance music, it soon expanded its offerings and became a potent force in raising musical standards throughout France. Choral societies and other institutions played similar roles in directing attention to other branches of musical literature; in this way Franck's pupils fulfilled the aim of their teacher and firmly established the dignity of nonoperatic music in French culture.

Saint-Saëns. Camille Saint-Saëns occupies an unusual place in the history of French music. In his long life he composed in virtually all fields, and Liszt's influence on him was strong and direct. He was an outspoken supporter of contemporary styles until about the midpoint of his career, and then he became equally strong in his conservative attitude. His technical facility as a composer was enormous, but his works are not distinguished by depth or seriousness.

Saint-Saëns was born in Paris in 1835. He showed great promise as a pianist at an early age and eventually became an outstanding performer

Saint-Saëns (piano) and Sarasate (violin) performing at a concert in the old Salle Pleyel, Paris, June 2, 1896. After a painting by J. Grigny.

on both piano and organ. From 1853 to 1877 he was a church organist in Paris, after which he toured Europe as a virtuoso pianist and conductor. He visited Russia, England, and the United States during the course of his concert tours, and in 1916, in his eighty-first year, he appeared in a number of South American cities. He remained professionally active as a conductor and composer until 1921, when he died in Algiers.

Of the more than two hundred compositions Saint-Saëns wrote across a seventy-year period from 1851 to 1921, scarcely more than a dozen have survived. In spite of his undoubted competence as a composer of vocal and piano music, the few works that are still performed are mostly in the orchestral field. The third symphony, in C minor (1886), two or three of his symphonic poems (1871–1874), several of his dozen concertos (1858–1895), and one of his operas (*Samson et Dalila,* 1877; see page 543)—these are the works for which he is still remembered.

The outstanding qualities in the music of Saint-Saëns are elegance and eclecticism. Phrases are balanced and invariably well proportioned. Emotional expression is restrained and in good taste. There are no crudities, but there are few surprises. The type of scherzo perfected by Mendelssohn is recaptured by Saint-Saëns, and many of his piano compositions recall the charm of Chopin. Solidly contrapuntal passages employing Baroque idioms stand next to passages akin to Liszt in their sonority and brilliance.

It is likely that the quality of Saint-Saëns's creative imagination was not equal to his technical prowess. Scarcely one of the surviving compositions is without a rhythmic or melodic figure that is repeated endlessly; one receives the impression that the composer was unable to progress beyond the figure he had invented, and thus had recourse only to literal repetition (see EXAMPLE 183). Yet so resourceful was he in matters of orchestration

EXAMPLE 183

Saint-Saëns, Rhythmic figures

and harmonic variety that these devices pass as stylistic idiosyncrasies rather than musical defects.

In his symphonic poems, of which *Le Rouet d'Omphale* ("The Spinning Wheel of Omphale," 1871), *Phaëton* (1873), and *Danse macabre* (1874) are the best known, Saint-Saëns adopted Liszt's form without his style. There is little of the chromatic harmony or theme transformation that are integral parts of Liszt's work and among his most important contributions to Romantic music. Saint-Saëns, even in these works, remained conservative in harmony and general idiom.

Fauré and his contemporaries. Among the host of contemporaries of Franck and Saint-Saëns, several may be mentioned briefly for their individual contributions to the various literatures. Édouard Lalo (1823–1892), French violinist and composer, is remembered especially for his *Symphonie espagnole* (1875), a violin concerto based to some extent on the rhythms of Spanish music. Lalo and Emmanuel Chabrier (1841–1894) were among the first composers to turn to Spain as a source of musical material. Chabrier's orchestral rhapsody, *España* (1883), was enormously successful and may have served to interest other composers in the exotic attractions of Spanish music. To the extent that Lalo and Chabrier continued the search for new source material, they were fulfilling their roles as Romantic composers.

Gabriel Fauré (1845–1924), a pupil of Saint-Saëns, exerted a strong influence on the development of twentieth-century music even though his own works have never been widely performed outside France. He was active as a teacher from about 1880 to 1920, his pupils including such composers as Maurice Ravel, Georges Enesco, Florent Schmitt, and the well-known teacher Nadia Boulanger, who was influential in shaping the styles of many outstanding contemporary composers of Europe and America. Primarily a lyricist, at home in the smaller forms, Fauré favored a restrained and elegant style. Five chamber-music compositions (1879 to 1924), a Requiem Mass (1887), and about a hundred songs (1865 to 1922) are his most representative works; other compositions include several stage works, many short piano pieces, sacred numbers, and others.

Fauré's great contribution to the music of his generation was a subtle, reserved, and wonderfully expressive harmonic style. At a time when many of his contemporaries adopted the richly emotional aspects of Wagner's idiom, he wrote with economy and clarity. The restricted range and great reserve of Gregorian chant are suggested by his music, and modal inflections derived from plainsong are basic to it. In a period characterized by strongly dissonant harmonies, he was content to employ major seventh chords and wide-ranging but fleeting modulations as means of achieving harmonic tension. An avoidance of the leading tone, characteristic of much of his music, is related to the underlying modal structure of his melodies. Chromaticism is often present, but the feeling of a tonal center is seldom obscured. And whatever his harmonic effect, Fauré employed it with taste and refinement.

The Romantic Period:
National Schools

I N T H I S book the history of music to about 1870 has been discussed primarily as it took place in a large, crescent-shaped area extending from
England southwest to Italy and embracing the Netherlands, France, and
Germany. The overwhelming majority of significant developments in
Western music from about the fifth century on occurred in that area.
With the turn into the last decades of the nineteenth century, however,
countries lying on the periphery of that crescent became more active
musically than before. Russia and Bohemia, for example, made concrete
contributions to the opera; these will be discussed in Chapter 26. In the
present chapter, equally significant activities in the field of instrumental
music in those and other countries will be discussed.

Several factors may account for the relatively late emergence of the
peripheral countries onto the musical scene. One factor is simply that for
many generations the musical audience in those countries favored the

Russian peasants dancing. Drawing by an unknown artist.

forms and styles in vogue in Italy, Germany, or France and were satisfied with imported compositions and composers; thus there was no demand for an indigenous music. Another factor is that several large regions (Hungary and Bohemia, for example) were essentially provinces of a dominant empire (the Austrian) and, as cultural outposts, were in no position to develop their own musical cultures. Summaries of the historical developments before about 1870 in Russia, Bohemia, and elsewhere, to be given below, will amplify this point.

After about the middle of the century political alignments in Europe changed markedly. Certain large cultural areas were united under central governments, and modern nations emerged: Italy and the German empire are examples. Some countries (Hungary, for instance) gained national stature, while others (notably Bohemia) were denied it. The feeling of nationalism, growing since the Napoleonic wars, was strengthened in countries of both types; the new nations could now look with pride on a renewal of their cultural autonomy, while the frustrated ones turned to their cultural heritage as a source of consolation.

Thus in the closing decades of the nineteenth century a number of regions began to make notable contributions to the cultural life of Europe. In the field of music, composers found inspiration and stimulation in the folk music, legends, and history of their own people, and national schools and national musical "dialects" arose to give a new variety to the field of music.

The Nationalist School in Russia

SECULAR art music played virtually no role in Russia before the end of the seventeenth century. Church music was based largely on a mixture of Byzantine and old Russian chant, called *znamenny,* and independent choral music was negligible in quantity and quality. Folk music, on the other hand, existed in extraordinary variety; it was characterized by strongly modal and Oriental inflections, irregular rhythmic patterns, and expressive content.

During the reign of Peter the Great (1672–1725), Russia was opened to influences from western Europe. For over a century thereafter Western music was imported by the court at St. Petersburg, and Italian opera became a staple of court entertainment. The long line of Italian composers who served as chapelmasters or directors of the Imperial orchestra wrote a large number of operas, ballets, and choral works in the Italian style of their respective generations. Baldassare Galuppi served in Russia from 1743 to 1748 and again from 1766 to 1768; he was followed in turn by Tommaso Traëtta, Giovanni Paisiello (who composed his famous *Barbiere di Siviglia* for Empress Catherine II), Domenico Cimarosa and others, to the very end of the eighteenth century. None of the works they composed in or for St. Petersburg made any use of indigenous materials, and consequently they had no effect on the evolution of Russian music.

In the time of Catterino Cavos (1775–1840), however, Russian folk materials began to find a place in art music. Cavos, a Venetian by birth, lived in Russia from about 1800 to his death; he was the first Italian composer to employ Russian subjects in his operas, of which the most notable is *Ivan Susanin* (1815). Twenty years later his work was amplified and completed by Mikhail Glinka, whose operas will be discussed in Chapter 26.

"The Five." In the 1860's in St. Petersburg a group of four young amateurs and one equally young professional musician did much to further Glinka's ideas and to establish Russian national music on a firm basis. The leader of the group of five was Mily Balakirev (1837–1910). Primarily a pianist, he became fired with enthusiasm for Glinka's ideals and subsequently wrote several pieces based on Russian tunes. From the study of Glinka's operas he acquired a flair for using folk idioms in orchestral contexts, and he went beyond the older composer in combining an Oriental idiom with the styles of Berlioz and Liszt.

Balakirev's principal achievement was to inspire and instruct his disciples, Alexander Borodin, César Cui, Modest Mussorgsky, and Nikolay Rimsky-Korsakov. He guided their first steps in composition, made suggestions, and even demanded changes in their works when he felt the results did not further the nationalism of which he was a fiery advocate. Much better trained in music than any of the four, he nevertheless lived to see their talents blossom and their musical accomplishments far overshadow his own.

Borodin. Alexander Borodin (1833–1887), the oldest of the group, was a student of medicine and chemistry and eventually became a prominent chemist and teacher. The demands of his scientific work kept him away from music for long intervals, and he composed slowly and carefully. His principal works are the unfinished opera *Prince Igor* (see page 545), two symphonies (1867, 1876; a third was left incomplete), a symphonic sketch called *In the Steppes of Central Asia* (1880), and two string quartets (1879, 1885). In addition, he composed about a dozen songs, some piano music, miscellaneous chamber-music pieces, and other operatic works.

While at his best as a lyricist, Borodin wrote in a variety of melodic styles. The descriptive sketch *In the Steppes* reflects an Oriental setting in its melodic outlines and skillfully suggests wide plains and remote places. His D-major string quartet, on the other hand, is written with the clarity of Mendelssohn and filled with sentimental melodies. Unlike many works by other composers of the time, his second symphony, in B minor, is based on thematic repetition rather than thematic development; yet it is exuberant, forceful, and sonorously orchestrated.

Cui. César Cui (1835–1918), of French ancestry, was a young engineering officer at the time his acquaintance with Balakirev began. Later he became an expert on military fortifications, taught at the Military Engineering Academy in St. Petersburg, and rose to the rank of Lieutenant-

General. Simultaneously, however, he wrote articles on musical subjects for Russian, Belgian, and French newspapers and was active as a music critic in St. Petersburg.

Cui was an ardent propagandist for the nationalistic music of his associates; his articles in foreign periodicals were the first to call attention to their compositions. Yet his personal taste seems to have inclined toward the music of Schumann and Liszt, and he was more French than Russian in his musical style. While he was perhaps the most prolific composer of the group, his music was to prove the least enduring.

Mussorgsky. Modest Mussorgsky (1839–1881), whose early musical training consisted only of piano lessons taken during a five- or six-year period, was a junior officer of the Guards when he met Balakirev. About 1858, having composed a few piano pieces and songs, he became fired by Balakirev's enthusiasm for the nationalist cause and resigned his commission to devote himself to music. For several years he studied music theory with Balakirev and began ambitious projects in composition only to lay them aside because of inadequate technique. From about 1863 to 1880 he intermittently held minor clerical positions in the government, composing assiduously but completing few works, and becoming increasingly addicted to alcohol. He died at forty-two of acute alcoholism.

Mussorgsky's principal works are the operas to be discussed in Chapter 26. In addition he composed about seventy songs, two or three works for chorus, about two dozen for piano, and a few orchestral compositions. The difficulty in enumerating these works precisely arises from Mussorgsky's habit of abandoning his compositions in an unfinished state,

EXAMPLE 184

Mussorgsky, Songs

[a] "The Peep Show"

Dropped from out ce - les - tial heights, a de - ni - zen of cloud - land comes to show to mor - tal minds myst' - ries that be - neath the sim - plest things are hid - den

[b] "Evening Song"

Eve-ning in si-lence falls on the fields, breeze gent-ly waft-ing cool com-fort yields.

later returning to them as source materials for other works in other media. Further, the majority of his compositions were posthumously "put in order" by Rimsky-Korsakov. The latter considered Mussorgsky's highly original and expressive harmonies the crude results of inadequate training. He therefore reharmonized and rearranged his friend's masterpieces, inserting new material of his own composition and otherwise adapting them in order to make them "acceptable" for publication and wider performance. Only in recent years have the original forms of many of Mussorgsky's compositions been made available and the qualities of his genius permitted to be seen.

Since Mussorgsky's revolutionary accomplishments in the field of opera will be treated elsewhere (see page 545), there remains only a discussion of his songs and two other compositions. The songs include three short cycles—*The Nursery* (1870), *Without Sun* (1874), and *Songs and Dances of Death* (1875–1877)—and about fifty single items, written from 1857 to 1879. Some express ironic humor and true comedy, others tragedy and grief. The broad declamatory style characteristic of the operas is found in some of the songs, while a simple folklike melodic idiom permeates others (see EXAMPLE 184). The forms are often free, following closely the forms of the texts, and the harmonies are skillfully chosen to express the varied moods. Taken as a whole, the songs reflect a clear picture of

"Ballet of the Chickens in Their Shells," one of the pictures by Victor Hartmann that inspired Mussorgsky's *Pictures from an Exhibition.*

PHOTO COURTESY ALFRED FRANKENSTEIN

Russian life and culture, and they testify to Mussorgsky's strong feeling for realism and drama.

Mussorgsky's principal work for piano is a set of descriptive pieces entitled *Pictures from an Exhibition* (1874). It includes ten short movements, each describing a picture by his friend Victor Hartmann; some of the movements are separated by a recurring "Promenade" that serves as a kind of *ritornello* to unify the composition. Extreme variety of moods characterizes the set, for the movements range from a deftly humorous "Ballet of the Chickens in Their Shells" through a mournful "Bydlo" to the spectacular "Great Gate of Kiev." The set was arranged for orchestra by Maurice Ravel in 1922 and has been widely performed in that version.

The orchestral work for which he is best known, *A Night on the Bare Mountain,* is largely the work of Rimsky-Korsakov. Mussorgsky first used the thematic material of this composition as incidental music for a play, *The Witches,* and later adapted it for use in two different operas, both left unfinished. After his death Rimsky-Korsakov reworked the material, employing the themes and general scope of the work but rearranging it in the form of a short symphonic poem. The program concerns an orgy of ghosts and witches that is brought to an end by the chiming of church bells. The work in its present form gives evidence both of Mussorgsky's macabre imagination and Rimsky-Korsakov's skill in orchestral arranging.

Rimsky-Korsakov. Nikolay Rimsky-Korsakov (1844–1908), the youngest member of the national school, went in a different direction from that of his associates. Whereas Balakirev, Borodin, and Mussorgsky turned primarily to Russian history as source material for their works, Rimsky-Korsakov found inspiration in the fields of fantasy and Russian legend; further, unlike the others, he became a successful professional composer. He entered the Imperial Naval School in St. Petersburg at the age of eighteen. Upon graduation in 1862 he was assigned to a cruise ship that remained away from Russia for almost three years, but he continued working on a symphony begun under Balakirev's direction in 1861, periodically sending it to Balakirev for correction. He completed it on his return, and it was performed as his Opus 1 in 1865.

In spite of his lack of formal training, Rimsky-Korsakov was appointed in 1871 to teach composition and orchestration at the Conservatory in St. Petersburg (founded by Anton Rubinstein in 1862), and two years later he resigned from the Navy to devote himself entirely to music. He soon made up for his insufficient training by concentrated self-study and became technically the best-equipped musician of the nationalist school. Even after giving up his naval commission he was appointed inspector of bands and orchestras in the Navy, doubtlessly adding thereby to his remarkable knowledge of instruments. He retained the naval post until 1884 but also remained active as a conductor in Russia, France, and Belgium and as a teacher in St. Petersburg until 1907, a year before his death. Among his illustrious pupils the names of Glazunov, Gretchaninov, and Stravinsky may be singled out.

In addition to composing more than a dozen operas (see page 546), Rimsky-Korsakov worked assiduously in the fields of choral, chamber, and orchestral music. Several of his orchestral works have won universal acclaim and have remained among the most brilliant compositions in the repertoire. Chief among them are his second symphony, *Antar* (1868, revised in 1897 and later called "symphonic suite"), a *Capriccio espagnol* (1887), another symphonic suite, *Scheherazade* (1888), and an overture, *The Russian Easter* (1888).

The first of these works, *Antar,* reflects Rimsky-Korsakov's interest in fantasy, for it describes episodes in the life of Antar, a legendary Arabian poet and desert hero; the Queen of the Fairies plays a role also. The work, modeled on the descriptive works of Berlioz, contains a recurring motive employed in the manner of the *idée fixe*.

In the *Capriccio espagnol* the composer sought to express a new idea in music: brilliant orchestral sound becomes the very essence of the composition rather than simply a garb for the themes. The five movements of the piece (of which the third movement is simply a note-for-note transposition and reorchestration of the first) are filled with cadenzas for various instruments, lively rhythms, and a variety of lyric melodies. It is a virtuosic piece, rising to sonorous climaxes and exploiting the color possibilities of the orchestra in brilliant fashion.

The symphonic suite *Scheherazade* is a longer and even more brilliant work than the *Capriccio*. Like *Antar,* it is based on tales from *The Arabian Nights*. Its four movements, concerned with Sinbad, the Kalendar Prince, and other legendary figures, are unified by two themes representing, respectively, the Sultan Schariar, who kills each of his wives after the first night of marriage, and Scheherazade, whose narrative ability so charms the Sultan for a thousand and one nights that he eventually abandons his murderous plan. In a modification of the technique of the *idée fixe,* the two themes, one forceful and imperious and the other suave and flowing, permeate the four movements; as the work progresses the transformation of the Sultan's harsh theme into a quiet and relaxed one subtly pictures the breakdown of his resolve.

A large amount of the thematic material contained in *Scheherazade* is derived from the two basic themes themselves. Simple thematic reiteration and sequence repetition with changed orchestration are the composer's chief technical means through long passages. In other passages lyric melodies or exciting accompanying figures are extended and repeated, again with constantly changing orchestral color. The result is a work unsurpassed in its variety of sound, and representing a virtuosic achievement in the area of orchestral writing.

On the basis of these and a few other works Rimsky-Korsakov revealed himself to be a consummate master of orchestration. His *Principles of Orchestration* (1896–1908) became a valuable textbook for generations of composers after him and showed how successfully he had studied the color possibilities of instruments alone and in combination. Yet he did not work just in the direction of brilliance and excitement, for his works also have quiet moods filled with sentiment and lyric charm. His essential character as a musician of good taste and refinement may always be sensed.

The Western School in Russia

THE NATIONALIST aspirations of Balakirev and his school, strongly supported in critical writings by an influential art critic and historian, Vladimir Stasov, were not shared by all Russian musicians. Another group of composers, many of them German-trained, emerged and set themselves in instinctive or conscious opposition to the artistic aims of the nationalist school. In contrast to the closely knit St. Petersburg school, these composers worked as individuals, most of them in Moscow, and were united only in their unspoken interest in Western culture generally—a culture largely synonymous with the German.

Alexander Serov (1820–1871), composer and government official, became the most prominent spokesman for the Western-oriented point of view, and the Rubinstein brothers were its most famous representatives in the fields of performance and teaching. Anton Rubinstein (1830–1894), a pianist of the highest quality and a prolific composer greatly esteemed in his lifetime, studied and lived in Germany and France for several years and made many tours to all parts of Europe, England, and the United States. Nikolay Rubinstein (1835–1881), also a pianist of great distinction who studied in Germany, worked primarily as a conductor and teacher in Moscow. He founded the Moscow Conservatory in 1866 and remained intimately associated with the musical life of that city during most of his career.

Tchaikovsky. Piotr (Peter) Ilich Tchaikovsky (1840–1893), the outstanding representative of the Western point of view, became one of the greatest of all Russian composers. His background resembled that of the nationalist composers, for he too arrived in St. Petersburg with little musical training and became a government clerk. His serious musical study began in his twenty-second year, when he entered the Conservatory; Anton Rubinstein was among his teachers. Four years later, in 1866, having graduated and given up his government position, he became an instructor of harmony at the newly established Moscow Conservatory under Nikolay Rubinstein. He remained in that position for about twelve years, meanwhile composing industriously and writing music cricitism for a Moscow newspaper.

In 1876, after a visit to the first Wagner festival at Bayreuth, he became acquainted with a wealthy widow, Nadezhda von Meck. Mme. von Meck admired Tchaikovsky's music, and learning about his precarious financial condition, she eventually offered him an annuity large enough to support him adequately. Now able to devote all his time to composition, he resigned his position at the Conservatory and moved about Switzerland, Italy, Germany, and Russia. He made his debut as an orchestral conductor in 1887 and thereafter undertook concert tours to

Germany, France, England, and, in 1891, the United States. In the fall of 1893 he traveled to St. Petersburg to conduct the first performance of his "Pathétique" Symphony. A week later he died, a victim of the cholera epidemic raging in the city.

Tchaikovsky worked in all the major fields of composition. Operas, ballets (see page 548), choral works, piano pieces, songs, chamber-music compositions, six symphonies, four concertos, and half a dozen descriptive pieces for orchestra are among the fruits of his constant industry applied for more than thirty years. Many of the works, especially those written before about 1870, are not representative of the mature composer and have long since been forgotten. Others were unsuccessful and were dropped even during the composer's lifetime. There remain, however, the last three symphonies (No. 4, F minor, 1877; No. 5, E minor, 1888; and No. 6, B minor, the "Pathétique," 1893), the violin concerto (D major, 1878), the first piano concerto (B♭ minor, 1875), several of the descriptive overture-fantasies, and two or three of the chamber-music works. It is on those works, along with the operas and ballets, that his fame rests securely today.

Tchaikovsky at the time of his American visit. 1891. Contemporary wood engraving, from a photograph.

CULVER PICTURES

Tchaikovsky did not entirely escape the appeal of nationalism, for two of his orchestral pieces (*Marche Slav* and *The Year 1812*) as well as much of his music for the stage are based on Russian subjects, and he quoted Russian folk material on occasion. But in general he employed Russian material in much the same way he had used Italian material (in his *Capriccio italien* and the string sextet, for example), as a flavor or exotic accent. In this respect he was a typical Romanticist rather than a nationalist, allied to the Rimsky-Korsakov of the *Capriccio espagnol*.

The orchestral works may be divided into two groups: the programmatic works, most of them cast as single movements, and the abstract works based on traditional forms. The best-known work of the first group, *Romeo and Juliet* (1869, revised 1880), is typical. It contains a slow introduction followed by a fast sonata-form with two themes, worked over both in the exposition and the development section proper, and it ends with a coda in slow tempo that refers back to the introductory material.

Three elements present in *Romeo and Juliet* are typical of Tchaikovsky's style: a vigorous, often agitated first theme (see EXAMPLE 185*a*), a mournful but eloquent second theme (185*b*), and a series of forceful run-

EXAMPLE 185

Tchaikovsky, *Romeo and Juliet*

(Condensed, and strings omitted)

ning figures extending across long passages. The third of these elements is here accompanied by a chord reiterated by all the wind instruments at irregular intervals in fast tempo and at a *fortissimo* dynamic level, to produce one of the most exciting passages in all of Tchaikovsky's works (see EXAMPLE 185c).

Tchaikovsky's abstract works are best represented by the last three symphonies, the violin concerto, and the ever popular B♭-minor piano concerto. The first movements of the symphonies are similar in form to the overture-fantasy *Romeo and Juliet;* the same type of extended development within the expositions is found, and thematic material from the introductions is generally employed in the main movements. In this respect he followed the pattern employed by many other Romantic composers.

One aspect of Tchaikovsky's themes, especially those in fast or moderate tempo, is characteristic of his works in general: the rhythmic structure is often based on syncopations, and the same type of syncopation will often mark an entire theme (see EXAMPLE 186). Much of the charm

EXAMPLE 186

Tchaikovsky, Symphonic themes

of his music is derived from the resourcefulness and imagination with which he handled the rhythmic element.

His method of manipulating themes is quite unlike that of his German contemporaries, and it has much in common with the methods of Borodin and Rimsky-Korsakov. Tchaikovsky's basic principles were reiteration and sequence repetition, often with different orchestral colors at each repetition. In a typical transitional passage he abstracted a small fragment of the theme and subjected it to the same kind of repetition that characterized thematic passages proper. EXAMPLE 187 illustrates the

EXAMPLE 187

Tchaikovsky, Symphony No. 4

method; the first three notes of the theme (compare the bracketed notes in EXAMPLE 186a) are taken out of context and repeated sequentially in a mood of growing excitement.

The moods evoked in the abstract works are identical with those found in the programmatic compositions, and it has been pointed out that the main movements of the symphonies are similar in form to the overture-fantasies. Thus an essential characteristic of Tchaikovsky's music emerges: the programs of the descriptive works apparently exerted little influence on either form or content; the feeling is justified that in programmatic and abstract works alike, he was expressing himself. The moods of his music cover a range from graceful to frenzied; individual movements may be described variously as delicate, sentimental, morbid, or hysterical.

One thing is certain, however; wherever the emotional content of the music permitted, Tchaikovsky revealed the extent of his lyric talent. Melodic eloquence is the key to his style, and an eloquent melody is usually to be expected, whatever the mood. The variety of moods, in turn, suggests that in spite of his Western orientation, Tchaikovsky could not deny his Slavic temperament. A reflective mind, a self-critical nature, and a controlled intellect were not among his strongest personal traits; but their lack is made up by honesty of expression and complete sincerity.

Bohemia

FOR MUCH of the time since the sixteenth century, music in Bohemia —or more especially in Prague, the capital of that ancient kingdom—was a reflection first of Italian music and later of Austrian. Many famous composers lived or were active in Prague, notably Philippe de Monte and Jacobus Gallus in the sixteenth century, and Mozart was a frequent visitor there in the late eighteenth. On the other hand, Bohemia produced a large number of eminent musicians of her own, some of whom returned there after being trained elsewhere (Bohuslav Czernohorsky, the teacher of Tartini, for example) and others remained in Western Europe (such as Johann Stamitz and Gustav Mahler). Until the twentieth century, however, Bohemia remained under the political rule of Austria, and Germanic musical culture dominated.

Toward the middle of the nineteenth century, the general political unrest that pervaded all of Europe took root in Bohemia and strengthened the hope of the Czechs for a restoration of their national integrity. Although political autonomy was denied them until the republic of Czecho-Slovakia was established in 1918, cultural nationalism became a potent force. A Czech Provisional Theater, founded in 1862, developed into the Czech National Theater in 1881, standing in opposition to the State theater which remained a stronghold of Germanic and Italian music.

Smetana. The outstanding musical figure of the time and the real founder of Czech national music was Bedřich Smetana (1824–1884). An excellent pianist, conductor, and composer, Smetana left Prague in 1856 because of limited opportunities there and settled in Gothenburg, Sweden, as a conductor. Several symphonic poems he composed in Gothenburg bear the stamp of Liszt and are unrelated to his later nationalistic interests. He returned to Prague in 1861 in anticipation of the opening of the Provisional Theater; he composed his Czech operas for it (see page 546) and was chief opera conductor there from 1866 to 1874.

Smetana's most representative orchestral work is a cycle of six symphonic poems. Entitled *Má vlast* ("My Country"), the cycle is based on subjects taken from Czech legend (*Vyšehrad* and *Šárka*), history (*Tábor* and *Blaník*) and topography (*The Moldau* and *From Bohemia's Fields and Groves*). Theme transformation occurs in each of the works, and each is divided into sections of contrasting tempo and texture, in a reflection of Liszt's manner. A motive representing Vyšehrad, the ancient castle of the Bohemian kings, is basic to the first symphonic poem and is quoted in the second and sixth, but the real unity of the cycle lies in the fact that all six of its components musically reflect the Czech heritage.

Dvořák. The music of Antonin Dvořák (1841–1904), who was closely associated with Smetana for two decades, transcends that of the earlier composer in variety and emotional content. Trained as a violinist and organist, Dvořák supported himself for about ten years as a viola player in the Czech Provisional Theater. He achieved local recognition as a composer in his late thirties, at which time Brahms became interested in his career and recommended him to publishers. The success of his choral works in England resulted in a number of trips to that country beginning in 1884, and his reputation as an excellent composer soon extended across Europe. From 1892 to 1895 he lived in New York as director of a conservatory and spent his vacations in a small Czech colony in Spillville, Iowa. Throughout his career he was active as a teacher and from 1891 to his death he was associated with the Prague Conservatory. He died in 1904, esteemed as one of the foremost composers of the nineteenth century.

A number of different influences came to bear on Dvořák at various stages in his career. His larger instrumental works were modeled on forms inherited from the Classical period, and his concern with musical organization and eloquent lyricism reflects the styles of Beethoven and Schubert, respectively. His close association with Smetana in the 1870's may be responsible for his turn to nationalistic material, seen in his four *Slavonic Rhapsodies* for orchestra and in the first set of *Slavonic Dances,* originally for piano but later orchestrated by the composer. His relationship to Brahms, beginning about 1878, was marked by a temporary casting out of Czech influences, an increase in thematic detail, and a more universal kind of expression. The majority of his finest instrumental works illustrate these aspects of his style. In his last years, after his return from the United States, he turned again to program music and composed several symphonic poems based on folk ballads.

Dvořák is represented in the repertoire primarily by two symphonies (Opus 70, D minor, 1885, called "No. 2" but actually his seventh; and Opus 95, "From the New World," E minor, 1893, called "No. 5" but his ninth); a concerto for violin (A minor, 1880) and one for cello (B minor, 1895); and several chamber-music works, notably the piano quintet (A

Antonin Dvořák,
1841–1904.
Engraving by
T. Johnson.

major, Opus 81, 1887), the "Dumky" piano trio (E minor, Opus 90, 1891),
and the "American" string quartet (F major, Opus 96, 1893). All of these
works reflect the variety of moods, excellent craftsmanship, and lyric
charm typical of Dvořák at his best.

In spite of the abstract nature and universal appeal of these compositions, various national materials are employed in them. The chamber-
music works (including several not mentioned in the above paragraph)
often contain inner movements labeled *furiant* or *dumka*. The first of
these terms refers to a fast, triple-meter Slavonic dance filled with cross
accents; the second is a Ukrainian lament in slow tempo alternating with
sections in gay mood and fast tempo. The piano trio of 1891, representing
one of Dvořák's rare departures from traditional form in the larger
works, consists of six such *dumky* (the plural of *dumka*) in which the
alternation of slow, elegiac sections and fast, lively ones is carried out
consistently. On the other hand, in the works composed in the United
States (Opus 95 and Opus 96, among others), American Indian rhythms,
the pentatonic scale, and the spirit of Negro folksong are reflected; but
they are given a Czech accent, so to say.

The thematic and rhythmic manipulations found in Dvořák's mature
works strikingly resemble those of Brahms, even if on a less concentrated
and profound level. Thematic similarities are seen especially in the D-
minor symphony of 1885, in which themes and theme fragments are
logically developed and various parts rise to well-proportioned and
controlled climaxes. The rhythmic similarity is especially notable in
the chamber music, in complex passages containing two or three different rhythmic figures simultaneously (see EXAMPLE 188 and compare page
486, EXAMPLE 176*b*).

E X A M P L E 188

Dvořák, Quartet, Op. 106

Dvořák's best-known work, the "New World" Symphony, departs from the forms of Brahms in several respects. Possibly because of the nature of its themes, which are meant to suggest folk material and hence are not suited to rigorous manipulation, the principle of sequence repetition plays a larger part than that of development. Cyclical form, rare in Dvořák, is employed here also, for themes from the first movement appear in the second and third, and the coda of the fourth summarizes themes from all three of the preceding movements. It is ironic that the one work that most often represents the composer on the concert stage today is perhaps the least representative of his mature style.

Scandinavia

As in the case of other peripheral countries, Denmark, Norway, and Sweden were receptive to foreign musical influences through much of the Baroque and Classical periods. In the first half of the nineteenth century, folksongs began to be collected and published in Copenhagen, Christiania (Oslo), and Stockholm, and a keen interest in the various national materials soon developed. Composers in those countries, many of whom had studied in Germany and become imbued with the spirit of Romanticism, turned to the folk-music collections as a new source of stimulation.

Niels Gade (1817–1890), trained at Leipzig and closely associated with Mendelssohn, brought the idioms and spirit of Danish folk music to his instrumental works without losing his innate elegant style. He was greatly esteemed during his lifetime both as a representative of Romanticism and as a leader of the Danish national school, but his works have largely disappeared from the repertoire.

Edvard Grieg (1843–1907), the foremost Norwegian composer of the nineteenth century, studied at Leipzig but did not entirely succumb to German Romanticism. He became interested in folk music about 1864 and turned his attention to the rich Norwegian material which had recently become available. In piano works, songs, choral works, and a few orchestral compositions Grieg recaptured the rhythms, melodic inflections, and general tone of folk music and combined them with his essentially lyric style. His many songs, written to German, Danish, and Norwegian texts, are characteristic of this fusion and are further distinguished by sensitive expression and imaginative accompaniments.

Grieg's ever popular piano concerto (A minor, 1868) and five chamber-music works represent his major excursions into the larger forms. He had little interest in thematic manipulation or in the careful planning required of a composer of sonata-forms, hence his larger works, in sectional form, exhibit the same lyricism and intimacy that characterize the smaller compositions.

The thoroughly individual style found in these compositions also pervades his choral works and other compositions. His use of sequence repetitions is perhaps its outstanding element; it is seen in concentrated fashion in the first movement of the piano concerto and throughout the

Suite No. 1 arranged from the incidental music to Ibsen's play, *Peer Gynt*. A second stylistic element is seen in the many melodies that hover around one tone (see EXAMPLE 189); this is a characteristic of much Nor-

EXAMPLE 189

Grieg, Cello sonata

wegian folk music. Finally, Grieg's melodies often contain a resolution of the leading tone to the dominant instead of the expected tonic. These elements, brought into a context of short phrases set in a predominantly homophonic texture and harmonized with many mediant chords, secondary seventh chords, and a few chromatic embellishments, constitute a style that illustrates Grieg's lyric temperament and colorful imagination.

The Romantic Period: Opera, 1850–1890

The period with which the present chapter is concerned was marked by no fewer than four distinct lines of operatic activity. There was first of all the continuation of the Italian opera tradition at the hands of Verdi. In opposition to that tradition, Wagner developed an entirely new philosophy of opera. In France, grand opera rapidly declined and a new operatic style took its place. And finally, the national opera emerged, especially in Russia and Bohemia. These four trends, which developed more or less simultaneously, will here be discussed separately.

Engraving by J. A. Mitchell, 1878. [PHOTO PIC, PARIS]

Verdi

WITH Rossini's retirement in 1829 and Bellini's premature death in 1835, only Donizetti remained to continue the production of significant Italian operas, and the sudden decline of his creative powers in 1844 soon threatened a gap in that production. A towering figure appeared in the person of Giuseppe Verdi, however, who continued the noble tradition of opera and led it to new heights. Dominating the operatic scene for almost half a century, Verdi accomplished his destiny through a unique combination of melodic and dramatic power and a feeling for humanity in his music.

Born in 1813 in Le Roncole, the son of an innkeeper, Verdi received his first musical instruction from local teachers. An application for admission to the Milan Conservatory having been rejected, he continued his studies privately in Busseto and Milan. After two minor attempts, his third opera, *Nabucco* ("Nebuchadnezzar," 1842), successful not only for its musical qualities but also for its political implications, launched him on his triumphant career; thereafter he became identified with the movement for Italian national rebirth. Although not all his later operas had lasting success, Verdi's worldwide fame was securely established by the 1850's. His operas were performed all over Europe and in the United States, and he traveled to Paris and London to oversee some of the productions. He became almost a national hero; he was elected to the first Italian national parliament in 1860, but he declined the King's offer to make him a marquis. The major portion of his royalties was devoted to philanthropic purposes, and he founded a home for aged musicians in Milan. A truly benevolent person of pure character, he died in 1901 in his eighty-seventh year, mourned by the entire musical world.

First-period operas. Verdi's twenty-six operas (six of which appear in revised versions) may be divided into three groups that roughly parallel his creative periods. The first group extends from 1839, the date of his first operatic attempt, *Oberto, conte di San Bonifacio,* to about 1850. Only three or four of the fifteen operas in that group, plus a few scattered arias, are known today. *Nabucco,* mentioned above, deals with the fate of the Jews in the Babylonian captivity; the Italian audiences saw in it a symbol of their own subjugation by foreign tyranny and hence the great popularity of the work. In dramatic power, however, *Nabucco* is inferior to *Ernani* (1844). The libretto of the latter work, written by Francesco Piave and modeled on a French romantic drama by Victor Hugo, concerns an episode from Spanish history filled with rebellion, intrigue, and tragedy; combined with exciting arias and ensembles, it assured the success of the opera. In these early works the influence of coloratura style and traditional forms (arias and recitatives) and harmonies is still present. The other surviving opera of this group, *Macbeth* (1847), is a transitional work and one that lay close to Verdi's heart, for he revised it eighteen years later for a Parisian production.

Second-period operas. The operas that contain much of Verdi's best-known music were composed in the years between 1850 and 1858. Three of the four were immediate international successes. In *Rigoletto* (1851), which also has a libretto by Piave based on a Hugo work (*Le Roi s'amuse*), the arias and ensembles transcend virtuosic coloratura style, for they depict genuinely human characters handled melodramatically: the unscrupulous duke, the innocent Gilda, the tragic, hunchbacked Rigoletto. Several of the arias and the famous quartet are known to every music lover. The music of Verdi's next work, *Il trovatore* ("The Troubadour," 1853) was responsible for this opera's success, for the book, a confusing story of mistaken identity, tragic love, and gypsy revenge, provides only a colorful background. Highlights of *Il trovatore* include the famous "Anvil Chorus," the "Miserere" with its extreme emotional contrasts, and the arias and duets sung by Leonora and Manrico. For the following opera, *La traviata* ("The Errant Woman," 1853), Verdi turned to a contemporary drama, again prepared by Piave, from Dumas's famous play, *La Dame aux camélias.* The drama of the courtesan Violetta's awakening to true love, her renunciation, and her death was pronounced by Verdi to be "simple and full of passion," but it had little impact at the first performance; the opera proved a failure, and several years elapsed before its beauty, sincerity, and intimacy were properly appreciated.

Verdi's next opera, *Les Vêpres siciliennes* ("The Sicilian Vespers"), was composed for Paris in 1855 and adapted for Italian performances in the

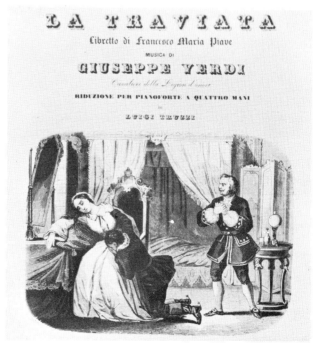

Title page of an
early edition of
Verdi's
La Traviata.

following year. Modeled upon the French grand opera, it is one of the few operas for which he wrote a full-fledged overture; significantly, Eugène Scribe, Meyerbeer's librettist, wrote Verdi's libretto also. *Les Vêpres* is performed less frequently than the next work, *Simone Boccanegra* (1857), which is concerned with the tragic fate of the *doge* of Genoa, offering ample opportunity for dramatic and gloomy music.

Third-period operas. Four operas on the highest musical and dramatic level were composed between 1859 and 1871. In the first of these, the celebrated *Un ballo in maschera* ("The Masked Ball," 1859), a historical political murder—that of Gustavus III of Sweden—is combined with a tragic love story.[1] Passionate and grisly sections (notably, a gallows scene) alternate in this work, but humor and elegance are also present. In spite of an unusually wide emotional range, Verdi preserved a unity of style and achieved new heights of artistic sincerity.

After a three-year gap, he composed *La forza del destino* ("The Power of Fate") for the St. Petersburg opera in 1862. The libretto, again by Piave, is unfortunately obscure and dramatically weak, but for it Verdi composed some of his most eloquent music. Leonore's aria, "Pace, pace, mio Dio," and her duet with the guardian are among the greatest treasures of operatic literature. *Don Carlos* (1867), based on Schiller's celebrated historical drama, is a grand opera in five acts written for Paris. The literary quality of the text permitted Verdi to develop lifelike musical characterizations here, and all the main characters are given music of the greatest expressiveness and pathos. Certain purely decorative elements included in the Paris version were eliminated in the four-act revision made for Milan in 1884.

Verdi's great masterpiece, *Aïda,* commissioned by the Khedive of Egypt to celebrate the opening of the Suez Canal, was first performed in Cairo in 1871. The libretto outwardly recounts an exotic Egyptian legend, but its essence is a series of universal emotional conflicts: patriotism and love, desire and duty, jealousy and compassion. While the festive purposes of the opera required that choruses, pageants, and even a ballet be included, these elements never obscure the intensely human drama. A subtle Oriental exotic touch gives the essentially Italian character of the music a special flavor. The individual numbers, here closely connected by continuous music, are all of the highest quality, and the opera ends with a duet that in its melodic power and grandeur may be compared with the closing scene of Wagner's *Tristan und Isolde.*

One of Verdi's most dramatic works is in the sacred rather than the operatic field. A Requiem Mass (1874), written in memory of the poet Alessandro Manzoni and including one number planned as part of a Requiem for Rossini, is stylistically similar to the second-period operas. Several extended solo passages recall the sustained lyricism of Verdi's

---

[1] The political censors of Verdi's time would not permit the dramatization of the work in this form. Verdi was compelled to transform the figure of the Swedish king into an English nobleman, and the locale of the opera was changed from Stockholm to Boston! Others of Verdi's operas were similarly modified to satisfy the authorities.

operatic scenes, and the choral setting of the Last Judgment ("Dies irae") provides one of the most dramatic moments in all of Verdi's works.

The last two operas. Verdi had always been stimulated by great literature; works of Dumas, Hugo, Schiller, Byron, and Shakespeare had provided him with librettos, and for his two last operas he turned again to Shakespeare. *Otello* (1887) represents the highest point of *opera seria* and *Falstaff* (1893) the perfection of *opera buffa*. Arrigo Boito, himself an eminent composer [2] and Verdi's close friend, provided excellent librettos for both operas and worked in close co-operation with the composer.

For purposes of the opera, Shakespeare's *Othello* was compressed and its episodic material eliminated, so that the three main characters, Othello, Desdemona, and Iago, stand out with utmost clarity. The famous "Credo" was added to reveal Iago as the personification of evil and nihilism, and the exciting storm in the introduction effectively symbolizes Othello's passion and jealousy. Although closed numbers still exist (notably the drinking song in the first act and the serenade, with its exotic orchestration, in the second), they are so tightly embedded in the scenes that the continuity of the several acts is assured. Verdi's melodic style had changed since the 1870's; while a folklike quality is still present, as in Desdemona's "Willow Song" and "Ave Maria," free dramatic sections replace the obvious melodic patterns encountered in the earlier operas. The impact made by *Otello* at its first performance in Milan was so great that many sections had to be repeated.

Otello was the greatest manifestation of Verdi's genius in the tragic genre; *Falstaff*, his only *opera buffa*, represents just as high an achievement in the field of comedy. An all-encompassing understanding of human frailty is reflected in the score of the opera, as humor triumphs over tragedy. Verdi's talent for musical characterization is nowhere shown more clearly; in a few measures he drew revealing portraits of Falstaff and of the tenderly loving Anne and Fenton (see EXAMPLE 190).

In *Falstaff*, Verdi departed from his earlier lyricism in several respects: there are few arias; the ensembles are in strict forms; lyricism is confined

EXAMPLE 190

Verdi, *Falstaff*

2 Boito's *Mefistofele*, composed in 1868 and later revised, is still performed.

to minor episodes; and, because of the content and tempo of the dialogue, *parlando* style is stressed. The orchestration is more subtle and sophisticated, and counterpoint is used more frequently than formerly; examples of the latter are seen in the satirical canon in the first act and the overwhelming vocal fugue in the finale, proclaiming *la risata final* ("the last laugh"). The unity between text and music, as well as between musical sections, is so great that no element can easily be separated from the body of the work. *Falstaff,* composed in Verdi's eightieth year, has no peers in the field of opera after the works of Mozart.

Verdi's style. Verdi's musical thoughts manifested themselves in operatic forms. At first the librettos showed a rather typical structure: three acts (sometimes with a prologue) or at the most four in operas composed for Italy, five in those destined for Paris. In the earlier operas Verdi retained the accompanied recitative and aria of his predecessors, but these were gradually replaced by through-composed sections. The grand scene and aria remained alive, however, along with the more lyric *cavatina* and *romanza,* and the *cabaletto,* a short and lively solo number, also found a place. These solo numbers were usually placed in dramatically strategic locations: a prayer or large aria often occurs near the opening of the fourth act, for example, a duet in the middle of the third act, and extended finales at the end of the second and third acts. In later works this somewhat schematic organization gave way to individualized treatment, especially in the last three operas, which are characterized by an almost continuous musical flow. In such sections certain motives sometimes recur, in the manner of a reminiscence, when the dramatic action justifies the practice. It may be pointed out that such remembrance motives, as they are called, are not at all related to Wagner's leitmotifs (see page 535).

Verdi's vocal and choral writing, always perfectly suited to the human voice, excels in dramatic power and individuality of contour and rhythm (see Example 191). The harmonic scheme supporting the melodies grew with his advance toward dramatic maturity; extended modulations and chromatically altered chords increased in number in the later works, without adversely affecting the directness of expression. The vocal lines always dominate the tonal complex and are never overshadowed by the instrumental accompaniments. The accompaniments are decidedly homophonic in the early works, whereas in later operas a more thematic tex-

EXAMPLE 191

Verdi, Melodic types

By courtesy of G. Ricordi & C., Copyright Owners.

TRANSLATIONS:
[a] Oh, what sweet shivers flood the enflamed heart;
oh, that I might still hear you answer me thus.
[b] One can never put such love into words.
[c] Oh, you must live! Yes, for my love you will live.
I have already undergone the agonies of death.

ture, polyphonic passages, and sparse accompaniments are found. The orchestra in general is dominated by the strings and woodwinds; but occasionally wide-ranging solo passages and unusual groupings of instruments are employed in characteristic Romantic fashion. Stage bands are used for special effects, and *Otello* contains passages for mandolins and guitars.

In all of Verdi's twenty-six operas, the human characters remain at the center of the action. Verdi was not concerned with aesthetic theories, myths, or symbols. In spite of the highly intellectual organization of his operas, more particularly the later ones, Verdi never lost a straightforward approach. Throughout his career he spoke directly to human hearts that could be touched by the quality of his melodies.

Verdi's Successors

EVEN during Verdi's lifetime and before his creative career had ended, a new movement of realism in Italian opera arose. Called *verismo* (from *vero*, "true"), it showed certain similarities to French naturalism. Whereas Verdi had proclaimed faith in mankind, even in his most tragic works, the new generation of composers distrusted men. They held that life, even in its most sordid aspects, should be represented on the stage, and that any glossing over or stylization of events for the sake of art should be rejected. In their work, technical rather than spiritual elements dominated; their librettos were filled with sensational drama and moods of excitement, and their music often became melodramatic and crude.

Though many composers wrote in the spirit of *verismo*, only two works in this style have survived to the present. Pietro Mascagni (1863–1945) produced his *Cavalleria rusticana* ("Rustic Chivalry") in 1890; it became a sensational success performed all over the world. A short, realistic drama of life among peasants, it presented jilted love, revenge, and murder but in incongruously tuneful, often sentimental melodies skillfully orchestrated. Ruggiero Leoncavallo (1858–1919), in his *I Pagliacci* ("The Clowns," 1892), revealed a higher level of talent than Mascagni. The opera, concerned with a triangle among a troop of clowns, also depicts jealousy, revenge, and murder but the characters are believable and the music sometimes reveals true individuality. The proper re-enactment of a *commedia dell' arte* within the opera is also a notable feature. The famous Prologue contains the basic thought of *verismo*, for it seeks to present the world as it really is.

The master who led Italian opera from this detour back to new successes on the traditional path was Giacomo Puccini. Although two of his best-known works were composed before the turn of the century, his style and technique relate him to the following generation; his operas will therefore be discussed in Chapter 30.

Wagner

RICHARD WAGNER (1813–1883), whose career and early works were touched upon in Chapter 22 (see page 451), became the dominant figure in German opera in the period after about 1850, just as Verdi, his exact contemporary, dominated the field of Italian opera during the same period. The success of *Der fliegende Holländer* in 1843 led to his appointment as musical director of the court of Saxony. During the following years he composed and wrote assiduously, but he also became active in a radical political organization and took part in the Revolution of 1849. After the uprising was crushed, he was forced to leave Germany. He spent eleven years as an exile in France and Switzerland and also visited Italy and England. In Switzerland he composed a large part of the Nibelung cycle and, under the spell of an infatuation for Mathilde Wesendonck, whose husband had offered Wagner a refuge in Zurich, he

Wagner conducting a performance of Beethoven's Ninth Symphony to raise money for the Bayreuth Festival House, 1872.

began work on *Tristan und Isolde*. Further travels took him to Vienna, Paris, and St. Petersburg until about 1862, when he was able to return to Germany.

Wagner's career had not been financially successful, and he was continually in debt. In 1864 Ludwig II, newly ascended to the throne of Bavaria, invited the composer to Munich and provided security and support for his creative work. Within less than two years, however, Wagner's political involvements and his liaison with Cosima, the daughter of Liszt and the wife of Hans von Bülow, forced him to leave Germany again. He and Cosima lived in Switzerland until 1872, and eventually his constant efforts on behalf of his music began to bear fruit in spite of his absence from Germany. His works were acclaimed, and Wagner Societies were established in many cities. With the support of the societies, King Ludwig, and many individuals, Wagner was able to realize a lifelong dream: the building of an opera house as a shrine for his own works. Bayreuth, in Bavaria, was selected as its location and in 1872, having married Cosima von Bülow, Wagner took permanent residence there. The first Wagner festival was held in 1876, and in spite of financial difficulties, the festivals have continued to the present day. In the winter of 1883 Wagner died in Venice; his permanent resting place is in Bayreuth.[3]

3 Ernest Newman's *Richard Wagner* is the most extensive and reliable biography.

Development of the Musikdrama. During his years of musical and political activity at Dresden Wagner composed *Tannhäuser* (completed in 1844) and *Lohengrin* (1848). *Tannhauser* is a Romantic opera based on a Medieval legend and brings abstract ideas to expression: the conflict between sensual and spiritual love, and salvation by prayer and intercession.[4] While it still contains pieces resembling the arias of "number operas," it reveals Wagner's gradual abandonment of traditional operatic forms. The overture, in free sonata-form, is programmatic in content, contrasting the "Pilgrims' Chorus" with the sensual "Venusberg music." The individual pieces in the opera are related by the use of recurring motives and connected by elaborate passages in which motive development, extensive modulations, and delayed cadences appear. And in the last act, Tannhauser's report of his pilgrimage to Rome is set in a free, declamatory style supported by many expressive motives in the orchestra, anticipating the style of the *Musikdrama* that emerged after *Lohengrin*.

The declamatory style introduced in *Tannhäuser* represents in effect a breakdown of the distinction between recitative and aria. The essence of the style is a fluid, nonperiodic melodic line (that is, one containing few regular, balanced phrases) in which strong internal cadences are avoided or delayed, giving the impression of music moving in long paragraphs rather than in concise sentences. This style, employed with greater frequency in *Lohengrin* than in *Tannhäuser* (see EXAMPLE 192), made possible the free and plastic forms that became characteristic in the later works.

Wagner completed *Lohengrin* in 1848; the work was produced by Liszt at Weimar in 1850, but Wagner did not hear it until 1860. This work marks a further step in the evolution of the *Musikdrama*. The libretto, a free mixture of historical fact and legend, concerns the conflict between Lohengrin and Elsa; but this conflict becomes a symbol of a larger conflict between Christianity and paganism and, on yet another level, between divine strength and human weakness. To an ever increasing extent

EXAMPLE 192

Wagner, *Lohengrin*

LOHENGRIN: Wie hehr er - kenn'ich un-srer Lie - be We-sen!   Die nie sich

4 For detailed synopses, see Newman, *Stories of the Great Operas and Their Composers.*

sah'n,   wir hat-ten uns ge-ahnt;   war ich zu dei-nem Strei-ter aus-er-
(lesen)

TRANSLATION:
I know the exalted spirit of our love! Without meeting,
each dreamed of the other. And called to be your
champion . . .

in later works, Wagner used the people and events of his operas as symbols of universal truths or universal forces.

Musical motives appear more often in *Lohengrin* than in Wagner's earlier works, and they are given a new function. No longer of the remembrance motive type, which had served other composers in reminiscent or retrospective passages, Wagner's motives now begin to have symbolical significance and to be attached to ideas or objects. One melodic motive represents Lohengrin and the Holy Grail, another the question concerning Lohengrin's origin, which Elsa is forbidden to ask, and so on. The motives are introduced whenever the idea or object is referred to or implied in the dramatic action. In many respects *Lohengrin* is a transitional work. It contains three preludes (one before each act), each of which gives a synopsis of the forthcoming action in the form of a brief symphonic poem. An equilibrium between melody and declamation is reached in the opera, and the traditional forms (aria, ensemble, and the like) are still recognizable in many sections. Finally, the orchestral writing prepares the way for the new sound of the later works; it requires a larger orchestra than before, stresses the lower brass instruments, and associates individual orchestral colors with the various characters of the work.

The gigantic tetralogy, *Der Ring des Nibelungen* ("The Ring of the Nibelungs"), stands at the center of Wagner's life work. He wrote the libretto (actually four connected epic poems) between 1848 and 1852, but the composition of the four separate musical scores required over twenty years, and long gaps intervened between composition and performance.[5]

5 The dates are as follows:

	COMPLETED	PERFORMED
Das Rheingold ("The Rhine Gold")	1854	1869
Die Walküre ("The Valkyries")	1856	1870
Siegfried, first part	1857	1876
second part	1871	1876
Götterdämmerung ("Twilight of the Gods")	1874	1876

RICHARD WAGNER GEDENKSTÄTTE DER STADT BAYREUTH

A scene from the first performance of Wagner's *Götterdämmerung*, Bayreuth, 1876. Painting by J. Hoffmann.

The first performance of the entire cycle was given at Bayreuth in 1876 and was then referred to as a *"Bühnenfestpiel* ("stage-festival play") in three evenings with a prelude." The complicated, often illogical, story of *The Ring* was compiled from many literary sources, all based on old Germanic myths.[6] The dramatic action is primarily a vehicle for the expression of philosophical ideas, however, and the characters are largely symbols. As the proper verse form to set the symbolical, mythological texts, Wagner chose the old Gothic alliterative verse form (*Stabreim*).

In *The Ring* Wagner attained his mature style and completed the creation of the *Musikdrama*. The essential feature of that style is the so-called endless melody, an expansion of the type introduced in *Tannhäuser* and consisting here of melodic lines set partly in lyric and partly in declamatory phrases. Extended monologues and dialogues replace the conventional arias, and the choral part is negligible. The melodic lines are heard over a continuous flow of thematic material in the orchestra, much of it in the form of leitmotifs ("leading motives").

The leitmotif as employed in *The Ring* differs in several respects from the type of recurring motive used in *Lohengrin*. The latter, most often a melodic phrase four or more measures in length, was treated as a special ingredient inserted into the general melodic structure from time

6 For details, see Hutcheson, *A Musical Guide to Richard Wagner's "Ring of the Nibelungs."*

to time, and was derived in form and function from the remembrance motives used by operatic composers a century before Wagner. The true leitmotif, on the other hand, is a short harmonic progression or melodic passage. It is raised to thematic importance throughout, and the complete system of leitmotifs becomes the basic thematic material out of which an entire *Musikdrama* (indeed, the entire tetralogy) is created. The various motives symbolize persons (Siegfried, for example), objects (the Sword, the Rhine gold), natural phenomena (the storm), emotions (love, hate, or greed), or attributes of character (faithfulness or treachery). Motives symbolizing similar thoughts or situations are related; a common contour or rhythmic pattern provides an intellectual connection between two or more motives, for example, and one can speak of motive families (see EXAMPLE 193).

The motives, which appear primarily in the orchestra, are manipulated, transformed, and combined in a continuous contrapuntal web. Since each

EXAMPLE 193

Wagner, Motives from *The Ring*

motive is associated with a specific character or other element of the dramatic action, the orchestra may be used to explain and comment upon the drama. Because of this, Wagner's vocal lines are less essential to the unfolding of the plot than are the vocal lines of conventional operas, with the result that large portions of *The Ring* and other music dramas can be performed successfully as orchestral works with the vocal parts eliminated. Wagner in effect suggested this possibility himself, for several dramatic episodes in *The Ring,* placed at moments of emotional climax, are purely symphonic in texture and medium: "The Ride of the Valkyries," "Forest Murmurs," and "Siegfried's Funeral March" are notable examples.

After decades during which analyses of Wagner's music dramas was confined to the observation of leitmotifs and their interactions, Alfred Lorenz developed a theory that the works illustrated certain architectonic principles as well.[7] Motives are organized into groups—that is, in strophic form, in *Barform: aab,* or in *Bogenform* (literally, bow form): *aba;* further, the groups themselves are repeated or combined in similar fashion into still larger entities. Groups of motives constitute scene segments, segments are combined into scenes, and scenes into acts. On a still higher level, according to Lorenz, the individual acts themselves are so related: the three acts of *Tristan und Isolde* (see below) constitute a gigantic *aba* form and the three acts of *Die Meistersinger* an equally large *aab.* Harmonic devices, key relationships, and tonalities, employed in symmetrical or contrasting fashion, serve to make these large formal relationships clear.

Between 1857 and 1859 Wagner broke off work on *The Ring* cycle (more specifically on *Siegfried*) to compose *Tristan und Isolde,* which represents largely a sublimation of his love for Mathilde Wesendonck. The story of Tristan and Isolde, one of the monuments of world literature, concerns the fulfillment of love through death, with the implication that complete bliss is achieved only after transfiguration to a spiritual life. In Wagner's setting, adapted from a Medieval version of the story by Gottfried von Strassburg, only the interplay of the emotions of Tristan and Isolde is important. The action is simplified to the utmost, the main characters alone assume dramatic significance (although Kurvenal, Tristan's squire, and Brangäne, Isolde's maid, play essential roles in the unfolding of the action), and King Mark's function is primarily to express renunciation.

The motive technique employed in *Tristan* is similar to that used in *The Ring,* except that the motives are fewer and are mainly concerned with thoughts and feelings instead of persons or abstractions. The orchestral writing reaches new heights of flexibility and color, and the heavy brass sonorities characteristic of *The Ring* are generally dispensed with in favor of solo passages for the woodwind instruments. But the element that sets *Tristan* apart from Wagner's other works, and indeed

7 In *Das Geheimnis der Form in Richard Wagner* ("The Secret of Form in Richard Wagner"), 1924–1937.

from every previous operatic composition, is its chromatic idiom. Chromatic melody and harmony had been used in many of his earlier works to express great emotional tension, but the harmonic idiom of those works remained primarily diatonic; in *Tristan,* however, chromaticism is raised to the level of a system. Chords are altered, connected, and resolved chromatically, with the result that the key shifts almost from measure to measure. Chromatic suspensions, passing tones, and other devices are introduced freely, and cadences are delayed or elided, to such an extent that the harmonic color is kaleidoscopic in its effect (see EXAMPLE 194).

E X A M P L E 194

Wagner, *Tristan und Isolde,* Act III

The tension and ambiguity innate in this harmonic type lend themselves admirably to the subject matter of *Tristan*—longing, passion, and tragedy. The chromatic style of this work represents simultaneously the end of the Romantic expansion of the tonal system and the beginning of the modern search for new harmonic systems. In its time *Tristan* was a difficult and incomprehensible work to many listeners, and public appreciation of its musical stature was long delayed.

Wagner's next composition, *Die Meistersinger von Nürnberg* ("The Mastersingers of Nuremberg," 1862–1867), found ready acclaim, for it was basically diatonic in harmonic idiom, with simple and direct emotional appeal. Although composed in the great tradition of comic opera, it is not essentially "comic"; only a few satirical scenes lampooning the composer's critics provoke laughter. The colorful story centers around the Guild of the Mastersingers and their leader Hans Sachs, who sacrifices personal happiness to altruism. In typical Wagnerian fashion, the theme is the conflict between novelty and tradition; the love story of the poet-knight, Walther, and the goldsmith's daughter, Eva, is of secondary interest in the course of the dramatic action. Wagner, who wrote the text as well as the music, also gave himself opportunity to express thoughts about art, politics, and even nationalism. His principal spokesman, Hans Sachs, one of the most appealing dramatic figures in all of Wagner's works, is shown as a warm-hearted man of great wisdom.

Although leitmotifs are employed in *Die Meistersinger,* the work has more in common with the traditional opera than any other *Musikdrama.* Several of its episodes are set as virtually independent numbers, notably the arias of Walther, the monologues of Hans Sachs, and the famous quintet. The songs of Walther and Sachs are cast in the old *Barform (aab)* of the thirteenth century. And the chorus plays an important part in such scenes as the Guild procession, the brawl, and the final apotheosis. The prevalence of diatonic harmony, the strong and regular rhythmic idiom, and the bright and transparent orchestral writing make this work more immediately approachable than any other late work of Wagner.

Philosophy and religion lie at the center of Wagner's last work, *Parsifal* (1877–1882). While it is based on old German epics, concepts drawn from both the West and the East are freely mingled in it. Penitence and salvation are intertwined with ideas of the existence of the human ego before birth and of reincarnation. The central dramatic ideas of *Parsifal,* the conflict of sensuality and spirituality and the redemption of sin by the Pure Fool made wise through compassion, are similar to those in *Tannhäuser* and *The Ring.* Many Christian elements, among them the Last Supper, the Holy Grail, and the sacraments of baptism and communion, are brought to the stage. Wagner's avowed aim in including these elements, which was to express a symbolical affirmation of his faith and not to demonstrate a theological dogma, makes *Parsifal* into a religious drama unique in the operatic literature.

Since there is relatively little dramatic action on the stage, the musical emphasis in *Parsifal* is on the orchestra. Leading motives are used copiously, although the contrapuntal texture is not as dense as in other works. Both chromatic and diatonic (quasi-modal) idioms are employed, often in sharply contrasting passages—one to express the sensual, penitent world and the other to suggest the mystical purity of which the Holy Grail is a symbol. Wagner's choral writing, notable in *Die Meistersinger,* here rises to its highest level and does much to express the religious moods that predominate in the first and third acts.

Wagner as writer and philosopher. Wagner's literary output, published across four decades and including articles on many nonmusical subjects, occupied ten volumes in the original German edition.[8] A group of treatises on various aspects of music culminating in an essay on Beethoven, another group dealing with art and politics (one of Wagner's favorite subjects), and a third dealing with religion and the state serve to indicate the diverse areas explored in his prose works. We need be concerned only with the theories that deal immediately with his musical work, its implications, and his hopes for its future.

8 An English edition translated by W. Ashton Ellis, *Richard Wagner's Prose Works* (8 vols., Reeves, London, 1892–99), excludes the texts of the operas and music dramas.

In *Oper und Drama* (1850), a long essay on aesthetics, Wagner presented the thesis that opera as an art form was unsatisfactory because a means of expression (music) had been made the object of opera, and the object of expression (drama) had become the means. Beethoven had introduced a new language (here Wagner referred to the device of combining voices and instruments in the chorale finale of the Ninth Symphony) that went beyond abstract musical thought. From this Wagner drew the conclusion that only a *unified* art work combining music with speech could be aesthetically satisfying. The problem of combining "tone language" with "word language" and the related problem of supplying both a feeling element (emotional response to the music) and an intellectual one (understanding of the ideas contained in the text) were solved, he felt, in his creation of the *Musikdrama*, the "total work of art" (*Gesamtkunstwerk*) that involves all the arts, including stagecraft. His strong national feeling, which included his belief in the intellectual and racial superiority of the German people, led him to assert, further, that the aesthetic goals of the *Musikdrama* could be reached only by employing the German language set in alliterative (*Stabreim*) verse forms. Wagner also asserted that the artist should use his ability to influence culture, to elevate and educate the people through art.

Wagner's thinking was molded by several German philosophers, especially Ludwig Feuerbach, Arthur Schopenhauer, and Friedrich Nietzsche. His aesthetic theories, obviously influenced by his nationalistic feeling, contributed to the ideas held by the cultural dictators of the German Third Reich under Hitler in the 1930's. But the subsequent historical development of music, especially that of opera, did not follow the direction anticipated in his theories. Thus Wagner was not the prophet of a new epoch of art, but the last great figure of German musical Romanticism.

Wagner's Successors

MANY German composers, adopting the techniques but not the spirit of Wagner, wrote operas that were widely performed in the period about 1880–1900 but have since been forgotten. Siegfried Wagner (1869–1930), the composer's only son, wrote such a work; entitled *Der Bärenhäuter* ("The Man in the Bearskin," 1899), it was only moderately successful. Other composers, however, brought original ideas to the Wagnerian technique and emerged with minor masterpieces. Engelbert Humperdinck (1854–1921), for example, composed romantic fairy operas in a modification of Wagner's style. His *Hansel und Gretel* (1893) is outstanding not only because of its eloquent melodies but also because of its skillful use of the leitmotif technique and its colorful orchestration. And Hugo Wolf in his Spanish opera *Der Corregidor* ("The Magistrate," 1896) combined Wagnerian techniques with the personal lyricism that was so eloquently cultivated in his songs (see page 557). Hans Pfitzner (1869–1949), a somewhat ascetic and conservative composer, wrote several successful operas, of which *Palestrina* (1917) has held a place in the German repertoire. In that work Pfitzner employed a mixture of leading motives, songlike sections, dramatic scenes, and choral passages in an archaic style. A slightly older composer, Richard Strauss (1864–1949), also began his career under the influence of the Wagner technique but soon found a personal style; his operas will be discussed in Chapter 30.

Wagner had considerable influence in France toward the end of the century, and Wagner cults were formed in both literary and musical circles. Among his literary apostles were Baudelaire, Verlaine, and Mallarmé. A number of French composers adopted the leitmotif technique, chromatic harmony, and the typical Wagnerian orchestral sound; Ernest Chausson, Vincent d'Indy, and Emmanuel Chabrier, known today primarily for their concert works, were well represented on the Parisian operatic stage during the last decades of the century, but neither their works nor Wagner's had a lasting effect on the course of French opera.

The *Drame Lyrique*

ABOUT the middle of the nineteenth century the two types of French opera began to lose their individuality. Serious subjects were sometimes treated in the field of comic opera, and lyric expression found a place amid the pomposity of grand opera. The essential difference between the two types lay in the fact that the separate numbers in comic opera were connected by spoken dialogue and in grand opera by recitatives or similar musical material. It seemed pointless to call a tragic opera "comic" merely because it contained spoken dialogue, or to refer to an unpretentious piece as "grand opera" because of musical connections between the arias. A new terminology was soon adopted, and an opera that contained continuous music, ballet, choral ensembles, and a fair amount of emotional expressiveness became known as a *drame lyrique*. One written in an unpretentious, popular style that stressed entertainment values developed into the type called light opera or operetta.

In the works of Ambroise Thomas (1811–1896) the change from comic opera to lyric drama may be seen clearly. The only opera of his still performed is *Mignon* (1866). The lyric and coloratura melodies and attractive ensembles of the work have little dramatic impact, but the romantic and sentimental tone of the text, adapted from Goethe's novel *Wilhelm Meister,* made it appealing. Some of the arias, notably Mignon's expression of longing for Italy and the brilliant polonaise, have not lost their charm even today.

The most celebrated representative of the lyric drama (or lyric opera, as it is generally referred to) was Charles Gounod (1818–1893). In spite of his deeply religious nature, he stressed sensuous and elegant effects in his music. His innate gift for melody and expression of sentiment enabled him to conquer the entire musical world: his opera *Faust* (1859) became the most popular and widely performed work in the entire operatic repertoire. The text of *Faust* contains few of the essential elements of Goethe's immortal drama, for it keeps only the names of Goethe's characters, the love story, and the intrigues of Mephistopheles. The many famous musical numbers that fill the score were originally separated by spoken dialogue; for a performance in 1869 recitatives were substituted and the famous ballet music was added. In later works, notably *Mireille* (1864) and *Roméo et Juliette* (1867), Gounod repeated his success on a smaller scale.

Leo Delibes (1836–1891) followed along the path marked out by Gounod, but with less success. Only one of his lyric operas has survived: *Lakmé* (1883), a story of India filled with exotic effects and rich orchestral color. His fame today rests largely upon three dramatic ballets that remain perfect vehicles for his elegant French waltzes and other vivacious dances: *La Source* or *Naïla* (1866), *Coppélia* (1870), and *Sylvia* (1876).

The exotic elements in Delibes's music may have been suggested partly by the style of Georges Bizet (1838–1875). Bizet's *Carmen* (1875) equals Gounod's *Faust* in popularity, but a great dissimilarity exists between the two, in that Bizet's music is genuinely dramatic. Traditional musical forms in *Carmen* were skillfully adapted to the changing moods of the drama, its melodies are striking (see EXAMPLE 195), and its harmony seldom

EXAMPLE 195

Bizet, *Carmen*

conventional. Bizet clearly delineated his characters and brought them to life, and he used Spanish color only as a means of increasing the realism. He had begun with more conventional works, but even in his early opera *Les Pêcheurs de perles* ("The Pearl Fishers," 1863), he revealed a fine sense of drama and color. Bizet's early death was an incalculable loss to French opera, for he had barely begun to develop a path away from the style of Wagner.

The generation that followed Bizet's was led by Jules Massenet (1842–1912), the most successful and productive French opera composer in the last decades of the century. Massenet's operas are difficult to classify because of an eclecticism that reveals the influence of many of his contemporaries. His orchestration is refined and immaculate, his melodies sentimental but intense (see EXAMPLE 196). He solved the problem of formal

EXAMPLE 196

Massenet, *Werther*

TRANSLATION:
Why this bitter word? Why not return?
When everyone awaits you here.

unity by closely knitting the various sections together with recurring motives. Because of their melodiousness one might assume that his operas lack depth and strength, but the fact remains that three of them—*Manon* (1884), *Werther* (1892), and *Thaïs* (1894)—are subtly dramatic as well. These works are still performed in the United States, and they and at least four others have found regular places in the French and Italian repertoires. Massenet continued to compose into the twentieth century, and his style was not without influence on the French Impressionists.

The imposing personality of Camille Saint-Saëns (see page 503) also left its mark in the field of French opera. In certain respects Saint-Saëns represents a late flowering of the ideals of Cherubini and Berlioz. His fabulous technical proficiency enabled him to write well-constructed arias and choruses, although his style was essentially nondramatic. In his work on a Biblical subject, *Samson et Dalila* (1877), appealing melodies, effective choral writing, and colorful orchestration substitute for dramatic intensity, hence the long-lasting place of this oratoriolike opera. Others of his stage works enjoyed only ephemeral success. Édouard Lalo (1823–1892) showed a similar conservative tendency in his *Le roi d'Ys* ("The King of Ys," 1888), an extremely popular opera in its time, based on the legend of the sunken island (and sunken cathedral) that was also treated in Debussy's famous prelude for piano. Jacques Offenbach, whose major importance lies in the field of the operetta (see below), composed one lyric opera, *Les Contes d'Hoffmann* ("The Tales of Hoffmann," 1881), that is still widely performed and enjoyed because of its melodic abundance.

Light Opera

COMPOSERS of comic opera in France sometimes tended towards light, almost frivolous operatic subjects and concentrated on pleasing the tastes of the larger public. The stage works of Louis Maillart (1817–1871) are usually considered the starting point for this trend, but its principal representative, who virtually dominated the Paris stage during the reign of Napoleon III, was Jacques Offenbach (1819–1880). Born in Germany, the son of a Jewish cantor, he went to Paris as a youth and soon created the so-called *opéra bouffe* or *musiquette*—a one- or two-act piece employing only three or four characters and a small orchestra, dispensing with the chorus. The ingenuity, incisive wit, and tunefulness he revealed in the new form soon made him enormously popular. His texts were sometimes risqué, often satirical, but always humorous, and the music was graceful and piquant.

Offenbach also composed standard operettas, the most successful being *Orphée aux enfers* ("Orpheus in the Underworld," 1858, revised 1874), and *La Belle Hélène* (1864). In both works he parodied classical antiquity and ridiculed the political and social conditions of his time. The public was enchanted with the incongruity of the gods of Olympus dancing the cancan, and the success of this type of operetta drew many other composers to the genre, notably Charles Lecocq (1832–1918) and Robert Planquette (1848–1903).

The Viennese school of operetta, established in the years after 1870, would not have been possible without the work of Offenbach in Paris. In Vienna, however, the satirical element was cast out and good-natured humor carried by waltzes and polkas became a major characteristic. The three outstanding composers of Viennese operettas were Franz von Suppé (1819–1895) and Karl Millöcker (1842–1899), whose works are confined to central Europe, and Johann Strauss, Jr. (1825–1899), called the "Waltz King," whose compositions won international acceptance. Among Strauss's fifteen operettas, *Die Fledermaus* ("The Bat," 1874) and *Der Zigeunerbaron* ("The Gypsy Baron," 1885) have held their places to the present day and are often performed in theaters dedicated to serious opera, notably the Paris, Vienna, and Metropolitan Operas.

The operetta in England reached a peak with the many works of Gilbert and Sullivan. The composer, Arthur Sullivan (1842–1900), attempted serious music also, but his fame today rests largely on such works as *H.M.S. Pinafore* (1878) and *The Mikado* (1885). Although his melodies lack the razor-sharpness of Offenbach's best tunes, they are ideal vehicles for the political satire that animates them.

National Opera

As we have seen in Chapter 25, one of the major characteristics of the Romantic period was nationalism. The large treasure of national melodies, rhythms, and dances found places in art music, especially in opera, and many composers wrote operas that established new national styles.

Russia. Mikhail Glinka (1804–1857), the founder of Russian national opera, was trained in Italy and Germany, where he mastered traditional operatic techniques; but he also sought to incorporate Russian folk idioms and rhythms into his works. His first successful opera, *A Life for the Tsar* (1836), was marked by secure handling of harmony and counterpoint and by the use of remembrance motives on the one hand, and by the use of mazurkas and polonaises on the other. In his second work, *Ruslan and Ludmila* (1842), he made more use of folk melodies. Alexander Dargomyshsky (1813–1869) followed the style of French grand opera in his early works, but in *Rusalka* (1856) he too turned to national material. His skillful use of declamatory recitative in this opera and in *The Stone Guest* (1872) was a remarkable feature of his style. Dargomyshsky left *The Stone Guest*, based on a version of the Don Giovanni legend by Pushkin, unfinished, but it was completed and orchestrated by Cui and Rimsky-Korsakov. Since its successful production in 1872 it has remained in the Russian repertoire. Alexander Borodin's *Prince Igor* (begun in 1869) also was left unfinished by the composer, but it was completed by Rimsky-Korsakov and Glazunov and performed in 1890. Only the overture and the brilliant "Polovtsian Dances" from the second act are still performed.

The principal composer of the nationalist group, Modest Mussorgsky (see page 510), made a complete break from Western tradition. His melodies reflected Oriental scales and speech inflections, his harmony was radically different from that of the West, his rhythms and forms spurned regularity and symmetry, and his orchestration was most unorthodox. Mussorgsky's masterpiece, *Boris Godunov* (1874), is not only the history of the Tsar and his adversary, the false Dmitri, but the tragedy of the Russian people. Real life comes to expression in his music; the death scene of Boris is a strong, masterful picture of passion. Mussorgsky's motto, "truth before beauty," pleased neither critics nor audience, and after the composer's death Rimsky-Korsakov felt impelled to modify the strongest elements of the music (see page 511).

Mussorgsky's other major opera, the unfinished *Khovanshchina* (1872–

1880), was also modified (and completed) by Rimsky-Korsakov. Less dramatic than *Boris,* this opera is more national and folklike in spirit (see EXAMPLE 197), and it contains sections of high quality and inspiration, notably the orchestral prelude and the choruses of the "old believers," based on ancient Russian church melodies.

EXAMPLE 197

Mussorgsky, *Khovanshchina*

Nikolay Rimsky-Korsakov, the great master of orchestration (see page 512), composed fifteen operas, most of them based on fairy tales. As in the orchestral works, the operatic melodies often contain exotic elements set in elegant fashion; they are harmonized in a style, often chromatic, that reveals the composer's fertile imagination. The forms include conventional arias and free and extended declamatory sections, and leading motives are often employed.

Several of Rimsky-Korsakov's most significant operas, though written in the twentieth century, are stylistically related to the nineteenth. *The Legend of the Invisible City of Kitezh* (1907) is a mystical pageant; *The Golden Cockerel* (1909), based on a fairy tale by Pushkin, is a humorous satire with political overtones. These works, by an eminent teacher who numbered Stravinsky among his pupils, were of considerable influence on the development of contemporary Russian opera.

Bohemia. Bedřich Smetana (see page 519) quickly cast off the influence of Liszt and established an individual operatic style by bringing Bo-

A scene from Rimsky-Korsakov's *The Legend of the Invisible City of Kitezh,* Prague, 1938.

hemian folk melodies and dances into contact with his innate lyricism. His style is also distinguished by his Romantic feeling for the spirit of nature, eloquently expressed. Most of his eight operas have been confined to the Czech repertoire, although a few have enjoyed isolated performances abroad, and only one has achieved international fame. *The Bartered Bride* (1866) is a comic masterpiece, picturing peasant life with mirth and good-natured humor tempered by realism and truly lyric elements. *Dalibor* (1867) was at first attacked as being "too Wagnerian" but eventually gained national acceptance. Among the remaining works, *The Kiss* (1876) has remained a Czech operatic favorite by virtue of its delightfully comic character.

Antonín Dvořák, whose importance is primarily in the field of instrumental music (see page 519), contributed ten operas to the Czech repertoire. Beginning in the vein of German Romanticism with *Alfred* (1870), he turned to the style of the nationalistic opera and composed several typically Bohemian works. With *Rusalka* (1901) he returned to the style of Romanticism; that work and *The Devil and Kate* (1899), a delightful comic masterpiece, deserve wider dissemination than they have today. A number of younger contemporaries of Dvořák, notably Zdenko Fibich (1850–1900) and the long-lived Josef Förster (1859–1951), composed operas for Prague that remained in the Czech repertoire for many decades.

Tchaikovsky

THE TEN operas and three ballets of Peter Ilich Tchaikovsky represent the Western point of view (see page 514) rather than the nationalist, and two of them are memorable. *Eugene Onegin* (1879), a sordid tragedy of Russian life, makes its appeal by reason of its lyric and dramatic qualities. The lyric element predominates, carried by graceful melodies imaginatively harmonized and orchestrated, and passages filled with honest sentiment heighten the effectiveness of the work. The opera is through-composed, with no recitatives as such, and distinguished by its ballets and choruses. *The Queen of Spades* (1890) represents the peak of his writing for the theater, for here a balance between lyricism and dramatic expressiveness is achieved.

Tchaikovsky's three ballets provided him with opportunities to give free rein to his melodic and rhythmic ideas. *Swan Lake* (1877), *The Sleeping Beauty* (1890), and *The Nutcracker* (1892) quickly became favorites and are still enjoyed by lovers of the ballet everywhere. They owe their effectiveness and fame primarily to the emotional strength and intensity of the music. In them as well as in the operas, the influence of the French lyric opera may be seen, but nationalistic elements are also found.

The Romantic Period:
Expanded Resources

THE VARIOUS musical developments we have been discussing in the last few chapters took place rather slowly in the middle and later years of the nineteenth century. In the last decades of the century, however, a vigorous acceleration of several major trends occurred, culminating in a last great outpouring of Romantic sound. The interest in variety of tone color and sheer weight of sonority, greatly extended by Wagner in his music dramas, now took hold in instrumental works as well. The expansion of harmonic resources to the point where the integrity of tonality was threatened, exemplified especially in *Tristan und Isolde*, continued past that point to lead to new harmonic styles. The very size of symphonic works increased greatly, both in length and in number of required instruments. As a last flowering of the subjective attitude, each composer ap-

"Arabesque over Right Leg." Sketch in bronze by Edgar Degas. [THE METRO-POLITAN MUSEUM OF ART, BEQUEST OF MRS. H. O. HAVEMEYER, 1929. THE HAVE-MEYER COLLECTION.]

proached the musical problems of his time in an individual way. Differences among composers' styles, increasingly apparent since Beethoven's time, now became so marked that virtually every composer wrote in a style of his own.

The key phrase in describing the period from about 1880 to 1910 is expansion of resources—in color, harmony, size, and intensity. Composers as unlike as Mahler, Wolf, Richard Strauss, Reger, and Scriabin contributed, each in his own way, to that expansion. Yet several of the style characteristics that became common after about 1880 were first employed in the music of Bruckner, a generation older than the composers just mentioned.

Austria

Bruckner. Anton Bruckner (1824–1896) spent his youth as a schoolteacher and organist in a number of Austrian villages. In 1856, competing against many rivals, he became organist of the cathedral of Linz, where he remained for twelve years. During that time he periodically traveled to Vienna for training in composition with Simon Sechter, court organist and teacher of organ and theory at the Vienna Conservatory. He succeeded Sechter as court organist in 1867, and a year later assumed his teacher's Conservatory duties also. His increasing fame as an organist was responsible for trips to France (1869) and England (1871), and his enthusiasm for the music of Wagner frequently took him to Bayreuth for visits with the composer. With these exceptions he remained close to Vienna until late in his life. He was almost fifty before his compositions began to attract favorable attention, and for decades after his death in 1896 his music remained a subject of controversy. He composed large quantities of choral music and many instrumental pieces, but he is re-

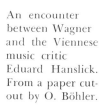

An encounter between Wagner and the Viennese music critic Eduard Hanslick. From a paper cutout by O. Böhler.

membered primarily for several enormous symphonies, three Masses, and a setting of the *Te Deum* for chorus and orchestra.

Bruckner's symphonies became controversial partly because of circumstances that prevailed in Vienna during his career in that city and partly because of their scope and content. Basically Bruckner was a victim of the differences of opinion that ranged about the music of Wagner. Eduard Hanslick (1825–1904), an influential music critic and partisan of abstract music, strongly opposed the music of Wagner and his followers and with equal strength and eloquence supported that of Brahms. Bruckner, an enthusiast of the Wagner style, sought to recapture the rich instrumental sound of that style in his works and dedicated his third symphony to Wagner. Thus he drew upon himself the critical wrath of Hanslick, even though his symphonies were not in the least programmatic, nor in the leitmotiv tradition. It is likely that Hanslick's opposition kept Bruckner's works from receiving unbiased hearings when they were first performed.

The ten symphonies [1] were felt to be strongly anachronistic in an age that prided itself on variety of mood, for one symphony greatly resembles another, three are in C minor, and three in D minor. The form of the first and last movements in all of them is virtually identical; each main section typically begins with a string tremolo over which a theme is proclaimed, usually by a brass instrument; it rises to a great climax and subsides quickly, after which the next section begins, following the same plan. Bruckner's first themes are clearly defined in harmony and are usually based on fifths or octaves, giving them an air of majesty (see EXAMPLE 198). These movements, usually in sonata-form, are greatly extended, both by the addition of a third-theme group (actually an expansion of the codetta of the exposition) and by the lengthening of transitions, developments, and theme groups themselves; the development and recapitulation are often connected.

EXAMPLE 198

Bruckner, First themes

[1] The first symphony is called "No. 0" and was not performed until 1924; the last, No. 9, was left with the finale unfinished.

In the internal fast movements Bruckner favored the scherzo form, thus reverting to Beethoven's practice, but his scherzos often contain trios in the style of the Austrian folk dance called *Ländler* that provide great contrast to the scherzo proper. Slow movements are broad, full of religious ecstasy; like some of the fast movements, they contain extended passages in the style of the Lutheran chorale (though Bruckner was a devout Catholic). Cyclical form devices are employed on occasion, primarily in the last movements, which carry the principal weight of the composer's musical thought (in contrast to the great majority of symphonies by earlier composers, in which the musical weight is on the first movement).

Bruckner's great Mass (F major, 1868 but revised in 1878 and 1890), the *Te Deum* (1881–1884), and his setting of Psalm CL (1892) represent an application of symphonic techniques to the choral field. Contrasting themes, orchestrally manipulated motives, passages based on sequence repetition, widely modulating harmonies—such symphonic devices are employed to provide the choral works with the same mood content and scope that is characteristic of the symphonies. An earlier Mass (E minor, 1866 but revised in 1885) is in a different category; written for eight-voice chorus accompanied by brass instruments, it stresses the vocal element in a contrapuntal context.

Bruckner's music often reached the public in other than its original form. He grudgingly permitted conductors to make large cuts in the scores of the symphonies and to reorchestrate passages in the style of Wagner, and he further permitted the works to be published in altered form in the hope of gaining quicker public acceptance. The distorted view thus established persisted for half a century; not until the 1950's were all the symphonies made available in a new edition that restored them to their original form and proportions.

Mahler. In the symphonies of Gustav Mahler the transformation of the Classical symphony was completed. In a typical four-movement symphony of the earlier period, the first movement had been characterized by a three-part form with well-defined harmonic sections (first-theme section in the tonic key, second in the dominant, and so on), clear distinctions between the two main themes and transitional material, and notable contrasts between dramatic and lyric moods. Other movements were similarly defined. During the Romantic period, virtually every important symphonic composer had departed in some degree from the Classical model by introducing additional themes, relating one theme to others, progressing far beyond harmonic duality, and increasing the sheer amount of contrast. The works of Mahler brought these tendencies to their highest point.

Mahler (1860–1911), born in Bohemia and educated in Vienna, began his career as an opera conductor in provincial towns and rose to positions in Prague, Budapest, Hamburg, and finally (1897–1907) in Vienna. His work as director of the Vienna Imperial Opera was outstanding, and he made it into one of the world's foremost operatic establishments. In 1907 he became principal conductor of the Metropolitan Opera and two years later also assumed the direction of the New York Philharmonic Orchestra. Internal dissension, overwork, and illness caused him to resign in 1911, and he died a few months after his return to Vienna.

Mahler's career was marked by noble and grandiose conceptions in the midst of personal unhappiness and spiritual isolation; few musicians could measure up to the demands he made upon them (and upon himself as well), and his tremendous idealism was often frustrated. His works include ten symphonies (the last unfinished) and several song cycles, several of them for voice and orchestra. The principal cycles are *Lieder eines fahrenden Gesellen* ("Songs of a Wayfarer," 1883), *Kindertotenlieder* ("Elegies on Infants," 1902), and *Das Lied von der Erde* ("The Song of the Earth," 1908). His symphonies reflect both the emotional turmoil in which he lived and the profound thoughts that inspired him. In a few cases he gave a clue to the meaning of a work—not by attaching a descriptive title but by indicating, often in his letters, the sources of his musical conceptions. Further, several of the symphonies contain vocal movements that give additional insights into his expressive intentions.

In contrast to the symphonies of Bruckner, which represent a single type, those of Mahler are more individualized works of art; nevertheless, they fall into several groups. The first four symphonies (1888, 1894, 1895, 1900) contain thematic material drawn from his songs to texts from *Des Knaben Wunderhorn,* a collection of German folk poems published early in the nineteenth century. The second symphony includes parts for soprano and alto solos and chorus, the third for alto and two choruses, and the fourth for soprano solo. Texts for those vocal movements are drawn in part from *Des Knaben Wunderhorn*, in part from works by Klopstock, Nietzsche, and others. The four symphonies of this group reflect such thoughts as the glory of resurrection, the joys of nature, the triumph of life over death, and the joy of heavenly life.

The fifth, sixth, and seventh symphonies (1902, 1904, and 1905) are abstract works inspired by a variety of philosophical and spiritual problems; the transition from despair to faith, the clash between destiny and the human will, and similar matters are suggested. The themes in these works are not conceived in the spirit of folk music, as were the themes of the first four symphonies, but independently conceived to express states of the soul. Mahler did not require vocal or choral forces in the works of this group.

The eighth symphony (1907), the so-called symphony "of a thousand," calls for a band, two choruses, a boys' choir, and seven soloists, in addition to a large orchestra. In its use of cyclical principles it completes the transfer of the symphonic idiom to choral writing and represents the highest point reached in late Romantic expression. The texts for the eighth symphony include a setting of the Latin hymn *Veni creator spiritus* and portions of Goethe's *Faust,* Part II, in German.

The last group includes the ninth symphony (1909), the unfinished tenth (1910), and the symphonic song cycle, *Das Lied von der Erde* (1908). The latter consists of six texts translated from a set of Chinese poems and

554

U. E. 2772.

A page from the printed score of Mahler's Eighth Symphony showing the massive instrumental and vocal forces used in this work.

composed for tenor and alto soloists in alternate movements (seven in all), accompanied by a large orchestra. The songs reflect all aspects of life, including gaiety, grief, defiance, beauty, and tragedy. A song cycle in the form of a symphony, *Das Lied von der Erde* expresses a farewell to life in a synthesis of vocal and instrumental music. That expression was amplified in the ninth symphony, a resigned and reflective composition of the highest spiritual worth.

In spite of the great length, varied content, and massive orchestration of Mahler's symphonies, their style is essentially lyric; the orchestration is arranged to enhance the lyric qualities by assigning a contrasting color to each voice in the contrapuntal context. The themes vary in length from short motives to extended melodies (see EXAMPLE 199). They are more numerous than in any previous music, and they are developed after each statement rather than only in development sections. These practices result in a variegated stream of motives, melodies, and transitions in which separate sections of contrasting harmony and mood are marked by changes of tempo and key but are thoroughly integrated. Thus, earlier concepts of first or second theme, transition, development, and the like lose some of their importance in this music. The harmonic idiom of the earlier symphonies was definitely derived from that of the Romantic period; the idiom of the last works, on the other hand, contained hints of polytonality and atonality and was of considerable influence on Schoenberg and members of his school (see Chapter 29). The effect of the whole is often overwhelming, so rich are the symphonies in thematic material and instrumental color.

Counterpoint, always a striking ingredient of Mahler's style, was employed with increasing frequency in the later symphonies, often culminating in fugal or canonic writing. Sometimes a number of themes, heard separately earlier in the work, are combined contrapuntally at climactic moments. Mahler showed a fondness for the old devices of *basso ostinato* and pedal point, which give his music a considerable degree of harmonic stability in spite of the modulations, cross relations, and unresolved dissonances that often take place in the other parts.

Mahler's attention to detail and his feeling for balance and proportion, notable attributes of his professional conducting, are also reflected in the symphonies. Specific directives to conductors and performers are often given in the score, to the extent of pointing out that a passage for soprano and orchestra "must be accompanied so discreetly that the singer may be heard without effort," or that under no circumstances may a particular tone (in the extremely low range of the bass part) be played an octave higher than written.[2] The instrumentation of Mahler's orchestra was often increased to Wagnerian proportions and beyond; four of each woodwind family (including E♭ clarinet and bass clarinet, for example) and additional brass and percussion instruments are usually required, and unusual instruments such as the posthorn and cowbells in the third symphony and mandolin and guitar in the seventh are sometimes called

2 These and many similar directives occur in the score of the fourth symphony.

EXAMPLE 199

Mahler, Symphonic themes

"Orchestre Symphonique," drawing by Raoul Dufy.

for. In the last works, however, the orchestration became more transparent, solo passages more common, and colors more subdued. All the instruments were handled with consummate skill; Mahler must be included among the great masters of orchestration.

Wolf. The declamatory song, in which a mood is psychologically developed or contrasting moods are brought into focus, was brought to its culmination by Hugo Wolf (1860–1903), the last of the great Germanic song composers. After decades of hardship and poverty accompanied by professional disappointments and lack of recognition, Wolf in 1883 became a music critic for the Viennese *Salonblatt.* In his idolization of Wagner and his intolerance of everything musical that displeased him, he used this position to publish vitriolic attacks against Brahms and his music. He resigned in 1887, however, to devote himself to composition, despite his continued lack of success. His first major recognition came in 1889, when some of his songs were published and subsequently widely performed. Late in 1897 he suffered a mental collapse, and he died in an asylum in 1903.

Wolf's great reputation is founded almost entirely on about three hundred songs, the finest of which were composed between about 1883 and 1896. He habitually concerned himself with one poet at a time, almost as if he wished to steep himself in the style and mood of one poet before progressing to the next.[3] After exhausting the works of German poets whose texts attracted him, he turned to translations of foreign poems. A set of forty-three texts from the *Spanisches Liederbuch* ("Spanish Song-book") and two sets of twenty-two and twenty-four, respectively, from the *Italienisches Liederbuch* (all in German translation) were followed by settings of three sonnets by Michelangelo, Wolf's last significant works.

The relationship between voice and piano, balanced by Schubert and modified in favor of the piano by Schumann, was radically altered by Wolf. In his songs the piano took the lead both in establishing moods and in expressing the inmost meanings of the texts. A typical Wolf song became not merely a musical setting of a lyric poem but a miniature dramatization that seemed to reflect the poet's sentiment at the time the poem was written. In effect Wolf went behind the text and directly to the mind of the poet. Thus in many cases the song is more expressive and significant than the externals of the text would suggest.

Although purely lyric songs occur, the majority of the vocal parts are set in a declamatory style closely reflecting the speech rhythms of the text. The musical rhythm and phrasing given to the piano are usually independent of the vocal element (see EXAMPLE 200), and often the piano has the main melody. Preludes, interludes, and postludes are common, contributing to the rounded form of the song. In his harmonic style Wolf was greatly indebted to Wagner; chromaticism in both voice and piano, altered chords, unprepared dissonances, and irregular resolutions of cadence-forming chords became notable features of his fluid style, which remained more economical and tonal than Wagner's, however. The range of expression extended from delicate humor to deepest tragedy, and

EXAMPLE 200

Wolf, *Morgenstimmung*

---

3 The period beginning in February, 1888, is typical: February 16 to May 18, forty-three songs on Mörike texts; May 24 to September 29, thirteen songs on Eichendorff texts; October 4 to October 11, nine songs on Mörike texts; October 27 to February 12, 1889, fifty songs on Goethe texts.

ge-macht,   schon   fühl ich Mor -   gen-lüf - te

changes of mood within a song were sensitively expressed through subtle harmonic changes from one section to another.

Germany

BY THE last decades of the nineteenth century, harmony had become so flexible and broad in its applications that it often ceased to function as a musical defining force. In earlier music the outlines of form, the limits of a phrase, period, or section, had been determined largely by the underlying harmony. That function of harmony was now minimized; nonperiodic phrases, motivic work, and the concept of continuous melody—all supported by harmony filled with chromatic embellishments, enharmonic structures, and free modulation—had led to a texture that may be called seamless. An interest in the clear delineation of formal divisions seemed remote, as may be seen in the symphonies of Mahler.

Faced with this turn in the development of music, German composers reacted in varying ways. Some turned away from contemporary developments and took refuge in the traditional Romantic style; Max Bruch (1838–1920) may serve as an example. Max Reger, who wrote primarily organ, piano, and chamber music, sought to graft the contrapuntal style of the Baroque, with its free, nonperiodic melodic types, onto the forms that Brahms had employed. And Richard Strauss, working in the field of the symphonic poem, came to terms with the amorphous texture by employing it in descriptive music, where titles and extramusical allusions could justify and explain the forms that resulted.

Reger. In a creative career that spanned scarcely twenty-five years, Max Reger (1873–1916) composed a large quantity of music in virtually every field except opera. He was born in Bavaria, educated principally at Wiesbaden, and, becoming an excellent pianist, toured as a soloist, conductor, and chamber-music player. In 1907 he became teacher of composition at the Leipzig Conservatory. He died in Leipzig in 1916 at the age of forty-three.

Almost half of Reger's 147 opus numbers represent chamber-music works, which include a number of suites for unaccompanied violin, for viola, and for cello. Some thirty-five opus numbers are given to organ pieces and sets, about twenty-one to solo piano compositions, and a dozen to miscellaneous works for orchestra, none of them symphonies. Many songs and choral compositions complete the list.

Reger's music is distinguished primarily by its adherence to the older forms, by its use of contrapuntal textures in some works and a concern for instrumental color effects in others, and by an involved, constantly shifting harmonic scheme (see EXAMPLE 201). The variation form and the

EXAMPLE 201

Reger, Gavotte from Op. 82, No. 5

fugue held important places in his works; his customary practice was to abstract melodic or rhythmic motives from the theme being varied, elaborate each motive in the manner of a fantasy, and crown the work with an extended fugue. This practice is illustrated in sets of variations on themes by Hiller and Mozart (for orchestra), by Bach and Telemann (for piano), and by Beethoven (for two pianos). In none of these works did he employ the figural variation technique of the Classical masters. And Reger's fugues differed greatly from the fugues of Bach, on which they were ostensibly modeled, for he brought a striking element of textural contrast into them—sometimes to the extent of introducing chordal passages or virtuosic figurations into the episodes. In both fugal and other works he showed a fondness for the Baroque device of a *cantus firmus,* over which the harmonies were permitted to move freely.

Reger's use of harmony became a matter of controversy during his lifetime and interfered with the acceptance and full recognition of his music, for he carried chromatic ornamentation and modulation further than any previous composer. As a typical practice in cadential passages, he began with a chromatically embellished dominant chord and resolved it to a key a second higher or lower than expected; the dominant of E, for example, would lead either to Eb or F. In other passages Reger constructed melodies so chromatic that the relationship to the underlying, essentially diatonic harmony was all but obscured. In still others he dispensed with pivot chords or connecting chords completely and wrote consecutive chords that showed no perceptible relationship to each other.

The unique sound of much of Reger's music is derived from such harmonic devices, set in thick textures in which the outer voices are contrapuntal and the inner voices complete the chords. These textures seldom provide contrasting sections or convey a wide range of expression. Without employing new material and without developing a new harmonic system, Reger succeeded in creating a kind of music that even today has both admirers and detractors.

Strauss. The form of the symphonic poem developed by Liszt in the 1850's contained a potential weakness; in comprising several contrasting sections, it stood in danger of diffuseness or loss of formal integrity. With the number and shape of its sections determined only by the wish of the composer, and the extent of the contrasts limited only by his taste, the symphonic poem could easily disintegrate into a set of tonal pictures arbitrarily selected and not bound by any higher unity. The problem was recognized by Liszt, but it was solved only later by Richard Strauss.

Born in Munich in 1864, the son of an eminent horn player, Strauss enjoyed a good academic and musical education and began composing even before his schooling was completed. His first two symphonies and a violin concerto were successfully performed before he was twenty, when he was offered a position as assistant conductor to Hans von Bülow at Meiningen. He succeeded von Bülow in 1885 and thereupon began his rise to a position as one of the foremost conductors of his time. The conductorship at Meiningen was followed by positions of growing importance at Munich, Weimar, Berlin, Vienna, and again at Berlin—all between 1886 and about 1922.

Strauss's reputation as a composer kept pace with his increasing fame as a conductor, and he traveled widely to perform his own works. Several visits to London (the last in 1947), two trips to the United States (in 1904 and 1922), and appearances in all the musical centers of Europe were undertaken during his long and active career. Although his orchestral style reached a peak about 1903 with the *Symphonia domestica* ("Domestic Symphony"), and his operatic style about 1910 with *Der Rosenkavalier* (see Chapter 30), he continued writing until a year before his death in 1949.

Strauss's first period of composition extended to about 1885; in that period he composed the symphonies and concerto mentioned above, a delightful serenade for thirteen wind instruments, several chamber-music works, and many other compositions. The works of this period, perfectly proportioned and abstract in nature, breathe a Classical melodious spirit and give eloquent testimony to the quality of the young composer's musical gifts.

During his stay at Meiningen Strauss became acquainted with Alexander Ritter (1833–1896), a violinist in the orchestra, the husband of Wagner's niece, and an enthusiastic adherent of the progressive tendency in music. Under Ritter's urging Strauss turned to the concept of "expressive music" exemplified in the works of Berlioz, Liszt, and Wagner. This was understood to mean a kind of music that went beyond abstract patterns, suggesting specific emotions and permitting a composer to recreate for his listeners the thoughts or feelings aroused by an extramusical idea or object. In other words, "expressive music" for Strauss meant program music—although he avoided the term. The link to Strauss's second

Richard Strauss
conducting.
Pastel drawing by
Alois Kolb.

period of composition was *Aus Italien* ("From Italy," 1886), a descriptive work in four movements.

In quick succession, then, he composed the symphonic poems that brought him to worldwide fame: *Don Juan* (1888), *Tod und Verklärung* ("Death and Transfiguration," 1889), *Macbeth* (completed in 1890), *Till Eulenspiegels lustige Streiche* ("Till Eulenspiegel's Merry Pranks," 1895), *Also sprach Zarathustra* ("Thus Spake Zarathustra," 1896), *Don Quixote* (1897), and *Ein Heldenleben* ("A Hero's Life," 1898). Two later orchestral works, *Symphonia domestica* (1903) and *Eine Alpensinfonie* ("An Alpine Symphony," completed in 1915), carried the style of the symphonic poems into structures composed of several movements. The *Alpensinfonie*, however, did not rise to the level established by the compositions of the period 1888–1903.

Strauss's symphonic poems are of quite different nature from those composed by Liszt some forty years earlier. In several of them the leitmotiv technique of Wagner is employed, and unifying elements may be found in the various motives that permeate their several sections. Others are cast into formal patterns derived from earlier music—sonata-form, rondo, and variations, for example. All of them reveal how greatly Strauss profited from Wagner's style of orchestration and how rigorously he developed the concept of orchestral virtuosity. And to a large extent he resolved in them the conflict between abstract and programmatic music.

The symphonic poems also reveal Strauss's ability to invent motives and themes that have the power to suggest specific elements or details. The impetuosity of a seeker for redemption (*Don Juan*), the breathing of a man on his deathbed (*Tod und Verklärung*), insolence and recklessness (*Till Eulenspiegel*), philosophical speculation (*Also sprach Zarathustra*)—such dissimilar programmatic elements are suggested in the various works, and for each Strauss found an appropriate musical counterpart (see EXAMPLE 202).

Each of the symphonic poems presented its own formal problem, and Strauss solved each one brilliantly. An extended sonata-form movement was suitable to express the mental conflicts, psychological development, and tragic end of the protagonist in *Don Juan*. By virtue of its basic idea, *Death and Transfiguration* fell naturally into two parts: the first, primarily in minor, presents the complex material representing life and death, the struggle for dominance, and the victory of death; the second, in major and with first-part themes suitably transformed (thus symbolizing transfiguration), balances the first part and serves roughly as a terminal development or coda that completes the musical form even as it summarizes the programmatic ideas.

Similarly, *Till Eulenspiegel's Merry Pranks,* which has a subtitle stating that the work is "in old-fashioned rondo form," exhibits formal regularity. It includes a prologue and epilogue that serve both to frame the work in a legendary "once upon a time" mood and to give it symmetry and unity. The various adventures of Till are suggested by recurrences of the theme associated with him (see EXAMPLE 202*c* and *d*) and by inter-

EXAMPLE 202

Strauss, Typical themes

vening episodes that develop and carry forward the musical counterparts of Till's pranks.

Don Quixote, based on the adventures of the "knight of the sorrowful countenance" and his squire, Sancho Panza, and cast in the form of variations, begins with an introduction establishing the mood of the piece and ends with an epilogue summarizing it. The themes representing the knight and his squire are introduced by solo cello and solo viola (sometimes bass tuba), respectively; various episodes suggested by events in Cervantes' masterpiece are treated in free sections based on the main themes that are themselves greatly transformed from one variation to the next.

The two longest and most complex works, *Also sprach Zarathustra* and *Ein Heldenleben,* most closely resemble the symphonic poems of Liszt in their formal aspects. Both contain a number of sections in contrasting tempo and a series of motives and themes that appear and reappear, suitably altered, in the various sections. In both works the sections are so arranged that they suggest the form of the cyclical symphony with its movements compressed and linked together. *Zarathustra,* for example, contains a long, slow fugal section corresponding to a symphonic slow movement and another section with scherzolike overtones. *Ein Helden-leben,* in addition to disclosing a similar structure, is distinguished by a long section (measures 686–780) in which themes from Strauss's other symphonic poems are quoted—in keeping with the autobiographical nature of the work.

Strauss's orchestral writing brought to its highest level the art of orchestration that had been developing for more than a century. His orchestra was enlarged even beyond Mahler's, and each of the many instruments, treated individually and with virtuosic requirements, was given its full share of thematic material. The unique tone color and technical capability of each member of the string, woodwind, brass, and percussion families were exploited to give his orchestra unprecedented flexibility and brilliance. Virtually every instrument from solo violin to solo cello, from E♭ clarinet to tenor tuba, is called upon, and most are given thematic material associated with a particular person, object, or idea derived from the literary work that lay behind the symphonic poem.

The great variety of moods expressed in these works is paralleled by the variety of textures. Monophonic, homophonic, and polyphonic textures and all conceivable combinations of them, ranging from the unsupported first theme of *Ein Heldenleben* to the fugue in *Zarathustra,* permitted Strauss to develop his ideas freely, subtly, and eloquently. The moods range from humor and irony to pathos and tragedy, yet in each case the corresponding texture is chosen.

With the composition of *Symphonia domestica* Strauss's style arrived at a plateau. His technical mastery remained at a high level, but for several decades the quality and appropriateness of his musical ideas seemed to regress. A large number of undistinguished orchestral works, including festival marches, commemorative waltzes, and suites drawn from his operas, were composed between 1905 and 1947. None of them showed the musical power and overwhelming imagination found in the eight great symphonic works. Gradually then, in his last instrumental compositions he adopted a more restrained style marked by relatively dissonant counterpoint and a neo-Classical harmonic idiom; the serious and eloquent *Metamorphosen* for twenty-three solo string instruments (1945) is one of the late masterworks in this style. And in the last songs for voice and orchestra (1948) the lyric sensitivity and musical imagery so copiously expressed in the symphonic works of the middle period were recaptured.

Russia

IN SPITE of the harmonic complexities found in the styles of Mahler, Reger, and Strauss, these composers did not habitually progress beyond the limits of the traditional tonal system. Key centers, key signatures, and chords built on thirds remained basic to their respective styles. In the twentieth century those limits were consciously abolished, as we shall see below, and nontriadic harmony became a striking element of the new music. A transition between the old and the new is seen in the music of Alexander Scriabin, an eminent Russian pianist whose career fell squarely across the stylistic boundary marked by the years around 1900.

Scriabin. Born in Moscow in 1872, Scriabin entered the Conservatory at the age of sixteen and began composing for the piano at about the same time. He made such rapid progress that he was able to undertake his first concert tour to Paris in 1895, during which he performed his own music. A series of subsidies from patrons and publishers enabled him to devote himself entirely to composition, although he taught piano at the Conservatory for five years. Subsequently he lived in Switzerland and played in many European musical centers between 1897 and 1914, but he eventually returned to Moscow, where he died in 1915 at the age of forty-three.

Scriabin's compositions consist of about seventy piano works, including ten sonatas and many sets of pieces (mainly preludes, mazurkas, and studies), and five orchestral works, of which three are symphonies and two resemble symphonic poems without being so named. The piano compositions up to about Opus 36 reflect the style of Chopin; in works above that number, as well as in the orchestral compositions beginning with the third symphony (*The Divine Poem,* Opus 43), Scriabin's unique and personal contribution to harmony may be observed. The later piano compositions are usually described as mystical, esoteric, and even diabolic;

E X A M P L E   203

Scriabin, Prelude, Op. 74, No. 5

they become ever more chromatic, free in form, and free of key signatures and tonal centers (see EXAMPLE 203).

In the orchestral works, which include *The Divine Poem* (1903), *The Poem of Ecstasy* (1908), and *Prometheus: the Poem of Fire* (1910), Scriabin sought to evolve a new type of harmony. He eventually developed a chord derived from the upper harmonics of the overtone series and arranged in fourths of various types, thus: C-F♯-B♭-E-A-D. To this chord and its many modifications he ascribed mystical attributes, derived from his interest in theosophical writings. *The Divine Poem,* for example, represented the soul and personality, and *The Poem of Ecstasy* reflected the spiritual joy found in creative activity. His last orchestral work, *Prometheus,* included a part for a "color keyboard" capable of projecting colored lights appropriate to the mystical qualities of the music, and this work was to be the first step toward a synthesis of all the arts.

Much of Scriabin's music constitutes a valuable part of the piano repertoire, and is prized for its subtle use of harmonic color as well as for its varied textures and mixed sonorities. The orchestral works may be enjoyed without reference to the philosophical concepts that inspired them; their restless harmonic style recalls the most advanced chromaticism of Wagner. Even though Scriabin's music, taken as a whole, serves as a link to the truly experimental and radical styles of the 1900's, it is basically subjective in spirit. It represents yet another facet of the urge to expand musical resources that marked the end of the Romantic period.

❧ 28 ❧

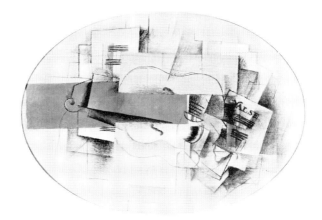

Emergence of
Contemporary Styles

I N A music-historical context the year 1900 is closely analogous to 1600, a year which, it will be recalled, marked one of the major turning points in the history of the art. Modal counterpoint reached its highest level of expressiveness and stylistic consistency at the end of the sixteenth century, only to be relegated to a secondary position and then obscured in the first decades of the seventeenth, its decline hastened by the emergence of a new way of composing homophonically that in the 1600's gradually strengthened the system of tonality. Thus the year 1600 represents a convenient point at which the crossing of the two stylistic paths, modal polyphony and tonal homophony, may be clearly observed.

In a similar manner, the year 1900 marks a major turning point. The expressive, subjective styles of Romanticism had run their course, increasing chromaticism had stretched the limits of the tonal system to the utmost, and further development of Romantic styles was not to be

"Composition with Mandolin." Painting by Georges Braque. [STADTMUSEUM, COLOGNE]

looked for. Some composers, sensing that subjective expression had reached the boundary of practicability and that forms had been expanded as far as possible, abandoned the basic tenets of Romanticism and sought new approaches to composition. The extent and results of their radical experiments will be discussed in Chapter 29.

Meanwhile, however, other more conservative composers in the early twentieth century held to a modified Romantic style or, adapting it to their expressive purposes, approached the problem of style from a different direction. This in turn brought about reactions from still other composers who, no longer content with the old but not satisfied with the new, were put in the anomalous position of developing a simple and objective new style that would retain its connections with traditional music.

Thus the twentieth century began in similar manner to the seventeenth: with a mixture of styles, some continuing the old, others departing from the old, and still others representing a tentative approach to the new. Romantic practices stayed alive in the music of Elgar, Rachmaninov, and many other composers; a post-nationalistic group emerged, headed by Sibelius; a new style derived from the old was developed by Debussy; and reactions to all these were set in motion by the neo-Classicists, whose leading figure was Busoni. These various stylistic lines, finally, stood in opposition to the truly radical experiments (see Chapter 29) that led to contemporary styles.

England

FOR TWO hundred years after the time of Purcell, England had held a minor role in the history of music. It had played host to a number of Continental musicians, some of whom—notably Handel—had become virtually English. It had adopted the styles of Italian and German music, in turn, and had developed competent performing groups in the instrumental, operatic, and choral fields. But its native composers and indigenous music—much of the latter written in small forms—had contributed little of historical importance or lasting value. William Sterndale Bennett (1816–1875), friend of Mendelssohn and Schumann, was among the few exceptions, for his music was known and respected both in England and Germany.

A renaissance of English music began in the last decades of the nineteenth century, however, and led to important achievements in the twentieth. Charles Hubert Parry (1848–1918), recognizing that the musical strength of England lay in the choral tradition, composed many oratorios in an effort to restore his country to a position of musical stature. *Scenes from Shelley's "Prometheus Unbound"* (1880), *Job* (1892), and *The Pied Piper of Hamelin* (1905), among the best and most enduring of his works, led the way to a revival of English music in general. Composing under the influence of Brahms but aware of the sonorities and power of Wagner's style, Parry revealed his sensitivity to good declamation and his understanding of the literary values of his texts.

Charles Villiers Stanford (1852–1924), Irish by birth but active principally in London and at Cambridge University, where he became professor of music, worked not only in the choral field but in chamber-music and symphonic music as well. The influence of Brahms is again noticeable in Stanford's instrumental works, but in an oratorio, *Eden* (1891), he reverted to the use of modal melodies. This work set in motion a renewed interest in all Renaissance music, and later English composers adopted modal inflections in a variety of works.

The compositions of Edward Elgar (1857–1934), filled with moods as rich and impulsive as those of Schumann, reveal a decided talent for orchestral writing. Most of his significant compositions were written between 1891 and about 1904. He wrote assiduously in a number of fields, and his oratorios and orchestral works were widely performed in England and the United States during his lifetime. Although his music still is heard regularly in England, only a few works have remained in the general repertoire elsewhere. Chief among them are the "Enigma" Variations for orchestra (1899), the oratorio *The Dream of Gerontius* (1900), and the violin concerto (1910)—plus, of course, the ubiquitous *Pomp and Circumstance* March No. 1 (1901).

Ralph Vaughan
Williams,
1872–1958.
Charcoal sketch
by Juliet Pannett.

Vaughan Williams. While Parry, Stanford, Elgar, and a host of lesser composers remained largely within the framework of German Romanticism, another group of English composers found their inspiration in English folksong. The interest in folk materials that developed in Russia, Bohemia, and other countries in the period after about 1870 found its parallel in England a few decades later. Irish, Welsh, and Scottish folksongs had been known and collected throughout the nineteenth century and even earlier, but English collections were not undertaken until the early years of the twentieth. Almost as a byproduct of the folklorists' activities, attention was also directed anew to the music of Elizabethan England, for that music contained a strong infusion of folk idioms and tunes. Thus the music of the new generation of composers was enriched by two ancient sources, seen in the use of modal melodic forms and cadential structures on the one hand and characteristic folksong rhythms, phrase structures, and melodic inflections on the other.

Ralph Vaughan Williams (1872–1958) became the foremost composer of the folksong-oriented group. A graduate of Cambridge University, he studied composition with both Parry and Stanford in London, spent a year with Max Bruch in Berlin, and in 1909, as a mature composer, studied with Ravel in Paris for a short time. Thereafter, except for military service during World War I, he devoted himself almost entirely to composition and to furthering his interest in folksong. He visited the United States in 1922, 1932, and 1954 to conduct his works and lecture at various universities, and he remained active to the very end of his long life. He died in 1958, in his eighty-fifth year, a few months after completing his ninth symphony.

Vaughan Williams remained an individualist throughout his career and modified his basic style from work to work as his expressive purposes required. In the orchestral *Norfolk Rhapsody* (1906), for example, he reflected the melodic turns and rhythms of folksong; without quoting existing tunes as such, he re-created the unsophisticated and direct spirit of English folk music. In the *Fantasia on a Theme by Tallis* (1910) for string orchestra, he steeped himself in the modal style of the English Renaissance period and wrote in a mystical, reserved, yet fervently expressive manner

EXAMPLE 204

Vaughan Williams, *Fantasia on a Theme by Tallis*

(see EXAMPLE 204). *A London Symphony* (1914, revised 1920) contains bits of musical illustration: the calls of street vendors, the chimes of Westminster, and the like. Those elements, it may be said, reflect Vaughan Williams' belief that art music may derive its strength, and even some of its content, from everyday sound without becoming programmatic. *On Wenlock Edge* (1909), a cycle of six songs for tenor and string quartet, with texts taken from A. E. Housman's *A Shropshire Lad,* is atmospheric and economically written in almost a Classical manner, yet it contains strong overtones of impressionism (see page 578).

Vaughan Williams' symphonies have been widely performed and have contributed to his reputation as the foremost English composer of the twentieth century. *The Pastoral Symphony* (1922, the third of his nine), a quiet and eloquent work, was followed by the Symphony No. 4 (1935), a severe and uncompromising composition full of harsh dissonances, chromaticism, and tremendous rhythmic drive. The contemplative Symphony No. 5 (1943) and the passionate and chromatically rich Symphony No. 6 (1948) offer an equally great degree of contrast. All of them reveal different aspects of his style, which sometimes approaches impressionism in its harmonic idiom.

Vaughan Williams' versatility in technique and variety of expressive content resulted in a style that, while basically Romantic in its subjectivity and harmonic structure, was essentially a manifestation of English nationalism. His choice of texts in his many vocal works reflected his interest in various facets of English life and character, and the folksong idiom was wonderfully absorbed into his melodic and rhythmic writing. His music, taken as a whole, gave evidence that after a gap of two centuries English composers had resumed their important place in music history; for in their espousal of national elements they had made vital contributions to the mainstream of international music.

Other composers. Gustav Holst (1874–1934), thoroughly English in spite of his Scandinavian name, brought a number of exotic strains into his music. Active as an organist, trombonist, and teacher, primarily in London, Holst is represented in a number of fields of composition. English folksong played a part in one group of his works, influenced by his friend Vaughan Williams: the orchestral *Somerset Rhapsody* (1907), two well-known *Suites for Band* (1909 and 1911), and the *St. Paul's Suite* (1913) for strings are typical of this group. In another group of compositions he revealed his interest in Eastern subjects: the *Choral Hymns from the Rig Veda* (1908–1912), two operas, and several smaller works are representative. A visit to Algiers in 1910 resulted in the *Beni Mora* suite for orchestra.

Although Holst continued to compose until 1933, his style reached its full maturity in two works written well before then. His best-known composition, *The Planets* (1914–1916), reveals the full resources of his imagination and technical mastery. The seven movements of this suite for large orchestra, each devoted to a different planet, are concerned with legendary astrological rather than astronomical associations.[1] *The Hymn of Jesus* (1917) for chorus and orchestra, based on texts from the Apocrypha, provides an extreme contrast to *The Planets* and suggests the range of Holst's musical interests. His style is characterized by a fluent melodic line often influenced by folksong idioms, a fondness for unusual meters ($\frac{5}{4}$ and $\frac{7}{4}$ appear frequently), a rhythm in which phrases are written without regard for bar lines, especially in text settings, and great harmonic flexibility to suit the varied expressive content of his works. The harmonies include modal inflections arising from folksong and standard Romantic harmonic devices but also an essay in polytonality in a concerto for two violins (1929).

The music of Frederick Delius (1862–1934) is not easily classified, for he was born in England of German parents, lived in Florida for several years, studied in Leipzig, and from 1890 to his death lived in France. In spite of long isolation from his homeland, he brought the spirit of English folksong into some of his works, notably the orchestral rhapsody, *Brigg Fair* (1907). Among his operas was one composed to a French text and another to a German text; the latter became known in England as *A Village Romeo and Juliet* (1907), and excerpts from it are frequently performed in orchestral concerts. A work for chorus and orchestra, *Sea Drift* (1903), has a text by Walt Whitman; and *A Mass of Life* (1905) is based on portions of Nietzsche's *Also sprach Zarathustra*. Other compositions are similarly diverse in conception and content. Delius's style, founded on traditional harmony, was characterized by a concern for the sound of isolated chords, a notable absence of counterpoint, and a rhapsodic form. He was at his best in small programmatic compositions that re-create a specific atmosphere; the orchestral piece *On Hearing the First Cuckoo in Spring* (1912) is a worthy representative of this class.

The music of William Walton (b. 1902) represents a style that may be called neo-Romantic, for rich tonal harmony, unashamed lyricism, and subjective expression find prominent places in it. His early works exhibit some of the satirical and humorous qualities that characterize neo-Classicism (see page 585). The first orchestral suite, based on his well-known piece for reciter and instruments, *Façade* (1926), and the brisk, pungent descriptive overture *Portsmouth Point* (1926) are typical of this phase of his career.

The power and sweep of Walton's imagination are revealed in a monumental oratorio, *Belshazzar's Feast* (1931). Florid recitatives for unaccompanied baritone soloist, dramatic and incisive passages for the chorus, and a wealth of brilliant writing for a large orchestra make this one of the most stirring choral works of the twentieth century (see EXAMPLE 205). In his viola concerto (1929), symphony (1935), violin concerto (1939), and cello concerto (1957), as well as in much of the music composed for films,

---

1 The movements are entitled "Mars, the Bringer of War," "Venus, the Bringer of Peace," "Mercury, the Winged Messenger," "Jupiter, the Bringer of Jollity," "Saturn, the Bringer of Old Age," "Uranus, the Magician," and "Neptune, the Mystic," respectively.

EXAMPLE 205

Walton, *Belshazzar's Feast*

Walton's mature style emerged. Writing with harmonies that are basically tonal but chromatically thickened, with long flowing melodic lines, and with free modifications of traditional forms, Walton has brought the expression of sentiment in line with contemporary developments.

Russia

WE HAVE seen that in the last years of the nineteenth century two separate schools of Russian music existed: the nationalistic school headed by Rimsky-Korsakov at the St. Petersburg Conservatory, and the Western-oriented school represented by Tchaikovsky but furthered principally by Taneyev at the Moscow Conservatory. The first generation of twentieth-century Russian composers, however, though trained at one or the other of those institutions, did not necessarily adhere to the line represented by their respective conservatories. Formalistic music was at times written by members of the St. Petersburg group, and nationalistic music emerged in the works of the Moscow-trained composers.

Sergey Rachmaninov, Reinhold Glière, Aram Khachaturian, and Dmitri Kabalevsky are among the prominent Moscow-trained composers; the St. Petersburg group includes Alexander Glazunov, Nikolay Miaskovsky, Sergey Prokofiev, Dmitri Shostakovich, and Igor Stravinsky.

The Moscow group. Sergey Rachmaninov (1873–1943) became one of the most accomplished piano virtuosos of the twentieth century; his concert tours throughout Europe and the United States extended from 1892 to the late 1930's. Driven out of Russia by the Revolution of 1917, he lived in France, Switzerland, and the United States and eventually became an American citizen. Of his many compositions, his second symphony (E minor, 1907), two piano concertos (C minor, 1903, and D minor, 1909), a *Rhapsody on a Theme by Paganini* (1934), and his preludes for piano (1892, 1904, and 1910) have remained in the repertoire.

Greatly influenced by Tchaikovsky, Rachmaninov brought the lyricism, power, and subjective utterance of that composer into the twentieth century. With them came a melancholy tone and a rhapsodic expansiveness that Tchaikovsky had not always revealed. Rachmaninov often derived his themes from short motives that gravitate about one tone, developing them in the manner of the German Romantic composers in thick, essentially diatonic textures that have little in common with the textures of truly twentieth-century music.

Reinhold Glière (1875–1956), a student of Taneyev in Moscow, taught in Kiev until 1920; thereupon he returned to the Moscow Conservatory, where he remained to the end of his life. During his long career as a teacher and composer he became interested in folksongs and traveled throughout Russia on collecting trips. Highly esteemed as a conductor as well, he undertook concert tours on which he conducted his works in all Russian musical centers. Glière is remembered chiefly for his monumental third symphony, entitled *Ilya Murometz* (1909–1911), and a ballet, *The Red Poppy* (1927). The symphony, Romantic in its conception and programmatic content, describes the adventures of a legendary Russian hero. In a style that remained within the bounds of traditional harmony and form, he revealed a disciplined imagination, an ability to invoke atmospheric moods, and a feeling for overwhelming orchestral sonorities.

Nikolay Miaskovsky (1881–1950) studied with Glière in Moscow and with Rimsky-Korsakov in St. Petersburg. From 1914 to 1921 he served in the Russian army and navy, after which he became a teacher of composition at the Moscow Conservatory. Unlike other Russian composers, he worked primarily in the field of abstract instrumental music; a dozen string quartets and no fewer than twenty-seven symphonies are his principal works. In his earlier compositions he expressed much of the melancholy and even pessimism that had marked the music of many of his countrymen: his sixth symphony (E♭ minor, 1924) is typical in this respect. His later works, however, reflect the "official" tone of optimism that perforce characterizes the music of Soviet composers.

Two younger Russian composers, both students of Miaskovsky, continued the tradition of solid craftsmanship and harmonic versatility of the Moscow school. Aram Khachaturian (b. 1903) has become widely known outside Russia through his piano concerto (1936). Of Armenian ancestry, he employs folk material of both Russia and Armenia and successfully expresses a variety of Oriental moods as well. Dmitri Kabalevsky (b. 1904) has remained close to the modern nationalistic strain of Russian music by composing operas and choral works on patriotic subjects.

The St. Petersburg group. Alexander Glazunov (1865–1936) was recognized as a talented and fully mature composer from about his twentieth year. As a pupil of Rimsky-Korsakov he first carried on the traditions of the Russian nationalist school, but his admiration for Classical forms soon turned him in the direction of abstract music. In eight symphonies, two violin concertos, and seven string quartets he disclosed masterful technical ability, an essentially lyric style, and a fondness for moods of restrained melancholy. His talent for brilliant orchestration was somewhat obscured by his tendency to work with full, detailed textures; as a consequence, his music often lacks variety of color. While his works are now considered unadventurous and thoroughly Romantic in general tone, they enjoyed great popularity during his lifetime and still deserve performance.

The younger members of the St. Petersburg group played important parts in establishing the various idioms grouped under the term neo-Classicism (see page 585). The music of Stravinsky, Prokofiev, and Shostakovich, the most prominent composers of the group, will be discussed in Chapter 29.

Sibelius

JAN SIBELIUS (1865–1957), the only Finnish composer to achieve international recognition, is in a sense related to the Russian composers discussed above. His music has certain similarities to that of Tchaikovsky,

especially in respect to its mood contrasts and dark tones. Some of it is nationalistic, such as the orchestral pieces *The Swan of Tuonela* (1893),
Finlandia (1899), and the *Karelia* suite (1893). However, his major works
—the seven symphonies composed between 1899 and 1924—are nationalistic only in the sense that they reflect some of the granitic hardness and
glacial sparkle of his native land.

After finishing his education in Helsinki, Sibelius studied in Berlin
and Vienna for about two years; thereafter, except for a few trips abroad,
notably one to the United States in 1914, he remained in Finland until
his death in 1957, in his ninety-first year. But his creative career had
ended in 1924, with the completion of the seventh symphony.

Sibelius's style was rooted in that of the nineteenth century, and few
twentieth-century developments are reflected in his music. Motive manipulation and cyclical form are its chief components; the motives are
not often placed in prominent positions, however, but rather emerge
from bits of introductory or transitional material. The themes developed
out of the motives are themselves changed on successive appearances, so
that an impression of constantly flowing material is created. The harmonies are those of the nineteenth century, but the typical quick fluctuations from one harmony to another are not often found. Long sections
based on one chord frequently occur, and many pedal points and *ostinato*
figures further stabilize the harmony. Passages consisting of a string
tremolo over slowly changing harmonies are typical of the later symphonies, notably in the finale of the fifth and the allegretto of the sixth
(see EXAMPLE 206).

Sibelius's orchestration, too, departs from the conventional practices of

EXAMPLE 206

Sibelius, Symphony No. 5

the nineteenth century. He often used instruments in families—the entire string section at one time, the entire woodwind at another, and so on—and changed rapidly from one family to another. He showed a fondness for dark woodwind colors, frequently employing those instruments in their lowest registers. Pizzicato passages for all the strings are also characteristic; the slow movement of the second symphony and the finale of the fourth are typical.

These style traits appeared gradually during the course of Sibelius's twenty-five year development as a symphonic composer. Found occasionally in the first two symphonies, they become characteristic of the last five. The increasing use of cyclical form and of fusion of movements provides an example. The first symphony contains four separate movements; in the second symphony the last two movements are connected, and in the third the scherzo and finale are intertwined. This process reaches its culmination in the seventh, which is in one long movement; while it contains sections contrasting in tempo and mood, the transitions from one to another are made gradually and a tightly unified composition based entirely on cyclical form emerges.

Impressionism

THE INEVITABLE revolt against the lush, inflated aspects of Romanticism began in France in the 1870's. It first manifested itself as a movement among French painters who sought to eliminate the heroic subjects, excess of realistic detail, and illustrative quality of Romantic painting. They worked toward recapturing the impression of an object or scene at a given moment, with particular concern for the quality of the light and atmospheric conditions that prevailed. Taking their name from a painting by Monet, they became known as "Impressionists"; the leaders of the group were Édouard Manet, Edgar Degas, Claude Monet, and Auguste Renoir.

About the same time a group of French poets, feeling that pathos and intellectuality were stifling the pure imagery and varied sound that represented the essence of poetry, led the way to a new kind of poetic expression. They sought to clothe poetic ideas in symbols, to suggest rather than state, and to stress the musical sound of the words rather than the intellectual aspects of the subject. Charles Baudelaire, Stéphane Mallarmé, Paul Verlaine, and Arthur Rimbaud, who became known as "symbolists," played leading roles in the development.

Debussy. French musicians too chafed under the weight, emotional richness, and technical excesses—as they considered them—of Romantic music, especially that of the Wagnerian school. The tenets of the Impressionist painters and symbolist poets greatly impressed Claude Debussy, a young musician who had earlier made pilgrimages to Bayreuth under the spell of his fervent Wagnerianism—an influence he was later to expunge entirely.

Debussy was born near Paris in 1862 and attended the Paris Conserva-

"Houses of Parliament," a painting by Claude Monet, one of the leaders of the Impressionist movement.

toire until his graduation in 1880. For parts of two years he was engaged as piano tutor in the household of Nadezhda von Meck, Tchaikovsky's patroness, and traveled and lived with her family in Switzerland, Italy, and Russia; in Russia he gained a firsthand acquaintance with the music of Mussorgsky. In 1884 he won the Prix de Rome and lived there until his return to Paris in 1887. Thereafter he lived in Paris, working as a part-time music journalist on occasion, but devoting himself principally to composition. He visited Vienna, London, and Bayreuth in 1887–1889, and between 1908 and 1914 conducted his works in London, Hungary, Russia, the Netherlands, and Italy. He died in 1918.

In 1888 Debussy became acquainted with the poets of the symbolist school. A year later he heard the music of Far Eastern groups at the Paris Exposition and was greatly impressed by the *gamelan,* the orchestra of Indonesia and Java. He still remembered his impressions of Mussorgsky's music gleaned in Russia in the early 1880's, and he encountered the musical ideas of Erik Satie (see page 586) about 1891. These diverse influences, superimposed upon a musical intellect that had already shown its disregard for outworn traditions at the Conservatoire in the late 1870's, played large parts in shaping his mature style.

Debussy's principal compositions were written in the period from about 1892 to 1913, with the major instrumental works falling in the first portion of the period, the piano works mainly in the second, and his single opera (see page 619), roughly in between. In a string quartet (1893), the orchestral *Prélude à l'après-midi d'un faune* ("Prelude to the Afternoon of a Faun," 1892–1894), and three Nocturnes for orchestra (1893–1899), the essential elements of the impressionistic style were established. Later orchestral works include chiefly a set of three symphonic sketches entitled *La Mer* ("The Sea," 1903–1905), the second of three *Images pour orchestre* (1906–1909), called *Ibéria,* and a number of works for piano, of which two sets of *Images* (1905, 1907) and two sets of Preludes, with twelve pieces in each (1910–1913) are the principal items.

One of the most striking features of Debussy's style is its harmony. Standard triads used in conventional fashion are present, but in addition, taller chords (sevenths, ninths, and elevenths) are often used in isolation

Pencil drawing of Claude Debussy, 1910. Artist unknown.

or in series, purely for the effect of their harmonic color (see EXAMPLE 207a), not resolving to consonances in traditional fashion. Chords thick-

EXAMPLE 207

Debussy, Harmonic devices

ened through the addition of dissonant seconds, fourths, and sixths are employed, as well as chords based on fourths or fifths used in parallel motion (EXAMPLE 207b) and chords derived from the whole-tone scale (C-D-E-F♯-G♯-A♯; see EXAMPLE 207c).

The forms of Debussy's impressionistic compositions—the string quartet and some of the piano pieces are not included here—are not subject to conventional analysis or diagramming. Traditional thematic development is largely abandoned, for Debussy's concern was with the color or mood of a particular moment, the sound of an isolated chord, the atmospheric effect of a specific passage. Bits of thematic material separated by other contrasting bits return periodically so that each composition is unified, but the effect of the whole is rhapsodic, fluid and colorful.

Among the devices used to suggest atmosphere are tremolos and rapid alternations of tones, harp glissandos that provide moments of shimmering color, *pizzicato* and guitarlike effects that enrich the percussive qualities of certain passages, and unusual instrumental colors heard in prominent melodies. The latter include such instrumentation as antique cymbals in *L'après-midi;* castanets, tambourine, and tamtam in *La Mer;* English horn and piccolo in *Ibéria;* and a semi-chorus of women's voices singing without text in "Sirènes," the third of the orchestral Nocturnes. Much of this material is employed in melodies of narrow range; some of the melodies are based on the diatonic scale, chromatically enriched, others on the whole-tone scale, and still others on the pentatonic scale.

Debussy's compositions are generally pictorial or descriptive in their effect, and his choice of titles—even in the short preludes for piano—indicates the nature of the impressions he sought to evoke. The three movements of *La Mer,* for example, are entitled "From Dawn to Noon on the Sea," "Play of the Waves," and "Dialogue Between the Wind and the Sea." Similarly, *Ibéria* contains movements entitled "On the Streets and Lanes," "The Perfumes of the Night," and "The Morning of a Festival Day." Among the Preludes for piano the following titles occur: "The Girl with the Flaxen Hair," "The Sunken Cathedral," "General Lavine—Eccentric," and "Fireworks."

It must be stressed that Debussy was concerned with re-creations of the moods or impressions suggested by the titles of his works and not with literal descriptions. Typical of his means were the sound of an isolated chord, the color of a particular instrumental combination, and the effect of a tremulous or murmuring background. In his ability to evoke the atmosphere out of which the impressions arose or to suggest emotional states, he was unmatched. He created his effects with great refinement and the finest of taste; there is not a touch of the commonplace or the vulgar in his work. In going beyond the harmonic and instrumental practices of his time he departed from the Romantic tradition, but in his adherence to subjective expression, to moods and impressions, he represents yet another aspect of the complex Romantic musician.

Ravel. Within a few years of its inception, and in spite of the opposition it aroused in official and academic circles, the impressionistic style began to exert strong influence on other composers. Chief among the French adherents of the style was Maurice Ravel (1875–1937), who was born in the Pyrenees but lived in Paris for the major part of his life. A product of the Paris Conservatoire, where he remained for several years of additional study after graduation, Ravel lived an outwardly uneventful life. His gradual acceptance as France's foremost composer led to a conducting tour to the United States in 1928. Except for this visit, he devoted himself almost entirely to composition, though he appeared occasionally as a pianist in his own works.

His larger orchestral works are a *Rhapsodie espagnol* (1907), two suites arranged from the ballet *Daphnis et Chloé* (1912), a "choreographic poem" entitled *La valse* (1920), the famous *Bolero* (1927), and two piano concertos (1931), one of them for the left hand. The principal piano compositions include *Jeux d'eau* ("Fountains," 1901), a sonatina (1905), and several sets of pieces, notably *Miroirs* (1905) and *Gaspard de la nuit* (1908). Several of his thirty songs and the cycle for voice and orchestra, *Shéhérazade* (1903), are representative of his Romantic vocal writing. His two operas will be discussed in Chapter 30.

Ravel's use of impressionistic techniques was quite different from Debussy's. He employed many of the same coloristic devices in the orchestra—tremolos, glissandos, unusual ranges, and the like—but his harmonic practices were more firmly rooted in the diatonic tradition (see EXAMPLE 208) and his forms were allied to those of the neo-Classical move-

EXAMPLE 208

Ravel, *Valses nobles et sentimentales,* No. 6

ment (see page 585). Debussy's music had favored the evanescent, fleeting moment and expressed quiet, dreamlike moods on occasion. Ravel's was more vigorous, and even more brilliant in orchestral coloring than Debussy's.

Ravel made major contributions to the idiom of the piano, and it is significant that several of his finest works in this field antedated Debussy's by several years. He exploited the upper register, introduced impressionistic orchestral effects—notably shimmering glissandos, clouded harmonies, and rustling arpeggios, and in effect brought the technical complexities of Liszt's style into contact with the impressionistic harmonic idiom. Although Ravel was one of the great masters of orchestration, he composed relatively little music originally designed for the orchestra; some of his best-known orchestral works were first written for the piano, chief among them the "Alborado del grazioso" from the *Miroirs* set and *Le tombeau de Couperin.*

Ravel's sense of form alerted him to the dangers inherent in Debussy's type of impressionism, for the impulsive, deliberately vague, and rhapsodic aspects of the older composer's style could have led to complete dissolution of form. Traditional forms, regular phrase structures, and even thematic development play a larger role in Ravel's music than in Debussy's. Further, in spite of descriptive titles, impressionistic effects, and coloristic harmonies, his music is objective and carefully worked out under the influence of a disciplined mind; thus it is thoroughly representative of the neo-Classical impulse.

Other composers. In the first decades of the twentieth century the impressionistic style influenced many composers, in France and elsewhere. A number of French musicians, adopting elements of the style, wrote distinguished works that have won respected places in the repertoire. Paul Dukas (1865–1935) was at his best in the larger forms; one opera (see page 621) and a symphonic poem, *L'apprenti sorcier* ("The Sorcerer's Apprentice," 1897) have survived. Albert Roussel (1869–1937) came to music after several years spent in the French navy, during which he became acquainted with Oriental music. Legends from the Far East provided him with source material for some of his works, notably for a three-movement composition for chorus and orchestra, *Évocations* (1910–1912), and an impressionistic opera, *Pâdmâvatî* (1914–1918), both of which contain mood pictures and veiled harmonies in the manner of Debussy. In later compositions he inclined toward the neo-Classical idiom and influences from the past; the suite from the ballet *Bacchus et Ariane* (1930) brings neo-Classical elements, pungent harmonies, and objective attitudes to expression.

Jacques Ibert (1890–1962), a pupil of D'Indy, winner of the Prix de Rome (1919), and director of the Academy of Rome (1937–1955), wrote many works in which impressionistic techniques were applied in neo-Classical contexts. An orchestral suite, *Escales* ("Ports of Call," 1924), a concerto for cello and wind instruments (1926), and *Angélique* (1927), the first of his operas (see Chapter 30), best represent his style.

The principal Italian exponent of impressionism was Ottorino Respighi (1879–1936). During his career as a professional violist he played in the Imperial Opera orchestra in St. Petersburg; there he studied with Rimsky-Korsakov. Later he moved to Berlin, where Max Bruch was his teacher. A few years after his return to Italy he became a teacher of composition in Rome and traveled widely as a pianist and conductor of his own works. He wrote copiously in many forms, but only a few works have retained places in the general repertoire: a string quartet, *Quartetto dorico* (1924), and two symphonic poems, *Fontane di Roma* ("Fountains of Rome," 1917) and *Pini di Roma* ("Pines of Rome," 1924).

Each of the symphonic poems contains four contrasting sections, in which Respighi's lyric gifts and orchestral virtuosity are fully revealed. His studies with Rimsky-Korsakov and his knowledge of the works of Richard Strauss are reflected in its brilliance and imaginativeness, use of recurring motives, and colorful orchestration. The pictorial elements in the respective sections (representing four different fountains in the one and four different groups of pines in the other) go beyond realistic description, for ideas lying behind the physical objects are invoked—for example, the tread of Roman legions in the section called "Pines of the Appian Way." Yet in another noteworthy passage Respighi requires a phonograph recording of the song of a nightingale, which is heard above the orchestral background.

In other countries, too, impressionism took root and merged with indigenous or personal styles. The works of Karol Szymanowski (1882–1937) in Poland were impressionistic in part, especially those written after 1917. In England, Arnold Bax (1883–1953) infused elements of the style into some works that are outspokenly Romantic and into others that make use of Celtic folksong idioms and are equally Romantic.

The compositions of Manuel de Falla (1876–1946) represent impressionism in Spanish music. Falla, coming under the influence of Debussy and Ravel in Paris in about 1907, adopted certain of their stylistic elements without losing the flavor of either his nationalistic writing or his neo-Classicism. His two operas and two ballets (see page 621) and a work for piano and orchestra, *Noches en los jardines de España* ("Nights in the Gardens of Spain," 1909–1915), reveal the colorful, atmospheric, and highly individual blend of impressionistic harmonies and Spanish rhythms. In his concerto for harpsichord and chamber orchestra (1926), on the other hand, objective expression and other neo-Classical idioms dominate.

Neo-Classicism

THE WORK of Debussy, as indicated above, began as a French reaction to the pathos-laden and subjective music of the late Romantic period, especially music in the general style of Wagner. The impressionistic style, however, was itself rooted in Romanticism, and a number of composers found it too vague and nebulous, too full of harmonic complexities, to provide the antidote they were seeking. Early in the twentieth century these composers moved in a direction opposite to that taken by Debussy, and under the aesthetic leadership of Erik Satie a reaction to impressionism itself set in.

About the same time the feeling arose in Germany that Romanticism had run its course and that a new spirit must be brought into music. An Italo-German pianist and composer, Ferruccio Busoni, led the way to a style that was objective, concentrated, sparse, and clear. Busoni turned back to the forms of the Classical period and sought to recapture the serenity and poise expressed by the masters of that period.

The two new aesthetic impulses, one French and the other German, had much in common, although their points of departure differed and they arrived at different solutions to the problem. The anti-impressionism of Satie and his followers and the anti-Romanticism of the Busoni group moved toward a revival of the aesthetic ideals of the eighteenth century. Eventually the term "neo-Classical" was applied to both groups, and neo-Classicism became a tent under which a great variety of composers with different stylistic outlooks could find shelter.

Satie and Les Six. Erik Satie (1866–1925) played an unusual role in the development of twentieth-century French music. After some piano instruction in his boyhood he attended the Paris Conservatoire for about a year when he was thirteen, and in his fortieth year he studied counterpoint with D'Indy and Roussel. Otherwise, he was self-taught. He earned a precarious living as a café pianist and became an intimate of the contemporary leaders in modern painting, poetry, and music.

Wit and irony were Satie's most potent weapons against what he considered the pretentiousness, extravagance, and vagueness of impressionism. To his piano pieces he gave fantastic and satirical titles: *Pieces in the Form of a Pear, Flabby Preludes,* and *Desiccated Embryos* are typical. His relatively few compositions are distinguished by absence of pathos, and the utmost economy of means. The melodies are in the style of popular café music, and the harmonies are based on chords built on fourths or on conventional chords employed in completely unconventional contexts.

Many younger musicians were strongly attracted to the eccentric Satie and his ideas, and in 1920 a journalist called critical attention to *Les Six,* six composers of the group who were united only by their opposition to the style of impressionism. Of the six only Darius Milhaud, Arthur Honegger, and Francis Poulenc assumed important places in French music; the others, Georges Auric, Germaine Tailleferre, and Louis Durey, played little part in later developments.

Milhaud. Darius Milhaud (b. 1892) turned against the nebulousness and subjectivity of impressionism early in his career. After completing his studies at the Paris Conservatoire he spent two years (1917–1918) as a secretary in the French legation in Rio de Janeiro; there he became acquainted with the rhythm and color of Brazilian folk music. He also visited the United States as early as 1922, taught in California for seven years (1940–1947) and made many trips to this country after that time; thus his familiarity with the jazz idiom was acquired at first hand. His

LEFT: A self-portrait by Darius Milhaud. RIGHT: A self-caricature by Erik Satie.

Etude pour un buste de M. Erik SATIE peint par lui-même, avec une pensée: Je suis venu au monde très jeune dans un temps bien vieux.

basic style, however, is polytonal with a strong infusion of dissonant counterpoint.

Milhaud's creative output has been enormous and covers virtually every field of composition. Fourteen operas, thirteen ballets (see Chapter 30), about twenty-eight choral works, some fifty orchestral compositions of many kinds, much chamber music for various combinations, innumerable piano pieces and songs, and music for films and plays are included, for a total of more than three hundred works. Two orchestral compositions, *Suite provençale* (1936) and *Suite française* (1944); a set of two-piano pieces, *Scaramouche* (1939); and a variety of other compositions represent Milhaud in the general repertoire.

The polytonal works are characterized by clearly defined diatonic melodies (see EXAMPLE 209); the textures in which they are employed

EXAMPLE 209

Milhaud, Symphony No. 3

range from transparent in the smaller compositions, to thick and ponderous in the works for chorus and orchestra. Jazz idioms find their most characteristic use in an early ballet, *La création du monde* ("The Creation of the World," 1923), and *Scaramouche* is filled with the rhythms of Brazil. In later works Milhaud abandoned some of the astringency of his dissonant counterpoint and restored a measure of lyric charm and sentiment.

Honegger. Arthur Honegger (1892–1955) was born in France of Swiss parentage. He studied at both the Zurich and Paris Conservatories, and the German-Swiss element in his background and training may be responsible for the generally serious tone and neo-Classical concern with form and proportion that mark all his works. Although not as prolific a composer as Milhaud, he wrote in the same wide variety of fields.

Two early orchestral pieces show different aspects of his style. A work for chamber orchestra, *Pastorale d'été* ("Summer Pastoral," 1920) is serene and melodious and written in a transparent tonal style. A larger composition, *Pacific 231* (1923), on the other hand, is a musical representation of a locomotive, with the gradual acceleration and deceleration carried out in skillful and imaginative fashion. The harsh dissonances of the work and the subject itself led to its being considered a symbol of the mechanical age, and Honegger's international reputation was long founded on that piece alone.

In a dramatic psalm (often performed as a kind of oratorio) *Le Roi David* ("King David," 1921), for narrator, chorus, and orchestra on a text by René Morax, Honegger achieved a unique blend of Biblical and contemporary moods. And in his fifth symphony (1950) a tone of tragedy and violence is established by dissonant counterpoint, touches of polytonality, and a variety of broad and dramatic melodies. Honegger's mastery of the larger forms is fully revealed here, and the work gives strong evidence of the neo-Classical tendencies that marked much of his music.

Poulenc. Although Francis Poulenc (1899–1963) composed in all the usual fields, his greatest contributions have been made in his choral and vocal works. A number of compositions for unaccompanied chorus, notably a Mass (1937) and a cantata, *Figure humaine* (1943), disclose his keen feeling for expressive melody, sensitivity to the nuances of the text, and highly developed harmonic sense. In his many songs and song cycles Poulenc succeeded in expressing the moods of the texts without departing from a cool, refined, and thoroughly contemporary harmonic idiom.

Busoni. Composers of many countries took part in the development of neo-Classical tendencies outside France in the first quarter of the twentieth century. Their activity was anticipated by a pianist and composer of Italian and German ancestry who spent most of his professional life in Germany. Ferruccio Busoni (1866–1924), one of the finest pianists of his generation, stressed clarity of line and form, transparent textures, and objective attitudes in his compositions.

It may be that Busoni's ideas simply reflected the spirit of his time, for neo-Classicism soon became a rallying cry for musicians generally.

Many younger composers found inspiration in the laws of music itself and abandoned their interest in literary works as source material. They sought to re-establish a balance of form and content—the essence of Classicism—and composed objectively in forms derived from the eighteenth century. Paul Hindemith was the most prominent German representative of the new tendency, and Sergey Prokofiev, among many others, was foremost among the younger Russian composers; their music will be discussed in Chapter 29.

Nationalism

T HE TREND toward the use of folk material in art music, introduced so effectively by Russian composers in the nineteenth century, gained strength and momentum in the twentieth. Many younger composers in the erstwhile peripheral countries continued to adhere to their respective nationalistic traditions. Countries that had not appeared on the national musical scene in the nineteenth century produced worthy representatives in the twentieth. And in many cases, composers who wrote chiefly in another style also showed nationalistic leanings. Sibelius in Finland, Vaughan Williams in England, and Falla in Spain were typical in this regard.

Hungary achieved a place of major importance in the twentieth century, primarily through the work of Béla Bartók (see Chapter 29) and Zoltán Kodály (1882–1967). By employing Hungarian legends and other folk material, Kodály added to the importance of the national school in his country. The orchestral suite arranged from his comic opera *Háry János* (1926) has held its place in the repertoire for decades; the orchestral *Dances of Galanta* (1934) and *Variations on a Hungarian Folksong* (1939) are other nationalistic works. His setting of Psalm LV for chorus and orchestra, *Psalmus hungaricus* (1923), however, is only indirectly in the nationalist tradition.

Nationalistic music in the western hemisphere is strikingly represented in the works of Heitor Villa-Lobos of Brazil and Carlos Chávez of Mexico. Villa-Lobos (1887–1959), one of the most prolific composers of recent times, dedicated himself to furthering Brazilian music in all its forms. In his educational work in the schools of his country he introduced his own choral arrangements of folksongs, and in many of his compositions he quoted indigenous tunes and wrote original tunes in the same style. He composed fourteen works of a type called *chôros,* containing syntheses of folk and popular music; virtually each *chôros* is set for a different instrumental combination—from solo guitar through small instrumental ensembles to a massive setting for chorus, band, and orchestra. In a number of *Bachianas Brasileiras,* again for various instrumental combinations, folklike melodies and rhythms are employed in more formal contexts; various movements are cast as preludes, arias, fugues, toccatas, and the like.

Carlos Chávez (b. 1899), working primarily in the larger forms, introduced many Mexican Indian percussion instruments into his orchestra. In a style that is related to the neo-Classical but finds its melodic and rhythmic material in the folksongs of his country, he has written a number of colorful, dissonant, and powerful compositions. His best-known work of this type, *Sinfonía India* (1935), employs Indian tunes and rhythms for thematic material, and gourds, rattles, rasps, and other Indian instruments to provide authentic color and rhythm. Some other works, including ballets, choral works, and chamber music, are nationalistic, and still others are not; but all convey the strength and vigor of Chávez' style and his mastery of contemporary, dissonant harmonic techniques.

The Twentieth Century:
New Horizons

THE FLIGHT from Romanticism, which led to the impressionistic style discussed in Chapter 28, took a further devious course before arriving at definitely new trends. As early as the first two decades of the century experiments were undertaken that were to change the entire basis of musical composition. Several of these experiments were ephemeral and left scarcely any trace in later twentieth-century music. The so-called futuristic movement, for example, stressing "music of the machines" and using factory and city noises as musical media, soon became dormant until the 1950's when it emerged again in a different form called "musique concrète"; Honegger's *Pacific 231,* mentioned in Chapter 28, was an early example of this style. And the microtonal school, which employed quarter-tones and even smaller intervals, soon shrank to a few experimenters, notably Alois Hába (b. 1893). Other movements, however, such as primitivism (set opposite the over-refinement of impressionism), jazz, and

"Three Musicians." Painting by Pablo Picasso, 1921. [MUSEUM OF MODERN ART]

Gebrauchsmusik ("functional music"), partially determined the course of musical developments. Many experimental elements can be traced in the music of the major composers, but they remained tangential to the general musical evolution of the time.

The two chief stylistic movements, existing side by side, that have continued into the present are the neo-Classical, whose earlier phases were described in Chapter 28, and the movement originally called expressionism but now identified with the employment of serial (twelve-tone) technique invented by Arnold Schoenberg. While Schoenberg and his immediate followers perfected this technique, other composers representing different styles have incorporated various aspects of it into their own work; the latest compositions of Stravinsky are examples. Still other composers remained within their own styles, developing their own harmonic and melodic idioms, and may be considered standard-bearers for the more traditional approach; Bartók and Hindemith are the most outstanding representatives of this tendency, and some of their works have already acquired the status of classics.

The Serial Style

Schoenberg. The artistic career of Arnold Schoenberg (1874–1951) encompasses the entire development from Romanticism to serialism. Born in Vienna into a middle-class family, Schoenberg had only a few months of formal instruction, which he received from his future brother-in-law, Alexander Zemlinsky (1872–1942), a well-known Viennese conductor and composer. Except for two short visits to Berlin, where he directed a musical cabaret and taught, he lived in Vienna as a free-lance theorist and teacher. In spite of the hostility directed against the unconventional nature of his music, his fame as a composer grew to such an extent that in 1925 he was appointed professor of composition at the Prussian State Academy of Music in Berlin. When the Hitler government came to power in 1933 he was compelled to leave Germany; after a short stay in Paris he migrated to the United States, first to Boston and then to a position at the University of California at Los Angeles. In his last years he saw a great change in the reaction toward his music; formerly ridiculed and despised, his works became appreciated and admired, but the change came too late to affect his bitterness.

The major stylistic changes in Schoenberg's music make a division into three periods natural and obvious. Ten works composed in his first decade of writing, to 1908, reveal his gradual abandonment of the Romantic style. The earliest of his songs show the influence of Brahms, whereas the well-known string sextet *Verklärte Nacht* ("Transfigured Night," 1899) illustrates the application of Wagnerian harmony, leitmotiv techniques, and programmatic purpose to the field of chamber music. The climax of his Romanticism was reached in the oratorio *Gurre-Lieder* ("Songs of Gurre," virtually completed in 1900–1901, with parts of the final section added in 1910); here Mahler's massive symphonic and choral style was brought to new heights. In the symphonic poem *Pelleas und Melisande*

(1903), elements of impressionism appeared, and in the *Kammersymphonie* ("Chamber Symphony," 1906) for fifteen solo instruments, a new harmonic idiom (chords based on fourths) and radical instrumental style (complete independence of each instrument) were initiated. The second string quartet (1908) represented the final break with traditional tonality, for references to a tonal center in the last two movements, to which a line for soprano voice, on texts by Stefan George, is added, are scarcely perceptible.

World War I and a pause in Schoenberg's writing extended his second or atonal period from 1908 to 1923, although the most important works in the period were composed before 1913. In those works thematic materials consist only of a few tones, which reappear in melodic and rhythmic variations. Wide intervals not based on harmonic relationships became characteristic, and accompanying figures or chords not in the shape of triads and seventh chords were derived from these and other intervals. New means of punctuation employing the rhythmic element were devised, and extreme brevity with concentrated expressiveness was typical. The most important works of this period, which include songs and piano pieces, were the two operas discussed in Chapter 30, *Five Pieces for Orchestra* (1908, 1909) and *Pierrot Lunaire* (1912). The latter is a cycle of twenty-one short poems in a mixed grotesque and ironic mood, set for speaker and a group of instruments. The texts are not sung but recited on indefinite pitches to which definite rhythmic values and general in-

"The Blue Circle, No. 242," painting by Vasily Kandinsky, 1922, an example of expressionism in art paralleling Schoenberg's work in music.

THE SOLOMON R. GUGGENHEIM MUSEUM

dications of melodic inflections are applied. This new method of text rendition was called *Sprechstimme* (translated as "speaking voice," but its function is more accurately rendered by "speech-song") by the composer. The forms of the songs in *Pierrot Lunaire* range from free aggregates of thematic material to strict polyphonic types such as passacaglias, canons, and fugues.

Schoenberg did not rest on his negative achievement, the dissolution of traditional principles of melody and harmony to create atonality, but went on to develop a technique of employing tones in new relationships that characterizes the works of his third period. Schoenberg called the new technique "the method of composing with twelve tones" and lived to see his invention adopted by many of the world's foremost composers.

In the application of this method, the twelve tones of the chromatic scale are arranged in a particular order determined afresh by the composer for each composition. No tone may be returned to before all of the others have been used, so that complete equality of all twelve tones is assured. The series, called a "tone row," may be employed in four forms: the original row (O), the inverted form (I), the retrograde form (R), and the retrograde inversion (RI), as shown in EXAMPLE 210. These four forms

EXAMPLE 210

Schoenberg, Suite, Op. 25, tone-row forms

may be used horizontally in melodic lines, vertically in chords, or simultaneously in both planes, and transposition of the entire row as well as octave transposition, doubling, and immediate repetition of any tone are permitted. In employing the technique, parts of rows (row groups) consisting of three, four, or six tones may be used. The row and all its variants must be embedded in rhythmic and sound patterns, so that true themes in a variety of textures result.

A page from the autograph score of Schoenberg's *Kammersymphonie,* version for full orchestra, Op. 9B.

The fundamentals of musical form remain unaltered in the third-period works (1923–1951) of Schoenberg, for the compositions embodying the serial technique are cast in sonata-form, variations, rondos, and the like. The most significant works of the group include the *Variations for Orchestra* (1928); several chamber-music compositions: the third and fourth string quartets (1927, 1936), a woodwind quintet (1924), and several other works; two concertos, one for violin (1936) and one for piano (1942); and the last two operas (see Chapter 30). Greater familiarity with Schoenberg's idiom has enabled today's audiences to understand many of these works, to derive aesthetic experiences from them, and to realize fully the emotional variety and spiritual content contained in them.

Berg. In his capacity as a teacher Schoenberg attracted students who became friends, disciples, and composers in their own right. Of his many pupils, the most outstanding were Alban Berg (1885–1935) and Anton Webern, who together with Schoenberg constitute the modern Viennese school. Berg, born in Vienna, belonged to an artistic family and was spared the financial problems that beset many composers; he was of frail health and almost neurotic, however, and realized his potential only as a pupil of Schoenberg. His externally uneventful life was tragically cut short in 1935.

Berg's main importance lies in the field of dramatic music (see Chapter 30), although his development from Romanticism to serial composition closely parallels Schoenberg's. The early period is represented by numerous songs and a piano sonata (1905–1908); the second, atonal period by a string quartet (1910), some orchestral pieces (1914), and a few songs for voice and orchestra based on postcard inscriptions (1912). Even as late as the chamber concerto for violin, piano and thirteen wind instruments (1925), he had not yet definitely adopted the serial technique.

That stage was reached in his second opera, *Lulu* (see page 624), and in three other late works: the *Lyric Suite* for string quartet (1926), *Der Wein* ("The Wine," 1930), a concert aria for voice and orchestra, and the celebrated violin concerto (1935), first performed after Berg's death. In Berg's twelve-tone works the emotional aspect is stressed (he was called the Romanticist among the expressionists), and the tone rows are so selected that traditional harmonies can be employed (see EXAMPLE 211;

EXAMPLE 211

Berg, Tone row from the *Lyric Suite*

the triadic possibilities are indicated by brackets). His themes are lyrical rather than angular, the forms are clear, and the instrumental sound is more mellow than Schoenberg's. Quotations from earlier music (*Tristan* in the *Lyric Suite,* for example, and a Bach chorale and a folksong in the violin concerto) contribute to making Berg's music generally approachable. His ability to combine divergent elements from various styles is a unique and personal aspect of his music.

Webern. Anton Webern was born in Vienna in 1883 into a noble (but not wealthy) family. He became the first of Schoenberg's pupils and also completed a Ph.D. degree in musicology at the University of Vienna in 1906. He was active as a conductor in minor posts and as a director of several choral organizations, and he also taught privately, often suffering from financial hardships. The German occupation of Austria after 1938 added to his personal difficulties, and during World War II he moved to a village near Salzburg. There he was killed accidentally by an American military policeman in 1945.[1]

---

[1] The circumstances of his death have only recently been discovered. See Hans Moldenhauer, *The Death of Anton Webern,* New York, Philosophical Library, 1961.

The Romantic compositions of Webern's youth, made available only recently, include numerous songs, chamber music, and an orchestral piece modeled on the styles of Mahler and Strauss. In his first published work, a Passacaglia (1908) for orchestra, Webern stood at the furthest edge of tonality and then, like Schoenberg, entered a period of atonal composition before adopting serial techniques. But Webern's music is quite unlike that of Schoenberg and Berg, and over thirty years elapsed before its message was grasped. The number of his works is small and their dimensions are minute, but they contain a maximum amount of expressiveness within their extremely small size. Called the "composer of the pianissimo espressivo," Webern possessed not only a sensitivity to sound and dynamics but also a great gift for intellectual organization; thus every note of his music has a special meaning and an individual function.

Webern's music is unique on several counts, for not only do the pitches fall into carefully worked-out patterns but the tone colors as well. Schoenberg had established the concept of *Klangfarbenmelodie* ("melody of tone colors") in some of his works by relating certain tones to specific tone colors. Webern completed that aspect of the technique, for in his music each instrument plays only a few tones before being relieved by another instrument; the result is a highly transparent and iridescent tonal fabric. The tone row itself becomes more concentrated, for certain row segments are themselves related to other segments or transpositions of segments; an example is seen in his Symphony, Opus 21, in which tones 7–12 constitute a transposition (augmented fourth downward) of tones 6–1. Dynamics are employed in a particular order, and rhythmic values are sometimes organized in a manner similar to pitches. Finally, the works are based on forms of the highest complexity, such as canons, mirror canons, and symmetrical variations.

The majority of Webern's compositions are songs or chamber-music works. In spite of the abstract and instrumental treatment of vocal lines and their jagged contours, their emotional component shines through (see EXAMPLE 212). During his lifetime he was considered a musical crank

EXAMPLE 212

Webern, *Die geheimnisvolle Flöte*

Strau - che,   und mein Lied   flog

Reprinted by permission of Universal Edition A.G., Vienna.

or worse in Vienna and was scarcely known elsewhere; today his music and his principles are responsible for the formation of a post-Webern school and have influenced many composers of electronic music (to be discussed below) and the latest period of Stravinsky's work.

Other composers. In the decades after its development the serial technique spread to other European countries and to the Americas. It has been used in part by some later composers and totally by others. Ernst Křenek (b. 1900), whose dramatic works will be discussed in Chapter 30, has become an active exponent of the twelve-tone style. Roberto Gerhard (b. 1896), of Spanish birth but a resident of England since about 1939, was a pupil of Schoenberg; in his tone rows he equates the width of the interval between the tones with the length of the tones and thus arrives at rhythmic series. Luigi Dallapiccola (b. 1904) has applied serial techniques to the lyricism of his native Italy; his instrumental and dramatic works (see page 626) have shown that this can be done successfully. Humphrey Searle (b. 1915), an English pupil of Webern, composed a symphony (1953) based on the tone row of his teacher's string quartet, utilizing traditional forms (sonata-form, rondo, etc.). The American adherents of serial techniques will be discussed in Chapter 31.

Bartók—An Individual Style

UNINFLUENCED by the currents of other contemporary music, Béla Bartók created a completely personal style. The uniquely original nature of his musical language remained intact, even though at times it seemed to resemble other parallel developments. Bartók is usually classified as a folklorist, for the basic rhythmic and melodic elements of his music can be seen as derived from the folk materials of his native land. But unlike Romantic nationalists, he created an idiom that reflected the spirit of peasant music and did not impose folksongs and rhythms on the forms of art music. He was aided in this achievement by his research in folklore, for together with Kodály (see page 589) and others he collected and analyzed thousands of authentic folk melodies from Hungary and neighboring countries, Rumania and Bulgaria, and also from Arabia, Egypt, and Turkey.

Born into a musical family in 1881, he received his first training from his mother. As an accomplished young pianist he attended the Budapest Academy, and in 1907 he was appointed an instructor of piano there, a position he retained for more than thirty years, taking leaves of absence for concert tours or collecting expeditions. When the political connections between Hungary and Hitler's Third Reich became imminent in 1940 Bartók migrated to the United States. But his hopes for a successful continuation of his career did not materialize, and neither teaching positions nor financial aid became available. He died almost indigent in New York in 1945; then, almost immediately, his fame as one of the greatest composers of the twentieth century began to spread around the musical world.

Compositions. Although the development of Bartók's style progressed in a straight line, certain stylistic aspects are seen more prominently at some times than others, permitting his works to be grouped into periods. The first period, to about 1908, includes compositions that still reveal the influences of Romantic and even impressionistic styles, somewhat combined with elements of his personal and nationalistic traits. His first string quartet (1908) is the best-known representative of the period.

Between 1908 and 1928 two tendencies dominated Bartók's composition: an emphasis on the material and spirit of folk music and experimentation with new sounds, rhythms, and harmonies. His works became astringent, harsh, extremely dissonant, and structurally complex, and in the early 1920's he approached the styles of expressionism. The piano compositions of this period include folkloristic pieces such as the *Rumanian Dances* (1910) and *Improvisations on Hungarian Folksongs* (1920), but they also include abstract works, of which the Suite (1916) and Sonata (1926) are representative. Between these two types lies the *Allegro barbaro* (1911), a piece rhythmically and structurally derived from the dance but experimental and dissonant in its harmony. The set of piano pieces entitled *Mikrokosmos,* a cycle of 153 graded pieces from the easiest to the most difficult, on which Bartók worked for eleven years (1926–1937), shows a transition from the second to the third period.

The universally admired masterworks were all composed between 1928 and 1943, and the latest of them reveal that Bartók's tonal orientation became stronger and his harmonic idiom more mellow without any loss of melodic or rhythmic strength. Two outstanding achievements of his last period are the *Music for Strings, Percussion and Celesta* (1936) and the *Concerto for Orchestra* (1943); the latter is distinguished not only by its contrapuntal ingenuity and a virtuosic treatment of the instruments that justifies its title, but also by a blend of humor, irony, and deepest emotion. The last four of his six string quartets (No. 1 was composed in 1908, No. 2 in 1917) are among the outstanding works of the literature. They reflect the harmonic and rhythmic idioms of the periods in which they were composed, but in addition they contain a wealth of fascinating experiments with string techniques and textures.

Several concertos among Bartók's third period works are important. The second piano concerto (1931) is virtuosic throughout and concise in form; adagio and scherzo are combined into one movement and the rondo finale is based on themes from the opening allegro. The more serene third piano concerto (1945, his last completed work) contains a chorale theme with elaborations as a slow movement and ends with a sprightly rondo with fugal sections. A violin concerto (1938) and an unfinished viola concerto (1945, orchestrated by Tibor Serly and performed in 1949), like the other concertos, are most valuable additions to the form.

Style characteristics. The melody and rhythm of Bartók's music have their roots in his national heritage. The folk melodies of eastern Europe are unlike the symmetrical melodies of the West. They are often modal or pentatonic, or they may show the influence of the Orient in their augmented seconds. Certain accentual patterns in the Hungarian language are quite different from those of Romance and Germanic languages, leading to irregular metrical and rhythmic patterns which are reflected in Bartók's music (see EXAMPLE 213). The best-known Hungarian dance,

EXAMPLE 213

Bartók, *Hungarian Peasant Songs*, No. 3

the *czárdás*, consists of two sections, one slow, improvisational, and rhythmically free (*lassu*), the other fast, rhythmically concise, and ferocious in mood (*friss*); both melodic types are used by Bartók. Whether his melodies are derived from folk material or entirely free, they are similar in contour, rhythm, and mood, and the rhythm is most often the dominating element.

Bartók's harmonic style is predominantly harsh and full of unresolved dissonances, although a turn to a milder style marked his last years. Chords built on seconds or fourths abound, octaves within chords are likely to be augmented or diminished (C–C♯ or C♯–C, for example), and even more extreme dissonances appear in clusters. All these devices are used for their expressive value, however, and never arbitrarily or illogically. A variety of textures is employed, ranging from dissonant contrapuntal passages in fugal and imitative style to homophonic passages in which melodies progress over a static chord group. The textural variety is balanced by Bartók's variety of instrumental colors; some movements are thick, percussive and dark, and others are based on transparent sonorities of delicate beauty. Such characteristics, combined with a wide dynamic range and ingenious use of form principles, give Bartók's music its strength and interest. Although he had no direct followers, he influenced the course of all music by his uncompromising development of a virile and consistently powerful kind of music.

The Neo-Classical Style

THE EARLY twentieth-century reactions to Wagnerianism on the one hand and impressionism on the other led to a vaguely defined style that had at its roots a desire to restore objectivity, balance, and restraint. Since some of the adherents of that style also restored traditional forms and even a degree of eighteenth-century thematic development, they were grouped under the term neo-Classical (see page 585). The French members of that school were discussed in Chapter 28, for their connections with the nineteenth century were still relatively close. Other, later neo-Classicists had a less tangible connection with that century and their styles are entirely products of the twentieth.

Hindemith. The central figure in contemporary German music is Paul Hindemith (b. 1895). In his works stylistic elements of the Baroque and Classical periods meet with modern harmonic practices and linear counterpoint, to result in a style that is personal and distinctive. Through his versatility as a professional musician—he has been active as composer, performer, conductor, theorist, and teacher—he has made his ideas widely known. Born in Hanau, near Frankfurt, he achieved a measure of fame in his youth as a viola virtuoso, chamber-music player, and conductor. As early as 1927 he was called to the Prussian State Academy of Music to teach composition. He filled this post with distinction until Hitler's government made his further activity in Germany impossible. Branded as a "cultural Bolshevik," he left in 1935 to reorganize the Turkish music-school system, and a few years later he moved to the United States, where he traveled widely and became a professor at Yale University. In 1953 he resigned that position and settled in Switzerland.

Hindemith has been a prolific composer in many musical fields and has been successful in all of them. Chamber music has attracted him most often, but orchestral, vocal, and dramatic works (see Chapter 30) are also numerous. His orchestral works include two full symphonies (E♭, 1941, and *Sinfonia serena*, 1947) and many smaller works such as sinfoniettas, a *Konzertmusik* for strings and brass (1931) and others; more than a dozen concertos, including several for viola, composed for himself; and the delightfully humorous *Symphonic Metamorphoses of Themes by Weber* (1944).

Among his chamber-music works are a series of about eight for various instrumental combinations, called simply *Kammermusiken,* seven string quartets, and a variety of miscellaneous works. To fill the need for solo literature for orchestral instruments he composed a series of sonatas for virtually all of the wind and string instruments, including viola d'amore and harp—each sonata with piano accompaniment. He has also written several piano sonatas, three for organ, and many other instrumental works. Of special importance is the *Ludus tonalis* ("Tonal Play," 1943) for piano solo, consisting of twelve fugues, one in each key, separated by interludes.

His choral works include the large oratorio, *Das Unaufhörliche* ("The Unending," 1931), several cantatas, and many choruses with and without accompaniment, including a madrigal cycle on poems by Weinheber (1958). A song cycle on texts by Rilke, *Das Marienleben* ("The Life of Mary," 1923, revised in 1948), is among his finest vocal works.

Another group of Hindemith's works is of the type called *Gebrauchs-musik* ("functional music"); it includes pedagogical pieces, works easy enough for amateurs but written with the same stylistic consistency that has marked his major works, and a few works with voices and instruments.

More than a decade was required for Hindemith to arrive at the style with which his name is associated. The influences of late Romantic composers, especially Brahms, Reger, and to a lesser extent Strauss, can be traced in the first ten works. A period of experimentation followed, in which he indulged in expressionistic outbursts, parodistic elements, and even jazz idioms. Gradually he absorbed the ideals of neo-Classicism—although the term neo-Baroque better describes his style, for in addition to Classical types he incorporated stylistic elements of Bach and earlier composers.

Hindemith defined the theoretical basis of his style in a book entitled *Unterweisung im Tonsatz* (1937).[2] In his system all intervals are arranged in ascending order of dissonance from the octave to the tritone; the degree of tension (dissonance) in them determines how they will be used. Chords are not necessarily constructed out of superimposed thirds, but all chords can be explained in reference to a tonal center, and Hindemith has never even approached serial writing. The interval of the fourth is prominent in his music, especially in melodic contexts (see EXAMPLE 214).

The texture and form of Hindemith's compositions are based on those of earlier centuries. Sonata-form, variation form, concerto grosso, passa-caglia, and fugue are all frequently represented. His contrapuntal technique is phenomenal, and the problems encountered in complex canonic and fugal writing are solved brilliantly. In spite of the preponderance of polyphonic textures, the phrases are well separated and cadences are

2 Translated into English as *The Craft of Musical Composition,* 1941–1942.

EXAMPLE 214

Hindemith, Trio No. 2

clearly defined. The rhythms are straightforward, but they often generate considerable momentum because of their steady flow; meters are changed freely if the moods of the music require. The dissonant melodies, contrapuntal textures, and free-flowing rhythms are embedded in an orchestral color that is neither Romantic nor impressionistic. Groups of instruments are pitted against each other; solo passages, especially in the winds, are generally placed opposite other passages in which a full or thick sound is characteristic; and the orchestral colors are made to blend rather than to stand out individually.

Hindemith's concept of music as a moral or ethical force has had a strong influence on his work. He emphasizes the importance of music in fostering the philosophical and spiritual nature of man and refuses the concept of art as mere entertainment. In his latest works he has stressed religious and even mystical thoughts; humor and lightness have been moved to the background. The consistency of his style across four decades and the varied expressive contents of his many works testify to the important place he holds in twentieth-century music.

Prokofiev. The long line of Russian post-Romantic music came to an end with the early works of Igor Stravinsky (see page 606) and Sergey Prokofiev (1891–1953). The subjective expression, rhapsodic utterance, and expansive emotionalism typical of Russian music of the 1880's found no place in Prokofiev's works. A capable pianist and industrious composer at the age of thirteen, he had already studied with Glière in Moscow when he entered the St. Petersburg Conservatory, where Rimsky-Korsakov was among his teachers. Within a few years after graduation in 1914, he was recognized as one of Russia's most brilliant pianists and had attracted much attention for the audacity of his music. From 1918 to 1933 he lived in various parts of Europe, visited the United States on several occasions, and made concert tours in Russia. In 1933, however, he returned to Russia permanently, except for another American tour in 1938. He was severely criticized by the Soviet authorities for what was considered his decadent musical tendencies (a synonym for a truly contemporary style), but eventually was restored to official favor. He died in Moscow in 1953.

The works that first brought Prokofiev to public notice already contained the elements that were to become characteristic of all his music. In the *Scythian Suite* (1914), the famous *Classical Symphony* (1917), and several of his early concertos and sonatas he introduced a quality of rhythmic propulsion, a harmonic scheme that avoided the traditional tonic-dominant relationships, and a melodic type that was sometimes angular, sometimes grotesque. In addition, the sense of humor that became a striking element of his later style was also present.

Later works, notably the fifth piano concerto (1932) and the fifth symphony (1944), brought a lyric quality to expression, but the vigorous rhythms and flexible harmonic scheme were retained. Melodies became less angular and often changed their harmonic direction in midcourse; in one typical passage, the melody gives the effect of touching on four different keys within eight measures (see EXAMPLE 215).

Among the elements that distinguish Prokofiev's music from that of the nineteenth century is a new economy in the use of material. Conventional transitions between themes are largely eliminated, and nothing is permitted to interfere with the clear and direct perception of the thematic material itself; further, recapitulations are generally shortened

EXAMPLE 215

Prokofiev, Symphony No. 5

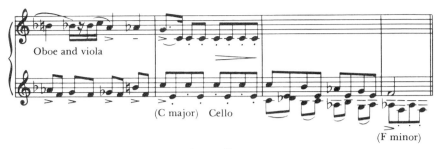

(C major)   Cello

(F minor)

or often only suggested instead of written out in full. In orchestral compositions the economy extends to the instrumental writing; the amount
of harmonic filling in the inner voices and the instrumental doublings
are greatly reduced, and a transparent, even sparse texture results in
which each instrumental color stands out clearly.

Another element of difference between nineteenth-century music and
the typically twentieth-century music of Prokofiev is in his use of rhythm.
The fast movements of Prokofiev are often vitalized by a regularly recurring or *ostinato* rhythmic figure that develops great momentum; in slow
movements triplets are often set against eighth notes, syncopations are
employed, and accents are placed on weak beats—all in order to heighten
the rhythmic tension.

While Prokofiev's harmonies remain within the tonal system, his simultaneous use of major and minor scales, chromatically conceived melodies,
and pungent dissonances give a fresh sound to his music. Tempo and
meter change freely within movements, phrases are typically five, six, or
more measures in length instead of the traditional four or eight measures, and frequent changes in the density of the texture give the music
a fluid, flexible expressive content.

Shostakovich. Half a generation younger than Prokofiev, Dmitri Shostakovich (b. 1906) was educated at the St. Petersburg Conservatory under
Glazunov and Steinberg. His first symphony (1925), written when he was
nineteen, was an immediate success in Russia and soon was heard in
musical centers in Europe and the United States. In subsequent compositions, however, he did not always realize the promise of that early work.
His fifth symphony (1937), a piano quintet (1940), and six string quartets (1938–1956) reveal him at his best. Many other works are uneven or
trivial.

Shostakovich's style, containing elements drawn from Prokofiev, Mahler, and even Beethoven, is based on contrasts of mood and texture.
Essentially tonal in its harmonic idiom, his music is alternately satirical,
sentimental, and flamboyant, but it always reveals the composer's technical competence. His orchestral writing, like that of Prokofiev, is trans-

parent and sparse (except in the so-called *Leningrad Symphony* of 1941) and testifies to his complete command of orchestral resources.

Other composers. The problem of finding a personal style that avoided Romantic excesses while salvaging techniques derived from traditional music has been solved in many different ways. In the music of Frank Martin (b. 1890), the most eminent contemporary Swiss composer, it was solved by adapting the twelve-tone technique of Schoenberg (see page 594) to diatonic, triadic harmony in a detailed contrapuntal texture.

Benjamin Britten (b. 1913), perhaps the most prominent English composer of the present time, found his solution by reverting to traditional forms. Sets of variations, passacaglias, and fugues are common in his works, but in each case the form is modified to suit the expressive requirements of the work of which it is a part. Britten is best represented in the fields of vocal music; his operas (see page 629) and choral works reflect his great sensitivity to the characteristics of English speech.

Stravinsky—A Panorama of Styles

THE CREATIVE career of Igor Stravinsky (b. 1882) covers a span of almost sixty years. All the styles and experiments of the twentieth century pass in review when we consider his music. From post-Romantic beginnings in a Russian nationalist context, through short essays in expressionism, he developed into the standard-bearer for international neo-Classicism; and in the last decade, he has embraced serial techniques which he had earlier rejected. In each period of his development he composed significant works, and as early as the 1920's he became a dominant figure.

Born near St. Petersburg, the son of a famous opera singer, Stravinsky grew up in a musical atmosphere; he was nineteen before he began the serious study of music, however, and twenty-five before he went to Rimsky-Korsakov for regular lessons. By 1909 several of his compositions had been performed. He began his association with the impresario Sergey Diaghilev, which resulted in a number of ballets, and Stravinsky's international career was launched. He had left Russia before World War I and spent the war years in Switzerland. When the Russian revolution made his return to his homeland impossible, he settled in France from 1920 to 1939. At the outbreak of World War II he moved to California, becoming an American citizen in 1945, but he has continued to make world tours as a conductor of his own works.

Compositions. Works for the stage, to be discussed in Chapter 30, lie at the center of Stravinsky's creative output. Instrumental and choral compositions are more numerous, however, dating from the beginning of his career to its latest phase, and chamber-music works and smaller pieces are also represented.

The symphonic works are abstract and without programmatic intention, although a few have titles to guide the listener. The first symphony (E♭, 1907) completed during the period of his studies with Rimsky-

Korsakov, is in the nationalist tradition and orchestrated in Romantic style. After a gap of over thirty years the *Symphony in C,* written for the Chicago Symphony Orchestra (1940), and *Symphony in Three Movements,* for the New York Philharmonic (1945), revealed the full flowering of neo-Classical formal and stylistic tenets. Single pieces for orchestra range from the youthful *Scherzo fantastique* (1909) to several works written in the 1940's of which the *Ode* (in memory of Natalie Kussevitzsky, 1943) and *Norwegian Moods* (1944) are the best known.

Stravinsky made extensive use of smaller orchestral groupings such as chamber orchestras, ensembles of solo instruments, and other combinations. The *Symphonies of Wind Instruments* (1920) in memory of Debussy, *Dumbarton Oaks Concerto* (1938) for sixteen instruments written in neo-Baroque style, *Danses concertantes* (1942), a set of dances without stage action, and *Ebony Concerto* (1946), composed for Woody Herman's dance band, are prominent in this category.

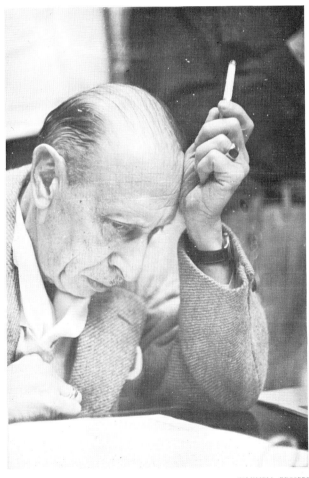

Igor Stravinsky,
b. 1882.

The earliest of Stravinsky's concertos are one for piano and orchestral wind instruments (1924) and a *Capriccio* for piano and full orchestra (1929, revised 1949). The latter is a virtuosic work in three movements; percussive effects, compulsive rhythmic figurations, and striking leaps are among the technical devices employed, and a rhapsodic slow movement shows the composer's percussive treatment of the solo instrument (see EXAMPLE 216). A violin concerto (1931) and a concerto for two pianos (1935) complete the list.

EXAMPLE 216

Stravinsky, *Capriccio*

The vocal works, some for solo voices and others for chorus, some with orchestra and others with smaller accompanying groups, vary in scope and importance. The *Symphony of Psalms* (1930) is undoubtedly Stravinsky's most celebrated choral work. Economically written, it dispenses with violins and violas and is consequently dark in tone. The three movements of the work, with texts drawn from the Book of Psalms, recall the forms of the Baroque period; a double fugue in the second movement is outstanding in this regard. A later choral work, the *Canticum sacrum* (1956), written for St. Mark's Cathedral in Venice, is vigorous and solemn in its neo-Classical first and fifth movements, while in the middle movements, each referring to one of the cardinal virtues of faith, hope, and charity, serial techniques are employed. A setting of the Lamentations of Jeremiah, *Threni* (1958), is entirely in the twelve-tone style; contrapuntal mastery is shown in the several canons in the work, in which a dry and bland orchestral sound is typical.

In a Cantata (1952) for two soloists, women's chorus, and five instruments, based on old English poems, Stravinsky employed such complex forms as ricercare and canon and devised a texture in which the manipulation of thematic material and the use of twelve-tone rows go hand in hand. In several short song cycles, the instrumental accompaniments are exceedingly diverse. *Three Poems from the Japanese* (1913) are for soprano accompanied by four wind instruments, piano, and string quartet; *The Cat's Cradle Songs* (1916) are for female voice and three clarinets; *Three Songs from Shakespeare* (1954), for mezzo-soprano, are accompanied by flute, clarinet, and viola; and *In Memoriam Dylan Thomas* (1954), a single work rather than a cycle, is set for tenor, string quartet, and four trombones.

The relatively few chamber-music works include several masterpieces. In *Three Pieces for String Quartet* (1914), Stravinsky experimented with radical sonorities and harmonies, while the contrapuntal and harmonic style of his middle period was established in the Octet (1923). *Ragtime* (1918), for eleven instruments, had brought the rhythms and melodic idioms of jazz into contact with the composer's personal style, and jazz elements were influential in his best known chamber-music work, *L'Histoire du Soldat* ("The Soldier's Tale," 1918), a work for seven instruments and a narrator, to which a dancer may be added if the work is staged as a pantomime. His Septet (1953) for three strings, three winds, and piano is representative of his latest period.

Stravinsky's piano pieces include two sonatas (1904, 1922), a sonata for two pianos (1944), and several smaller pieces. *Piano Rag-Music* (1919), a virtuosic piece based on syncopations, was composed for Artur Rubinstein; a *Circus Polka for a Young Elephant* (1942) is full of grotesque humor; and a collection of piano pieces for children, *The Five Fingers* (1921), is intended as a set of teaching pieces. His flexibility in the face of the most divergent compositional problems is unmatched among contemporary composers.

Stravinsky's styles. Three clearly defined styles of writing can be seen in Stravinsky's music. In his earliest works he represented Russian nationalism, composing in a post-Romantic idiom; his euphonious orchestral sound and luxuriant harmonic scheme, encompassing extensive modulations, revealed his ties with tradition. Even at that stage, however, his rhythmic sense was highly developed, for he largely abandoned standard patterns and employed regular and irregular meters ($\frac{2}{4}$, $\frac{3}{8}$, $\frac{5}{16}$, and $\frac{4}{16}$, for example) in close succession; in addition he made considerable use of other irregular groupings, such as $\frac{5}{4}$ and $\frac{7}{4}$. Further, he used traditional patterns in nonsymmetrical forms: the eighth notes in a $\frac{4}{4}$ measure were often arranged in patterns of $2 + 3 + 3$ or $3 + 2 + 3$ instead of $4 + 4$. He invested these irregular units with a strongly motoric drive and used many rhythmic *ostinati* and polyrhythms.

Stravinsky's subsequent evolution led him first to intensified chromaticism and increasingly dissonant chord structures. About 1911 he touched briefly on atonality, as seen in the cantata *The King of the Stars* (1911), for male chorus and orchestra; and an affinity with the style of Schoenberg came close in such works as *Three Poems from the Japanese* (1913) and *Three Pieces for String Quartet* (1914). This transitional, tentative period came to an end early in the 1920's, when the neo-Classical phase of his career began.

In the neo-Classical works Stravinsky used less chromaticism and turned increasingly to a diatonic idiom, employing it in a highly individual way. Intervals of thirds, fifths, and sixths replace seconds and fourths as chordal building material. Triads and seventh chords are employed in major and minor forms simultaneously, so that their harmonic functions are canceled, and two diatonic chords (tonic and dominant, for example, or supertonic and mediant) are often sounded together, to give rise to the device called "pandiatonicism." Keys are juxtaposed rather than connected through modulations. And in the music which results from the use of these harmonic devices and which retains the rhythmic and metrical irregularities of the earlier period, the sound ideal is radically altered. Thin and transparent textures, sometimes with only two voices, replace the full-sounding instrumental combinations of the works written before 1920. Wind instruments, especially oboes and bassoons, are prominent and the expressive string instruments are either omitted or relegated to subordinate roles.

Stravinsky's acceptance of Classical and Baroque forms does not imply imitation but reflects his use of the earlier principles of organization in his own music. Song forms and sonata types are found, as well as contrapuntal types such as fugues and canons. The melodic structures sometimes assume the triadic patterns characteristic of eighteenth-century music. Stravinsky's attitudes toward such use of older materials and toward his art in general have been expounded in several of his books and lectures. He is concerned essentially with the clear organization of the musical material he creates in his imagination, with the intellectual aspects of the creative process; the emotional element is less important, for the sounds and melodies contain expressive values within themselves.

In his most recent period, in which he has gradually altered his basic techniques, Stravinsky's aesthetic attitude has not changed. The modification of his technical processes may in part be due to his awakened interest in music of the Renaissance. His Mass (1948) and *Monument for Gesualdo* (1960) represent landmarks in this development. He has also been attracted by the highly developed intellectual processes of Webern, feeling that Webern's music (see page 597) is less Romantic (that is, less emotional) than that of Schoenberg and Berg. This adoption of a new method has not entirely changed his personal idiom, however, and even in works based on serial techniques the highly individualized Stravinsky style is still present, tonal relationships can be established, and rhythmic manipulation dominates.

The evolution of Stravinsky's serial style came about gradually. Tone rows of five to seven or more tones are used in some works (*In Memoriam Dylan Thomas*, for example), even while in other works contemporary with them tone rows are missing. In still other compositions of the same period, notably the *Agon* ballet (1957), twelve-tone sections occur. Thus

Stravinsky arrived at a fully developed serial technique, carrying further elements that were suggested in the music of Schoenberg and Webern. Transpositions and interactions of the four forms of the row (O, I, R, and RI; see page 594) are employed freely, and the rows are so constructed that certain tone groups called "invariants" reappear in transpositions of the row (see EXAMPLE 217), thereby facilitating modulations. Further, the rows are used in segments and the order of the notes is changed.

EXAMPLE 217

Tone row with invariants

An analysis of Stravinsky's serial techniques alone does not explain the structure of an entire composition, however, for a typical work contains a definite form and its sections are sometimes repeated literally. According to Stravinsky, the real meaning of twentieth-century music is to be found in the full development of serial techniques and the related principle of perpetual variation. Thus he has shown no interest in the use of nontraditional tonal material of the type currently being explored by a group of younger composers.

Latest Experimental Styles

THE ORGANIZATIONAL techniques of Anton Webern have stimulated many experiments designed to achieve complete intellectual control of all aspects of music. Some composers have sought to transcend traditional tone-producing media by abandoning instruments and voices and turning to electronic devices for creating and manipulating sound. Such devices make possible a greater differentiation of the tonal system, dynamics, and rhythms. Edgar Varèse (b. 1885), a French composer long active in the United States, was a pioneer in this field. As early as the 1920's he composed works for unorthodox instrumental groups in which percussion instruments played leading parts; these works, of which *Hyperprism* (1923) and *Ionization* (1931) are the best known, are essentially essays in rhythm and sonority that dispense with traditional forms. Later Varèse turned to electronic sound generators and tape recorders and in 1958 contributed a *Poème électronique* for the Brussels Exposition.

Olivier Messiaen (b. 1908), prominent French composer, has arrived at his innovations by adapting serial techniques in an individual way. Selecting certain scale segments (later, rows) for his melodies and chords, he invented new rhythmic patterns by augmenting or diminishing the rhythmic values of each note in a musical fragment; for example, each note might be lengthened by half or by quarter (see EXAMPLE 218). He

EXAMPLE 218

Rhythmic patterns

has also introduced Hindu melodies and rhythms as well as occasional sounds of nature (bird calls, for example) into his music; in spite of these extraneous elements, a refined sound derived from impressionism is basic to his music.

Pierre Boulez (b. 1925), a pupil of Messiaen and the undisputed leader of the French experimentalist school, took his point of departure from serial techniques, working toward the complete integration of music by incorporating duration rows, dynamic rows, and articulation rows as well as tone rows. In the application of a duration row, the length of each tone in a series is determined by a formula employed like a tone row; the loudness level and articulation quality (staccato, legato, slurred, etc.) of tones in that series are derived in similar fashion. Boulez has also employed the exotic rhythmic patterns introduced by his teacher. He has recently been attracted by "musique concrète," which attempts to treat nonmusical sounds (that is, noises) electronically and employ them coloristically. He also permits the performer to change the arrangement of sections in a work during a performance; this principle is called "chance music" or "aleatory music" (from *alea, dice*).

Karlheinz Stockhausen (b. 1928), the leading German composer of electronic music, has fully exploited the principle of "chance music." In his *Klavierstück XI* ("Piano Piece No. 11," 1956) he has assembled fragments of musical ideas, leaving to the performer the order and number of times (up to three) each fragment is to be played. Stockhausen's earlier works, based on Webern's techniques, are for conventional instruments; in later compositions tonal material produced by electronic generators is occasionally combined with the sound of the human voice. The complexity of this music is such that charts and graphs are required to supplement the musical notation. Critical opinion is still divided on the extent to which it will influence the path of music into the future.

The Twentieth Century: Opera

C OMPOSERS of opera at the turn of the century stood in the shadow of Wagner and Verdi, whose work had profoundly affected all aspects of the musical theater. The new generation of opera composers, forced to meet the stylistic challenges offered by those masters, reacted in a number of different ways, and the twentieth century began with a variety of operatic styles. Four distinct lines of musical thought can be traced: post-Romantic, impressionistic, expressionistic, and neo-Classical. In the most recent operas, however, the lines have become blurred to some extent, for composers have tended to assimilate elements drawn from two or more of the basic styles.

"Maestro," silver sculpture by Paul Lobel.

Post-Romantic Operas

THE INFLUENCE of Wagner's achievements in the fields of harmony and structure lasted through the first decades of the twentieth century. Direct imitation of his style had abated, but certain features persisted to such an extent that the term post-Romantic is justified in referring to many operas of the time.

Strauss. During a long career extending from 1889 to 1942, Richard Strauss (1864–1949; see page 561) composed fifteen operas [1] and two ballets. Ten of the operas have remained in the German repertoire, the majority gaining international recognition as well. The first four of the fifteen reveal a development and intensification of Wagner's techniques but none of his philosophical ideas. In later works, Strauss employed closed musical forms more frequently than he did Wagner's types of open forms, and his harmony became more conservative, though he did not abandon the leitmotif technique. The librettos are dramatically stronger and more sophisticated, sometimes even introducing symbolism without losing their direct and immediate appeal.

Strauss's first outstanding opera was *Salome* (1905), based on a German translation of Oscar Wilde's play in which the Biblical story became a drama of psychological perversion. This was followed by *Elektra* (1908), the first of the six operas Strauss wrote in collaboration with Hugo von Hofmannsthal (1874–1929). Through its intensity, excitement, and passion, *Elektra* marked the virtual end of the Romantic music drama.

In the operas from *Guntram* to *Elektra,* Strauss employed an orchestral polyphony which is even thicker than that found in Wagner and sometimes lacks the mellow orchestral color of the earlier composer's style. The harmony is more advanced and the dissonances are generally more extreme than Wagner's, resulting from combinations of distant harmonies, suggesting polytonality, or from tone clusters having no tonal relationships. Chord resolutions are often either delayed or missing entirely, but in such cases tonal passages with strong cadences are then inserted to provide contrast. Tonalities are associated with particular characters or situations, and tonal contexts are adjusted to suit the background; for example, Oriental elements are suggested in *Salome* and harsh quasi-modal or polymodal harmonies in *Elektra*. All this harmonic variety is placed under the prevailing declamatory arioso resembling Wagner's "endless melody."

The most celebrated of the collaborations with Hugo von Hofmannsthal, *Der Rosenkavalier* (1910), marked a change in Strauss's style, ap-

---

1 *Guntram* (1893), *Feuersnot* ("Fire Famine," 1901), *Salome* (1905), *Elektra* (1908), *Der Rosenkavalier* ("The Cavalier of the Rose," 1910), *Ariadne auf Naxos* (1912), *Die Frau ohne Schatten* ("The Woman Without a Shadow," 1917), *Intermezzo* (1923), *Die aegyptische Helena* ("The Egyptian Helen [of Troy]," 1927), *Arabella* (1932), *Die schweigsame Frau* ("The Taciturn Woman," 1935), *Friedenstag* ("Day of Peace," 1936), *Daphne* (1937), *Die Liebe der Danae* ("The Love of Danaë," 1940), and *Capriccio* (1941).

proaching the clarity and relative restraint of the neo-Classical manner. From this work onward, Strauss customarily added other forms to the Wagnerian structure. His larger pieces resemble arias or ensembles in their over-all form; set in well-defined tonalities, they often contain regular symmetrical phrases. Folklike melodies and dances often appear. The orchestral sound is still that of Romanticism, and as in the symphonic poems, Strauss's great mastery of orchestration is always evident. The glittering motive of the rose in *Der Rosenkavalier,* consisting of a chord sequence played on the celesta, is one of his finest achievements.

The operas from *Ariadne auf Naxos* to *Capriccio* are increasingly filled with stylistic experiments. In *Ariadne* (1912) a chamber orchestra accompanies the action, and elements of stylized *opera buffa* (including coloratura effects and ensemble writing) are combined with the expressive and melodious style of *opera seria*. In *Intermezzo* (1923) the main musical content is in the extended orchestral preludes and interludes, while the action itself is carried forward in *recitativo* style. The two symbolic operas, *Die Frau ohne Schatten* (1917) and *Die aegyptische Helena* (1927), become increasingly involved and hyper-Romantic, but the literary element predominates and the approach is intellectual. Extended choral writing and even scene-and-aria form are found in the later operas, notably in *Friedenstag* (1936). The last opera, *Capriccio* (1941), contains movements of dance suites, a number of quotations from other works, and, in the center of the opera, a true fugue on a theme derived from a recitative (see Example 219). In all the operas Strauss applied amazing skill to the solution

EXAMPLE 219

Strauss, *Capriccio*

of technical problems and remained within his personal, highly developed musical idiom; a completely satisfying dramatic style results.

Puccini. The achievements of Verdi and the naturalistic tendencies of the school of *verismo* (see page 531) left their mark on Italian opera production well into the twentieth century. Since the Italian public demanded easy comprehensibility, operas that attempted a more advanced approach were not successful. Giacomo Puccini (1858–1924), the latest of the Italian opera composers to enjoy worldwide fame, took this requirement into account. With very few exceptions his operas cast a magic spell over his audiences, not only because their music was directly appealing but also because his texts worked freely on the emotions; sentimentality, shock, stark drama, and even horror, placed in fascinating settings, are characteristic.

The mere enumeration of Puccini's works recalls their triumphs. *Manon Lescaut* (1893) is based on the same story that Massenet had used, and in setting it he succeeded in matching the French composer's accomplishment. A moving account of the lives of Parisian bohemians, *La Bohème* (1896), and a story of sordid political intrigue, *Tosca* (1900),

EXAMPLE 220

Puccini, *La Bohème*

A scene from Puccini's *Turandot*.

were equally successful. In *Madama Butterfly* (1904) he introduced an exotic setting for the tragic story of the love of a Japanese girl for an American naval officer. A truly American "western," *La fanciulla del West* ("The Girl of the Golden West," 1910), did not reach the high level of the earlier operas, but Puccini hit his stride again in three one-act operas (1912), of which *Gianni Schicchi,* his only comedy, is one of his masterpieces. His last, musically most advanced work, *Turandot* (1924, unfinished), with its last scene completed by Franco Alfano in 1926, continued the chain of successes.

All of Puccini's works, like Verdi's, are of the type called "singers' operas"; that is, they are essentially melodious. The melodic lines are not often long, however; the musical thoughts are compressed into short, characteristic motives that are manipulated and extended in modified sequences and rarely dissolve into coloratura passage work. Other opportunities for vocal display are provided, however: "sobbing" motives, long high tones at climactic points, and similar devices fill his most exciting pages. In arias the vocal part is often doubled in the orchestra, and in the frequent duets the voices sometimes sing in unison, thus making the texture dominantly homophonic. A single line (vocal and instrumental in unison) in the middle range is often accompanied only by a few syncopated chords in the same range (that is, the passage is without a true bass), providing a unique and effective texture almost monophonic in its effect (see EXAMPLE 220). The skillfully written and flawlessly declaimed solo numbers and vocal ensembles are connected by through-composed sections in which leading motives often occur. Recapitulation of large sections—for example, in the closing scene of *La Bohème*—provides an effective dramatic device.

Puccini's harmonic idiom is thoroughly individualistic. On occasion he employs chord sequences similar to those used in impressionistic works. Dissonant chords containing compound appoggiaturas or added tones (see EXAMPLE 221) and chords suggesting a pseudo-Oriental primitivism

EXAMPLE 221

Puccini, *Turandot*

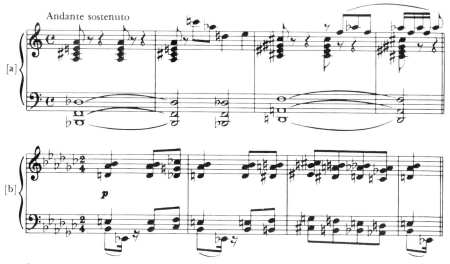

are frequently used. His orchestral writing is equally personal; it includes many free mixtures of unlike colors (brass and strings, for example) and a great variety of sonorities from delicate to overwhelming. With all its color and variety, however, the orchestral writing never interferes with the clarity of the vocal lines.

Other composers. Two operas roughly contemporary with Puccini's achieved international recognition almost equal to that of the older composer's works. Umberto Giordano (1867–1948) composed his finest opera, *Andrea Chenier*, in 1896; Italo Montemezzi (1875–1952) produced his famous *L'Amore dei tre re* ("The Love of Three Kings") in 1913. These are thoroughly dramatic works containing a wealth of melody and many passages full of emotional tension; they provide excellent roles for the singers and are consequently appealing, although neither work is notable for stylistic consistency or great originality.

Composers in countries other than Germany and Italy also worked in the post-Romantic tradition. Dmitri Shostakovich (b. 1906; see page 605) composed several operas that reflect Russian nationalism. These works are relatively simple and strongly tonal in style, and have therefore won acceptance in his homeland, where "understandable music" is virtually required of composers. His opera, *Lady Macbeth of the Mtzensk District* (1934), a grim drama of Russian life, shows the same stylistic eclecticism, gift for parody and caricature, and technical competence that are found in his symphonies. Other Russian composers have also been active in the field, although few of their works have become known outside Russia. Perhaps the best-known such work, written in a conservative and popular style, is *Quiet Flows the Don* (1935) by Ivan Dzerzhinsky (b. 1909); this opera became a kind of national display piece.

Twentieth-century Czech opera has followed two divergent paths. One path, representing a continuation of the Romantic tradition of Smetana and Dvořák, has led to *Schwanda the Bagpiper* (1927), a folk opera filled with singable tunes and dances, by Jaromir Weinberger (b. 1896). The Polka and Fugue from *Schwanda,* arranged for concert performance, have been widely performed and have kept the name of this opera alive. The other path attracted Leos Janáček (1854–1928), who drew his style from the natural inflections of speech and whose style in this respect departed from the Romantic. The best known and most appealing of his eleven operas is *Jenufa* (1904), a moving tragedy of peasant life.

Impressionistic Operas

THE REACTION against Romanticism in France, especially against the Wagnerian influence, began long before the turn of the century; the straightforward, nonsymbolic music of Bizet's *Carmen* had pointed the way as early as 1875. Not until musical impressionism became influential, however, did a new type of French opera emerge, and that type is represented by comparatively few examples.

The new type was foreshadowed by *Louise* (1900), composed by the long-lived Gustave Charpentier (1860–1956). This work, called naturalistic, realistic, and symbolic by various commentators, was labeled a "musical novel" by the composer, who wrote his own libretto. A story of everyday life in Paris, it is filled with sentimental melodies of the Massenet type, a continuously flowing texture containing leitmotifs (though not used in Wagner's symbolic manner), melodramatic passages, and realistic imitations of street cries. The orchestra is subdued but full of glowing color; the music is based on a harmonic idiom that has many points in common with the style of Debussy. In spite of the stylistic mixture found in this opera, *Louise* reflects a specifically Parisian atmosphere. Its realistic portrayal of life was felt to be a welcome antidote to the symbolic works of Wagner.

Debussy. Symbolism of another kind was introduced into Debussy's *Pelléas et Mélisande* (1902). The first performance of this work was an event of historical importance, for it was a new type of opera, entirely French, and equally remote from operatic tradition and extraneous influences. The text, based on Maeterlinck's symbolic play, contains very little action; the love and death of Mélisande, caught between the jealousy of her husband Golaud and the affection of his brother Pelléas, are its principal elements. The surface events of the action do no more than mirror mystical, psychological events, while the characters symbolize vague and often subconscious emotions. Debussy was virtually compelled to create a new technique in setting this play to music.

The dialogues and monologues follow the natural flow of the French language. They are intense rather than eloquent, free rather than stylized into arias, but sometimes, at emotional climaxes, they give way to song. The orchestra, neither symphonic in the Wagnerian style nor accompanying in the traditional manner, is given recurring motives during the short scenes comprising the work; the scenes themselves are connected by extended orchestral interludes. The unreality of the atmosphere is expressed in the iridescent colors of the orchestra, the modal and exotic elements in the harmony, and the augmented and altered chord structures. Restraint takes the place of pathos and dramatic passion, but the intensity increases in the scenes between Mélisande and Pelléas and decreases in Mélisande's

A scene from Debussy's *Pelléas et Mélisande*.

encounters with Golaud. The refinement of this work did not inspire imitation, nor did it create a large following. Even Debussy did not find a worthy successor to it; his later stage works comprise only two minor ballets, *Jeux* and *Khamma,* both composed in 1912.

Dukas. The only other truly impressionistic opera, *Ariane et Barbe-bleue* ("Ariadne and Bluebeard"), was composed by Paul Dukas (see page 584) in 1907. The text, also by Maeterlinck and based on the familiar legend of Bluebeard, is treated in the same symbolic manner that was typical of *Pelléas.* In general, Dukas employed the harmonic and declamatory style of Debussy, but elements of César Franck's style—notably transformation of themes and restless modulation—also found a place. The symphonic element and sheer quantity of sound are more pronounced in Dukas's work, and choral writing is prominent as well.

Ravel. The operas of Maurice Ravel (see page 582) are impressionistic only in their harmony and orchestration; their aesthetic concept and structure show a turn to the neo-Classical school. The comic opera *L'Heure espagnol* ("The Spanish Hour," 1911) is melodious and full of dances and rhythmic animation, and its Spanish color blends perfectly with the French *esprit.* Ravel shared the fondness of other twentieth-century French composers for writing ballets. His famous dance-drama *Daphnis et Chloé* (1912) is today most often performed as an orchestral suite, however. Impressionistic elements are stronger in this work than in his second opera, *L'Enfant et les sortilèges* ("The Child and the Sorceries," 1925), a fairy tale written in an advanced harmonic idiom and called a lyric fantasy by the composer.

Other composers. The impressionistic style left its mark on the operas of several composers outside France. Two of several Italian operas by Franco Alfano (1876–1954), *Risurrezione* ("Resurrection," 1904), based on Tolstoi's novel, and *Madonna Imperia* (1927), combine traces of impressionism with some of the strength of the style of *verismo.* The rich sound and expert handling of voices in these works do not compensate for the lack of genuine melodic and dramatic power. Of the operas of Ildebrando Pizzetti (b. 1880), *Assassinio nella cattedrale* ("Murder in the Cathedral," 1958), based on T. S. Eliot's drama, is the most successful. Ottorino Respighi (see page 584) combined impressionistic and traditional elements in his stage works with varying degrees of success. Only three of his eight operas and several ballets were performed outside Italy: *Belfagor* (1923), a comic fairy tale; *La campana sommersa* ("The Sunken Bell," 1927), based on Gerhard Hauptmann's celebrated German fairy tale; and the mystery play *Maria Egiziaca* (1932). In these works as in his symphonic poems, impressionism is reflected primarily in the orchestral writing.

Only one dramatic composer of renown, Manuel de Falla (see page 585), emerged in contemporary Spain. His name was carried across the world by two operas and two ballets, all written in the idiom of his native country, combined with impressionistic color effects. The strongly rhythmical dances in these works recall the many dance forms for which Spain is noted, and their orchestral accompaniments often include guitar and castanets. Falla's vocal writing, impressionistic in melodic idiom but partly Romantic in sentiment, is in turn elegant, brilliant, and melancholy. Dances drawn from his first opera, *La vida breve* ("The Short Life," 1913), and from his first ballet, *El amor brujo* ("Love the Magician," 1915), have become widely known in a variety of instrumental arrangements.

Early in his career Belá Bartók (see page 598) composed one opera, *The Castle of Duke Bluebeard* (1911), a symbolic drama filled with somber and tragic moods. As in most other non-French impressionistic operas, the impressionistic touches are found most strikingly in the orchestral writing: shimmering colors, a variety of glissandos and tremolos, and a great degree of restraint in employing the heavier instruments characterize the score.

Expressionistic Operas

THE MOVEMENT called expressionism, whose chief early exponents were Arnold Schoenberg and Alban Berg, led to a number of operas in which intense expression is combined with technical novelty. Expressionism, roughly contemporary with the middle phase of impressionism, had an opposite intention; for whereas the French impressionists were interested in representing external objects as they appeared to the beholder, the Germanic expressionists tried to reflect the inner life of feeling. From the psychological viewpoint adopted by the expressionists, the inner life of twentieth-century man is clouded by tensions, fears, and a variety of subconscious urges. Thus expressionism as a musical style was preoccupied with setting intense, conflicting, and sometimes irrational thoughts and emotions.

Schoenberg. A monodrama, *Erwartung* ("Expectation," 1909; first performed in 1924), Schoenberg's first work for the stage, is a predecessor of the expressionistic style. The composer had passed beyond the influence of Wagner's harmonic idiom and had entered his period of atonal writing; but Wagner's concept of attaching psychological significance to musical motives is reflected in Schoenberg's work. His next opera, *Die glückliche Hand* ("The Lucky Hand," 1910–1913), is concerned with the illusory forms of happiness as contrasted with true spiritual happiness. Many of the vocal lines of the atonal score, containing little thematic material as such, are based on a kind of half-spoken, half-sung recitation of the kind later employed in *Pierrot Lunaire* (see page 593). Other lines are angular, combining natural declamation with dramatic expression (see EXAMPLE 222). In addition, the score contains stage-lighting directions for the use of green light on the faces of the chorus to symbolize unearthliness.

Schoenberg's last two operas, written almost two decades later, were

EXAMPLE 222

Schoenberg, *Die glückliche Hand*

DER MANN: Wie du läch - elst! Wie dei - ne Au - gen lach - en! Dei - ne

schö - ne See - le!

TRANSLATION:
How you smile! How your eyes laugh!
Your beautiful soul!

composed after the twelve-tone system had been established. In the one-act *Von Heute auf Morgen* ("From Today to Tomorrow," 1930), he applied the system to a conventional lighthearted play of everyday life. The last opera, *Moses und Aron,* is a sacred drama of philosophical depth and highest ethical significance. He completed the first two acts in 1932, resumed work on the score in 1951, but died in that year before it was completed. First performed in 1954 in its unfinished state, it has gradually been recognized as Schoenberg's masterpiece.

Concerned with the founding of a Promised Land, *Moses und Aron* depicts the eternal conflict between thought and action, between the visionary and the interpreter of the vision. The entire work is based on a single twelve-tone row that is used in declamatory recitative as well as in strict, traditional forms; the choral fugue in the Interlude is an example of the latter. The work is filled with dramatic effects of the highest order: large-scale orchestral dances contrast with extended passages in speech-song, a semichorus (seated in the orchestra pit rather than on the stage) represents the Voice of God, and an elaborate scene of the worship of the Golden Calf brings orchestral color and rhythmic excitement together in outstanding fashion.

Berg. Alban Berg (1885–1935), pupil and disciple of Schoenberg (see page 595), became the most important dramatic composer of the expressionistic school. He absorbed the stylistic traits of his teacher and brought them to fruition in his operas. *Wozzeck,* completed in 1922 and first performed three years later, has gradually won recognition as the prototype of the new, twentieth-century musical drama. Its text, adapted from a work by Georg Büchner (1813–1837), an early Romanticist whose writings stressed the darker side of life, is gripping in its intensity. It goes beyond the human drama of a soldier who kills his wife and drowns himself, in its sociological emphasis on the tragedy of the downtrodden, underprivileged poor. Berg's music moves in free, atonal harmonies, but tonal relationships are also present. The predominantly declamatory vocal lines are angular, the wide leaps effectively underscoring the emotional tensions of the work. Many uncanny orchestral effects serve the same end.

The formal organization of *Wozzeck* has been widely discussed, for the forms of abstract music are used throughout; the table on page 625 gives an outline of the work. This plan of organization is probably not noticed by the listener, who is held only by the impact of the drama and music.

Berg's other opera, *Lulu*, not quite completed at his death in 1935 and first performed in 1937, represents a free application of the twelve-tone system. In contrast to *Wozzeck*, which in text and music is still somewhat dependent upon Romanticism, it is completely abstract. The drama of the elemental, almost animal-like Lulu and her disintegration was written by Franz Wedekind, a typical representative of German literary expressionism. The small number of performances of this work have made historical evaluation difficult, but the music has been thoroughly studied by German scholars. Among stylistic discoveries made so far is an identification of various characters with different versions of twelve-tone rows.

Other composers. Expressionistic tendencies and twelve-tone organizations are found in many later operas, of which *König Hirsch* ("King Stag,"

A scene from
Berg's *Wozzek*.

THE FORMAL ORGANIZATION OF *WOZZECK*

Drama	*Music*
ACT I	
Exposition: Wozzeck seen in relation to his environment	*Musical form:* five character pieces
SCENE 1. Wozzeck and the Captain	Suite in eleven sections
2. Wozzeck and Andres	Rhapsody on three chords
3. Marie and Wozzeck	Military march, lullaby, and scene
4. Wozzeck and the Doctor	Passacaglia with twenty-one variations
5. Marie and the Drum Major	Quasi-rondo: Andante affetuoso
ACT II	
Development: Wozzeck becomes convinced of Marie's unfaithfulness to him	*Musical form:* symphony in five movements
SCENE 1. Marie, the Child, Wozzeck (Wozzeck's first suspicions)	Sonata movement
2. Captain, Doctor, Wozzeck (Wozzeck is derided)	Invention and fugue
3. Marie and Wozzeck (Wozzeck accuses her of unfaithfulness)	Largo, free form for chamber orchestra
4. Garden of a country inn (Marie dances with the Drum Major)	Scherzo with three trios and two recapitulations (two orchestras)
5. Guardroom: Soldiers, Andres (the Drum Major manhandles Wozzeck)	Introduction and Rondo marziale
ACT III	
Catastrophe and Epilogue: Wozzeck murders Marie and atones by committing suicide	*Musical form:* six inventions
SCENE 1. Marie and her child (remorse)	Invention on a theme
2. Marie and Wozzeck at the pond (Marie's death)	Invention on one note
3. The tavern (Wozzeck seeks forgetfulness in drink)	Invention on a rhythm
4. Wozzeck's death in the pond	Invention on a chord of six tones
5. Epilogue: Orchestral interlude	Invention on a key (D minor)
6. Children playing, Marie's child among them	Invention on a continuous movement of eighth notes

1956) by Hans Werner Henze (b. 1926) is representative; in this work these elements are combined with surrealism. Ernst Křenek (b. 1900) has written stage works in many different styles. In his thirteen large and small operas, expressionistic (both atonal and twelve-tone), neo-Classical, parodistic, and even experimental styles are represented. He achieved worldwide success with *Jonny spielt auf* ("Johnny Strikes up the Band," 1927), an opera containing jazz elements and with a Negro jazz musician as its hero. It has played in more than four hundred theaters around the world. His *Karl V* (1933) represents his shift to an expressionistic twelve-tone idiom.

Expressionistic techniques have come into Italian opera only recently. Luigi Dallapiccola (b. 1904), distinguished Italian exponent of the twelve-tone system, scored two notable successes with *Volo di notte* ("Night Flight," 1940), based on a book by the well-known aviator Antoine de St.-Exupéry, and *Il prigioneri* ("The Prisoner," 1950), a psychological tragedy influenced by the style of Alban Berg. In spite of the complexity of Dallapiccola's idiom and forms, his melodies remain eminently singable and his style conveys genuine dramatic emotion.

Neo-Classical Operas

IN SPITE of its new technical means and revolutionary effects, expressionism is related to Romanticism. Both styles are subjective in their aesthetic purpose, the chief difference between them being that expressionism reflects a different world of feeling (the subconscious), and does so with greater intensity, than Romanticism. In the early twentieth century many opera composers sought a new approach that was objective rather than subjective; the neo-Classical style, which cast out hyperemotional and overly dramatic effects, was the result.

Ferruccio Busoni (see page 585) is generally credited with formulating the aesthetic ideals of neo-Classicism: clarity of structure and sound, achieved by the use of traditional operatic forms and smaller orchestras; economy and restraint in emotional content, in spite of the incorporation of harmonic and other technical advances of contemporary music; and an objective attitude toward the drama. These ideals are seen clearly in his three operas, especially *Doktor Faust* (completed by his student Philipp Jarnach and performed in 1925), which have served as models for many of the later neo-Classical opera composers.

Hindemith. One of the century's most significant composers of instrumental music (see page 601), Paul Hindemith (b. 1895), has also taken a leading position in the field of the music drama with eight operas and four ballets. The neo-Classical style is represented in three serious operas. In *Cardillac* (1926), an intense, dissonant contrapuntal style is employed; the composer concentrates on the linear aspects of the texture, leads the several voices with regard for their melodic implications above all, and apparently disregards the vertical component of the music. The result is an objective, nonexpressive idiom.

In *Mathis der Maler* ("Mathis the Painter," 1938), an opera based on the story of the celebrated German artist, Matthias Grünewald, the texture is somewhat less contrapuntal but equally dissonant. Archaic elements such as modal inflections, chords without qualifying thirds, and passages in parallel voices are combined with the earlier idiom. Three symphonic interludes from this work have won a respected place in the concert repertoire. His latest opera, *Die Harmonie der Welt* ("The Harmony of the World," 1957), reveals a further lessening of the rigorous counterpoint and an increase in the warmth of expression. The text, written by the composer, deals with the astronomer Johannes Kepler, and stresses symbolical and spiritual elements.

Another aspect of Hindemith's personality is seen in the humor and irony of his comic opera, *Neues vom Tage* ("News of the Day," 1929, revised 1944). Here he composed in a witty style, parodying the idiom of Romantic opera and even including modern dance music. An example of his *Gebrauchsmusik* ("functional music") is the children's opera, *Wir bauen eine Stadt* ("Let's Build a Town," 1930), a work suitable for performance in schools.

Weill. The operatic career of Kurt Weill (1900–1950) was divided between Europe and the United States. Weill began as a pupil of Busoni in Berlin, where he composed short operas on both serious and comic subjects. An association with the playwright Berthold Brecht led to a new type of musical play containing lyric episodes, dialogue interspersed with orchestral interludes, and simple but forceful harmonies. *Die Dreigroschenoper* ("The Threepenny Opera," 1928), a modernized version of the old English *Beggar's Opera,* became their greatest success. Short, satirical, and harsh songs in modern dance rhythms, accompanied in jazz idioms by a small orchestra, are interspersed between the episodes of the play, which is a political and social satire. Weill and Brecht's satirical *Aufstieg und Fall der Stadt Mahagonny* ("Rise and Fall of the Town of Mahagonny," 1930) represents the same general style.

Weill settled in the United States in 1935 and continued to make valuable contributions to the repertoire of the musical theater, both in comedy and genuine folk opera. His American works include *Knickerbocker Holiday* and *Lady in the Dark;* the famous folk opera, *Down in the Valley* (1948), based on Kentucky mountain songs; and a serious opera, *Street Scene* (1947).

Other German composers. With about one hundred permanent opera houses, Germany has remained a fertile field for contemporary opera composers. Several have won acclaim in Germany and a number have been represented on foreign stages as well. Carl Orff (b. 1895) has revived a chantlike declamation carried by strong rhythms and dissonant harmonies, but he has also given new life to the spirit of comic opera. His works include *Die Kluge* ("The Clever Woman," 1943), based on a fairy tale by Grimm, and *Antigonae* (1949); they and his scenic cantatas, *Carmina Burana* ("Songs of Beuren," 1937) and *Catulli carmina* ("Songs of Catullus," 1943), along with his work as a music educator, have brought him international fame.

Boris Blacher (b. 1903) has experimented widely in opera and ballet and has introduced a system of "variable rhythm" based on arithmetic progressions, permutations, and the like. In collaboration with Werner Egk (b. 1901), his predecessor as director of the Academy for Music in West Berlin, he composed *Abstract Opera No. 1* (1954), a work in which the action is based on an allegorical diagram and the music is based on metrical rows, mirror images of those rows, and other complicated, abstract forms. Probably the most significant dramatic talent among Germanic composers is Gottfried von Einem (b. 1918), an Austrian pupil of Blacher, who has two successful operas to his credit: *Dantons Tod* ("The Death of Danton," 1947) and *Der Prozess* ("The Trial," 1953); in the latter, Kafka's novel is used as the basis for eclectic music of great dramatic power.

Les Six. Operas in the impressionistic style, as indicated above, were not numerous; nor did they do much to combat the influence of Wagnerianism in French music. A stronger and truly contemporary counter-influence was at hand in the neo-Classical style, and that style in its various manifestations has dominated French opera since the 1920's. Jazz idioms are employed in some of the operas and even more of the ballets that were composed in France; but in most cases jazz has remained a tangential stylistic element.

The change to a new style had been suggested in the operas of Ravel; that change became an actuality in the works of *Les Six* (see page 585). Increasing infiltration of popular elements in the comic operas and ballets on the one hand, and emphasis on heroic themes drawn from Biblical stories and history on the other, marked the new style. The operas did not represent the old grand operas, however, but a kind of ceremonial drama that sometimes bordered on the oratorio.

In the dramatic works of Darius Milhaud (see page 586) several aspects of the new style are represented. Among his fourteen operas and many ballets are the opera *Esther de Carpentras* (1925), comic and even satiric in tone, and the ballet *La création du monde* ("The Creation of the World," 1923), in which satire and jazz elements are characteristic. His more important works are serious and sometimes even esoteric, however, and are distinguished by his mastery of structure, his polytonal harmonic idiom, and the literary excellence of their texts. The most successful works are *Christophe Colomb* (1928), with narrator and chorus; *Maximilien* (1930), the tragic story of the unhappy emperor of Mexico; the classical drama *Medée* (1938); and the drama of the great South American liberator, *Bolivar* (1943). For the celebration marking the third millenium of Jerusalem, Milhaud composed a Biblical pageant, *David* (1954), which reveals the full resources of his personal, expressive style. In quite another vein are the three "minute operas" of 1927, in which the drama is compressed into a thirty- or forty-minute span.

The operas of Arthur Honegger (see page 588), not as numerous as Milhaud's, are equally important from a dramatic standpoint. His best-known musical dramas, the Biblical *Judith* (1926) and the classical *An-*

tigone (1927), contain closed forms, complex choral writing, and dramatic declamation of great intensity. His uncompromising harmonic idiom is prominent in these works, whereas the ballets and operettas are characterized by a more amiable and lighthearted style.

In recent years a third member of *Les Six*, Francis Poulenc (see page 588), enjoyed remarkable operatic success in spite of an eclectic style composed of elements of Classicism, Romantic sentimentality, and even quasi-primitive simplicity. In his farce *Les mamelles de Tirésias* ("The Breasts of Tiresias," 1944) his music is satirical, parodistic, and entertaining. *Les dialogues des Carmélites* ("The Dialogues of the Carmelite Nuns," 1955) is a tragic horror opera of the French Revolution but spiritually motivated. Poulenc's most recent dramatic work, *La voix humaine* ("The Human Voice," 1958), is a monodrama in which one singing actress carries the entire action during the course of a telephone conversation. The work is in recitative style throughout but organized in strict forms, producing great dramatic impact.

Other French composers. Jacques Ibert (1890–1962) and Jean Françaix (b. 1912) avoid pretentiousness and write amusingly. Among Ibert's many ballets, operas, and operettas, the ironic farce with spoken dialogue, *Angélique* (1927), enjoyed considerable success. A generation later, Françaix's opera *La princesse de Clèves* (1953) won acclaim for its amusing qualities and maintenance of the French tradition of clarity and singability. None of the French composers have so far been touched by the expressionistic tendency.

English composers. Neo-Classicism mixed with other ingredients, mainly nationalistic and post-Romantic, has characterized the operas of two prominent English composers. Ralph Vaughan Williams (see page 571), skillfully incorporating folk-music idioms into his vocal writing, enjoyed one major operatic success with *Riders to the Sea* (1937), a tragic story set in an austere and archaic style. Benjamin Britten (see page 606), the outstanding English opera composer of the present day, has seen five of his operas gain international acceptance. His style is neo-Classical in all essential aspects, and he reveals a structural craftsmanship far above that of many other opera composers; his latest opera, *The Turn of the Screw* (1954), for example, is a variation cycle. *Peter Grimes* (1945) is perhaps the best known of his other operas; Britten's ability to create moods, a mark of great compositional ability, comes to full expression here. The three "Sea Interludes" from this work have become an extremely effective addition to the concert repertoire.

Prokofiev. An outstanding pupil of Rimsky-Korsakov, Sergey Prokofiev (see page 604) adhered throughout his writing for the musical stage to his artistic ideal of elaborating folklike melodies in neo-Classical contexts. His seven ballets met with mixed reception; only two, *Romeo and Juliet* (1940) and *Cinderella* (1945), are still performed occasionally. His first ballet (1920) is worth mentioning if only because of its intriguing title:

A Tale of a Buffoon Who Outwitted Seven Buffoons, also known as *Chout.* This work is representative of Prokofiev's unfailing sense of humor, in which satirical expression is a major ingredient.

Prokofiev's sense of dramatic characterization and effective climax, coming to full expression in his operas, was not recognized until after his death. His early opera, *Love for Three Oranges,* was successful at its first production in Chicago in 1921 and in European cities after that date. The serious operas composed after his return to Russia were not immediately acclaimed, however; *Simeon Kotko* (1940), a story of the Russian revolution, was the last operatic success he enjoyed during his lifetime. His most important opera, the colossal *War and Peace,* based on Tolstoi's novel, is an heroic work with extended choral sections and several descriptive instrumental numbers; begun in 1941 and revised after a 1946 performance, it was not produced in its definitive version until 1955.

Stravinsky. The late-Romantic and nationalistic style of Rimsky-Korsakov influenced the early work of Igor Stravinsky (see page 606), his most prominent pupil. Stravinsky showed a preference for the ballet in his early works, possibly because his personal style was so strongly centered on rhythm. His ballets, many of them well known in concert versions, can be classified into three groups. The first group, composed in Paris in the period about 1910–1918, reveal post-Romantic trends that soon gave way to a more dissonant style while retaining folkloristic content. The best-known works of this period are *L'oiseau de Feu* ("The Firebird," 1910), *Petrushka* (1911), and *Le sacre du printemps* ("The Rite of Spring," 1913).

These were followed by a neo-Classical period, lasting to about 1950, during which works of two kinds were written: original works and those based on themes by other composers. Of the first kind, the classical ballet *Apollon Musagète* (1928, first performed in Washington, D. C.) is representative. The second type is seen in works such as *Pulcinella* ("After Pergolesi," 1920), and *Le baiser de la fée* ("The Fairy's Kiss," 1928), based on music by Tchaikovsky. Of the works of his most recent style period, which includes the adoption of serial techniques, his ballet *Agon* (1957) is outstanding.

The field of opera also engaged Stravinsky's attention. His early works, primarily short chamber operas with comic or burlesque content, are those of a composer experimenting with new sonorities and problems of staging. His neo-Classical period is represented by *Oedipus rex* (1927), a static opera-oratorio in classic form, written to a Latin text in order to increase the feeling of objectivity; and *The Rake's Progress* (1951), a major work in English on a text by W. H. Auden and Chester Kallman. The latter work contains arias, recitatives, ensembles, choruses, and instrumental numbers conceived in the spirit of the Baroque period (with touches of Mozart), and it does not violate the composer's unique musical personality or interfere with his use of pandiatonic harmonies (see EXAMPLE 223).

EXAMPLE 223

Stravinsky, *The Rake's Progress*

TOM: Since _ it _ is not by mer - it we rise or we fall, but the

Stravinsky's latest work for the stage is *The Flood,* a ballet pantomime with narrative passages and sections in the style of melodrama. Written as an experiment for television and produced in mid-1962 as part of the observance of Stravinsky's eightieth birthday, *The Flood* reveals the continued vitality and stylistic flexibility of this great composer.

American composers. The contribution of a large number of American composers to the fields of opera and ballet, which dates from the late nineteenth century to the present day, includes works in many forms. Operas written under the influence of Italian or German works, operas based on the jazz idiom, folk operas, and the genuinely American musical comedy are represented. In the interest of presenting a comprehensive survey of American contributions to all branches of music, the discussion of stage works written for audiences in the United States will be placed in Chapter 31.

৵৵ 31 ৵৵

Three Centuries of American Music

As VIRTUALLY the last major nation to appear on the musical scene, the United States played little part in the formation of an international music before the twentieth century. Music was cultivated by the earliest settlers, however, and became a significant factor in their lives. While it did not at first follow the paths taken in European countries with older musical traditions, it enriched the religious and social life of the time. Separated from Europe by an ocean and struggling against a hostile environment, the early colonists drew upon their innate musicality and a few traditions they had brought with them and developed the kinds of music that met their needs at the time. In the eighteenth century, as later generations renewed cultural ties with their forefathers' homeland and

Engraving from cover of *The Western Minstrel,* a collection published in Philadelphia, early 19th c. [CULVER PICTURES]

gained new recruits to help in building a nation, they imitated the developments of European music. And not until the early twentieth century did American musicians contribute substantially to those developments.

Music in the Colonial Period

WHEN the colonization of the North American continent began early in the seventeenth century, the two sources of patronage that had helped to shape European art music were of course not available. The influence of the Catholic church had been a vital factor in determining the forms and content of sacred music since about the thirteenth century, and the support of the aristocracy had been equally strong in the field of secular music since the fourteenth. Neither of these sources being available in the new land, American musicians were forced to make their own way from the beginning.

Musical practices. The first music in the colonies came from *The Booke of Psalmes, Englished both in Prose and Metre* (the "Ainsworth Psalter," Amsterdam, 1612), and *The Whole Booke of Psalmes* (the "Sternhold and Hopkins Psalter," London, 1562), brought respectively by the Pilgrims, or Separatists, who settled in what is now Plymouth in 1620, and the Puritans, or non-Separatists, who founded the Massachusetts Bay Colony in 1630. Both psalters contained translations of the 150 Psalms and a number of one-line tunes—thirty-nine in a variety of metrical patterns in the "Ainsworth" and forty-two in more regular metrical patterns in the "Sternhold and Hopkins"; many of the melodies in both psalters were derived from those composed or arranged by Louis Bourgeois for the Genevan Psalter (completed in 1562), published by Jean Calvin (see page 163).

Within a few years the Boston Puritans, becoming dissatisfied with the translations in Sternhold and Hopkins, made a new version. *The Whole Booke of Psalms Faithfully Translated into English Metre* (the "Bay Psalm Book," 1640), the first book to be printed in America, was eventually (in 1692) adopted by the Pilgrims as well. The first several editions, containing only the texts, referred in an "Admonition to the Reader" to suitable melodies found in other psalters, notably one published by Thomas Ravenscroft with four-part settings by composers such as Thomas Tallis, Thomas Morley, and other prominent Elizabethans. In the ninth edition of the Bay Psalm Book (1698) thirteen tunes were included, and from then on, the number and variety of psalters in New England increased steadily.

By the beginning of the eighteenth century the strict singing of psalms had given way to a free, quasi-improvisatory, and heterophonic style, especially in the villages and rural areas, and the same psalm was sung differently from one church to another. In other words, the psalms had entered the realm of folksong and were treated to the kinds of transformations that have always distinguished the folksong tradition. This tra-

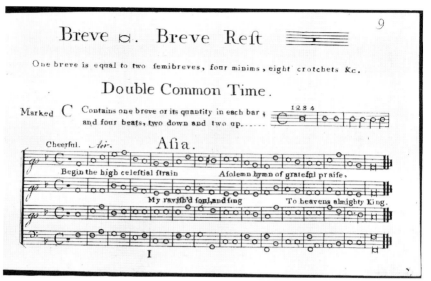

A page from Andrew Law's *The Art of Singing*, 1794.

dition was opposed by some of the clergy in the larger towns and cities; they sought to enforce the practice of "singing by note," that is, singing according to the printed notes themselves. To further their aim, they helped to establish singing schools, in which note reading was to be taught and the strict tradition of singing psalms encouraged.

The first singing schools were founded before the middle of the eighteenth century, and the movement spread up and down the east coast and into the west wherever the wilderness had been opened. Often taught by itinerant musicians who had little musical education themselves, the schools frequently contributed to maintaining the folk tradition rather than erasing it, and in later years they became the centers for spreading the type of gospel-hymn singing that grew to be characteristic of rural America.

Music for recreation also existed in the colonies from the beginning. Instruments, while rare, were known. Psalm settings in three or four parts and designed for home or other social use were often sung, to such an extent that the widely circulated belief in the Puritans' opposition to the recreational use of music can be proved false.[1] Concerts seem to have been a late arrival on the New England scene, however; the first on record was a public concert given in Boston in 1731, of which neither the program nor the names of the performers are known.

The musical life of Philadelphia and the surrounding area was greatly enriched by the presence of various religious communities established early in the eighteenth century. Chief among them were the Ephrata Cloister, established by the German-born Conrad Beissel (1690–1768) in 1735, and that of the Moravian Brethren (composed of German-Bohemian

---

1 Chase, *America's Music*, pp. 6–15.

Protestants, followers of John Hus) at Nazareth and Bethlehem, Pennsylvania in 1740–1741. Other Moravian settlements were established elsewhere, notably at Salem (now part of Winston-Salem), North Carolina.

The Moravians cultivated many varieties of music and instituted performances of orchestral and chamber-music works of Stamitz, Johann Christian Bach and, later, Haydn, Mozart, and other composers. In their church services the organ was often supplemented by string and wind instruments, and in addition to hymns their choirs sang anthems written by members of the church. Johann Friedrich Peter (1746–1813), born in Holland but a member of the Bethlehem community from 1770, was outstanding. He composed a large number of anthems, some with orchestral accompaniment, and six string quintets (1789, composed at Salem); the latter, written in the general style of Haydn, were probably the first chamber-music works to be composed on American soil. The strength of the Moravian musical tradition continued through the nineteenth century, and the performances of the famous Bethlehem Bach Choir at the present day are a direct outgrowth of it.

Philadelphia and New York enjoyed the services of music teachers from about the 1730's and the production of dramatic works and ballad operas from about 1750; public concerts began in 1736 in New York and 1757 in Philadelphia. Performances became frequent in later years, often consisting of mixed orchestral and solo (violin, vocal, flute, and others) numbers, although a large portion of Handel's *Messiah* was given in New York as early as 1770. Some of the leading citizens of Philadelphia were competent amateur musicians; they played chamber music in their homes frequently and were not averse to playing in public on occasion.

BETTMANN ARCHIVE

An early nineteenth-century singing school.

In the south, Charleston, South Carolina and Williamsburg, Virginia were the most important musical centers through much of the eighteenth century. A public concert in Charleston in 1732 (a year after the first-known performance in Boston) was followed by others; as in the other musical centers, the works of Rococo and early Classical composers formed the bulk of the repertoire. In Williamsburg, the seat of English gentry and of Americans who maintained the English traditions, amateur performers took part in a variety of private concerts and cultivated music as assiduously as they would have done in London.

The first composers. In 1759, at the commencement exercises of New Jersey College (later to become Princeton University), an ode by one of the graduating students, James Lyon (1735–1794), was performed; that music has been lost. Lyon in 1762 published *Urania*, a collection of anthems, psalms, and hymn tunes, including six of his own settings. Nine later compositions by Lyon, who became a Presbyterian minister in 1764, appeared in other collections to 1807. In 1759 Francis Hopkinson (1737–1791), a lawyer in Philadelphia, composed a song, "My days have been so wondrous free," and copied it, together with five other songs of his, into a manuscript volume containing about a hundred items (including works of Purcell, Handel, Pergolesi, and other eminent composers). He had composed other songs earlier and was to write eight more in 1788.

Thus Lyon and Hopkinson, one a minister in Nova Scotia and Maine and the other a signer of the Declaration of Independence, became the first native-born American composers. They were followed by a Boston tanner, William Billings (1746–1800), who was more imaginative and more gifted. In contrast to Hopkinson, who confined himself to two-part writing (melody and bass), and to Lyon, whose style was basically chordal, Billings wrote four-part settings in imitative and even canonic texture,

EXAMPLE 224

Billings, *Lebanon*

known to him as "fuguing"; his compositions employing that texture became known as "fuguing tunes."

Billings' works included *The New England Psalm-Singer* (1770), *The Singing Master's Assistant* (1776), and four other collections to 1794, in which hymns and anthems are in the majority. With a melody suited to the sense of the text, a harmony that made considerable use of secondary triads (but rarely seventh chords), a texture that is either chordal or imitative, Billings developed a strong and spirited mode of expression (see EXAMPLE 224). A fine mixture of reverence and humor, of sensitivity and rough vigor, characterizes his music.

Music after the Revolution

THE PERIOD from about 1785 to 1860 was marked by an influx of European musicians to the United States, a great increase in the number of published song collections, and a proliferation of the various song traditions in rural areas. The Europeans, professionally trained, became active primarily as teachers and performers and did much to superimpose European styles and standards on American music. The number of consumers of music grew steadily, and the publishing of music and manufacturing of instruments became profitable business ventures. And as the musical life of the cities became ever more a reflection of European taste, it became separated from that of the rural areas, where folksong singing was colored by the influence of religious sects.

The European influence. Even before the Revolution, America had attracted a number of eminent European musicians, of whom the most notable were probably Carl Theodore Pachelbel and Alexander Reinagle. Pachelbel (1690–1750), son of the famous Nuremberg organist and composer, worked in Rhode Island and South Carolina as a church organist from 1733 to his death. Reinagle (1756–1809), born in England of Austrian parents, settled in New York in 1786 and soon thereafter moved to Philadelphia. A pianist, conductor, and composer, he contributed to raising standards of keyboard performance and took an active role in producing and conducting a variety of concerts and ballad operas.

Among the many foreign-born musicians active in the early decades of the nineteenth century, a few rose to prominence. Raynor Taylor (*c.* 1747–1825) worked as an organist, composer, and musical entertainer in Philadelphia; James Hewitt (1770–1827) was similarly active in New York and Boston; and Benjamin Carr (1768–1831) established the first music store in Philadelphia and became the first publisher of American music.

The accomplishments of such men, solid rather than spectacular, helped to lay a foundation for the successful tours of a number of European virtuosos who visited the United States in the middle years of the century. Ole Bull (1810–1880), a Norwegian violinist, made five American tours between 1843 and 1879. An eccentric performer with fabulous technical skill, he played mainly his own compositions, some of which were

Jenny Lind singing at Castle Garden in New York, 1850.

based on American themes (*To the Memory of Washington, Niagara*, and the like). Jenny Lind (1820–1887), Swedish-born soprano and one of the finest singers of her time, spent the years from 1850 to 1852 concertizing on the east coast and as far west as St. Louis. A number of brilliant pianists, notably Henri Herz (1803–1888) and Sigismund Thalberg (1812–1871), and other performers undertook similar tours, and by the late 1870's the United States was regularly included on the itineraries of many of Europe's most successful artists.

The political events in Europe in 1848, which led to revolutions in France, Austria, and Germany, were followed by the migration of a host of German musicians to the United States. Unlike the earlier generation, however, many of them moved inland. Soon cities such as Cincinnati, St. Louis, Chicago, and Milwaukee came under the musical influence of well-trained, competent German performers and teachers and began to rival the eastern cities as centers of musical culture. The predominant Germanic flavor of American music was thus assured and remained its chief characteristic through the second half of the nineteenth century.

American composers. The national interest in hymn singing, which had gradually taken the place of psalm singing in the eighteenth century, provided a springboard for the career of Lowell Mason (1792–1872), composer, publisher, and teacher, and the most successful of the many purveyors of church music of his time. Born in Medfield, Massachusetts, Mason was a bank clerk in Savannah for fifteen years (1812–1827). He was largely self-taught in music, but he became a successful organist and choirmaster in a Savannah church. Moving to Boston, he became active as a music teacher to children as well as to adults, as choir director, and as propagandist for a higher level of church music. His work in teaching children led to the adoption of his principles by the public schools of Boston in 1838 and thus laid the groundwork for America's unique system of music education in the schools.

Mason's publications had begun even before his return to New England; the first of his many collections, *The Boston Handel and Haydn Society Collection of Church Music* (1822), went through seventeen editions. *The Juvenile Lyre* (1831), the first secular song book for children in America, *Lyra Sacra* (1832), *The New Carmina Sacra* (1852), and literally dozens of other collections were successful in edition after edition, and Mason was probably the first American musician to become wealthy.

Mason's interest in improving church music led him to adapt melodies from the secular works of eminent composers and fit them to hymn texts; composers as far apart as Handel and Weber, and including most of the Classical masters, are represented in his arrangements. And judiciously mixed in the collection are many hymns of his own composition. Tunes such as "Nearer My God to Thee," "From Greenland's Icy Mountains," "My Faith Looks Up to Thee," and "Work for the Night is Coming" are still remembered; and his arrangements include, above all, "Joy to the World," adapted from Handel.

Of interest, too, is the fact that Mason's descendants became prominent in other musical fields. One of his sons, Henry, became a founder of the firm of Mason and Hamlin, manufacturers of pipe organs and pianos; another son, William, was one of America's finest pianists and teachers in the period after 1860; and his grandson Daniel Gregory Mason (1873–1953, the son of Henry) was an eminent post-Romantic composer, author, and teacher almost to the middle of the twentieth century.

The careers of two other American composers ran in directions quite different from that of Lowell Mason. Stephen Collins Foster (1826–1864), born near Pittsburgh, owes his place in American history to perhaps a dozen of his two hundred songs. And Louis Moreau Gottschalk (1829–1869), born in New Orleans, became the first of America's virtuoso pianists and a composer of many descriptive piano pieces based on Caribbean subjects.

Foster came from a family background in which genteel sentimentality was a virtue, and he grew up and worked in cities (Pittsburgh and Cincinnati) where the last traces of frontier primitivism and simplicity had not yet been cast off. He became acquainted with the songs of Negro dockworkers and the entertainments of the blackface minstrels that were a feature of the American stage through much of the nineteenth century. He also lived in New York during the first years of the Civil War, where lack of financial success contributed to his death in his thirty-seventh year.

Foster's songs reflect these varied experiences. Some are filled with the sentimental expression typical of much popular music: *Poor Beautiful Maiden, Come Where My Love Lies Dreaming,* and *Beautiful Dreamer* are of this type. Others are war songs, of which *We Are Coming, Father Abraham* is the best known. Many of the songs were written for minstrel groups such as the Christy Minstrels, which did much to popularize them; *Massa's in de Cold Ground, My Old Kentucky Home,* and *Old Black Joe* are his most famous songs of this type. The songs of all types are simple in structure, melody, and harmony. Four-measure phrases predominate and repetition of phrase elements, entire phrases, or both, is common; *Oh! Susanna,* with an *aa′ba* form and *Old Black Joe,* with *aa′ab,* illustrate this feature. Harmonies seldom progress beyond I, IV, and V triads, modulations are rare, and the rhythms are regular except for the many brief syncopations. Foster's art lay in his ability to employ tastefully the simplest of materials and to write with unashamed sentiment; his best works resemble folksongs in their naturalness and immediate appeal.

In contrast to Foster, who represented the field of popular song, Louis Gottschalk lived and worked in the sophisticated world of concerts and large-scale compositions. He grew to adolescence in New Orleans, was taken to Paris (1841), became a phenomenally successful pianist, and made concert tours in Europe from 1850 to 1852. Returning to the United States, he gave hundreds of concerts, interrupted by a six-year stay (1856–1862) in the Caribbean area, until 1866. Then he traveled in South America, where he died in 1869.

Gottschalk composed about ninety works for piano, two operas, two symphonic poems, and several miscellaneous pieces. Many of the piano works are small salon pieces of no enduring value. Others, however, bring to music the exotic world of the Caribbean and are early representatives of American nationalistic music based on mixed racial themes. A work for chorus and orchestra, *Escenas campestres Cubanas* ("Scenes of the Cuban Countryside"), piano pieces such as *Souvenir de la Havane, Ojos crillos* ("Creole Eyes") and the well-known *La Bamboula,* based on an Afro-American dance, are typical of the style.

Nationalism. A few works by Ole Bull and Louis Gottschalk had been in the general tradition of nationalistic music, although Gottschalk had favored Caribbean subjects. Initiating a truly American nationalism in music was in large part the work of Anthony Philip Heinrich (1781–1861). Born in Bohemia, he came to the United States about 1818, settling first in Philadelphia and then in Kentucky. His many compositions, primarily for large orchestra, had little musical value; but the titles of some of them indicate the direction of his musical interests: *Pocahontas, the Royal Indian Maid; Grand American Chivalrous Symphony;* and *The Wildwood Spirit's Chant.*

William Fry (1813–1864), a native of Philadelphia, became active in the cause of American music and sought to have American composers represented on concert programs. His music, however, did not always employ American subjects and thus ran counter to the general trend. His works include *Leonora* (1845), one of the first operas written by a native-born composer, a symphonic poem *Niagara* (1854), and four symphonies that were descriptive (*Santa Claus* and *A Day in the Country,* for example) in the tradition of the time but were not specifically American.

Leopold Damrosch conducting a performance of the Berlioz Requiem in the Seventh Regiment Armory in New York, 1881.

1860–1920

THE LAST decades of the nineteenth century were marked by an increase in the stability and quality of American concert life. Traveling orchestras carried portions of the standard repertoire to towns and cities that had known little concert music previously, and permanent orchestras were founded in the larger cities. A growing number of American composers, most of them still trained in Germany, wrote music that enjoyed a fair number of performances. The period ended with the formation of a school of composers in New England, the rise of individual composers elsewhere, and a decline of the German influence on American music.

Musical performances. America's rich orchestral life was built on a foundation provided by Theodore Thomas (1835–1905), violinist and eminent conductor. Born in Germany, Thomas came to the United States in 1845 and for several years earned his living as a violinist. He organized an orchestra of his own in New York in 1862, and from 1869 traveled throughout the country giving many concerts distinguished by a wide range of music and exemplary performance standards. Together with William Mason (1829–1908), the son of Lowell Mason, he instituted a series of chamber-music concerts that brought the musical public into contact with yet another branch of the art. In 1872 Thomas helped organize and later conducted the biennial Cincinnati music festivals, setting a pattern for programming large works for chorus and orchestra that lasted for more than seventy-five years. In 1891 he moved his musicians to a permanent home in Chicago and founded the Chicago Symphony Orchestra, which became one of the country's outstanding musical organizations.

Thomas's work in Chicago added to the growing list of permanent major orchestras in the country. The New York Philharmonic Orchestra, founded in 1842, was the oldest, and a second orchestra, The New York Symphony, had been established by Leopold Damrosch in 1878; the two groups merged in 1928. Orchestras were founded in Boston, St. Louis, Cincinnati, and elsewhere in the last decades of the century and in increasing numbers during the early years of the twentieth century, until today virtually every city of any musical pretension supports its own orchestra on a reasonably permanent basis.

Chamber music of the highest quality was introduced to the growing American public through the work of an American violinist, Theodore Spiering (1871–1925). Born in St. Louis, Spiering studied in Cincinnati and Berlin, returning to play in the Chicago Symphony Orchestra under Thomas. He founded a string quartet in 1893 and for twelve years traveled to all parts of the United States and to many Canadian cities, extending to remote parts of the country the work done by Thomas and Mason in New York three decades earlier. Spiering then became concert master of the New York Philharmonic under Gustav Mahler and in the last months of Mahler's life conducted that orchestra in his place, thus be-

CULVER PICTURES

A band concert in Woodward's Gardens, San Francisco.

coming one of the first native-born conductors of a major musical organization.

The field of band music was represented and furthered primarily by
Patrick Sarsfield Gilmore and John Philip Sousa. Gilmore (1829–1892),
born in Ireland, established his famous band in Boston in 1859; he was
active as bandmaster during the Civil War and later organized enormous
festivals (1869 and 1872) in Boston in which thousands of performers took
part. He traveled throughout the country with his band and did much
to popularize concert band music on his many tours.

John Philip Sousa (1854–1932), born in Washington, became director
of the U.S. Marine Band in 1880 and organized his own band in 1892.
Sousa's Band became perhaps the best known of all American touring
organizations. Annual trips throughout the United States up to the late
1920's, four concert tours to Europe, and a world tour in 1910–1911 carried
the name of Sousa to all parts of the musical world. His many marches,
with their attractive melodies and rhythms, skillful instrumental writing,
and varied tone colors, introduced a musical quality that military music
had rarely possessed earlier. Among his famous marches, *Stars and Stripes
Forever, The Washington Post, Semper Fidelis,* and *El Capitan* are the
most representative.

Growth of the nationalist tradition. George Frederick Bristow (1825–
1898), violinist, composer, and teacher in New York, extended the work
of William Fry and sought to have American composers represented on
concert programs. Four symphonies and several of his shorter works were
performed by the New York Philharmonic Orchestra, of which he was
a charter member, between 1847 and 1874; and his opera *Rip Van Winkle*

(1855), enjoyed a run of four weeks. Other works include oratorios entitled *The Great Republic* (1879) and *Niagara* (1898). Bristow's opera, the first on an American subject, gave evidence of his belief that American legend and folklore contained suitable subjects for musical treatment and that the continued German domination was to be resisted at all costs.

Arthur Farwell (1872–1952) still found it necessary to continue the struggle for the recognition of American composers well into the twentieth century. Born in St. Paul, he was active as a teacher in various parts of the country before settling in New York. In 1901 he established the Wa Wan Press for the publication of American music—other composers' as well as his own. He made several transcontinental tours as a lecturer on American music and collected Indian music and other folk material. Many of the compositions published by the Wa Wan Press during its eleven years of life reflect his interest in that music. Among them are his sets of piano pieces called *American Indian Melodies* (1901), *Impressions of the Wa Wan Ceremony of the Omahas* (1906), and *From Mesa and Plain* (1905).

Other composers, although not directly connected with Farwell's activities, also turned to Indian music and arranged or elaborated Indian themes and rhythms in their works—most of them in small forms written for piano or piano and voice. Harvey Worthington Loomis (1865–1930), Charles Sanford Skilton (1868–1941), and Frederick Jacobi (1891–1952) are among the best-known names in this group.

The New England school. The influence of German music on American composers, strongly felt since the early days of the republic, grew even stronger in the second half of the century; the work of Fry, Bristow, and later, Farwell, was in itself insufficient to change the patterns of American music. Aspiring composers studied with German or German-trained musicians in this country, then traveled to Germany to complete their education, and returned to the United States as representatives of the prevailing German Romantic style.

John Knowles Paine (1839–1906) became the most eminent composer of his generation. Born in Portland, Maine, he spent three years as a student in Berlin and in 1862 became an instructor at Harvard University. In 1875 the first professorship of music in any American university was established there, and Paine was promoted to that position. His students included many who later played significant roles in the development of American music, notably the author and critic Henry T. Finck (1854–1926), the composers Arthur Foote (1853–1937), Frederick Converse (1871–1940), and John Alden Carpenter (1876–1951), and the versatile teacher, author, and composer Daniel Gregory Mason (1873–1953).

Paine's compositions, often in the style of Schumann and the young Brahms, include two symphonies, symphonic poems, several pieces of chamber music, a Mass, many choral works in the larger forms, a number of pieces for piano, and some for organ. He was one of the first American composers to demonstrate technical competence in the larger forms, and he set standards of structure, texture, and orchestration for an entire generation of composers.

Arthur Foote, one of Paine's students at Harvard, became closely associated with several contemporary Boston musicians who carried forward the work of Paine by composing in the larger forms in a Brahmsian style. The members of this group, George W. Chadwick, Arthur B. Whiting, and Horatio W. Parker, together with Foote, brought about a late flowering of the Romantic style and formed a distinctive German-oriented New England school.

Foote was the only member of the school who did not study in Germany. Active as an organist, pianist, and teacher in Boston for fifty years, he became a noted chamber-music player as well. His compositions showed a wider range of influences than those of his friends: orchestral works are programmatic in the general style of Liszt, the chamber music resembles that of Brahms in its involved textures and full sonorities, and two cantatas, *The Wreck of the Hesperus* (1888) and *The Skeleton in Armor* (1893), recall Wagner's colorful harmonic style.

George W. Chadwick (1854–1931), after preliminary training in Boston, studied in Leipzig and Munich for three years and returned to Boston in 1880. Thereupon he became active as a teacher of composition at the New England Conservatory of Music, where he numbered Parker and Whiting among his students. He was a prolific composer in many fields, writing operas, symphonies, quartets, cantatas, songs, piano pieces, and other works as well.

Chadwick's music, in which conventional feeling and exuberant Romanticism are imaginatively blended, reveals his complete command of compositional techniques, but it rises above much music by other New England composers in its humor, vitality, and rhythmic charm. Chadwick was a master of orchestration, and his flowing melodies and rich Romantic harmonies are set in vivid orchestral colors; among his most representative works are a symphonic sketch, *Tam O'Shanter* (1915), and a set of four *Symphonic Sketches* (1895–1908).

Horatio Parker (1863–1919), following the path established by a generation of American musicians, studied in Munich for three years and received a thorough training as organist, conductor, and composer. He returned to Boston in 1885, then spent eight years in New York as a teacher and church organist. In 1894 he was made professor of music at Yale University, but he remained active as a choral conductor in New York.

An oratorio, *Hora novissima* (1893), brought Parker fame as a choral composer, and his fame was extended to England when the work was performed there in 1899. He composed about fifty songs and more than thirty other works for various combinations of voices, and his instrumental works include a symphony, a symphonic poem, and miscellaneous orchestral works, chamber music, piano pieces, and organ works. In 1912 he won a ten-thousand-dollar prize, offered by the Metropolitan Opera, with his *Mona* and a year later in another competition won a similar prize with another opera, *Fairyland;* neither work has survived in the repertoire. Parker's first major success, *Hora novissima,* remains his best-known composition. It is distinguished by stylistic variety, including Renaissance, Baroque, and Romantic elements, and by effective use of contrapuntal writing and rhythms adapted to the sense of the text (see EXAMPLE 225).

Hora novissima represents the New England school at its best and suggests that Parker and his colleagues had assimilated everything they found appealing in the music of Europe. They did not duplicate the step taken by Mahler and Strauss in the direction of expanded resources —and this may be taken as evidence of the basic conservatism of the group.

MacDowell. The career of Edward MacDowell (1861–1908) as a composer in America embraces only the years from 1888, when he returned to New York after many years spent in Germany, to 1905, when mental illness brought his work to an end. In those seventeen years he rose to a position of fame and was called America's greatest composer; yet today all but a few of his works have disappeared from the repertoire.

Born in New York, he received his musical training from local teachers and, for a brief period, from the Venezuelan Teresa Carreño, the most brilliant woman pianist of the time. He was taken to Europe in 1876 and after two unsatisfactory years at the Paris Conservatoire moved to Germany. He studied with Joachim Raff at Frankfurt from 1879 to 1881, taught at Darmstadt for a year, and then settled in Wiesbaden as a piano teacher and performer. He returned to the United States in 1888 and taught music in Boston, where his orchestral works were performed by the Boston Symphony Orchestra. His fame as a composer, buttressed by his European reputation, spread rapidly, and in 1896 he was called to New York as professor of music at Columbia University. In 1904 he resigned that position, and in the following year he suffered a mental collapse that ended in insanity. He died in 1908.

MacDowell's compositions include two piano concertos, three symphonic poems, two orchestral suites, four piano sonatas, about twenty sets of piano pieces, and some songs. The piano pieces and sonatas give evidence of his Romantic leanings; titles such as *Woodland Sketches, Sea Pieces, New England Idyls, Sonata tragica,* and *Sonata eroica* are typical. The orchestral suites are similarly revealing, for the first suite contains movements called "In a Haunted Forest," "Summer Idyl," and the like, while the second ("Indian") suite includes "In Wartime," "Dirge," and "Village Festival."

MacDowell's historical place is that of a composer who brought to its highest peak the refined, sturdy, but derivative style of American Romanticism. At times his music is rhapsodic and vigorous, colorfully harmonized in the tradition of Dvořák; at other times it is sensitive, sentimental, and atmospheric in the general style of Grieg. Short phrases set in homophonic textures are most typical. The harmony is chromatic, in the Romantic manner, in the vague and dreamy passages with which the works are filled, and squarely diatonic in more forthright passages.

EXAMPLE 225

Parker, *Hora novissima*

Ives. At the turn of the century the most original of all American composers began writing a body of music that is unique in the literature. For almost twenty-five years (1907–1930) he was a successful businessman in New York and composed only as an avocation. His reputation spread very slowly, and his full stature was not recognized until he was in his seventies. Charles Ives (1874–1954) received some musical instruction from his father and played in the latter's band in Danbury, Connecticut, after which he attended Yale University and studied with Horatio Parker. For a few years he served as a church organist in New York and neighboring cities and then founded the insurance firm that occupied him until 1930. His compositions, written from about 1888 to 1927, include five symphonies, many descriptive pieces for orchestra, miscellaneous chamber-music works, four violin sonatas, two piano sonatas and other piano pieces, choral music, and 114 songs.

The majority of Ives' descriptive pieces are strongly related to the American scene. Titles such as *Three Places in New England, Central Park in the Dark,* and *Lincoln, the Great Commoner* are found in his orchestral works; and the four movements of his second piano sonata, subtitled *Concord, Massachusetts, 1840–1860,* are called "Emerson," "Hawthorne," "The Alcotts," and "Thoreau." Other works reflect typically American activities: a fireman's parade, gospel-hymn singing (with faulty ensemble and intonation), camp meetings, and the like. And in still other compositions a variety of American tunes, popular songs, and hymns are quoted, most often with humorous or parodistic effect.

Some of Ives' works are written with conventional melodies, harmonies, and rhythms; others employ polytonal effects, free and unmetrical rhythms, tone clusters, quarter tones, and a variety of neo-primitive percussive devices (see EXAMPLE 226). Remarkably enough, these extreme stylistic elements were introduced years before Bartók, Stravinsky, or other European experimenters had entered the scene. Improvisation was a factor of his music also, for performers are directed to rework certain

EXAMPLE 226

Ives, *The Cage* (1906)

his cage from one side back to the oth - er side; he

stopped on - ly when the keep - er came a - round with meat;

etc.

(All notes not marked with sharp or flat are natural.)

phrases according to their inclinations. And the orchestration is sometimes free, in that certain parts may be added or subtracted at will.

The delay in the recognition and performance of some of Ives' music
has had the effect of minimizing its startling originality. For example,
his second symphony, composed in 1902, was first performed in 1951;
the second piano sonata, written between 1904 and 1915, had its first
public performance in 1939. Many works composed before 1920 have
not yet been performed, notably the fourth symphony (1910–1916). Thus,
many discoveries about the inventiveness, humor, sense of tone color, and
all-embracing emotional content of Ives are yet to be made by the public.
Further performances of his music will solidify his position as a composer who reflected all facets of American life in his music, who brought
American history to musical expression in a style that is in turn strong,
raucous, humorous, satiric, sentimental, and profound. His place as one
of the most original and forward-looking composers of the twentieth
century is already assured.

Other composers. In the early years of the century, as the long-lived
Germanic influence gradually began to lose its effectiveness, a French

influence briefly took its place. The impressionistic style of Debussy, it-self a reaction to German musical domination, was employed by many American composers in a variety of works. The outstanding American impressionists were Charles Martin Loeffler and Charles Tomlinson Griffes.

Charles Martin Loeffler (1861–1935), of Alsatian birth, came to the United States in 1881; he was a member of the Boston Symphony Orchestra from 1882 to 1903, after which he remained active as a teacher and composer. Many influences converged in his music, German, Russian, and French among them. Although his style was basically impressionistic, it was modified by personal elements that included Gregorian chant, modal inflections, and free and rhapsodic forms, carried by colorful and resourceful orchestration. His best-known work, *A Pagan Poem*, in its final form for piano and orchestra (1907), illustrates the richness and refinement of his style.

Charles Tomlinson Griffes (1884–1920), born in Elmira, New York, studied and taught in Germany from 1903 to 1907, then returned to become a teacher in Tarrytown, New York. The influence of his German training, perceptible in his early works, quickly disappeared as he became interested in impressionistic music, Oriental idioms, and the style of Mussorgsky. The compositions written after about 1910 illustrate his complete identification with the style of Debussy. *The White Peacock*, originally for piano (1917) but recast for orchestra (1919), makes use of chromatic lines, unresolved series of ninth and eleventh chords, and similar impressionistic devices in forms that are characterized by quick alternations of irregular metrical patterns: $\frac{5}{4}$, $\frac{3}{2}$, $\frac{7}{4}$, etc.

The Pleasure Dome of Kubla Khan, another work originally for piano (1912) but arranged for orchestra (1916), adds an Oriental melodic flavor to the basic impressionistic style. In later works, notably a piano sonata (1919), he turned to the harmonies of Scriabin but retained Oriental touches by using scales containing augmented seconds. Had Griffes lived beyond 1920, it is likely that he would have embraced a thoroughly contemporary style, for the turn away from subjective tonal writing became marked in the compositions of his last years.

Music after 1920

THE GERMANIC influence, weakening in the first decade of the century, was canceled completely by World War I (1914–1918), after which American musicians who felt the need of European study worked in France instead of Germany. In subsequent decades, however, American educational facilities improved to such an extent that many of the younger composers received their entire education in the United States. The various stylistic trends found in the music of contemporary European composers, from post-Romantic to serial writing, are reflected in many combinations and with personal deviations in the music of hundreds of recognized American composers of serious music.

The composers mentioned in the following pages represent the styles and combinations of styles that give twentieth-century music its variety and vitality. They cannot easily be grouped; many have changed gradually from one style to another during their careers, while others have moved freely from style to style in consecutive works. In the following pages they are arranged roughly in a stylistic order from Romantic (or neo-Romantic) through neo-Classical to experimental. It is likely that the younger composers among them have not yet reached their definitive styles; any attempt to categorize them at the present time is unwarranted.

Hanson. One of the most venerated figures in American music, Howard Hanson (b. 1896) has been a stalwart supporter of American composers and, as director of the Eastman School of Music since 1924, the teacher of many of them. His works include five symphonies, a group of symphonic poems, many extended choral works, and other compositions, most of them on a large scale and in a style that may be compared with that of Sibelius. Hanson is an avowed Romanticist; his music is tonal and full of melodic inventiveness, and it reveals his fondness for the lush sound of the Romantic orchestra. Among his best-known works are the second symphony ("Romantic," 1930) and two choral works, *The Cherubic Hymn* (1949) and *The Song of Democracy* (1957).

Barber. The music of Samuel Barber (b. 1910) follows the same Romantic trend, but elements of other styles are also present: Baroque touches are evident in his *Capricorn Concerto* (1944) for flute, oboe, trumpet and strings, for example, and experiments with a twelve-tone row are seen in his sonata for piano (1949). The basic character of his music has remained constant, however; lyricism and emotionalism, effective orchestral writing, fine craftsmanship, and tonal harmony in spite of greater dissonance in the later works—these have been stable elements in his music. Two of his early works have continued in the repertoire: the *Adagio for String Orchestra* (1936) and the *Essay for Orchestra* (1938), both often performed in Europe as well as in the United States. Other works include symphonies, concertos, many songs, and an opera, *Vanessa* (see page 662).

Piston. The music of Walter Piston (b. 1894) reveals an emphasis on formal elements and the intellectual process, but Piston's innate lyricism is also present. As a student of Nadia Boulanger in Paris (1924–1926), he divested himself of any interest in nationalistic thematic material. Abstract music, especially in the forms of symphony and string quartet, has been his major interest, and his style has a strong neo-Classical flavor—except that traces of jazz-derived syncopated rhythms may be detected in his early works, and lyricism has become more pronounced. Each of his seven symphonies, dating from 1938 to 1961, has a different character brought about by the composer's fertile imagination and structural ingenuity. Certain movements in the symphonies are decidedly austere and

EXAMPLE 227

Piston, Quintet for Flute and Strings

lacking in drama, for Piston practices the greatest economy in the use of thematic material (see EXAMPLE 227, in which the cello outlines the first measure of the first-violin theme); others represent neo-Romanticism at its best. The refined and subtle qualities of his music are always apparent, however. His most frequently performed works include the fourth symphony (1950), the piano quintet (1949), and the third and fourth string quartets (1947 and 1951). An earlier work, the orchestral suite from the ballet *The Incredible Flutist* (1938), shows Piston in a light and humorous vein; frequent performances of this unrepresentative but delightful work have made Piston's name known to audiences everywhere.

Schuman. William Schuman (b. 1910), well known as president of the Juilliard School of Music and more recently as president of the Lincoln Center for the Performing Arts in New York, is related to the neo-Classical group in spite of his intermittent concern with folkloristic elements and American subjects. He has written seven symphonies, the most recent one in 1960, various choral works, three ballets, and a "baseball opera," *The Mighty Casey* (1953). Schuman's style is detailed; polyphonic writing takes precedence over homophonic, and the harmonic sound is often harsh and dissonant. His sense of formal organization and orchestral sonority, his flair for devising attractive rhythms, and his ability to write melodically contribute to the stature of his music.

Harris. Schuman's teacher, Roy Harris (b. 1898), is one of the most complex figures on the American musical scene. He has written a large quantity of music, much of it frequently performed in the 1940's, and has won numerous prizes and honors for his outstanding works; but his music is difficult to classify. Although certain personal elements are basic to his style, his plans of construction have changed from time to time and his thematic material is sometimes folkloristic and sometimes abstract. His talent is revealed most strikingly in the larger forms, which have been employed in seven symphonies, several concertos, three string quartets, and other chamber music.

Harris's harmonic style is essentially diatonic, although chords are sometimes based on fourths. Modality and polymodality often take the place of major or minor tonalities. His melodies are usually tuneful and uncomplicated, although they may be set in asymmetric rhythms, and they sometimes are constructed out of motives or motive groups. The forms of his works reveal considerable diversification: each movement of the third string quartet (1939) consists of a prelude and fugue; an overture, *When Johnny Comes Marching Home* (1935), is based entirely on manipulations of one folksong; and the third symphony (1939) consists of several sections in contrasting moods and forms that are all connected into one long movement. In spite of the great variety of form and content in his music, Harris has remained true to his basic style and has not permitted himself to be influenced by other contemporary developments.

Cowell. Henry Cowell (b. 1897) represents an experimentalist tendency. In the 1920's he won a measure of fame by exploiting tone clusters—groups of tones played on the piano with the fist or forearm—in his piano concerto and other works; later, together with an inventor of electronic musical instruments, he developed the Rhythmicon, a device for playing several complex rhythms simultaneously. Despite these excursions into extramusical areas, he has composed industriously and has over a thousand works to his credit.

Cowell has often employed American folk material, the fuguing tune of William Billings (see page 636), Celtic and Anglo-Saxon tunes, and, most recently, Oriental and other exotic material as well. In all his works he has maintained a high level of craftsmanship, writing in an easily comprehensible style that often contains touches of honest sentiment. In addition to composing he has written several books, among them a biography of Charles Ives.

Thomson. Virgil Thomson (b. 1896), like Cowell, has made considerable use of folk material, but while Cowell has employed it in a Romantic spirit, Thomson has introduced it with a bantering air. Born in Kansas City, he studied at Harvard and then went to Paris, where Nadia Boulanger was his teacher. Finding a strong affinity with France, he remained there fifteen years, became acquainted with the younger French composers, and began to compose in a neo-Classical style. The detached objectivity of that style was retained in later works, but the seriousness gave way to irony, wit, and the kind of primitivism found in the style of Erik Satie. An association with Gertrude Stein, who wrote the librettos for his two operas (see page 662), increased his tendency to compose in an aphoristic, sophisticated style. Some of his pieces are meant to be serious, others are written with tongue in cheek. His talent for descriptive writing is best seen in his music for films, of which *Louisiana Story* (1948) was the most successful. And although Thomson's style is economical and purposely obvious, he has been a strong supporter of more experimental American composers and more dissonant styles; his position as a music critic in New York gave him opportunities to write valiantly on behalf of American music of all types.

Copland. Aaron Copland (b. 1900), one of America's most distinguished composers, used jazz idioms in many of his early works. Born in Brooklyn, he received his early training in New York and in 1921 studied with Nadia Boulanger in Paris. After composing his earliest works in a style that shows French influence, he felt the need to establish a closer relationship with his audiences; the inclusion of jazz idioms in his post-1925 compositions represents a step toward that goal. An orchestral work, *Music for the Theater* (1925), a piano concerto (1927), and *Symphonic Ode* (1932) are among typical works of the period. The *Ode* is notable for a new transparency of texture, achieved by omitting unessential harmonic "fillers" in the inner voices.

A brief experimental period followed in the early 1930's, in which abstract expression came to the fore. The characteristics of this period are strikingly revealed in *Piano Variations* (1930), a massive and austere composition filled with ingenious manipulations of form and sound. Harsh dissonances, angular melodic lines, percussive effects and a wide emotional range are found here, yet in spite of the technical difficulty of the piece, the texture remains clear. Another orchestral piece, *Statements* (1935), is written in the same general style; polytonality and linear complexity reach new heights here, but the partial quotation of an Irish folksong heralds a fundamental change in Copland's style.

In the works of the following period Copland abandoned his experiments temporarily, composing in a simpler and more conservative idiom, and one that offered fewer difficulties to performers. The many compositions of this period may be grouped in four classes: patriotic works, such as *A Lincoln Portrait* (1942) for speaker and orchestra; reflections on foreign travels, in which indigenous materials are employed, such as *El Salón México* (1937), a fantasy on Mexican songs and dances (see Example 228), and in *Danzón Cubano* (1942), a two-piano piece (later orchestrated) filled with Latin polyrhythms and native themes; theater works (see page 661), incidental music, and film music, the latter best represented by *Of Mice and Men* (1939); and functional music, ranging from *An Outdoor Overture* (1938) to children's piano pieces and including a children's opera, *The Second Hurricane* (1937).

After his international fame was securely established, Copland returned to the composition of stylistically unrestricted and nonfunctional

E X A M P L E 228

Copland. *El Salón México*

music. The piano sonata (1941) and third symphony (1946), both among
his strongest works, as well as the clarinet concerto (1946) and a group of
intense songs on texts by Emily Dickinson (1950), best represent this phase.
In the symphony one may still hear reminiscences of earlier stylistic elements such as American melodies or Latin rhythms, but they are now sublimated, melodically and harmonically transformed, and embedded in
large forms.

In the years since about 1950 Copland has intensified his quest for new
techniques by incorporating serial writing into his music. The piano
quartet (1950) is based on an eleven-tone row so arranged that the com-

E X A M P L E 229

Copland, Piano Quartet

poser can employ its scale portions and chord intervals without essentially changing his personal idiom (see EXAMPLE 229). A similar structure is seen in the monumental Fantasy for piano (1958), except that here a ten-tone row is used, the two remaining tones being reserved for cadence points in a tonally oriented context.

Riegger. Recognition of Wallingford Riegger (1885–1961) as a significant composer was delayed until he was almost sixty. Born in Georgia, he lived in Germany from 1907 to 1917, first as a student and later as a conductor, after which he was active as a teacher and composer in various American schools. His early works, to about 1924, were conservative in style, and he rejected contemporary techniques almost entirely. After 1924, he took an interest in serial writing, but he did not hesitate to modify the system to meet his needs. Some of his works employ strict twelve-tone rows, while others introduce the rows mixed with traditional melodic material. Riegger's feeling for symmetry of phrase structure was almost Classical, and lyric warmth and immediate appeal are seldom missing from his works. The effect of rigid discipline in his music is softened by his personal, transparent orchestral style, in which only a few instruments are employed at any one time. His best-known works include the *Dichotomy* (1932) for chamber orchestra, the third symphony (1948), several piano pieces, and the tonal, jazzy *New Dance* (1942) for orchestra.

Bloch. The career of Ernest Bloch (1880–1959), eminent Swiss-American composer, unfolded principally in the United States. Trained in Germany and Switzerland, he came to this country in 1916 and remained, except for a nine-year interval (1930–1939), until his death in 1959. Bloch's music, essentially post-Romantic in feeling and content, was strongly colored by his Jewish heritage. He consciously sought to recapture the intensity, sensuality, violence, and despair emanating from the Old Testament, and his most successful works reflect the complex nature of the Jewish soul.

Bloch's first major success in the United States came with the orchestral *Trois Poèmes Juifs* ("Three Jewish Poems"), performed in Boston in 1917. A symphonic poem, *America,* brought him national fame, for as the winning entry in a contest sponsored by a musical magazine, it was performed by five orchestras across the country within a two-day period in 1928. Other works, however, have proved more lasting and have contributed to Bloch's reputation as an imaginative, intense composer with superb technical competence: *Schelomo* ("Solomon," 1916), a rhapsody for cello and orchestra; a piano quintet (1923), in which quarter-tones are employed; a concerto grosso (1925), for strings and piano; and the second string quartet (1945). Bloch's style was subjective, rhapsodic, and harmonically rich.

Sessions. Bloch was active as a teacher during much of his career and made vital contributions to the education of a whole generation of

American composers. Among his outstanding students was Roger Sessions (b. 1896), whose works have commanded great respect in spite of infrequent performances. In highly literate articles on the contemporary musical scene, Sessions has rejected any attempt to place him within a particular school or group of composers; his individual style, neo-Classical in general scope but surcharged with emotion, is strongly dissonant and filled with moments of great tension. Sessions composes primarily abstract music in the larger forms; his principal works include four symphonies (1927 to 1958), concertos, and chamber music. His style is not reducible to a "system," although the influence of Schoenberg can be detected at times. The seriousness, utmost sincerity, and impeccable craftsmanship of his music place him in a leading position among American composers.

Other composers. Two special ingredients of American music, the Negro spiritual and the syncopated dance, have been widely employed both in popular and serious music. William Grant Still (b. 1895) succeeded in creating an idiom that brings the melodies of his race into contact with contemporary harmony and counterpoint; his *Afro-American Symphony* (1931) and other orchestral and vocal works give evidence of his artistry and skill in making this unlikely connection.

George Gershwin (1898–1937) sought to make jazz "respectable" by superimposing this idiom on forms derived from Classical forms. His *Rhapsody in Blue* (1924), *Concerto in F* (1925) for piano and orchestra, and the symphonic suite *An American in Paris* (1928), in all of which jazz idioms are copiously employed, became landmarks in the history of American music. His jazz opera *Porgy and Bess* (see page 659) provides yet another example of this amalgamation.

Leon Kirchner (b. 1919), a pupil of Schoenberg and Sessions, has written a number of orchestral and chamber-music works that have captivated listeners by their expressive power, which shines through the rhythmic and textural complexity of the music. In his major works, such as the piano concerto (1953) and the second string quartet (1957), he has assimilated elements of several contemporary styles, employing them in an intensely personal way.

Elliott Carter (b. 1908), a pupil of Walter Piston and Nadia Boulanger, holds a prominent position among younger American composers. Beginning with elements of the neo-Classical style, he soon developed an individual mode of writing that embraced the asymmetrical tone-aggregates of expressionism and a preoccupation with rhythmic development. He employs not only great rhythmic freedom and variety but also a principle he calls "metrical modulation," in which both the accents and value of the metrical units are frequently changed (see EXAMPLE 230). He also speaks of "dramatizing" the parts of the ensemble, by which he means writing in a fluid, extremely complex, and almost improvisational idiom. His two string quartets (1951 and 1960) have attracted international attention.

Ross Lee Finney (b. 1906), a pupil of Boulanger, Alban Berg, and

EXAMPLE 230

Carter, String Quartet No. 1

Sessions, represents a group of composers who at first combined neo-Classical structures with nationalistic content; successful concertos for piano (1934) and violin (1944) illustrate this phase of his development. About 1950 his style changed to include serial writing, but his individuality as a composer has not been affected. His sixth and seventh string quartets (1957, 1960) are outstanding examples of his style, and a fantasy for unaccompanied violin (1961) reveals new sonorous possibilities and resources in this rare type.

Attempts to alter the entire course of music by applying new processes of tone selection and production have been made in the United States as well as in Europe. Harry Partch (b. 1901), an exponent of microtones, has divided the octave into forty-three instead of the usual twelve tones. His works, among them a ballet, incidental music to plays, and various descriptive pieces, offer great difficulties in the field of intonation, but they are not at all problematical in rhythm or emotional content.

Otto Luening (b. 1900), originally a composer of conventional neo-Classical music, has joined with Vladimir Ussachevsky (b. 1911) in experimenting with new methods of manipulating vocal and instrumental tone by using a tape recorder. Conventional tones and phrases have been recorded, then altered in pitch and quality by re-recording at other speeds. The tapes are then spliced, superimposed, and combined in various other ways to produce completely new sounds and sound complexes. The tape recorder has been used in such works as *Poem in Cycles and Bells* (1954) for tape recorder and orchestra, composed jointly by the two men.

The experiments conducted at the Electronic Music Center, operated in New York by Columbia and Princeton universities, are an outgrowth of this earlier work. An electronic tone synthesizer permits complete control of the elements of pitch, quality, duration, rhythm, and dynamics, and conventional instruments need not be employed. In working with the synthesizer, the composer selects the exact components of each tone he wishes to work with and manipulates them in accord with his expressive requirements. Milton Babbitt (b. 1916), a pupil of Sessions and a composer of serial music for conventional instruments, and Luening and Ussachevsky are the leaders in this development. The full impact of electronic experiments on the future course of music cannot yet be assessed.

Opera in the United States

OPERA companies were active in the United States in the last decades of the nineteenth century, primarily in New York, New Orleans, and Chicago. Italian, French, and German operas were produced in many cases only a few years after their first European performances, and as indicated above, American composers of the time imitated the European models. American operas well into the twentieth century were of this type; the sources of operas by Walter Damrosch (1862–1950), Horatio Parker (see page 645), and Deems Taylor (b. 1885) are to be found in Europe. None of the operas by these composers contributed to the formation of a distinctively American opera, and not even Howard Hanson's *Merry Mount,* commissioned by the Metropolitan Opera and performed in 1934, could break free of traditional European styles.

The first opera in which a new style was attempted, *The Emperor Jones* (1933) by Louis Gruenberg (b. 1884), based on Eugene O'Neill's play and written in a highly idiomatic, declamatory style, contained jazz idioms, Negro spirituals and dances. Two different types of opera stemmed from *The Emperor Jones:* the American jazz opera, which remained genuine and consistent in style without employing the popular idiom of the musical show, and the folk opera, in which the melodic and harmonic material is Anglo-Saxon rather than Afro-American.

The most important work of the jazz opera type was *Porgy and Bess* (1935) by George Gershwin (see page 657). Unlike many other stage works by Gershwin, this is a true opera. Stylized jazz elements, colorful orchestration, and humorous numbers and several choral sections set in syncopated rhythms are prominent features of *Porgy and Bess.* In addition, sentiment and tragic emotion as well as tension and drama come to expression, notably in the prayer during the storm scene. *Porgy and Bess* is still in the repertoire.

Leonard Bernstein (b. 1918), known as a conductor, pianist, composer, and lecturer, may be considered Gershwin's successor. Although he has written much serious music, his real gift seems to be in the fields of ballet and light opera. Melodic ingenuity and excellent craftsmanship characterize his idiom, in which he successfully introduces dramatic tension into the rhythms of the modern dance. His best-known works, the ballet *Fancy Free* (1944) and the musical show *West Side Story* (1957), reveal a tasteful, self-assured style.

The folk opera is characterized by unpretentious music, clearly defined forms, direct emotional appeal, and an American subject. Among successful examples of the type, *The Devil and Daniel Webster* (1939) by Douglas Moore (b. 1893) may be mentioned. The work contains musical numbers separated by dialogue, in the manner of the *Singspiel,* but the music is genuinely American with its ballads, fiddle tunes, and country dances alternating with lyric melodies; the score is filled with humorous and

A page of the "manuscript" of *Ensembles for Synthesizer,* by Milton Babbitt. The numerals, in binary form, are key-punched onto the paper roll which, through brush contacts, controls the relays of the R.C.A. Electronic Sound Synthesizer. Four time-parallel control tracks are notated here, each with five independent controls of the sound event: frequency, octave, envelope, spectrum, and volume. The notation is incomplete in the sense that the numerals have no predetermined signification, but designate only what they have been assigned to designate for this particular run of the Synthesizer. The frequency numerals denote frequency classes or noise sources. The octave numerals designate the registral members of the frequency classes. The envelope numerals designate the growth and decay characteristics. The spectrum numerals designate choices

ironic passages. Moore's *Ballad of Baby Doe* (1956), based on an historical episode in the West, is more serious than his earlier work; lyric and dramatic moods prevail, but the melodies remain folklike and singable.

The Tender Land (1954), the folk opera by Copland (see page 654), is modeled upon the earlier work of Moore, although Copland had employed folk materials in several of his ballets, notably *Billy the Kid* (1938), *Rodeo* (1942), and *Appalachian Spring* (1944). Carlisle Floyd (b. 1926) has continued the tradition of folk opera with his *Susannah* (1955). In the hands of other composers, the genre has sometimes taken on smaller dimensions and emerged as a chamber opera: *A Tree on the Plains* by Ernst Bacon (b. 1898) is an example.

American operas have found their way to Europe in recent decades. It is ironic, however, that the works that represent American composers abroad are not essentially nationalistic in style. Some are post-Romantic, others are in a naturalistic idiom, and still others contain elements of serial and neo-primitive styles. In *Vanessa* (1956) by Samuel Barber (see page 651), for example, arias, ensembles and large finales are written in a tonal idiom carried by a sonorous and colorful orchestration.

Barber's libretto was written by Gian-Carlo Menotti (b. 1911), who is himself a notable dramatic composer and several of whose operas have been successful in American and European opera houses as well as on Broadway. Born in Italy but a resident of the United States since 1927, Menotti began with two comic operas, *Amelia Goes to the Ball* (1937) and *The Old Maid and the Thief* (first staged performance, 1941). Later works show an affinity with the school of *verismo* (see page 531), an understandable relationship since Menotti is his own librettist and has an excellent sense of theatrical effect.

In the selection of his subjects Menotti has broken down the artificial barrier between popular opera and "learned" opera. His librettos are sound from the theatrical standpoint, and sometimes the dramatic values rise above the purely musical ones, which do not often stand alone. His flexibility as a dramatist has enabled him to compose one-act chamber operas suitable for radio and television performance; the tragic and ghostly *The Medium* (1946) and the delightfully comic *The Telephone* (1947) are performed often. Other works include a dramatic opera, *The Consul* (1950), a chamber opera for Christmas, *Amahl and the Night Visitors* (1951), and the full-length *The Saint of Bleeker Street* (1954).

---

of resonators, equalizers, filters, etc. The volume numeral denotes relative intensity. The duration of each component is not digitally specified, but is determined in analogue: duration is distance along the paper roll. In the notation, duration is indicated by the number of vertical squares occupied, with each square representing a hole, in this case representing $\frac{1}{32}$ of a second. The complete manuscript contains a description of the wirings and settings of the Synthesizer, with their associated code numbers, for each run. This page is more accurately described as an excerpt from a part than from a score, since it does not indicate all that is occurring during this temporal interval, but merely one "part" or four "parts" to be mixed with other such parts.

A scene from Copland's ballet *Rodeo,* choreographed by Agnes de Mille.

Virgil Thomson (see page 653) incorporates yet another operatic tendency into his operas: an attempt to find a style suitable for surrealistic
texts. He composed two works to texts by Gertrude Stein, *Four Saints in
Three Acts* (1934) and *The Mother of Us All* (1947), deliberately using
commonplace formulas, parodistic elements, and even musical clichés
with startling effect; the idiom in a sense resembles that of Erik Satie
(see page 586) and is filled with the same kind of French irony.

Serial writing also finds a place in opera. Louise Talma (b. 1906),
beginning her work in a neo-Classical style, gravitated to twelve-tone
writing in a collaboration with Thornton Wilder based on the classical
drama *The Alcestiad.* Completed in 1959, the opera was successfully
produced in Frankfurt in 1961. Hugo Weisgall (b. 1912 in Czecho-
Slovakia but an American resident since 1920) has employed serial writing in some of his operas, notably in his setting of Pirandello's *Six
Characters in Search of an Author* (1956). The composition of American
operas in serial style as well as in other idioms is being stimulated by
commissions offered by various philanthropic foundations. This justifies
the hope that other important operatic works will be composed and performed in the years ahead.

Summary

For two centuries after the first settlements were established on the American continent a tradition of American music did not exist. The earliest musicians in the colonies necessarily began with the European tunes and rhythms they had brought with them. Their music grew slowly at first, periodically absorbing fresh infusions of European material, and developed in the shadow of the European culture from which it was derived. It showed little originality and did no more than reflect the styles then current in the dominant musical nations. But it was helping to establish an American tradition.

Gradually American composers became aware of the wealth of source material that lay close at hand: English, French, Spanish, and Negro folksongs; gospel tunes and hymns; indigenous dances and Indian melodies; and exotic elements from the Caribbean. American legends grew as the land was mastered, providing additional material for composers whose interests lay in descriptive music. But still European techniques and aesthetic standards dominated, and only a few composers were able to free themselves from the restrictions and conventions imposed by the old traditions.

Not until well into the twentieth century did American composers rise above foreign domination and emerge with styles that were not derived from the European. Technical elements common to the world's music were employed, of course, but the emotional content, rhythmic sweep, and harmonic color began to be sensed as belonging to this nation. Folk idioms, folk material, and the rhythms of popular music lay at the base of many of the new compositions; but these elements were assimilated or transformed, and works that were distinctly American resulted.

It is obvious that much of the music composed in the last half century has few claims to immortality, and a large portion of it, performed once if at all, has long since been forgotten. But all of it was necessary to lay the foundations of a tradition out of which truly American works could be written. Today's composers are well trained, imaginative, and industrious; periodically they provide new insights, techniques, and expressive content that strengthen the position of our country's music. They have reached the point at which European composers had arrived centuries ago, for they now possess a substantial musical heritage out of which to draw sustenance. How much of the music composed in this century will endure cannot be determined now. But regardless of its destiny, it will have served an essential purpose: to provide a background out of which American composers can create music that truly reflects the aspirations, ideals, and spiritual complexity of America.

ᘒᓕᔓ BIBLIOGRAPHY ᘒᓕᔓ

THIS highly selective bibliography contains only a few of the thousands of items that bear on the subject of music history. It seeks to call attention to the books that the reader will find most immediately useful and most generally available. It emphasizes books in English, but it also includes some of the outstanding works in foreign languages. Since many of the books listed contain extensive bibliographies, articles in periodicals have not been given; however, major English-language periodicals dealing with music history are included.

I: General References and Periodicals

APEL, WILLI, *Harvard Dictionary of Music,* Harvard University Press, Cambridge, 1944.

Baker's Biographical Dictionary of Musicians, 5th rev. ed. by Nicolas Slonimsky, G. Schirmer, New York, 1958.

BESSARABOFF, NICHOLAS, *Ancient European Musical Instruments,* Harvard University Press, Cambridge, 1941.

BLUME, FRIEDRICH, ed., *Die Musik in Geschichte und Gegenwart,* 10 vols. to date, Bärenreiter, Cassel, 1949– .

COBBETT, WALTER W., ed., *Cobbett's Cyclopedic Survey of Chamber Music,* 2 vols., Oxford University Press, London, 1929–30.

DARRELL, RICHARD D., *Schirmer's Guide to Books on Music and Musicians,* G. Schirmer, New York, 1951.

DAVISON, ARCHIBALD T., and WILLI APEL, eds., *Historical Anthology of Music,* 2 vols., Harvard University Press, Cambridge, 1947, 1950. **Abbr.: HAM.**

DUFORCQ, NORBERT, ed., *Larousse de la Musique,* Librairie Larousse, Paris, 1957.

GEIRINGER, KARL, *Musical Instruments: Their History in Western Culture from the Stone Age to the Present,* tr. by Bernard Miall, Oxford University Press, New York, 1945.

Grove's Dictionary of Music and Musicians, 5th ed. by Eric Blom, 9 vols., 1 suppl. vol., Macmillan, London; St Martin's, New York, 1954, 1960.

HAYDON, GLEN, *Introduction to Musicology,* Prentice-Hall, Englewood Cliffs, N.J., 1941.

HEYER, ANNA HARRIET, *Historical Sets, Collected Editions, and Monuments of Music: A Guide to Their Contents,* American Library Association, Chicago, 1957.

Journal, American Musicological Society, Boston, 1948– .

JULIAN, JOHN, *A Dictionary of Hymnology,* rev. ed., Murray, London, 1925.

LAVIGNAC, ALBERT, ed., *Encyclopédie de la Musique,* 11 vols., Delagrave, Paris, 1913–39.

Lowenberg, Alfred, *Annals of Opera, 1597–1940,* 2d ed., Societas Bibliograph-
ica, Geneva, 1955.

Modern Music, League of Composers, New York, 1924–46.

Moser, Hans Joachim, *Musiklexikon,* 4th ed., 2 vols., Sikorski, Hamburg, 1955.

Music and Letters, London, 1920– .

Music Review, Cambridge, England, 1940– .

Musical Quarterly, The, G. Schirmer, New York, 1915– .

Notes, Music Library Association, Washington, 1943– .

Parrish, Carl, ed., *A Treasury of Early Music,* Norton, New York, 1958. **Abbr.:
TEM.**

———, and John F. Ohl, eds., *Masterpieces of Music Before 1750,* Norton, New
York, 1951. **Abbr.: MoM.**

Pulver, Jeffrey, *Biographical Dictionary of Old English Music,* Dutton, New
York, 1927.

Reese, Gustave, *Fourscore Classics of Music Literature,* Liberal Arts Press, New
York, 1957.

Riemann, Hugo, *Musiklexikon,* 12th ed. by Willibald Gurlitt, 2 vols. of biog-
raphies published; 3d vol., general reference, in preparation, Schott, Mainz,
1959– .

Sachs, Curt, *The History of Musical Instruments,* Norton, New York, 1940.

———, *World History of the Dance,* Norton, New York, 1937.

Schering, Arnold, ed., *Geschichte der Musik in Beispielen,* Breitkopf & Härtel,
Leipzig, 1931; reprinted, Broude Bros., New York, 1950. **Abbr.: GMB.**

Scholes, Percy A., *The Concise Oxford Dictionary of Music,* Oxford University
Press, London, 1952.

———, *The Oxford Companion to Music,* 9th ed., Oxford University Press, London, 1955.

Strunk, Oliver, ed., *Source Readings in Music History,* Norton, New York,
1950. **Abbr.: SRMH.**

Thompson, Oscar, ed., *The International Cyclopedia of Music and Musicians,*
8th ed. by Nicolas Slonimsky, Dodd Mead, New York, 1958.

Winternitz, Emanuel, *Musical Autographs from Monteverdi to Hindemith,*
Princeton University Press, Princeton, 1955.

II: Music Histories

Adler, Guido, ed., *Handbuch der Musikgeschichte,* 2d ed., 2 vols., Keller, Berlin-
Wilmersdorf, 1930.

Allen, Warren D., *Philosophies of Music History,* American Book, New York,
1939.

Bücken, Ernst, *Geist und Form im musikalischen Kunstwerk (Handbuch der
Musikwissenschaft* series), Athenaion, Potsdam, 1929.

———, ed., *Handbuch der Musikwissenschaft,* 13 vols., Athenaion, Potsdam, 1928–
32.

Burney, Charles, *A General History of Music,* 4 vols., London, 1776–89. New
ed. by Frank Mercer, 2 vols., Harcourt, Brace & World, New York, 1935;
reprinted, Dover, New York, 1960.

CHASE, GILBERT, *The Music of Spain,* Norton, New York, 1941.

COMBARIEU, JULES, *Histoire de la musique,* 3d ed., 3 vols., Colin, Paris, 1948–50.

EINSTEIN, ALFRED, *A Short History of Music,* Knopf, New York, 1947.

GROUT, DONALD J., *A History of Western Music,* Norton, New York, 1960.

———, *A Short History of Opera,* 2 vols., Columbia University Press, New York, 1947.

HAAS, ROBERT, *Aufführungspraxis der Musik (Handbuch der Musikwissenschaft* series), Athenaion, Potsdam, 1931.

HEINITZ, WILHELM, *Instrumentenkunde (Handbuch der Musikwissenschaft* series), Athenaion, Potsdam, 1932.

KINSKY, GEORG, ed., *A History of Music in Pictures,* Dent, London, 1937.

LACHMANN, ROBERT, *Die Musik der aussereuropäischen Natur- und Kulturvölker (Handbuch der Musikwissenschaft* series), Athenaion, Potsdam, 1931.

LANG, PAUL HENRY, *Music in Western Civilization,* Norton, New York, 1941.

LEICHTENTRITT, HUGO, *Music, History, and Ideas,* Harvard University Press, Cambridge, 1938.

MILLER, HUGH M., *History of Music* (College Outline series), 2d ed., Barnes and Noble, New York, 1953.

MOSER, HANS JOACHIM, *Geschichte der deutschen Musik,* 5th ed., 3 vols., Cotta, Stuttgart, 1930.

NEF, KARL, *An Outline of the History of Music,* rev. ed., tr. by Carl F. Pfatteicher, Columbia University Press, New York, 1957.

New Oxford History of Music, The, ed. by Egon Wellesz and others, 3 vols. to date; other vols. in preparation, Oxford University Press, London, 1957–

Oxford History of Music, The, 2d ed., 7 vols. and intro. vol., Oxford University Press, London, 1929–38.

PRUNIÈRES, HENRI, *A New History of Music: The Middle Ages to Mozart,* tr. by Edward Lockspeiser, Macmillan, New York, 1943.

STEVENSON, ROBERT, *Music in Mexico: A Historical Survey,* Crowell, New York, 1952.

WALKER, ERNEST, *A History of Music in England,* 3d rev. ed. by Jack Allan Westrup, Clarendon Press, Oxford, 1952.

WESTRUP, JACK ALLAN, *An Introduction to Musical History,* Hutchison, London, 1955.

III: Selected Complete Editions

BACH, JOHANN SEBASTIAN, *Werke,* ed. by Moritz Hauptmann and others, 47 vols., Bachgesellschaft, Breitkopf & Härtel, Leipzig, 1851–1926; reprinted, J. W. Edwards, Ann Arbor, 1947.

BEETHOVEN, LUDWIG VAN, *Werke,* ed. by Guido Adler and others, 25 vols., Breitkopf & Härtel, Leipzig, 1864–90; reprinted, J. W. Edwards, Ann Arbor, 1949.

BERLIOZ, HECTOR, *Sämtliche Werke,* ed. by Charles Malherbe and Felix Weingartner, 20 vols. (incomplete), Breitkopf & Härtel, Leipzig, 1900–07.

BRAHMS, JOHANNES, *Sämtliche Werke,* ed. by Hans Gál and Eusebius Mandyczewski, 26 vols., Breitkopf & Härtel, Leipzig, 1926–28; reprinted, J. W. Edwards, Ann Arbor, 1949.

BYRD, WILLIAM, *Collected Works*, ed. by Edmund H. Fellowes, 20 vols., Stainer and Bell, London, 1937–50.

CHOPIN, FRÉDÉRIC, *Werke*, ed. by Johannes Brahms and others, 14 vols. and 3 suppl., Breitkopf & Härtel, Leipzig, 1878–80. New ed. by Ignacy J. Paderewski and others, 13 vols., Fryderyk Chopin Institute, Warsaw, 1949.

CORELLI, ARCANGELO, *Oeuvres*, ed. by Joseph Joachim and Friedrich Chrysander, 5 vols., Augener, London, 1888–91.

COUPERIN, FRANÇOIS, *Oeuvres complètes*, ed. by Maurice Cauchie, 12 vols., L'Oiseau-lyre, Monaco, 1932–33.

DES PREZ, JOSQUIN, *Werke*, ed. by Albert Smijers, 41 vols. to date, Alsbach, Amsterdam, and Kistner & Siegel, Leipzig, 1925– .

DUNSTABLE, JOHN, *Complete Works* (Musica Britannica series), ed. by Manfred Bukofzer, Stainer and Bell, London, 1953.

HÄNDEL, GEORG FRIEDRICH, *Werke*, ed. by Friedrich Chrysander, 102 vols. (incomplete), Breitkopf & Härtel, Leipzig, 1858–1902.

HAYDN, FRANZ JOSEPH, *Sämtliche Werke*, ed. by Eusebius Mandyczewski and others, 10 vols. published, Breitkopf & Härtel, Leipzig, 1907–33; ed. by Jens Peter Larsen and others, 4 vols. published, Haydn Society, Boston, 1949–52. A new edition is in preparation, Haydn Institute, Cologne, 1954– .

LASSO, ORLANDO DI, *Sämtliche Werke*, ed. by Franz X. Haberl and Adolf Sandberger, 21 vols. published, Breitkopf & Härtel, Leipzig, 1894–1927. A new edition is in preparation, Bärenreiter, Cassel, 1956– .

LISZT, FRANZ, *Musikalische Werke*, ed. by Ferruccio Busoni and others, 39 vols. to date, Breitkopf & Härtel, Leipzig, 1907–25.

LULLY, JEAN BAPTISTE, *Oeuvres*, ed. by Henri Prunières, 10 vols. to date, Société Française de Musicologie, Paris, 1930– ; Stainer and Bell, London, 1930–39.

MACHAUT, GUILLAUME DE, *Musikalische Werke*, vols. 1–3 ed. by Friedrich Ludwig, Breitkopf & Härtel, Leipzig, 1926–28; vol. 4 ed. by Heinrich Besseler, Breitkopf & Härtel, Wiesbaden, 1954. Another ed. by Leo Schrade (see under Section IV).

MENDELSSOHN, FELIX, *Werke*, ed. by Julius Rietz, 36 vols., Breitkopf & Härtel, Leipzig, 1874–77.

MONTEVERDI, CLAUDIO, *Tutte le opere*, ed. G. Francesco Malipiero, 16 vols., Universal, Vienna, 1926–42.

MOZART, WOLFGANG AMADEUS, *Sämtliche Werke*, ed. by Gustav Nottebohm and others, 24 series in 75 vols., Breitkopf & Härtel, Leipzig, 1876–1905; reprinted, J. W. Edwards, Ann Arbor, 1955.

OBRECHT, JACOB, *Werke*, ed. by Johannes Wolf, 30 vols., Breitkopf & Härtel, Leipzig, 1908–21. New ed. by Albert Smijers in preparation, Alsbach, Amsterdam, 1953– .

OKEGHEM, JOHANNES, *Complete Works*, ed. by Dragan Plamenac, 2 vols., 1927, 1947; 3d vol. in preparation, Columbia University Press, New York.

PALESTRINA, GIOVANNI PIERLUIGI DA, *Werke*, ed. by Franz X. Haberl and others, 33 vols., Breitkopf & Härtel, Leipzig, 1862–1900. New ed. in preparation, 27 vols. to date, Scalero, Rome, 1939– .

PURCELL, HENRY, *Complete Works*, 26 vols. to date, 6 vols. not yet published, Novello, London, 1878–1928.

RAMEAU, JEAN PHILIPPE, *Oeuvres complètes*, ed. by Camille Saint-Saëns and others, 18 vols. (incomplete), Durand, Paris, 1895–1924.

SCARLATTI, DOMENICO, *Opere complete per clavicembalo*, ed. by Alessandro Longo, 11 vols., Ricordi, Milan, 1947–51.

SCHUBERT, FRANZ, *Werke*, ed. by Johannes Brahms and others, 41 vols., Breitkopf & Härtel, Leipzig, 1884–97.

SCHUMANN, ROBERT, *Werke*, ed. by Clara Schumann, 31 vols., Breitkopf & Härtel, Leipzig, 1881–93.

SCHÜTZ, HEINRICH, *Sämtliche Werke*, ed. by Philipp Spitta, 18 vols., Breitkopf & Härtel, Leipzig, 1885–1927.

SWEELINCK, JAN, *Werke*, ed. by Max Seifert and others, 12 vols., Nijhoff, The Hague, 1894–1901.

VIVALDI, ANTONIO, *Le opere*, ed. by G. Francesco Malipiero, 290 fascicles to date, Ricordi, Milan, 1947– .

IV: Chapters 1–7, The Ancient and Medieval Periods

ABRAHAM, GERALD, and DOM ANSELM HUGHES, eds., *The New Oxford History of Music*, Vol. 3, *Ars Nova and the Renaissance*, Oxford University Press, London, 1962.

APEL, WILLI, ed., *French Secular Music of the Late Fourteenth Century*, Medieval Academy, Cambridge, Mass., 1950.

——, *Gregorian Chant*, University of Indiana Press, Bloomington, 1958.

——, *The Notation of Polyphonic Music, 900–1600*, 5th ed., Medieval Academy, Cambridge, Mass., 1961.

AUBRY, PIERRE, *Trouverès and Troubadours*, tr. by Claude Aveling, G. Schirmer, New York, 1914.

BECK, JEAN BAPTISTE, *Les chansonniers des troubadours et des trouvères*, University of Pennsylvania Press, Philadelphia, 1927.

BEDBROOK, G. S., *Keyboard Music from the Middle Ages to the Beginnings of the Baroque*, Macmillan, London, 1949.

BESSELER, HEINRICH, *Bourdon und Fauxbourdon*, Breitkopf & Härtel, Leipzig, 1950.

——, *Die Musik des Mittelalters und der Renaissance* (*Handbuch der Musikwissenschaft* series), Athenaion, Potsdam, 1931.

BUKOFZER, MANFRED F., *Studies in Medieval and Renaissance Music*, Norton, New York, 1950.

FYZEE-RAHAMIN, ATIYA BEGUM, *The Music of India*, Luzac, London, 1925.

GALPIN, FRANCIS W., *Music of the Sumerians and Their Immediate Successors, the Babylonians and Assyrians*, University Press, Cambridge, England, 1937.

HUGHES, DOM ANSELM, ed., *The New Oxford History of Music*, Vol. 2, *Early Medieval Music up to 1300*, Oxford University Press, London, 1958.

IDELSOHN, ABRAHAM ZEVI, *Jewish Music in Its Historical Development*, Holt, New York, 1929.

LACHMANN, ROBERT, *Die Musik des Orients*, Hirt, Breslau, 1929.

LEFEBURE, DOM GASPAR, ed., *St. Andrew Daily Missal*, Lohmann, St. Paul, Minn., 1945.

LEVARIE, SIEGMUND, *Guillaume de Machaut*, Sheed and Ward, London, 1954.

Liber usualis, ed. by the Benedictines of Solesmes, Desclée, Tournai, 1950.

MARROCCO, WILLIAM T., *Fourteenth-Century Italian Cacce*, 2d ed., Medieval Academy, Cambridge, Mass., 1961.

PANÓFF, PETER, *Die altslavische Volks- und Kirchenmusik (Handbuch der Musikwissenschaft* series), Athenaion, Potsdam, 1930.

PARRISH, CARL, *The Notation of Medieval Music*, Norton, New York, 1957.

PIERIK, MARIE, *Gregorian Chant Analyzed and Studied*, Grail Publications, St. Meinrad, Ind., 1951.

PIRRO, ANDRÉ, *Histoire de la musique de la fin du XIV siècle à la fin du XVI*, Laurens, Paris, 1940.

REESE, GUSTAVE, *Music in the Middle Ages*, Norton, New York, 1940.

RIEMANN, HUGO, *History of Music Theory*, tr. by Raymond Haggh, University of Nebraska Press, Lincoln, 1962.

ROCKSETH, YVONNE, ed., *Polyphonies du XIII siècle*, 4 vols., L'Oiseau-lyre, Monaco, 1935–39.

SACHS, CURT, *Die Musik der Antike (Handbuch der Musikwissenschaft* series), Athenaion, Potsdam, 1928.

———, *The Rise of Music in the Ancient World*, Norton, New York, 1943.

SCHNEIDER, MARIUS, *Geschichte der Mehrstimmigkeit*, Bard, Berlin, 1934–35.

SCHRADE, LEO, ed., *Polyphonic Music of the Fourteenth Century*, 3 vols. of music, 2 vols. of commentary, L'Oiseau-lyre, Monaco, 1956.

STUMPF, KARL, *Die Anfänge der Musik*, Barth, Leipzig, 1911.

TRUMBLE, ERNEST, *Fauxbourdon: A Historical Survey*, Institute of Medieval Music, Brooklyn, 1959.

WAITE, WILLIAM G., *The Rhythm of Twelfth-Century Polyphony*, Yale University Press, New Haven, 1954.

WELLESZ, EGON, *A History of Byzantine Music and Hymnography*, 2d ed., Clarendon Press, Oxford, 1961.

———, *The New Oxford History of Music*, Vol. 1, *Ancient and Oriental Music*, Oxford University Press, London, 1957.

WERNER, ERIC, *The Sacred Bridge*, Columbia University Press, New York, 1959.

V: Chapters 8–11, The Renaissance Period

ABRAHAM, GERALD, and DOM ANSELM HUGHES, eds., *The New Oxford History of Music*, Vol. 3, *Ars Nova and the Renaissance*, Oxford University Press, London, 1962.

BOETTICHER, WOLFGANG, *Orlando di Lasso und seine Zeit*, 2 vols., Bärenreiter, Cassell, 1958.

BORREN, CHARLES VAN DEN, *The Sources of Keyboard Music in England*, tr. by James E. Matthew, Novello, London, 1913; Gray, New York, 1914.

BUKOFZER, MANFRED, *Studies in Medieval and Renaissance Music*, Norton, New York, 1950.

COATES, HENRY, *Palestrina*, Dent, London, 1938; Farrar, Strauss, New York, 1949.

DAVID, HANS T., *The Art of the Polyphonic Song*, G. Schirmer, New York, 1949.

EINSTEIN, ALFRED, *The Golden Age of the Madrigal,* G. Schirmer, New York, 1942.

——, *The Italian Madrigal,* 3 vols., Princeton University Press, Princeton, 1949.

FELLOWES, EDMUND H., *The English Madrigal,* Oxford University Press, London, 1925.

——, *English Madrigal Composers,* 2d ed., Clarendon Press, Oxford, 1948.

——, *Orlando Gibbons and His Family,* Clarendon Press, Oxford, 1951.

——, *William Byrd,* 2d ed., Oxford University Press, London, 1948.

GRAY, CECIL, and PHILIP HESELTINE, *Carlo Gesualdo, Prince of Venosa,* Kegan Paul, Trench, Trubner, London, 1926.

HEWITT, HELEN, ed., *Harmonice musicae odhecaton A,* Medieval Society, Cambridge, Mass., 1942.

JEPPESEN, KNUD, *Counterpoint: The Polyphonic Vocal Style of the Sixteenth Century,* tr. by Glen Haydon, Prentice-Hall, New York, 1939.

——, *The Style of Palestrina and the Dissonance,* tr. by Margaret Hamerik, 2d ed., Oxford University Press, London, 1946.

KINKELDEY, OTTO, *Orgel und Klavier in der Musik des 16ten Jahrhunderts,* Breitkopf & Härtel, Leipzig, 1910.

KRENEK, ERNST, ed., *Hamline Studies in Musicology,* 2 vols., Burgess, Minneapolis, 1945.

——, *Johannes Okeghem,* Sheed and Ward, London, 1953.

LESURE, FRANÇOIS, *Musicians and Poets of the French Renaissance,* tr. by Elio Gianturco and Hans Rosenwald, Merlin, New York, 1955.

LOWINSKY, EDWARD E., *Secret Chromatic Art in the Netherlands Motet,* tr. by Carl Buchman, Columbia University Press, New York, 1946.

——, *Tonality and Atonality in Sixteenth-Century Music,* University of California Press, Berkeley, 1961.

REESE, GUSTAVE, *Music in the Renaissance,* rev. ed., Norton, New York, 1954.

VI: Chapters 12–15, The Baroque Period

ABRAHAM, GERALD, ed., *Handel: A Symposium,* Oxford University Press, New York, 1954.

ARNOLD, FRANCK THOMAS, *The Art of Accompaniment from a Thoroughbass,* Oxford University Press, London, 1931.

ARUNDELL, DENNIS, *Henry Purcell,* Oxford University Press, London, 1927.

BACH, CARL PHILIPP EMANUEL, *Essay on the True Art of Playing Keyboard Instruments,* tr. by William Mitchell, Norton, New York, 1948.

BLUME, FRIEDRICH, *Die evangelische Kirchenmusik (Handbuch der Musikwissenschaft* series), Athenaion, Potsdam, 1931.

BUKOFZER, MANFRED, *Music in the Baroque Era,* Norton, New York, 1947.

CARSE, ADAM, *The Orchestra in the XVIIIth Century,* Heffer, Cambridge, England, 1940.

DANNREUTHER, EDWARD, *Musical Ornamentation,* 2 vols., Novello, London, n.d. (*c.* 1895).

DAVID, HANS T., and ARTHUR MENDEL, eds., *The Bach Reader,* Norton, New York, 1945.

DAVISON, ARCHIBALD T., *Bach and Handel: The Consummation of the Baroque in Music*, Harvard University Press, Cambridge, 1951.

DEAN, WINTON, *Handel's Dramatic Oratorios and Masques*, Oxford University Press, New York, 1959.

DENT, EDWARD J., *Alessandro Scarlatti: His Life and Works*, Longmans, London, 1905; St Martin's, New York, 1961.

———, *Foundations of English Opera*, Cambridge University Press, London, 1928.

———, *Handel*, Duckworth, London, 1947.

DEUTSCH, OTTO E., *Handel: A Documentary Biography*, Norton, New York, 1955.

DOLMETSCH, ARNOLD, *The Interpretation of the Music of the 17th and 18th Centuries*, Novello, London, 1915; Gray, New York, 1915.

EMERY, WALTER, *Bach's Ornaments*, Novello, London, 1953.

GEIRINGER, KARL, *The Bach Family: Seven Generations of Creative Genius*, Oxford University Press, New York, 1954.

HAAS, ROBERT, *Die Musik des Barocks (Handbuch der Musikwissenschaft series)*, Athenaion, Potsdam, 1929.

HINDEMITH, PAUL, *J. S. Bach: Heritage and Obligation*, Yale University Press, New Haven, 1952.

HUTCHINS, FARLEY, *Dietrich Buxtehude: The Man, His Music, His Era*, Music Textbook Co., Paterson, N. J., 1955.

KIRKPATRICK, RALPH, *Domenico Scarlatti*, Princeton University Press, Princeton, 1953.

LAURENCIE, LIONEL DE LA, *Rameau*, Laurens, Paris, 1908.

MELLERS, WILFRED H., *François Couperin and the French Classical Tradition*, Dobson, London, 1950.

MEYER, ERNST H., *English Chamber Music*, Wishart, London, 1946.

MOSER, HANS JOACHIM, *Heinrich Schütz: His Life and Work*, tr. by Carl F. Pfatteicher, Concordia, St. Louis, 1959.

PINCHERLE, MARC, *Corelli*, tr. by Hubert E. M. Russell, Norton, New York, 1956.

———, *Vivaldi: Genius of the Baroque*, tr. by Christopher Hatch, Norton, New York, 1957.

PRUNIÈRES, HENRI, *Lully: Biographie critique*, Librairie Ronouard, Paris, 1909.

REDLICH, HANS FERDINAND, *Claudio Monteverdi*, Oxford University Press, London, 1952.

SCHMIEDER, WOLFGANG, ed., *Thematisch-systematisches Verzeichnis der Werke von Johann Sebastian Bach*, Breitkopf & Härtel, Leipzig, 1950.

SCHRADE, LEO, *Monteverdi: Creator of Modern Music*, Norton, New York, 1950.

SIGTENHORST-MEYER, BERNARD, *Jan Pieterzoon Sweelinck*, 2 vols., Servire, The Hague, 1946, 1948.

SPITTA, PHILIPP, *J. S. Bach: His Work and Influence on the Music of Germany*, 3 vols., tr. by Clara Bell and J. A. Fuller-Maitland, Novello, London, 1899; reprinted, Dover, New York, 1951.

STEVENS, DENIS, ed., *A History of Song*, Norton, New York, 1961.

STEVENSON, ROBERT, *Music Before the Classic Era*, Macmillan, London, 1955.

TERRY, CHARLES SANFORD, *Bach's Orchestra*, Oxford University Press, London, 1932.

ULRICH, HOMER, *Chamber Music*, Columbia University Press, New York, 1948.

URSPRUNG, OTTO, *Die katholische Kirchenmusik* (*Handbuch der Musikwissenschaft* series), Athenaion, Potsdam, 1931.

WESTRUP, JACK ALLAN, *Purcell,* Dent, London, 1937; Farrar, Strauss, New York, 1949.

WHITE, ERIC WALTER, *The Rise of English Opera,* Lehmann, London, 1951.

YOUNG, PERCY M., *The Oratorios of Handel,* Dobson, London, 1949.

VII: Chapters 16–20, The Classical Period

ANDERSON, EMILY, tr. and ed., *Letters of Beethoven,* St Martin's, New York, 1961.

——, tr. and ed., *The Letters of Mozart and His Family,* 3 vols., Macmillan, London, 1938.

BÜCKEN, ERNST, *Die Musik des Rokoko und der Klassik* (*Handbuch der Musikwissenschaft* series), Athenaion, Potsdam, 1931.

BURK, JOHN N., *The Life and Works of Beethoven,* Random House, New York, 1943.

CARSE, ADAM, *The Orchestra from Beethoven to Berlioz,* Heffer, Cambridge, England, 1948.

DENT, EDWARD J., *Mozart's Operas,* 2d ed., Oxford University Press, London, 1947.

EINSTEIN, ALFRED, *Gluck,* tr. by Eric Blom, Dutton, New York, 1936.

——, *Mozart: His Character, His Work,* tr. by Arthur Mendel and Nathan Broder, Oxford University Press, New York, 1945.

EVANS, EDWIN, SR., *Beethoven's Nine Symphonies,* 2 vols., Scribner, New York, 1923–24.

GÁL, HANS, *The Golden Age of Vienna,* Parrish, London, 1948.

GEIRINGER, KARL, *Haydn,* Norton, New York, 1946.

GIRDLESTONE, CUTHBERT M., *Mozart's Piano Concertos,* tr. from the French by the author, Cassel, London, 1948.

HOBOKEN, ANTHONY VAN, *Joseph Haydn, thematisch-bibiographisches Werkverzeichnis,* Vol. 1, *Instrumental Works,* Schott, Mainz, 1957– .

JAHN, OTTO, *W. A. Mozart,* 6th ed. by Hermann Abert, 2 vols., Breitkopf & Härtel, Leipzig, 1923–24.

KINSKY, GEORG, and HANS HALM, *Das Werk Beethovens: Verzeichnis seiner sämtlichen vollendeten Kompositionen,* Henle, Munich, 1955.

KOECHEL, LUDWIG RITTER VON, *Chronologisch-systematisches Verzeichnis sämtlicher Tonwerke Wolfgang Amade Mozarts,* 5th rev. ed. by Ernst Reichert, Breitkopf & Härtel, Wiesbaden, 1960.

LANDON, H. C. ROBBINS, ed., *The Collected Correspondence and London Notebooks of Joseph Haydn,* Essential Books, New York, 1959.

——, *The Symphonies of Joseph Haydn,* Macmillan, New York, 1961.

LARSEN, JENS PETER, *Die Haydn Überlieferung,* Munksgaard, Copenhagen, 1939.

LEVARIE, SIEGMUND, *Mozart's Le Nozze di Figaro: A Critical Analysis,* University of Chicago Press, Chicago, 1952.

MACARDLE, DONALD W., and LUDWIG MISCH, eds., *New Beethoven Letters,* University of Oklahoma Press, Norman, 1957.

MARLIAVE, JOSEPH DE, *Beethoven's Quartets*, tr. by Hilda Andrews, Oxford University Press, London, 1928; Dover, New York, 1961.

NEF, KARL, *Geschichte der Sinfonie und Suite*, Breitkopf & Härtel, Leipzig, 1921.

POHL, KARL FERDINAND, *Joseph Haydn*, with additions by Hugo Botstiber, 3 vols. in 2, Breitkopf & Härtel, Leipzig, 1927.

RIEZLER, WALTER, *Beethoven*, tr. by G. H. D. Pidcock, Dutton, New York, 1938.

SAINT-FOIX, GEORGES, *The Symphonies of Mozart*, tr. by Leslie Orrey, Dobson, London, 1947.

SULLIVAN, JOHN W. N., *Beethoven: His Spiritual Development*, Knopf, New York, 1927.

TERRY, CHARLES SANFORD, *John Christian Bach*, Oxford University Press, London, 1929.

THAYER, ALEXANDER W., *The Life of Ludwig van Beethoven*, ed. by H. E. Krehbiel, 3 vols., Beethoven Assn., New York, 1921; reprinted, Southern Illinois University Press, Carbondale, 1960.

TOVEY, DONALD S., *Essays in Musical Analysis*, 6 vols.: Vol. 1, *Symphonies;* Vol. 2, *Symphonies, Variations, and Orchestral Polyphony;* Vol. 3, *Concertos;* Vol. 4, *Illustrative Music;* Vol. 5, *Vocal Music;* Vol. 6, *Miscellaneous Notes, Glossary, Index;* Supplement, *Chamber Music*, ed. by Hubert Foss; Oxford University Press, New York, 1935–39.

ULRICH, HOMER, *Chamber Music*, Columbia University Press, New York, 1948.

VEINUS, ABRAHAM, *The Concerto*, Doubleday, New York, 1944.

VIII: Chapters 21–27, The Romantic Period

ABRAHAM, GERALD, *Chopin's Musical Style*, Oxford University Press, New York, 1946.

———, ed., *Grieg: A Symposium*, University of Oklahoma Press, Norman, 1950.

——, *A Hundred Years of Music*, 2d ed., Duckworth, London, 1949.

———, ed., *The Music of Schubert*, Norton, New York, 1947.

———, ed., *The Music of Tchaikovsky*, Norton, New York, 1946.

———, ed., *Schumann: A Symposium*, Oxford University Press, New York, 1952.

BARZUN, JACQUES, *Berlioz and the Romantic Century*, 2 vols., Little, Brown, Boston, 1950.

———, *Darwin, Marx, and Wagner: Critique of a Heritage*, Little, Brown, Boston, 1941.

———, ed., *New Letters of Berlioz, 1830–1868*, Columbia University Press, New York, 1954.

BERLIOZ, HECTOR, *Memoirs*, tr. and annotated by Ernest Newman, Tudor, New York, 1935.

———, *Treatise on Instrumentation*, rev. by Richard Strauss, tr. by Theodore Front, Kalmus, New York, 1948.

BROWN, MAURICE J. E., *Schubert: A Biography with Critical Digressions*, St Martin's, New York, 1958.

BÜCKEN, ERNST, *Die Musik des 19ten Jahrhunderts (Handbuch der Musikwissenschaft* series), Athenaion, Potsdam, 1928.

CALVOCORESSI, MICHEL DIMITRI, *Modest Mussorgsky*, Rockliffe, London, 1956.

CURTISS, MINA, *Bizet and His World*, Knopf, New York, 1958.

DEUTSCH, OTTO ERICH, *The Schubert Reader*, tr. by Eric Blom, Norton, New York, 1947.

——, and DONALD R. WAKELING, eds., *Schubert Thematic Catalogue*, Norton, New York, 1951.

EINSTEIN, ALFRED, *Music in the Romantic Era*, Norton, New York, 1947.

——, *Schubert: A Musical Portrait*, tr. by David Ascoli, Oxford University Press, New York, 1951.

EVANS, EDWIN, SR., *Handbook to the Works of Brahms*, 4 vols.: Vol. 1, *Vocal Works*; Vols. 2 and 3, *Chamber and Orchestral Works*; Vol. 4, *Pianoforte Works*, Reeves, London, 1912–36.

GEIRINGER, KARL, *Brahms: His Life and Works*, 2d rev. ed., Oxford University Press, New York, 1947.

HULL, A. EAGLEFIELD, *A Great Musical Tone Poet: Scriabin*, Kegan Paul, Trench, Trubner, London, 1916.

HUTCHESON, ERNEST, *A Musical Guide to the Richard Wagner "Ring of the Nibelung,"* Simon and Schuster, New York, 1940.

KAPP, JULIUS, *Giacomo Meyerbeer*, rev. ed., M. Hesse, Berlin, 1932.

KRACAUER, SIEGFRIED, *Orpheus in Paris: Offenbach and the Paris of His Time*, tr. by Gwenda Davis and Eric Mosbacher, Knopf, New York, 1938.

KROLL, ERWIN, *Ernst Theodor Amadeus Hoffmann*, Breitkopf & Härtel, Leipzig, 1923.

LORENZ, ALFRED, *Das Geheimnis der Form bei Richard Wagner*, 4 vols., Hesse, Berlin, 1924–33.

LYLE, WATSON, *Saint-Saëns: His Life and Art*, Dutton, New York, 1923.

NEWLIN, DIKA, *Bruckner, Mahler, Schoenberg*, Columbia University Press, New York, 1947.

NEWMAN, ERNEST, *The Life of Richard Wagner*, 4 vols., Knopf, New York, 1933–46.

——, *The Wagner Operas*, Knopf, New York, 1949.

NIEMANN, WALTER, *Brahms*, tr. by C. A. Phillips, Knopf, New York, 1947.

RADCLIFFE, PHILIP, *Mendelssohn*, Farrar, Strauss, New York, 1954.

REDLICH, HANS F., *Bruckner and Mahler*, Farrar, Strauss, London, 1955.

RIMSKY-KORSAKOV, NICOLAY, *My Musical Life*, tr. from 5th rev. Russian ed. by Judah A. Joffee, ed. by Carl van Vechten, Knopf, New York, 1942.

——, *Principles of Orchestration*, tr. by Edward Agate, Kalmus, New York, 1933.

ROBERTSON, ALEC, *Dvořák*, Pellegrini & Cudahy, New York, 1949.

SEARLE, HUMPHREY, *The Music of Liszt*, Williams and Norgate, London, 1954.

SITWELL, SACHEVERELL, *Liszt*, rev. ed., Cassel, London, 1955.

SUCKLING, NORMAN, *Fauré*, Dent, London, 1946; Farrar, Strauss, New York, 1952.

TOVEY, DONALD F., *Essays in Musical Analysis*, see under VII: The Classical Period.

TOYE, FRANCIS, *Rossini: A Study in Tragi-Comedy*, new ed., Barker, London, 1954.

——, *Verdi: His Life and Works*, Knopf, New York, 1946.

VALLAS, LÉON, *La véritable histoire de César Franck*, Flammarion, Paris, 1955.

WAGNER, RICHARD, *Opera and Drama,* tr. by Edwin Evans, Sr., Reeves, London, 1913.

WALKER, FRANK, *Hugo Wolf: A Biography,* Knopf, New York, 1952.

WEINSTOCK, HERBERT, *Chopin,* Knopf, New York, 1949.

IX: Chapters 28–31, The Twentieth Century

ABRAHAM, GERALD, ed., *The Music of Sibelius,* Norton, New York, 1947.

ARMITAGE, MERLE, *George Gershwin: Man and Legend,* Duell, Sloan, New York, 1958.

BEECHAM, SIR THOMAS, *Frederick Delius,* Knopf, New York, 1960.

BRODER, NATHAN, *Samuel Barber,* G. Schirmer, New York, 1954.

CARNER, MOSCO, *Puccini: A Critical Biography,* Knopf, New York, 1959.

CHASE, GILBERT, *America's Music,* McGraw-Hill, New York, 1955.

COPLAND, AARON, *Our New Music,* McGraw-Hill, New York, 1941.

COWELL, HENRY and SIDNEY, *Charles Ives and His Music,* Oxford University Press, New York, 1955.

DEBUSSY, CLAUDE, *Monsieur Croche: The Dilettante Hater,* tr. by B. N. Langdon Davis, Lear, New York, 1948.

DEMUTH, NORMAN, *Musical Trends in the Twentieth Century,* Rockliffe, London, 1952.

———, *Ravel,* Dent, London, 1947; Farrar, Strauss, New York, 1949.

DENT, EDWARD J., *Ferruccio Busoni: A Biography,* Oxford University Press, London, 1933.

EIMERT, HERBERT, ed., *Die Reihe,* Vol. 1, *Electronic Music;* Vol. 2, *Anton Webern;* Universal, Vienna and London, 1957.

FOSS, HUBERT, *Ralph Vaughan Williams: A Study,* Oxford University Press, London, 1950.

FRANK, ALAN, *Modern British Composers,* Dobson, London, 1953.

HANSEN, PETER, *An Introduction to Twentieth-Century Music,* Allyn and Bacon, New York, 1961.

HARTOG, HOWARD, ed., *European Music in the Twentieth Century,* Praeger, New York, 1957.

HINDEMITH, PAUL, *A Composer's World,* Harvard University Press, Cambridge, 1952.

———, *The Craft of Musical Composition,* 2 vols., Vol. 1 tr. by Arthur Mendel; vol. 2 tr. by Otto Ortmann, Associated Music Publishers, New York, 1941–42.

HODÉIR, ANDRÉ, *Since Debussy: A View of Contemporary Music,* Grove, New York, 1961.

HOWES, FRANK, *The Music of William Walton,* 2 vols., Oxford University Press, London, 1942.

JOHNSON, HAROLD E., *Jan Sibelius,* Knopf, New York, 1959.

KOLNEDER, WALTER, *Anton Webern: Einführung im Werk und Stil,* Tonger, Bodenkirchen am Rhein, 1961.

KRAUSE, ERNST, *Richard Strauss: Gestalt und Werk,* Breitkopf & Härtel, Leipzig, 1955.

LEIBOWITZ, RENÉ, *Schoenberg and His School,* tr. by Dika Newlin, Philosophical Library, New York, 1949.

MACHLIS, JOSEPH, *Introduction to Contemporary Music,* Norton, New York, 1961.

MAISEL, EDWARD M., *Charles T. Griffes: The Life of an American Composer,* Knopf, New York, 1943.

MARTYNOV, IVAN, *Dmitri Shostakovich: The Man and His Work,* Philosophical Library, New York, 1947.

McVEAGH, DIANA, *Edward Elgar: His Life and Music,* Dent, London, 1955.

MERSMANN, HANS, *Die Moderne seit der Romantik (Handbuch der Musikwissenschaft* series), Athenaion, Potsdam, 1931.

MILHAUD, DARIUS, *Notes Without Music,* Knopf, New York, 1953.

MYERS, ROLLO H., *Erik Satie,* Dobson, London, 1948.

NESTYEV, ISRAEL V., *Sergei Prokofiev: His Musical Life,* tr. by Florence Jonas, Stanford University, Stanford, 1960.

NEWLIN, DIKA, *Bruckner, Mahler, Schoenberg,* Columbia University Press, New York, 1947.

PAHISSA, JAIME, *Manuel de Falla: His Life and Works,* tr. by Jean Wagstaff, Museum Press, London, 1954.

PERLE, GEORGE, *Serial Composition and Atonality,* University of California Press, Berkeley, 1962.

PERSICHETTI, VINCENT, *Twentieth-Century Harmony,* Norton, New York, 1961.

Problems of Modern Music, ed. by Paul Henry Lang, Princeton Seminar in Advanced Musical Studies, Norton, New York, 1962.

REDLICH, HANS F., *Alban Berg: The Man and His Music,* Abelard-Schuman, New York, 1957.

RUBBRA, EDMUND, *Gustav Holst,* L'Oiseau-lyre, Monaco, 1947.

SEARLE, HUMPHREY, *Twentieth-Century Counterpoint,* 2d ed., De Graff, New York, 1954.

SCHOENBERG, ARNOLD, *Style and Idea,* Philosophical Library, New York, 1950.

SESSIONS, ROGER, *The Musical Experience of Composer, Performer, Listener,* Princeton University Press, Princeton, 1950; reprinted, Athenaeum, New York, 1962.

SLONIMSKY, NICOLAS, *Music Since 1900,* 3d ed., Coleman-Ross, New York, 1949.

SMITH, JULIA, *Aaron Copland,* Dutton, New York, 1955.

STEVENS, HALSEY, *The Life and Music of Belá Bartók,* Oxford University Press, New York, 1953.

STRAVINSKY, IGOR, *Exposition and Development,* Doubleday, New York, 1962.

———, *Poetics of Music,* Harvard University Press, Cambridge, 1947; reprinted, Vintage, New York, 1956.

———, and ROBERT CRAFT, *Conversations with Igor Stravinsky,* Doubleday, New York, 1959.

STROBEL, HEINRICH, *Paul Hindemith,* 3d ed., Schott, Mainz, 1948.

VALLAS, LÉON, *Claude Debussy et son temps,* Michel, Paris, 1958.

VLAD, ROMAN, *Stravinsky,* Oxford University Press, London, 1960.

INDEX

Compositions with distinctive titles (e.g., Brahms' *Deutsches Requiem,* Verdi's *Otello*) are listed by title; other compositions (sonatas, symphonies, etc.) are listed by composer. Italicized folios refer to illustrations and musical examples; folios followed by "n" refer to footnotes.

A

a cappella concept, 269; birth of in Josquin's time, 128; misconception of term, 253
Abaco, Evaristo dall', 292, 294
Abbatini, Antonio, 222
Abraham and Isaac (oratorio, Carissimi), 265
Academic Festival (overture, Brahms), 481
Académie de poésie et de musique, 189, 208
Académie Royale de Musique, 228, 344
Accentualists, 38
accentus, 27
acoustics in Pythagorean theory, 16–17
Adam, Adolphe, 464
Adam de la Halle, 50
Adlgasser, Anton, 365
Aegyptische Helena, Die (opera, Strauss), 615
Aeschylus, 15
Affetti musicali (Marini), 217
Africaine, L' (opera, Meyerbeer), 460
Agostino, Paolo, 254
Agrippina (opera, Handel), 238
Aïda (opera, Verdi), 460, 527
Ainsworth Psalter, 165, 633
air, 189
air de cour, 189, 227, 277
Albert, Heinrich, 252, 440
Albert V, Duke of Bavaria, 139
Albinoni, Tommaso, 295, 300
Albrechtsberger, Johann, 405
Alceste (opera, Gluck), 337, 338
Alcestiad, The (opera, Talma), 662
Alcidiane (ballet, Lully), 227
aleatory music: *see* chance music
Alessandro Stradella (opera, Flotow), 452
Alfano, Franco, 617, 621
Alfonso X, 50
Alia musica (anon.), 41
Allegri, Gregorio, 253
Allegro, L' (oratorio, Handel), 270
Alleluia chant, 40, 47–48, 61
allemande, 204
Alma redemptoris mater (motet, Dufay), 110
Almira (opera, Handel), 238
Alpensinfonie, Eine (Strauss), 563
Also sprach Zarathustra (symphonic poem, Strauss), 564–65
Amahl and the Night Visitors (chamber opera, Menotti), 662
Amazons, Les (opera, Méhul), 340
Ambrose, Bishop of Milan, 28
Ambrosian chant, 28
Amelia Goes to the Ball (comic opera, Menotti), 662

American music, 631; in Colonial period, 631, 633–37; Moravian Brethren's influence on, 634–35; early concerts in New York and Philadelphia, 635; in Colonial South, 636; first composers, 636–37; post-Revolutionary, 637–38; Lowell Mason's contributions to, 638–39; influence of Europeans on, 637–38; Foster, 639–40; nationalistic composers, 640; Gottschalk, 640; first orchestras, 642–43; growth of band music, 643; Paine and the New England school, 644–46; MacDowell, 646; Ives, 648–49; impressionistic influence on, 649–50; after 1920, 650–59; Copland, 654–56; jazz in, 657; Negro spiritual in, 657; electronic experiments in, 658–60; opera, 660–62; summary of, 663
Amfiparnasso, L' (madrigal comedy, Vecchi), 212n
Amor brujo, El (ballet, Falla), 622
Amore dei tre re, L' (opera, Montemezzi), 618
An die ferne Geliebte (song cycle, Beethoven), 441
Anacreon, 15
Andrea Chénier (opera, Giordano), 618
Anerio, Felice, 152, 253, 254
Anerio, Giovanni Francesco, 253, 264
Anglebert, Jean Henri d', 285, 286
Années de pèlerinage (Liszt), 495
Antar (symphony, Rimsky-Korsakov), 513
anthem, 168, 256–59
Antica musica ridotta alla moderna prattica, L' (Vicentino), 179
antiphonal singing, 296; in primitive music, 7; in Hebrew music, 11; in Venice, 153–56; in G. Gabrieli, 180–81; in pre-Classical Mass, 362
Apel, Willi, 62n
Apollo, 14, 15, 16
Apothéose de Corelli, L' (Couperin), 315
Apothéose de Lully, L' (Couperin), 315
Aquinas, Thomas, 207
"Archduke" trio (Beethoven), 420
Archilochos of Paros, 14
Archytas, 17
Arditta zanzaretta (madrigal, Gesualdo), 184
aria di bravura, 243
Ariadne (opera, Monteverdi), 220
Ariadne auf Naxos: melodrama, Benda, 349; opera, Strauss, 615
Ariane et Barbe-bleue (opera, Dukas), 621
ariette, 345, 346
arioso, 224
Ariosto, Lodovico, 183, 191
Aristoxenus, 17
Armide (opera, Gluck), 337, 339

F
G
H
I
J
K   2